A Sociology of Ireland

FOURTH EDITION

A Sociology of Ireland

FOURTH EDITION

Perry Share, Mary P. Corcoran
& Brian Conway

GILL & MACMILLAN

Gill & Macmillan
Hume Avenue Park West
Dublin 12
with associated companies throughout the world
www.gillmacmillan.ie

© Perry Share, Mary P. Corcoran and Brian Conway 2012
978 07171 4984 1

Index compiled by Rachel Pierce
Print origination by Carole Lynch
Printed by GraphyCems, Spain

A CIP catalogue record is available for this book from the British Library.

Frontispiece

It is a definition of a sociologist that he/she is someone who analyses his/her own society. There are no sociologists who do not also live through the complexities and incoherencies of a concrete historical situation and who do not try at the same time to bring out and define general processes of functioning or transformation. I claim for all sociologists not only the right but the duty to be both committed and uncommitted, partisan and independent, realistic and prophetic. How could we set apart the unity of our thought from the history of our personal lives and the experience of profound historical transformations? We not only work on our societies; we work on ourselves.

Alain Touraine (1996)
'A sociology of the subject' in J. Clark and M. Diani (eds)
Alain Touraine. London: Falmer Press, p. 326.

Acknowledgements

We would like to acknowledge the input of Hilary Tovey, co-author of previous editions of A *Sociology of Ireland*, whose influence remains evident in this one. We were also ably assisted in the preparation of this volume by research assistants Kati Lemba (IT Sligo funded by ISSP) and Aoife Campbell (NUI Maynooth SPUR programme). Marion O'Brien, Catherine Gough and Kristin Jensen at Gill & Macmillan provided excellent editorial support at all times. We thank our colleagues and students, who continue to inspire us.

Abbreviations

AIRO	All-Island Research Observatory
ACP	Association of Catholic Priests
BRIC	Brazil, Russia, India, China
CAP	Common Agricultural Policy
CCTV	Closed circuit television
CORI	Conference of Religious of Ireland
CSO	Central Statistics Office
DDDA	Dublin Docklands Development Authority
DES	Department of Education and Skills
DTEDG	Dublin Travellers' Education and Development Group
ERI	Economic Research Institute
ESR	*Economic and Social Review*
ESRI	Economic and Social Research Institute
EU	European Union
FDI	Foreign direct investment
FGM	Female genital mutilation
GAA	Gaelic Athletic Association
GDP	Gross domestic product
GDI	Gross domestic income
GNP	Gross national product
GUI	Growing Up in Ireland (study)
HEA	Higher Education Authority
ICT	Information and communications technology
ICTU	Irish Congress of Trade Unions
IDA	Industrial Development Authority
IJS	*Irish Journal of Sociology*
ILO	International Labour Organisation
IMF	International Monetary Fund
IPA	Institute of Public Administration
JBR	Jumbo breakfast roll
JNLR	Joint National Listenership Research
MNC	Multinational corporation
MRBI	Market Research Bureau of Ireland
NAPS	National Anti-Poverty Strategy
NESC	National Economic and Social Council

NIC	Newly industrialising country
NIRSA	National Institute for Regional and Spatial Analysis
NGO	Non-governmental organisation
OECD	Organisation for Economic Co-operation and Development
PISA	Programme for International Student Assessment
PRTLI	Programme for Research in Third Level Education
RSE	Relationships and sexuality education
RTÉ	Radio Telefís Éireann
SAI	Sociological Association of Ireland
SSIS	Statistical and Social Inquiry Society
TILDA	The Irish Longitudinal Study on Ageing
TNC	Transnational corporation
UN	United Nations
VEC	Vocational Education Committees
WTO	World Trade Organisation

Contents

Part III   Cultural Forms and Trajectories

Part I

Origins, Dynamics and Contexts

1
Sociology and Modernity

Sociology is a robust discipline in our higher education institutions and in civil society. For more than 100 years, the sociological perspective has inspired students, informed policy debates and provided trenchant critiques of society. It may be helpful to clarify here at the outset what sociology does that other social science disciplines, such as economics, generally speaking, do not do.

According to the renowned Swedish sociologist Gorän Therborn (1991, p. 188), the key difference between sociology and other disciplines lies in the conceptualisation of the relationship between the individual and their context. Rational choice models of behaviour (favoured by economists) treat actors as given and situations as discriminating, so 'people act the way they do because their situation is such and such, and they act differently when their situation changes'. In contrast, sociology treats the cultural belonging and structural location of actors as the principal explanatory variable. Thus, 'people act the way they do because they belong to a particular culture and and/or because they have certain resources to draw upon'.

When sociologists come to interpret society, or a particular process or problem in a society, they tend to be attuned to the particular cultural and social locations of people. They pay attention to the structural context of people's action and the kinds of resources they can draw upon that help to shape their courses of action. The recent past and present – the provenance of sociologists – is challenging to analyse because sociologists observe, investigate and write from inside the maelstrom of everyday life. Gathering evidence is often cumbersome; disturbing taken-for-granted understandings is tricky. Challenging the viewpoints of those in powerful positions and, in particular, exposing power differentials in society is a fraught business, but there is a long tradition of such critical observation in the discipline. Key 19th-century thinkers in particular have bequeathed useful frameworks for theoretical and empirical analysis to present-day sociologists. They were incessantly curious about their society and contemporary sociologists maintain this quizzical stance.

In this chapter we provide a brief and necessarily highly selective introduction to sociology. It contains little specifically Irish material (that comes later in the book) except for some illustrative examples. We sketch the historical context in which the study of social matters was first formalised into the discipline of sociology and outline some of the key ideas that emerged during that formative period. These ideas remain central to sociological thought today. We aim to connect with 'the high tradition' in sociology that can be traced back to the revolutionary discoveries about society by thinkers such as Karl Marx, Max Weber and Émile Durkheim in the period from 1850 to 1920.

The nature of Irish modernity is a key theme of this book and in this chapter we focus in particular on how sociology has interpreted this concept. The classic sociological debates about modernity offer a degree of intellectual vigour, emotional depth and engagement rarely found in Irish discussions of the topic. But given its origins in large powerful societies like Britain, Germany, France and the US, sociology has also contributed to a metropolitan conception of 'modern society' that can marginalise or confuse the experience of modernity in societies like Ireland. Our brief discussion of the classic sociological theorists and how their ideas related to particular issues of social change form the basis of this opening chapter.

THE ORIGINS OF SOCIOLOGY

Sociology, as a distinct form of enquiry, is a product 19th-century Europe. The term itself was coined around 1838 by the French writer Auguste Comte. A long tradition of thought about the nature of society and social change can be traced back to the ancient Greeks and to Islamic culture, but most of this earlier thinking was philosophical (depending on reasoning from basic assumptions), theological (drawing from divine revelation) or psychological (in the sense that it started with some first principles about human nature and argued from these to an account of society). Writers like Comte sought a new approach with its own distinctive label that took society rather than human nature as its starting point and that used systematic methods to collect empirical evidence. Harriet Martineau is also increasingly being recognised as a major founder of the discipline of sociology (Giddens, 2006, p. 20). As well as translating the work of Comte into English, and thus introducing his work to the English-speaking world, she was a significant theorist and social analyst in her own right. Her book, *How to Observe Morals and Manners* (1838), was an early primer in social research and she also carried out extensive study tours, including a number of visits to Ireland (Hill, 2005).

Harriet Martineau: A pioneering sociologist in Ireland
Sociology is generally seen as a discipline that owes its major debt to key founding fathers of the 19th century, yet a number of women writing in that century clearly showed themselves capable of applying a powerful sociological imagination to their explorations of the social world. Harriet Martineau (1802–76) was an English-born writer and sociologist who lived in Dublin for several months during 1831. Her observations of a political economy in Ireland that maintained the country in a state of colonial subjugation led her to identify herself as 'an indignant witness of [Ireland's] wrongs'. Martineau later continued her travels in North America, producing a number of

sociological accounts based on her detailed observations there. She returned to Ireland in 1852 to observe and write about the Great Famine and its aftermath. In researching her dispatches from Ireland, she travelled throughout the country making empirical observations, read profusely and consulted with experts, including making visits to the Dublin Statistical Society (Conway, 2006).

Two features of the 19th century help us to understand the emergence of sociology, its subsequent development and the central issues that remain of concern to sociologists. First, this was the age of industrial and political revolution. Second, it was also the age of science. Together, we could say these made it the age of control: of people and of nature. The application of science, particularly through industrial technology, enormously increased the scope of human control over the natural environment and its resources. In politics, radical thinkers similarly tried to bring the institutions of the state under the control of human reason. Inevitably the desire to control through the accumulation and application of knowledge would be extended into the field of society.

The British sociologist Bryan Turner suggests that it was then that the idea of 'the social' as a human creation separate from 'nature' became widely accepted:

modern industrial society was not a natural community ... it dealt with needs and the satisfaction of wants in a wholly revolutionary and unique fashion. Natural communities were bound by tradition and by the traditional or conventional satisfaction of wants and needs. (1996, p. 3)

The discipline of sociology, Turner suggests, developed in order to analyse this new concept of a 'separate and autonomous world of the social'; indeed, the ideas of society, modernity and sociology emerged together. For some, sociology was a science that could be used to control both human behaviour and the development of societies. For others it offered a form of reasoning that could emancipate humans from external control and, by helping them to understand their own social situation and circumstances, increase their autonomy. These dual – often competing – views of sociology persist. They often meet in debates over whether sociology is a science and, if so, what sort of science it should be.

The growth of sociology was part of the formation of modernity. By the early 19th century, the conviction was widespread in Europe and North America that the most profound changes yet experienced by humanity were underway. The Industrial Revolution, first in Britain and later in France, Germany and the United States, precipitated new economic processes that seemed likely to forever alter the organisation of societies and social relationships. The 'democratic revolutions' in the United States (1776) and France (1789) provoked intense debates about human nature, legitimate authority and the proper relationship between the individual and society. The speed of social change seemed to have accelerated tremendously and social thinkers became preoccupied with trying to identify modernity and to chart its likely future path. Contemporary sociology has inherited a view of itself not just as the study of society, but of *modern* society. By contrast, the cognate discipline of anthropology is often defined as the study of pre-modern, or traditional, social forms, though many contemporary anthropologists would challenge this distinction.

Nineteenth-century social thinkers disagreed over how to characterise and evaluate modern society. They differed in their emotional and moral responses to social change. Some feared that the modern world posed a threat to social order; their aim was to discover how social stability could be restored and secured. This preoccupation has developed within contemporary sociology as *the problem of social order*: the attempt to explain how the organisation of society is maintained and reproduced over time. Other thinkers were far more excited by the potential of modernity to expand human control over social arrangements and to overcome existing constraints on human freedom. Their response shaped contemporary sociology's second core preoccupation: *the problem of social inequality*.

Most sociologists today see both these concerns as central to sociological inquiry. We may better understand what is common to all in a society (such as beliefs, values, shared identity and social consensus) when we recognise what divides individuals and social groups (unequal access to power and social respect, conflict over beliefs and values). We cannot explain social order in any society unless we can show how social inequality is managed within it; equally, the type and experience of social inequality are deeply influenced by how the society is ordered and organised.

We have considered above the emotional and moral responses to modernity of the social thinkers of the 19th century and their intellectual or analytic responses. We shall now see how the ideas and interpretations of modernity of some major sociological theorists of the period have influenced the way all of us today, sociologists or not, think about and interpret the world in which we live.

SOCIOLOGY AS THE STUDY OF MODERN SOCIETY

The 19th-century writers who tried to interpret the changing world around them agreed on one thing – it was new and unique in historical experience – but they differed on how to describe and characterise it. As a result, their writings offer at least four distinct themes for characterising modern society. Three derive from attempts to identify the most important effects of the economic transformation introduced by the Industrial Revolution, while the fourth is more concerned with tracing the social effects of cultural change. We might summarise them as follows:

- Modern society as *industrial* society.
- Modern society as *capitalist* society.
- Modern society as *urban* society.
- Modern society as *rational* society.

Modern society as industrial society

The Industrial Revolution is normally understood to be the transformation of an economy dominated by agriculture to one based on manufacturing. It was a process that spread from 18th-century Britain to the rest of the Western world. The technological changes involved, such as the invention of new machines and new ways of harnessing power for the production and transport of goods, had far-reaching effects on people's livelihoods and on the social organisation of work. In the early 19th-century British cotton industry, for example, the introduction of power looms brought weavers out of their cottages and small workshops and into factories where they experienced new work routines (the 'tyranny of the clock') and new work relationships of authority and control (Thompson, 1982).

The French thinker Émile Durkheim interpreted the social changes that accompanied industrialisation as an increase in the *division of labour* in society. This refers to how work tasks are divided and shared among the working population. Durkheim argued that in pre-industrial societies, one worker or workgroup (such as a family) did a range of different work tasks necessary to meet survival needs and work was organised sequentially so that each stage in the production process was completed before the next was begun. This allowed a single worker to see the whole process through from beginning to end and to have a wide range of skills with limited specialisation.

By contrast, in industrial society, each worker now specialises in a single activity that has to be complemented by those of other specialised workers. With the shift from handicraft to machine production and from the workshop to the factory, all the processes necessary to produce a given item can be carried out simultaneously. The industrialisation of agriculture and food provides a good example of Durkheim's thesis. In Ireland in the earlier part of the 20th century, butter was produced manually by farm families who also tended, fed and milked the cows. Today the labour of producing butter is divided between the farmer who produces the raw milk, the factory that processes it into butter, the factory that produces feed for the cows, the factory that produces the computer programmes to regulate the timing and content of the cows' meals and so on. We can see the same process in other areas of society. The job of 'teacher' has become divided into first-, second- or third-level teacher and into educator, career guidance advisor, counsellor or youth worker. A 'knowledge worker' may refer to a programmer who works with computers, to an engineer who is developing phone technology, to the sales assistant who sells you a phone or to the call centre worker who responds to your account query. The outcome is a much more complex and detailed system of occupational divisions and identities in modern industrial society.

A question that preoccupied Durkheim was how a society with such an advanced division of labour could retain the social bonds between individuals that he thought necessary for social order. Such societies tend to be very individualistic, with a danger that those within them may lose a sense of social connectedness or obligation to others. Pre-industrial societies were unified on the basis of similarities – most people shared the same sorts of skills, responsibilities, values and life experiences. This unity is destroyed by industrialisation. For Durkheim, an answer could be found in the fact that as people become more specialised occupationally, they become more dependent on their fellow citizens. As each of us provides only a specialised service to others, we rely on them to provide us with their services and skills. In a modern industrialised society, collective social order depends more on the acceptance of difference and on co-operation between individuals and groups than on feelings of sameness and collective identity.

Durkheim sometimes went so far as to suggest that industrial society is synonymous with 'civilisation' because of the new order of *moral individualism* that a highly developed division of labour can create. This moral code reverses earlier understandings of the proper relationship between the individual and society. It shifts the emphasis from the duties the individual owes to society to the duties society owes to the individual. Moral individualism treats the individual as the source of all ethical value and encourages the organisation of society to ensure the maximisation of individual rights.

Durkheim realised that individualism could sometimes be amoral rather than moral. He argued that modern society constituted an abnormal form of the division of labour and a breeding ground for amoral individualism. The industrial society that emerged at the end of 19th-century Europe did not extend equal rights to all of its citizens. It was full of arbitrary inequalities and severely restricted the opportunity for an acceptable lifestyle for some social groups. Instead of generating feelings of solidarity and mutual respect between specialised and differentiated individuals, it tended to encourage either unbridled egoism (selfishness) or what Durkheim termed *anomie*.

This concept is one of Durkheim's most significant contributions to sociology. He used it to identify a condition of society that arises when the rules by which social life is organised are incoherent, incomplete or widely disregarded. Examples might include a society that publicly prides itself on its impartial exercise of justice but where everyone knows that in practice there is one law for the rich and another for the poor; or a society that legitimises divisions between rich and poor on the grounds that anyone can succeed if they work hard enough, yet systematically discriminates against some groups so they can never succeed no matter how hard they try. The result of living in an *anomic* society is that people may suffer a deep sense of isolation and meaninglessness in their lives and work. In certain social conditions, anomie can, as Durkheim famously argued, lead to suicide, the ultimate statement of the collapse of the bond between the individual and society.

Durkheim's insights retain their currency in the modern era. Much commodity production is now characterised by a division of labour that occurs on a global scale. Thus, it is in factories in China that the in-demand commodities such as smartphones and tablet computers desired by Western consumers are produced. An investigation into the conditions of Chinese workers in these factories reveals the enormous human cost of working in situations characterised by excessively long working hours and draconian workplace rules. A report (Chamberlain, 2011) based on research carried out by two non-governmental organisations (NGOs) uncovered an 'anti-suicide' pledge that workers at the two plants were urged to sign after a series of employee deaths. The investigation reveals a detailed picture of life for the 500,000 workers at two factories owned by Foxconn, which produces millions of Apple technology products each year. Foxconn was accused of treating workers 'inhumanely, like machines'.

Modern society as capitalist society

The society that has emerged over the past two centuries is often described as industrial capitalist society. Though the terms 'industrial' and 'capitalist' are often used in tandem in this way, they are not synonymous. Instances of capitalism can be found prior to the development of modern industry. Some forms of agricultural production in 18th-century Britain were capitalist, as were many business enterprises in 15th-century Italian city states. Similarly, the 20th century has seen the development of industrial societies that were not capitalist, such as the former Soviet Union. Sociologists generally use the term 'capitalist' to describe a particular way that economic production is organised: it is oriented to exchange on markets; we produce things in order to sell them; the wealth or resources used in production are held in private ownership; and these resources are invested and reinvested to produce the greatest possible profit. Capitalist societies are those where this type of economic organisation predominates.

The major interpreter of modern society as capitalist society was Karl Marx. Marx understood capitalism very specifically as an economic system in which profit is made by those who own the means of production (land, money or credit, machinery, buildings) through exploiting the labour of those who do not. Owners, or 'capitalists', realise a profit when they can sell products on the market for more than they cost to produce. This is possible mainly through paying those who labour to create the product less than the true value of their contribution to its final market price. This is only possible in a society where private ownership of wealth is concentrated in the hands of a minority and the rest of the population, reduced to owning nothing but their own capacity to work (their labour power), have to sell this to the capitalists in order to survive. Capitalism as an economic system, Marx argued, both produces and depends on a particular type of social structure peculiar to capitalist societies – division into two major and opposed classes, the capitalist class, or *bourgeoisie*, and the working class, or *proletariat*.

While the concept of industrial society led Durkheim to ask questions about social order and stability, the concept of capitalist society enabled Marx to focus on questions of inequality and conflict. In his view, it is the relationship between the two major classes – a relationship of conflict – that determines the form and development of modern society. Capitalist economies are very dynamic and characterised by continual technological innovation as capitalists strive to reduce production costs, increase profits and diminish their dependence on human labour. But capitalist society is also a society that alienates human beings from each other and its structures reduce human freedom.

The Marxist concept of *alienation* is as significant to sociologists as Durkheim's notion of anomie. Marx used the term to attack what he saw as the profoundly dehumanising effects of capitalism. Under capitalist conditions, workers become *alienated* – separated – from the products of their work, much as is suggested in the example of the Chinese workers above. What they produce does not belong to them but to the capitalist, the owner of the means of production who has bought their labour. Instead of being a recognisable outcome of their own human creativity, what they produce appears foreign to them, disconnected from their identity and lives. But alienation does not stop here, on the production line. The result of a capitalist division of labour is that people become alienated from work itself as it is subdivided into fragmented tasks, mechanised and managed from above, thus denying workers the use of their own skills and knowledge or control over the timing and sequence of their work. In these conditions, work becomes a meaningless activity undertaken for purely instrumental reasons – to make money to survive. Inevitably, workers also become alienated from each other. They no longer see themselves as engaged in a joint productive task but merely as atomised individuals.

Ultimately, since Marx believed that it is creative interaction with the environment through meaningful work that makes us human, this means that capitalism alienates people from their own essential humanity. Finding no meaning in their working lives, people become obsessed with material possessions and work harder and harder in order to acquire more and more, whether or not the possessions have any intrinsic value. They learn to see themselves as no more than consumers. It is inevitable that capitalist societies are dominated by an ideology that glorifies material possessions unless the working class can find the means to mobilise against it and regain humanity for modern human beings.

Marx and crisis

In the 19th century, Karl Marx and his collaborator Frederick Engels identified capitalism's propensity to periodically overextend itself and fall into crisis. They believed that while capitalism would right itself in the short term, in the long term the system would essentially be destroyed. Since the onset of the global financial crisis in 2008 and the consequent downturn in economic growth, sluggish stock markets, rash of mortgage foreclosures and failed banks, many commentators have sought to explain what went wrong.

Writing in the *Financial Times* (18–19 October 2008), journalist John Plender suggested that it was none other than Karl Marx who, in 1893, had provided as good an account of today's financial implosion as any living commentator. He went so far as to quote from Marx's key work, *Das Kapital*: 'to the possessor of money capital, the process of production appears merely as an unavoidable intermediate link, as a necessary evil for the sake of money-making. All nations with a capitalist mode of production are therefore seized periodically by a feverish attempt to make money without the intervention of the process of production.'

These are prophetic words indeed given that the financial crisis was engendered at least in part by the development of sophisticated financial commodities such as 'credit default swaps': highly complex, abstract products that were poorly understood even by those who traded in them. Marx would probably have been quite unfazed by the spectacle of greedy bankers laying waste to the international financial services sector, since in his theory of capitalism he had predicted just such a scenario (Plender, 2008).

Marx's analysis of social change is often described as *materialist*. He understood the development of modern capitalism to be the result primarily of changes in economic organisation. While not denying the key role of the economy, Max Weber stressed that ideas and values also influence social change. Weber thought it important to ask how people could come to accept the new economic relations and behaviour that capitalism demands. In particular, he asked how they could accept the search for profit as the central, overriding goal of life, when in previous 'traditional' societies work was more often simply a means to achieve an acceptable standard of living, to be abandoned once that was reached. How do we explain this change in people's values?

Weber argued that a key influence here was religion. He focused in particular on the religious changes that took place in the 17th and 18th centuries in Western Europe, especially the emergence of a puritan type of Protestantism (most clearly seen in Calvinism) whose followers came to believe that an austere, self-denying life of unremitting work was the best way to glorify God and to calm anxieties over whether they were one of the 'saved' who would find a place in heaven. Weber's sociology is laced with irony. The frenetic materialism of modern capitalist society can be traced back to the 'work ethic' of an ascetic religious world view.

Weber, like Marx, saw modern capitalist society as characterised by inequality. But whereas Marx's focus was on the material bases of inequality, Weber was more interested in the *ideas* that are used in modern society to explain and to justify inequality. Weber's view of sociology as the study of human action and of the meanings that actors give to their world has been highly influential on sociologists ever since.

Modern society as urban society

Industrialisation is widely associated with a switch from an agricultural to a manufacturing economy. It is also associated with urbanisation: the growth of towns and cities and the depopulation and decline of rural areas. Of course, cities existed in pre-industrial societies, but industrialisation boosted and accelerated their development as well as transforming their character in important ways. The concentration of factories in urban areas attracted migrants from the countryside and immigrants from overseas (mainly to the United States) and the number of working-class inhabitants in cities swelled enormously. Rapidly expanding, badly built and overcrowded working-class housing areas were prone to epidemics and seen by many upper- and middle-class urban people as symbolic of the threat to social order posed by a chaotic and uncontrolled poor.

Urbanisation was perhaps the most visible of the massive changes that modernity brought to society. It attracted the attention of many social commentators, including some sociologists who saw it as evidence of regress rather than progress. They mourned what was being lost with the passing of 'traditional' rural society. The influential German sociologist Ferdinand Tönnies, for example, wrote that urban industrial society was characterised by a loss of community. He argued that industrialisation increases the scale and thus the impersonality of society. With urbanisation, the close personal relationships of small-scale pre-industrial local societies are replaced by impersonal calculative relationships where others may be seen as no more than a way to achieve one's own aims. Though Tönnies did not explicitly identify 'community' (*Gemeinschaft*) with rural areas or a rural way of life, nor 'impersonal association' (*Gesellschaft*) with urban areas, many writers subsequently did, with the result that 'rural society' is often confused with 'traditional' or 'pre-industrial' society, while the urban is inevitably linked to modernity.

Another important German social theorist, Georg Simmel, wrote about the city as the key location of the everyday experience of modernity. For him, modern individuals are formed within and by an urban or metropolitan world. In cities, people are constantly involved in interactions with strangers that engage only fragments of the individual personality, leaving most of it unknown. On the city streets, people are bombarded by a constant stream of impressions and are brought into contact continuously with anonymous others. City dwellers typically respond to this by developing stratagems of defence such as inward retreat, social distance and an attitude of blasé indifference towards everything they encounter (Simmel, 1971, p. 326):

> The metropolitan type of man ... develops an organ protecting him against the threatening currents and discrepancies of his external environment which would uproot him. He reacts with his head instead of his heart ... Metropolitan life, thus, underlies a heightened awareness and a predominance of intelligence in metropolitan man.

But if city living is associated with intelligence and heightened self-consciousness in a way that rural living is not, Simmel (1971, p. 326) also emphasised that the city is the seat and the visual representation of the modern money economy:

The metropolis has always been the seat of the money economy … money economy and the dominance of the intellect are intrinsically connected. They share a matter-of-fact attitude in dealing with men and with things; and in this attitude, a formal justice is often coupled with an inconsiderate hardness … Money … reduces all quality and individuality to the question: How much?

Simmel recognised that the money economy – that is, the model of modernity, the very basis of the modern global marketplace – has a particularly corrosive power. He warned that the utilitarian ethos and calculative frame of mind that it promoted was ultimately subversive of individual and group identities. For Simmel, a key aspect of the modernist project was the individual's attempt to keep the objective culture produced by the money economy at bay and to develop, through myriad forms of belonging, a subjective identity. The elaboration of one's individuality became in modernity the only guard against the loss of subjectivity. The dominance of the money economy can be seen in our global world as more and more spheres of social life are subject to a utilitarian ethos (how much?) and to processes of economisation and financialisation wherein money becomes the measure of all things. Privileging an exclusively economic perspective rules out others and has implications not only for our notions of collective identity, but how we shape our institutions. An economistic perspective promotes the economic self over the social or reflexive self.

While Simmel's fascination with the metropolis was tempered with ambivalence, subsequent sociological characterisations of the urban way of life were far more trenchant. The American sociologist Louis Wirth, writing in 1938, claims the city to be the source of innovation in the modern world and the dominant, controlling centre of modern society. But he also believed that 'the urban way of life' created through the variables of size, density and heterogeneity made for a world of strangers in which social relations were characterised by impersonality, transience and anomie. The supposed absence from urban life of a sense of community was and is used to explain the high rates of crime and other social problems that seem to be a feature of modern society.

In fact, there is little evidence to support the idea that settlement patterns, whether concentrated and large scale, as in urban settings, or dispersed and small scale, as in rural ones, determine either social relationships or psychological characteristics. The belief that there is a characteristically 'urban way of life' to be contrasted with the 'rural way of life' has come to hinder sociologists when investigating the very different ways that different social groups experience life, as we shall see when we explore studies of communities in the Irish context (Chapter 4). Nevertheless, the modern city distinguishes our world from that of earlier periods in history and the experience of modernity in the urban setting remains a focus of research for contemporary sociologists.

Modern society as rational society

Political revolutionaries in late 18th-century Europe tried to replace tradition with reason and law as the basis for societal organisation. They claimed, for example, that rulers should no longer govern by inheritance or divine right, but should be selected in accordance with clear, formal and universally acceptable procedures. Behind this lay the belief that human beings are naturally sociable, co-operative and reasonable; if they often appeared to be the opposite, this was due to the distorting effects of oppressive and unreasonable forms of social organisation. With the removal of these distortions, people would be freed to create the type of society in which these natural qualities would gain full expression. The spread of democracy, universal education and beliefs in individual rights seemed to indicate the benign progress of reason in society, as did the development of law, science and, as suggested earlier, sociology itself. Nevertheless, not all sociologists were convinced that the increasing rationalisation of social life equated to undiluted progress, nor that it necessarily advanced human happiness.

Simmel, as we have already noted, connected the hard-headed rationality of the inhabitants of large cities with the colonisation of all areas of urban life and experience by the money economy and monetary values. Weber argued that one important form of rationalisation in modern society was the development of bureaucracy as a way to administer and control large organisations. Modern bureaucracies are organisations whose official functions are set out in writing (for example, in 'rules and procedures') and are divided into sets of distinct tasks allocated to specific officials. These officials are given the necessary authority and resources to carry out these tasks, but no more; they do not 'own' their positions within the organisation but are selected for them on the basis of explicitly specified qualifications. Positions within the bureaucracy are organised in a hierarchical way with each position being under the control and supervision of a higher one; administrative actions, decisions and rules are recorded in writing and organisational records provide the basis for continual review and improvement of the organisation's performance. This type of administrative apparatus is quite different from any found in earlier societies and is above all a rational way to organise administration. Though today we often use the term 'bureaucratic' to mean 'inefficient', Weber believed this type of rational administrative system to be extremely efficient at the time.

For Weber, rationality refers primarily to a way of acting. *Rational action* is taken on the basis of a calculation of the relationship between means and ends: 'I choose to do X because I want to achieve Y, and doing X is the most effective way to achieve Y.' This contrasts with *customary action*: 'I'll do X because this is how our people have always done it.' Modern society, according to Weber, is one where rational action, involving the application of knowledge, calculation and rules, increasingly replaces customary action. This spread of instrumental rationality undermines religious belief and fundamental values. A rationalised world thus threatens to become secularised, 'disenchanted' and, ultimately, meaningless.

Weber associated the growth of rational systems of administration with the development of large-scale capitalist enterprises but linked it in particular to the state. Modern capitalist society characteristically involves an expanded bureaucratic state which, in Weber's view, means that modern states possess the power to supervise, assemble information on, monitor and organise citizens to a degree unprecedented in the pre-capitalist world. Bureaucracy and democracy are in conflict, since the former centralises power and concentrates it in the hands of those who control the bureaucratic organisation. Ironically, therefore, the very advance of reason may lead to a reduction in human freedom and happiness.

Sociological theorising did not, of course, end in the 1920s. Later in this book you will encounter further references to Weber, Durkheim, Marx and Simmel and also modern theorists such as Habermas, Bourdieu, Giddens, Foucault and many Irish authors whose work is cited and discussed. They continue to carry forward the task of understanding the world in which they live, if not always by building on, then at least in dialogue with the ideas of the classical social theorists.

SOCIOLOGY AS A SCIENCE OF SOCIETY

Restivo (1991, p. 4) describes sociology as 'a field of inquiry simultaneously concerned with understanding, explaining, criticising and improving the human condition'. We have already devoted some attention to the 'understanding', 'criticising' and 'improving' aspects of sociological work, but not much to 'explaining'. Sociological inquiries are not only about exploring theories and ideas. Theories and ideas must be tested against reality if they are to be any use as explanations. Sociology is an empirical discipline that makes discoveries about social reality through the application of theoretical ideas and methods of research. Here we discuss briefly the practices and status of sociology as a research-based discipline or what many would call a (social) science.

There are many ways to research social life, such as large-scale questionnaire surveys, structured or unstructured interviews, ethnographic observation or the collection and analysis of documents. For most sociologists, research is not just a matter of choosing a technique – it involves reflection on the fundamental issues of how we 'gain our knowledge of the social world, the relationships that are held to exist between theory and research, and the place of values and ethics in research practice' (May, 1997, p. 1). The attention paid to these issues makes sociology somewhat unique as a research discipline.

The assumption that doing sociological research is just a matter of selecting appropriate tools implies an unproblematic relationship between researcher and social reality. Early sociologists such as Comte or Durkheim may have held such a view, but it is not easily accepted by contemporary sociology, with decades of reflection on the difficulty of trying to do good social research. Durkheim, who in 1895 authored one of the first textbooks of sociological research (*The Rules of Sociological Method*), said that the social researcher should study social phenomena 'in the same state of mind as the physicist, chemist or physiologist when he probes into a still unexplored region of the scientific domain' (1964, p. xiv). Here he was following Comte, who believed that sociology could and should be modelled closely on the methods and procedures of the natural sciences to produce similar systematic knowledge of and control over the social world. Comte thought the social world could be explained as the natural world could – by deriving objective laws or generalisations about the behaviour of phenomena (in the case of sociology, people and groups) that would allow us to predict their future behaviour patterns. Prediction was important to him because the capacity to predict enhances the potential for control. In reality, sociologists since then have rarely been interested in prediction (now more a concern of economists) and have tended to concentrate on close description and interpretation of what has already occurred.

There are major difficulties with any attempt to treat the social and natural worlds identically or to argue that sociology can only be scientific if it models itself on the natural sciences. Indeed, it has become increasingly clear (see Woolgar, 1988 and many others who have studied the social world of science) that there is no single model of natural scientific inquiry that all scientists agree on and follow. Rather, it is important for social researchers to be reflexive, that is, *critical of their own methods of generating knowledge*. As a result, sociology has had to devise its own distinctive methods and procedures for research.

A number of key considerations govern the practice of sociological research. First, people within the social world already understand to some degree how their world operates. As a consequence, they cannot be treated as would the elements that make up the natural world. Objects in the natural world such as atoms, molecules or ecological systems 'behave' – they are governed by the laws of cause and effect. Humans 'act' – they have reason and purpose, they make choices and they confer meaning on their world. They have their own theories about why their world is as it is and these are also empirical facts for the sociologist to study. Second, sociologists are members of the world they research. Indeed, without access to the social world as participants as well as researchers, it would be extremely difficult, if not impossible, for sociologists to understand anything about it. Social reality is a product of people's ideas and interpretations and is not automatically accessible to the senses or to measuring tools in the way that natural phenomena are. To grasp someone's interpretation of reality, we need to participate, even in a minimal way, in their culture.

Sociologists differ in their responses to these difficulties. We can distinguish three main positions. *Positivism* refers to those who, in the tradition of Comte, hold the view that for the purposes of research, people can be seen to react to their environment as molecules react to heat – without conscious knowledge of what they are doing. Positivism implies that we do not need to ask people *why* they do what they do – we can learn this from our own observation of them. Thus, for example, we need not ask heroin users why they take the drug since we can see that they are 'addicted' to it. More broadly, positivism assumes that there are 'facts' about the social world that are independent of how people define them. It may deduce, for example, that Irish society is class divided, though many people in Ireland would claim that class is irrelevant and that people rise or fall largely on their own merits. It is argued that social facts can be revealed to us by research and it is possible to generate an 'objective' knowledge of social reality. This does not depend on the researcher's feelings about or interpretations of that reality, but is produced by detached and impartial observation and measurement.

Subjectivism insists that 'the only thing we can know with certainty is how people interpret the world around them' (May, 1997, p. 13). It rejects the positivist claim that research can provide privileged access to 'facts' that people in the social world are not themselves aware of. Extreme versions of subjectivism abandon the idea that there are such facts – indeed, that there is *any* external reality beyond people's ideas and definitions of it. Less extreme versions redefine the goal of sociological research as description – it should reveal how interpretations are constructed and how people reach mutual agreements on working definitions of reality. A subjectivist approach to environmental problems, for example, might focus on how the idea that we are threatened by global catastrophe in the form of global warming has come to dominate contemporary environmental politics, rather than on how the 'fact' of global warming is a result of collective human behaviour.

Subjectivist positions have been boosted by feminist critiques of conventional or positivist research. In particular, feminists have revealed how much supposedly objective and impartial knowledge generated by sociological research has been gender blind or gender biased. It has produced accounts of the social world that are only 'real' from a male point of view. Feminist sociologists have forcefully challenged the positivist claim that the good researcher is disengaged from the subject they study. They argue that research is in fact a two-way process where the findings are as influenced by the social identity, status and biographical experiences of the researcher as those of the 'researched'. Research knowledge is always the product of collaboration between researcher and researched and is thus relative to the conditions under which it was generated. There is no detached vantage point from which the absolute truth can be discerned.

A third position, *critical realism*, or as it is often called, *critical theory*, is mainly associated with Marxist sociologists, though it also shares elements with Freudian approaches to researching human behaviour. Both take as a starting point the idea that there are underlying mechanisms in society or in people's subconscious that operate outside consciousness and generate surface phenomena (losing your job; a 'Freudian slip') that we cannot fully explain just by looking at the surface. Critical theorists share with positivists the idea that research should do more than just describe how people act towards each other and how they develop shared ideas about reality. Research should go beyond description to explanation and should try to identify the conditions that allow such interaction and interpretation to happen. This does not mean we should ignore the sense that people make of their world, but we should recognise that it is often distorted or incomplete. Critical theorists part company both with positivists and subjectivists over the issue of detachment and disengagement in research. For them, the purpose of research is to reveal what needs to be criticised in contemporary society, for example oppression and inequality. Their standpoint is engaged and passionate, not detached. They do ultimately accept, with caution, the notion that ordinary people can sometimes be wrong about how they understand and evaluate their own social world. The insights of critical research can help to illuminate more adequately the 'true' nature of the world.

Apart from the issues raised above, others that sociological researchers face include the place of ethics and values in research and the relation between theory and research. It was held as orthodoxy for many years that 'objective' research, in the social as in the natural sphere, does not allow an attachment to values to bias the gathering and interpretation of data. We have seen that there is now far less consensus among social researchers that this is possible or even desirable. The emphasis has shifted from trying to keep values out of research to developing codes of *research ethics*.

Ethical research is honest and avoids manipulating or exploiting subjects, readers, sponsors or funders unless there are, in rare cases, compelling reasons for deception. Reflection on ethics encourages researchers to examine the research process as a whole, in particular the values and interests, often unanticipated or unconscious, that shape it. Also of importance are the circumstances under which the research is being carried out: who has funded it, to what end, who has defined the core 'research problem' and what is to happen to research findings. The fact that a government department, for example, has funded a piece of research and has an interest in how it is done and what it discovers does not necessarily make the research invalid, but it is important for researchers to keep in mind that they are operating in a world where there is unequal power, both in the definition of 'a problem suitable for researching' and in avoiding the intrusions of the researcher. The rich and powerful are far less often the subject of social research than the poor and marginalised. Social scientists are encouraged with promises of funding, media attention and participation in policy-making spheres to do research that is 'relevant', even fashionable. For the sociologist, the construction of a relevant research topic is itself a social phenomenon that can be researched.

The sociologist of education Kathleen Lynch (1999a, 1999b) has argued strongly that even critical models of sociological research typically exclude the 'researched', who usually have no control over the research project and may never see the final product. Successful instances of genuinely participatory research are rare and if those researched have some control over the research methodology, this seldom extends to participation in the development of theory or analysis. The lack of any real engagement with those who experience inequality means, for Lynch, that sociologists are debarred from moving beyond a critique of existing systems towards any truly transformative or emancipatory practice.

Much social research is done without reference to theory. C. Wright Mills (1961) described this as 'abstracted empiricism' and Restivo (1991, p. 1) calls it the 'low tradition' in sociology. The career world of the modern sociologist is organised so as to widen the gap between research and theorising. There are strong pressures to specialise in one or the other and those whose areas of competence are the most specialised tend to receive the highest rewards. Publication outlets such as journals and books are divided according to the specialised markets they serve. A widening gap between research and theorising leaves sociology vulnerable to a process whereby its research problems are determined by others. A sense of development or cumulation of knowledge about social reality becomes difficult to achieve. The discipline tends to fragment into a series of disconnected sub-fields of research that lack interconnection or possibilities for dialogue, for example the sociology of childhood, urban life, economic development, food, religion, management, health and illness and so on. But research *can* draw on theory and contribute to the rebuilding and refinement of theoretical frameworks in many different ways. There is no single right way of relating the two, yet some mutual engagement appears to be essential to a dynamic and coherent sociology.

SOCIOLOGY, MODERNITY AND POST-MODERNITY

Our brief review of the early sociological responses to the massive social changes of the 18th and 19th centuries showed how the experience of these changes led to interpretations of modern society that are still potent and continue to largely define what sociology is about. Sociologists are now aware that the development of modernity is not only a series of historical changes or processes in the material world, but also involves intellectual assumptions that legitimate and sanction these changes. They are captured particularly in the taken-for-granted identification of modernity and progress.

It is part of the modern attitude to assume that human history has a meaning and a destiny and that it consists of a sequence of movements towards a higher, more civilised, more orderly, more humanly satisfying way of organising social and individual life. It is characteristic of modernity to assume that people have developed ways to research reality that allow them to arrive at truth and that the uncovering of truth aids and expands the realisation of human freedom. It is part of modernity to take for granted that revolutionary changes in society – political (the French Revolution) and technical (the Industrial Revolution) – are incremental advances in the unfettering of human reason so that it can be put to use to improve the world. It is, finally, a quintessentially modern belief that the development of science and its application in the empirical world through industrial technology enhances human control over and capacity to manage the natural environment for the greater benefit of all.

Such assumptions are so ingrained in modern thinking about the world, including sociological thinking, that we have come to accept them as largely unquestioned. Sociologists have begun to draw attention to the novelty of such ideas, in historical terms, and what we might call their fragility. Kumar (1995) points out that to 17th-century Europeans, the very idea of historical change would have been strange, as most believed that human life was fundamentally unchanging. For them, the objective of studying history was primarily to discover, as the Scottish philosopher David Hume put it, 'the constant and universal principles of human nature' under varying sets of circumstances. The idea of progress – that human history could be thought of as, in effect, a movement towards the realisation of heaven on Earth – would have struck them as downright blasphemous. Similarly, the idea that underlay the advance of science – that nature is made up of inert matter that can be partitioned, manipulated, combined and recombined to realise human ends – contrasts markedly with earlier understandings of nature as an unpredictable and explosive living system to be placated through ritual or co-operated with through long experience and observation (Merchant, 1980).

Ironically, perhaps, the excavation of intellectual history in the period before modernity has helped the emergence of what is today widely referred to as *post-modernity*. Post-modern thinking contextualises and relativises modernity. Instead of believing, with the modernisers, that the intellectual assumptions of modernity are objectively true and absolute in all historical eras, it emphasises how they are historically quite novel, unique and contingent. The concept of post-modernity is notoriously difficult (Rose, 1991) and we do not propose to go into it in great depth here. We will simply try to disentangle some of the different ways that it has been understood in order to indicate some of its impacts on contemporary sociology.

It is most common to understand post-modernity as a historical period that comes *after* modernity. Thus, if we are now post-modern, it is because we have moved into an era characterised by new social, economic, political and intellectual conditions. Therefore, while existing sociological analyses may not be entirely out of date in post-modern society, they may fail in some crucial ways to capture its core experiences. Ulrich Beck (1992), for example, argues that societies today are increasingly organised around struggles to escape from 'bads' (such as threatened environmental disasters) instead of struggles for access to 'goods' (social equality, well-paid work, education, housing). In the 'risk society' that is now replacing industrial society, your position in relation to environmental risks is more significant than your position in relation to the class structure. Class analysis, central to modern sociology, no longer tells the full story of how people's 'life chances' are shaped.

Zygmunt Bauman (1992) suggests that contemporary society has shifted from a society organised centrally around work to a society organised around consumption. In modern society, work provided people with their core identities and the important relationships that tied them to the larger society. In post-modern society, we locate our identities and social ties in our patterns of consumption – what we acquire and how we display it (see Chapter 15 for an extended discussion). While much classical sociological theorising about modernity emphasises shifts in the world of work as basic to social change, we need to move beyond this to develop new theories for post-modern society. Sociologists do not necessarily agree on these points, in particular on whether contemporary society is so fundamentally different that it needs a radical revision of existing theories.

According to a second interpretation, post-modernity is about the abandonment of the intellectual assumptions of modernity, especially the notions that human history has a discoverable meaning and that science can uncover absolute truth. While modernity took it for granted that we can establish 'overarching narratives' of history and progress, post-modernity involves turning our backs on any such attempt since all truth is relative and thus no interpretation of the course of history can ever claim absolute correctness. While the idea that truth is relative is perhaps hard for some scientists to accept, it may be easier for sociologists, especially those who work in the Weberian tradition. They are interested in the meanings that people use to guide their actions rather than in establishing whether those meanings are correct or incorrect. But the call to abandon *all* overarching narratives is rather more difficult. The impetus to do sociology reflects a desire to interpret the world in ways that make it meaningful, even if these are only fragmentary and partial interpretations. Sociology involves the construction of narratives and depends on a belief that these narratives are more than just 'stories', that they have some scientific basis. Faced with this way of understanding the concept of post-modernity, many sociologists deny that it makes any sense or has any relevance for their discipline.

A third approach to post-modernity sees it not as a historical successor to modernity nor as a rejection of its intellectual assumptions, but as an occasion to reflect on the experience of modernity (Kumar, 1995, p. 67) or, in Bauman's words, 'as modernity conscious of its true nature – *modernity for itself*' (1992, p. 187). Bauman argues that while modernity struggled to order and organise the world, much of the time this struggle gave rise to chaos, to 'variety, contingency and ambivalence'. Instead of trying to repress these outcomes as evidence of the failure of modernity, we should embrace and reflect on them in order to develop new sociological understandings of the contemporary human condition. From this point of view, post-modernity is best understood as a *stance* adopted by the sociologist. It involves an acceptance of social and cultural difference, a readiness to revise interpretations and an openness to competing perspectives. Above all, it implies a willingness to stand back and rethink the bases on which judgements and interpretations are made and the fundamental ideas that the discipline has developed. This approach is often called *reflexive sociology*. It is one that we try to maintain throughout this book as far as we can.

NEO-LIBERALISM, PUBLIC SOCIOLOGY AND ECONOMIC CRISIS

In the late 1990s and into the first decade of the 21st century, countries across Europe and the United States experienced an economic boom largely predicated on the availability of cheap credit. As financial and credit markets experienced deregulation, money became more available and speculation became rife. People who hitherto would have been considered 'credit risky' were encouraged to invest in home ownership, while the debts that they signed up to were repackaged as financial commodities that could be traded in the international marketplace.

When the financial markets began to fail in 2007 it became clear that capitalism had over-extended itself and a period of adjustment ensued. This is a rather anodyne way of describing a series of catastrophic events that has included the failure of long-established blue chip banks, mass foreclosures of housing, rising rates of personal indebtedness and growing unemployment. One way to understand the current crisis is to refer back to the classic work of Marx on the crisis-ridden nature of capitalism. But the current crisis also provides an opportunity for sociologists to reflect more critically on the social processes that underpin the crisis and how sociology itself may be implicated in them.

Michael Burawoy, former president of the American Sociological Association, has been promoting a form of 'public sociology' that he argues is a response to 'the growing gap between the sociological ethos and the world we study' (2005, p. 259). Burawoy advances an analysis of sociology based on a disciplinary division of labour that brings four different types of knowledge into a kind of antagonistic interdependence with each other: professional, critical, policy and public. Sociology, he asserts, operates in a field of power and it is primarily the role of sociology to engage with and defend the interests of civil society against the deleterious enchroachments of the market and the state.

Burawoy (2011) argues that the modern public university where sociology has flourished over the last 100 years is in crisis, a crisis that has its genesis in what he describes as 'a third wave marketisation'. This extends to every domain of life but has been especially visible in the financial sector. Marketisation associated with neo-liberalism and deregulation has laid the groundwork for the commodification of land and the environment, labour, capital and money and also knowledge. The decline of the public university system in the United States and the introduction of tuition fees in the United Kingdom are trends that point toward the privatisation of access to knowledge. Ironically, at a time when we talk with ease about the information economy and the knowledge society, access to knowledge itself as a publicly available good is in some respects becoming more difficult.

The recent financial implosions tellingly reveal that the financially savvy remain thin on the ground. Many people remain caught in what Ungar (2008) describes as a knowledge-ignorance paradox. Ironically, while society has become more economised, the individual capacity to actually grasp economic and financial information has declined. Innumeracy and economic illiteracy are widely found in modern 'advanced' societies (Ungar, 2008, p. 309). In the United States, the subprime mortgage market was premised on the principle that foolish clients would neither read nor understand the terms of the mortgage contained in the small print. In Ireland, a National Adult Literacy Agency study (NALA, 2010) revealed that 40 per cent of Irish people had difficulty with everyday maths. British research demonstrates that more than 6 million people in England do not understand numbers or how those numbers have an impact on their lives: 'they are confused by supermarket offers and bamboozled by tracker mortgages, calorie labels and petrol prices' (Leith, 2010).

As universities become more privatised (subject to the market and in particular the knowledge needs of corporate donors) they have also become more regulated (by the state) through the imposition of new standards of accountability, 'value for money' evaluation and increased pressure to raise university funding from the private sector. Burawoy sees this as leading towards an *instrumentalisation* of the research process, with a pathological emphasis on the quantification of outputs. He proposes an alternative model of the modern university that would re-embed the discipline of sociology in civil society.

Drawing on the insights of Weber and the critical theorists of the Frankfurt school, Burawoy argues against the pursuit of instrumental knowledge and in favour of reflexive knowledge that would involve a discussion of 'ends': in other words, 'what kind of values and goals should we pursue in society?' His ideas take on a new urgency in an era of economic crisis, when the economic growth models relentlessly pursued by neo-liberal governments around the world have crumbled to dust. Writing in a similar vein from an Irish perspective, Kirby and Murphy (2008) argue that Ireland's model of development as the Celtic Tiger era came to a close rested on values of individualism, income maximisation and economic growth as an end in itself rather than as a means to social development. The alternative model, they suggest, requires that values of social solidarity take priority, that economic growth becomes a means to sustainable and equitable social development and that decision-making processes be broadened to include a much wider range of stakeholders, exercising their franchise through a much broader set of means. Perhaps it is time for sociology to take on this task by situating itself more fully in the public sphere and seeking a more organic integration of its public, policy, professional and critical forms of knowledge.

2
Irish Sociology

There is currently much talk in professional and other sectors about the need for *reflexivity*. In other words, we need to be conscious of what we know, but also how we know it. Amongst other things, this means developing an understanding of where disciplinary areas of knowledge come from. A discipline, whether physics, geography or sociology, is a social construct and has its own history. In this chapter we attempt to piece together the data – which remains patchy and is still evolving – that can give us an idea of where Irish sociology has come from.

In Ireland sociology has never had the official status or public recognition that adheres to dominant discipline areas such as history, economics or psychology (Conway, 2006). It is a common complaint of sociologists that they do not have the media profile of their counterparts in other fields – there is as yet no Irish sociological equivalent of a Diarmaid Ferriter, David McWilliams or Maureen Gaffney. Sociologists are rarely called upon to offer commentary or expert critique, even on what might be regarded as 'social' matters, nor are their books to be found in the best-seller lists. On the other hand, it can be argued that the discourse of sociology has had quite a pervasive effect on Irish society, helping to frame many current debates and insinuating itself into the language of policy and critique.

In her analysis of the role of social scientists in Irish public life, anthropologist Eileen Kane (1996, p. 136) distinguishes between 'the intelligentsia' and 'intellectuals'. The former, she suggests, are in the business of producing easily identifiable knowledge that is useful for public administration, whereas the latter provide independent critical commentary about the state of the world, including how it is administered. It is tempting to see the first as acting within the system and the second as somehow outside of it, but Kathleen Lynch (1999b, p. 53) reminds us that in Ireland, as elsewhere, many intellectuals, even 'radical' ones, are relatively privileged and part of the structures of power. Sociologists may occupy either of these positions or combine them in different ways. Often, for example, they are employed by the state, in educational institutions, research centres or government agencies, but at the same time they do strive to develop a critique of the system of which they are a part. Needless to say, this can be a difficult balancing act.

Sociology has mainly been viewed in Ireland as an applied social science. Governments, funders of research, professional bodies and media commentators expect it to provide empirical data by which public policy can be guided. Its task is to analyse patterns and predict trends and to help the powerful to manage society, solve social problems and bring about desired forms of social change. It is also recognised as adding a useful dimension, even a human element, to the study for certain professions, such as medicine, nursing, law or education. But of all the social sciences, sociology is probably regarded as the least satisfactory and reliable public servant, less serious than other more 'scientific' disciplines like economics and political science. Kane suggests that for the public and policymakers, 'social scientists are seen to be, at best, jaywalkers, losing fact to science and meaning to literature' (1996, p. 133).

This understanding of the discipline is one-sided and '[slights] both the nature and potential of public life and the importance of other, more critical and theoretically informed versions of sociology' (Calhoun, 1996, p. 429). Sociology can do more than provide the data needed to carry out the 'technical activities' of ruling elites. It can also generate and inform public debate on the important issues of the day and subject 'the concepts, received understandings and cultural categories constitutive of everyday life and public discourse to critical theoretical reconsideration' (Calhoun, 1996, p. 429). As British sociologist Ken Plummer (2010, p. 3) poetically puts it:

> sociologists stand in awe and dreading, rage and delight at the humanly produced social world with all its joys and its sufferings. We critique it and we critically celebrate it. Standing in amazement at the complex patterns of human social life, we examine both the good things worth fostering and the bad things to strive to remove. Sociology becomes the systematic, sceptical study of all things social.

This chapter briefly outlines the variety of approaches in sociology before exploring the development of the discipline in Ireland. This development can be clearly linked to three main areas: the state, the Catholic Church and the interest of 'visiting' scholars. Each of these strands has had a long history in Irish social thought. Then the chapter describes the processes whereby the discipline of sociology has institutionalised itself, largely through the work of the Sociological Association of Ireland and the employment of sociologists in the tertiary education system. It examines the stimulus to sociological research provided by Ireland's increased focus on academic and scientific research, so much a part of the emergent 'knowledge economy'. Overall, we hope to provide a framework within which the nature and extent of contemporary Irish sociological work can be located.

VARIETIES OF SOCIOLOGY

There can be a variety of reasons for 'doing sociology'. These include a *managerial* objective to make government more effective and rational; a *critical* or *democratic* objective to inform and develop individuals so they can participate more fully in society and its government; and an *intellectual* objective to critically examine the social world and better understand it; this may even extend to a 'playful' objective, where the analysis is intellectually stimulating in itself. In Table 2.1 we can see the connection between these objectives and the four 'founding theorists' of sociology whose ideas about modernity and its development we outlined briefly in Chapter 1.

Table 2.1: Sociological approaches of the founding theorists

Playful/intellectual	Managerial	Critical/democratic
Simmel	Weber, Durkheim	Weber, Marx

Durkheim's writings reflect an instrumental and positivistic approach to sociology: it can provide the state with diagnoses of social trends that help it to manage society in a more rational and progressive and less conflictual manner. Marx offers a very different model: the sociologist as politically engaged critic who seeks to awaken and shape the consciousness of the public, in particular that part of it – the working class – that can bring about revolutionary social change. Simmel offers a third model. He was the first theorist to suggest that sociology should examine and analyse society at play as well as at work. It is possible to see his sociological work as a form of 'play' – a disengaged intellectual activity that sees playing the game as its own reward. The hardest person to locate in this simplified scheme is Weber. Less optimistic than Durkheim about the benefits of rationality and rational social management, Weber is closer to Marx in his attempts to develop sociology as a critical reflection on the long-term processes of social 'modernisation'. But Weber, unlike Marx, had no alternative vision to capitalist modernity. His work often seems, like Simmel's, to provide only its own reward in the intellectual pleasures of understanding and creative interpretation.

From its earliest days, sociology has been characterised by disagreement over its nature, purpose and social role. When we look at the history of the discipline in Ireland, we may expect to find similarly competing views as to what it is or should be about. This chapter is an attempt to sketch that history. It argues that sociology in Ireland has tended most often to reflect the Durkheimian managerial model. Its desired contribution has been to help improve, reform and rationalise how Irish society is governed, but there have been occasional flights from this position towards the critical/democratic stance, particularly in the late 1970s, and towards the playful/intellectual approach, particularly since the 1990s. We will try to explain, sociologically of course, why this has been the case.

THE DEVELOPMENT OF SOCIAL INQUIRY IN IRELAND

In 1934 the visiting American anthropologist Conrad Arensberg reported that he 'could not source any material on Irish sociology, indicating the absence of sociology (or anthropology) as a professional discipline at that time in Ireland' (Byrne et al.,

2001, p. XXXVn). Despite this valid claim, social inquiry has had a long history here. In recent years there has been an emerging literature that has sought to trace the history and development of sociology in Ireland. Though a full-length study has yet to emerge, a number of important writers, documents and institutions have been identified.

Conway (2006, p. 8) asserts that (as in other countries) 'Irish sociology was likely born sometime during the 19th century' and that this was 'outside the university setting' (p. 12). Writers such as Byrne et al. (2001), Hill (2005), Garvin and Hess (2006), Conway (2006), Murray (2005, 2009) and Murray and Feeney (2009, 2010) have begun to explore the development of sociological analysis of Irish society in quite considerable detail. They have helped to describe and analyse the three main sources of early sociological knowledge: the state; the Catholic Church; and overseas writers, including sociologists and anthropologists. The next part of this chapter outlines these three sources in more detail. The combination of these three powerful influences – state, church and external influence – produced a landscape of sociology in Ireland that was quite distinctive for many years. By contrast, in Sweden sociology developed very much from the discipline of philosophy (Larsson, 2008), whereas in Latin America it emerged from the study of law, with a specific focus on nation-building (Pereyra, 2008, p. 269).

OFFICIAL KNOWLEDGE

The emergence of sociology in Ireland, particularly the generation of 'statistics', was, as in other countries, inextricably linked to the operation of government and the development of the modern nation state. The word 'statistics' originally related to the study of how a state should be organised and embraced the legal, educational, public health, welfare, criminal and economic aspects of society. It gradually came to mean, more narrowly, quantitative information or 'figures' as states began to collect ever more numerical data as a way to monitor and regulate populations.

The first population census in Ireland (a 'private census of Mr Dobbs') was attempted in 1732 (Kennedy, 2001, p. 10) and was followed by another in 1821. The year 1824 saw a detailed educational census and in 1847 the first agricultural census was carried out. In 1854 there was an exhaustive census of landholding (Griffith's Valuation) throughout the country. These statistical exercises were an important element in the colonial administration of the country.

The first association in Ireland devoted to empirical social inquiry, the Dublin Statistical Society, was formed in 1847. Fifteen years later it was renamed the Statistical and Social Inquiry Society (SSIS). It celebrated its 150th anniversary in 1997 and continues its work to the present day (Daly, 1997, 1998; www.ssisi.ie). As Daly notes (1997, pp. 19–28), it was no coincidence that the Society was founded at the height of the Great Famine, which was a major challenge of governance to Britain's oldest colony.

An instrumental, state-sponsored view of social inquiry would have been widely shared across 19th-century Europe, but for Ireland there was an additional factor: it was a colony of Britain and disruptive and difficult to control. As with military technology, the technology of social inquiry found colonial Ireland a good terrain on which to experiment. The early formation of the discourse of social inquiry in Ireland occurred in circumstances where it was deemed important not only to increase the rationality of the state, but also to increase its control over society.

The early membership of the Dublin Statistical Society was drawn from the city's affluent male professional and intellectual elite – lawyers, Trinity College academics, businessmen, senior Dublin Castle officials and leading members of the Church of Ireland (Daly, 1998, p. 2). Few were interested in statistical techniques as such. Rather, they believed that systematic and objective, or 'scientific', information would help to answer the great social questions of the day and suggest a direction for reformative action by the state. Daly describes them as people who were generally optimistic about how Ireland was progressing economically in the wake of the Famine and who tended to share the 'assimilationist' view that 'the best recipe for further prosperity was to bring Irish laws and administrative practices into line with those in England and Wales'. For Boylan and Foley (1992), the social scientific inquiry that the Society fostered was not a 'value free universalistic science', but a key part of the 'civilising' project launched by a colonial elite that aimed to transform Ireland into, as Archbishop Whateley put it, 'a "really valuable portion of the British Empire" rather than a sort of "morbid excrescence"'(quoted in de Guistino, 1995, pp. 228–9).

During the first 25 years of its existence, the SSIS had a considerable impact on the United Kingdom's Irish legislation and on matters such as the management of poverty and of children in need. From the 1870s, its influence was undermined by the rise of nationalist and labour movement politics and none of those actively involved in these social movements was a member of the Society. Yet within a few years of the establishment of the Irish Free State, the SSIS was a significant political arena once again. It established close links with the new civil service and many senior public officials were active members (Daly, 1998, p. 4). Like its predecessor, the new Irish state continued to measure, count and analyse its population as part of its system of government. It found in the SSIS an appropriate forum for the generation of data and advice on the direction of policy.

By the 1950s the SSIS had become a prominent advocate of 'economic planning', particularly through the papers read to it and published in its *Journal* by T.K. Whitaker. By the 1960s, it was entering into 'a golden age … Many views first aired at its meetings had now been accepted as official policy. Economics and statistics appeared to offer a blueprint for a modern and prosperous Ireland, precisely as the Society's founders had hoped in 1847' (Daly, 1998, p. 7). In the process, 'social inquiry' had become largely redefined as economic and statistical inquiry. Most of the papers presented to the SSIS came from economists and statisticians, especially those employed by government departments and semi-state bodies, the Central Bank and the Central Statistics Office (Daly, 1997, p. 165). The marginalisation of sociology in the SSIS foreshadowed the marginal position it would occupy in the larger society but, simultaneously, it was also set free from the business of government to develop different understandings of its role and purpose.

Nevertheless, the instrumental and applied nature of social inquiry espoused by the SSIS strongly influenced the subsequent shaping of Irish sociology. With funding assistance from the American Ford Foundation, in 1959 the Society was central in the establishment of the Economic Research Institute (ERI). The foundation of the ERI was directly linked to the economic and social development in Ireland that was taking place under the 1960s Programmes for Economic Expansion (Murray, 2009, pp. 164–86). The ERI's early concerns – European integration, productivity and tariff protection – mirrored the concerns of the government of the day (Daly, 1997, p. 161). Despite this congruence, the ERI was explicitly 'non-political'. Following a review by the Danish social scientist Henning Friis (Jackson, 2004, p. 25; Murray, 2009, p. 180), it had 'social' added to its remit and became the ESRI in 1966. It became a key location for sociological research in the country and the chief employer of professional sociologists.

The ESRI has specialised in conducting large-scale social research that is predominantly numerical or quantitative in form. Research is addressed to issues seen as significant social or policy problems by the state and is undertaken with a view to making public policy and action more rational and effective. ESRI research has contributed in particular to our knowledge of class structure and mobility patterns in Ireland and of inequalities (particularly gender related) in access to education. The influence of the ESRI in defining what constitutes useful sociological knowledge has been felt in other state-funded research institutions such as Teagasc, the Health Research Board, the Educational Research Centre and the National Economic and Social Council (NESC). Over time, sociology has acquired a footing in all these sites, but what constitutes the discipline is fairly tightly defined.

In the new century the ESRI has continued to conduct policy-driven research, some of it in established fields where it has a well-merited international reputation, such as social mobility, poverty and disadvantage, education and labour market studies. It has also been active in areas that reflect the concerns of Ireland of the 2000s, such as immigration, sport, ageing, social capital and sexuality. It continues to have a strong influence on social research in Ireland, not least through the migration of some of its key sociologists to the universities, though it has had to engage in a much greater amount of externally funded activity.

SOCIOLOGY AND CATHOLIC SOCIAL TEACHING

In an analysis of the emergence of sociology in the West, Langer suggests that Catholicism has been less than helpful to the development of sociology, drawing attention to the comparative lack of development of the discipline in countries such as Austria and Spain. He argues that:

> Catholicism always generated its own 'social theories' which are usually less
> individualistic and less complex than the dominating theories of sociology. On
> the other hand they have more normative implications ... when sociology
> developed in a Catholic milieu it was either occupied with the question of 'social
> order' (especially how to stabilise the state) or strongly empirically oriented
> (usually in a later stage). Sociology as the secularised self-consciousness of
> modern society did not flourish on Catholic foundations. (Langer, 1992, p. 5)

The development of a Catholic-influenced sociology in Ireland reflected aspects of
the experience elsewhere. Sociology made sporadic appearances in academic circles
in Ireland from as early as 1910, when it was taught in University College Dublin
under the name of 'social philosophy'. Its adoption in the National University of
Ireland reflected the interest in social ethics stimulated by the papal encyclical *Rerum
Novarum* (1891) and later by the encyclical *Quadragesimo Anno* (1931), 'with its
concern for a counter to the trades unions and what was perceived as a drift on the
part of the working class towards socialism and communism' (Jackson, 1998, p. 1).

In 1944 the Catholic Truth Society published Father Peter McKevitt's book, *The
Plan of Society* (McKevitt, 1944). This textbook was intended to underpin the
course in Catholic sociology at the Maynooth seminary, where the Knights of
Columbanus had endowed a Chair of Sociology and Catholic Action in 1937.
However, the book had very little to say about Irish society per se. It was based on
an interpretation of aspects of European society in the context of papal encyclicals
and on the works of prominent European Catholic writers, with references to a very
small number of American and British sociologists. It also reflected the fact that
apart from some state-derived statistical information, there was a dearth of
indigenous sociological research within Ireland.

By the 1950s, the Catholic Church's interest in pastoral and community issues
and its strong involvement in voluntary associations and voluntary service
provision had led a number of its members to take an interest in the discipline of
sociology. The Christus Rex Society organised the teaching of sociology to selected
groups of religious in the late 1950s. It also published a journal, *Christus Rex*
(renamed *Social Studies* in 1973), that became an important outlet for Irish
sociological writing during the 1970s and 1980s. In addition, Catholic sociology
continued to exert considerable influence through its role in journals, institutions
and even the locations where sociologists met (Conway, 2006, pp. 13–15). It was
also involved in adult education through the Dublin Institute of Catholic Sociology,
founded in 1950 by Archbishop McQuaid and headed up by the Rev. James
Kavanagh, author of the widely read text *Manual of Social Ethics* (Kavanagh, 1954),
an outline of Catholic social thought on topics such as human rights, the family,
private property, capitalism and communism. The Institute organised an annual
Social Study Congress with prominent speakers (Conway, 2006, p. 14).

As in Spain (Langer, 1992, p. 12), clerics and former clerics were prominent as
early sociologists in Ireland. Thirty years after the appointment of Father Peter

McKevitt at Maynooth, the first chairs in university sociology departments were also given to Catholic priests – at University College Dublin, where James Kavanagh (later to become Archbishop of Dublin) was appointed in 1966, and at University College Galway. Clerics with a strong interest in sociology, including Professor Edward Coyne and Father Bill McKenna, were also instrumental in the establishment and development of the Jesuit-run College of Industrial Relations, now the National College of Ireland (Kennedy, 2001, pp. 181, 205). The first lay professor of sociology in the Republic of Ireland, Professor Damien Hannan, was appointed to University College Cork in 1971 and the second, Professor John A. Jackson, came to Trinity College Dublin in 1974.

In Irish universities, in contrast to the research institutions, Catholic social teaching and philosophy heavily influenced sociology, particularly in terms of the 'Catholic corporatism' that had developed in other European societies such as Belgium, Italy and the Netherlands. Whereas the positivist tradition in sociology inherited from the SSIS and similar organisations emphasised social research that served the state, the Catholic corporatist tradition focused on civil society. This referred to core institutions outside the state, for example the family, the community and the parish.

The relationship between the 'Catholic' and the 'official' elements in Irish sociology is interesting. Both tended to be positivistic and rather uninterested in theoretical issues and debates. Each took for granted that they could easily identify the proper objects of sociological research in the 'real world' (social problems) and tended to encourage empirical research rather than theoretical or conceptual development. Lynch (1987, p. 117), talking about the sociology of education, though her remarks can be applied to the discipline as a whole, suggests that 'the Catholic view of the good – in terms of social order – has been transformed from being a religious ideal into a conceptual model of the world that purports to represent empirical reality'. Yet the perceived consumers of 'official' and 'Catholic' research were quite different in each case: for the former, the state and its agents; for the latter, 'the people', variously defined.

The extent to which early Irish sociology approached any form of social critique or defined social problems independently of a statist perspective was due to the influence of the Catholic tradition. It remains a discernible influence on the activities of bodies like Focus Ireland, Social Justice Ireland and the Jesuit Centre for Faith and Justice. Catholic social teaching, on the other hand, had provided considerable opposition to the enthusiasm among members of the SSIS during the 1940s for the introduction into Ireland of a British-style welfare state (Daly, 1998, p. 6; Kennedy, 2001, p. 192). There is also no doubt that some Catholic clergy sought to appropriate Irish sociology so as to prevent it from becoming a vehicle for the importation of socialist or Marxist ideas into Irish society.

FOREIGN VISITORS

Today we think of Ireland as a particularly globalised society, but in fact it has long been a society of interest to thinkers and writers across the world. After a period of historical neglect, the work in and on Ireland of some major international thinkers of the 19th century has begun to attract attention. The work on Ireland of writers such as Harriet Martineau, Gustave de Beaumont and Alexis de Tocqueville is beginning to be explored, while there is a renewed recognition of the importance of Marx's and Engels's work on Irish society (Hazelkorn, 1980; Slater and McDonough, 2008; Ó Síocháin, 2009; see 'Marx on Ireland' below). Analysis of these works has helped to locate the analysis of Irish society within a broader sweep of European and American social and political analysis.

Martineau, de Beaumont and de Tocqueville visited Ireland in the first half of the 19th century (between 1831 and 1852) and reported on their experiences to an international audience: they 'applied a sociological lens to Ireland's then impoverished situation' (Conway, 2006, p. 10), which was of international interest. As we outlined in Chapter 1, Harriet Martineau is increasingly being recognised as a major founder of the discipline of sociology. Her writings spanned many topics and fields, but Ireland was a significant one. Her work can mainly be found in *Ireland: A Tale* (1832), which, like much of her other work, made use of the novel form to express her observations, and in *Letters from Ireland* (1852), based on a series of letters she dispatched from post-Famine Ireland to the London newspaper, the *Daily News* (Conway, 2006, p. 9).

In 1835 the French writer Gustave de Beaumont travelled to Ireland with his friend and fellow writer Alexis de Tocqueville, the celebrated author of *Democracy in America*. He returned in 1837 and two years later his observations and analysis of pre-Famine Ireland were published in two volumes as *L'Irlande Sociale, Politique et Religieuse*. This book was republished (in English) in 2006 with an introduction by Tom Garvin and Andreas Hess (2006), who describe it (p. vi) as 'one of the first sociological bestsellers in France'. De Beaumont was highly critical of the role of landowners in Ireland and noted the poverty and inequality brought about by an inequitable society. He argued that 'Ireland was to the United Kingdom what slavery was to the United States' (Garvin and Hess, 2006, p. xi). He prophesied 'the emergence of an Ireland of small owner-occupier farmers'. His book is 'a classic account of the painful birth pangs of Irish democracy, Ireland providing in miniature a model of the struggle for democracy against feudalism in Europe' (Garvin and Hess, 2006, p. xiii).

De Beaumont's analysis is reminiscent of anthropologist Clifford Geertz's notion of 'thick description', i.e. 'a wide range of readings and possible interpretations, usually derived from a broad variety of sources. Detailed note-taking, interviews with experts and other knowledgeable sources, direct observation, the collection and careful study of secondary sources such as journals, government reports, books and studies, as well as detailed notes from travel books and diaries, all contributed to the final draft' (Garvin and Hess, 2006, p. xiv). Similar approaches were to be taken by the many anthropologists who subsequently visited Ireland.

Marx on Ireland

According to Slater and McDonough (2008), Marx had a far more complex understanding of the colonialisation of Ireland than can be accounted for by dependency theory. They develop this argument on the basis of a close examination of Marx's 1867 *Outline of a Report on the Irish Question to the Communist Educational Association of German Workers in London*, which was delivered during the height of Fenian activity in Britain.

In the case of Ireland, Marx argued that colonialism – from the Plantations to the 1860s – impacted on all aspects of Irish civil life, including political representation, the legal code between the landlord and tenant, the economy, the population structure, emigration, the ecology of agricultural production and the physical and mental health of the native population.

Marx's account implies that colonialism can violate the ecology of the colonised society as well as its economic, political and social integrity. Slater and McDonough argue that the control exercised by the colonising regime meant that a colonial agenda became inescapable. In the Irish case, the colonial agenda meant supporting a feudal landlord caste and a feudal mode of production.

Marx's account of Irish history indicates that there cannot be a general theory of colonialism, with a single 'prime mover', because colonialism depends on the conjunction of the forces operating in the political regime with those in the local economy and civil society. Marx provides the theoretical tools for conceptualising colonialism as a social process, making it possible to trace the *particular* colonial tendencies operating within a *specific* colonised society.

An important influence on the formation of Irish sociology has been the subsequent work of foreign sociologists and anthropologists, particularly the latter. Anthropology normally deals with 'other' societies perceived to be very different to our own. We are familiar with the idea of anthropologists leaving the Western world to go and inquire into the 'primitive' peoples of Africa or the South Pacific, but for anthropologists in Britain, Europe, the United States and Australia, Ireland itself often provided a suitably exotic, or even 'primitive', location for research, made even more attractive by the fact that the society was (mainly) English speaking. This generated a steady stream of anthropological researchers, from Browne and Haddon in the 1890s (Curtin and Wilson, 1989, p. ix) to Eipper, Wilson, Peace, Saris and others in the 1980s and 1990s, seeking to understand our mysterious ways (Wilson and Donnan, 2006).

The most influential of such anthropological research remains that by two American social anthropologists, Conrad Arensberg and Solon Kimball, conducted in a farming locality in north Co. Clare in the early 1930s. The striking feature of their work, compared to other social research carried out in Ireland at that time or in the following 40 years, was that it addressed a problem set not by the state, church or any other 'external' body, but from within the discipline of anthropology itself (Byrne et al., 2001). Arensberg and Kimball, following the research practices developed in America by Lloyd Warner (in his 'Yankee City' studies) and Robert and Helen Lynd (*Middletown*, 1929), wanted to discover how communities work. How do people who live in them behave towards each other? How does this behaviour add up to a set of patterns or 'social system' that can reproduce itself over long periods of time, even when the individuals involved have gone and have been replaced by new ones? Warner and others had developed the idea that communities can be analysed as integrated systems made up of interrelated parts that are 'functionally interdependent'. They had tested this theory through research in American, largely urban, communities. Arensberg and Kimball wanted to see if the theory held true in a remote and isolated rural community. Their interest was not initially in Irish society at all but in testing and developing a theoretical idea about how societies should be understood.

We could thus locate Arensberg and Kimball towards the playful/intellectual end of the spectrum outlined in Table 2.1, but it was their detailed observations about rural Ireland that made the greatest impact on Irish social researchers. Almost inevitably, given how social inquiry has been understood in Ireland, they were seen to be writing about a 'social problem': small or marginal farming in the underdeveloped western periphery. Arensberg and Kimball's work set the agenda for sociological research into urban (Humphreys, 1966) as well as rural Ireland and the context for analyses of the 'modernisation' of Irish social and cultural development for much of the next 40 years. It was only in the 1970s that critical assessment and discussion of their approach began to take place, marking a watershed in the development of sociology as a discipline in Ireland (Tovey, 1992).

Sociology on the buses: The 1967 Tavistock Dublin Bus Study
In 1946, just one year after the Second World War, a London-based non-profit research institute under the title of the Tavistock Institute of Human Relations was established to carry out empirical research on various aspects of industrial life in England. It conducted a range of studies of work and working lives ranging from the social organisation of employment in coal mines and textile mills to evaluation research. *Human Relations*, the journal of the research institute, provided an outlet for much of its published work.

Industrial unrest among Dublin bus workers in the 1960s provided the impetus for the then chairman of Coras Iompair Éireann (CIE), Todd Andrews, to enlist the help of the Tavistock Institute to better understand the factors influencing work morale among busmen in Dublin city. This was a period marked by industrial unrest in relation to a new 'one man one bus' policy introduced by the national transportation company. The Tavistock study – based on interviews with drivers, union officials and managers carried out by five researchers and guided by socio-technical systems theories emphasising shared rather than hierarchical decision-making in work contexts – was envisaged to involve a data collection phase followed by a strongly practical-minded phase aimed at bringing about on-the-ground changes in industrial practices. Empirically, the study focused on the nature of the work of the Dublin bus drivers and their relations with managers and union officials. The findings of phase one confirmed what bus workers already knew – that morale was low and declining.

The second practical phase of the Tavistock study ran aground, however, as a result of the politics of research publication. Even when the partially completed study was published, media pundits and CIE representatives homed in on the study's dated empirical material. The wider – if neglected – lesson of the study was that it highlighted what it termed a 'privatisation' trend among Dublin bus workers by which was meant a tendency to put individual needs and interests ahead of those of the collectivity (Murray, 2005).

THE INSTITUTIONALISATION OF IRISH SOCIOLOGY

By the 1970s, Irish sociology was becoming consolidated as a distinct discipline, developing the features, such as career paths, standardised curricula, organisations and publication outlets, that help to establish a field of academic endeavour. In this it was very similar to comparable countries, such as New Zealand (Crothers, 2008) and Sweden (Larsson, 2008). By the mid-1970s there were four or five sociologists in each of the departments in University College Dublin, University College Cork and Trinity College Dublin (TCD) and two in the Department of Political Science and Sociology at the National University of Ireland, Galway (NUIG) (Jackson, 1998). Lecturers in sociology began to be appointed to the teacher training colleges and the Regional Technical Colleges (RTCs). Publication outlets for sociological work were increasing. The *Economic and Social Review* (ESR), a journal produced under the auspices of the ESRI, was first published in 1970. Though it published more papers from economists than from any other discipline (O'Dowd, 1988, p. 20), it did publish an increasing number of sociological papers over time. In 1973, *Social Studies* rose out of the ashes of the previous *Christus Rex* journal (Conway, 2006, p. 15).

The international influence continued to make itself felt. The ESRI employed a significant number of researchers who had received their sociological training abroad, especially in the United States. In the university sector, while many staff had taken a first degree in Ireland, virtually all had received postgraduate sociology training abroad (including later President of Ireland, Michael D. Higgins). Staff employed in the National University colleges had generally trained in America; in TCD the links were predominantly with Britain.

Both foreign and foreign-trained sociologists were instrumental in carrying out a form of 'technology transfer' in the importation to Ireland of (particularly) British and American models of sociological theorising and research. It could be argued that the development of sociology in Ireland was dependent, in a similar way that the sociology of other less powerful Western countries was, for example in Australia, Scandinavia and Canada. The sociology of the core countries, in particular the United States, the UK, Germany and France, has long dominated the development of the discipline in smaller peripheral countries. In the latter the resources devoted to sociology are comparatively small and these countries rely heavily on their 'big brothers'. This is especially the case when, as with Ireland and Britain, the similarities between the countries (not least linguistically) appear at least on the surface to be substantial. This may explain why Irish sociologists have long drawn on the work of those in the core economies (principally the UK and the US) rather than in countries that we may have more in common with economically, politically and socially, such as Finland, Austria or New Zealand.

American-trained sociologists working in Ireland largely adhered to structural functionalist theoretical models, while staff from Britain were largely followers of one or another variant of Marxism, which enjoyed a revival in Britain and Europe in the late 1960s and 1970s. During the following decade, other theoretical perspectives began to emerge and be used, such as symbolic interactionism, phenomenology and ethnomethodology. These interpretive approaches challenged both Marxist and functionalist realist worldviews. A growing interest in qualitative rather than quantitative methods, stimulated by feminist thought as well as by anthropology, challenged the dominance of positivist orientations in research. This theoretical and methodological pluralism stimulated new topics for research and new issues for debate. O'Dowd notes (1988, p. 4) that some sociologists feared that this 'hindered the development of the discipline' and, in particular, 'undermined its potential contribution to policy-making'. It seemed likely to alienate prospective funders who saw a discipline riven with internal controversies and arguments about its own theoretical assumptions and research practices.

A highly significant milestone in the institutionalisation of sociology was the establishment in 1973 of the Sociological Association of Ireland/Cumann Socheolaíochta na hÉireann (SAI). The SAI has carried out the normal range of activities of a professional association: hosting annual conferences and occasional seminars, maintaining a website (www.sociology.ie) and, from the 1990s, publishing an academic journal, the *Irish Journal of Sociology*. The impact of the SAI as a forum for debate and self-recognition has been invaluable. During its first decade, its conferences were the site of lively arguments that pitted Marxism against functionalism; modernisation theory against dependency theory; revisited Arensberg and Kimball and the conception of Irish 'peasant' society; or disagreed over how to interpret the place of 'community' in Irish life.

In the 1980s the SAI sought to further professionalise sociology. It established principles of employment for research workers and developed a research code of ethics. At one point the Association appeared to be moving towards becoming an exclusive professional body that would monitor and regulate the right to practise. This initiative raised issues about access to membership – which had always been very open – and there were stormy debates about the purpose of the SAI and, more broadly, of sociology itself. For some there was still the idea that the prestige of the discipline depended on its 'relevance' to society, defined in statist or social problems terms, while others were committed to a more critical and detached orientation.

An important contribution by the SAI to the consolidation of the discipline was its sponsorship of publication of the 'Studies in Irish Society' collections: *Power, Conflict and Inequality* (1982), *Culture and Ideology in Ireland* (1984), *Gender in Irish Society* (1986) and *Whose Law and Order? Aspects of Crime and Social Control in Ireland* (1988). It also commissioned two Irish sociology textbooks in 1986 and 1995. Together with Peillon's *Contemporary Irish Society* (1982) and the ESRI book *Understanding Contemporary Ireland* (Breen et al., 1990), these texts were widely used in teaching and significantly shaped the development of Irish sociology.

IRISH SOCIOLOGY SINCE THE 1990s

In 1991, after a decade of economic stagnation, the Irish government agreed to make funds available for a programme of educational expansion in response to demographic and social pressures on third-level places. This supported the expansion of sociology across the tertiary sector and saw the emergence of more opportunities for graduate study in particular. At the same time, new sources of funds for research became available, mainly from the EU. For the first time, large-scale research became a possibility for Irish sociologists. After decades of state resistance (Murray and Feeney, 2009, 2010) government departments began to fund research either through the employment of researchers or by commissioning research from the universities and research institutes. Small, independent research consultancies were set up by sociology graduates and flourished in the new research climate. In 1995 the Royal Irish Academy set up a Social Science Research Council to support research projects and postgraduate training (Jackson, 2004, pp. 35–8).

In the late 1990s the billionaire Irish-American philanthropist Charles 'Chuck' Feeney, through his organisation Atlantic Philanthropies, pumped large amounts of money into the development of academic research in Ireland, significantly shifting Irish state policy in the process (O'Clery, 2007, p. 269). The resulting Programme for Research in Third Level Institutions (PRTLI) underpinned significant investment in social research, including sociology, through the establishment and funding of bodies such as the National Institute for Regional and Spatial Analysis (NIRSA), centred at NUI Maynooth; the Institute for the Study of Social Change at UCD; and the Institute for International Integration Studies at TCD. Since 1999 the state has funded scholarships for postgraduate social research, thereby greatly expanding the opportunities for Irish students to conduct sociological research. Whereas formerly the narrowness of the funding base meant research had tended to be closely tied to specific policy issues (Lynch, 1999b, pp. 44–6), a more generous funding environment has led to the emergence of a broader approach to sociological research.

Though figures are hard to come by, sociologists have increasingly been employed in both the state sector and in private industry, such as market research and consultancy companies. Sociologists made a significant impact through the policy-oriented research programmes of state advisory and advocacy bodies such as the Combat Poverty Agency and the National Consultative Committee on Interculturalism and Racism (both bodies were closed down by the Fianna Fáil/Green coalition government in 2008–9) and the Crisis Pregnancy Agency (merged into the Health Service Executive in 2010).

The investment in research funding has seen the number of sociology books and articles published in and about Ireland significantly increase, reflecting the dynamic nature of contemporary Irish society. Subjects have included 'established' topics such as education, religion, inequality, housing, the family and community, but have also explored topics of popular interest such as globalisation and the mass media; Travellers and Irish society; immigration, multiculturalism and racism; sport; and sexuality. These issues continue to reflect matters that are of immediate concern to politicians, public servants and opinion formers: they might be interpreted as sociologists' attempts to address public issues that have arisen in contemporary Ireland. But there have also been attempts to analyse the perhaps more everyday and mundane indicators of change in Irish society and culture, such as food and drink, traffic, popular music, public art, shopping and celebrity culture. The series published by the Institute of Public Administration, *Sociological Chronicles*, has provided a platform for this type of analysis in particular.

Despite this expansion of output, it is perhaps surprising that sociology has not really managed to establish itself within Irish life as a significant or stimulating guide to how that life is changing. While Langer (1992, p. 1) suggests that in Western society as a whole 'sociology has become the most popular way for society to interpret itself … firmly integrated into … everyday communication', in Ireland such influence seems to rest more clearly with historians, literary critics and, increasingly, psychologists. How then, with its history to date, should we evaluate the contribution that Irish sociology has made to Irish society? Does Irish society need Irish sociology at all?

Bonner (1996) has suggested that Irish sociology has been good at producing substantial factual knowledge about Irish society but has left questions of sociological theory largely unexplored. He reflects the claim of historian J.J. Lee (1989, pp. 562–643) that there has been an underdevelopment of philosophy or theorising in contemporary Irish life compared to our much stronger aesthetic and literary traditions. History and psychology are very popular ways to interpret reality, given their emphasis on the narrative and on the individual.

Similarly for Kane (1996, pp. 139–45), positivistic thinking has been endemic within Irish society. It has 'shaped not only the social sciences, but official and public expectations about the nature of reality and what constitutes credible evidence as a basis for action'. The result is a 'stultifying empiricism'; a sociology oriented towards 'social engineering' that has seen as its primary audience the state and, formerly, the Catholic Church. As a result, Kane argues, Irish sociology has emphasised pathology, crime and deviance; poverty and unemployment; violence, drugs and alcohol; the conditions of some minorities; and the problems of rural areas. These are all fields that 'have symbolic and political resonance for both church and state'. A further consequence for Kane is that Irish sociology (like most others) studies 'down, in class and power terms, rather than up', with very little, if any, research being done on the powerful social groups in society. That is left to (a few) investigative journalists and, in recent years, various public tribunals of inquiry.

Kane contrasts this type of sociology with critical theory, which sees research as part of an attempt 'to facilitate transformation towards a desired end' (1996, p. 140). For critical theorists, knowledge is always embedded in its socio-historical context. They ask 'knowledge for whom?'; 'knowledge for what?' Inquiry is thus 'a political act'. Kane remarks that critical theory can also produce a top-down or paternalistic perspective on the subjects studied. It sees others as in need of truth and empowerment, not the theorists themselves. It 'seeks to transform the world view of others, while failing to seek the insights of those whose thinking we are liberating to liberate our own' (1996, p. 141). Kathleen Lynch has also been a major critic of contemporary Irish sociology from within the discipline and has urged sociologists to adopt an approach to research that empowers those researched and overtly addresses issues of power within the research process (1999b).

In the decade and a half since Kane and Bonner made their critiques of Irish sociology, there has been substantial growth in publishing in the discipline. The terrain of Irish sociological research and writing has expanded to embrace a more diverse and eclectic range of approaches, ranging from state-sponsored, large-scale quantitative research to more speculative, qualitative and interpretive work. Much of this work is outlined and discussed in the remainder of this book, though it is not possible to span the whole field and we have not had the space to consider some important work. Nevertheless, we would suggest that there is enough relevant and interesting contemporary research in Ireland to ensure that sociology remains a significant and valuable element of the social sciences, even if it sometimes has to struggle for its place in the sun.

3
The Dynamics of Irish Development

In Chapter 1 we introduced sociology as *the study of modernity*. We suggested that to sociologists, a 'modern' society is one that is rational, industrial, urban and usually capitalist. Clearly, Irish society has become more urbanised and more industrialised (or more post-industrialised) in the past 35 years. But in comparison to other European states like Britain, Germany or France, it is doing so considerably later. As a consequence, Ireland is often described as a 'late moderniser', i.e. a latecomer to modernity. There is an assumption that there is a condition called 'being modern' or 'modernity' and that change in Irish society represents a shift towards this condition. But when we consider this further, some interesting questions are raised. If we say Ireland is becoming modern, what are we comparing it to? Are we implying it has become more like those societies that industrialised early? Or is there a different, specific way of 'being modern' that characterises late modernisers like Ireland? And if we say that Ireland is modern now, what are we implying about the past and about the processes of change that have occurred? There are also broader questions that might be raised about Ireland as a modern capitalist state at a time when capitalism itself is facing serious crisis.

We begin this chapter with a brief overview of sociological accounts of how societies 'become modern'. These are usually referred to as theories of social change or theories of development. Two general points can be made about these before we go on to look at specific examples. First, the question of how to explain change or development has been central to the growth of sociology as a discipline. It has produced much disagreement between sociologists, not just about details of the theory, but also about the theories themselves as ways to understand social life. These are also more than just academic disagreements. In the contest between sociological theories of change, we find resonances of the clash of ideas between elites in Irish society about how to understand our history and how to locate Ireland as part of the contemporary world. Sociological theories both influence and are influenced by the ideas held by important social groups in society. Nowhere is this more obvious than in relation to social change, as interpretations of the past are often used to explain and justify movements towards a particular sort of future.

The second point relates to the concept of development itself. Until recently, much sociology identified 'development' with 'becoming modern', but this is increasingly seen as simplistic. As sociologists become more reflexive in thinking about society, they have become less certain that modernity is the most 'developed' condition to which societies can or should aspire. The values that underpin the ideal of modernity, discussed in Chapter 1, no longer command automatic allegiance, as the problems generated by the continuous pursuit of 'progress' threaten to outweigh its benefits. This is brought into particularly sharp relief during times of crisis, when the pursuit of growth as an end in itself proves unsustainable – as we have witnessed in the crash in the Irish (and indeed global) economy since 2008.

The sociological debate over development is itself characteristic of modernity and may lose its rationale as our faith in continual progress is eroded. We may have to approach it in a more questioning and critical way than before and recognise that there is more than one way for a society to be modern. This is especially helpful to a society such as ours that has for so long felt the pressure to see itself as 'unmodern' or backward compared to the rest of the world. If there are *varieties of modernity*, then there is the potential to make real choices about how we want to develop in the future. We may also rediscover the value of our past instead of downgrading it as 'less than modern'. Sociological theorising helps us to examine not only how the world is, but also how we think about the world.

THEORIES OF DEVELOPMENT

In this section we outline the three dominant ways of thinking about social change and development: the theories of *modernisation*, *dependency* and *globalisation*. We will not discuss them in great detail, as we are mainly interested in providing a context within which to examine recent change in Irish society.

Sociological studies of development long assumed the best way to understand social change was to take a single society, analyse it in detail and then compare it to others to see what resemblances could be found on selected dimensions. This seemed a natural way to proceed, as theorists took for granted that the societies of the world could be ranked on a *continuum* of development, from the most developed or 'modern' to the least. It was suggested that if we knew the main structural or cultural features of the most modern societies, we could interpret change in other societies as evolution towards these. This approach underpins *modernisation* theory. It has shaped the ideas of elite social groups, academics such as sociologists and historians, policy-makers and ordinary people, in Ireland and in many other countries, during much of the period since the Second World War.

In the 1980s and 1990s a very different perspective on development emerged in sociology. It argues that to understand the changes taking place in particular societies, we must start with an examination of the relationships that connect countries and regions into an international 'system'. It implies that no society exists in isolation: all are influenced in very significant ways by international trends and relationships. This approach underpins both *dependency* and *globalisation* theory. Below we note some contrasts in how these theories explain social change in general before going on to look specifically at Irish society.

MODERNISATION THEORY

Modernisation theory is used in sociology to mean a complex set of interconnected ideas, but two of its key features are:

- An evolutionary account of social change.
- The belief that all societies in the world are converging at different speeds and from different starting points towards the same point – modern industrial society.

Many of the 19th-century social thinkers we met in Chapter 1 (including Comte, Tönnies and Durkheim) were greatly influenced by Charles Darwin's ideas about evolutionary change in nature. They sought to apply these ideas to an understanding of social change, suggesting that we could treat societies as analogous to natural species that developed through the process of 'survival of the fittest'. More complex forms of social organisation are better adapted to survival within their environment and thus replace simpler forms. Therefore, nation states replace tribal societies; factory production replaces the craft worker; the supermarket replaces the local grocery store; and social networking supersedes the limitation of face-to-face interaction. Evolutionary interpretations of social change encouraged the assumption that change is unidirectional – that there is one pattern of change, from primitive (simple, 'traditional') to modern (highly complex, highly adapted to survival) – and that all societies must eventually follow this pattern. They also encouraged the belief that development is 'an imitative process, in which the less developed countries gradually assumed the qualities of the industrialised nations' (Hettne, 1990, p. 60). Ultimately they reflected a belief that change equals progress, thus establishing the most 'modern' societies as the model that developing societies should try to emulate. Since the social theorists involved were all from the West and took for granted that this was where the most 'advanced' countries were found, this approach encouraged an ethnocentric view that saw 'modernisation' in terms of 'Westernisation'. Thus, modernisation theory defined a clear task for development analysts (including sociologists, economists and political theorists): identify the qualities of modern societies that are to be imitated and suggest ways to facilitate their imitation.

Rostow (1960) was a particularly influential modernisation theorist. He argued that as societies converge towards modernity, they pass through a sequence of distinct stages of development ('traditional', 'pre-modern', 'modernisation take-off' and so on). We can take a society and by looking at specific features within it (does it have a mass education system? how developed is its banking system? how urbanised is it?) we can say what stage of modernisation it has reached. We can then use this finding to explain other features, such as its type of family structure or the extent of secularisation. This indicates further changes needed to move the society to the next development stage. We can see that modernisation theory can be not just an explanation for social change, but a justification to direct social change in a particular way. Its influence on leaders of both modern and modernising societies has made it something of a self-fulfilling prophecy.

If societies change by evolving through particular development stages into the 'modern' form, what starts the process off? Some modernisation theorists see *technological innovation*, perhaps imported by a modernising elite, as the starting point. Technological change in agriculture, such as the introduction of mechanical harvesters or tractors, may set off a process in which many agricultural workers become redundant, move to urban centres and contribute to the development of industry. Modernisation theorists argue that social change follows a 'logic of industrialisation': once the technology is present, industrialisation and its accompanying social changes inevitably follow. In turn, the division of labour becomes more complex, as large-scale industrial production requires a wide range of specialised and technical skills. The society becomes more 'open' or meritocratic as jobs need to be assigned to people on the basis of their skills, rather than any inherited social position. There is increased equality of opportunity and social mobility and reduced social conflict as different class, ethnic or regional groups come to share the goals of further development and higher standards of living. Other cultural changes follow, for example a decline in the influence of religion, or secularisation (see Chapter 13). In short, once the technological changes occur that let industry 'take off', social changes follow the same logic in all industrialising societies and they become more and more alike.

For other modernisation theorists, social change is driven by cultural change, especially in *social values*. It is the values and attitudes of the developed West, rather than its technology, that must be implanted into more traditional societies before industrial development can begin. There is a parallel here with Weber's theories about the relationship between particular sets of ideas and capitalist development. The term 'traditional' was used to imply that societies not only lacked the science and technology of the advanced world, but were trapped within traditional culture. For example, they valued people more for their 'ascribed' than their 'achieved' characteristics; preferred face-to face, personalised relationships to impersonal, detached ones; and social interaction was influenced more by kinship or familiarity than by universal rules. Modernisation theory implies that such values are an obstacle to cultural and economic development.

In summary, modernisation theory suggests that the social organisation and cultural features of a society can largely be explained by identifying the 'stage of development' it has reached on the path towards modernity. It seems to offer a powerful analysis of change because it treats societies as integrated systems where change in one part (for example, the organisation of work) leads to changes in almost every other part. While its roots go far back into the thinking of the 'classical' social theorists, particularly Durkheim and Weber, in the hands of later theorists, discussions of modernity have often narrowed into checklists of technical and cultural criteria. A major concern of the classical theorists had been to understand specific historical patterns of change in the countries of early Europe, but modernisation theorists universalised these analyses into an account of global evolution. They eschewed the strong sense of ambivalence towards modernity that had characterised the classical theorists' discussions, such as Weber's concerns about the effect of increasing bureaucratisation and rationalisation on the human spirit, Durkheim's analysis of anomie or Marx's scathing analysis of the roots of alienation.

The most damaging legacy of modernisation theory may be the simplistic conception of change as a transition from 'traditional' to 'modern'. The term 'traditional' took on pejorative overtones. It no longer simply referred to societies whose culture and ways of organising political, social or economic life were different from those of the most powerful European societies; rather, it suggested such societies were inferior, as they had failed to develop modern forms. This position of innate superiority became a particular target in the critique of modernisation theory launched by dependency theorists.

DEPENDENCY THEORY

Modernisation theory treats traditional societies as unchanging and isolated from contact with the outside world, and once technological or cultural change is introduced, the process of differentiation and evolution towards higher stages of development unfolds according to its own logic, independent of relationships with other societies. The theory has been heavily criticised on both counts, particularly by dependency theorists.

The first to outline dependency theory was a German-born economist working in South America, André Gunder Frank. It is significant that he came from Latin America, a part of the world that has had long experience of colonial domination. To Frank, it was inconceivable that the pattern of social change in any single society could be explained without reference to its past and present relationships with others. Moreover, by the late 1960s, when he put forward his theory, Latin American countries were no longer colonies. Most had been politically independent since the 19th century and had been trying to develop and modernise themselves, yet most remained economically underdeveloped. To Frank, it was clear that there was no universal, linear pattern of change by which less developed countries 'converged' with more developed ones. He argued (1967) that all countries are part of an international system that affects societies in different ways. Some, mainly early-industrialising Western countries that had been colonisers, have been able to establish relationships with others, particularly those that had been colonised. These are essentially relationships of exploitation. Through these relationships, the dominant or core countries systematically funnel out the wealth created in the underdeveloped countries. The wealth accumulates in the developed countries, both as capital and as 'human capital'. Frank argued that it was wrong to see underdeveloped societies as being behind or outside the development process; rather, both developed and underdeveloped societies are part of a single international system. Underdeveloped societies have been underdeveloped and maintained in a state of underdevelopment by the core countries that have developed at their expense. Lack of development is not the result of the value systems or technologies of the underdeveloped countries, but lies with the core countries and the resultant relationships.

Frank refused to label less developed societies 'traditional'. For him, this was a term that 'denies all history' to the society concerned. Developed societies do not have a monopoly on history. Underdeveloped ones also have a history, usually one of colonisation where the economy and social institutions were restructured to suit the colonisers. Their agriculture was reorganised, for example, to produce cash crops such as coffee, soybeans or rubber for export as industrial raw materials rather than food for home consumption. Thus, Brazil became a major exporter of coffee, the Middle East of oil and Malaysia of rubber. Irish agriculture under colonial rule specialised in the production of live beef cattle for export and processing in Britain. The history of colonised countries was therefore one of restructuring resulting in dependency. They became increasingly dependent on the core countries that profited from their underdevelopment for the sale of their agricultural exports and the import of industrial products. For Frank, this was 'the development of underdevelopment'. He argued that even when such countries gained political independence, they remained locked into international relationships that promoted the process of underdevelopment.

Modernisation theory saw world development as a process where modern societies helped traditional societies to develop through the transfer of new technology, social values or capital. Dependency theory challenged that account. It argued that the transfers were primarily in the opposite direction, from the poor countries to the rich. This generated much debate on whether it was ever possible for underdeveloped countries to break free from underdevelopment. But in the 1970s and 1980s it became apparent that many previously underdeveloped countries *were* experiencing social change in the form of industrialisation. By the late 1970s, for example, there were nearly a million workers employed in industrial production, including car-making, in Brazil, many earning well above the minimum wage. This phenomenon seemed to contradict the claim that development was impossible in dependent societies. But what sort of development was it?

Dependency theorists point out that transnational corporations (TNCs) – companies that operate across national boundaries rather than within several or many nations – have played a significant part in the new industrialisation process. TNCs do not just replicate their firms in different countries: their operations are underpinned by a structured division of labour. The production process is broken down into more and less skilled parts, or into stages further from and nearer to the finished product. These are located in different parts of the world depending on what a region has to offer. The TNC may be able to draw on a large unemployed or underemployed workforce, which is cheap to employ or docile to manage, or raw materials or access to a specific market. TNCs engender a new *international division of labour* that operates on a global level and shapes the possibilities for development of both the industrialised and the newly industrialising societies.

TNCs operate on a huge scale, with annual turnover often greater than the gross national product (GNP) of the country where they locate their branch plants. They can influence government policies on trade unionism or prevent the introduction of controls on environmental degradation if these are likely to push up production costs. Many sociologists refer to this as a form of *dependent development*.

In summary, dependency theorists put forward a number of theses that contrast sharply with the modernisation paradigm. For them, the most important obstacles to development are *not* internal characteristics of technology, capital or culture, but are external to the underdeveloped society and relate to its position in the international division of labour. In the international system, value is transferred mainly from the peripheral/underdeveloped societies to the core/developed societies. Development in the core *produces* underdevelopment in the periphery. Development and underdevelopment, taking place in different regions or spaces of the world, are parts of a single process.

FROM DEPENDENCY TO GLOBALISATION

During the 1970s and 1980s, dependency theory was exposed to intense discussion and debate. Critics asked if it was really possible to distinguish between dependent and independent economies and to allocate societies unequivocally to either category. The problems experienced by peripheral economies, as outlined by Frank, were said to be the product of a particular and temporary stage in global capitalist development: they did not represent a permanent relationship of exploitation. It was argued that the focus on external relationships encouraged dependency theorists to ignore relevant social or cultural features *internal* to dependent societies that could help explain their situation. Dependency theory was criticised for its failure to analyse class and power structures within dependent societies that could help to explain underdevelopment.

So intensive was the criticism of dependency theory that by the 1990s, it was seen by many to be no longer relevant. Nevertheless, it has had a major impact on social theorising, on the decline of the modernisation paradigm and on resistance to theories of development that simplistically equate modernisation with Westernisation and equate 'traditional' societies with societies that are non-Western in practices and culture. As a thesis about social change, the dependency approach has now evolved into theories of globalisation that shift the focus of analysis towards *interdependence*. These recognise that no country can exercise wholly autonomous control over its economy or society and that development cannot be said to result purely from internal factors. To understand change in any society or region, we must start from an overview of the world system and locate the networks of cross-national relations in which a particular country is enmeshed.

O'Hearn (1998, p. 14) argues that the concept of *interlinking commodity chains* is useful, where 'a global division of labour spans distinct core, semi-peripheral and peripheral regions'. World regions are organised into a hierarchy in terms of what they can offer to the commodity chain of a TNC, for example different forms of 'human capital': expensive research and development skills in one region; cheap factory labour in another. 'Economic development' then relates to how well a country or region can move towards higher-value, more sophisticated and more profitable activities. There are tensions and competition *within* the core, for example between the US and Europe, and between different regions within each of these, such as the 'sunbelt' and 'rustbelt' of America. Processes of global change continuously give rise to the peripheralisation of some core areas (Detroit) and the development of some peripheries into core economies (the BRIC – Brazil, Russia, India and China – economies in the 21st century). Indeed, it is widely suggested that in recent decades the world has become globalised in ways that are both quantitatively and qualitatively new. Thus, earlier approaches influenced by dependency theory may need to be replaced by new theories of globalisation.

Globalisation is a very broadly used concept and may be losing its explanatory power. Even at the end of the last century, British sociologist David Held and his colleagues noted the term had come to encompass everything from global financial markets to the Internet. For Held et al. (1999, p. 1), globalisation is:

> a widespread perception that the world is rapidly being moulded into a shared social space by economic and technological forces and that developments in one region of the world can have profound consequences for the life chances of individuals or communities on the other side of the globe.

It is linked to a pervasive sense of insecurity and uncertainty, as the forces that propel it forward are perceived to overwhelm the capacity of nation states and citizens to respond; globalisation demonstrates the limits to national politics.

Held et al. (1999) proffer a framework for thinking about globalisation that distinguishes three broad schools of thought: the *hyperglobalisers*, the *sceptics* and the *transformationalists*. The hyperglobalisation perspective sees global capital as the engine of economic growth and is a cheerleader for the possibilities offered by a neo-liberal global economic market. From this perspective, the old North–South division outlined by dependency theorists is 'an increasing anachronism as a new global division of labour replaces the traditional core-periphery structure with a more complex architecture of economic power' (p. 4). The emergence of Brazil, Russia, India and China on the economic world stage is evidence that globalisation can create new winners, albeit many countries remain losers in the system. Hyperglobalists see the nation state as declining in power, to be replaced by new forms of global governance and a global civil society.

In contrast, the sceptics argue that current globalisation must be seen in an historical context and that an international system of trade in labour and capital has been in place for several hundred years. For sceptics, Held et al. suggest, globalisation is no more than a process that enables interactions between economies that remain predominantly national. The nation state is not in decline: the power of national governments endures. World trade is dominated by regional alliances structured around the Americas, the Pacific Rim, China and the European Union. Many Third World countries remain excluded. Globalisation is less about creating greater interconnectedness between states and more about reproducing entrenched economic inequalities.

The transformation perspective is espoused by sociologists such as Castells, Giddens and Sassen. They see globalisation as a powerful transformative force, not deterministic but emergent, contingent and subject to contradiction. It is 'a long-term historical process inscribed with contradiction and shaped by conjunctural factors' (Held et al., 1999, p. 7). The current era of globalisation is marked by the emergence of new patterns of global stratification in which some states are incorporated more fully into globalised economic relations while others are excluded. Globalisation does produce relations of inequality, but these are recast over time. Furthermore, the position of the nation state is transformed: sovereignty, territoriality and state power no longer coincide as labour and capital circulate globally and new forms of regulation and governance emerge at the supranational level.

Contemporary globalisation has evolved through ideologies and policies of neo-liberalism such as marketisation and deregulation. These have come under intense scrutiny in the wake of the worldwide financial crash of 2008. It has also been shaped by global events such as the 9/11 attacks in New York, the wars in Afghanistan and Iraq and the emergence of the BRIC economies as key players on the world economic stage (Stiglitz, 2006). According to the US economist Joseph Stiglitz, trade and capital market liberalisation were key components of the 'Washington Consensus' brokered by the International Monetary Fund (IMF), World Bank and US Treasury to promote development in the 1990s. This policy was shown to have had a deleterious effect on many economies, leading not to growth but to greater economic instability. It focused too much on raising GDP with little regard for issues of sustainability in the economic, political, social and environmental realms.

Reich (2007) argues that what emerged during the period of market liberalisation from the 1980s to the crash of 2008 was a form of *supercapitalism* that privileged consumers and investors. They were given more choice and more flexibility in making those choices. This intensified competition amongst companies, who in turn produced cheaper products (for the consumer) and higher returns (for the investor). The negative social consequences of this supercapitalism are manifold and include widening inequality, as most gains from economic growth favour those at the top; reduced job security; instability or loss of community; environmental degradation; and hyperconsumerism (Reich, 2007, p. 209). As the first decade of the 21st century came to an end, the effect of rampant neo-liberalism and weakly regulated supercapitalism reverberated throughout economies around the world, engulfing both the US and the EU in unprecedented financial crises.

Stiglitz (2003, 2006) adds further negative consequences of globalisation: an unfair global trade regime that impedes development; an unstable global financial system that results in recurrent crises that particularly impact on poor countries; and a global intellectual property regime that denies access to affordable life-saving drugs, even when AIDS stalks the developing world. But Stiglitz is not anti-globalisation per se, preferring to see the enormous potential of globalisation to be a force for change. He suggests (2006) that investments in education and research, together with a strong social safety net, can lead to more productive and competitive economies, with more security and higher living standards for all. What is lacking is that while countries have become more economically interdependent, the institutional frameworks for acting together effectively and democratically are absent. Stiglitz argues that it is possible to make globalisation work, but only if political regimes seek to actively manage the process.

DEVELOPMENT IN IRELAND

The major economic and social changes that occurred in Ireland in the 1990s and into the 21st century – the rise and precipitous fall of the Celtic Tiger – have given rise to many attempts to describe and understand what has been happening. Journalists (Hourihane, 2000; McWilliams, 2005; O'Toole, 2009, 2010; Cooper, 2010), social psychologists (O'Connell, 2001; Gaffney, 2011) and environmentalists (Clinch et al., 2002) as well as the economists and sociologists discussed in this chapter have all attempted to provide a framework of analysis for the Irish 'economic miracle' and its demise. Though these works have often reflected the complexity and contradictoriness of the processes of change, an underlying modernisation theme can be detected. It is widely assumed – indeed, it has been argued – that the lifestyles, values, occupational structures and political concerns and challenges of the Irish people increasingly resemble those of 'modern' societies of Europe and North America. This process is universally linked to economic change: as our economy increasingly resembles that of the more 'advanced' societies, so does our way of life mirror theirs. Similarly, when an economic tsunami hits in the United States, as happened in 2008, the effects are felt around the world, including Ireland.

Ireland has often been described as a 'late industrialising society'. O'Hearn (1998, p. 34) notes that the connection between industrialisation and modernity has a long history in Ireland; Marx remarked that 'every time Ireland was about to develop industrially, she was crushed and reconverted into a purely agricultural land'. This pattern became a powerful element in Irish nationalist mythology. For nationalist leaders such as Sinn Féin's Arthur Griffith, if Ireland was ever to compete as a nation on equal terms with Britain, industrialisation was essential. The struggle of the independent Irish state to develop an industrial economy may thus have been as much an expression of modernity as a response to material conditions. As a consequence, agricultural activity has tended to be relegated to the realm of the 'traditional' and O'Hearn is not alone in his neglect of the role of agricultural industries in the development of the Irish economy. Whereas these were 'written off' by the 1990s, the food and agriculture industries have emerged as one of the key areas of economic potential in the early years of the 21st century.

AGRICULTURAL DEVELOPMENT

The agrarianisation of Ireland

The society that gained political independence in 1922 was highly specialised in agriculture. Some 58 per cent of the male labour force at the time worked in agriculture. Agricultural commodities made up the bulk of Irish exports, and as an earner of foreign currency and source of livelihood for many Irish families outside as well as inside farming, agriculture was a key sector, both economically and politically. In this respect, Ireland was not unique: Denmark and Finland had similar economic profiles. Moreover, despite the reliance on agriculture, by world standards Ireland was a comparatively wealthy country.

Ireland was not 'naturally' agricultural but became so as a result of historical processes, in particular the long relationship with Britain. In the 18th century, British rule contributed to the spread of the Industrial Revolution throughout Ireland with the development of rural industries such as linen and milling and urban-based wool and food-processing industries (Cullen, 1987). By 1821, there were reported to be more people engaged in 'manufacture, trade and handicrafts' than in agriculture in one-third of Irish counties (Haughton, 1995), but during the 19th century, this blossoming of 'proto-industrialisation' was rapidly reversed outside the north-east. A key factor was the incorporation of Ireland as a region of the British economy following the 1800 Act of Union. Thus, for a century prior to political independence, Ireland was part of a single market centred on England. In this context it underwent specific and deliberate processes of de-industrialisation and agrarianisation.

Ireland's agricultural economy was not a 'traditional' economy if by that we mean one that was uncommercialised and isolated from markets. From the 17th century, Irish farmers were integrated into global food markets through their incorporation into British colonial and imperial trade relations. By the end of the 17th century, almost half of Irish agricultural exports went to continental Europe, mainly to France (Haughton, 1995). Over the next 200 years, exports became more focused on Britain as Ireland became an important source of labour and food for British industrial expansion.

Irish agriculture has a long history of commercialisation and integration into international markets. Much of what happened in Irish social and economic history can be explained only in terms of this external integration. Sociology in Ireland has generally been slow to recognise this and its implications for theories of development. This is partly because of the frequent dismissal of agrarian or rural Ireland as 'traditional' through overenthusiastic use of modernisation theory and partly because the form of farming that was inherited by the Irish state, and that has since persisted, was family based. Family-based forms of production tend to be wrongly linked with 'subsistence' agriculture, regarded as non-capitalist and remote from the modern, urban, capitalist and rationalised economy.

Irish farming in the 20th century

This does not mean that Irish agriculture at the point of political independence was entirely commercialised or that all Irish farmers were equally involved in market relationships. On the contrary, what the new state inherited was a *dualistic* agrarian economy, characterised by wide gaps in wealth, income and political power between large and small farmers and between different farming regions. Smaller, poorer farm households were concentrated in the north and north-west of the country and the midlands, while larger, richer farmers were found predominantly in the east and south.

While this dualism has persisted and strengthened up to the present, in the early part of the century it was less obviously a problem. Though there were extremes of size at each end of the scale, Irish farms overall tended to be small, at least compared to those in Britain. They were also less specialised than today in terms of output. Despite the massive dominance of cattle production, most farms operated a mixed production regime with some tillage, dairying, pigs and poultry, either for consumption by the farm family and farm animals, or for sale, or both. They mostly had common tenure conditions and organisation of farm production. It was therefore possible to view farmers as forming a fairly homogenous class. By the 1920s, as a result of land reforms commenced by the United Kingdom government, the great majority of farmers were owners of their land, rather than tenants. Most worked their farms with family labour or, on the larger farms mainly to be found in the east and south of the country, with the addition of a small number of hired labourers.

Arensberg and Kimball (2001 [1940]) show how familial relations on family farms were shaped by the fact that they were also relations within a farm business. The father of the family was also the boss of an enterprise in which the main workers were his wife and sons. This led to complex and often tense relationships between family members. For example, the marriage of a son had major implications for the continuity of the farm enterprise and so involved business considerations as much as personal choices in terms of timing, choice of partner and the nature of the contract between the new couple. Similarly, family needs influenced the form of farming. In particular, it encouraged the type of mixed farming outlined above. Class differentiation between farmers was already marked by 1900 and became more pronounced over the course of the 20th century.

The 'modern farming' approach to agriculture coincided with the interests of the food industry and agribusiness, which since the 1960s have become increasingly powerful actors in world agriculture. For example, the Kellogg food company has been an important agent in the global diffusion of modern techniques of farming through the funding of research centres. These powerful new ideas about farming formed part of a complex of beliefs about modern, rational economic behaviour whose adoption was fostered by the close relationships that grew up between American and Irish agricultural professionals in the post-war period. Indeed, just like Irish sociologists, a number of agricultural scientists received postgraduate training in American universities during the 1960s (Tovey, 1992a). Subsequently, as part of the Irish state's interventions into agriculture, they helped to introduce the new sets of beliefs and practices associated with 'modern farming'.

These processes fed into a policy orientation, now termed 'productionism', that concerned itself in an increasingly narrow way with the productive function of agriculture: its capacity to produce food or raw materials for a food-processing industry. This approach disregarded other important functions, such as the provision of employment, the underpinning of a vibrant rural community or the care and management of the environment. Productionism reflects a particular conception of modernity. It has not been peculiar to Irish agricultural policy but has dominated agricultural thinking in most parts of the 'developed' world since the late 1950s. It underpinned the EU's Common Agricultural Policy (CAP) for some two decades from the 1970s until the 1990s.

Employment in agriculture in Ireland has declined sharply. The proportion of the labour force engaged in agriculture fell from around half in the 1920s to less than an eighth in the mid-1990s to just one-twentieth today. In 2010, the agrifood sector in Ireland (including agriculture and the related food, drink and tobacco industries) accounted for 7.4 per cent of national employment (www.teagasc.ie). Until the early 1980s, the fall in agricultural employment was primarily among farm labourers and 'relatives assisting' (family members who lived and worked, often unpaid, on the farm) rather than among farmers themselves, but since then there has also been a marked decline in the number of farmers. The main reason for declining numbers of farmers is not that they are moving into other jobs, but that those who retire are not being replaced. Increasingly, farm sons (this was always true of daughters) aim to secure educational certification and a place in a broader labour market rather than leave school early, go through an agricultural apprenticeship under their father and in time succeed to the farm. Farm heirs already in work outside farming when their father retires or dies are increasingly likely to continue their existing job and work the holding part time, if at all, though this depends on the size and value of the farm and where it is located.

Changes in farming practices

Some key changes will be discussed here. First, and most striking, is how far Irish agriculture has moved away from mixed farming to *specialisation*. When Ireland joined the EEC in 1973, dairying was still carried out on almost two-thirds of farms. Today this has fallen dramatically, from 40,000 in 1996 to just 18,294 in 2010. Average herd size has increased at the same time, suggesting increasing scale and intensity of production (Teagasc, 2007; www.teagasc.ie). Pig-keeping was once widely dispersed on Irish farms and small in scale, but by the 1990s had become a concentrated enterprise: by 2007, holdings specialising in pigs had consolidated to just 600 (Teagasc, 2007). Specialists in the more profitable types of farming, such as cattle fattening, dairying and cereals, tend to be large farms in the east and south-east, while specialisation on the small farms of the north-west and west is in virtual monocrop production of 'drystock' (young beef cattle raised for selling on), a specialisation that provides one of the lowest incomes in Irish farming (Tovey, 1982).

A second important change is the *commoditisation* of farming. Farmers are increasingly involved in and dependent on markets, not just to sell their produce, but to obtain the resources or inputs they need to complete each round of production. This can be regarded as a critical change, as it means farmers lose skills and substantial amounts of control over the farm production process. They become more dependent on the manufacturers whose resources or commodities they now buy rather than self-produce on the farm. An example is the switch in Irish farming in the 1960s and 1970s from the production of fertilizer on-farm to buying in bags of industrially produced chemical fertilizer. Other examples include no longer keeping seeds from previous crops but buying them in from seed companies and buying in young dairy calves or lambs instead of raising replacements on the farm itself.

We argued earlier that Irish agriculture has been commoditised for centuries through the sale of its output on domestic and international markets. But input commoditisation has developed into the norm only in the period since the 1960s. It is linked to processes of increasing specialisation on farms and to the trend away from mixed farming. It appears to have been deliberately encouraged by the state through the agricultural advisory service (Leeuwis, 1989). Agricultural economists and other specialists believed that the best way to solve the problem of low income in the sector was to increase the level of farm output (an example of 'productionism') and that this could be best done by moving farmers towards a 'high input/high output' regime that required extensive use of bought-in inputs. Commoditisation of agriculture, especially of inputs, exposes farmers to external influence and control.

Commoditisation is accompanied by a third key process: *scientisation*, a process of technological intensification where tasks once carried out by farm family members, perhaps using farm animals, such as ploughing, are taken off-farm, mechanised, made amenable to industrial production and sold back to the farmer in the form of new tools such as tractors. Technological intensification has been a feature of Irish farming since the 1950s, particularly on larger farms. Scientisation also refers to how the knowledge needed to carry out farm tasks is removed from farmers and farming communities and brought under the control of scientific 'experts', from where it is returned to farmers in the form of state regulations or industrially produced 'technological packages'.

Co-opting organic knowledge

The process of scientisation has occurred in the organic farming sector, even while many farmers and consumers are turning to organics as an alternative to the industrialised production systems of conventional agriculture. Jorgensen (2006) observes that organic farmers are not just producers of food but also of knowledge – that they extract, debate and develop on an ongoing basis. Such farmers are aware of and do draw on scientific advancements as well as locally derived knowledge. But there are also particular ways that information is passed on in the organic movement that differ from how knowledge is diffused in the conventional food system. Jorgensen argues that when the state takes over the responsibility of passing on knowledge about organic production to interested individuals, it has the potential to reach a greater number of people than the organic movement. But its very involvement in that knowledge diffusion process reverses the traditional system of knowledge transfer, thereby disempowering organic farmers rather than empowering them. Although encouraging organic conversions, state agents still seem to be caught up in the system of knowledge transfer in which their role is that of authoritative expert, giving instructions and providing templates for action. The danger, as Jorgensen sees it, is that local knowledge, with its potential for sustainability, is silenced in this process.

As a consequence of such trends, dualism and inequality have intensified. Farmers are increasingly polarised between those who can survive and make a good living under these new conditions of production and those who cannot. Increasingly, farmers outside the elite are categorised as 'part-time farmers' even if they do not receive any earnings from off-farm work nor have any other occupation to put time into. They are essentially those who lack the capital or access to educational and informational opportunities needed to adopt scientised, commoditised, specialised forms of farming. They are increasingly seen as surplus to the requirements of an efficient food industry and so available to be diverted into other, non-competing farm activities such as farm tourism or non-intensive, 'environmentally friendly' agriculture like organic farming.

From co-ops to global players: The rise of the Irish food industry

Agriculture can no longer be thought of as a set of independent, separate farming units but as part of an extensive, globalised food system. Links, direct and indirect, are growing between farmers and the food industry as well as between farmers and manufacturers of farm inputs. This process of *integration* is encouraged by state policy, where food industry interests, particularly those of large food processors, transport companies and retailers, come to take precedence over those of farmers. Agriculture in Ireland is increasingly referred to as the agrifood industry. This sector is worth €24 billion to the national economy and is one of the most important indigenous manufacturing sectors. It accounts for around 8 per cent of GDP, with agriculture alone accounting for 3 per cent of GDP (www.teagasc.ie). In 2011, the state-funded industry support agency Bord Bia announced a record year for Ireland's food and drink sector: food and drink exports increased by 12 per cent in that year to reach an all-time high of almost €9 billion; they increased at three times the rate of Ireland's merchandise exports in the first three quarters of 2011.

In Ireland, the farmers' co-operatives (co-ops), established in the 19th century, have historically played an important role as food processors or as intermediaries between farmers and food processing companies. Since co-ops are legally made up of their farmer members, it is inappropriate for them to engage in contracts with farmers, but they have been able to use other strategies to achieve integration and control over selected producers, such as giving them privileged access to professional farm development advice or to the purchase of inputs for the farm on credit from the co-op as well as paying bonuses to farmers who meet particular requirements of quality or timing of supply. Use of such practices signals the transformation of the co-ops from social organisations to increasingly capitalistically oriented enterprises.

Since the early 1970s, co-ops have become increasingly concentrated. A new stage in this concentration process was reached with the 1997 merger of Waterford and Avonmore Foods to form Glanbia, claimed to be the fourth largest dairy food company in the world. Over the same period, the co-ops have been increasingly transforming themselves into conventional companies quoted on the stock exchange, thereby opening themselves up to influence from a growing numbers of non-farmer shareholders. Though still nominally farmer controlled, the extent to which they can or wish to act on behalf of local farmers is doubtful. A small number of co-ops (such as Glanbia and the Kerry Group) are now substantial food corporations in their own right, operating at a global level. From its humble beginnings – its first dairy and ingredients plant was commissioned in Listowel in 1972 – the Kerry Group has grown into a leading multinational company with annual sales of approximately €5 billion. The corporation sees itself as a world leader serving the food and beverage industry and a leading supplier of branded foods into the Irish and UK markets. With its headquarters in Tralee, the group employs over 20,000 people across Europe, the Americas, Australasia and Asia. It operates manufacturing facilities in 23 different countries and international sales offices in 20 other countries across the globe. It has grown to become one of the largest and most technologically advanced manufacturers of ingredients and flavours in the world (www.kerrygroup.com). Development of this increasingly integrated food system also reflects consumers' changing food preferences, or perhaps more accurately, changes in the sorts of food made available to them by retailers. Chief among these is the change from relatively unprocessed to highly processed foods.

INDUSTRIAL DEVELOPMENT

A comprehensive body of work on Irish industrial development already exists (Allen, 1997, 2000, 2009; Jacobson, 1989; Kirby, 1997, 2002; Kirby and Murphy, 2011; O'Hearn, 1992, 1998; Ó Riain, 2004; Wickham, 1983, 1986, 1997) and we offer only a summary account here. Breen et al. (1990, p. 5) suggest 1960 as an initial vantage point from which to survey earlier and more recent developments. This was a time when Ireland:

> could be characterised economically as one of the peripheral regions of the United Kingdom. British capital was the major source of foreign investment. Two-thirds of all exports went to the British market. Entry into the labour market for each new generation often meant emigration to Britain.

At a time when most of the developed industrial economies in Europe were experiencing economic growth, the Irish economy was stagnant and emigration rates were very high. During the 1930s, the Fianna Fáil government had tried to reduce economic dependency by protecting Irish industry against foreign competition and by encouraging domestic production in both agriculture and industry to replace imported goods. This period of protectionism and import substitution could be interpreted as an early attempt by the Irish state (anticipating dependency theory by some 30 years) to achieve 'independent development' by disengaging the Irish economy from the international exchange relations in which colonialism had entangled it. Allen describes Fianna Fáil's strategy as 'building native capitalism' (1997, pp. 33–4) and in this it reflected policies pursued in other parts of the world, most notably Latin America. Protectionism sought to construct a 'tariff wall' inside which Irish indigenous industries could be nurtured. In terms of its own objectives, the strategy was quite successful, but government intervention in the economy did not go far enough to be entirely successful: it 'never induced new producers to step in and produce things that were needed by existing companies', nor did it 'induce domestic capitalists to reinvest after they exploited the profitability of a few "easy" sectors' (O'Hearn, 1998, pp. 36–7).

In 1958, protectionism was abandoned and a decision was made to open up the economy to foreign investment and promote export-oriented industrialisation. Barriers to foreign firms selling goods on the Irish market were also dismantled, especially with membership of the EEC in 1973, allowing companies that located in Ireland direct access to the European market. The impact of the new strategy was quickly visible: manufacturing output grew by 5 to 6 per cent per annum in the 20 years from the end of the 1950s and employment in industry increased from 179,000 people in 1961 to 237,000 in 1981. Manufactured goods as a proportion of exports rose dramatically, from less than one-fifth in 1958 to nearly two-thirds in the early 1980s, while exports of live animals and other foodstuffs fell equally dramatically. By 1984, one-third of exports were going to EC countries other than Britain, with only 28 per cent going to Britain (Wickham, 1986). The main contributors to this industrialisation process were foreign-owned companies and TNCs. Who were the main beneficiaries?

Allen (1997, p. 108) argues that the '1958 turn' to an 'open economy' was undertaken by Fianna Fáil governments who still pursued the goal of 'building native capital'. Grant aid and subsidies for foreign firms went to those that were export oriented and did not compete with native capitalists in the home market. TNCs were perceived as bringing a new dynamism into the economy that could 'revive the Irish business class'. O'Hearn disagrees: he suggests that Irish companies selling in the home market lost out to foreign competitors and were unable to compensate through expansion into exporting (though some, such as food processors, did develop into major exporters, as we saw above). By the mid-1980s, employment in Irish-owned manufacturing companies was at its lowest since the 1940s and the Irish industrial economy had become heavily dependent on foreign investment for development. The main beneficiary, according to O'Hearn, has been global capital.

THE GEOGRAPHY OF INDUSTRIAL DEVELOPMENT

The spatial and social impacts of the industrialisation strategy of the 1970s and 1980s have been the subject of much debate. On the spatial side, the regional distribution of growth has attracted considerable attention. During the protectionist period, industrial growth took place mainly in larger urban centres and its distribution was largely unplanned or uncontrolled, despite de Valera's 'ideology of ruralism' (Breathnach, 1985). It was not until the early 1970s that regional planning became an overt part of development policy. The pattern of regional growth then began to change markedly. In the early 1970s, the eastern 'core' regions of the country had been the most attractive to new manufacturing firms, both foreign and indigenous. But the IDA spurred on manufacturing employment in the other regions, particularly the west and mid-west, in rapidly expanding industries such as electronics and chemicals. Thus, by 1990, the highest proportion of high-tech firms was in the mid-west region, followed by the Dublin area and the western region (Boylan, 1996, p. 186). Foreign companies contributed most to the change. By the late 1980s they accounted for almost half of total employment in the 'western periphery of Ireland', that is, in all regions outside the three 'core' eastern ones, compared with about a third in 1973 (Drudy, 1991, p. 166).

Regions that had consistently lost population since the 1950s (or indeed 1850s) began to experience population growth, particularly through immigration or return migration. But while the more peripheral areas of the country clearly needed the additional employment, the regional policy left the core areas, particularly Dublin, 'in serious difficulty in relation to manufacturing employment' (Drudy, 1991, p. 167). Even within the peripheral regions, the success of the policy is debated. The social impact of industrialisation on the Irish countryside, for instance, has been much discussed. International research on the effects of 'industrialisation by invitation' has stressed its gendered nature and addressed in particular the significant part played by women in the process. O'Donovan and Curtin (1991) note that in Ireland during the 1960s and 1970s, the IDA publicly stressed that jobs in the new factories were for adult males, suggesting that they would be high quality, full time, well paid and highly skilled. In practice, many of the workers recruited were women, particularly rural women. Breathnach (1993, p. 23) notes that in the 25 years after 1961, women's employment in manufacturing outside of Dublin, Cork, Limerick and Waterford increased by 139 per cent (it decreased by 35 per cent in these urban centres) and concludes that 'access to female labour from a rural/small town background has been a locational determinant of considerable significance to foreign firms investing in Ireland'. Breathnach argues that TNCs employed women as part of their broader strategy to locate the lower-skilled assembly stages of the production process in Ireland.

TNCs are relatively mobile and can respond quickly to global economic change. Kirby (1997, p. 131) notes that although over 390,000 new industrial jobs were created in Ireland in the two decades to 1994, over 400,000 were lost, leaving the country with a net reduction in industrial employment despite massive expenditure of taxpayers' money on job creation. But it could also be argued that this investment had improved the 'quality' of the jobs and that shoe manufacturers and biscuit bakers had been replaced by 'modern' personnel engaged in computing and the manufacture of healthcare devices. But not even those relatively skilled jobs in the new information economy are secure. There is intensified competition for TNC investment, particularly in the new accession states in Europe, and some firms have moved out of Ireland in response. In 2009, for example, the Dell corporation closed its Limerick manufacturing facility and transferred the assembly plant's functions to a Polish plant in Lodz. Employment in a range of industries is becoming more precarious (see Chapter 6).

Dependency theorists generally believe that industrialisation in Ireland has contributed more to the growth of skilled and semi-skilled manual jobs than to managerial and R&D positions. They argue that the expansion of foreign-owned industries has not led to a corresponding growth in indigenous Irish industry or in industry-related services. For them, foreign industries remain an enclave within the Irish economy, importing most of what they need for production and exporting most of the products (Kirby, 1997; O'Hearn, 1998). Within the new international division of labour, TNCs organise production across borders: most of the highly skilled work and the profits remain in the core countries, while the less-skilled tasks are distributed to the periphery.

Since the early 1980s, industrial policy has largely been oriented towards 'encouraging investment, both foreign-owned and indigenous, in high technology manufacturing sectors such as electronics, pharmaceuticals and biotechnology, as well as in internationally traded services including financial services, software, shared services and e-commerce' (McCafferty, 2007, p. 69). Ireland's more recent industrial experience has generated new arguments. During the late 1990s, the economy experienced a remarkable boom, described by many as an 'economic miracle'. For several years, Irish growth rates were the highest in the (then) 15 EU or 29 OECD member states. Between 1993 and 1997, national income rose by around 44 per cent and there was a 16 per cent rise in employment. Many of the new jobs were in services, but manufacturing employment also grew, against international trends: industrial production grew by 15 per cent in 1997 alone. In the mid-1990s Ireland attracted 30 per cent of new TNC investments in the EU, compared to 19 per cent going to Britain. Company profits soared, tax revenues increased and the national debt was dramatically reduced (Sweeney, 1998, p. 3). This interlude appeared to represent a new departure in Irish industrial history.

According to Sweeney (1998, p. 15), the growth recorded up to the turn of the 21st century had a foundation in 'good infrastructure, investment in that important capital – human beings – and a healthy demographic structure'. For Sweeney, the key factors that led to the boom had largely been 'internal' and included good planning and state management; a tighter fiscal regime; investment in education; IDA success in 'picking industrial sector winners'; and acceptance of 'flexible' work practices by Irish workers and trade unions. He places particular emphasis on the social partnership established in 1987 between the state, employers and trade unions that, he argues, helped to maintain Irish competitiveness. Important external factors included EU Structural Funds, the attractiveness of Ireland to TNCs looking for a location within the EU market and the revolution in telecommunications.

Ó Riain (2000) describes the growth of 'a significant sector of indigenous Irish-owned companies, often working in knowledge-intensive, high technology products and services' as perhaps the most surprising outcome of the Celtic Tiger economy. He points to the Irish-owned computer software sector, which, along with Israel and India (interestingly, both societies with a high number of English speakers and with a global diaspora), is one of the world's largest. Out of fragmentary beginnings in the 1970s, a dynamic industry was forged by the 1990s, largely due, Ó Riain argues, to developmental interventions of the Irish state that created the economic and social conditions for the industry's success. Key figures in state agencies such as the National Board for Science and Technology, Eolas, Forbairt and the National Software Directorate created and maintained networks among the social actors that helped foster this new industry: educators, policy-makers, new employers and employees.

Although the state played an important role in attracting TNCs like Microsoft and Lotus into Ireland in the 1980s, this in itself did not lead to the development of an Irish-owned software industry. The most critical contribution was the active role taken by the state in 'building up a web of associations and social ties that supported information-sharing and co-operation' across and between the new firms and the centres of innovation and advanced technology programmes, located mainly in the universities (Ó Riain, 2000, p. 243).

In contrast, Allen (2000) argues that Ireland's economic success in the early years of the Celtic Tiger arose from conditions in the global economy and had little to do with 'planned modernisation'. He notes that growth rates have fallen in all major industrial economies since the mid-1970s, reflecting falling rates of profit. This has led to increased competition between both firms and states. It has been particularly felt in the US, where business has responded in two ways: first, it has attacked the employment conditions of US workers, and second, it has expanded investment abroad in search of better profit opportunities. As a consequence, investment abroad by American-based TNCs quadrupled between 1982 and 1997 (Allen, 2000, p. 22). Ireland benefited, as it was an attractive location for US investment into Europe. Particularly attractive was the 'spectacularly low' rate of corporate taxation in Ireland (10 per cent as against 34 per cent in the US); a young, English-speaking workforce that 'could be hired at rates of pay which stood at the bottom of the European league'; and the dominance of a stable pro-business government (Allen, 2000, p. 25).

For Allen, then, the birth of the Celtic Tiger had little to do with Irish initiatives, and in 2000 he predicted – rightly, as it happened – that it would not be sustained into the future. For him, the Irish economy was a 'capitalist success story'. But by other, more important, criteria, such as equality and social justice, he judges it an abysmal failure. In a similar vein, Kirby and Murphy (2011) argue for an interpretation of the Irish state as competition oriented rather than developmentally based. While they concede that pockets of developmentalism are evident in the Irish state, 'the overriding logic that can be identified in the uneven nature of its actions is one that gives priority to the maximisation of competition and profitability over the investment in the welfare state or society' (2011, p. 77).

Crisis had been a hallmark of Irish economic reality almost since the foundation of the state, but during the boom years, crisis went out of fashion as the country revelled in unprecedented growth rates. While sociologists raised questions about the distribution of wealth, the equity of the tax regime and the economisation of everyday life under the Celtic Tiger, the band played cheerfully on. Yet there were ominous signs that growth was unsustainable. In his interrogation of the recent crisis, Ó Riain (2010) dissects the illusory quality of the Irish economic boom. He traces the economy's derailment to a set of policy decisions taken in the late 1990s under the banner of economic liberalism. The particular strand of liberalism pursued by the Irish government placed markets at the centre of society. In the absence of robust political regulation, speculation and corruption ensued.

Ó Riain observes that the booming Celtic Tiger economy of the late 1990s depended on a set of co-ordinated measures, including significant initial spending on social and regional infrastructure, social wage pacts, taxation and employment, a developmental industrial policy and public subsidies for social services. However, at the point when these measures could have been strengthened and consolidated in the early 2000s, Ireland's leaders turned away and rode a wave of property and financial speculation, eventually leading to economic collapse. According to Ó Riain, 'what distinguishes Ireland is its openness to the world economy, exposing it to the volatility of global capitalism' (2010, p. 24). While Ireland is affected by the global economy, the extent of the instability unleashed in Ireland has been much greater than in the global economy as a whole. The Irish crisis was generated by the old-fashioned overextension of banking loans to property developers (see Chapter 5).

Table 3.1: Financial institution lending (resident non-government) in selected sectors, 1998–2007

Sector	2007 percentage of total lending	% increase in lending, 1998–2007	% of the lending increase accounted for by this sector
Agriculture and forestry	1.3	72	0.7
Manufacturing	2.2	105	1.4
Computers and office machinery (also included in manufacturing)	0.0001	–3.5	–0.00001
Construction	7.0	1,538	8.0
Financial intermediation	16.2	224	13.6
Real estate activities	20.9	2,417	24.4
Computer and related activities	0.05	389	0.05
Research and development	0.02	1,928	0.03
Education (schools and colleges)	0.2	714	0.2
Health and social work	0.7	1,105	0.7
Other community, social and personal services	0.8	313	0.8
Personal house mortgage finance	33.6	542	34.5
Other personal housing finance[2]	0.3	161	0.2
Personal finance for investment	1.6	593	1.7
Other personal	5.0	283	4.5

Source: Ó Riain, 2010.

According to Ó Riain, Irish government policy played a key role in precipitating the crisis: in 1998, capital gains tax was cut from 40 to 20 per cent in an effort to boost growth through increased (and undirected) flow of capital into markets. Capital surged into the economy, with bank lending between 1998 and 2007 increasing dramatically (2010, p. 30). Table 3.1 indicates where this capital went: two-thirds into loans to the property sector, while a further 16.2 per cent of the increase went into lending between financial institutions. Ó Riain notes that relatively little investment went into the productive sector. For instance, in 2007 (the year before the Celtic Tiger burst), less than 1 per cent of bank lending went into high-tech (computer hardware, software and research and development). Ó Riain concludes that the net effect of the capital gains tax cut was to increase speculative lending in real estate and finance relative to the productive long-term investments needed in the high-tech sectors, which could only attract a tiny proportion of Irish investment.

Worryingly, 'beneath the veneer of the boom, the financial, speculative economy was suffocating the productive, innovative economy' (Ó Riain, 2010, p. 31). Moreover, the low-tax growth strategy pursued by the Fianna Fáil/Progressive Democrat administrations had created a dangerous shift in the structure of tax revenues. More and more taxes were raised from turnover and growth and less from incomes. When growth slowed in 2008, the returns from capital gains, corporate taxes and stamp duty collapsed, leading to a huge hole in the national finances. The banks were exposed as being undercapitalised, to be saved by government guarantee, and the seeds were sown for the eventual bailout by the IMF and the EU (see Chapter 5). The contraction of the economy after the Celtic Tiger boom period has presaged a new era of high unemployment, renewed emigration for many of Ireland's educated and skilled labour force and what Allen (2009, p. 17) has termed 'shock therapy' for the Irish citizenry as a whole.

IRELAND – WHERE IN THE WORLD?

Throughout the 20th century, industrial development strategies had a significant effect on Irish society. The economy became less reliant on a single external 'core' market – Britain. It reduced its heavy dependence on agricultural commodities, though food-based exports remain highly significant. The occupational structure became much more diversified: white-collar work in industry, services and the professions has expanded, as has skilled or semi-skilled manual work, while agricultural employment has contracted. The class structure also changed: in the 1950s, about half of each new generation of young people who remained in the country and found work found it in family-owned businesses, particularly farming. Today, people's jobs are related more to their educational qualifications than to their family connections. The Irish economy has been transformed from one based on agriculture and traditional forms of manufacturing to one increasingly based on the high-tech and internationally traded services sector. In 2011, the services sector accounted for three-quarters of employment, industry a fifth and agriculture just a twentieth. Ireland's remarkable growth performance throughout the late 1990s and into the new millennium led to the rapid convergence of output per capita with the world's wealthiest economies, but this changed dramatically with the economic crisis of 2008, when global capitalism entered the deepest recession that it has experienced since World War II (Allen, 2009).

Clearly, the extent to which 'modernisation' in the form of rapid growth within the economy should be seen as progress can be questioned, as we have seen above. Two further aspects of current occupational and sectoral structures may be mentioned here. First is the position that service employment now holds in Ireland. The record growth in employment since the mid-1990s, as has been pointed out, is primarily in service rather than manufacturing jobs. While some service work, particularly in the professions, is very well paid, much new service employment is low paid and casualised. Many of these sectors were dominated by immigrant labour during the first decade of the 21st century. Second, the sectoral organisation of the economy has changed greatly since the early attempts at industrialisation under protectionism. Economic growth and exports have become increasingly concentrated in a small number of economic sectors dominated by TNCs: the so-called '3 Cs' of computers (electronics and engineering), chemicals and cola concentrates. At the turn of the century, these accounted for around one-third of *all* value added in Irish manufacturing (O'Hearn, 1998, p. 73).

The dominance of a narrow range of economic sectors that are not deeply 'embedded' in the host society is of concern to both O'Hearn and Kirby. Kirby favours an industrialisation process that involves increasingly sophisticated value-adding to indigenous raw materials. His ideal is Denmark, where agricultural processing contributed to the development of a high-quality food processing industry and associated engineering, mechanical and high-tech manufacturing. Such a process 'is far more embedded in that country's social structure than an industrialisation process largely dependent on multinational companies setting up plants' (Kirby, 1997, p. 142). One of the consequences of Ireland's high dependence on TNCs is that much of the wealth generated in the country is expatriated. As a result, Ireland scores well on measures of gross domestic product (GDP) but less well on measures of gross domestic income (GDI). GDP is a relatively straightforward measure of output and, according to the OECD, gives a measure of how well off a country is compared with competitors and past performance. Ireland's position moved up the GDP rankings since 1999 and it was in the top five countries in the OECD by 2003 (OECD *Observer*, March 2005). In 1995, Ireland's GDP per capita was 12 per cent below the OECD average, whereas in 2003 it was 22 per cent above the average. In 2008, GDP sharply declined (see Figure 3.1).

But the question is: does GDP measure the country's actual wealth? The property bubble (which led to the collapse of the real estate sector), foreign direct investment (FDI) (which repatriates profits) and immigrant labour (generating income, a part of which is remitted to the country of origin) may all have inflated the revenue and investment available to the state. The GDI measure accounts for these inward and outward flows, and on this ranking Ireland dropped to seventeenth place in the OECD. The gap between GDP and GDI in Ireland is significant and reflects the reality that a significant proportion of the income generated in the country does not stay here.

Figure 3.1: Growth rates, 2006–2010

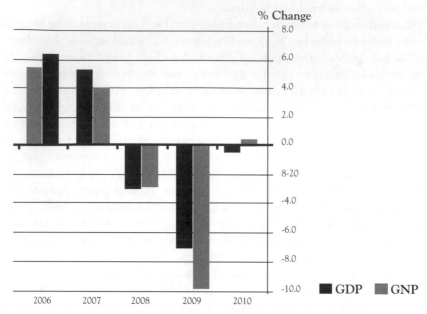

Source: Central Statistics Office.

Globalisation theorists argue that we cannot understand the pattern of change in Irish society unless we use a 'global approach'. We must discuss Ireland not as a locally bounded society, but as an increasingly integrated element of a global capitalist system. Global processes lead to the incorporation, peripheralisation and reincorporation of different zones within the global economy. By placing Irish experience in relation to these trends, we can better understand our own recent history. O'Hearn (1992, 1998) and Allen (2000) argue that the global system is dominated by the United States; Irish history has been shaped, far more than we realise, by changes in the US society and economy and in America's understanding of how the global system should be managed.

According to O'Hearn (1992, pp. 22–8), the US began to consolidate its position as a world power in the 1950s, as the British empire declined. American interests required the expansion of a world order based on interdependence through trade, backed by American military might. The global system was to be maintained through a triangular system of trade, wherein the US would sell industrial products to Europe and modernising parts of Asia; the Europeans would sell their own industrial output to their former colonies; who in turn would supply raw materials to the US. This centred the whole system on America and was actively pursued through the Marshall Aid plan for European restructuring. The Irish state, far from choosing to participate in free trade within the system, was unable to remain outside it even if it so wished. Over the following 30 years, this regime proved remarkably tenacious, despite its failure to resolve unemployment, stagnation and poverty in Ireland and other incorporated countries.

The context within which Ireland is situated has been shifting in recent decades, however. From the Irish point of view, O'Hearn suggests, the most important change is in European integration strategies. These have shifted from 'a primarily US-inspired plan to reintegrate Europe' into global trade to a project by the European core itself to increase its economic and military power. The EU has expanded steadily in recent years and has 'sought to strategically reformulate the roles of its territories so that they could collectively contribute to the creation of a more globally competitive Union' (Kitchin and Bartley, 2006, p. 11). Ireland has benefited greatly from its association with the EU since 1973. Kitchin and Bartley (2007, p. 9) contend that the growth experienced in Ireland (during the early period of the Celtic Tiger) owes much to Ireland's membership of 'the evolving European mega-region'. In the early years of EU membership, Ireland benefited substantially from transfers from Brussels and was later to avail of Structural Funds. These funds have played a significant role in underpinning the multi-annual National Development Plan (NDP) spending programmes. Ireland was also able to tap into European markets, thereby significantly reducing trade dependence on Britain. The virtual elimination of trade barriers after the passage of the Single European Act in 1992 impacted positively on the Irish economy. In particular, Ireland provided not just a reliable way for US companies to enter the larger European market, but was also English speaking. More recently, Ireland has had to rely on its relationships within Europe to secure significant transfers associated with the IMF bailout.

Increasingly, the economic centre of gravity is shifting toward Asia and Irish government delegations, the IDA and Irish entrepreneurs are developing strategies for tapping into the markets of the BRIC countries (Brazil, Russia, India and China). O'Hearn might argue that Ireland is undergoing a period of 're-peripheralisation' in the context of shifting cores within the global economic system. We can argue with details of this portrayal of the recent period in Ireland and we might question the one-dimensional view of change it offers, where the impact of globalisation on Ireland is confined to the economic level, with politics and culture essentially ignored. But while O'Hearn's 'globalised dependency perspective' can be perceived as narrow, it does point to some of the inherent weaknesses in the Irish economic model that remain to be addressed.

The debate between versions of modernisation theory and versions of dependency theory as contrasting ways to understand societal change is clearly not settled (see Kirby, 2002 and Kirby and Murphy, 2011). We have argued that modernisation theory provides only a partial, and in some respects distorted, understanding of social change in Ireland, as it overlooks the external relationships that have so strongly influenced how we have developed. At the same time, it is not helpful to assume that Irish social change has been totally externally imposed either: powerful groups within Irish society, and particularly the Irish state, have also shaped our development experience.

4

Associational Life: Community and Civil Society

In the last chapter we examined the broad scale of Ireland's economic growth and how Irish sociologists have sought to locate Ireland within a global context. In recent years this type of macrosocial analysis has lost some of its appeal. Alexander (1998, p. 6) notes a greater sociological interest in 'informal ties, intimate relationships, trust, cultural and symbolic processes, and institutions of public life'. This turn towards intimacy and the microsocial has stimulated an interest in the sociology of popular culture and everyday life, from Putnam's (2000) discussions of card-playing and ten-pin bowling to emerging analyses of food, eating and drinking, clothes and fashion (see Chapter 12). The pervasiveness of the Internet and the growth of social networking, with its potential to bring new forms of expression and communication within reach of all, are also proving fertile ground for sociological researchers (see Chapter 14). Allied to this is a revival of interest in the idea of civil society, partly driven by disenchantment with formal politics.

Informal associations, trust and the institutions of public life are the stuff of civil society. For Alexander this is a sphere in society 'marked by civility, equality, criticism and respect'. In this chapter we discuss the concept of civil society and seek to connect it with Irish sociology's longstanding focus on community. Community researchers and civil society analysts share an interest in *associational* life in society, from informal relations of everyday civility to more formal movements and organisations outside the state.

Peripheral or late-developing societies (as Ireland has been described) are thought to exhibit a weak civil society. Society is structured around the state, unable to organise itself independently (Peillon, 2001, p. 171). In Chapter 3 we suggested that the state has played an important role in shaping social change in Ireland, but this should not be taken to mean that associational life has been weak. The continuing strength of 'community' as a basis for mobilisation and voluntary action in Irish social life indicates the vitality of associational life. Here we ask whether community can be seen as the Irish way to achieve civil society or whether it is in some respects a barrier to this process. Arguably, too strong a tradition of studying community has deterred Irish sociology from entering into broader debates about the nature of citizenship and how people may engage with political and public life.

CIVIL SOCIETY

Civil society is a concept with a long history in Western thought (Keane 1988, 1998; Seligman, 1992; Alexander, 1998). In the 18th century it referred to social institutions that fell 'between' the family (the sphere of private life or intimate relationships) and the state (formal public action). In particular it included voluntary associations and forms of collective co-operation, marked off from both state and family by virtue of their voluntary form of participative social engagement. In the 19th century the idea came under powerful attack, particularly from Marx, who argued that civil society, far from being an arena of co-operative, associative and democratic action, was simply another terrain within capitalist society on which the capitalist class could enact its dominance under a veneer of civilised and philanthropic concerns. The Marxist critique had 'fateful effects' (Alexander, 1998): the concept of civil society went out of fashion. It came to be seen as a historical curiosity with little relevance to actual societies and was superseded in the 20th century by an interest in 'citizenship', understood as a set of rights held by individual citizens rather than an active engagement in civic life.

In the 21st century, the expansion of the Internet as an open space for potential mobilisation, social networking and communication has revived an interest in the potential of civil society to act as a countervailing force to the state. But the Internet is also the object of debate. Striking a cautionary note as to its potential, the American writer Malcolm Gladwell has argued that the kind of weak ties favoured by social media networks seldom lead to high-risk activism. The Internet, he suggests (2010):

> makes it easier for activists to express themselves, and harder for that expression to have any impact. The instruments of social media are well suited to making the existing social order more efficient. They are not a natural enemy of the status quo.

The Internet is not a universally accessible medium and many of the uses to which it is put do not fall within the high-minded aspirations of those who would see it as a new digital public sphere. While the work of groups such as Wikileaks may facilitate the diffusion of information, the Internet is also the progenitor of cyber-bullying and facilitates the circulation of child pornography. Sociologists must take care to robustly analyse the social conditions that enable or disable civil society in the control of tendencies towards violence, abuse and repression.

Those interested in civil society stress that we must be careful not to idealise it. As Powell observes, civil society sits in an uneasy relationship between the state and the market. It can be viewed as part of 'the conservative restoration by those who see it as a weapon against modernity ... while equally critics on the political left fear that civil society may be used as a weapon for welfare reform at the expense of the dispossessed' (Powell, 2010). In a similar vein, Alexander argues that contemporary societies provide civic spaces for solidarity among citizens, even while these very spaces can themselves be exclusionary: society is much more complex and conflictual than the idealised versions of civil society often recognise.

SOCIABILITY AND DEMOCRACY

Civil society theorists have been particularly concerned with the negative effects of power and hierarchy, seeing power as the opposite of individual autonomy and self-realisation. They have also focused on the trend towards social atomisation and the tendency in late modernity to deny collective identity and solidarity.

Recent writings on civil society thus contain two key themes. The first is an interest in the forms of relatively informal and intimate *sociability*. Sociability is seen as a valuable dimension of social life that protects against the anomie of excessive individualism. Analyses of sociability look for conditions that may help to prevent social atomisation; it is where everyday feelings of solidarity with others are fostered and a sense of belonging to a larger collectivity is created and sustained. Here, civil society is described as that realm of social experience where we learn to reconcile the conflicting demands of individual interest and the collective social good. This approach follows Durkheim (see Chapter 1) in its concern for the social formation of the individual, relations between the individual and society and how societies manage (or fail to manage) individual and collective difference. It points to the possibility of a social order organised around social solidarity rather than instrumental relations of power or money.

From within this approach to civil society has emerged an interest in the widely used concept of social capital. The best-known proponent of this term is the American sociologist Robert Putnam in his influential work *Bowling Alone* (2000). Putnam uses the term to try to capture the idea that social contacts and connections 'add value' to society in many spheres, from economic productivity to better health (see Chapter 9). Social capital is indicated by networking in a society, where dense networks of reciprocal social relations mean high social capital, and by social norms of reciprocity and trust. A network can either be 'bonding' (facing in towards creating a tightly knit and exclusive social group) or 'bridging' (facing out to create contacts and relationships with other networks). Each is an important source of social capital, despite the danger that the bonding form can have negative social effects (such as racism).

Putnam is particularly interested in the links between social capital and social connectedness, or what he often calls 'civic engagement'. He argues that in modern America, political, religious, workplace and philanthropic forms of civic engagement are declining and people now increasingly go 'bowling alone' instead of in informal friendship teams. We can see in Putnam's work an account of the collapse of American civil society, understood specifically as sociability or social connectedness. But while his analysis is often powerful, it is questionable whether the term 'social capital', with its instrumental and economic connotations, is a valid replacement for 'civil society'. For most civil society theorists, sociability and solidarity are goods in their own right. The renewed interest in civil society expresses a desire to avoid treating people as 'functions' in or resources for the benefit of a larger social system, but rather to see individuals as having autonomous value (Hess, 2000).

A second theme links civil society to *democracy*. Civil society is seen here as a diverse set of non-governmental organisations and institutions that can act to counterbalance the state and prevent it from dominating the rest of society. Here, the most important characteristic of civil society is its public nature: it is in civil society that citizens engage in public debate and argument about issues of concern to them and where genuine 'public opinion' can be formed (Habermas, 1971). Keane (1998) argues that strong, participatory civic society is essential to ensure the state continues to abide by democratic principles. Powell (2010) suggests that civil society provides an ethical framework for sustainable development because it represents the active voice of citizenship.

Theorists of civil society understand democracy in a rather specific way. A democratic society is not simply one where governments are subject to periodic elections, with competition between political parties and majority rule. Rather, it is one that enables and facilitates public engagement of citizens in shaping their own society. Its defining characteristic is that it contains one or many 'public spheres' (Habermas, 1989) – occasions for citizens to come together as equals to exchange and debate opinions in an atmosphere oriented to reaching agreement and compromise. 'Public spheres' are created by the associational life of citizens and can be found in voluntary and professional organisations, in trade union meetings, in the mass media (for example, radio phone-ins, newspaper letters pages, social network sites, blogs) and in social movements. Though created from the sociable life of citizens acting outside the state, they depend for their vitality and continuance on state support and guarantee. Through its public order legislation, a state may restrict the use of open spaces (parks, streets, public halls) by assemblies of citizens, it can enact legislation to recognise the rights of citizens to join together in trade unions or it can ensure the vitality of public broadcasting, media diversity and the free flow of information. The significant role of the state as a facilitator or constraint on civil society was brought into sharp relief during the so-called Arab Spring of 2011. Peaceful protest movements spread through North African countries and to the Middle East demanding democratic reforms and accountability. In a desperate attempt to thwart public protest against the ruling regime in Egypt, the government initially blocked Facebook and Twitter access before bowing to public pressure for political reform. In Libya the state took repressive measures against the protestors, resulting in a long-drawn-out violent struggle for power.

In theory, at least, the two key themes about civil society are interconnected. Some level of sociability and solidarity among citizens and a sense of a shared identity seem to be an essential basis for the public, collective engagement that secures a democratic society. In reality, the connections are often less straightforward: solidarity among citizens may be highest where democracy is denied, as in the opposition movements alluded to above. Indeed, some argue that in Western societies, the political trappings of democracy and the institutionalisation of individual citizenship rights have contributed to the decline of social solidarity and collective identity (the rise in public apathy noted by many commentators and evidenced in poor turnouts in elections).

Despite its difficulties, the concept of civil society allows sociologists to raise interesting questions about contemporary social life. These include questions about voluntary organisations, their persistence and their impact on social solidarity; about social exclusion or inclusion; about citizenship and the meanings attached to this in different social settings; and about the practices and institutions – both real and virtual – that help us to enact citizenship as a public role. Current debate on the development of new media technologies overlaps strongly with questions being asked about the nature of community (Stevenson, 1999). The means of communication are diversifying (for instance, we now communicate frequently through text, Facebook comments and tweets) just at the point when old communal relations are increasingly open to question.

The question raised by Stevenson and others is whether new media technologies are responsible for undermining a sense of community by robbing people of participatory public spaces or whether they are the sites where more diversified relations of solidarity can be formed. It is difficult to answer this question. One set of theorists sees new electronic media as destroying communal forms of identification, promoting the progressive privatisation of everyday life and the commodification of public life. People are encouraged to be passive rather than active within civil society. On the other hand, it is argued that new technology opens possibilities for bringing in voices from the margins; that it helps to create new forms of social networks; that individuals are now empowered to choose their communities rather than to be passively assigned to them; and the new means of communication can presage an era of new radicalism. According to Stevenson (1999), a genuinely sociologically informed account of the opportunities and dangers heralded by the development of new media technologies should seek to develop some of the more ambivalently conceived aspects of the relationship between media and society and move beyond this kind of binary thinking.

In this chapter, we raise some of these questions in the Irish context. How does 'real civil society' operate in Ireland? This question is difficult to answer, as there has been little discussion of democracy, or even of citizenship, amongst Irish sociologists, at least until very recently. There is, however, much work on sociability and association. In particular, Irish sociology has a long history of studying *community*. It is perhaps within the tradition of community studies that Irish sociology has best been able to raise questions about the relationship between the individual and society. How does a national concern about community and communality shape democratic action in Ireland? Does it contribute to or does it discourage the vigorous participation in public spheres and suspicion of unaccountable power? Has it shaped how 'citizenship' has been defined and actualised in Ireland? We look now at the Irish sociology of community in light of such questions.

SOCIOLOGY AND COMMUNITY

While philosophers debated civil society, an interest in community was central to early sociology. As sociological thought developed, two sociological problems emerged, each carrying ideas about community. One was Durkheim's concern to foster moral individualism: a relationship between the individual and society that encourages individual autonomy but does not collapse into egocentrism as societies differentiate and become more complex. For Durkheim, the advancing division of labour had the potential to leave individuals without a sense of moral obligation to any social group or collectivity. Contemporary civil society theorists reflect this concern by regarding community as a collectivity that can provide a sense of shared identity and mutual dependence and a basis to act for the common good.

The second sociological problem was seen in Tönnies's concern that industrialisation encouraged new types of social relationships that could suppress or even destroy human communality. In the pre-industrial world, Tönnies argued (2001 [1887]), most of the relationships that engaged people were communal (*Gemeinschaftlich*): intimate, face to face, enduring and based on detailed knowledge of others, their biography and their place in local society. But the rise of industrial capitalism replaced these by associational (*Gesellschaftlich*) relationships: impersonal, contractual, calculative or instrumentally rational, based on limited or no knowledge of the personal circumstances of others but on formalised rules for associating with those with whom we may have only distant, partial or transient contact.

Both Tönnies and Durkheim were responding to the profound social and cultural changes that result from industrialisation. But where Tönnies's ideas have underpinned a modernisation thesis that assumes the decline of community to be a key 'fact' about the modern world, Durkheim reminds us of the human need for community and its continual recreation in social life.

For Tönnies, the concepts of *Gemeinschaft* and *Gesellschaft* did not identify particular social groups, but articulated how industrial society had altered social relationships and rendered them less personal and emotional – less human. But sociologists later took up his critique in ways that substantially changed it. First, they assimilated it into the armoury of modernisation theory to help detail the process – seen as positive – whereby 'traditional' societies give way to 'modern' ones (see Chapter 3). Second, they turned Tönnies's analysis of changing relationships across time into an analysis of contrasting relationships across space. *Gemeinschaft* or community became associated with rural space, while *Gesellschaft* (following Simmel; see Chapter 1) was linked with urbanity. Captured by an ideology that equated the city with the modern and progressive and relegated rural society to the backward and traditional, they took for granted that community was linked to 'the rural way of life' while urban living meant a loss of community.

Community became a popular but increasingly confused sociological concept. In the mid-1950s an American sociologist (Hillery, 1955) set out to examine how his colleagues had defined and used the concept. He counted over 90 definitions and concluded, tongue in cheek, that the only common element was that they were all 'about people'. The term causes confusion, as it is commonly used to refer both to place (as in 'the local community') and to a type of relationship (some prefer to call this 'communality' or even 'communion').

Community implies that social as well as spatial features hold people together, that those in a community know each other and share a sense of being part of a defined social group (of course, this may not be true!). Here, 'community as place' shades into 'community as relationship': we assume that what moulds an aggregate of individuals into a community is a special sense of identity, a 'communality' of spirit that derives from shared interests and position in society. Indeed, this consensus may be so significant that we can talk of 'the community' itself as an entity over and above its members, with its own opinions, history and needs.

It is also possible to talk of a community in a social sense without tying it to any location. People may have feelings of shared identity as members of a community that has no common geographical base, such as professional and occupational groupings (the academic community, the business community), religious denominations (the Muslim community) or groups who share a common lifestyle interest (Facebook groups). Clearly, community has a tendency to be a complex and confusing concept in both sociological theory and everyday usage.

THE ECLIPSE OF COMMUNITY AND THE RISE OF 'INDIVIDUALISATION'

Many sociological accounts of community are tinged with nostalgia, a sense that the world of communities is past. The critiques of modern urbanism and industrialisation by writers such as Tönnies and Simmel gave rise to an enduring tradition of sociological thought that superimposed a series of binary oppositions on social development. Thus, modernity was opposed to tradition, large scale to small scale, impersonal to intimate and city anonymity to rural community. Within this conceptual framework, the development of modernity inevitably meant the loss or 'eclipse' of community.

The 'eclipse of community thesis' (Stein, 1964) combines a number of ideas that need to be examined separately. The eclipse of locality argument suggests that attachment to local place, and its significance for one's social identity, declines in modern society. Modern social identities, it is argued, are now constructed from universal categories such as gender, occupation, profession or social class. But this assumption has been strongly challenged within sociology. While it is true that territorial boundaries may be redrawn in the process of development, they do not necessarily disappear (Tovey, 1985); people continue to see their own locality as a basis for collective identification, even collective action. In the Irish context we can see this clearly in the tremendous reach and currency that Gaelic games have through the presence of the GAA in every corner of Ireland.

The GAA and community ethos

A serious dispute arose between GAA players and administration in Cork in the 2008 and 2009 seasons, threatening the advance of the team through the national championship.

In his analysis of the genesis of the dispute and its aftermath, sociologist Paddy O'Carroll (2010) throws light on the wide-ranging importance of the local club for GAA sport generally. The stand-off between the central GAA administration, the Cork County Board and the local clubs brought Cork GAA to an abrupt halt but also kick-started a mobilisation of grass roots supporters that ultimately contributed to the resolution of the crisis.

O'Carroll dissects the yawning gulf between a GAA organisation that is increasingly rational and technocratic in orientation and the local clubs for whom the encounters on the playing fields are the lifeblood of their communities. The Cork players' strike and its outcome direct our attention to the significant (if frequently latent) role that the local club and the community play as a fundamental building block of the GAA.

According to O'Carroll, the mobilisation of local clubs in support of the players demonstrates a *locally generated* resolve to oppose the institutional GAA when the members perceived the communal GAA to be under threat. O'Carroll documents the GAA's unique contribution at local level, which has rendered it a sports association probably unsurpassed among voluntary organisations anywhere. He concludes that competition, winning and identity maintenance form the matrix in which locality and community are infinitely re-created.

Sometimes when people talk of the eclipse of locality they mean that in the contemporary world, local societies can no longer be regarded as self-contained or isolated. We may think of the past as a time when most of people's interactions were with their kin and neighbours, in a circumscribed space. Lives were conducted within the overlapping social boundaries of the local parish, the catchment area for the local school and shops and the local labour market (see, for example, Leyden, 2002). This may not be universally true: while in some previous historical periods people did live in fairly immobile societies, there have been many societies long characterised by large-scale movement of populations, whether as individual migrants or as displaced groups. But it is true that our daily lives are now conducted across a greatly enlarged space, made possible by continual developments in the technology of transport and communications, from the telephone to cheap air travel to Skype. But this differs by class position and income level. Bauman (2001, p. 58) remarks that 'the successful ... do not need community'. Some social groups in Ireland may experience 'community' more than others and the eclipse of locality thesis may not apply equally to different social groups.

A second aspect of the eclipse of community thesis relates to the eclipse of local autonomy. Stein (1964) coined the phrase 'eclipse of community' to express concern with the spatial distribution of power. He argued that throughout the previous century, the local autonomy enjoyed by small American communities had steadily declined, resulting in a concentration of power in the state and the federal 'centre'. Such centralisation was a result of urbanisation, industrialisation and bureaucratisation. These had combined to reduce the capacity of local decision-making institutions such as local government, local education committees and health boards and local parish organisations to determine their own affairs.

A third dimension of the eclipse of community thesis could be called 'eclipse of communality'. It is argued that modern individuals find it hard to establish authentic relationships with others or to develop a secure sense of identity to a degree not found in pre-modern societies. Those aspects of personal identity that used to be preordained by membership of social groups and institutions are now increasingly open to individual choice. We may now choose our religion, nationality, family membership, even – still with some difficulty – our gender. As such identities can increasingly be selected, constructed and manipulated, it seems less easy to accept them as being authentic. Turkle (1999), for example, has argued that the Internet allows for a more flexible self to engage in identity play by cycling through cyberspace. Wellman and Hampton (1999) propose the idea of a networked society, where online interactions provide people with a means of living simultaneously online and offline, allowing them to move between virtual and face-to-face communities. O'Connor and MacKeough (2007) analysed the postings on a women's magazine discussion board in Ireland and found that contributors enjoyed a feeling of 'virtual togetherness' through their interactions on the website. Communality was reproduced virtually rather than through co-presence.

For Beck and Beck-Gernsheim (2002), the key experience of individuals in late modernity is *individualisation*. Whether we like it or not, contemporary institutions impose on people the obligation to live as individuals and to construct their own 'do-it-yourself' biography: 'we live in an age in which the social order of the national state, class, ethnicity and the traditional family is in decline. The ethic of individual self-fulfilment and achievement is the most powerful current in modern society' (Beck and Beck-Gernsheim, 2002, p. 22). Those charged with managing society continue to talk as if people can be assigned to collective groups and identities, but the experience of people themselves is that their identity is not assigned, but self-created. This raises very difficult questions about the possibility of continuing social integration, even of 'society' itself as a meaningful term.

The 'eclipse of community' thesis has shown remarkable staying power in sociology and Putnam's work is a modern and highly popular version of it. But in much contemporary sociology it is being replaced with a search for shared, communal identity: what we might call the quest for community (whether on- or offline). The communitarian orientation in sociology, for instance, seeks to develop new ways to organise social, economic and political life. There are similarities with the 19th-century co-operative movement (which in Ireland led to the establishment of co-operative creameries and other food processing organisations and credit unions). Adherents believe that 'co-operative communities' that respect and care for all their members are necessary for social well-being and that social and political progress depends on finding 'a third way' between right and left, or between individualism and authoritarianism. This communitarian sentiment found its way into US President Obama's inauguration speech in January 2009:

> For as much as government can do and must do, it is ultimately the faith and determination of the American people upon which this nation relies. It is the kindness to take in a stranger when the levees break, the selflessness of workers who would rather cut their hours than see a friend lose their job which sees us through our darkest hours.

Communitarians are particularly concerned by the growth of individualism and see rebuilding communities as a way of fomenting social bonds 'to sustain the moral voice' (Etzioni, 1995, p. 122). In reality, this position is conservative: it focuses on the obligations of the individual to the community at the expense of the rights of the individual against community controls. Communitarians are also criticised for their failure to recognise community's capacity for intolerance or repression. For feminist theorist Iris Marion Young (1990, p. 300), communitarianism favours 'unity over difference, immediacy over mediation, sympathy over recognition of the limits of one's understanding of others from their point of view'. It ignores how communities can make illegitimate moral claims on their members. Many find the 'paradigm communities' that communitarians invoke – family, neighbourhood and nation – troubling in this respect. Such communities can never be genuinely inclusive: their identity always depends on the exclusion of some people, since 'any definition of what members have in common necessarily implies some form of closure against "outsiders"' (Day, 1998, p. 235).

In his appraisal of Helmuth Plessner's *Limits of Community*, Hess (2007) argues that it is the public sphere alone and not communities per se that can tolerate contradiction and social distance. Hess argues that the deployment of community rhetoric often conceals authoritarianism, bullying and other predatory behaviour that has a deleterious effect both on the social fabric of Irish society and its public life. Given these ambiguities, it is not surprising that civil society theorists also experience difficulties with the concept. Communal solidarity needs to be counterbalanced in civil society by a well-established public sphere where people can recognise themselves as citizens, not just as members of a particular community. We return to this important issue after a brief discussion of community and its analysis in Ireland.

COMMUNITY IN IRISH SOCIOLOGY

Community is a popular word in Ireland. We like to think our society is made up of communities and permeated by a spirit of community. Public discussions assume that communities are desirable forms of social organisation. Those without a community are said to lead impoverished lives or are believed to be unstable and unreliable members of society. Leaders of church and state favour community responses to social problems like poverty, unemployment and crime. Local residents combine to defend the interests of their community against outsiders, whether property developers, road engineers or Travellers. Health professionals, media personalities and educators claim to serve the community. People all over Ireland engage in intense virtual interactions via Facebook, blogs and multi-player interactive computer games. Our communality is part of our image of Irishness, reflected in literature, sport, media and politics. So we would expect community to be a core concept in Irish sociology. Not surprisingly, community studies have played an important part in Irish sociology as well as in the collective self-representation of Irish society.

There is a long tradition of ethnographic research on communities in Ireland (Bell, 1982). Such studies include Arensberg and Kimball (2001 [1940]), Humphreys (1966), Cresswell (1969), Messenger (1969), Symes (1972), Leyton (1975), Sacks (1976), Fox (1978), Scheper-Hughes (1979), Harris (1984), Brody (1986), Curtin and Varley (1986), Eipper (1986), Peace (1986, 2001), Tucker (1987), Curtin (1988), Ruane (1989), Silverman (1993) and Shutes (1991). In this chapter we focus on only a small number of these. Much of this research has focused on rural and peripheral areas. Some newer studies have redressed this imbalance somewhat. See, for example, Humphreys's (2007) work on urban and small-town neighbourhoods in Munster and Corcoran et al.'s (2010) work on suburban localities in and around Dublin.

The best-known – indeed, the archetypal – account of 'the Irish community' was by American anthropologists Arensberg and Kimball, who over a period of two years in the early 1930s lived in (though not at the same time) and studied a rural area in Co. Clare. Their work gave rise to a number of publications, amongst them the celebrated *Family and Community in Ireland*, originally published in 1940. A third edition, with an informative introduction by the sociologist editors, was published 60 years later (Byrne et al., 2001).

The study area was quite remote – a good distance, in those car-less days, from the market town of Ennistymon – and was inhabited predominantly by small farmers. Arensberg and Kimball's description of small farming in the locality stressed its familial nature. They showed how the fortunes of the farm enterprise were entwined with the survival of the family on the land and how the relationships of family members were also those of boss and workers within an enterprise. They emphasised how this type of farming gave rise to and relied on particular sorts of local relationships outside the immediate family. Individual farm households, which independently met their own needs by working their privately owned land, were drawn into relationships at the local level through two community institutions: kinship (many households in the area were related by marriage) and the practice known as *cooring* (the exchange of labour between households, either routinely or at particular points of the year such as haymaking, when labour needs were high).

According to Arensberg and Kimball, these institutions reflected the strong value that the local culture placed on the obligations of neighbourliness. They also helped to ensure a level of equality between the farm households in the local area and prevented any from falling into severe poverty or debt, or indeed from becoming particularly wealthy. For Arensberg and Kimball, Irish rural life in the 1930s was strongly shaped by the local community and the feelings of mutual identification, mutual dependence and collective solidarity to which it gave rise.

The gaze of the young American researchers on the community they studied was quite austere, yet they were able to find not only collective solidarity but also some spontaneous sociability. Soon after arrival they remarked (2001 [1940], p. 173) how 'night after night, the day's work done, [our] new acquaintances, at least the males among them, walked out upon the roads to this house and that in search of recreation and companionship'. At first unable to interpret this behaviour, they later came to see that these visitings were structured by gender and age. Women were largely confined to the area around the home and had little opportunity for everyday sociability with others outside the family. Men found their friends mainly among their kin, and even here the dominant impression is of relationships that were work oriented and serious. The old men's 'cuaird', which gathered to smoke, drink tea, tell stories and debate the issues of the day, saw itself as responsible for the well-being and order of the community. But among the young men, free of responsibility for farm and family, high spirits and playfulness could find expression. Arensberg and Kimball decided that recreational patterns reflected and consolidated a man's status in the community.

Over the years, Arensberg and Kimball's methodology and conclusions have been heavily critiqued (see Gibbon, 1973). They have been condemned for failing to anticipate how quickly Irish rural life would change as the 20th century wore on. The editors of the 2001 edition, however, suggest that the work points to 'the developing crisis of modernity' (Byrne et al., 2001, p. lxxxi). In the society they studied, individuals were still:

> bound into their family and local settings. Personal preference [was] a secondary question in comparison with the well-being of the people among whom one lives. But ... by the end of the century in which they wrote, Irish people had come to have a much stronger sense of their individual rights to make decisions affecting their own lives – but within a socio-economic setting often experienced as immune to control.

Arensberg and Kimball bequeathed a potent image of the rural Irish community to later Irish sociologists. Three features had particular force. First, they refer often to the isolation, remoteness and self-containment of the local area, reinforcing the idea that its people constituted a naturally distinct and boundaried local society. Local households are shown as economically isolated from the rest of Ireland, as even though they were part of a countrywide system of cattle production, much of their farming was to meet their own consumption needs. The people are also depicted as culturally distinctive from those living in the more anglicised eastern counties.

Second, the account tends to emphasise the similarities between households and local residents much more than the differences between them. For example, there are few non-farming households in the locality and there is no big variation in the size of local farms. Though there were both big and small farmers in Ireland at the time, Arensberg and Kimball suggest that each tended to be found in different localities and thus in different communities.

Third, in a local economy there are many occasions for conflict, such as between father/farm boss and sons/farm labourers, between family members around inheritance or between households over ownership of land, but the strongest impression in the study is of agreement and harmony. This image of the rural community – self-contained and separate from 'society in general', homogeneous, bound together by local institutions and characterised by co-operation and consensus – has dominated contemporary community discourse in Ireland. It permeates public belief about what Irish society was like in the past and what – ideally – it should be like today.

Curtin (1988, p. 77) has argued that Arensberg and Kimball did not entirely ignore conflict, but for 'theoretical and methodological reasons' were more interested in exploring social harmony, stability and integration. The problem was in how their research was taken up by others: 'for long, the generally uncritical acceptance of their account ... discouraged the discovery and analysis of conflicts of interests as normal social structural features of rural communities'. Subsequent sociological and anthropological study of Irish communities has tended to ignore conflict and the management of difference between community members.

A potential source of dissimilarity, difference and conflict within communities is that of gender. Arensberg and Kimball largely sidestep this phenomenon: while recognising the very different lives led by women and men in rural Ireland, they treat gender roles as complementary and mutually reinforcing. Brody, in a study of a western small-farm area carried out in the late 1960s, depicted men and women as living in virtually separate communities, so different were their life experiences, identities and aspirations. According to Brody (1986), the local institutions at the core of rural social life in the late 1960s were the shop and the pub. Those whose social life revolved around the shop were the most marginal to the 'traditional' community: young single women expecting to emigrate and older married women who, despite active involvement in farm work, were not regarded as having any particular farming skills or knowledge. The pub was frequented by men identified with the agricultural life of the area: the older farm owners and some younger expectant heirs. Indeed, for young men to visit the shop rather than the pub was an indication that they were seeking an identity outside the local farming community and were highly likely to emigrate in the near future. While the shop was a centre for sociability, the pub, as Brody describes it, was silent and repressed, particularly during the winter months.

For Brody, rural Ireland had undergone a process of urbanisation since Arensberg and Kimball's visit. Younger rural people had adopted an urban view that saw little to value or conserve in rural life. Those left behind in rural areas had become profoundly demoralised. Brody, like many earlier sociologists, linked urbanisation to a weakening in the bonds of community. For Brody (following Tönnies), modern life or 'urban capitalism' tolled the death knell of community. Interestingly, this theme is reanimated in a recent commentary on the impact of the post-Celtic Tiger property crash in the West of Ireland. Commenting on the 'ghost estates' that now haunt the rural landscape of Leitrim, Sparks and Duke (2010, p. 106) observe that:

> The 'gold-rush' style pursuit of the speculative value of houses disembedded the commercial enterprise of building from the social function of houses as homesteads and of town centres as locales of community living, fundamentally damaging the latter and ensuring the ultimate futility of the former. Here the individualistic pursuit of profit through unsustainable development projects partly financed by state provision of tax incentives is seen to have laid waste to the landscape and fabric of rural community life.

Peace's (2001) community study *A World of Fine Difference* offers a very different picture of contemporary rural life. Set in 'Inveresk', a mixed fishing, farming and small business locality in the south-west, its interest is in how 'a small Irish community maintains its sense of social distinction, notwithstanding the comprehensive process of modernisation to which it has been subject in the late twentieth century' (2001, p. 1). Despite being economically and socially transformed over the previous 30 years, Inveresk retains 'a strong, indeed pervasive, sense of its own distinct identity, of being a special place in the world'. It is actually a diverse place of different occupational groups and spatial domains. Local inhabitants are keenly aware of this diversity: they respect and wish to maintain it and fear pressure from outside to homogenise their local society.

Peace is interested in how Inveresk people can both express local diversity and celebrate a distinctive common identity. He identifies a 'politics of identity' that is performed on different local occasions, sometimes emphasising difference, sometimes collective identity – as in the hilarious annual local concert, where a sense of collective distinction is both savoured and shared (2001, pp. 104–5). Peace does not wish to generalise from his local study, as he sees Ireland 'as a richly diverse and heterogeneous economic and political landscape, a multiplicity of spaces and places in which the proliferation of cultural difference is the order of the day' (2001, p. 7). Yet his reworking of 'community' adds considerably to our understanding of its meaning and its expression. Community, he argues, is not a given; rather, it is performed by the locals involved, on particular occasions and through particular relationships. The actors concerned are self-conscious and self-critical. Much of the performance of community in Inveresk occurs through conversation, slagging and *craic*. This picture of how 'community' is reproduced differs greatly from that suggested by Brody or Arensberg and Kimball.

Why should Inveresk people wish to perform or constitute their community? Peace suggests this may be an exercise of local control, a response to feelings of powerlessness and alienation from wider Irish political structures. Those in Inveresk are aware that regional politicians accord them little importance, even while trying to build up clientelist relations (see Chapter 5). For them, power is concentrated in Dublin and exercised on behalf of the wealthy and powerful. Inveresk people create a local communal world where they themselves can be powerful as a response to the centralisation of power in the wider society. Here, centralisation of power does not inevitably lead to Stein's 'decline of community'. Peace's account of Irish rural modernity is not one of a 'crisis' of (impotent) individualism, as in Byrne et al.'s reading of Arensberg and Kimball, but rather one of collective, if circumscribed, empowerment. As noted earlier in this chapter, O'Carroll's dissection of the GAA players' strikes in 2008 and 2009 points to the latent power of local communities when confronted with what they perceive to be bureaucratic intransigence.

A more recent 'community' study shifts focus to early 21st-century suburban development in the Dublin hinterland. Corcoran, Gray and Peillon's (2010) investigation presents a picture of new suburban communities that is much less bleak than that of the popular imagination. Generally speaking, respondents in four different suburban localities in the Dublin hinterland 'electively belonged' to their communities: they felt attached to the place where they lived. People saw the suburbs as good places to raise children. They derived sustenance from close relations with others, particularly those at similar stages of family formation. The research also suggests relatively modest but not negligible levels of social and civic participation. In all these respects, local residents are socially embedded in their respective localities. Such a conclusion goes against the dominant perception of suburbs.

Nevertheless, while the findings from the four suburban locations did not register a fundamentally deficient social fabric, the very intensity of suburban development creates its own difficulties. The built and natural environment, an important signifier of place, may be obliterated by development that proceeds unabated. Attachment to place may be undermined. The family-friendliness of suburbs appears to be linked to a pattern of demographic homogeneity that marginalises those at divergent family stages while reinforcing traditional gender roles.

Furthermore, such suburbs face immediate and pressing problems that have a negative effect on the quality of life. Local residents clearly identified the main problems they faced in the locality: these related mainly to the unregulated nature of development, the lack of a range of basic amenities, the school situation and heavy traffic on inadequate roads. Although many residents stated that they had done something to address these problems, they were also aware of the ineffectiveness of their action. Local residents in the suburbs found it difficult to deal collectively with the many problems they faced. The lack of local government institutions at neighbourhood level meant that they were struggling in their efforts to manage their own local affairs. Much like Peace's respondents, they felt alienated and powerless in relation to wider political structures. While there are many ties that bind in suburbia, those ties are in danger of being eroded by the intensification of development and its attendant problems on the one hand and the absence of locally embedded institutional structures for responding to community needs on the other.

Irish community studies suggest that local solidarity and shared collective identity based on locality have a long and dynamic history. As Peace describes it, locals construct community as a framework in which a vibrant, autonomous, self-empowering social life can be played out. In this respect, community clearly is and remains an important dimension of civil society in Ireland. Community studies suggest that collective solidarity depends on particularisms and on the perceived distinctiveness of a specific social group or way of life as compared with others. Particularistic communities have a place in civil society, but must be able to co-exist with other forms of civil life, in voluntary associations, friendship networks, social networks, social movements and so on. We return to this issue below, but first we discuss contemporary uses of 'community' by the Irish state and its agencies.

COMMUNITY AS RHETORIC AND AS IDEOLOGY

For Peace, the vocabulary of community is owned and shared by the everyday local actors of Inveresk. Other sociologists have been less sanguine: they argue that the discourse of community in Ireland has been produced, used and appealed to by specific social actors, usually those with social and economic power. Community has indeed been 'eclipsed', but they suggest a rhetoric of community is alive and well and is persistently and frequently reproduced in public debates and discussions. It persists because it is useful to powerful groups in Irish society, including the state and its agents. Evocations of community, and of what 'the community' wants and needs, are an effective way to legitimise the actions of those in power and to minimise challenges from those who may be disadvantaged.

Harris's (1984) anthropological study of industrial development in north Mayo reflects this approach. The development was a product of globalisation and the new international division of labour: with IDA support, two TNC branch plants located in the area and soon came to dominate the local economy in terms of jobs. This brought about some important changes in the local society, not least a large growth in the number of women working outside the home, as the factories mainly sought female workers. In addition, the development benefited some locals more than others: it brought most benefits to those who were property owners or entrepreneurs who could sell land or other commodities to the new factories or could profit from the increased spending power in the area. Harris argues that economic globalisation fractures the unity of the national economy: local areas may become more oriented to the global horizon of the TNC than to other localities within Ireland. As the reality of 'the nation' becomes ephemeral and change becomes ubiquitous, it becomes necessary to find an alternative source of collective identity. 'Community' provides such an alternative. Harris argues that this strategy to create a local consensus around economic development does not equally favour everyone in the community; indeed, when overt conflict arose, local leaders responded by redefining the boundaries of the community.

In contrast to Harris's thesis, a more recent analysis of the impact of industrial development on an Irish town argues that economic globalisation can have the effect of encouraging a reassertion of local identity through a reappropriation of history and a symbolic revival of the indigenous (Irish) language (Van Der Bly, 2007). Van Der Bly selected Leixlip, Co. Kildare, as a case study of economic globalisation within a nation state that itself is strongly globalised. Leixlip has the highest per capita proportion of foreign direct investment (FDI) in Ireland, largely because it is home to both the flagship Intel Corporation and Hewlett Packard (HP). Drawing on extensive ethnographic fieldwork in the locality, Van Der Bly pinpointed two identities that are expressed in response to the dominant globalisation that characterises Leixlip. On the one hand, she observed a global, *expansive* identity largely created through the presence of the American multinationals and their introduction of a culture that homogenises local life experience. On the other hand, she noted a local *explanatory* identity that instructs both residents and outsiders on what Leixlip represents in terms of language, national belonging, shared history and with whom they share their present (Van Der Bly, 2007, p. 251). This explanatory identity is not only local but also cosmopolitan, incorporating 'global connections, references and imaginations in local identity.' For Van Der Bly, the dynamic that exists between these two co-existing forms of identity creates a homogeneous culture on the local level. But crucially, in the town of Leixlip, processes of globalisation are not completely dominant, but 'create their own antithesis, to such an extent that the counter-reaction becomes part of the process itself'.

Irish state and other agencies most commonly use the term 'community' in connection with aspects of service delivery, for example in the areas of welfare, health, education or development. Community services are generally not organised by the local community on the basis of a diagnosis of its own needs, but are nearly always services delivered to residents in a locality. Community policing is a case in point – it refers not to policing by the community of itself, but to policing by the state, delivered to those living in a particular area with the co-operation of local organisations such as residents' associations. Indeed, if a community does attempt to police itself, this is defined as 'vigilantism' and is condemned. The use of 'community', for O'Carroll (1985), is a rhetorical flourish: it obscures the fact that the state does no more than deliver services to the Irish population on a territorial basis – by locality, rather than by gender, class or age. Its primary purpose is to confer legitimacy on state activities.

Claims such as these bring a useful scepticism to bear on the rhetoric of community. But insofar as they assume that community is only a rhetoric and may have little 'on the ground' reality for Irish people, they seem to suggest that Irish society is largely penetrated by state power or globalisation, unmediated by civil society institutions and associations. The history and practice of 'community development' in Ireland suggest that the situation is more complex.

COMMUNITY DEVELOPMENT

'Community development' as an idea may have emerged from grass roots movements, but today it is increasingly being adopted by states as a key dimension of development policy – and nowhere more so than in Ireland, at least until the economic downturn that occurred in 2008. Curtin and Varley (1995) argue that in Ireland, community action has taken two forms: one that attempts to work with the state for local development, which they term *integrationist*, and one that mobilises against the state, in particular against its taking of power from the local level, which they term *oppositional*. An example of integrationism can be found in the Muintir na Tíre movement and its structure of Community Councils. Curtin and Varley (1995, p. 379) see this movement as remarkable for its 'all together' ideology. It has an ability to project itself as concerned only with the common good and to transcend divisions of class, party or gender – even of religion. It claims to speak for the locality as a whole and that all locals stand to benefit from its activities. The strategy of the Community Councils is to build partnership ties with the state and to work through established political networks.

A good example of the oppositional tendency is the community-based Shell to Sea campaign in north Mayo. A large number of activists have been campaigning vigorously since the early 2000s against the siting of a gas pipeline in the locality. As Garavan (2006) points out in relation to the oral hearing into the building of an on-shore gas pipeline, attempts are constantly being made by figures in authority to write risk and unpredictability out of social space. But risk, uncertainty and contingency continue to assert themselves and can be articulated through local knowledge in order to challenge the arguments derived from rational science. According to Garavan, the Corrib Gas oral hearing gave rise to an intriguing effort by local residents to contest the monopoly usually enjoyed by scientific reasoning and to attempt to engage Shell in a real deliberation about the issues that were at the heart of their opposition.

As Garavan demonstrates, the burden of the argument advanced by community activists at the oral hearing lay in contesting the validity, or appropriateness, of relying only on scientific forms of knowing in arriving at an understanding of place. Community speakers did not attempt to contest the scientific reasoning on its own ground; rather, they attempted to show that it simply was not a sufficient basis by which one could come 'to see' their local place accurately or comprehensively. They asserted the value of local discourses, local knowledge and forms of reasoning grounded on 'common and local senses'.

The two approaches to community action are distinguished by their attitude towards the state: part of the solution or part of the problem? But the Irish state's orientation to community development groups has varied over time. Until the 1980s, it saw such groups as having no more than a marginal contribution to make to local social service provision and as largely irrelevant to economic development.

Since then, the community sector came to be constituted as a significant actor in its own right – in policy discourse if not in the political process itself. The change was visible in, for example, the development of the FÁS community enterprise and social economy programmes, the Third EC Programme to Combat Poverty and a series of EU-inspired 'area-based development programmes' since the late 1980s. These institutional mechanisms helped to place terms like 'partnership' and 'participation' at the centre of contemporary development discourse in Ireland and internationally (Sabel, 1996). They reflected an attempt by national and EU institutions to 'institute a formal structure of co-operation between the state and local actors' (Curtin and Varley, 1995, p. 383).

After 2008, in the wake of the economic crisis, the state has withdrawn much of its support for the 'community pillar'. It has dismantled the Combat Poverty Agency and the National Consultative Committee on Racism in Ireland and has downsized the Equality Authority. Funding for many community programmes, particularly the community development programmes based in disadvantaged neighbourhoods, has been severely curtailed. A community sector that expanded rapidly during the Celtic Tiger years now finds itself starved of resources. In the face of such adversity, will we see a return to community activism?

There have been instances since the late 1970s where local communities have flexed their muscles in oppositon to industrial development initiatives promoted by the state. Examples include the opposition by residents of Killeagh, Co. Cork to the siting in their locality of a Merrill Dow chemicals plant (Peace, 1993; Tovey, 1993) and the campaign (mentioned above) mounted by the people of Rossport against the construction by Shell of a gas pipeline (Garavan, 2006). The campaign against fracking for gas in the north-west of the country is just beginning to emerge. It similarly pits elements of the local community against a particular type of energy-related development. At stake in such struggles is the question of how local resources should be used and what 'development' should mean: should this be determined by local people or by the central state and its agencies?

Other examples of opposition are found in campaigns against hospital closures or the erection of mobile phone masts. The focus of such campaigns tends to be on resisting the impact of national planning strategies on a specific locality rather than attacking the strategies themselves. Yet the distinction is not clear cut. Murray's (2007) study of the opposition to an incinerator in Ringsend demonstrates the important interplay between local, national and global levels in the evolution of the community's campaign. In the course of organising community awareness of the government's proposal for the incinerator, activists made use of both transnational discourses on incineration that emanated principally from transnational NGOs as well as the NGOs themselves. In other words, there was little evidence of reticence on the part of members of the community in reaching out to 'outsider' help if it would be useful in resisting the incinerator. But residents do 'critically filter' the impact that transnational factors have on their resistance to the incinerator and the primary determinant in this is attachment to the locale or community. Essentially, global or transnational flows are negotiated in this context, with residents unwilling to 'buy in' to the global agendas of the NGO, preferring to focus on the specific issue of salience to their own locality. Integrationist and oppositional tendencies can be linked together in particular campaigns in complex ways.

A key feature of western European governance since the 1990s has been the evolution of new state strategies to grapple with the problem of uneven development (Brenner, 2004). The challenges faced by European states in this period have been identified by Mingione (1996, 1997, 2005) as the industrial restructuring and the attendant intensified pressure of competitiveness, the crisis of welfare and public services and the reshaping of patterns of political representation and citizenship. Taken together, these challenges have forced a reworking of both the regulatory regime within which the state does its business and the form and functions of state practices. According to Mingione, Europe is set on a path toward social regimes that are centred on more unstable, fragmented, flexible and non-standardised rationales than in the past (2005, p. 67).

Partnership emerged as a popular strategy deployed by the state at national and local level in order to address problems of accumulation, redistribution and social exclusion. Urban regeneration strategies in particular have embraced the idea of partnership between stakeholders in attempts to boost economic development, refashion neighbourhoods for the tourist gaze, address deficiencies in the housing market and reinvent public space. The experience of Fatima Mansions in Dublin, regenerated through a public-private partnership, is a case in point.

Community action and urban regeneration: The case of Fatima Mansions

Fatima Mansions was built between 1949 and 1951 by Dublin City Council to rehouse people living in tenements. The development originally consisted of 15 four-storey blocks with an average of 27 units per block. The complex was configured inwardly, which had the effect of cutting off Fatima Mansions from the neighbouring locale, both physically and symbolically. In the 1970s a confluence of factors propelled the estate into a spiral of decline: deindustrialisation in the city centre reduced employment opportunities; fiscal cutbacks in the local state resulted in a decline in maintenance and services to the estate; and many residents moved out when incentives were made available through a government programme to buy a home elsewhere. This gradually produced a residualisation effect, as less reliable tenants frequently replaced those who had moved on. They were unable to exert moral authority on the estate and it became vulnerable to problems of social disorder – vandalism, joyriding and, later, drugs. Fatima Mansions earned a reputation as an undesirable place to live.

Since 1998, a local development coalition – Fatima Groups United (FGU) – has undertaken a series of innovative and strategic actions to drive forward a programme of regeneration for the community. This has involved a visionary and courageous approach to very real challenges set against the backdrop of deprivation and the failures of previous public policy interventions. The original flat complex was demolished in the early 2000s. A public-private partnership involving a private developer and Dublin City Council working together through the Fatima Regeneration Board brought to fruition a new development consisting of a mix of social housing units (150), affordable housing units (70) and private apartment units (396) configured around a state-of-the-art Neighbourhood Centre and an all-weather football pitch.

From the start, the presence of a cadre of residents and local community workers willing and committed to the project of regenerating the estate was crucial to the changes it experienced. With this cadre in place, it worked hard to develop its own leadership, build allies with and links to community power nodes, leverage resources from other community groups and communicate its efforts to wider publics. In short, residents became more professional and sophisticated in their claims-making. All of this is made clear in Fatima United Groups' document *Dream Dare Do*, in which the estate sets out the lessons it learned via its attempts to bring about positive social and economic change from the early 1990s onwards (Conway, Corcoran and Cahill, 2011).

Partnerships are seen as a palatable alternative to hierarchies and markets (Benington, 2001, p. 203). Partnership is not new, as it builds on a history of inter-agency collaboration and participation by local communities in the implementation of programmes and delivery of services in many countries (Geddes and Benington, 2001, p. 25). In tackling poverty, the focus has increasingly been on integrated, multidimensional and geographically targeted approaches. This reorientation toward the local reflects the kind of spatial turn that Brenner and others have identified within western European governance. The mobilisation of spatial strategies is articulated through policy initiatives such as urban neighbourhood regeneration schemes. According to Geddes and Benington (2001), local partnership approaches, particularly those aimed at tackling social exclusion, are attractive to policy-makers, as they are seen to be highly adaptable, flexible and applicable at different levels of scale.

For Walsh et al. (1998), partnership brought a 'radical new localism' into Irish public policy. To the grass roots tradition of community development, they argue, the Irish state added its own interest in 'social partnership' as a way to achieve consensus on economic and social objectives. Larragy (2006) suggests that part of the extension of social partnership in its early days into social policy, and the concomitant incorporation of the community and voluntary sector, was due to a legitimation crisis. The economic crises of the 1980s and its problems of social marginalisation required a multi-sectoral response. Larragy found that the community and voluntary sector was able to significantly moderate neo-liberal tendencies in policy and place issues such as unemployment on the partnership agenda during the 1990s and into the early 21st century.

Local partnerships are required to promote social inclusion. While involving representatives of disadvantaged local groups in partnerships does give them some input into decision-making, Walsh et al. (1998) note that such groups remain marginal to mainstream development policies. Local partnerships have brought a 'new positive dynamic' to many localities: they have attracted new resources; delivered services more effectively and efficiently; created new assets with a commercial as well as a social value; and encouraged dialogue and consensus-building at the local level. But local participation in their decision-making may be narrow and the rules for deciding their membership are inflexible. Walsh et al.'s reservations are echoed in other discussions of community development. Curtin (1996, p. 268) suggests that 'empowerment of the poor is now to be achieved not through protest and conflict with power-holders, but through consensus-based partnerships'. Local groups that are not included in the local coalition of community and state agencies may find themselves excluded from local development strategies.

COMMUNITY DEVELOPMENT AND CIVIL SOCIETY

Strictly speaking, partnerships are not 'civil' associations, as they are tightly tied to the state, but they can provide a medium in which social interests can crystallise and the public sphere can be extended. As Ó Riain (2006, p. 315) points out, 'the constant dialogue and struggle between the horizontal and vertical dimensions of partnership is central to the outcomes of partnership negotiations and processes'. Local partnerships use the language of community, but the local actors are often not communities but rather spatial coalitions whose territorial boundaries have been marked out by the state. This can help to overcome particularistic attachments to a locally boundaried social group and offers a possibility of 'civil repair' to a society characterised by competing and rival local solidarities.

The term 'civil repair' comes from Alexander (1998, p. 7) and relates to a particular type of relationship between civil society and other spheres in society (the state, the economy, the family). 'Civil repair' is where economically underprivileged members of the capitalist economy make claims for respect and power on the basis that they are also members of civil society and make use of institutions like the law, the mass media, trade unions or the vote to force the state to intervene on their behalf against overweening economic interests. An example of such claims-making was the 2010 campaign run by residents in Dolphin House, Rialto, Dublin, in conjunction with the Irish Human Rights Commission to highlight sub-standard housing conditions. To the extent that local partnerships or other civil society coalitions make a claim for the spatially and socially excluded in Irish society to be recognised as equal members of civil society, they have at least the potential to become vehicles for 'civil repair'.

Peillon is less optimistic about the contribution to civil society that local partnerships can make. He says that the partnership discourse that has emerged amongst local groups and community development professionals draws from a model of civil society that envisages 'a communal association of people that is largely self-governing and does not allow the state to exercise too much power' (2001, p. 134). But the actual practice of partnerships operates according to a different logic of civil society: an 'administered' rather than a democratic civil society, shaped by the state and for its purposes.

Powell (2000, p. 90) also warns that civil society, like community, is a term that has been embraced not only by academics but also by politicians as a prescriptive model of the future organisation of society. Calls to reinvigorate both these concepts have coincided with a withdrawal from the welfare state and a loss of belief in its capacity to solve social problems. This 'new' kind of politics may be little more than 'neo-conservatism': a view that expects the disadvantaged in society to prevail through their own resources, without any structural change in society.

COMMUNITY, CIVIL SOCIETY AND CITIZENSHIP

Civil society is not identical with community. It is both a realm of collective solidarity and an institutional realm that includes the law and the courts, the mass media, 'dignitaries' and 'public servants' who exercise power and identity through their work within voluntary organisations and 'movement intellectuals' who articulate new ideas through their involvement in social movements (Alexander, 1998, p. 97). We have focused on community because the strength of the community studies tradition in Irish sociology provides a way to explore the issues of sociability and association. To end, we look briefly at two other central elements of a developed civil society: the 'voluntary' or 'third sector' and citizenship rights institutionalised in law.

According to Bauman (2001, p. 139), 'a republic is inconceivable without the well-entrenched rights of the individual citizen'. He suggests that individual citizens need protection from both communal and anti-communal pressures. Marshall (1950) distinguished between three forms of citizenship or citizen rights: civil, political and social. Elements of civil rights (of individual freedom, including freedom of the person against state violence; freedom of faith, thought and speech; the right to own property or make contracts; and the right to justice before the law) existed before political rights (the universal franchise; the right to organise collectively as a political party, trade union or interest group). The latest of the three, and still the most contested, is social citizenship rights, which provide a basis for social inclusion of all members of society through, for example, rights to healthcare, employment, a pension or environmental protection. Most of these rights have been institutionalised in Irish law.

Some have argued that citizenship rights, while indispensable, have not rendered society fully 'civil'. According to Seligman (1992, p. 130), the contemporary idea of a society based on equality of citizenship 'has somehow denuded citizenship of that universal solidarity of mutual affections and natural sympathy … at the core of the idea of civil society'. It is the autonomous individual, not the shared realm of sociability, which now forms the ethical foundations of society. For Seligman, this has led to a situation where ethical and moral issues are now seen as the concern of the private individual. The contradiction between the rationalised civil society of individual citizenship rights and a moral world of social solidarity is one that Seligman fears theories of civil society cannot resolve.

Powell (2000, pp. 96–8) distinguishes between two forms of citizenship: 'entitled citizenship' and 'active citizenship'. Entitled citizenship leads to a view of the citizen as an individual entitled to a range of social and economic welfare rights. The assumption is that these entitlements free the citizen to live an active, informed and associational life in society, but in practice it has led to increased individualism, often of a hedonistic and self-oriented form. The institutionalisation of citizenship rights does not necessarily produce the 'active citizen' who 'pursues moral commitment through involvement in the community', supports democracy and indeed is 'the cornerstone of civil society'. 'Active citizenship' can be manifested through the presence of strong voluntary associations and social movements in a society. Indeed, the first report of the Task Force on Active Citizenship (Department of An Taoiseach, 2006) maintains that voluntary and community organisations are the backbone of active citizenship, with an ability to achieve trust and cohesion in a way that governments cannot. However, the report also identified cynicism and a lack of confidence in democratic and some other consultative structures, particularly at local level.

Civil society theorists emphasise the importance of the voluntary sector in society in ensuring social pluralism. While the state tends to homogenise society and culture, voluntary organisations and movements sustain a diversity of ideas, opinions, institutions and interests. Some seek close partnership relations with the state in return for statutory funding, while others 'challenge the state through vigorous social movements that may be seen as constituting "a people's opposition"' (Powell, 2000, p. 103)

During Ireland's Celtic Tiger years, Irish society arguably veered toward a highly individualised conception of citizenship. Indeed, Murphy and Kirby (2008) argue that Ireland's model of development at this time rested on values of individualism, income maximisation and economic growth as an end in itself rather than as a means to social development. The policy-making process was dominated by a narrow political and economic elite. The shock of the economic collapse and its consequences has created conditions conducive to mobilising a 'people's opposition'. This has not taken the route of bloody protest in the streets, as in Greece throughout 2010 and 2011. Rather, there has been a new emphasis on political reform and greater democratic accountability. Murphy and Kirby argue for an alternative model of development that would require values of social solidarity to take priority, economic growth to become a means to sustainable and equitable social development (rather than an end in itself) and the decision-making processes to broaden to include a much wider range of stakeholders, exercising their franchise through a much broader set of means. Two recently emerged civil society groups highlight this trend.

ACTIVATING CIVIL SOCIETY

Claiming Our Future, a progressive movement for an equal, sustainable and thriving Ireland, emerged in 2010, linking many different voluntary and community pillar organisations under a single rubric. One of the first events it organised was a novel civil society 'think-in' that took place at the RDS in Dublin on 30 October 2010. One thousand people took their places at one of the 100 roundtables set up in the hall. Throughout the day, each table debated the kind of values they wanted to underpin Irish society, the priority that should be accorded to a range of policy objectives and the sorts of initiatives and actions that could be taken to achieve the agreed objectives. Using a software package, every table was able to exercise their votes and all the votes were aggregated to come up with an overall, consensual result. For details on the deliberative process and the outcomes, see the movement's website (www.claimingourfuture.ie). The most innovative aspect of the proceedings was the emphasis on deliberative engagement. This has become a hallmark of Claiming Our Future as they continue to organise deliberative democracy events around the country.

Similarly, 2011 saw the establishment of another national initiative aimed at encouraging more active citizenship. The idea underpinning We the Citizens is to explore new ways of public decision-making that might help to restore trust in politics in the aftermath of economic and social crisis. The organisation has hosted town meetings around Ireland and a national Citizen's Assembly in order to garner public views on an agenda for reform and change.

It is too early to tell the extent to which these kinds of initiatives can contribute to a more robust voice for civil society in the shaping of the national political agenda. Nevertheless, they are indicative of a more engaged polity and a demonstrable interest in fomenting change in the aftermath of crisis.

Part II

Social Divisions

5
Who Rules Ireland?

STATE, POWER AND SOCIETY

To understand the structures, institutions and dynamics of any society, the processes of power must first be understood (French and Raven, 1959). The concept of power has been widely examined, theorised and critiqued in sociology because power relations (either covert or overt) invariably lie at the heart of most social processes. In this chapter we seek to examine power relations in Irish society, focusing in particular on who has access to power, who exercises power and the consequences that flow from those arrangements. We provide a macrosociological overview of the structures and institutions in society in which power is embedded and which facilitate the reproduction of inequalities. Three case studies focusing on access to power and inequality are then reviewed, exploring dimensions of class, gender and ethnicity. We begin with a discussion of the relationship between the state and society. Ireland as a representative democracy vests power in the institutions of the state (the executive, the legislature and the judiciary), but as we shall see, power is also wielded elsewhere, most notably in the marketplace, with serious consequences for both the polity and the society.

If the state acts on and influences society, society must act on and influence the state (Peillon, 1995). There are at least two ways that society can influence the state. First, as a set of social institutions the state reflects and is shaped by the power hierarchies and social divisions that exist in society. Over a period of time we find that some social groups have been better able to access state positions than others. Irish society contains different (and competing) social classes, genders, regions, religious and cultural groups and we could expect the Irish state to recognise and represent the values and interests of some of these more than others. This view of the state still sees it as being able to take independent action on society but suggests that how the state defines and selects its favoured projects is strongly influenced by its own history and by the various groups that played a part in its construction. A second, alternative viewpoint queries whether the state is a significant actor at all. It suggests that far from being an autonomous agent for change, the state is controlled by more powerful and less obvious interest groups within society. Variations on these views produce four main types of argument in sociology about the nature of state rule and about who the 'real power-holders' in society are.

The first can be called the *ruling class thesis*. This derives directly from Marx's analysis (see Chapter 1) that portrays capitalist society as sharply polarised between two opposed social classes: capitalist/bourgeoisie and working class. Ruling class theorists contend that capitalist society is ultimately ruled by the capitalist class – the owners of capital and of large productive property. Though the state may appear to be independent, in practice it always acts in the interests of capital. Despite occasional apparent conflict, the state has no goals of its own separate from those of the capitalist class. It may pursue goals that appear to militate against ruling-class interests, such as introducing a wealth tax or property tax, but these are ultimately in the long-term interest of capital because the monies raised are likely to be reinvested in the economy and in public services. This approach is resisted by many state theorists. Peillon (1995, p. 363) remarks that while the state may emphasise 'the project of the bourgeoisie', this does not automatically make it 'an instrument of this particular class. The conflicts of interest that erupt from time to time between state and bourgeoisie simply rule out such a possibility.' While Peillon agrees that the state does generally privilege the interests of the capitalist class, in his view this is because the capitalist class controls a scarce resource (capital) required for economic growth, not because the state is merely its agent or mouthpiece.

A second argument is the *power elite thesis*. This maintains that society is ruled, not by a ruling class, but by a coalition of elites that includes owners of capital or their representatives. This group, termed the 'power elite' after a 1956 book of the same title by American sociologist C. Wright Mills, may include top financial advisors, employer association lobbyists, military leaders and opinion leaders such as politicians, journalists and even academics. The precise make-up of this group varies from society to society. In contemporary Ireland, we might see military leaders as relatively unimportant but business leaders as a key element of the power elite (see 'An Irish power elite?' below). The power elite differs from the ruling class: a class consists of people who share the same economic position and economic interests but who may have few social contacts with each other; an elite is a social group whose members share similar backgrounds, educational experiences and lifestyles. They move in the same social circles, often intermarry and share a common sense of group identity and a belief in their right to lead society.

One of the by-products of the tribunals of inquiry into payments to Irish politicians has been the illumination of the kind of 'golden circles' that formed an intrinsic part of the Irish political establishment, particularly in Fianna Fáil under the leadership of Charles J. Haughey, and more recently in the Fianna Fáil-dominated governments led by Bertie Ahern. In the wake of the economic crisis, analysts have begun to marshal evidence to prove the existence of such a ruling elite in Irish society (see below). Both ruling class and power elite theorists see power as being sharply divided in society: the rulers have all or most of the power while the rest of society has little or none.

A third approach rejects this view of power and argues that modern societies contain a plurality of relatively equal interest groups who compete with each other to influence the state. If ruling class theories have their roots in a Marxist analysis of capitalist society, *pluralist theories* owe much to Durkheim's argument that the transition to modernity involves a process of increased differentiation and specialisation of social and occupational roles. According to this view, modern society is highly complex and diverse, made up of many pressure groups and associations that represent the outlooks and interests of people in different positions within the division of labour. Pluralist theorists regard the state as outside and above this interplay of interests. The state is a neutral referee that oversees the competition and decides which demands to favour at any given time. The state is portrayed as a rational actor responding primarily to the reasonableness of the case made by an interest group rather than to traditional loyalties or to threats. The rational state thus reflects the general *rationalisation* of society that accompanies modernisation.

The fourth analysis of power in modern society is often called the *corporatist approach*. This suggests that society is ruled by the state acting in conjunction with a small number of specific interest groups that it has taken into a privileged form of 'partnership'. Employer groups, farmers' associations and trade unions are allowed to participate with the state in the process of policy formation and implementation while this is denied to other interest groups such as the unemployed, consumers or the voluntary sector. In return, the privileged organisations guarantee to secure the support of their own members for state policies, which benefits the state by reducing the level of social conflict.

An Irish power elite?

In Ireland as elsewhere, sudden economic decline combined with the dramatic collapse of the banking system has focused attention on 'a golden circle', a small number of board directors (and others) operating at the highly lucrative apex of Irish business. A strong perception existed well before the present economic crisis that Ireland is run by a small pool of well-connected individuals sitting on the boards of Ireland's top companies (Clancy et al., 2010, p. 1).

This statement is drawn from a study that aims to reveal Ireland's ruling elite. Clancy et al. focus on the zenith of the Celtic Tiger (2005–2007) and examine the annual reports of 40 companies that play an important role in the Irish economy. Twenty-six are private companies and 14 are state-owned bodies. By examining the composition of the boards of directors of these companies, the authors are able to identify the extent to which the same people serve on multiple boards (multiple directorships) and the extent to which companies had directors who were members of two or more boards simultaneously (interlocking directorates). Such practices, according to the authors, signal two key issues of concern: a single individual holding multiple functions and responsibilities may not be in a position to provide the necessary attention required by any individual business or activity; and a concentration of directorial responsibilities amongst a small elite group may undermine the independence of boards and militate against good corporate governance generally.

The key findings of the analysis include the following.

- A network of 39 individuals held powerful positions in 33 of the 40 top public organisations and private Irish businesses and held more than 93 directorships between them in these companies during this period.
- Each of the 39 members of this 'Director Network' held multiple directorships on at least two boards across 33 of the 40 companies concerned.
- More than a quarter (11) of the 39 members of the Director Network were particularly well connected. They had 10 or more links, via these multiple directorships, to other members of this network and/or sat on three, four or even five boards of the top 40 companies simultaneously.
- In addition to holding multiple directorships, a significant proportion of the Director Network held very senior full-time positions, either as CEOs or executive directors or equivalent positions.
- Over half of the members of the Director Network held board positions in at least one of Ireland's four largest financial institutions: Anglo Irish Bank, AIB, Bank of Ireland and Irish Life and Permanent. The three most tightly interwoven boards were all financial institutions.
- There was a significant lack of diversity among members of the Director Network; for example, only one in nine directors was a woman.

While Clancy et al. were looking at these companies from the outside in, a rare glimpse from the inside out was provided in the *Irish Times* by Donal Casey, a former bank executive (19 February 2009). Casey offers a trenchant account of the failures of the Irish banking system that resonates with the 'golden circle' analysis of Clancy et al. Casey's explanation relies heavily on sociologically grounded insights. He outlines three reasons for the failure of Irish corporate entities to anticipate or avert the crisis:

1. Excessive power was invested in individual, largely autocratic chief executives. There is any amount of sociological research on the nature of power, authority and bureaucracy. A century ago, Max Weber warned of the dangerous tendency of bureaucracies to centralise power and for the means to an end to take precedence over the end in itself, leading to a form of instrumental rationality.

2. Casey points to the narrow gene pool from which Irish non-executive directors are drawn. He might just as well have directed the reader to the body of evidence marshalled by Irish sociologists that demonstrates how social reproduction through class position is a given in Irish society and has survived almost unblemished throughout the Celtic Tiger years. This evidence has pointed to the tendency for those who are born into the same social class, who attend the same schools and who play golf together to form a power elite. We should not therefore be surprised that the one coterie of people shows up on the same boards, to support each other's ambitions through interlocking directorates and to ensure that the system is ultimately reproduced in their interest. Casey points out that when you have such a closed system and a culture of deference to a CEO overlord, it is difficult, particularly for underlings, to step outside the frame and offer criticism. In a similar vein, Ross (2009) has argued that cross-directorships in the banking sector fuelled a culture of common purpose: light-touch regulation gave carte blanche to the bankers to lend in a dangerous and excessive fashion. The latter found willing 'co-conspirators in Ireland's rising band of property developers' (Ross, 2009, p. 92).

3. Casey points out that non-executive directors were ignorant about what was going on in their organisations. They accepted the views presented to them from the top. What they should have done was adapt an ethnographic approach to their jobs, trying to get a handle on the organisation from the ground up. This is the lesson the eminent sociologist Howard Becker taught his students in his seminal essay 'Whose Side Are We On?' (Becker, 1967). The view from below is just as important as the view from the top and allows one a better overall understanding of the workings of the organisation. From understanding comes insight and the capacity to act in an informed and reasoned way.

WHO RULES IRELAND?

Do any of these theories help us to answer the question, 'Who rules Ireland?' Do they assist in our understanding of the persistent direction taken by Irish state policy in relation to, for example, social equality? The taxation policies followed in recent decades might suggest to us that power in Irish society is held by a ruling class. Research on the redistributive effect of taxation in Ireland in the 1970s and early 1980s (Rottman et al., 1982; Peillon, 1995) shows that redistribution occurred primarily among people who lived from income: professionals on high incomes, for example, lost substantial amounts of their income in tax that was redistributed in the form of state services and welfare payments to those on very low incomes. The government coalitions from 1997 onwards, however, that involved Fianna Fáil and the Progressive Democrats championed low taxation policies. For instance, the 2000 Budget made the incomes of the poorest 20 per cent of the population rise by less than 1 per cent, those of the middle income groups rise by 2 to 3 per cent and those in the top 30 per cent by about 4 per cent. Priority was given to tax cuts over everything else (O'Toole, 2009, p. 23).

Over the decades since the foundation of the state, virtually no redistribution at all has occurred from those who own property (large business owners, large farmers) to those without property. In 2007, Bank of Ireland Private Banking estimated that including private residential property, the top 5 per cent held 40 per cent of the wealth. If residential property was left out of the equation (and it was considerably inflated during the boom years), the top 1 per cent held 34 per cent of the wealth (O'Toole, 2009, p. 76). While this seems to be evidence of a bias in state policy towards owners of capital, it does not necessarily show that Irish capitalists constitute a ruling class. Much of the capital invested in Ireland has been foreign owned in recent decades and several leading businesspeople are domiciled outside of the country. The debt owed by the Irish state is to international, largely faceless bondholders. Does this fact then force us to conclude that the class that rules Ireland is located *outside* the country and that capitalists within Ireland are not a ruling class but merely the local representatives of an international capitalist class?

The pluralist thesis offers a less conspiratorial account of who rules Ireland but does not fully explain why some interest groups, even when organised into formal associations, obtain little effective recognition in state policy-making. These tend to be the groups already most disadvantaged – the unemployed or tenants of under-resourced public housing complexes. A corporatist analysis may better explain the mechanisms at work. Corporatism in one version or another has a long history in Ireland. It was first experienced in the form of Catholic corporatism – a programme that sought to minimise state intervention in civil society so that people could express their Christianity through the voluntary organisation of their own economic and social lives. It was popular across much of Europe at the beginning of the 20th century and reached its zenith in the 1930s to 1950s (Kennedy, 2001). Catholic corporatism encouraged people to form local or sectoral organisations to take over the management of their daily lives and saw these as natural units through which people could participate in the political process. The impact of this teaching in Ireland is evident in the Constitution of Ireland drawn up under de Valera's leadership. However, it failed to make any other significant impact on the Irish social or political system, a fact that Whyte (1979, pp. 74–6) attributes to the influence of entrenched political and civil service structures. In an analysis of Ireland from the mid-1930s to 1960, Garvin (2004) has argued that economic, social and cultural stagnation was exacerbated by the lack of imagination on the part of policy-makers as well as the power exercised by the Catholic Church, the strength of the small farm community and what he describes as the 'gerontocratic' tendencies in the political elites and in society as a whole.

Corporatism was revitalised, in a secular mode, in the late 1950s as a way to organise development planning and to provide a system of consultation and conciliation between the state and major interest groups. It has been extensively used since then as a means to secure industrial peace (through national partnership programmes, for example – see Chapter 4) and to ensure that state development goals are widely disseminated and promoted among significant social groups.

Corporatist accounts of the state help to explain how it can maintain social order in an unequal society – in other words, how the state solves the legitimation problem. To involve the main, and often opposed, interest groups in society in the process of policy formation ensures that both will ultimately accept state policy.

A good example of this was the Croke Park Agreement brokered in 2010 between the government and the Public Services Committee of the Irish Congress of Trade Unions (ICTU). Under the terms of the agreement covering the period 2010 to 2014, a commitment was made by public servants and their managers to work together to change how the public service does its business so that both its cost and the number of people working in it would fall while continuing to meet the need for services and improve the experience of service users. In return for these savings, certain guarantees were made to workers, in particular that pay rates would not be reduced after 2010 and that there would be no compulsory redundancies in the public sector.

In recent decades the Irish state, like most other Western states, has become progressively more interventionist. It now seeks to undertake the leading role in modernising not only the economy, but also other institutions, such as education and welfare, that can influence economic performance. Thus, it has become an increasing target for its citizens' demands and aspirations; it is expected not only to organise economic growth but also, for example, to prevent environmental pollution that results from industrial production. This widens the arena of conflict and makes corporatist strategies more difficult to maintain.

So far we have said nothing about Irish politics. Where do they fit into theories of state power? If we take the view that Irish society is ruled by a ruling class or power elite, party politics and electoral processes effectively become irrelevant. The only function of the political process is to provide an appearance of democratic control that masks where the real power resides. Even corporatist theories may support that conclusion. But in Irish politics there are some features that may help to explain how the society has developed in recent decades and why there has been little opposition to the form of that development. Political scientists have suggested that the structure of political parties in Ireland during this period has been unusual when seen from the perspective of core societies. Parties have divided not along a left/right axis like those in most European countries, but around a nationalist cleavage inherited from the early years of the state's foundation (Garvin, 1998). Furthermore, Irish parliamentary processes are thought to be particularly influenced by clientelist relationships between politicians and citizens where electoral support is traded for the real or apparent granting of favours or assistance by politicians (see Sacks (1976) and Higgins (1982) for classic analyses and Komito (1984) for an alternative view). Whether either of these features is peculiar to Irish politics or is common to semi-peripheral societies is open to debate, but both processes arguably help to prevent people from recognising or organising themselves in opposition to social inequality.

What remains is the power elite analysis, but this has been relatively little researched in Ireland. Without more research it is difficult to determine if there is an Irish power elite: recent tribunal findings suggest, at least, close connections between elements of the political and business elites. For example, the Moriarty Tribunal, established in order to investigate payments made to politicians, found that payments received by former Taoiseach Charles J. Haughey during his political career devalued the quality of a modern democracy. The tribunal found that during the period 1979 to 1996, Mr Haughey lived a life and incurred expenses vastly beyond the scale of public service entitlements. His income during this time was supplemented by clandestine donations. The Mahon Tribunal of Inquiry into Certain Planning Matters and Payments, published in 2012, found that while Taoiseach, Bertie Ahern had acted with impropriety in relation to the management of party funds. The power elite thesis is rich in the possibilities it brings to a discussion of power in Irish society. It focuses less on structures than on processes. The power elite is understood as a collective agent and what is of interest are the processes through which this agent assembles, manages and exercises power in particular situations.

WHEN THE IMF CAME TO TOWN

> *Knock knock!*
> *Who's there?*
> *IMF.*
> *IMF who?*
> *IMF-ing serious! Your country is broke, your government are liars and I am already in your house!*

In December 2010, staff from the International Monetary Fund (IMF) visited Dublin to meet with Irish government officials and work out a bailout plan. An iconic picture of Ajai Chopra, head of the IMF's mission to Ireland, walking past a homeless man begging in a Dublin street became a leitmotif for all that had gone wrong with the Irish economy. After two years of financial fire-fighting, speculation and denial, the government admitted that it could not solve the problems generated by the crisis by itself. The Irish people had to come to terms with the fact that the country was effectively insolvent and that in order to continue to function, the government would have to seek external support. The bailout plan accepted by the Irish government is part of a financing package amounting to €85 billion, also supported by Ireland's European partners through the European Financial Stabilisation Mechanism, the European Financial Stability Facility, bilateral loans from the United Kingdom, Sweden and Denmark and Ireland's own contributions. Under the terms of the bailout, the government is required to cut spending by €12.4 billion by 2015.

The bailout prompted considerable debate in the country, not least about the status of Irish sovereignty. Writing in the *Irish Times* one year on from the bailout, Paul Cullen questioned whether the government of Ireland has any control over its destiny ('Some years before Republic can join sovereign nations of the world', *Irish Times*, 22 November 2011). National sovereignty, a core value at the foundation of the state, Cullen writes, was eroded on joining first the EU and then the eurozone. Most significantly, it has been challenged in the course of the recent crisis. Irish finances have to be supervised on a quarterly basis by an appointed troika of financial experts. Cullen notes that the finance committee of the Bundestag (German parliament) discussed Irish budget details before the Oireachtas had sight of the information. He says that the idea that the Irish government is in control is now somewhat illusory: the oversight of Ireland's finances is effectively managed beyond the state boundaries.

One of the outcomes of the current economic crisis has been a focus on the concept of power and privilege in Irish society. Numerous books have been published in the wake of the Celtic Tiger that seek to analyse the anatomy of the current crisis and to apportion blame to a power elite that had remained virtually unquestioned for decades. In his dissection of the rise and decline of the Celtic Tiger economy, journalist Fintan O'Toole (2009) argues that a culture of cronyism thrived during the boom years, largely as a result of Fianna Fáil's tenure in office and the party's fixation on gaining and holding power. The years of the Celtic Tiger, he suggests, lacked the social and political ambition that could have prevented the overheating of the property sector and ensured a more sustainable growth model for the country.

O'Toole is particularly incensed by what he describes as the corrupt relationship that flourished between business and politics under Fianna Fáil's stewardship. From the mid-1990s, corruption – particularly in the form of the bribery of public officials – lay at the heart of the development of the capital city. A small group of businessmen, through their close ties with the political elite, were able to direct how the city was planned (see the Mahon and Moriarty Tribunals of Inquiry). Unlike in other democracies, O'Toole observes, when this corruption emerged into the public domain, there were no real consequences. Almost nobody served a custodial sentence, there was no real change in the political culture and more importantly, 'the Irish electorate showed an extraordinary degree of tolerance towards politicians who were known to have engaged in dodgy dealings' (2009, p. 32). This reflects the overall response in Ireland to white-collar crime (see Chapter 10).

According to O'Toole, the Irish political system is fundamentally built around often fanatical local loyalties and organised through clientelistic political relationships: 'there is a strong impulse to vote ... for someone who will successfully manipulate the system on behalf of both constituents individually and the constituency as a whole' (2009, p. 33). In many respects, the modern organisation of constituency politics is not that different from the party machine that Weber noted in his analysis of the 19th-century US ward system. This means of doing business through the cultivation of local networks of support continues to thrive in 21st-century Ireland. Political leaders as well as political representatives maintain staff whose job it is to manage the constituency office and to ensure that the hand of 'the boss' is seen to be across all queries directed to and processed by the office. Such values are an embedded part of Irish political culture and mirror (or more accurately, distort) the technocratic, rational-legal administrative systems through which national and local government operate.

Thrity years ago, Higgins (1982) that relationships based on clientelism and patronage are inherently coercive and exploitative in character and seriously undermine the notion of the common or public good. The persistence of this form of traditional political domination makes it hard to conceive of a transformative politics emerging from within the Irish political system. The current configuration is not conducive to encouraging independent thinking or the expression of forceful beliefs. Come election time, many politicians must compete against party colleagues in multi-seat constituencies. They dare not neglect their constituents or espouse views on the national stage that might not play well locally. The adversarial system in the Dáil and Seanad encourages symbolic point-scoring politics rather than substantive and deliberative exchange.

The flouting of the ethic of responsibility in politics has been a major factor in the civic disillusionment evident among the general public. Tribunals of inquiry have lain bare some of the weaknesses of recent political leaders who have been shown to have been deficient in exercising responsible judgment. Golden circles and cosy cartels flourished. When Taoiseach Bertie Ahern was asked why he appointed people who had given him money to state boards such as Aer Lingus, Dublin Port and Enterprise Ireland, he answered that he had done so 'because they were my friends'. For O'Toole this encapsulates the taken for granted cronyism at the heart of Irish political culture.

Close relationships between leading politicians and business figures do not necessarily depend on a crude cash-for-favours basis. Rather, 'it was all about being on the inside track, being in the know, getting your calls returned, being able to have that quiet word' (O'Toole, 2009, p. 41). It paid to be seen as a friend of those in power, and those who did not pay might at least perceive themselves to be at a disadvantage. Thus, O'Toole concludes (2009, p. 43) that both a push factor (fear of not being on the inside) and a pull factor (the promise of being 'sorted out') combined to tilt the relationship between money and politics, business and the state away from the public interest and toward the mutual benefit of businesspeople and politicians. The apotheosis of this arrangement was seen in the Fianna Fáil fundraising tent at the annual Galway Races, a favourite meeting place for property developers, builders and the party elite.

Covering similar territory to O'Toole, Ross (2009) traces a watertight circle encompassing politicians, mandarins (senior civil servants) and senior figures in the banking sector. He argues that the interests of each group coalesced during the Celtic Tiger period around a form of economic growth fuelled by speculative developers. As he observes, 'once the bankers had identified the builders as a vehicle, the regulators turned a blind eye to the orgy of lending, the Department of Finance collected the property taxes and the government used the windfall to win elections' (2009, p. 136).

The ethic of irresponsibility that infected the political culture also set the tone for business and bank dealings. A number of schemes operated by the main banks (such as the opening of 'non-resident' savings accounts by people who were clearly local to the community) actively encouraged tax evasion. They were largely ignored by the regulators and proceeded with neither legal accountability nor managerial responsibility. Shane Ross (2009, p. 33) concludes from his survey of banking practices in Ireland over decades that:

> Ireland's banks have operated in a world where rules were there to be circumvented; where officialdom turned a blind eye to breaches of codes and laws alike; where customers were cattle; where governments underwrote the activities of cowboys in pin stripe suits.

A culture was created and maintained in which people tended to go about their business on the basis of an unwritten code that accepted and respected that 'people in the know' could do things differently, including flouting the tax system: 'in the very small and overlapping worlds of Irish banking, business, politics and public service people knew … that there was a system of networks and connections with the ruler of the country at its centre' (O'Toole, 2009, p. 72). As Casey has noted (see above), such power relations require compliance by those lower down the food chain.

An array of tax reliefs, loopholes and schemes were made available during the Celtic Tiger years that enabled significant tax avoidance by an elite group of businesspeople. By 2008 there were more than 5,000 Irish businesspeople who were 'non-resident' for tax purposes, including 440 'high net worth' individuals defined by the Revenue Commissioners as those with net assets of more than €50 million (O'Toole, 2009, p. 85). The upshot was that government policy under the Fianna Fáil/Progressive Democrat leadership had created two classes of citizens: 'those at the bottom for whom taxation was compulsory and those at the top for whom it was voluntary' (O'Toole, 2009, p. 89). One of the most significant tax schemes in operation during the boom years was the Section 23 relief, which allowed for most of the cost of building rental accommodation in designated areas to be set against tax liability. According to O'Toole (2009, p. 117), 'the state ended up subsidising – to the tune of around €2bn in all – the building of houses whose purpose was to provide shelter, not for real people, but for the taxes of their builders'.

Sparks and Duke (2010) trace the impact of this rampant development in the villages and towns of Co. Leitrim, the county with the highest proportion of so-called 'ghost estates' in the country. They suggest that under the terms of Section 23 and similar schemes, there was a conflation of the symbolic home with the economic house, of the community town centre with the commercial retail park. Crude processes of commodification and marketisation came to replace the traditional notions of 'homestead' and 'community ethos', with their connotations of place attachment and local embeddedness. Land was perversely revalorised in the form of bricks and mortar investments. When the crash hit, these bricks and mortar investments turned to dust.

POWER AND SOCIAL CLASS

One of the most insightful and theoretically developed analyses of power and social class in Ireland from an ethnographic perspective remains that of Australian anthropologist Chris Eipper (1986). His work provides a 30-year perspective on who rules Ireland and thus enables us to reflect on how things have changed or remained the same in the intervening period. His study focused on the town of Bantry in Co. Cork in light of the impact of Gulf Oil, a multinational oil company that had established an oil refinery close to the coastal town in the mid-1960s. Eipper's analysis of local community interaction sought to examine the changing nature of class domination in Irish society in its local, national and international forms. Although he treats the lived experience of class as a key issue for understanding local social life, Eipper does not believe that class and class processes can ever be fully understood if they are treated as purely local. At the same time, he argues, class cannot be treated, as has sometimes been the case in locally based studies, as no more than 'external factors' that provide a 'context' for local experience. Rather, what Eipper calls the 'nexus between church, state and business' (the 'ruling trinity' that provides the title for his study) is forged and operates *simultaneously* at the local and national level (1986, p. 3). We can only understand 'how class worked in Bantry' if we link this up to 'how it worked in a number of other places too'.

Eipper's approach is ambitious in that it tries to look at the macro and the micro at the same time, which is unusual in sociological analyses of class. It also tries to keep in sight both issues of structure and of agency. As a result, Eipper has perhaps been the most successful at constructing a theoretical perspective on class in Ireland that integrates the three key dimensions of class analysis: interests, cultural meanings and political action. To develop this perspective, he makes an essential distinction between two ways that people can act in their relations with others: as 'acting subjects' and as 'social agents'. 'Class', he argues, 'has to be analytically grasped as both an ideological encounter and as a material condition' (1986, p. 12). Class is understood as a material condition when we treat people's behaviour as a result of the material constraints under which they operate, or the economic location they occupy or as an expression of their pursuit of material self-interest. The problem is how to translate abstract categories of class, such as capital or wage labour, into substantive classes that have cultural and political histories, such as the bourgeoisie or the working class.

To understand social experiences 'in all their lived complexity', we cannot 'satisfactorily treat people as merely personifications of economic relations ... the actual flesh and blood people who empirically relate to one another in real life' relate to one another 'as persons' (1986, p. 12). They are formed by social and cultural experiences as well as by economic position. Their interaction is shaped by notions of status and social honour, and in turn expressions of the dominant ideological beliefs about the types of persons and ideas that are entitled to respect and deference. Eipper then argues that class analysis has to combine the analysis of two forms of class relationship:

1. People act as the 'social agents' or representatives of economic class locations, for example as the representative of the interests of owners of capital.
2. They are acting subjects, real people living a distinctive way of life within a given social habitat.

Both ways of acting involve struggles for power and control, particularly for control of people's class consciousness, 'which is the acme of class struggle, of class formation' (1986, p. 14).

Eipper uses these theoretical concepts to produce an analysis of class and power relationships in Bantry before and after the arrival of multinational capital in the area. As we have already suggested, he sees Irish society as dominated by a ruling bloc comprising church, state and business, though from the perspective of the 21st century we might note that the church has largely lost its power to the other two members of the trinity. He closely examines both the personal power exercised by each of these groups in Bantry life, historically and contemporaneously, through the clergy, politicians and local business elites and, at a national level, the relationships between the church 'as a corporate body', the state and business institutions, particularly as these involve the control of 'development' and its ideologies. But spanning both these levels is a third form of class power: 'the impersonally instituted authority of corporate property, of capital accumulated and organised on a world scale, as a more imperious version of class domination than that confronted in the analysis of the ruling bloc dominating Irish society' (1986, p. 203). This is the class power of multinational corporations or TNCs. The penetration of this global form of class power into Irish society, Eipper argues, leads to the subordination of local and national class processes to international ones. The arrival of Gulf Oil in Bantry not only signalled a realignment of class forces, locally and nationally, but also a reconstruction of the dynamics of social change in Irish society. In future, the capacity of classes to reproduce themselves and their relationships with other classes would increasingly be mediated by and dependent upon the class interests of global capital.

A similar point is made in the urban context by Corcoran (2002) and Benson (2007). Conflicts within communities over proposed development can sometimes bring everyday understandings of class into sharper relief. Corcoran (2002) explored this process in relation to a proposed docklands development project in the Dublin north inner city. In 1998, the first proposal submitted for the development of 51 acres of the brownfield site (Spenser Dock) on the north side of the Liffey emerged from a property consortium led by Treasury Holdings. An American-based architect designed a 26-building complex for the site, including a national conference centre, apartment blocks, office buildings, hotels, parkland and the refurbishment and change of use of several listed buildings and structures. Dublin City Council granted partial planning permission in the first instance, but the decision was appealed by a range of parties that included local residents, the DDDA (Dublin Docklands Development Authority) and the development consortium itself. Due to the unprecedented scale of the scheme and the interest it had generated, an oral hearing was conducted by An Bord Pleanála in the spring of 2000. In July of that year, it rejected the bulk of the scheme, granting planning permission for the National Conference Centre only.

The hearing on the Spencer Dock development project provides some insight into how the idea of the city can become the focus of contested claims between different class groupings. Conflicts between commercial interests (the Spencer Dock Development Company) and community values (docklands residents' associations) were largely grounded in arguments over the significance of place. On the one hand, the proponents of the scheme argued that the development would represent the most comprehensive urban project in the history of the state. The scheme was defended on economic grounds, with the suggestion that since Dublin was already part of the global information economy, it could capitalise on growth in that area by providing commercial buildings such as those proposed in the Spencer Dock scheme. On the other hand, the residents (and a variety of other interested parties and groups) opposed the development on the basis of its architectural inappropriateness, excessive scale, environmental impact, disregard for the past and negative social implications for the community. Opposition to the proposed development crystallised around the clash between the global and the local, with the Treasury Holdings plan viewed as a kind of battering ram of globalisation that ultimately threatened to obliterate the 'local' in Dublin. Local docklands opposition to the proposed development may be interpreted as a questioning of the city's new globalised status, neatly summed up in the term 'the Manhattanisation of Dublin'. Among docklanders and their supporters, there appears to be a growing awareness that unfettered development that ignores the vernacular of the city can only lead to a Dublin that is much the same as anywhere else and, therefore, a 'nowhere place'.

In her exploration of the process of gentrification in the traditional working-class community of Ringsend in Dublin, Benson (2007) argues that deindustrialised spaces in prime locations close to the city centre become ripe for development as a neighbourhood oriented towards the needs of middle-class professionals. Apartment blocks have been built on sites once dominated by industry and not only represent a shift to a post-industrial landscape, but also a shift in the social and spatial relationships that were embedded in Ringsend as a particular place. The marketing of these new apartment blocks draws on Bourdieu's notion of *distinction* in order to appeal to the consumer desires of prospective buyers (see Chapter 15). Ringsend is no longer the domain of Dublin's traditional working class. Rather, the process of gentrification represents a new phase of capital accumulation in the city that excludes the working class on many levels: economic, social and cultural. The emergent forms of community that exist in the new apartment complexes differ from the everyday understanding of the practice of community by Ringsenders. For the old-timers, community is grounded in co-presence and locality, while for the newcomers, community is not necessarily place based: social networks and attachments extend well beyond the reach of Ringsend. Benson (2007) concludes that the sustainability of Ringsend as a neighbourhood with a particular history, landscape and social fabric is not contingent on integration, but on ensuring the vitality of a mosaic of co-existing micro communities.

GENDER AND POWER

> When we talk about women's power, we are still talking about potential rather than reality (Walter, 1998, p. 3).

Conflicts over gender, sexuality and the family have been a significant part of the Irish political and public discursive landscape for at least the last 30 years. For many people, the shift towards modernity in Ireland is symbolised not only by the development of the economy and the physical infrastructure, but also by how people think, talk and act in relation to moral issues. In Ireland, this often means issues related to gender. Thus, as Jenny Beale argued (1986, p. 184), 'as Irish society has industrialised and urbanised, and as traditional values and ways have been challenged and questioned, every aspect of women's lives has been subject to scrutiny and change'.

For Beale, the image was one of progress, of overcoming the barriers to women's full equality in Irish society. Twenty-five years later, the picture is perhaps more complex. While many of the challenges faced by the women's movement have been addressed, the more intractable issues related to gender remain. In an analysis of women's political mobilisation in Ireland, Galligan (1998b, p. 106) points to an apparent contradiction: 'there is little doubt that the role of women in Ireland today is very different to the social role and function assigned to their mothers, even if attitudes towards that new role remain staunchly traditional'.

Furthermore, in Ireland as elsewhere, the direction of change is being questioned. Is 'having it all' in a consumer heaven the aim of Irish people – particularly women – or does a more equal opportunity to work and to consume only serve to paper over the deeper layers of inequality within Irish society, such as occupational segregation, family violence and the unequal burden of domestic labour and childcare (see Chapter 6)? Discussion of gender and family issues in the public sphere continues to reflect the long-term issues of gender inequality and the unresolved uncertainties of moving rapidly towards a post-modern society. It is often around gender- and family-related issues that the tensions and connections between the personal and the political are made most apparent, whether in relation to, for example, state support for childcare, responses to male youth suicide or the recognition of same-sex marriage.

It would be superfluous here to list the many public debates – usually heated, often sensationalised – that have taken place over such issues as child sexual abuse and same-sex marriage. They are very well known to people in Ireland through saturation media coverage and continual public and private debate. The very frequency and ubiquity of such debates, scandals and revelations are evidence to many people of the speed and depth of the processes of modernisation within Irish society. Peillon (1998, p. 117) suggests that 'through these crises Ireland is being propelled, at an incredible pace, into what Anthony Giddens has called *high modernity*'. Through the sheer speed and depth of change, Irish people are being forced to adopt a thoroughly modern stance of reflexivity, to be increasingly self-conscious about the sort of changing society they inhabit. It is thus hardly surprising that, as suggested by Foucault, our society has become highly involved in perpetual talk of gender, sexuality and morality.

From the 1930s to the 1960s, women in Ireland suffered from legal discrimination in a broad range of areas, including employment, property rights, family law, inheritance, social welfare, taxation and access to, and protection of, the law (Galligan, 1998a, p. 30). The legal system explicitly and implicitly favoured men. Women in this sense stood outside of the key power relations underpinning Irish society. The early second wave feminist movement in Ireland was not particularly radical in its challenge to prevailing social and political values compared to the women's movement of many other countries of the West. But given the conservative nature of Irish society, the limited liberal agenda of the majority of Irish feminists was seen by both the public and politicians to be a radical challenge to established power relations. The strategies and outcomes of the Irish women's movement had less in common with the more advanced movements of northern Europe and Britain and much similarity with those of countries such as Greece and Italy (economies with a strong agricultural sector and powerful institutionalised churches) and the United States (with a comparatively small public sector) (Galligan, 1998a, p. 54). As a result, according to Galligan (1998a, p. 29), 'women's public participation [was] clearly predicated on traditional social attitudes reinforced by the ideology, institutions and structures of an authoritarian Roman Catholic Church and a conservative, nationalist State'.

Women remain under-represented in decision-making structures at both national and regional levels in Ireland. According to blogger Fiona Buckley writing on the National Women's Council of Ireland website (5 May 2011), the 25 women returned to the Dáil in the 2011 election represents a numerical and percentage (15 per cent) high in terms of women's political representation in Ireland, but when compared internationally, the new 'record', she writes, is meagre. Ireland currently lies in 74th position in a world classification table of women's representation in parliament compiled by the Inter-Parliamentary Union (IPU). While women constituted a minority of candidates in the 2011 general election (86 out of a total 566 candidates), the average success rate for all candidates was 29 per cent. According to Buckley, this indicates that there is no bias against female candidates amongst the Irish electorate.

The question remains that if the chances of getting elected are equal, why do so few women put themselves forward in the first place? Buckley says 'the answer lies in what is often termed the "4 Cs" of care (childcare or otherwise), culture, cash and confidence. A fifth "C" – candidate selection – is also used to explain the low numbers of women contesting election on behalf of political parties. Together, these are the main barriers facing women when entering politics.' Even if there is no overt discrimination against female candidates – and some parties, such as Labour, have moved toward affirmative action in candidate selection – it is nevertheless true that other factors militate against female involvement. The timing of political meetings pays little attention to women's domestic obligations; male networks of political power and influence often exclude women, even if inadvertently; women generally have lacked power in other fields that 'produce' politicians, such as business, law and the trade unions; and male-dominated political agendas may be of little interest to women.

While women's success in Irish party politics may be limited (though still highly significant), they may have had more impact within local, grass roots and community-based politics, the emergence of which has been an important part of the Irish political scene over the last decade. While Galligan suggests that 'the nature, quantity and outcomes of women's public activities at grass-roots level have yet to be analysed in any form' (1998a, p. 58), she points out that the experience in Ireland parallels that of other European countries. Such involvement tends to be 'specific and issue-driven', for example in the areas of adult education and drugs issues. 'It is seen as an end in itself, not necessarily the start of a broader level of political involvement, as the dearth of women in local politics does not reflect the extent of women's participation in local political activities' (Galligan, 1998a, p. 59). This also suggests that the highly adversarial and ritualised nature of local politics may have little attraction for publicly minded women.

Despite the barriers facing women within both the formal and informal political processes, it is apparent that the specific raising of gender issues and input by women have had significant effects on the form and the content of political debate and policy-making. Thus, suggests Galligan (1998a, p. 21), the 'mainstreaming of feminist priorities has made a significant contribution to the increased output of public policies with a women-centred focus in modern times'. If nowhere else, this is reflected in the support that women's groups have received from the state. At the same time, the women's movement is experienced and expressed very differently within groups that are experiencing racism, poverty and social exclusion. Movements around gender, despite the sometimes universalising nature of their object, can be as exclusive and divisive as any social or political movement. Lentin, among others, has argued (1998, pp. 6–7) that:

> Most studies addressing citizenship and Irish women ... presume a homogeneity of 'Irish women' and of feminist struggle, and fail to address the impact of both

racist discourses and the multi-tiered access to citizenship on women of ethnic minorities. In other words, mobilisation around the categories of gender can occlude other important divisions and differences in Irish society.

THE VOICE OF TRAVELLERS IN IRISH SOCIETY

Travellers are one of the most significant minority groups in Irish society. With Ireland's increasing religious, political, cultural and sexual diversity, greater attention is now being paid to the experiences and human rights of minority groups. The pressure to adapt to diversity is exerted both from within elements of the majority – not least sections of the state – but also from minority groups. One view suggests that there has been an increased tolerance of diversity in Irish society and that Travellers have benefited from this. This optimistic view would point to expanded educational provision, the role of the media, EU membership, foreign travel and a general improvement in living standards as positive factors. According to this view, greater tolerance of diversity is another mark of a successfully modernising society.

A more pessimistic view of the position of Travellers in Irish society would draw attention to the increasing *in*tolerance of diversity in Ireland, as indicated in the racist response to refugees, asylum seekers, New Age Travellers and any others who display 'visible difference' (Kuhling, 1998; McVeigh, 1998; Pollack, 1999; MacLahlann and O'Connell, 2000). It would stress the continuing difficulties experienced by Travellers in gaining basic human rights and how legal and bureaucratic structures help to maintain an institutional structure of discrimination.

Generally missing from either the positive or negative accounts is any recognition of how Travellers themselves have helped to shape their incorporation into modernity. It is widely recognised that there has been a radical transformation of how the position of Travellers has been interpreted over the past 25 years: from a subgroup of the poor or subculture to a distinct ethnic group. Hayes has described in detail the complex and comprehensive range of discourses whereby Travellers have been constituted as 'others' in Irish society, in terms variously of their 'secrecy, dishonesty, licentiousness, violence and "a society within a society"' (2006, p. 230). Hayes shows how these constructions of Traveller identity have persisted over an extended period of time (at least since the 19th century) and are also reflected in the discursive construction of nomadic peoples elsewhere in Europe. He also outlines how in more recent times, Travellers' own actions have consciously sought to re-create common notions of Traveller identity and community and in particular to assert a distinct ethnic identity. According to McCann et al. (1994, p. xi), 'the concept [of ethnicity] has radical implications for the study of Irish Travellers because it approaches Traveller culture as distinct and valuable in its own right with its own historical path of development, rather than as a short-term adaptation to poverty or marginality'. It has also, they claim, encouraged major changes in policy towards Travellers, identifying 'the need for policies which respect cultural differences, rather than ones which seek to erode them in the name of the settled community's image of "social improvement" or its administrative convenience' (1994, p. xii).

The claim that Irish Travellers constitute a distinct ethnic group is controversial within academic research and in Traveller/state relations. For Ní Shúinéar, ethnicity is a matter of possession of objective social and cultural characteristics that can be used as criteria to decide, in relation to any social group, whether it is an 'ethnic group' or not. The main characteristics are:

- Biological self-perpetuation.
- Racial difference.
- Shared fundamental cultural values and cultural difference.
- Social separation from other groups.
- The presence of language barriers.
- Hostility or antipathy between the group and members of other groups.

In her view, Irish Travellers can be shown to exhibit all of these and thus 'meet all the objective scientific criteria of an ethnic group' (1994, p. 54).

There is an alternative way to understand ethnicity that has received attention from sociologists and anthropologists. It focuses on the *subjective* dimensions of ethnic group membership rather than on an objective possession of racial or cultural characteristics. Here, ethnicity resides:

- In the belief by members of a social group that they are culturally distinctive and different from outsiders.
- In their willingness to find symbolic markers of that difference (for example, food habits, religion, forms of dress, language) and to emphasise their significance.
- In their willingness to organise relationships with outsiders so that a kind of 'group boundary' is preserved and reproduced.

McLoughlin (1994) treats ethnicity not as a set of objective characteristics, but as a *claim* that groups make about themselves or about others. Claiming to be an ethnic group is, in her view, part of a larger social and political agenda. Instead of asking: does this group really meet the objective criteria that constitute ethnicity?, we should ask: does it help this group's situation to be pursuing this agenda – to 'play the ethnic card' – rather than some other one? A group can seek to establish its cultural worth even if it does not appear to possess anything that clearly distinguishes it culturally from others; conversely, groups that may be culturally very distinctive may not embark on an ethnicist movement at all.

This discussion suggests that the debate around Travellers' ethnicity is misplaced to a degree. It may be more useful to study how an ethnicist movement has arisen among Travellers in recent years and how this has profoundly affected both Travellers themselves and policy-makers and members of Irish society more generally. We can investigate whether this change in the Traveller discourse has been of benefit. For example, has the shift from a 'culture of poverty' discourse towards ethnicity helped to empower Travellers themselves? Hayes's study does go some way to showing how Travellers have actively sought to develop expressions of distinctive cultural identity. One of these is through autobiography, and he outlines a number of books that have allowed individual Travellers (e.g. Nan Joyce and Pecker Dunne) to talk about their lives and Traveller culture. Hayes (2006, p. 259) argues that these autobiographical accounts represent an expression of ethnicity that can be linked to broader patterns: they have, he suggests, 'coincided with a re-engagement on the part of Irish people with the questions of identity and cultural difference in an era where increasingly globalised societies are seeing transformations and new complexities in the cultural interactions between different peoples and cultures'. They form a marked contrast with some of the media perceptions of Travellers, which have tended to recycle the dominant negative 'myths' and 'stereotypes' of the past.

Pavee Point, formerly the Dublin Travellers' Education and Development Group (DTEDG), was significant in the development of ethnicism within the Travellers' movement. It developed in the early 1980s as an organisation that involved equally both settled people (mainly social workers or researchers with a professional interest in Travellers) and Travellers. This signalled a major difference from previous bodies, such as the National Council for Travelling People, which had been set up by and included only settled people and which worked *for* rather than *with* Travellers. John O'Connell (1992, p. 7), director of the DTEDG, described this difference: 'When we formally established the DTEDG in 1985 we acknowledged Travellers as an ethnic group. We decided that any work with Travellers should support their right to retain and develop their identity … We also wanted to offer our skills in support of Travellers in their struggle for justice and acceptance in Irish society.' Gmelch (1989) has noted the growing politicisation and mobilisation among Travellers during the 1980s. For perhaps the first time, Travellers began to see themselves as a distinctive ethnic group that counted possession of a distinct language as a central symbol of this distinctiveness (see Binchy, 1994; Ó Baoill, 1994).

Although language has emerged as a significant marker of ethnicity for Travellers, for them a more significant symbol that summarises and captures their essential identity and difference from other groups in Irish society is *nomadism*. There is a certain irony in this, given Gmelch's suggestion that the emergence of ethnicism among Irish Travellers is linked to their transformation from a predominantly rural, mobile group in the 1960s to a substantially urban, 'immobile' group in the late 1980s. Gmelch argues that the experience of urban migration has been a particularly important factor for the emergence of the Traveller movement. It contributed to a situation where settled people's anger and hostility towards Travellers greatly increased, which in turn helped to politicise Travellers themselves. It also helped to create the conditions under which collective mobilisation of Travellers was made easier. In their pursuit of recognition and social justice, Travellers have forged contacts with other Irish Travellers and Traveller and Gypsy organisations elsewhere in Europe and have also engaged in creating ethnic identity systems to symbolise their own distinctiveness.

The 'culture of poverty' approach to interpreting their situation, first developed by McCarthy (1971), profoundly influenced how ordinary Irish people thought about Travellers and helped to shape the policies that were introduced to deal with 'the itinerant problem' during the 1970s. McCarthy has since rejected this approach and admitted that it 'has done them a great disservice in so far as the theory has been used by certain people to discredit Travellers and to negate their separate cultural identity' (1994, p. 128). Although the development of a different theoretical approach to Travellers, based on the idea of a distinct ethnicity, has partly been a result of the fact that Travellers have become more vocal and that researchers have begun to listen, it is also clear that outside professionals and intellectuals have contributed in no small way to the elaboration of ethnic identity and ethnicist claims that Travellers have experienced. To a certain extent, concepts of cultural oppression and ethnicity were already gaining currency among sociologists and social activists in Ireland as a way of understanding social exclusion and marginalisation in general before they were specifically used to understand the situation of Travellers. The role of intellectuals both from within and outside social movements in developing movement ideas and practices is an issue that has generated much interesting sociological research in recent times. We mention it here to show that sociology itself, inasmuch as it helps to develop conceptual tools, has a potential role in bringing about social change.

PUBLIC INTELLECTUALS – SPEAKING TRUTH TO POWER?

Power elite theory sees an important role in society for the intelligentsia. These are the people who translate the sectional interests of other members of the elite coalition – the political class or big business – into a project for society that appeals to and appears to embrace the interests of all the people. The role of the intelligentsia is to legitimate the elite's hold over power by providing it with ideas and concepts to help mobilise the support of the people it rules. Is this how the Irish intelligentsia has acted? The term 'intelligentsia' covers a complex reality. At its broadest, it includes the increasing number of workers who create and communicate knowledge rather than material goods and resources and is often referred to as the 'knowledge class'. Here, however, we are using the term much more narrowly to refer to those often called *intellectuals*. Intellectuals are arguably a particularly important group in peripheral and dependently developing societies. Intellectuals participate significantly through their contribution to the process of state-building – a process that post-colonial countries like Ireland have gone through as seek to transfer the allegiance of their populations to the new state institutions that replace those of the ousted colonial rulers.

At the time of political independence, the main intellectuals influencing Irish life came from the nationalist movement and the Roman Catholic Church (there was also a significant tradition of Anglo-Irish or Church of Ireland intellectuals, such as the Kilkenny-based writer Hubert Butler, but their influence on society was limited and oppositional). In the following three decades or so, up to the 1950s, the values and goals of this group dominated Irish life: a vision of a social order organised around small to medium property (farms and manufacturing concerns), distinctively Irish in language and values, with a dominant voice for the church in education, health and welfare and a limited role for the state (O'Dowd, 1992).

From the late 1940s, however, a new intelligentsia was developing – senior civil servants, journalists, professional economists and other government advisors – who gradually replaced the established intellectual elite of nationalists and clerics. This 'modernising elite', as it saw itself, believed that the state could play a much greater role in achieving development and it gave significant support to the state when it adopted the strategy of industrialisation through foreign investment in the late 1950s. In turn, these intellectuals benefited from the expansion of state and semi-state activities that accompanied modernisation in the subsequent decades. A considerable proportion of the almost exclusively male (O'Connor, 1998, p. 83) intellectual elite was to be found in some form of state employment: as university teachers, members of the judiciary or as managers and scientists in semi-state organisations.

With the advent of RTÉ Television in 1961 and the general expansion of media and cultural activities in the 1960s and beyond, the composition and orientation of the intellectual elite changed again. Encouraged by Ireland's membership of 'Europe', the focus of younger intellectuals and media personalities increasingly alighted on the 'opening up' of the local society to cosmopolitan values and ideas. After the nation-building intellectuals and the modernising intellectuals came the globalising intellectuals. Much of the power exercised by intellectuals and the respect they command derives from their claim that the knowledge they produce is 'free floating', that is, unbiased by any particular social memberships (class, gender, local community, age group or generation) that the intellectual may have. Intellectuals, when speaking as such, claim to be able to transcend social positions, political affiliations and socialisation and produce ideas that are universal and timeless. Intellectuals present themselves as non-partisan and therefore take for granted that their efforts to shape state policy are made in the public interest and not in their own.

Yet international research suggests that intellectuals tend to be drawn overwhelmingly from middle- or upper-middle-class families of the sort where education is highly valued and where there are plenty of resources available to obtain it. In Ireland, the picture is a little different since both the strength of the Catholic and nationalist intelligentsia in the early years of the state and the expansion of technical and professionalised intelligentsia in more recent decades has meant that many Irish intellectuals came from a lower-middle-class background. But the argument that their class background makes their world views less than 'universal' and non-partisan still stands.

A second sociological position argues that class of origin is less important in terms of explaining the particular values and orientations that intellectuals articulate than class of orientation. The French sociologist Bourdieu (1984, p. 176), on the basis of research into intellectual and academic life in France, argues that intellectuals should be seen as part of the bourgeoisie, the dominant class in capitalist society, albeit a rather 'dominated' part of that class. They may own little material capital but do possess 'cultural capital' and this encourages them to see their interests and those of the bourgeoisie as intertwined. This class position, in Bourdieu's view, profoundly shapes intellectuals' judgements about what is to be regarded as genuine intellectual activity; what political ideas, artistic products and so on should be given serious critical consideration and which should be simply ignored, ridiculed or marginalised.

Many Irish historians, psychologists and economists recognised as intellectuals or 'opinion-formers' would be seen primarily as professionals, and these are the intellectuals who dominate national discourse. Commentators like John Waters in the *Irish Times* or Kevin Myers in the *Irish Independent* frequently adopt an oppositional or contrarian position on the key issues of the day. Waters, for example, has regularly taken issue with the feminist movement, which he holds responsible for the emasculation and marginalisation of men in Irish society. Myers has clashed frequently with those who take a nationalist or republican position on the North. On the other hand, there are now a number of 'professional' intellectuals who make a living from dispensing opinion through various media channels. Eddie Hobbs draws on his financial expertise to develop a critique of personal spending habits and David McWilliams has used a variety of platforms, including a regular newspaper column, a book and a TV series, to promulgate his views on the transformation of Irish society. His book *The Pope's Children* (2005) offers a pseudo-sociological dissection of the new class system in Irish society. McWilliams celebrates what he saw as the newfound confident, sassy, go-getting middle class, whose identity was expressed primarily through what and how they consume. Psychologist Maureen Gaffney provides frequent media comment on lifestyle, gender and health issues, often from a social psychological perspective. Her popular book *Flourishing* (2011) argues that positive thinking can be life-changing and that in post-Celtic Tiger Ireland, ensuring that the positives of one's life outweigh the negatives is an important component of managing one's everyday life. In other words, the power to change one's life lies in one's own hands.

There is some basis for the claim by power elite theorists that intellectuals' main contribution to society is to legitimate the activities of those in power. A number of studies (for example, O'Dowd, 1996; Lynch, 1999b) suggest that Irish intellectual life has been characterised by a lack of significant criticism of or dissent from existing social arrangements. We can explain this by reference to the class background of Irish intellectuals or to their links with the modernising state, or both. But this is not a criticism that Irish sociologists can make of other Irish intellectuals without being willing to turn it on themselves. Sociology in Ireland is remarkable for the slight influence it has had on mainstream intellectual life in comparison with that of other academic disciplines or of artists and writers. But whatever influence it *has* achieved has failed to significantly expand the role of intellectual as alienated outsider or as protagonist of human emancipation.

INTELLECTUALS AT A TIME OF CRISIS

Public intellectuals become really public and influential in quite specific settings at times when political order and moral certainties are shaken, according to Lodge (2009). Similarly, Garvin (2012) has argued that intellectuals tend to be valued only when things have become unstuck. In the good times, they tend to be ignored. The first role of the public intellectual is to encourage or even force people to think, but according to Garvin there has always been a strain of anti-intellectualism in Irish life. In his view, the value of education, as distinct from practical training for earning one's living, has never been fully grasped in independent Ireland. Garvin decries a trend that he sees underway (and not exclusively in Ireland) whereby many universities are coming under increased pressure to engage in applied, intellectually derivative and profitable research at the expense of free enquiry. He sees this as tantamount to the destruction of imagination and a veritable assault on university intellectual life.

Drawing on Sartre's aphorism that if an intellectual is to understand his society he must adopt the point of view of its most underprivileged members, O'Connor (2012) argues that public intellectuals, at least in theory, should be concerned with creating new agendas and raising issues that those in power seek to avoid. Moreover, she suggests that public intellectuals have a key role to play in transforming 'private troubles' into 'public issues'. Against the backdrop of the economic crisis, O'Connor raises concerns about the crisis of legitimacy within the state and what she sees as the key fault lines of gender and class. She questions the normalisation of a patriarchal political system and documents the myriad ways in which gender inequality is still reproduced – often unquestioningly – in Irish society. She argues that since the institutional elite has remained relatively stable across time (despite economic, social and cultural change), there is little likelihood of it producing from within its ranks critical public intellectuals who might question the basis of elitism. Even if academics and public intellectuals are motivated to engage in critique there is, according to O'Connor, an absence of a public arena in which to do so. She calls on public intellectuals to promote the notion of fairness as a cornerstone of society. She asks that public intellectuals address themselves to issues of gender and class and strive to mobilise greater community awareness through a more robust media presence.

The concept of accountability is central to O'Dowd (2012). He notes that with the global and local crises of financial capital, the contradictions associated with abdicating accountability to the capitalist markets have become more apparent. While acknowledging the important role public intellectuals may play in exposing corruption and malfeasance, O'Dowd forensically traces structural and historical factors in Ireland that serve to limit the influence of public intellectuals and diminish the possibility of their mounting a sustained critique of the existing political and economic system. He notes the formative influences of the Irish national movement and its relationship with nationalism and British imperialism and the Catholic Church on public intellectuals. Furthermore, O'Dowd delineates four key crises in the history of the state that have been critical to the formation of Irish intellectuals and the debates that have preoccupied them: the economic collapse of the 1950s, the eruption of the Troubles in Northern Ireland in the 1970s, the economic recession of the 1980s and the current global capitalist crisis. He concludes that the progressive economisation of public debates, the general enthralment to consumer capitalism and its co-optation of the state, politics and culture have combined to marginalise the role of public intellectuals in accountability and democracy. As a result, there has been insufficient scrutiny and critique of the power elite in Irish society.

6
Work and Livelihood

For many people, work occupies the largest part of their waking hours, and sometimes even their dreams! For others, a lack of work is the most compelling aspect of their lives. Much of the world's population labours for no pay, in the home, the community or the economy, their activities not even recognised or measured as 'work'. Yet all of us are dependent on work for our livelihoods: either our own work, that of family members or the fruits of others' work redistributed as social welfare payments or profits and dividends. Work – or the lack of it – can and does shape our physical and emotional health, provides our friends and enemies, shapes our identities and environments and locates us in social hierarchies. It contributes much to our popular culture and our everyday social interactions. Work is a central element of contemporary social life in Ireland, as in most other societies.

This chapter explores the world of work from a sociological perspective. It starts by defining work, revealing it to be less obvious a phenomenon than we might initially expect. It then reviews how work has been of interest to sociologists from the beginnings of the discipline; it examines some influential concepts in the sociology of work and introduces the concept of 'precarity', which expresses much about contemporary thinking in the field. It then turns its attention to the sociology of work in Ireland, with a brief overview of some key trends, including flexibilisation and globalisation of employment. It considers issues related to gender and work, and considerable space is devoted to an examination of paid and unpaid care work. The final section raises some issues about the possible future(s) of work. We also explore some of the ways in which work and personal life overlap and intertwine, for better and for worse, in the contemporary workplace.

WHAT IS WORK?

What is work? The answer to this question is not as obvious as it might appear. We can think of work fundamentally as a *purposive form of human activity*, though such a definition can also be applied to other activities, such as sport or a hobby. Indeed, there is probably little that humans do that we think of as completely 'purposeless'. 'Work' might mean activity that is carried out for *pay, salary or wages*, and this is a common and commonsense way to think of it. Nevertheless, feminist sociologists and economists in particular have emphasised the massive amount of work carried out in society for no direct monetary reward, such as housework, caring work in the home or voluntary work in the community. Work is also linked to the notion of *occupation*: 'what do you do?' is not just a question about your daily activities, but about the type of person you are and where you 'fit' in the social world. Like many sociological concepts, we can conclude that 'work' is complex and contested.

Nevertheless, it is necessary for a broad range of practical, policy and governmental reasons to define work and related terms such as employment, unemployment and part-time work. The International Labour Organization (ILO) and other bodies such as Eurostat define work as follows:

> persons in employment are those who, during the reference week, did any work for pay or profit, or were not working but had a job from which they were temporarily absent. 'Work' means any work for pay or profit during the reference week, even for as little as one hour. Pay includes cash payments or payment in kind (i.e. payment in goods or services rather than money), whether payment was received in the week the work was done or not. (Eurostat, 2011, p. 21)

Here the emphasis is on work for reward, and these bodies define those not at work or seeking work as 'economically inactive'. This is not a very illuminating term, as in most cases such people *are* actively involved in the economy through their consumption activities – even if they are lying in a hospital bed. They may also be providing a valuable service, such as carrying out unpaid care for a dependent family member.

Keith Grint, in his standard text on the sociology of work, reflects the complexity and difficulty of clearly defining what 'work' is:

> Work tends to be an activity that transforms nature and is usually undertaken in social situations, but exactly what counts as work is dependent on the specific social circumstances under which such activities are undertaken and, critically, how those circumstances and activities are interpreted by those involved. (Grint, 2005, p. 6)

Such interpretations are closely related to issues of culture and power, which means terms like 'work', 'leisure', 'housework' or 'unemployment' must be located in a social, historical, discursive and political context. In this sense, for Grint (2005, p. 7) work is 'indexical': how it is understood tells us much about the society we are looking at. Thus, rather than trying to categorise types of activity as 'work' in any formal way, it may be more useful to understand work as a type of activity that is identified, assessed and constructed in particular social situations, in themselves shaped by relationships of power. We will see that this approach is useful when we come to consider contested areas such as domestic and caring work later on in this chapter.

KEY SOCIOLOGICAL UNDERSTANDINGS OF WORK

The study of work has been a central part of the discipline of sociology. It is inevitably linked to macrosociological analyses of the economy and social class and to the broadest levels of social change that entail the productive basis of societies, such as the distinction between preindustrial and industrial society. It is also important to the more intimate understanding of everyday social life, though sociological writing at this level is much less common – for some vivid examples, see the works of American sociologists Richard Sennett (2008) and Arlie Hochschild (2003). It may be that novelists, visual artists and filmmakers have given us a more compelling insight into how people experience work in their daily lives.

In the 18th century, social and political theorists (such as Adam Smith) began to examine the economy as a separate sphere from the political and other aspects of society. Particular types of social activity began to be identified as having economic value and this helped to shape what we might now think of as 'work'. At the same time, the economic sphere began to achieve a privileged place in society and came to be seen as the determining feature of social life. This was reflected in the writings of the founding figures of sociology. Thus, for Marx, economic production became the 'base' on which society was erected and the 'relations of production' determined the political and cultural 'superstructure'. Similarly, Durkheim gave great weight to the impact of economic relationships in society, particularly in his concept of the 'division of labour'. For Weber, the elevation of work to a 'moral duty' was part of the process whereby ascetic Protestantism contributed to the evolution of capitalism (Grint, 2005, p. 16).

For Durkheim, the growth of specialised economic activities and the increased distinction between occupations was a fundamental aspect of modern societies. Such specialisation – the 'division of labour' – was a consequence of the forces of industrialisation and urbanisation that accompanied the emergence of capitalist society. The division of labour led to the breakdown of traditional ('mechanical') forms of social solidarity and their replacement by what Durkheim termed 'organic solidarity': relationships of economic reciprocity and interdependence that the new industrialist social organisation needed to function effectively. These many-stranded networks of relationships were potentially stronger and more resilient than the simpler and authoritarian sets of social relationships that they replaced. Conversely, they also allowed for the development of individual freedom from the overwhelming constraints of traditional society. The downside was potential disengagement and rootlessness: the particular condition of modernity that Durkheim termed *anomie*. It was thus necessary for industrial society to develop new forms of regulation that could manage the emergent division of labour and prevent the development of anomic relationships (Grint, 2005, p. 97).

For Marx, work was central to human dignity and identity. Humans were *homo faber* – it was only through engagement in fulfilling work that people could express their 'species being' (Grint, 2005, p. 20). For workers in capitalist economies, the fragmentation of tasks and the lack of control over their work contributed to the phenomenon of *alienation*, where workers were divorced from the product of their labours and, by extension, from full participation in human society. Nevertheless, Marx was a believer in material production as the measure of human progress, a notion very much associated with his European 19th-century origins. Thus it came to be that Marxist-inspired governments, such as those of the Soviet Union and Maoist China, celebrated work itself through their officially sanctioned arts and culture and sought to maximise agricultural and industrial production through centralised planning.

Notwithstanding the celebration of labour we can see in Marxist thought, for most of human history work has been seen as something to endure rather than a pleasure or the most meaningful thing in life. Grint (2005, p. 15) points out that, linguistically, many of our words for work, like 'labour', and 'travail', are linked with ancient expressions of pain, torture and lack of freedom. Dislike of manual labour (and of those who had to engage in it) goes back to the ancient Greeks or, more accurately, to those privileged ancient Greeks (such as Aristotle and Plato) whose feelings on the matter have been passed down to us through history, unlike those of the slaves who left behind no written record of their experiences.

Not surprisingly, then, historically many social and political movements have been concerned to reduce the overall burden of work and to improve the conditions under which it is performed. Most notable has been the labour movement, which has included trade unions and labour parties. The feminist movement has also concerned itself with work, partly in seeking to improve the conditions for women workers in paid employment, but also to gain recognition for types of work, such as unpaid caring work and housework, that have not tended to be recognised as 'work' within modern industrial societies. Social movements based in immigrant communities have also strongly focused on workers' rights at times.

Perhaps the most interesting aspect of Weber's sociology in relation to our understanding of work was his path-breaking analysis of *bureaucracy*. For Weber, the rise of bureaucracy was an effect of the 'rationalisation' of social life. This was the 'disenchantment' of the traditional world and the replacement of magical and spiritual understandings with those derived from scientific thought and calculability. In modernity, human action was based on calculations of means and ends rather than a belief in fate or destiny. Bureaucracy was the dominant principle of the organisation of modern society that embraced and expressed the rationalist ethos. Rather than being based on tradition, it was founded in legal relationships and expert knowledge (Grint, 2005, p. 104).

For Weber, bureaucracy allowed for the emergence and development of the modern organisation – and workplace. Bureaucratic organisation depended on a number of key principles: hierarchical authority, written rules, full-time and salaried career officials, a clear separation of home and work, and the separation of ownership and control of an enterprise. According to Weber, an organisation with these features would be more rational and effective, and we can see in his analysis an image of many contemporary workplaces such as factories and offices, schools and hospitals. Weber also acknowledged the drawbacks of such a method of organisation: its tendency towards depersonalisation, boredom and lack of initiative. Nevertheless, his analysis has been influential in terms of our understanding of the contemporary workplace.

More recently the American sociologist George Ritzer has sought to 'make Weber more contemporary' (2011, p. xii) through the concept of 'McDonaldisation'. This approach reflects how the eponymous hamburger chain organises its production: by taking the process of food preparation and subjecting it to a highly organised division of labour within which any specific step, such as toasting a bun or flipping a burger, can be achieved with minimal skills through following a set of instructions or 'script'. Through the widespread adoption of the McDonald's approach to work, Ritzer sees the Weberian concept of rationalisation being applied to a myriad of fields of social life, from religious expression and sport to healthcare and higher education (Ritzer, 2011).

FORDISM AND POST-FORDISM

In a capitalist economy like Ireland's, work can be seen as the production of commodities – physical things like medical devices or services like healthcare – for profit. For Marx, as we saw in Chapter 1, the fundamental division in capitalist society was between the class of the *bourgeoisie* – those who own the means of production, such as land, factories or capitalist firms – and the *proletariat* – those who do not own productive capital and have only their labour power, physical or mental, to sell. Despite the extensive welfare system that typifies modern societies, we can say that this fundamental division continues to exist. Marx showed how it was the generation of *surplus value* – the added value that employees create over and above what they are paid – that constitutes the profit for the owner of productive property. Capitalist firms also determine the range of commodities to be made available. This helps to drive innovation in the form of new and improved products, but may also mean that certain types of useful or necessary products may not be produced or marketed (e.g. particular types of housing, drugs for certain conditions) as there is insufficient opportunity for a profit to be made. Thus it is the owners and controllers of the 'means of production' who wield the most power in the workplace and how it is organised.

The organisation of work around profit, and the consequent need to maintain productivity, means that issues of control (by employers) and resistance (by workers) are central to the workplace. This struggle has driven much of the sociological interest in work: 'where workers are troublesome, organized in strong unions, demanding high wages and strike-prone then the sociology of work is sure to follow' (Curtis, 2007, p. 72). While the history of the labour movement is coloured by strikes, lockouts and violent protests, direct confrontation between capitalists and workers is now relatively rare; rather, management intervenes.

Management seeks to control work in a range of formal ways (such as contracts, clocking-in and training) and informal ways (such as tacit dress codes, expectations about working after hours, praise and criticism) in order to increase productivity and efficiency and to subordinate workers into a degree of compliance while maintaining flexibility. Workers may in turn resist these efforts in a number of ways, from formalised union bargaining backed up by industrial action, to personal negotiation, to informal methods such as go-slows, working to rule and absenteeism – even sabotage (Curtis, 2007, p. 73).

The celebrated American sociologist Harry Braverman has had a significant influence on the sociology of work through his book *Labour and Monopoly Capital* (1974). Braverman focused interest on the *labour process* – how production was organised by bringing human labour and technology together in specific and often dynamic ways. For Braverman, a key element of the capitalist labour process was the 'deskilling' process whereby traditional 'craft' skills (such as ironworking or furniture-making) are lost through the transfer of workers' hard-won skills to management, usually through the operation of increasingly sophisticated technologies (such as the assembly line and, more recently, computer technology). Many sociologists have further explored the phenomenon of deskilling, including in areas of the human services like social work and medicine.

A particularly influential way of thinking about the labour process is through the use of the term 'Fordism' (after the key proponent of the assembly line method of manufacture, US car-maker Henry Ford). Fordism is the quintessentially 'modern' way of organising not just industrial production, but a whole industrial society. It is based on the assembly line; mass production of standardised goods; high use of specialised technology; close control and measurement of workers; and a mass consumerist society. The 'Fordist' period is often taken to refer to the triumph of 'modernity' in the 20th century, but we have seen how similar themes have been explored in today's society by Ritzer through his McDonaldisation concept: he argues that many jobs in our society continue to be deskilled and subjected to managerialist fragmentation and control.

The most recent phase has been identified by sociologists as 'post-Fordism'. It is argued that the mass production approach typified by Ford – and indeed by McDonald's – has passed, as well-educated and savvy consumers demand more choice and more personalisation of products, such as clothing, cups of coffee, glasses of beer or cars. The development of computer-based technology has made 'flexible specialisation' easier and it is argued that many industries have shifted to smaller-scale 'batch production' (e.g. microbreweries) rather than a 'one-size-fits-all' approach (e.g. Budweiser). But Ritzer (2011, pp. 43–7) argues that even if there has been a move to post-Fordist production in some areas, the McDonaldisation of society continues with the use of a rationalised, hierarchical assembly line and closely managed labour process, where 'the last thing on the minds of most people hiring for jobs is creativity' (Ritzer, 2011, p. 44). It appears that both types of production co-exist in contemporary societies, though arguably much of the 'assembly line' work has been outsourced to places like India, China and other comparatively low-wage economies, and not just in manufacturing, but in some areas of the service industries, such as call centres and data processing. Advanced economies (like Ireland) can then focus on the higher end, lower-quantity production of niche or luxury products.

An influential way of looking at labour markets is in terms of *labour market segmentation*, a concept that was developed in economics in the 1970s (Reich et al., 1973) and which has subsequently been much explored within sociology. This approach argues that there is not a single market for jobs, but rather that the totality of available employment is divided into a dual labour market with 'primary' and 'secondary' sectors. Each has its own characteristics (see Table 6.1). Without the requisite educational and social resources, it is difficult to move from one labour market to the other.

Table 6.1: Labour market segmentation: The dual labour market

	Primary labour market	Secondary labour market
Pay	Higher	Lower
Job security	More secure	Less secure
Working conditions/fringe benefits	Good working environment; range of fringe benefits	Less pleasant working environment; few or no fringe benefits
Career ladder	Present	Absent
Unionisation/ membership of professional organisation	High	Low or absent
Autonomy	Higher	Lower
Availability of employment	Consistent	Intermittent
Examples	Teacher, nurse, lawyer, maintenance technician, hotel manager	Cleaner, casual university tutor
Features of workforce	Older, male, citizen, formal qualifications, stable	Young, female, immigrant, lacking formal qualifications, mobile

Labour markets can be segmented in different ways. For example, gender is a powerful factor, as we will see later in this chapter. Ethnicity is also important, with members of subordinate ethnic groups often carrying out the dangerous, demeaning or 'dirty work' that 'nobody else wants to do'. Educational qualifications as well as social and cultural capital (such as the right connections, accent or address) also help to provide admission to the favoured 'primary' labour market. For Ireland, Ó Riain and Murray (2007, p. 251) note that the Irish secondary labour market is 'more feminised, less unionised and more part-time'.

A MORE PRECARIOUS WORLD?

An influential concept that has emerged within the sociology of work is that of 'precarity'. This word, associated with the writings of European sociologists such as Bourdieu, Paugam and Castel (Dörre, 2006), means precariousness or a lack of security. It reflects the impact of post-Fordist patterns of production on people's experiences, not just of work, but of their lives more broadly. It is the outcome of the destabilising effects of globalisation and neo-liberal economic policies. It refers to contemporary trends of job insecurity, flexibilisation, deskilling and deprofessionalisation.

Precarity means 'seeing the future as fundamentally uncertain' (Ross, 2009, p. 212). The concept of a clear and permanent career track, the idea of a job for life or a single and secure career trajectory is becoming a far less realistic expectation. Areas of work that, in Ireland as elsewhere, would have been seen as offering such a trajectory, such as working for a bank, in the public sector or for a blue chip company, are shrinking, to be replaced with far more dynamic and insecure types of employment relationship, such as contract or freelance work or subcontracting. These relationships differ depending on the resources that a worker brings to the relationship and the sector within which they seek to be located: 'the indefinite life may soon be the new standard, warily embraced by "free agents" and high-wage professionals at the jackpot end of the New Economy, and wearily endured by the multitude of contingent, migrant, or low-wage worker at the discount end' (Ross, 2009, p. 212). Within this environment, workers may therefore find themselves experiencing a welcome flexibility (for so-called 'portfolio workers' who have desirable skills they can sell on the open market) or, alternatively, a world of 'flexploitation' for those lacking the requisite skills, experience or other desirable attributes, such as many in the retail or hospitality industries.

Precarity is a consequence of people's limited access to secure and stable employment. Rather, they find themselves in 'contingent work and temping, fixed-term contracts and forced part-time work along with mini- and midi-jobs, dependent self-employment or state-subsidised work schemes' (Dörre, 2006). These are the types of jobs that were formerly labelled 'atypical', but it is argued by sociologists of work that such jobs are becoming all too typical. In effect, a greater number of people are finding themselves in situations that reflect the features of the secondary labour market.

Precarity of employment does not just impact on the experience of working itself. It has much broader implications for the individual and for the nature of society. For example, in the Fordist system, wage labour has been linked with key aspects of occupational and broader social protection, including pensions, health and safety protection, protection against unfair dismissal and incremental pay scales. These benefits to workers have been won through decades of industrial and political struggle, backed up by the power of the labour movement. They are also part of the trade-off between employers and workers that has provided for a stable and relatively predictable regime of production. Neo-liberal politics and economics reject such notions of stability, seeing the global market as the sole legitimate determinant of employment conditions.

Precarity impacts on people's ability to make long-term plans about their lives, for example in relation to housing or raising a family. Arguably, it is contributing to the plummeting birth rates across many European societies, particularly in parts of southern Europe (Baizán, 2005). It impacts not just on those directly involved, but also has a 'disciplining effect' on those who are in more secure, better-rewarded or long-term positions.

As Dörre (2006) notes, post-Fordist working society has now become divided into zones of varying levels of security. Although the majority of employees are still to be found in a 'zone of integration' with regular working conditions and a more or less intact social safety net, there is another zone that is growing all the time – the 'zone of precarity'. Within this part of society across the Western world, there is a disappearing social safety net and a growing disconnection from, and disaffection with, mainstream society. This can be seen, for example, in the rapidly rising and increasingly persistent levels of youth and long-term unemployment across Europe, including in Ireland. It has been suggested that increasing precarity lies behind social unrest amongst young people, for example the riots that took place in British cities in the summer of 2011 and the global 'Occupy' movement that emerged across many Western cities in the same period.

For some types of workers, flexibility can be seen as positive, offering a more congenial relationship to work, but for the majority it is 'flexploitation'. Most temporary or precarious workers do not go on to achieve security or permanency. Another consequence is that precarity for men sees them moving into areas of part-time work that were formerly the preserve of women, thus threatening women's employment opportunities. Precarity also ultimately impacts on the longer-term success of companies themselves by stifling innovation and motivation and threatening the quality of output (Dörre, 2006).

WORK AND IRISH SOCIETY

Following from Grint's point about the 'indexicality' of work, what does 'work' mean in a society like Ireland and what do our understandings of work in Ireland say about the type of society we think we inhabit? To understand work in the Irish context, it is important to be aware of Ireland's particular trajectory of economic development, as discussed extensively in Chapter 3.

For much of Ireland's history, the majority of the male population worked in the agricultural sector. Since the early 20th century, this has predominantly been as farm owner/occupier, though a significant class of agricultural employees did persist into the 1960s. Until the 1980s many men worked in indigenous manufacturing industries, often based on agricultural output (e.g. baking, brewing, dairying and meat factories), in transport (docks, railways, local road maintenance) and the retail/wholesaling sector. Both men and women worked in private and public services like banking, postal services, education and health as well as the relatively small civil service.

Manufacturing industry saw a long-term decline from the late 18th century, to be revived under the protectionist policies of Irish governments in the early to mid-20th century, which sought to revive and develop indigenous industries, and subsequently moved towards foreign direct investment (FDI) that aimed to attract overseas manufacturing and assembly firms to Ireland. More recently, the development of the 'smart economy' has focused on global firms in the knowledge industries (e.g. Google, Facebook), the 'creative industries' (such as computer games and animation) and value-added in the food and agriculture industries. These broader economic patterns help to shape Irish people's experiences of work.

In many ways the landscape of work in Ireland reflects that in other advanced Western economies. As in those economies, the majority of jobs (about three-quarters) are to be found in the service sector, which spans very broadly from the cleaning of offices and serving of meals, to the painting of pictures (and houses), to the invention and selling of financial products. About a fifth of those with jobs work in manufacturing, helping to make tangible goods from whiskey to Viagra to laptop computers, while just a twentieth work in the sector that, until relatively recently, employed the majority of Irish people: agriculture. What are some of the key questions to ask about the Irish workforce? Important aspects relate to its size and composition, the balance between full-time and part-time work, the sectoral distribution of employment, the quantity of work (as in hours per week worked and overall hours worked), pay and conditions and unemployment.

The so-called Celtic Tiger years (1997 to 2007) saw a significant expansion in the number of people in paid work in Ireland. The labour force increased from 1.3 million in 1988 to 2.2 million in 2008 – a two-thirds increase over two decades, while the population increased by only a quarter (Timoney, 2010, p. 4). This remarkable expansion is associated with a number of linked factors, including a major increase in economic activity and output, as measured by GNP and GDP; a higher rate of participation in the labour force, especially amongst women; net immigration of workers from outside of Ireland; and a high level of job creation, which provided a demand for these potential extra workers. There were particularly large increases in numbers employed in services (especially private services like finance, real estate and retail) and construction during these years (Timoney, 2010,

p. 7). This surge in paid employment was a remarkable transformation in a society that, for almost all of its existence as an independent state, was unable to provide employment for a substantial proportion of its people and forced them to emigrate in search of a livelihood. Regrettably, in the wake of economic crisis and a collapse in employment in many sectors, the need to emigrate has emerged in Ireland once again.

At 69.5 per cent, the 'activity rate' (which measures the proportion of the population actively involved in the paid workforce) in Ireland is slightly below the average of the EU27 (71 per cent). The highest rates are in Iceland and Switzerland, at over 80 per cent (Eurostat, 2011, p. 14). Both of these countries have a high rate of part-time work that tends to draw more women, especially those with dependents, into the workforce. Timoney (2010, p. 5) suggests that the overall participation rate in Ireland is in line with global averages. Ireland has a relatively high level of part-time work, especially for men – 22 per cent of all workers are part time: 12 per cent of men and 35 per cent of women (Eurostat, 2011, p. 28). Eurostat (2011, p. 30) reports that about one-tenth of workers in Ireland are on limited-term contracts – that is, in a relatively precarious situation.

In terms of sectoral distribution of employment, Ireland is in that group of countries that has a high proportion in the services sector: 76 per cent compared to an EU27 average of 69 per cent; 20 per cent are in manufacturing industry (EU27 is 25 per cent) with just 5 per cent in agriculture, which is around the EU average but represents a halving of the significance of this sector in terms of employment over the decade since 1998 (Timoney, 2010, p. 7; Eurostat, 2011, p. 32). Providing some support to government rhetoric about the 'smart' economy, Ireland has the highest proportion in the EU with tertiary education, at 42 per cent of the workforce (EU27 average is 29 per cent) (Eurostat, 2011, p. 33).

In terms of hours worked, Ireland has the second lowest average number of hours worked per week at 39.6 hours (Denmark is the lowest at 38.8) (Eurostat, 2011, p. 35) and it has the lowest average number of hours worked per year across the whole of Europe (1,479 hours per annum, compared with an EU27 average of 1,746 and a figure for the UK of 2,108). The UK is the real home of the 'long hours' culture in Europe (Eurostat, 2011, p. 84). Despite this, pay in Ireland is the sixth highest in Europe (Eurostat, 2011, p. 76) and in terms of purchasing power parity (PPP) has the sixth highest legal minimum wage (introduced in 2000) – almost identical with that of the UK (Eurostat, 2011, p. 84). Nevertheless, according to Timoney (2010, pp. 14–15), in the manufacturing sector Irish wage costs have remained very competitive on a global basis since the mid-1990s, helping to attract FDI and drive economic growth.

The rise of precarity, as outlined above, can be linked to unemployment, especially youth unemployment. This phenomenon has once again become a major social and political issue across Europe, including in Ireland. During the Celtic Tiger period, unemployment rates in Ireland fell to historically low figures (4.6 per cent in 2007), but since the development of the economic crisis the rate has increased sharply. In late 2011 it stood at 14.3 per cent (seasonably adjusted standard unemployment rate, December 2011, www.cso.ie), which resembled the very high rates of the 1980s and early 1990s. The increase has been more significant for men (4.9 per cent to 16.9 per cent) than for women (4.1 per cent to 9.7 per cent), reflecting the virtual collapse of the construction and related industries (Eurostat, 2011, pp. 42–3).

Youth unemployment is a major problem across Europe, with a fifth of young people aged 15 to 24 unemployed. They are twice as likely as older workers to be without work (Eurofound, 2011, p. 1). The rate is as high as 42 per cent in Spain, while it is just 10 per cent in Denmark. In Ireland the rate is 28 per cent, and again males suffer disproportionately, with 34 per cent of young males unemployed compared with 22 per cent of young women (Eurostat, 2011, p. 44). Ireland has the lowest employment rate in Europe for single parents (49 per cent) compared to the EU27 average of 67 per cent (Eurostat, 2011, p. 52). This indicates that this group is significantly excluded from the labour market and helps to explain the high level of poverty experienced by single parents.

FLEXIBILISATION OF THE WORKFORCE

A noted trend in Ireland, as in other advanced economies, has been the increased 'flexibilisation' in the Irish workforce. Sociologists have linked this trend to concepts such as post-Fordism and precarity. Work patterns that differ from full-time, permanent employment (itself always only one of a number of work patterns) have been labelled 'atypical'. Ó Riain and Murray (2007, p. 252) note that such 'atypical' work arrangements may include practices such as 'part-time work, temporary employment, self-employment and contracting out'. The growth of such work patterns can be driven both by the desires of employers for a more 'flexible' workforce they can deploy in various ways, but also by workers who want more control over the timing and location of their work, as in 'flexitime' and home-based or mobile working. The growth of flexible work is linked to a number of factors, such as the expansion of the service sector; the increased role that information and communication technologies (ICT) have had in the workplace, with social media and mobile telephony amongst the recent drivers of change; and an increased focus on issues of 'work–life balance', often associated with the increase in the number of women in the paid workforce. Young workers are also more likely to be found in 'flexible' work situations (Eurofound, 2011, p. 1). The flexible worker, suggest Ó Riain and Murray (2007, p. 249), has now become the desired form of employee in the Irish context.

Ó Riain and Murray (2007, p. 252) note that 'flexibility' is underpinned by a dual labour market within firms: 'the flexible firm has a core of multi-skilled workers that it seeks to retain through satisfaction with tasks, seniority within the organisation and monetary rewards. It also has a periphery of workers pulled into or pushed out of the firm according to the needs of the situation.' Thus, different groups of workers experience 'flexibility' in different ways. For the much sought-after skilled 'knowledge' worker (such as a designer, programmer or consultant) it may provide the rewards that can come from 'portfolio' working across firms or even countries; for most workers it offers a more precarious existence and reduced pay and conditions. Ó Riain and Murray (2007, p. 253) argue that such patterns of work are an important element of Irish society: 'having missed the Fordist era of mass production, Irish workers are for the first time participating at home in an advanced industrial economy in which flexible work and employment loom large'.

Ó Riain and Murray point to one of Ireland's economic 'success stories' – the software sector – as a place where we can witness the realities of the flexibilised workplace. They argue that it is here, in this highly globalised industry, that such patterns are most manifest in Irish society: 'with high turnover, individualised human resource management strategies, and non-union approaches' (2007, p. 259). Only 5 per cent of those employed in the software sector are members of trade unions, compared with a national rate of 34 per cent (CSO, 2010c). The industry features US models of workplace organisation that feature 'relatively little employee autonomy and close managerial control' (Ó Riain and Murray, 2007, p. 260). Companies emphasise the crucial role of the 'team', which results in a combination of long hours and high pressure to get work done but also permits a high level of work autonomy – a feature of many 'knowledge-based' jobs. Despite the focus on the 'team', reward structures are individualised through performance-related pay; relatively high pay rates in the sector are combined with a 'pervasive job insecurity'. There is much about the economically important software sector in Ireland that reflects the most contemporary global trends in how work is organised.

Always On?

One long day at the computer. You can just absorb your whole life in work. (young female office worker quoted in Gregg, 2011, p. 110)

It is 4.30 p.m. on a wet and windy Thursday evening in Dublin. In a local outlet of a global coffee shop chain, dozens of people are dotted around tables, on couches and in booths, with an array of longer and shorter coffee-based drinks or herbal teas and infusions. Many are using laptop or notepad computers to surf the Internet, taking advantage of the 'free' wireless Internet (wi-fi) in the café; some are clearly working, with papers and documents to hand; others are checking email or Facebook; others again are doing similar things, but on hand-held smartphones. Here and there are groups of people, mostly young, chatting to each other, but always with a phone in hand, switching backwards and forwards from text-based to 'live' chat. One or two people are reading (paper-based) books, magazines or newspapers. The atmosphere is partly workplace, partly meeting place, partly refuge.

In pre-capitalist societies, and in much of the world even today, the borderline between 'work' and 'non-work' is blurred. In traditional agricultural societies, in family-based and sole operator businesses such as pubs and small shops, and in street-based economic activities, personal, family and economically productive time and activities often overlap. 'Work', 'leisure' and 'family life' are mutually supportive, integrated and, of course, often in tension. The meanings that participants derive from such activities are also complex and intertwined. 'Home life' and 'work life' are not so easily separated.

In modern industrial urban and suburban societies, 'work' and 'home' became increasingly discrete areas of activity. People left a place called home and travelled (commuted) to other places – shop, office or factory – where 'work' took place, amongst a group of people (workmates, colleagues) that were separate and different from 'family' life in the domestic environment at home. Numerous aspects of contemporary culture (transportation systems, emotional life, popular entertainment, interior architecture, suburbia) are supported by, and support, this spatial and temporal separation. It is the classical pattern suggested by 'leaving home to go to work' and 'leaving work to come home'.

According to recent sociological research in Ireland and elsewhere, contemporary modes of technology-supported work, for example in the IT, creative, academic and business sectors, are, for some, contributing to new forms of work/non-work relationship. In particular, key features of contemporary technology and work organisation are leading to a *reintegration* of the workplace and the domestic place; of work time and non-work time, particularly for so-called 'professional' workers. These changes, termed 'work's intimacy' by Australian writer Melissa Gregg, have both positive and negative repercussions for work and for workers.

'Work has broken out of the office, downstairs to the café, in to the street, on to the train, and later still to the living room, dining room and bedroom' (Gregg, 2011, p. 1). In such ways, work increasingly comes to dominate the physical and emotional worlds of contemporary professionals. This is a group that has long put work at the centre of their lives – at least as long as the modern corporation has existed: they say they enjoy or even 'love' their work. Yet modern information technology – smartphones, wi-fi enabled computers, laptop and notebook computers, text messaging and telephone answering machines – do much to support an 'always on' culture where one is potentially 'at work' any time, any place, even in bed. This is referred to by Gregg as 'presence bleed'.

This phenomenon reflects a work culture that has become ever more demanding. Contemporary work, particularly in the so-called knowledge-based industries, penetrates ever more aspects of life. It may even displace the family as a source of friendship, solace and emotional connection, a trend exacerbated by social media services like Facebook, where the lives of 'friends', 'family' and 'contacts' intertwine. Add this to the emphasis on 'working for the team', the 'long hours culture' and the constant need to be 'in touch' and 'up to speed' and it is not surprising that Gregg (2011, p. 145) suggests that one's relationship with work can become a form of 'adultery'.

Since the 1980s, telecommunications providers (including Eircom and other Irish-based firms) have sold the promise of 'working from home', of 'telecommuting' or home-based working. Many public and private sector companies now have specific policies to support such work, though in practice most such arrangements are informal. There can be great attractions in such a set-up. As blogger Niall Doherty puts it, 'it's great because there's wireless Internet, a stocked fridge, and nobody telling me to wear pants' (O'Doherty, 2011). Homeworking may be particularly attractive for women, as it offers the opportunity to combine paid work with domestic work, like childcare and housework. The home (one's own or others') has long acted as a workplace, even in contemporary capitalist society. There are long-established forms of homework, such as piecework in the clothing industry (such as knitting Aran jumpers), home-based hairdressing (Cohen, 2010) and party-selling of product lines such as Avon and Tupperware.

Homeworking can indeed provide for a more 'family friendly' lifestyle. But it has its drawbacks. Cohen (2010), in her analysis of home-hairdressing services, notes the difficulty in keeping work-based and other relationships separate, as hairdressers are always open to requests for services, even when 'off' work. Gregg focuses on the tensions within the household when 'domestic' spaces – the kitchen table, the couch in front of the TV, the bed – are commandeered for work purposes. Similarly, she also notes how working at home, usually with electronic devices, can negatively impact on the quality of family interaction: 'it was ... common for children to be competing for attention from tired and busy parents, whose own computer use continued on their return home' (Gregg, 2011, p. 135).

Furthermore, homework is a major benefit to employers in that many of the costs (such as phone bills, development and maintenance of home networks, heating and lighting) are absorbed by the employee; it can also be very difficult for employees to put limits on what constitutes 'work'. Gregg reports many examples of employees using their own (non-paid) time in order to 'catch up' with what's happening back at the office, to clear accumulated emails or to participate in 'team' projects even on days off.

Gregg is particularly critical of email: both the facilitator and the scourge of today's information-based workplace. She notes that 'what begins as a democratic communication platform just as often becomes an opportunity for co-workers to force their own agendas on to others' schedules, obstructing individuals' capacity to manage their workload' (2011, p. 79). The need to send, read and constantly monitor email is not included in workers' schedules or contracts, so this often has to be done in 'free' time, often at home. Ironically, such is its demanding nature that email, together with widespread use of social media such as Facebook and Twitter, serves to reduce the amount of face-to-face communication that takes place. Email penetrates into people's private space, as it impacts on meal breaks, disrupts sleep patterns and even follows employees on their holidays as they take along phones and laptops to 'keep in touch' with the workplace.

The Nomadic Work/Life in the Knowledge Economy project at the University of Limerick examined the work of ICT professionals in the Shannon region. It found that lower-level ICT professionals (mainly white, male, middle aged, with technical backgrounds), perhaps surprisingly, continue to work conventional nine-to-five jobs, with a 'clear demarcation between work and life spheres' (d'Andrea, 2010, p. 3). The situation is different for ICT company owners and directors, who experience considerable overlap between work and family life:

> More time must be dedicated to business tasks, as work is taken home over nights and weekends. Physical time is not only dedicated to concrete business activities, but it also translates in the almost permanent availability normally expected from such top professionals. In terms of mental time, dedication to work and worrying over it are intangible examples of a subjective dedication to work regimes, as the latter overflows into times and spaces otherwise dedicated to personal, family, leisure and social spheres. Wireless communication devices, the flexibilisation of work across time-space, and the internationalisation of work teams and clients, have greatly contributed to the encroachment and pressures of work over life.

As for the Australian scene described by Gregg, it is the younger workers in the Limerick study who are more likely to immerse themselves in work, to make heavy use of 'always on' electronic equipment, to work 'anywhere' – 'home, trains, airports, hotels' – and to actively blur the boundaries between family and work life. Like the workers in Gregg's study, these workers 'whenever asked about their subjective states ... express a mix of excitement with passion for high-tech business as well as an underlying anxiety and stress over daily tasks, business future and life possibilities' (d'Andrea, 2010, p. 4).

The research reported by Gregg, Cohen and d'Andrea all points to the complexity of modern work patterns in advanced economies such as Ireland's. The role of information technology is key. On the one hand it promises freedom, autonomy, creativity, control over the place and timing of work, even excitement and fulfilment. But the reality is more complicated. For many workers, such as sales reps, public health nurses and merchant seamen, mobile working is nothing new (Cohen, 2010). For others, the capacity of communications technologies to 'seep into' other aspects of everyday life just makes work more demanding, especially when it comes into conflict with, or even dominates, family life and leisure time. Conventional labour movements find it difficult to respond to these trends, particularly as the time needed to check email, update one's Facebook page or respond to telephone messages is rarely counted in workload assessments. A new form of work-based politics may be necessary.

GLOBALISATION AND THE IRISH WORKFORCE

One of the key features of the development of the Irish workforce in recent years has been globalisation. We have seen that since the 1960s, foreign direct investment (FDI) has become a central element of the Irish economy. Similarly, Irish corporations and companies have increased their levels of investment overseas, with the emergence of a number of Irish-based or Irish-linked multinational corporations. During the Celtic Tiger period, a major new trend for the Irish workforce occurred: inward labour migration. While this phenomenon has been part of most Western economies since the middle of the 20th century (e.g. Commonwealth-based immigration to the UK; 'guest workers' in Switzerland and Germany), it is a significant change for Ireland.

At the same time, Irish people became increasingly conscious of the global competition for corporate investment and consequent employment. This contest was starkly illustrated by the relocation in 2009 of nearly 2,000 computer assembly jobs by multinational computer manufacturer Dell from their factory in Limerick to one in Lodz, Poland. The logic for this was the availability of significantly lower pay rates in Poland. Nevertheless, a range of more skilled positions was maintained in Limerick.

Global labour migration takes a number of forms and may involve a number of relatively discrete job markets. At the 'top' we find a global marketplace for high-level employees of multinational corporations, global bodies and academic institutions. This has been referred to as the 'international class of knowledge workers who are valued almost entirely for their ability to apply or create new bodies of knowledge' (Ó Riain and Murray, 2007, p. 252), who may be developing a career profile through international experience or opportunity. Such highly qualified specialists are often referred to as 'ex-pats' rather than economic migrants and may be attracted by lifestyle and relationship issues as well as by more 'extrinsic' aspects, such as money or organisational status (Crowley-Henry, 2010).

At the 'lower' end of the labour hierarchy, there is significant migration of people across the globe to fill the requirements of the agricultural, manufacturing and service industries. Ireland has experienced an influx of workers into parts of the agriculture industry (e.g. Latvians and Lithuanians into the border counties' mushroom industry, Brazilians into the meat factories of Gort, Co. Galway), Poles and Slovaks onto the building sites of every town and townland in Ireland and Filipina and South Asian women into the healthcare and aged care industries. It can be easy to overstate the level of labour mobility, however. Research by the European Foundation for Living and Working Conditions indicates that only 4 per cent of EU citizens have changed countries in search of work; this is still (perhaps surprisingly) more than twice the rate of inter-state mobility in the US. Ireland is one of the EU countries with a relatively high level of labour mobility, compared to Italy, where less than a tenth of the working population has even moved into a different region to the parental home (Eurofound, 2008).

Barrett et al. (2008) found that immigrants from the 'accession' or newer EU member states earn 10 to 18 per cent less than comparable Irish-born workers, depending on whether we control for sector or occupation. Those from the newer member states have greater disadvantages than other immigrant groups. This may be related to the fact that those from the accession countries are the newest arrivals or to differential levels of education. Immigrants with the lowest education did not have a pay gap with Irish-born workers, but the pay gap rises along with educational attainment (Barrett et al., 2008, p. 16).

GENDER AND WORK

Possibly one of the most significant and influential shifts in Irish society over the past 50 years has been the movement of women into the paid workforce. This change has been seen as a key indicator of the modernisation of Irish society and has been broadly welcomed, though its implications are often contested.

To be sure, Irish women have always worked, but for married women in particular, this work was hidden and undervalued, located firmly within the family and the household. As women have increasingly taken up paid jobs in the economy, this has had repercussions for their power in other spheres, such as the law, consumption, personal relationships and cultural representations. Yet a firmly delineated 'gendered division of labour' (O'Sullivan, 2007, p. 268) remains in Irish society. This is reflected in unequal rewards for work, differing ways of combining work and other aspects of life and occupational segregation, whereby women and men continue to engage in different patterns of work activity.

In 1971, just 28 per cent of Irish women were in the paid workforce; now that figure stands at 56 per cent (Eurostat, 2011, p. 24). At the same time there has been a marked reduction in the number working exclusively in the home. Over the Celtic Tiger years in particular there was a marked increase in women's participation in paid work in Ireland, with almost 300,000 women joining the workforce between 1996 and 2006 (Russell, 2010, p. 15). As a consequence, Ireland has a rapidly narrowing gender gap in relation to workforce participation. In 2000 the gap in participation was 22 per cent, while in 2010 it had decreased to 8 per cent. It is now one of the narrowest gaps in Europe outside of the Scandinavian and Baltic countries (Eurostat, 2011, p. 24). Sexton et al. (cited in Russell et al., 2007, p. 3) suggest that women will comprise 45 per cent of the total employment in the Irish workforce by 2015. As O'Sullivan remarks (2007, p. 273), 'a normative expectation is emerging that to be an adult is to be a worker, irrespective of one's gender or marital status'. In other words, women, whether married or single, are no longer 'allowed' to exempt themselves from participation in the paid workforce.

A range of factors has been identified as the cause of the significant increase in Irish women's participation in the labour market: changes in the nature of employment, with a major expansion of the services sector; changes in family structure, including smaller family size, more family breakdown and lone parenting; the impact of feminist thought and feminism as a social movement; higher family indebtedness and consumption, including higher housing costs; greater availability of childcare; and better educational access for women. O'Sullivan (2007, p. 271) points to the impact of both the 'demand' and 'supply' sides of the consumerist culture of Celtic Tiger Ireland: 'the rise of consumer culture has led to the triumph of the idea that couples "need" two incomes to service their mortgage and other consumption ... [while] the economy's need for the extra capacity offered by women workers, including mothers, is the macro-level driver behind recent changes rather than any restructuring of gender roles'.

This shift has changed the culture of work in Ireland. O'Sullivan (2007, p. 270) describes how this impacts on the students she encounters in a metropolitan university:

> there is optimism amongst the majority of female students about their life chances; they believe they can 'have it all', they can see their advantageous position in the educational system and are looking forward to combining successful careers, children and marriage. They believe in a fair and meritocratic society – a gender-blind society – where exam results, qualifications and hard work count and gender does not.

She sees this as overly optimistic, as it does not envisage any type of structural change – or assumes that the necessary changes have already occurred. The system is still set up for the worker with no family responsibilities, or rather with strong domestic support.

Notwithstanding the increasing proportion of women in the workforce, a gender gap in pay remains. According to Eurostat (2011, p. 79), in Ireland there was a gender pay gap of around 16 per cent in 2009, which is less than the average of about 18 per cent for the EU as a whole. While this is some improvement over the figure of 22 per cent in 2003, the differential has a significant impact:

> Despite progress in terms of women's overall participation in the labour force, and some progress in terms of promotional prospects, women's economic power remains weaker than men's overall and this disadvantage begins early in women's working lives. In a heterosexual couple, this makes it seem logical and economically rational to define a woman's work as less important than a man's. This can, over time, lead to a situation where the woman's primary role is defined as mother and homemaker, and the man's as breadwinner. (O'Sullivan, 2007, p. 277)

What is the cause of this 'glass ceiling'? This is a matter for much debate and analysis. On average, men have more years of work experience than women, and this appears to be the single biggest contributor to the pay gap. The discrepancy may be exacerbated by time out of work to raise a family or periods of part-time work. In the United States and United Kingdom, the gender wage gap also remains in the range of 20 to 30 per cent (McGuinness et al., 2009, pp. iii–2), though much smaller gaps can be found in some European countries, such as Slovenia, Belgium and Poland (Eurostat, 2011, p. 79).

While women in Ireland have moved substantially into the paid workforce, in common with most other societies they remain responsible for (and carry out most of) domestic and caring labour within the home, as outlined later in this chapter. It has been argued that this 'double shift' – which involves not just domestic labour, but the moral pressure to assume the care responsibility for children and other dependents – militates against gender equality in the workplace. As Murphy (2009, p. 181) notes, even though 'women are being asked to change their expectations and place themselves on a work continuum ... little has been done to change the world of care or work to accommodate women's care and employment needs'. This failure to address the broader issues that impact on women's paid workforce participation means that they are more likely to be directed, or forced, into part-time, 'atypical' or more precarious work situations.

Gender segregation remains a key factor in the Irish labour market. As O'Sullivan (2007, p. 273) points out, in Ireland 'professional work is the only area with an even gender balance'. Male-dominated areas of work include machine operatives and craft workers, whereas women dominate clerical, secretarial and sales workers. Despite its pervasive nature, labour market segmentation is a dynamic process and the marketing of jobs and occupations as 'men's work' or 'women's work' can change over time (in the 19th century, 'secretaries' were inevitably male; now that occupation is almost exclusively female). In Ireland, sectors like education are becoming increasingly feminised, especially in primary and secondary teaching.

CARE WORK

As we have suggested, much of the world's work is not recognised as such and receives little or no financial reward. Across the globe, including in Ireland, countless hours are spent working to care for others – often by family members, but also by a large, predominantly low-status and largely hidden paid care workforce. In the last three decades, largely through the work of feminist and other sociologists, philosophers and economists and the advocacy of carers themselves (e.g. Pahl, 1985; Waring, 1989; Nash, 1995; Lynch 2007; McGinnity and Russell, 2008; Care Alliance Ireland, 2010), this highly significant aspect of work has come to be recognised, theorised, measured and better understood. The emergent understanding of care work has had important implications for the analysis of work more broadly and has been recognised as central in expanding the sociological conception of work (Gallie, 2011, section 2.5).

Care work has been defined as an activity that 'demand[s] intensive relational work that is geared toward improving the personal well-being of others' (Duffy, 2011, p. 9). It might be paid or unpaid. While paid work is often seen as taking place in the 'public' sphere, much of the world's unpaid work is found in the 'private' sphere of families and domestic settings. It is a feature of modern societies that these two spheres are formally separated (Armstrong and Armstrong, 2005, p. 169). Paid care work (such as nursing, formal aged care or early childhood education) takes place in workplaces such as hospitals, nursing homes or crèches, while the unpaid work of 'carers' happens in private living spaces. In practice, this distinction is blurred: much paid care takes place in private homes, such as home help, community nursing or occupational therapy, while formal caring institutions draw on a considerable amount of unpaid voluntary labour and support from relatives and friends.

The relationship between the 'private' and 'public' spheres of work is dynamic. In some cases, private activities have moved into the 'public' sphere, as reflected in the increased level of dining outside the home, the re-emergence of paid domestic labour such as cleaning and nannying services and an increased use of paid-for aged care (Ó Riain and Murray, 2007, p. 253). On the other hand, there is a move to privatise some formerly public services, often in the guise of moving people from institutional care (for example, large disability facilities) 'into the community', which in practice usually means unpaid care by family members.

Care work, paid or unpaid, has been identified by sociologists within the Marxist tradition as 'reproductive work' – work necessary to ensure the current and future population (as workforce and consumers) can survive and flourish in the present and into the future. As such it is a crucial element of society and 'what may at first glance appear to be private and removed from the world of market work is actually intimately and inextricably connected to it' (Duffy, 2011, p. 11). While care work continues to be routinely ignored by many economists and those who measure a nation's GDP, it is of fundamental economic importance in any society. In Ireland, the Care Alliance (2010, p. 2) has estimated that unpaid care work contributes €2.5 billion to the economy every year.

Mignon Duffy, an American sociologist who has carried out a recent analysis of paid care work, identifies two key forms: *nurturant* care work is relational and involves direct caring work with another, as in nursing or early years education and care; while *non-nurturant* care work is 'labour that is often out of sight or at least does not involve explicit relationship with those being cared for' (Duffy, 2011, p. 6). It includes the work of people like hospital attendants, cleaners and catering workers whose work is the relatively 'hidden' element of care work but is nonetheless crucial. She includes both these aspects in her analysis of paid care work in the US, as there are important gender, class and ethnic cleavages between the two parts of the care workforce.

There can be a tension in seeing care work predominantly in terms of 'work', as this may be seen to downplay or even negate the affective or 'caring' dimension. Duffy (2011, p. 13) argues that it is important to develop an understanding of this field of activity that can capture both aspects in tandem: the reproductive function and the affective dimension. She cautions against a reading that sees a straightforward move in the provision of care from the family to the market, reminding us that historically, those with sufficient wealth or power have always been able to employ others to carry out domestic and caring work, whether inside or outside the home.

What we see emerging now in advanced societies like the US and Ireland is a complex blend of domestic care, commoditised private or public care (such as nursing homes) and the involvement of a range of expert and professional carers, for example in the fields of health and aged care. Thus, 'a system which relied on family members and hired help to face one set of care challenges has been transformed into a system that combines family care and expert workers to address the radically different care challenges of today' (Duffy, 2011, p. 131). This complicated picture is partly the consequence of significant demographic changes, not least a much greater proportion of people living well into old age. The complex world of care is reflected in a differentiated care workforce, which continues to be segmented on long-established gender, ethnic and class lines and on the basis of educational and professional credentials.

Care work is often seen – ideologically and in practice – as 'women's work', but in reality it is carried out by people across all categories, both male and female. The unpaid care workforce in Ireland has been shown to include children and grandparents (Share and Kerrins, 2009; Fives et al., 2010) as well as those we generally think of as 'working age'. A substantial number of men are prepared to identify themselves as carers: nearly 40 per cent of Ireland's 161,000 self-reported 'family carers' are male (Care Alliance Ireland, 2010, p. 3), while in some sectors of the paid care workforce (e.g. nursing) the number of male employees is slowly increasing, though not without challenges (Keogh and O'Lynn, 2007).

Notwithstanding these trends, there is a strong association in most modern societies between femininity and caring. Men continue to be viewed as the breadwinners within families while women are held, or left to be, responsible for the planning, organisation and delivery of caring. In Ireland, women's increased participation in the paid labour market has not been mirrored by a corresponding increase in men's participation in unpaid care work (O'Connor and Dunne, 2006, p. 59).

Given that domestic and care work have historically been little analysed, recent studies of everyday time use in Ireland (McGinnity and Russell, 2008) reveal interesting patterns. A national time use study sponsored by the Equality Authority and carried out by staff of the ESRI (McGinnity and Russell, 2008, pp. 36–7) shows that within households with children, women typically spend 5 hours 16 minutes per weekday on primary childcare activities (such as physical care and supervision), while for men the average figure is just 1 hour 55 minutes (see Table 6.2). Though the gap is closer at the weekends, women are still doing twice as much unpaid care work.

Table 6.2: Participation in and time spent on caring activities on weekdays and weekend days (per cent)

	Weekday			Weekend		
	Childcare 1: Physical care supervision	Childcare 2: Play, talk, homework, etc.	Adult care	Childcare 1: Physical care supervision	Childcare 2: Play, talk, homework, etc.	Adult care
	% doing activity			% doing activity		
Men	12	15	3	13	17	5
Women	35	31	12	28	29	8
All	24	23	8	21	23	6
Significance	***	***	***	***	***	n.s.
	Time among those who participate (hh:mm)			Time among those who participate (hh:mm)		
Men	1:55	1:51	2:47	3:22	2:25	1:43
Women	5:16	2:11	3:34	6:21	2:45	3:42
All	4:25	2:04	3:25	5:27	2:38	3:01
Significance	***	n.s.	n.s.	***	n.s.	*
	Average time all (hh:mm)			Average time all (hh:mm)		
Men	0:14	0:17	0:05	0:26	0:25	0:05
Women	1:50	0:40	0:25	1:49	0:48	0:18
All	1:03	0:29	0:16	1:08	0:37	0:12
Significance	***	***	***	***	***	**

Note: If two activities are recorded simultaneously, the time is recorded for both activities. Therefore, the total time includes care as a primary activity and as a secondary activity. Stars refer to statistical significance of gender differences using Pearson's chi-square test for the proportion participating and Anova for the time spent. ***$p < 0.001$ **$p < .01$ * $p < .05$.

Source: McGinnity and Russell, 2008, p. 36.

The ESRI time use study also confirms that due to their disproportionate involvement in unpaid care work, employed women in Ireland continue to work a 'second shift' – their work in the paid workforce is on top of the burden of work within the household. Men enjoy more leisure time at weekends, while women's domestic tasks continue. The consequence is that Irish women work on average around 40 minutes longer per day than men, including both paid and unpaid labour and travel time (McGinnity and Russell, 2008, pp. x–xi). The most egalitarian division of domestic labour is in households where both partners are engaged in paid work outside the home, though women still do more work. The arrival of children tends to increase women's involvement in unpaid work while increasing men's in paid employment. Compared to other European countries, Ireland maintains a relatively 'traditional' gender division of labour, with a high proportion of male breadwinner couples (McGinnity and Russell, 2008, p. xi).

Sociologists have explored this gendered dimension of care. Why is it that care work has been so strongly identified with women and what are the implications of this for the women themselves and for society as a whole? Is it a 'timeless' phenomenon or can we trace the 'feminisation' of care work? Should more men be involved in care work, and if so, what would this mean? McGinnity and Russell identify 'factors like national policies, cultural norms and past practices to account for the rather traditional division of domestic labour in Ireland compared to other countries' (2008, p. xi).

It has been suggested that there are links between women's overwhelming responsibility for unpaid domestic work and their domination of many sectors of the paid care field. Duffy (2011, p. 2) points out that 'many of the jobs in which women have been concentrated have been seen as paid versions of the jobs they do at home – taking care of children, watching over the sick, and cleaning people's houses and hospital rooms'. But a broader and historical examination of the care workforce illustrates that there is no 'natural' association between women and caring jobs. For example, it is only in the last half-century that women have come to dominate primary teaching; men have long been dominant in psychiatric nursing and many medical fields; and areas of 'non-nurturant' care like cleaning and catering work are as likely to be segmented on class and ethnic grounds as on a gender basis.

It is important to carefully examine any aspect of care work to see if and how it becomes associated with a particular gender, class or ethnic category. For example, why has there been such an increase in the number of Filipina nurses in Ireland in the 21st century? Why did Irish women constitute almost half the domestic servant workforce in the northern United States at the start of the 20th century (Duffy, 2011, p. 23)? Why has there been such a marked 'feminisation' of primary teaching across the Western world in the last 50 years? Why is it difficult for men to get involved in nursing or professional childcare?

Theorising care work

The Irish sociologist with the most consistent interest in the area of care work has been Kathleen Lynch. With her UCD colleagues (Baker et al., 2004) she has theoretically and empirically explored what she terms 'love labour'. This term points to the *affective* nature of caring work – how it relates to emotions, feelings and love – particularly what Lynch (2007) terms 'primary care relations' – those that typically involve close family members. She argues that this type of nurturing care work is centrally important to human existence and to society, in domestic relationships but also more broadly:

> The inevitability of interdependency does not just apply in personal relationships, but also in work places, in public organisations, in voluntary groups or other social settings. While it is obvious that we cannot flourish personally without support, encouragement and affirmation, even in our paid work lives we can only flourish fully if we work with others who are nurtured, fed and supported so they are willing and able to work. (Lynch, 2007, p. 554)

Lynch argues that care work is also 'hard work', involving emotional work, moral commitment, mental work (such as planning), physical work (such as lifting or washing) and cognitive work (the skills of caring). Caring thus has the potential to involve the expenditure of significant physical and emotional energy; it can be a pleasure but also a burden. It also involves people in making decisions and value judgements about how to balance their own interests with those of others.

Lynch sees care work as taking three distinct forms: love labour, general care labour and solidarity work (see Table 6.3). She sees all three of these forms of care work as 'vital for human self-preservation and self-realization, both collectively and individually'. She points out that in contemporary societies, care work is 'low-status work' and those who perform it are labelled accordingly, especially if they are doing it full time. According to how the Central Statistics Office (CSO) categorises workers (CSO, 2003, cited in Lynch, 2007, p. 551), those employed in the care sector have the same status as semi-skilled workers such as bar staff, goods porters and mail sorters – the second lowest occupational ranking. Those employed in private households as domestic staff are classified by the statisticians as unskilled workers – at the bottom of the occupational ranking.

Love labour is the most demanding form of care work, involving high levels of physical activity, expenditure of time, degree of attentiveness and relationships of trust. Commitments can be very long term and emotional engagement is likely to be intense. The scope of such work is broad and not easily limited. While the caregiver may gain material benefits (e.g. ultimate inheritance of property, reciprocal care in old age), love labour tends to be other-focused and may involve considerable cost to the provider. Notwithstanding this, there are also strong interdependencies and mutualities and love labour is nearly always a two-way process, unlike many other forms of service work. Such relationships involve power and can sometimes involve exploitation or abuse.

Table 6.3: Mapping other-centredness: Love, care and solidarity

FORMS OF CARE WORK			
Features of care work	Love labour	Secondary care labour*	Solidarity work**
Using the skills of knowing how to care (cognitive work)*	Having knowledge of what love is and what it is not	Knowing how to care	Knowing how to do solidarity work (as opposed to charity)
Emotional engagement (emotional work)	Intense and prolonged (may be positive or negative)	Moderate and variable	Politically emotional rather than personally emotional
Commitment and responsibility	Long standing and sustained but may be reneged upon	Temporary and contingent	Variable – can be long standing or temporary
Spending time	Prolonged time	Variable time	Variable time
Moral imperative	Strong and compelling, especially for women	Limited and bounded	Determined by law, culture and personal values
Trust	High (expectation)	Moderate and variable	Variable but can be reasonably high
Belongingness	High (expectation)	Moderate and variable	Variable but can be reasonably high
Attentiveness, including advance planning (mental work)	High (expectation)	Variable	High at the political level if it is to be effective
Scope	Extensive	Bounded	May be bounded or extensive
Intensity	High	Low and bounded	Variable
Mutuality	High interdependency whether voluntary or not	More circumscribed	Not necessarily present
Practical tasks, including physical work	High (expectation)	Moderate and variable	Variable but can be reasonably high

* Secondary care work varies considerably depending on whether or not it is set in the context of professional care relationships or voluntary relationships.

** Solidarity work also varies in character depending on whether it is determined by state action, custom or culture and whether it is voluntary.

Source: Lynch, 2007, p. 558.

Lynch argues that unlike other types of care relationship, love labour is non-transferable and thus non-commodifiable, as it is 'given in the contexts of pre-established relationships with a unique history and assumed future involving continuity and attachment' (Lynch, 2007, p. 560). Thus, this particular type of primary caring is not subject to the 'commercialisation, commodification [and] marketisation of care' more generally identified by Duffy (2011, p. 4) – for Lynch, it cannot be provided by the market. For her, 'secondary care' and more general care relationships (such as those we might generally have for relatives outside of the immediate family, neighbours or friends) do not involve the same degree of personal commitment and moral dimension of love labour. The same applies, according to Lynch, in relation to paid care work. While it may well have a significant emotional component and degree of commitment, it is curtailed by the existence of an employment contract. She concludes that 'one cannot pay someone to love someone else; one cannot pay someone to make love to one's partner and claim that this is a substitute for oneself; one cannot pay someone to visit or talk to a friend in hospital and claim that the visit is from oneself' (Lynch, 2007, p. 566).

Finally, Lynch, like Duffy, draws attention to how divisions of gender, class and ethnicity lead to unequal participation in care work – especially in the more burdensome aspects of commitment and heavy emotional and physical work – the 'visiting, tending, lifting, feeding, collecting or delivering'. The more privileged can become 'care commanders', able to avoid all but the most pleasant or symbolic aspects of care (attendance at key rituals, playing and so on). Lynch argues that:

> high status for both men and women is inversely related to the doing of love, care and solidarity work as the idealised workers are 'zero-load' workers: these are without care, be it by being detached from dependency relations by ignoring them, delegating dependency work to others (paying others to do it), or by commanding others to do their dependency work. (Lynch, 2007, p. 564)

The receipt of good-quality care and attention can also contribute to what Lynch calls 'nurturing capital' – a form of capital in society that is little discussed from a sociological or economic perspective.

THE FUTURE OF WORK

What does the future of work hold? Prediction about social trends, even by well-informed commentators, is always a risky business. In 1982 the then Australian shadow minister for Science and Technology, Barry Jones (he later became science minister in the Labour government of the 1980s), confidently asserted that 'even with a computer in every household – as seems probable in the future – it is unlikely that much more employment would be generated than in the existing television industry' (Jones, 1982, p. 117). While Jones was very prescient about the domestic-ation of the computer (at that time, computers were generally large, bulky and very expensive machines, not the sort of thing you would have in your house), he was way out in terms of employment in the computer industries. More recently, Irish sociologist Mary Murphy (2009, p. 180) suggested that in Ireland, 'it is reasonable to accept that, for most people of working age, participation in paid employment is possible'. How quickly things can change!

Jones's work, like many conjectures about the future of work, give much salience to the role of technology. There is much 'technological determinism' in such discussions: technology is seen as the key driver of change rather than the other way around. In the post-Second World War period there was a strong belief that labour-saving devices would usher in a period of untold leisure and that a major problem for advanced societies would be how to use up all the free time. In some ways, technology has had such an effect and working hours have in fact declined in most European societies. But the picture is not necessarily benign: the impact of technology is also experienced as workplace stress, unemployment and increasing precarity.

Grint (2008, p. 355) sees the future of work as being overwhelmingly shaped by the emergence of global capitalism – the development of a fundamentally unequal global division of labour. He sees the key players as global TNCs that can manipulate world markets through techniques of branding and financial transfers that can evade the governance of individual states. Within this scenario the experience of 'work' across the world will be widely divergent; indeed, Grint (2008, p. 377) draws our attention to the persistence in the world of a number of forms of completely unfree labour: slavery.

In the Irish context there is uncertainty about the future of work. Analysts (e.g. Miles, 2005) frequently paint Ireland as a 'knowledge society', echoing the governmental rhetoric of the 'smart economy'. The features of such a society are a strong influence from the field of information and communication technologies (ICT), a focus on innovation and a strong service industry sector. Knowledge itself, in the form of intellectual property (IP), becomes a key resource. But the experience of economic crisis has battered the faith in the capacity of the knowledge economy to guarantee a livelihood for all Irish people. The expenditure on research and education that is required to create the basis for such an economy is being cut back and the country is once again experiencing a 'brain drain' as many of the best educated leave to form part of the global knowledge class. For those in jobs in Ireland, as elsewhere in the advanced economies, it appears that significant change is imminent (Bollier, 2011).

In 2009 a *Time* magazine feature (*Time*, 2009) addressed the future of work and identified many of the features that have been discussed in the social scientific and business literature. It stressed the central role of cheap and ubiquitous information and communication technologies in changing the nature of work, in particular the capacity of the Internet and cloud computing to support the globally distributed organisation of work. This effectively ushers in a new international division of labour where much of the routine component of service work can be outsourced to low-cost economies in convenient time zones. The work that stays in advanced economies like the US (and perhaps Ireland?) will be 'high tech, high touch' – advanced technology-based manufacturing and high-value-added services that require personal interaction.

The nature of people's working lives will change, with later retirement ages (something we are already witnessing in Ireland), less linear career paths with a shift towards more 'contractors and consultants', changes to how pensions and other benefits are managed and financed, and higher participation rates amongst older people and women. There will be a move towards a more 'fluid and virtual' experience of work that may involve much less time spent in a conventional 'workplace' and more at home, in 'third places' like cafés and airports, and more mobile and distance working. In the language of the consultants, work will become 'something we do, rather than a place we go' (Dixon and Ross, 2010). It is even suggested that the model of the workplace of the future might be found in online video games:

> Rob Carter, chief information officer at FedEx, thinks the best training for anyone who wants to succeed in 10 years is the online game World of Warcraft. Carter says WoW, as its 10 million devotees worldwide call it, offers a peek into the workplace of the future. Each team faces a fast-paced, complicated series of obstacles called quests, and each player, via his online avatar, must contribute to resolving them or else lose his place on the team. The player who contributes most gets to lead the team – until someone else contributes more. The game, which many Gen Yers learned as teens, is intensely collaborative, constantly demanding and often surprising. 'It takes exactly the same skill set people will need more of in the future to collaborate on work projects,' says Carter. 'The kids are already doing it.' (Fisher, 2009)

7
Education

Education stands at a central point in our discussion. On the one hand, it is about the creation of particular forms of knowledge and how certain understandings of life and society are generated, transmitted and debated in Irish society. On the other hand, education is intricately bound up with questions about modernity: it is seen as a key to modernisation and a driver of social, economic and personal change.

Sociological analysis of education faces an institution of great complexity. Formal education involves a huge proportion of Ireland's population – an estimated one-third of the people as learners, educators or parents (Drudy and Lynch, 1993, p. ix). Education is an umbrella term that covers a broad range of activities and sites from pre-school to primary and post-primary, through to third-level and adult education. It can include public and private sector training and professional development and even extend to processes of self-education that take place outside of any formal structure. Furthermore, many other activities, from tourism to sport to the mass media, also have a significant, and sometimes quite self-conscious, educational component.

The range of actors and institutions involved in education is similarly broad – it includes children and parents, students and lecturers, pupils and teachers. Also of major importance are the personnel and institutions of the state – the bureaucracy of the Department of Education and Skills (DES) and the numerous official bodies involved in education, from the school inspectorate to parents' groups and third-level accreditation bodies. Education is connected to other institutions, such as the world of employment, law, the mass media and social administration. Like many of the aspects of Irish society discussed in this book, education as a separate field of analysis is constituted at an abstract level while the social reality of education is in many ways inseparable from the totality of the fabric of social life.

Education has always been closely connected to the project of modernity. As Clancy (1995, p. 467) points out, this is for at least two reasons. First, education stands for our ability to develop society in ways that can lead to the betterment of populations through economic growth, spiritual enlightenment, aesthetic appreciation and social progress. The measurement of educational development in terms of, for example, levels of literacy, numbers of schools or the output of scholarly articles is used as a way to gauge social development. Ireland's success as a western European economy is often linked with its well-educated workforce and high levels of cultural achievement. This connection has become even more pronounced in the age of the knowledge-based 'smart economy'. Second, education reflects modern humanity's urge to shape nature through the application of rational knowledge: through learning about and knowing the world, we can better control it. Education can thus contribute to a more efficient use of physical resources, for example through better farming practice, and can also help in the creation of a more ordered and rational society through consumer education, environmental awareness and so on.

In this chapter we examine some key aspects of education that have been of interest to Irish sociologists. First, we examine some of the mythology that has grown up around education. On the one hand, state institutions and the popular media trumpet our levels of educational achievement, while on the other hand a range of international statistics indicate that Ireland compares quite poorly on a number of indices, or perhaps more accurately, that the country has declined from a formerly elevated position. We then provide a brief overview of the main sectors of education, focusing on issues of management and control. The content of education is discussed: what is taught in schools and other educational sites and why? We may be better able to answer these questions by exploring how educational outcomes and processes are related to issues of social inequality, gender, sexuality, class and ethnicity. These issues feature in the final part of the chapter.

EDUCATION IN IRELAND: MYTH AND REALITY

Ireland presents itself as a modern country with a highly educated and literate population, yet even a brief survey of some of the relevant statistics reveals a more complex picture. Table 7.1 indicates the proportion of the population with upper secondary education (to Leaving Certificate level or equivalent) in the OECD countries in 2009. We can see that Ireland, at 72 per cent, is just below the OECD average in terms of completion of upper secondary education. However, the position has improved rapidly – in 1995 the comparable figure was only 47 per cent. In the younger age group (25–34), Ireland is above the OECD and EU average but still very far behind countries such as Canada, the Czech Republic and Korea, which, according to the statistics, have achieved almost universal completion of upper secondary education. Another empirical indicator of educational attainment is reading literacy. When compared to other countries, the literacy levels of 15-year-old Irish students are unremarkable, though still above the OECD average (Table 7.2).

Poor resourcing helps explain Ireland's generally mixed performance in international studies of education. For example, the most recent *Education at a Glance* report (OECD, 2011) compares countries on a range of education indicators and shows that while Ireland is above the OECD average in the proportion of its population with a secondary education, public expenditure on education, at 5.6 per cent of GDP, is below the OECD average of 5.9 per cent (OECD, 2011, p. 230).

Table 7.1: Population that has attained at least upper secondary education, percentage by age group (2009)

Age group	25–64	25–34	35–44	45–54	55–64
Australia	71	83	73	67	58
Austria	82	88	85	80	72
Belgium	71	83	78	67	54
Canada	88	92	91	87	80
Czech Republic	91	94	94	91	86
Denmark	76	86	81	71	68
Finland	82	90	88	84	67
France	70	84	77	64	55
Germany	85	86	87	86	83
Greece	61	75	69	57	40
Hungary	81	86	83	80	72
Iceland	66	70	71	64	57
Ireland	**72**	**86**	**77**	**65**	**48**
Italy	54	70	58	50	37
Korea	80	98	94	71	43
Luxembourg	77	84	79	74	70
Mexico	35	42	37	32	21
Netherlands	73	82	78	71	63
New Zealand	72	79	75	70	62
Norway	81	84	83	77	79
Poland	88	93	92	88	77
Portugal	30	48	31	22	14
Slovak Republic	91	95	94	90	83
Spain	52	64	58	46	30
Sweden	86	91	91	85	76
Switzerland	87	90	88	86	83
Turkey	31	42	28	25	19
United Kingdom	74	82	76	72	64
United States	89	88	88	89	89
OECD average	73	81	77	71	61
EU21 average	75	83	79	72	63

Source: OECD, 2011, p. 39.

Table 7.2: Cross-national ranking in PISA* performance in reading among 15-year-old children (2009)

Korea	539
Finland	536
Canada	524
New Zealand	521
Japan	520
Australia	515
Netherlands	508
Belgium	506
Norway	503
Estonia	501
Switzerland	501
Iceland	500
Poland	500
United States	500
Germany	497
Sweden	497
France	496
Ireland	**496**
Denmark	495
Hungary	494
United Kingdom	494
OECD *average*	493
Portugal	489
Italy	486
Slovenia	483
Spain	481
Czech Republic	478
Slovak Republic	477
Israel	474
Luxembourg	472
Austria	470
Russian Federation	459
Chile	449
Mexico	425
Brazil	412

* PISA refers to Programme for International Student Assessment. The PISA surveys have been carried out every three years since 2000.

Source: OECD, 2011, p. 282.

Major problems and barriers persist in primary education, notwithstanding considerable investment in recent years. There are still many schools operating in substandard accommodation. Primary school class sizes are larger than virtually all other European countries except the United Kingdom – in an OECD league table of average primary school class sizes, Ireland ranks twenty-fourth (OECD, 2011).

In Ireland, one in six (or 9,000) young people leave school every year without a Leaving Certificate qualification. They are considerably more likely to have poor labour market outcomes, health outcomes and other life prospects (Smyth and McCoy, 2009). Although Irish early school-leaving rates are lower than the European average, they are considerably higher than in parts of Europe such as Austria, Germany and the Nordic countries. Social divisions strongly influence Irish early school-leaving patterns, as young men and children from working-class backgrounds are more likely to leave school early (Byrne and Smyth, 2010).

There remain major problems of adult literacy and numeracy and comparatively few resources have been dedicated to tackling this issue. It impacts on people's ability to communicate adequately in certain situations. OECD data (2009) has shown that Ireland has significant mathematical performance problems compared with most other OECD countries. In a 2009 OECD survey, Ireland was placed amongst the lowest of the 64 countries studied.

It is now commonplace for educationalists, sociologists and policy-makers to make explicit the connections between education and the information economy. McBrierty and Kinsella (1998, p. 8) assert that knowledge, information and associated skills have displaced labour as the primary source of productivity and competitiveness. Indeed, the post-industrial 'knowledge' or 'smart' economy is the watchword of policy discourse (Department of the Taoiseach, 2008). Trinity College Dublin sociologist James Wickham (1998) criticises aspects of Ireland's educational performance from this perspective. He throws cold water on the notion of the 'intelligent island' and argues that even though we have a lot of education in Ireland, we are far from being a learning society (1998, p. 82). In particular, he suggests the links and networks between education and industry need to be much better developed. In this criticism he is carrying on the long tradition that has existed since the late 19th century of calling for 'more technology' in Irish education (Drudy and Lynch, 1993, p. 217). Ireland suffers, according to Wickham, from a highly academic approach to teaching and learning, as reflected in the focus of our secondary schools, exam system and universities. In contrast, our vocational education is too narrowly focused, aiming to meet the needs of firms and single industries rather than the requirements of society as a whole. There is little company-based training and academic research is poorly funded. All this adds up to a weak national system of innovation and means that, as a society and economy, we are likely to remain dependent on others to do our thinking for us.

While Wickham is correct to highlight the shortcomings of the Irish system – some of which, such as research funding, have since been addressed – he also reflects a rather narrow view of education in Ireland. For example, he pays little attention to the range of courses offered in the non-university third-level sector. Though often vocationally oriented, these offer a broad range of employment options, from the training of make-up artists for the film and TV industries to multilingual secretaries for the financial sector as well as the more familiar education of computer programmers and laboratory technicians. Furthermore, while he acknowledges the importance of the cultural sector, he does not recognise the importance of academic knowledge in the generation of growth and investment in this field. Such non-instrumental knowledge is crucial to the development of industries as diverse as computer games, tourism and teleservices. If technical, scientific and rational knowledge are the hallmarks of modernity, it may be that a post-modern society and economy demands more critical thought, creativity and flexibility.

The arguments over the extent and nature of education give some indication of its centrality not only to economic growth and development, but also to the creation of national identity, personal fulfilment and the institutionalisation of power. As a major institution in all contemporary societies it will always be at the centre of emotive and extended debates. We examine some of these debates in this chapter, but first we provide a brief sketch of the main contours of the Irish education system.

THE IRISH EDUCATION SYSTEM

It is conventional to divide the provision of education into four stages: primary, post-primary, tertiary and adult education. We will keep this convention even though it omits consideration of important aspects of the educational process, such as early childhood education and vocational and professional training. The Irish education system provides a unique amalgam of state, religious and other interests. It is also dynamic, responding in different ways to changes in social attitudes, the strength and influence of other institutions, industry-based pressure groups and competing expert discourses, including sociological and educational research. This section can therefore only provide a snapshot of the system.

Primary education

The 1937 Constitution specifically acknowledges the role of parents in Irish education. It asserts that the family is the primary and natural educator of the child. Article 42.1 states that it is the 'inalienable right and duty of parents to provide, according to their means, for the religious and moral, intellectual, physical and social education of their children'. While a very small number of parents have claimed their rights under the Constitution and have opted for home-based education, virtually all children in Ireland are educated from an early age in national school; there are over 3,300 national schools in the state and only 37 non-state-funded primary schools (DES, 2011; www.schooldays.ie).

Despite the intention of those that set up the Irish national school system in the mid-19th century, it rapidly became a de facto and de jure religious denominational system, with its denominational nature explicitly recognised and supported by the state (Curry, 2003, p. 85). The churches secured the dominant position in the provision of primary education in the country and Ireland maintained a largely state-financed but religion-controlled system. This position of power has been actively protected by the churches and it is only since the 1970s that others, such as teachers and parents, have had any formal role in the management of national schools. Even this role remains heavily circumscribed, with effective power still in the hands of a heavily centralised government department, the patron of the schools (normally the local bishop) and industrial agreements between the teachers' unions and the state. As O'Higgins-Norman (2011, p. 119) remarks, 'at no stage from 1831 until quite recently has the official Church sought to promote or develop any other form of schooling except that over which it has complete or decisive influence'.

This control of the school system only began to be challenged in the mid-1970s. In the face of both Catholic Church and state opposition, some parents sought to establish inter-denominational national schools. The first of these, the Dalkey School Project, opened in the late 1970s and was followed by similar institutions, often having to operate out of unsuitable temporary premises, in towns like Sligo and Galway. A second challenge to church control has come from a perhaps unlikely source: the expansion of primary education through the medium of the Irish language, in the *gaelscoileanna*. Like the multidenominational project schools, these are managed by boards of people committed to a specific educational and social objective rather than by nominees of the local Catholic or Protestant bishop.

Now the Irish educational landscape is characterised by a multiplicity of education providers and patrons, including Foras Pátrúnachta, Educate Together, Gaelscoileanna and religious providers. A small number of national schools under a new model of governance, the 'community national school', have been established. This means that the Catholic Church's monopoly position has been weakened, an issue that has recently become a live public policy issue. Regardless of the governance concerns of adults, however, Irish children attending primary school report high levels of satisfaction with their schooling experiences (Williams et al., 2009).

A social portrait of the schooling experiences of Irish children: Findings from a national study
The Growing Up in Ireland (GUI) study (2007–2014) (www.growingup.ie) is a government-funded national study. It is the first detailed nationally representative longitudinal study of Irish children, conducted by researchers at the Children's Research Centre, Trinity College Dublin and the ESRI. It involves studying two groups of children, 11,000 nine-month-old infants and 8,500 nine-year-olds, over a seven-year period. It covers almost every facet of children's lives, from their family situations to their health outcomes and education experiences. The study involves collecting qualitative and

quantitative data over an extended period of time in relation to about 20,000 Irish children.

One report of the study provides a portrait of the education experiences of nine-year-old children. It found that about 20 per cent of Irish nine-year-olds attend a single-sex school, that 29 per cent are taught in multi-grade classrooms, that over 85 per cent are taught by female teachers and that 54 per cent had a male principal.

Significantly, Irish children report high levels of satisfaction with school, as 93 per cent reported they liked school 'sometimes' and more than half said they 'always' liked school. Almost all children in the study reported that they received homework several times a week and of the subjects in the curriculum, Irish children disliked Irish the most, preferring Maths and reading (Williams et al., 2009).

The Catholic schools question has come under renewed scrutiny as the church engages in dialogue with the state over the future status of schools under its patronage. A Forum on Patronage and Pluralism in the Primary Sector was established by the government in 2011 as a mechanism for reaching agreement on the future direction of Catholic schools in the context of increasing pluralism in Irish society (see 'Managing structural change in Irish education in an era of religious and ethnic pluralism' below). Increasing ethnic and religious diversity is a fact in Irish schools. Research by Smyth et al. (2009) shows that a tenth of the primary school-going population and 6 per cent of the second-level population is made up of immigrant students. Against international trends, immigrant children in Irish schools tend not to be segregated from other children.

A cross-national study (Smyth, 2009) of religious education in multicultural contexts found that among Irish parents, proximity to a school was the most important factor in decision-making around school choice but that religion was the most important consideration for parents of a minority faith or no faith. The study found that while parental choice is emphasised in Irish education policy discourse, these choices are constrained by the structural realities of the education system. Multidenominational Educate Together schools, for example, operate only in some counties, so this choice is not available to many parents who must therefore send their children to the local denominational (usually Catholic) national school. The study found cross-national variation in on-the-ground religious teaching practices: in Irish Catholic primary schools, the emphasis on religious education tends to be more from a faith development than a 'learning about' religion viewpoint. Irish children attending Catholic schools were also less likely than children in other school contexts – such as Educate Together schools – to learn and know about religious traditions other than their own (Smyth, 2009).

Managing structural change in Irish education in an era of religious and ethnic pluralism

The Forum on Patronage and Pluralism in the Primary Sector was established by the Irish government on 19 April 2011, under the chairmanship of Professor John Coolahan, to consider proposals for dealing with the management of Irish primary schools against the background of an increasingly pluralistic society. This pluralism has three facets:

- An increase in the number of people who self-identify as non-religious.
- The presence of a greater diversity of faith traditions than before.
- Declining commitment in the dominant faith tradition, Catholicism.

The forum's task involves a careful consideration of the historic role of the Catholic Church in educational provision in Ireland. It received about 220 submissions from a variety of stakeholder groups representing a diversity of interests and views, from the Muslim community to Catholic and Gaeltacht schools. Its work also draws on relevant existing research and documentation. The forum's final written report – under seven general headings of overview of background context, current school and demographic context, planning towards future patronage arrangements, towards divesting school patronage, Irish medium schools, stand-alone schools and issues – was published in April 2012 (www.education.ie).

Post-primary education

Historically, post-primary education in Ireland has been provided by a mix of church, state and other private bodies, with the first of these agencies being dominant. Participation rates in post-primary education have risen markedly since the introduction of free secondary education in 1967. The post-primary sector now serves over 350,000 students (CSO, 2011b, p. 96) in a variety of school types: secondary, vocational, community and comprehensive. Though almost completely funded by the state, this level of education remains organisationally dominated by religious bodies, principally the Catholic religious orders. Of a total of 728 second-level schools, 383 are secondary, 253 are vocational and 92 are community or comprehensive (DES, 2012). The four types of school differ mainly in their ownership, management structures and funding arrangements, but offer a common curriculum determined by the state.

Unlike most other European countries that have, or have had, a binary system (a technical/academic divide) of post-primary education, the greater proportion (around 55 per cent) of post-primary education in Ireland takes place in academically oriented secondary schools. These are privately owned and managed institutions under the control of religious communities, boards of governors or individuals, but are formally recognised, funded and regulated by the DES. Vocational schools and community colleges educate just over a quarter of post-primary students. They are administered by and funded through the Vocational Education Committees (VECs) of local government. Community and comprehensive schools, containing about 16 per cent of post-primary students, are managed by boards of management of differing compositions: those of community schools are representative of the local VEC, religious communities, parents and teachers. Those of comprehensive schools represent the relevant diocesan religious authority, the local VEC and the Minister for Education and Science, with no formal input from the other partners in education, that is, students, parents or teachers.

There are significant differences between the privately owned secondary schools and the others in the sector. The former are far more likely to be denominational and single sex while the latter are non-denominational (in the case of vocational schools) and coeducational (in the case of vocational, comprehensive and community schools and colleges). The secondary schools have a tradition of providing an academic curriculum while in the past the vocational schools have had an explicit mission to offer technical education. This distinction is overlaid by a class distinction: secondary schools (with a number of important exceptions) have been oriented towards a middle-class clientele, with vocational schools being for working-class students. The more recently developed comprehensive and community schools and colleges explicitly aim to bridge this division with varying degrees of success.

The 'points race' for access to third-level education has given rise to a significant private, unregulated post-primary education sector, as in countries like Japan and Italy. This manifests itself in private colleges that cater to repeat exam candidates and provide personal private tuition or grinds. According to the Commission on the Points System (1999, p. 100), a high number of students report attendance at grinds. Research on 'grind schools' (Smyth, 2009) suggests that children of middle-class backgrounds are more likely to take up private tuition and such children are more likely to attain better educational outcomes in terms of Leaving Certificate performance. But if we control for prior academic ability and student motivation, the effect of private tuition on educational attainment is much weaker. This suggests that broader social processes are more influential in shaping academic achievement than private tuition (Smyth, 2009). Though small in comparison with the fee-paying sector in countries such as the UK, the US and Australia, the emergence of private institutions at upper-second and third level, and the entry of major players like the US Kaplan corporation (owners of Dublin Business School and part of the *Washington Post* group), is nevertheless evidence of the incipient marketisation of Irish education (Smyth, 2009) and raises important questions about access and equality.

As in the primary sector, the influence of the churches is diminishing in the post-primary sector, but for different reasons. The main causative factor is the precipitous decline in membership of the religious orders, such as the Christian

Brothers and the Mercy Sisters, who had such a key role in the establishment and management of secondary schools and who also secured influence over community schools and colleges. A considerable number of Catholic secondary schools are already under the direction of lay principals and this will increase greatly in the next two decades. The orders have begun to establish alternative structures that may permit them to retain a management role in such schools into the future (Clegg, 2003).

Higher education

Like many other Western countries, Ireland has effectively moved into a period of mass higher education. Almost two-thirds (approximately 60 per cent) of Leaving Certificate students now go on to some form of third-level education. In 2011 there were 190,000 students (157,000 full time and 32,000 part time) enrolled in state-funded Irish third-level institutions (DES, 2011). A decade earlier there had been just 116,000 full-time students, though the number of part-timers has hardly increased over the same period, from 31,000 in 2000 (DES, 2012). The higher education sector includes seven universities, 13 Institutes of Technology and a number of other institutions, including teacher-training and some private colleges. Unlike some countries (e.g. Australia and the UK), Ireland has deliberately maintained a 'binary system' of higher education, with academic and professional studies in universities and vocational and applied studies in Institutes of Technology, though this distinction is becoming increasingly difficult to sustain as each sector encroaches on the other's territory. In 2011 there were 89,273 students enrolled in universities, 62,885 in Institutes of Technology and 9,489 in teacher-training and other publicly supported colleges. This compares with a figure of just 21,000 full-time students in all tertiary institutions in 1965 (CSO, 2006c, p. 111; DES, 2011). At the time of writing, the Institutes of Technology are all actively intending to merge into a new class of institution, the 'Technological University', with the likely emergence of four such institutions at some point in the future.

Adult education

Adult learning has been one of the more neglected elements of educational provision in Ireland – not least by sociologists – but is now one of the most rapidly growing. According to DES data, in 1999 there were 17,158 people involved in adult literacy programmes compared to 54,288 a decade later (DES, 2009). Adult education has recently begun to acquire a higher profile, particularly in relation to economic and community development. Lynch (1997, p. 118) suggests complex causes behind this expansion, but the most influential 'is probably the changing trends in thinking among educationalists, a movement both physical and psychological – a movement for education to go out into the community, rather than the community coming to it'. Adult education is now seen as 'the route to empowerment for many marginalised groups in modern Irish society', including those in poverty, substance abusers and those suffering from educational disadvantage (Connolly, 1997, p. 40). Women in particular are central to the provision and use of many aspects of adult education. It is seen by many as an opportunity for people to make up for the poor educational provision of previous years and to move beyond the considerable inflexibility of the Irish school system (Hannan et al., 1998, p. 127). However, the sector remains heavily underfunded and has a low political profile compared to other aspects of education.

As Slowey (1987, p. 118) points out, the adult education sector is highly diverse and it may be misleading to talk about it as a 'system' at all. It continues to reflect its origins in 'the labour movement, church activities, university extension, women's associations, scientific and literary groups and community activities'. As a consequence, the range of activities that fall under the rubric of adult education is vast, from the person completing a PhD with the Open University to the community activist undertaking training in advocacy skills and the retired person learning how to make their own wine. The motivations for engaging in adult education may include social involvement and contact, acquisition of specific knowledge and skills, career change, general self-development and a means of assessing one's potential (Slowey, 1987, pp. 131–3). For women in particular, adult education may also provide an opportunity to move out of a purely domestic role and to (re)enter the paid workforce.

Notwithstanding the extreme diversity of the adult education field, there is now a greater interest in the concept of *lifelong learning*, where the process may be as important as the outcome. This is not a new concept: Buachalla (1974) was talking about the opportunity for 'permanent education' in Ireland nearly four decades ago. The Irish government has argued for support for lifelong learning on the basis that it can address six key areas: consciousness raising, citizenship, cohesion, competitiveness, cultural development and community building (DES, 2000). It has yet to be seen whether the policy rhetoric is accompanied by practical outcomes and whether there is a real appreciation of the barriers to access that actively militate against wider participation in adult education, such as funding, accreditation and provision of childcare.

THEORETICAL BASES FOR THE STUDY OF EDUCATION

We have seen that the Irish education system is both large and complex. It involves a great proportion of the population and consumes vast resources. But what is it for? And how should we understand it? This is where the differing theoretical orientations towards education come into play. Reflecting as they do the broader shapes of sociological theorising, they sometimes differ sharply as to how we should interpret the educational enterprise. There are also some important areas of commonality between them, as we shall see.

A functionalist (or Durkheimian) analysis of education focuses on how it contributes to the stability of society. The education system, from primary school to third level, is seen to have a range of functions. These include a socialisation and training function, providing people with the basic and more developed skills required to operate effectively within society (such as literacy), and more specialised skills that support the functioning of the economy (such as computing skills). Schools and other educational institutions are also a key location for the creation and maintenance of national and cultural identities. This function is perhaps most starkly illustrated in the US system, where the teaching of national symbols, songs and historical narratives is particularly overt, but this process is mirrored in all societies.

Education also has a major allocative function, based on the notion of meritocracy: it functions to distribute jobs and social positions to individuals based on their capacity, abilities and performance. In this way the education system is an essential basis for social stratification in society. A further set of functions includes the integrative functions of education, such as the maintenance of language communities and the development of social networks.

Like most manifestations of functionalist thinking, its place in educational sociology has been sharply criticised from conflict and interpretative viewpoints. But like other functionalist arguments, it continues to have great resonance with common-sense accounts of social life, and as it does not challenge to any extent the existing power relationships within society, it enjoys considerable support among governments, policy-makers and many researchers.

One of Max Weber's main concerns in the analysis of Western society was the spread of rationalisation – the development of calculative and technical ways of thinking about the world, most clearly expressed in science and economics (see Chapter 1). Though Weber did not deal at length with the issue of education, it is clear that the themes underpinning his analyses of social life are of considerable relevance to an understanding of this topic. For example, his analysis of bureaucracy and bureaucratic systems of societal management stressed the importance of particular forms of rational, specialised and disinterested knowledge. This type of knowledge may be contrasted with magical or religious knowledge and with the notion of cultivation, whereby a person is socialised in a more general way for a particular station in life.

In modern societies the acquisition of specialised knowledge becomes a key to social standing and, increasingly, to wealth and power. Members of society are able to perceive the importance of such knowledge and to pursue it. Access to education becomes a crucial aspect of personal development, and in as much as resources are scarce, is of benefit to those individuals and groups that can gain access to specialised knowledge. In Ireland, a neo-Weberian approach to education, which sees education very much as a resource that individuals and groups can access to varying degrees, has been influential. Drudy and Lynch (1993, p. 39) argue that a neo-Weberian approach 'also draws our attention to concepts such as power, domination and authority; to the conflict over economic resources and rewards; to the competition for status and prestige; to the struggle for control; and to the role of bargaining, negotiation and compromise'.

Whereas a neo-Weberian approach stresses the choices and strategies that social groups may adopt, the Marxist approach to education reflects an economically determinist position. Clancy (1995, p. 469) points out that both functionalism and Marxism, as varieties of structuralism, share a determinist, macrosociological view of education. The main difference is in the normative assessment of the situation. The Marxist approach focuses on how the education system operates as an institution for the creation and transmission of social inequality and the maintenance of the class system. Schools are seen as a site for social control, both through the overt activities of reward and punishment and through the hidden curriculum that stresses and rewards punctuality, obedience and respect for authority – the very attributes required of a productive workforce. For Marxists, the school is also a site for the transmission of capitalist ideology, particularly values related to private property, nationalism and individualism. Of the theorists who operate within a Marxist or neo-Marxist paradigm, the most influential in the last quarter century has been Pierre Bourdieu. He moved away from the mechanistic determinism of more traditional Marxist arguments about education and emphasised the cultural sphere and the notion of cultural capital as a significant source of inequality.

A feminist analysis focuses on gender inequalities in education. The main issues for feminists are the sexism of both the hidden and overt curricula, discrimination against girls and women within the education system, the male control of educational institutions and other aspects of gender inequality. Early feminists saw education as having the potential to radically transform the nature of gender relationships and to provide women in particular with a means to redress discrimination against them in public and private spheres. Later feminist research recognised that entering the institution of education was insufficient in itself to bring about wholesale social change. They argued that not only were girls and women disadvantaged in terms of access, but that the system was a key site for the creation of dominant ideologies about masculinity and femininity. The school was therefore not an arbiter and transmitter of neutral knowledge, but a mechanism for the maintenance of patriarchal social relations. More recently feminists have enthusiastically adopted post-structuralist theories in an attempt to better understand the operation of discourse and the creation of subjectivities within the educational field. This has led to a fundamental critique of the philosophical basis of schooling and of knowledge as well as analysis of educational processes and practices.

An interactionist approach to education is microsociological and focuses especially on what happens in the classroom or other educational sites. It emphasises the importance of schooling itself. It is concerned with the meanings and interpretations that people bring to social situations, including those related to education. Interactionist and other interpretative approaches argue that structuralist approaches, whether functionalist or Marxist in nature, ignore the realities of teaching and learning. Post-structuralist approaches are also highly critical of the notion of the participants in education being viewed as fixed identities. They emphasise the processes of personal growth and development that occur within the system and point out that identities are multiple and dynamic, rather than singular and static. This approach pays a great deal of attention to issues of language and discourse. The overall thrust of these types of sociological approach is away from determinism. The experience of education can be neither read off from notions of ability or attitude nor deduced from class, gender or ethnic position. Rather, it is something that needs to be examined in detail, in context and with an openness to its dynamism and capacity for change.

° One influential approach is rational action theory, which suggests that people make calculations about the value of education to themselves or their children. While this approach emphasises the capacity of people to make choices about the paths and options available to them, it can be said to largely ignore broader patterns of inequality and meaning that shape the choices that people face. Of greater importance has been resistance theory. This approach suggests that oppositional behaviour of some within the education system (most importantly, working-class students, especially males) is a rational response to the situation in which they find themselves. It tries to combine the determinism of structuralist theories of education with the voluntarism of the more interpretative approaches. Resistance theory grew out of the work of ethnographers who closely studied everyday behaviour in schools – especially the work of writers at the University of Birmingham, such as Angela McRobbie and Paul Willis, whose 1977 book, *Learning to Labour*, has been one of the most cited books in British sociology and cultural studies.

While resistance theory does help to make sense of the rejection of education by a significant minority of those within it, it does little to point towards an alternative. Fagan (1995, p. 94) concludes that '[while it] certainly draws a more politically enabling picture of early school leavers, and does not construct them in positions of subordination, it leaves them without a political strategy or political project for emancipatory social change'. Lynch and O'Riordan (1999, p. 92) are more positive. They suggest that resistance theory 'has identified spaces and places to challenge unequal social relations through education. It has enabled people to see beyond the limits of structures and to identify modes of thinking and analysing that can facilitate change. It has offered hope for change, which is important in and of itself'. But most resistance theory is developed by middle-class people on behalf of marginalised groups and not in conjunction with such groups or individuals themselves.

Post-structuralist approaches focus on the role of language in the creation and power of definitions of educational reality. An early example in Ireland was the work of Denis O'Sullivan (1989, 1992), who examined how the American economist Dale Tussing helped to shape the discourse of Irish education in the late 1970s. An extensive analysis of Irish education that has consciously adopted a post-structuralist viewpoint has been that of Honor Fagan (1995). This study attempts to deconstruct the discourses that constitute the social category of early school leaver. Fagan outlines and deconstructs the dominant discourses within education, including the sociology of education itself. Through her post-structuralist approach, she aims to question the assumptions made about existing realities and furthermore, how sociology itself constructs the objects of its analysis. The political aim is to open up alternatives to how issues are posed and thus to shape the action that flows from analysis. The early school leaver is shown to be constructed within a range of powerful discourses, each of which seeks to explain the phenomenon. These include the genetic discourse that sees educational problems as inherited; the cultural deprivation discourse that locates the problems in working-class culture; and the structuralist Marxist discourse that sees the issue as a reflection of the power of capital. Each of these discourses serves to disempower and oppress its object – those that leave school early. Fagan argues for what she terms the political discourse: one with a radical and emancipatory aim that seeks to actively change the situation, not just describe or explain it.

The post-structuralist approach favoured by Fagan (see also Ryan, 1997) has a distinctive methodological approach. It combines extensive but selective use of the voices of the researched with a complex and dense theoretical exegesis that seeks to make sense of the phenomena being analysed. It is as if the complexity of the social world is reflected in the very language being used to talk about it. It is not surprising that it is a mode of discourse that is deeply unattractive to policy bodies and government agencies who seek clear, concise information that appears to incorporate common sense with a scientific style of presentation. Thus, while a post-structuralist approach challenges the orthodoxies of education on many fronts, as yet it has had little impact on the policy-making or management processes around Irish education.

THE SOCIOLOGY OF EDUCATION IN IRELAND

Though there has been some history of sociological research into education in Ireland, until the 1990s public debate in the area was largely the preserve of historians and economists. Sociological analyses tended to be rather narrow and instrumentalist. A review of the field by Drudy in 1991 identified the dominant approach as functionalist and positivist. Research tended to be shaped by the predominance of policy-related issues and there was a lack of independent research funding. This tended to severely circumscribe educational discourse, and in the vivid terminology of O'Sullivan (1992, p. 434), alternative viewpoints were notable by their absence: 'to utter the unsayable is to invite marginalisation, exclusion or communicative dismissal'. According to Drudy (1991, p. 110), this lack of theoretical diversity led to 'considerable paradigmatic insulation and lack of debate on the nature of the educational system and its relation to other major social institutions'. In other words, there was little impact on educational sociology from the broader theoretical and methodological debates within the sociology discipline, in particular in relation to more interpretative and critical approaches. The dominant interest was in the relationship between socio-economic status and educational attainment. A more critical approach has since developed that has focused on the nature and role of the educational system and its relationship to the state (Drudy, 1991, p. 112) and on people's attitudes about aspects of the system, but there is still a dearth of research within the Irish sociology of education that can tie together the experiences of students, teachers, families and the broader community.

Despite their limitations, sociological analyses have been of key importance in exploring the relationship between education and society, though for a variety of reasons (Kelleghan, 1989, pp. 202–5), it is difficult to relate research directly to policy. It has been crucial in expanding thought about education and schooling beyond the psychologistic interpretations that dominate much educational discourse (Lynch, 1999a, p. 3). In Ireland, it has provided comprehensive data with which activists and policy analysts can push for reforms to educational provision, particularly for disadvantaged groups, and it has provided educators with an alternative to individualistic and fatalistic accounts of school failure.

On the other hand, it has done little to incorporate any input from the objects of research. In this sense, the sociology of education, like much sociological discourse, has been a 'colonising activity' (Lynch, 1999a, p. 40). It has had little space for the voices or interests of children and young people, the main consumers of education. For example, research by Lynch (1999a, pp. 217–59) has identified the lack of democracy within schools as a key issue for students, but this has never been the focus of large-scale, government-funded research, nor is it likely to be.

The ESRI has been a major site of sociological research into Irish education. In common with its programme of research into socio-economic inequality, it has largely adopted a so-called neo-Weberian focus (Drudy, 1991, p. 112; Drudy and Lynch, 1993, p. 39). It sees social inequality as an outcome of the skewed distribution of resources in Irish society, such as property, skills and credentials, and adopts a largely pluralist model of power. The ESRI has focused on the two main issues that have dominated the international literature: the relationship between social inequality and education (especially as this relates to questions of intergenerational social mobility) and the links between gender and education, including such issues as subject choice, coeducation and exam performance. ESRI research tends to be quantitative and policy oriented (e.g. Smyth and McCoy, 2011); indeed, it has contributed significantly to recent educational policy documents.

For critics such as Lynch, the major shortcoming of Irish educational sociology is that it has failed to challenge the broader structural issues of poverty and class inequality. Research such as that carried out by the ESRI and the Education Research Centre at Drumcondra tends to focus on the distribution of chances within the existing unequal and hierarchical system. Within this dominant liberal model of meritocratic individualism (Drudy and Lynch, 1993, pp. 49–50), issues of class or gender are not analysed as generative forces of action within the education system, but as attributes of individuals. This shortcoming has been replayed more recently in the shift of theoretical interest from issues of inequality to issues of difference and a concern for other types of disadvantage based on ethnicity, culture and gender. Lynch (1999a, p. 29) argues that this shift further marginalises fundamental issues of inequality. The move within the Western sociology of education from class to difference may in fact represent an avoidance of the most intractable issue in education, arising perhaps from a frustration with reformist approaches as well as reflecting a response to the demands of marginalised groups. In other words, three decades of educational reform, including the development of comprehensive education, widespread coeducation, extensive curriculum reform and changes in teaching practice, have left patterns of class inequality in education largely unchanged.

A major contribution to the sociological analysis of schooling in Ireland has been the extensive study conducted by Lynch and Lodge (2002). This attempts to address some of the positivistic shortcomings that these authors and others have identified in prior Irish educational research. The study focuses on the key educational institutions themselves – the schools – and aims (2002, p. 1) to 'explore the inside life of schools, in classrooms and staffrooms, in corridors and recreational spaces where students and teachers live out the practice of education on a daily basis'. This involved interviews with teachers and pupils, analysis of essays written by pupils and, crucially, observation of the social interaction that took place in the classrooms, playgrounds and meeting rooms. While observation of teaching practices is an important part of the training of teachers, such micro-level analysis is rare in the Irish sociology of education. Lynch and Lodge then attempt to locate this micro-level interaction within a macro-level theoretical framework that addresses issues of power and control as central in Irish education, not least issues of structured class and gender inequality and injustice.

Lynch and Lodge's research attempts to show how and why the class basis of Irish schooling has been maintained as well as other inequalities based on gender, ability and ethnicity. They also draw attention to the importance of affective relationships of caring, interdependence, solidarity and belonging, though unfortunately they did not explore this aspect in the research (2002, p. 12). An important aspect of their extensive study is that it focuses on issues of power and justice in schools – issues that normally tend to be neglected or sanitised. Thus they raise a key question (2002, p. 2):

> if all students are not treated with equal respect and enabled to develop their capabilities to the full, this raises important moral questions about the right of the State to confine people in an institution that may have enduring negative effects, be that culturally, economically or socially.

This important research challenges many aspects of both the common-sense and sociological understandings of contemporary Irish secondary schooling.

DEFINING KNOWLEDGE: SHAPING THE CURRICULUM

The content of the curriculum – what is taught – is a key site of struggle in education (Conway, 2002). In Ireland this was particularly the case within the primary system. Historically the national schools were the locus of a battle over the hearts and minds of Irish children between the colonial state and the Catholic/nationalist opposition to it. According to Clancy (1995, p. 473), 'issues of moral socialisation took precedence over issues of technical socialisation' and the teaching of subjects such as Irish, history and religion assumed great importance in the independent state.

Many critics (though few sociologists) have drawn attention to the religious domination of the Irish education system. It is certainly true that Irish schools have to an extent been saturated with religion: 'religion may be fully integrated into the rest of the curriculum and ... the ethos and hidden curriculum fully reflect the religious ideals of the school' (Clancy, 1995, p. 476). The denominational character of Irish education poses particular challenges in the context of increasing cultural diversity (Smyth and Darmody, 2011). This is manifest in ongoing public debate about the place of religion in the school curriculum and how it should accommodate religious diversity and parents and children who do not identify with the Catholic or indeed any other faith tradition (Catholic Schools Partnership, 2011; Smyth and Darmody, 2011). One study using survey data and case studies of 14 schools in urban and rural locations in Ireland found that some non-Catholic parents were concerned about the religious instruction received by their children in a Catholic school. Children themselves had broadly positive views of religious instruction, mentioning in particular the possibilities provided to opt out of it and the emphasis on global religions in the religious education programme (Smyth and Darmody, 2011).

Some research suggests that the denominational character of Irish education has in fact been diminished significantly in terms of curriculum content. As Drudy and Lynch point out (1993, p. 82), greater numbers of students now study:

> scientific, commercial and technological subjects, that teach students to seek empirical proof for the existence of phenomena, to maximise profit, and to rely on technological solutions for human problems. Such principles are very much at variance with a faith based on dogma or belief in the efficacy of divine intervention for the resolution of human difficulties.

Apart from religious ideas, the education system seeks to inculcate a number of other qualities and values and key among these is that of achievement. As Clancy (1995, p. 470) suggests, 'the differentiation which teachers make between students within the school prepares students for the differential allocation in the labour market'. The demands of the labour market are directly (in the gearing up of the Institutes of Technology to respond to skills shortages identified by industry) or indirectly fed through to the education system. Through this process, the value placed by the labour market on particular subjects is reflected in the status or rewards that accrue to different occupations; this then shapes the evaluation of particular types of knowledge. The limited fields of endeavour that are recognised by the system are then further narrowed according to notions of ability. Ability is reduced to one's performance according to a set of standardised tests: ultimately the exam-based Leaving Certificate. There is little or no recognition that ability is discursively created, dynamic, contingent and shaped by broader issues of class, ethnicity, age and gender. Nor is sufficient attention given to understandings of learning that emphasise the influence of socio-cultural contexts on ability (Conway, 2002).

Clancy alerts us (1995, p. 479) to the growing instrumentalism of the Irish education system. The official discourse on Irish education has come to be suffused with a concern for labour market issues and competitiveness to the detriment of more humanist concerns. Do business and industry have too much influence over what is taught and learned through the Irish education system? Clancy suggests that it is not just a matter of successful interest groups, but that the discourse of education itself has shifted from its humanist base – 'the growth in provision and take-up of economically utilisable subjects on the post-primary school curriculum reflects the centrality of economic self-interest as a cultural value' (1995, p. 480). Similar trends exist in the tertiary sector, where the language of total quality management, with its emphasis on benchmarking, best practice, stakeholders and the student as customer, has come to dominate policy- and decision-making (HEA, 2011).

A Marxist approach to education looks critically at the content of the curriculum. It sees the focus on achievement as an ideological process that helps to underpin the logic of the capitalist system. There has been little such critical research examining the assumptions that underlie the curricula of Irish education or how they reflect the interests and views of the powerful in Irish society. This conclusion is hinted at by Clancy, though he does not mention capitalism per se when he says that the educational system is 'an instrument of cultural domination; its real function is best understood in terms of the need for social control in an unequal and rapidly changing social order' (1995, p. 471).

Lynch (1999a, p. 260) argues more fundamentally that because of the power of ruling-class male social groups, 'only particular forms of knowledge have been legitimated within education'. These are based on linguistic and, to a lesser extent, mathematical skills and abilities. Other competencies and qualities, such as artistic and creative ability, caring and empathetic skills, kinetic (movement) skills, lateral thinking and what Lynch terms personal intelligences (1999a, p. 275), are routinely neglected or ignored by the examination system that dominates Irish education. Lynch finds this deeply ironic (1999a, p. 260), as:

> the educational institution has, in certain respects, become cut off from many of the lifeworlds and labour markets which it serves at the very time that educational credentials are being used more than ever to select and satisfy people within the labour market.

In other words, in a time when cultural diversity and creativity are becoming key economic resources in themselves, it can be said that education is in some ways becoming less functional for Irish society. This also applies to the skills required for 'love labour' – increasingly required activities of caring, nurturing and looking after others (see Chapter 6).

McSorley's (1997) Clondalkin study suggests that the content of the curriculum is unattractive and irrelevant to working-class students. Fagan's (1995) findings are very similar. She points out that the education system completely fails to reflect the reality of students from poor families. Thus, 'by not using the life experience of the young people as a basis from which to educate and by not linking the background of the young people to the curriculum, the curriculum is irrelevant and meaningless' (1995, p. 100). The result is a very high level of conflict between students and teachers and also between families and teachers.

GENDER AND EDUCATION

Gender is central to the experience of education. People's experiences of 'being a boy' or 'being a girl' are shaped in many ways by the experience of schooling (Ryan, 1997). Drudy (1991, p. 115) suggests that gender has only become an issue in Irish educational research since the 1980s. There has been an extensive amount of sociological research on gender and education in Ireland since then, but this has tended to take place within a limited number of institutional contexts and from a rather narrow theoretical position. Lynch (1999a, p. 135) points out that the dominant discourse in the Irish sociology of gender and education has been the liberal feminist discourse of equality of opportunity. In other words, it has been about identifying barriers to equality of opportunity within existing structures rather than challenging them in any fundamental way. Lynch suggests there has been 'no substantive analysis of mainstream compulsory education in terms of its pedagogical, organisational or curriculum practices from a critical feminist standpoint' (1999a, p. 134). Nor, it must be said, has there been any extensive analysis of the relationship between masculinity and education. Perhaps ironically, this has only now started to occur as girls have begun to significantly outperform boys in public examinations. It can be said that the orthodoxy of hierarchical and meritocratic educational structures and discourses has not been effectively challenged.

Given that educational research has, as we have seen, tended to work within the system, there has been a tendency, reinforced by positivist models within social research, to measure equality through indicators such as the number of women participating in particular educational courses; the number of men and, especially, women in non-traditional areas; or the number of images of men and women depicted in texts (Lynch, 1999a, p. 135). In addition, though we have an increasing quantity of information about gender in Irish education, this is rarely combined with sensitivity to issues of class or ethnicity.

Irish women have a history of high participation in second-level education (partly due to a lack of alternative employment opportunities). Males and females are now equally represented in many aspects of education, with females now making up a slight majority (in the range of 51 to 55 per cent) at post-primary level (Lynch, 1999a, p. 141). Women have increased their level of participation in third-level study and now represent a slightly higher proportion of new entrants to universities than males, while their representation in teacher-training colleges is nearly four times greater than that of males (DES, 2010). Males have a higher representation than females in Institutes of Technology. In 2009/ 2010, for example, 10,836 new entrants to Institutes of Technology were males compared to 8,074 females (CSO, 2011b, p. 105). Taking all higher education institutions together, the number of males and females entering for the first time is basically the same. Rates of participation across socio-economic groups are similar for males and females. Girls now outperform boys in virtually all subjects in second-level public examinations (Junior and Leaving Certificates), including applied mathematics and engineering, though the perception of male subjects (such as Design and Communication) and female subjects (such as Home Economics) persists and is reflected in the distribution of exam candidates in these areas.

As pointed out by Lodge and Lynch (2004, p. 13), gender issues in education are very complex and range across questions of access, curriculum, affective issues of human relationships and major issues related to power. There is a growing body of research in Ireland on such issues and the strong positivist framework in relation to the sociological research on education is being expanded into more critical and micro-level analyses.

Coeducation

Sociologists have demonstrated that educational institutions are key sites for the construction of gender identities. The work of researchers such as the Australian post-structuralist sociologist Bronwyn Davies (1990) has shown that gender is being formed from very early on in the education process, that is, in pre-school or play group. There is some evidence that by the time they reach second-level school, girls have a poorer academic self-image (Lynch, 1999a, p. 142). While high levels of stress have been identified in both male and female students, especially in exam classes (Hannan et al., 1996, p. 199), levels appear to be particularly high in all-girls secondary schools, perhaps related to the strongly academic focus combined with a strong emphasis on the personal formation of students in particular directions (Lynch, 1999a, p. 229).

There has been considerable debate about the merits of coeducation in terms of its overall benefits and whether it favours boys, or girls, or both. While Ireland has had a long history of segregated single-sex schooling at post-primary level, now the majority of pupils (about 70 per cent at primary level; 62 per cent at post-primary) are educated in coeducational environments (Lodge and Lynch, 2004, p. 16). This applies particularly to those in the vocational, community and comprehensive school sectors. It has been argued that girls suffer from coeducational schooling, especially as they have been shown by some research to receive less attention and encouragement from teachers than boys (Lynch, 1999a, p. 143). A study carried out in Irish schools by Emer Smyth and Damien Hannan (1997) sought to examine the effects on girls of coeducation, particularly whether a shift to non-segregated schooling adversely affects their educational and occupational achievements.

According to the authors of the study (1997, p. 10), coeducation changes the patterns of interaction and the 'engenderment' of schools. As Lodge and Lynch (2004, p. 17) point out, the unusually large (in international terms) proportion of young people in Ireland who are educated in single-sex settings means that many 'cannot avail of the day-to-day learning about gender relations that takes place in coeducational environments'. A 1996 Irish study found that male and female former students of coeducational schools were positive about the social and personal education they received (Smyth, 2010). International research remains inconclusive as to the impact of single-sex education. It is a complex issue – complicated by variation in national context (Smyth, 2010) – that requires careful disentanglement of the multitude of factors that shape students' school experiences. These include the social background and prior ability of students; school history, management, ethos and organisation; policies of selectivity of schools; and coeducation itself (Hannan et al., 1996).

Irish research (Smyth and Hannan, 1997) that looked at performance in Junior and Leaving Certificate examinations showed that after other factors had been taken into consideration, the effects of coeducation on performance were minimal and were certainly less important than other factors such as social class and ability. One finding that did stand out was that girls in coeducational settings underperformed in the area of mathematics. While this finding will take further research in the Irish context to explain, it is suggested that this may be the outcome of dominant ideas among pupils, teachers and parents about the gender appropriateness of certain subjects. This applies in particular to the range of subject choice that is made available in the first place. Boys' single-sex schools are much less likely to offer subjects such as Home Economics and Music, whereas girls' schools rarely make more technical subjects available (Lodge and Lynch, 2004, p. 17). This inevitably shapes the subsequent third-level options available to students, as reflected in the comparatively low numbers of males who enter health and welfare-related courses and the significantly lower number of females who opt for technological programmes at this level. Given the central importance of educational experiences and qualifications, these patterns clearly have a major impact on the career pathways of males and females.

Schools and sexuality

There has been little research in Ireland that addresses the issue of sexuality in schools. O'Higgins-Norman (2009, p. 2) has argued that the topic 'is something that has yet to find an appropriate forum for discussion and learning'. Yet schools are highly sexualised locations where as well as engaging in the more formal curriculum, young people explore and create their identities, including their sexual identities. Similarly, much of the popular culture – in popular music, magazines, the Internet, films and TV – related to schools and schooling is focused on issues to do with sex, sexuality and sexual relationships, so this blind spot is somewhat surprising. Fragmented elements of sociological research in Ireland have revealed some information in this area.

A small-scale study by Ryan (1997) focused on the experiences of girls attending six coeducational schools in the Dublin area. The aim was to explore how sexuality is involved in the development of gender identity in the school context. The research revealed the importance of 'reputation' and how it is understood in different ways for boys and girls. Girls reported that they had to be seen to be attractive and interested in sex, but not so interested that they could appear to be easy or branded a slut. On the other hand, they could not appear to be too uninterested in sex or boys for fear of being branded frigid, stuck-up or lesbian.

Other small-scale research by Inglis (1998b, pp. 145–6) had similar findings, though presented in a more optimistic context. He concludes that 'pupils may be far more experienced and adventurous in their sexual attitudes and practices than either the teachers or the parents believe. Sex has become part of their lives. It is a central aspect of their everyday relations … sexually active is seen as being the norm.' Young people gained information from the mass media and (occasionally) from parents, but the main sources were friends and siblings. Teachers, and especially religious personnel, were generally seen as being irrelevant. The key issues for students related to what to do in situations like 'relationships, bad experiences, being drunk and having unprotected sex' (1998b, p. 138). The main fears, especially for girls, were pregnancy and getting a reputation. But Inglis found evidence of ultimate female control: 'there was a sense that while avoiding pregnancy and a reputation was a girl's responsibility, girls ultimately had the final say as to what would and would not happen sexually' (1998b, p. 143).

There is evidence that even if sexuality has become less hidden within schools, it still must be expressed within a limited framework. O'Higgins-Norman (2009) conducted research into homosexuality in five second-level schools in the greater Dublin area and revealed much about the broader expression of sexual matters in the educational environment. Based on interviews with students, parents, teachers and managers, as well as observation in the schools themselves, he found six key recurring themes related to sexuality:

1. Being normal means being heterosexual and clearly masculine or feminine.
2. Fear of all things homosexual.
3. Negative stereotyping of gay men and lesbians.
4. Name calling and the minimising of its significance.
5. Religious influence on teachers' attitudes and behaviour.
6. Non-recognition of any fluidity of sexual orientation.

There was a strong element or 'heteronormativity' within schools: heterosexuality was viewed as 'normal' and any other expression of sexuality as 'abnormal', even if accepted. Very few of the interviewees had any direct contact with gay or lesbian people and they tended to display a rigid and stereotyped understanding of non-heterosexual sexualities, often based on media representations:

> Will and Grace has a lot to answer for. Gay guys are seen as cool; they are not a threat (to girls), it is like having a guy who knows about being a girl. Girls cannot understand a gay woman, they are not as understanding of them, and most of the girls seen as lesbian on TV are sad or uncool. (Parent quoted in O'Higgins-Norman, 2009, p. 10)

O'Higgins-Norman (2009, p. 14) finds that 'schools accept homophobic bullying [in particular, 'slagging'] as a normal part of school life and that many teachers do little to address it'. This supports earlier research by Lodge and Lynch (2004, p. 37) who, based on retrospective accounts of gay and lesbian people's experiences, identify outcomes of isolation, depression and loneliness among students because of their sexual orientation. They report (2004, pp. 37–8) that many lesbian and gay young people have had experiences at school that impact on their academic success. They may suffer from harassment, stress, depression or even violence and this may lead them to achieve less well academically or even drop out of school. Perhaps more insidiously, the identity of gays and lesbians – whether pupils or teachers – is rendered almost invisible in the curriculum: it is just not talked about. For O'Higgins-Norman (2009, p. 12), 'it is the power of silence that ultimately controls how teachers and students alike react to the issue'. In O'Connor's analysis (2008) of teenagers' essays about their lives, there is hardly any mention of sexuality, possibly as they were written in a school environment, though this did not stop participants from writing about their experiences with drink or drugs (e.g. pp. 122–3).

In areas such as SPHE (social, personal and health education) or RSE (relationships and sexuality education) there is a failure to address sexual orientation and universal heterosexuality is assumed. O'Higgins-Norman (2009) suggests that the possibility of a diversity or malleability of sexual identity is not even considered, perhaps as it is a threat to the binary gender order. Both Lodge and Lynch as well as O'Higgins-Norman trace the reticence of schools when it comes to matters of homosexuality to the continued pervasiveness of religious influence.

It is perhaps not surprising then that research by Hyde and Howlett for the Crisis Pregnancy Agency found little evidence that the dominant educational discourse had any place for positive images of female sexual desire or agency. Rather, it was about protecting girls from dangerous male sexuality (Hyde and Howlett, 2004). This aims to render girls as passive and also as responsible for all teenage sexual behaviour. Nevertheless, the research suggests (2004, p. 79), following Inglis, that things are changing and that teenagers have become more liberal about sexuality in recent decades. They suggest that this shift may be:

closely related to young women's increasingly liberal stance in relation to sexual intimacies. At a broad level, it appears to be the agency of young women, facilitated through the processes and knowledge acquired in their social circle, primarily through friends and the media, that has redefined and re-shaped adolescent sexual norms.

Both Ryan and Lynch, in separate research exercises, have observed behaviour in Irish schools that they would define as sexual harassment, including verbal denigration and unsolicited touching of female students and teachers. Ryan argues that there is no acceptable framework within schools for dealing with such abuse or harassment. Lynch (1999a, p. 236) argues that gender inequality was not part of most students' daily vocabulary of analysis and thus harassment was neither identified nor recognised in the institutions concerned. Hyde and Howlett also call for an overt focus on issues of gender and sexuality in schools and remark (2004, p. 46) that in a school where a gender studies programme was offered, attitudes to gender and sexuality appeared to have changed.

In Chapter 8 we outline the relative neglect of issues of masculinity within Irish sociology. The same critique can be made in the area of education, for much the same reasons: there has been little examination of the specific experiences of boys or of the construction of masculinity ('doing boy' as O'Connor, 2008, p. 12 terms it) through the practices and discourses of Irish education. Lynch (1999a, p. 233) has suggested that in boys' schools she studied, 'the equation of superior masculinity with physical prowess and sport was particularly evident in schools where sporting success was central to the school's sense of identity'. There is a perception that (especially working-class) male peer groups adopt a culture that is hostile to education. A cultural milieu of this type was described in Britain in Willis's *Learning to Labour*, but there has been no equivalent Irish study. A similar milieu is described in Fagan's analysis of early school leavers, but this does not make any particular attempt to bring gender issues to the forefront. One study by the National Council for Curriculum and Assessment (Mac an Ghaill et al., 2002) of the Exploring Masculinities programme in Irish schools found that teachers were broadly supportive of its attempts to develop the social and personal education of boys.

At the primary level, Lodge (2005) has examined the gendered nature of middle childhood (that is, around the age of seven to eight years) within the school environment, in particular the school playground. She found that while many of the children exhibited stereotypical patterns of play and friendship, 'others (of both sexes) had more ambiguous gendered styles of behaviour and interaction' (2005, p. 181). Nevertheless, most play was sex segregated, with most boys being involved in football (the highest-status activity) and 'apparently haphazard games of chasing'. Play between the sexes was generally sexualised, in the form of kiss-chasing. In the school studied by Lodge, the gendered patterns were reinforced by broader institutional structures of sex-segregated education. It may well be that children in a less sex-segregated environment might exhibit different patterns of gendered behaviour. Indeed, the most popular boys in the group studied reflected less stereotyped, more androgynous behaviour that embraced both skills at sport but also 'kindness to peers and a willingness to engage in games played by girls' (2005, p. 188). This suggests that gendered identities in schools are perhaps more malleable than is generally perceived and that not all boys seek to express themselves through displays of dominant masculinity.

EDUCATION AND CLASS INEQUALITY

> What is remarkable about the debate about class inequality in education is its almost ritualistic character. While there is probably no single subject that has been researched in as much detail as class inequality in education, there have been no serious attempts at policy level to radically alter the class outcomes of education. (Lynch and Lodge, 2002, p. 38)

There has been a major shift in the class basis of Irish society. Where formerly property was the main determinant of social wealth and position, this has now been at least partly replaced by the ability to secure wages or salary in a competitive and dynamic labour market (Breen and Whelan, 1996, p. 98). As a result, there is now a closer link between educational attainment and labour market position. A key concern of sociologists of education, in Ireland as elsewhere, relates to how schools operate as a selection mechanism for future occupational positions: how do people acquire the qualifications that will provide them with the means to access scarce resources in the future?

There is now a considerable body of Irish sociological research that examines issues of educational opportunity and economic and class inequality. According to Lynch and O'Riordan (1999, p. 93), this, as with other educational research, has been from within a positivist framework. They argue that the 'equality empiricists' have dominated the debate around educational inequality, framing it within a liberal political perspective and a broadly functionalist sociological tradition. Within this approach, the problem of class inequality in education is defined as a lack of opportunity to move upwards within an already class-stratified society. Lynch and O'Riordan conclude that while this liberal model helps to show how educational resources within the existing system are (mal)distributed, it does little to challenge the hierarchical nature of the system itself. It fails to critique the content and objectives of education and the broader systems of inequality that shape the nature and priorities of the system. For Lynch (1999a, p. 252), 'while distributing more education to those groups who want it is crucial, it may also be necessary to change the education system itself to take account of the differences which various groups bring to that system. Schooling needs to recognise and respect difference if it is to treat all people with equality of respect. It cannot assume that all people will fit the one mould.'

As indicated by Lynch and O'Riordan, the Irish equality empiricists (largely located within, or connected to, the ESRI) have produced a sizeable body of data in relation to the links between social inequality and educational participation and outcomes. This research continues a process of research that has been taking place in Ireland since the mid-1960s (Drudy and Lynch, 1993, p. 141). The government-sponsored *Investment in Education* report published in 1965 (carried out by economists, not sociologists) revealed the links between educational and class inequality. The considerable investment in education that took place in the wake of this report (including the introduction of free secondary education) led to a growth in educational participation, but this was not equitably distributed across the population. Research by Clancy (1982, 1988) during the 1980s showed that in terms of access to tertiary-level education, investment in secondary education had actually contributed to an increase in inequality: those favoured in class terms were better able to make use of the new educational opportunities that had been opened up.

Research into (male) social mobility in Ireland by Whelan and Whelan (1984) also demonstrated the links between education and class. It suggested that access to educational opportunity was a major factor in the inheritance of class inequality and that this pattern was particularly marked in Ireland, at least during the 1970s. Subsequent research by Breen and Whelan on data from the late 1980s revealed that little had altered: a modest change for men and none at all for women. They concluded (1996, p. 126) that:

> Despite increasing overall levels of educational attainment the pattern of educational social fluidity has remained unaltered. There is a continuing strong link between class origins and educational attainment.

The relationship between educational attainment and subsequent labour force outcomes has also endured and exhibits 'a relatively straightforward pattern … whereby class origins are largely translated into educational qualifications which then determine the distribution of relative chances of access to the more desirable classes' (Breen and Whelan, 1996, p. 126). Overall, while investment in education in Ireland has led to an increase in educational attainment and performance at all levels, the differentials between classes have not diminished. Rather, the increased emphasis on education as a mechanism for social advantage has seen the already advantaged groups in Irish society further secure their position.

A Higher Education Authority report (TWG, 1995), drawing on the work of a number of sociologists, has identified three crucial schooling transition points at which the effects of socio-economic background are particularly significant. The first of these relates to whether a student continues in school long enough to take the Leaving Certificate or becomes an 'early school leaver'. While one-fifth of all students left school without reaching Leaving Certificate level, only 3 per cent of those with higher professional backgrounds failed to make this transition compared with almost half of those from unskilled manual backgrounds. This pattern is long established. Research by Rudd on early school leavers in 1966/7 (cited in Clancy, 1995, p. 484) revealed that the 15 per cent of students who left after primary school (note the change in measurement) were predominantly from the unskilled/semi-skilled working-class and farming groups. One determinant of early leaving is reading ability, which has been shown to be linked to social class background. McSorley (1997, p. 39) reports large differences between children who attended schools in outer-suburban Clondalkin and inner-city Dublin, where 19 to 35 per cent of children were two to three years behind in reading ability, and those at school in Rathgar, a wealthy suburb, where no children were below their expected ability for age.

A second key educational transition relates to the level of achievement of those who remain to complete the Leaving Certificate. Here, the level of achievement varies widely according to socio-economic group. As Smyth and Hannan (1997, p. 16) point out, 'most of the difference between schools in average Leaving Certificate performance is due to differences in the social background and prior performance characteristics of their pupils'. While fewer than one-third of those from unskilled and semi-skilled manual backgrounds attained at least two grade Cs at Higher Level, over three-quarters of those from the higher and lower professional groups did so. This raises many issues in relation to the neutrality of the examination system as a measure of merit. The third transition relates to the destinations of those who successfully complete the Leaving Certificate.

Retention in the second-level system and performance in the Leaving Certificate are important determinants of entry to higher education, and retention and performance are in turn heavily influenced by socio-economic background. Data from the School Leavers' Survey shows that social class background is a key determinant of Leaving Certificate achievement and transition to higher education. The survey found that among 2006 and 2007 school leavers, 58 per cent of students from higher professional social class backgrounds – compared to 16 per cent in semi-skilled or unskilled manual social class groups – achieved four or more honours in their Leaving Certificate. Unsurprisingly, students from professional backgrounds also do much better in terms of transition to higher education – 70 per cent transition to third level compared to only 30 per cent of students from the semi or unskilled manual category (Smyth and McCoy, 2009).

As in most Western countries, overall participation in third-level education has increased dramatically in Ireland since the 1970s, but significant social class differences persist. Indeed, the trends identified in Clancy's earlier research have been largely sustained in studies carried out by successive researchers. They conclude that patterns of entry to higher education by socio-economic background reflect both continuity and change. The more powerful social classes are still favoured, but participation across the board has increased, with the important exception of those from a lower non-manual (low-level service) background, who make up 10 per cent of the national population. Qualitative research among members of this group has attempted to unpack the 'why' question in relation to low third-level participation rates among non-manual groups. It has found that those who do not progress to third level have negative school experiences and that these play into their negative identification with education in secondary school. These negative experiences include a lack of perceived choice about subject options and levels, low teacher expectations and an unfavourable school atmosphere (McCoy and Byrne, 2011).

Such differences may be expressed in spatial terms (Table 7.3). In Dublin, admission rates to third-level education vary significantly. Consider, for example, that admission rates are just 0.10 for students from Ballyfermot compared to 0.71 for those from the wealthy neighbourhood of Dublin 6. Taking Ireland as a whole, the Dublin region, with its high concentration of working-class people, and Donegal have the lowest participation rate in higher education, while the western counties, such as Galway, Sligo and Leitrim, have the highest. For those that make it to college, Clancy found significant social class selectivity between different types of institution and, within institutions, between fields of study: elite groups are disproportionately able to access the elite courses such as law, medicine and dentistry. Institutes of Technology, while they have been crucial to the widening of educational access (especially outside Dublin), are disproportionately accessed by the less well off. This leads Clancy to warn (2001, p. 177) that 'what is essential is that a concern for equality of opportunity requires us to monitor not just the overall admission levels, but also the differentiation within the third-level sector'.

Table 7.3: Admission rates to higher education for select Dublin postal districts and counties in Ireland, 1998 and 2005

Postal district/county	1998	2005
Dublin 11 (Finglas-Ballymun)	0.14	0.27
Dublin 12 (Crumlin-Kimmage)	0.20	0.32
Dublin 8 (Kilmainham-Inchicore)	0.29	0.21
Dublin 22 (Clondalkin-Neilstown)	0.13	0.19
Dublin 14 (Rathfarnham-Clonskeagh)	0.68	0.79
Dublin 6 (Rathmines-Terenure)	0.70	0.71
Dublin 18 (Foxrock-Glencullen)	0.77	0.73
Dublin 4 (Ballsbridge-Donnybrook)	0.59	0.49
Dublin	0.38	0.45
Laois	0.39	0.52
Galway	0.57	0.62
Mayo	0.56	0.65
Clare	0.50	0.66
Sligo	0.56	0.62
Donegal	0.35	0.39

Source: Fitzpatrick Associates and O'Connell, 2005.

A final set of barriers may exist for those who wish to engage in adult education. There is consistent evidence (Drudy and Lynch, 1993, pp. 261–7; Department of Education and Science, 1998) that those already disadvantaged in the education process, such as early school leavers, are also excluded from adult education. Barriers to participation include financial constraints, lack of childcare provision, entry requirements and lack of appropriate information and guidance. Thus, Drudy and Lynch (1993, p. 262) suggest that adult education has not become a viable second-chance option for the majority of those that have already been let down by the education system.

ETHNICITY AND EDUCATION

Irish educational settings are increasingly marked by ethnic and cultural diversity. This provides challenges for educators and is beginning to be increasingly recognised in sociological and educational research. Important issues relate to the participation of the Travelling community in education and in the challenges of the increased ethnic diversity that have resulted from large-scale immigration to Ireland.

The negative educational experience of Travellers is beginning to attract more sociological and policy attention, though this is hampered by the lack of reliable data, especially in relation to Travellers' educational attainment. Traveller participation in mainstream education is improving (see Table 7.4) and about 90 per cent of Traveller children make the transition from primary to secondary education (Hourigan and Campbell, 2010). Nevertheless, serious barriers to full participation remain. Research by Hourigan and Campbell (2010) reveals that prejudice, welfare dependency, lack of Traveller participation in school management and early marriage patterns are significant factors hindering Traveller participation in the Irish education system.

The formal education system (especially second level) is experienced in a negative way by many Travellers for a number of reasons: feelings of difference and discrimination; lack of flexibility towards nomadic lifestyles; the higher levels of family responsibility of Traveller girls; and the potential role of the education system in undermining Traveller culture (Lodge and Lynch, 2002, p. 96). The perception of likely discrimination or hostility is borne out in Lynch and Lodge's findings in relation to settled secondary students' attitudes. They report that 'deep-seated prejudice towards Travellers was encountered across most of the schools … many students were quite willing to express their dislike and antagonism towards Travellers in public' (2002, p. 138). Nevertheless, this was not universal and the discriminatory discourse was challenged by some students, especially those who had actual contact with Travellers in educational settings. Amongst the educators, research has indicated that nearly two-thirds of pre-service teachers have had no contact with the Travelling community (O'Higgins-Norman, 2011, p. 117) and this must impact on how they subsequently interact with members of the community in the school setting.

Table 7.4: Participation of Travellers in mainstream Irish education

Primary education	
1988	3,953
2007–8	8,158
Post-primary education	
1999–2000	1,000
2007–8	2,596

Source: Hourigan and Campbell, 2010.

The phenomenon of substantial immigration to Ireland has also had major implications for the education system, as does the development of an international education industry. O Loingsigh (2001, p. 115) states that there is a lack of recognition of cultural diversity in our existing system. This is reinforced by existing structures, for example the denominational aspect of the primary school system. The need to respond to ethnic diversity will require a change of management structures, of school ethos and of the level of resourcing. For example, there is virtually no teaching of mother tongue languages to immigrants or the children of immigrants, despite the existence of legislation in the Education Act that indicates that cultural and linguistic diversity must be recognised. An intercultural education system is required, suggests O Loingsigh (2001, p. 119), that is:

> not about integrating ethnic minorities into our culture so that they become more Irish than the Irish themselves but rather about educating people about tolerance, human rights, democracy and, most of all, respect for difference.

Recent research points to the challenges of involving parents of immigrant children in their schooling in Ireland. One study based on survey and case study data found that a lack of cultural capital – for example, lack of language competency – constrained immigrant parental involvement in their children's education (Darmody and McCoy, 2011).

CONCLUSION

Lynch and O'Riordan (1999, p. 122) remind us that educational disadvantage in Irish society can only be fully understood in terms of the advantages enjoyed by others:

> The financial, cultural and educational experiences of working-class students need not, in and of themselves, create educational inequality; what creates

inequality is the fact that others have differential access to resources, incomes, wealth and power which enables them to avail of opportunities presented in education in a relatively more successful manner.

In many ways, the education system has been structured by the advantaged in order to maintain their position. As well as operating in a system that reflects their economic and cultural interests, wealthier students are able to purchase goods and services (grinds, computers, books, foreign travel) on the private market that give them an educational advantage. They also enjoy access to extra-curricular activities like sport, clubs and debating that have been shown to increase their educational and social capital (McCoy et al., 2012). They enjoy better study conditions and experience fewer pressures to take up part-time or full-time work.

The facilities and opportunities available to more advantaged groups in education relate to how the process itself is perceived. Allen (1998, p. 202) makes the point, for example, that whereas training for the long-term unemployed is seen as a social cost, similar education provided for graduates is defined as an investment. Such analysis may help to explain the consistent enactment of education policies (such as free fees in secondary and, more recently, third-level education) that disproportionately benefit the already well-off (Clancy, 1995, p. 485) and the neglect of areas (particularly primary and adult education) that have a greater capacity to lead to social equality.

Lynch and O'Riordan (1999, p. 122) argue that 'those whose own class are the definers of what is culturally and educationally valuable in the first instance are strongly positioned to be the major beneficiaries of educational investment'. Historically in Ireland there is a strong discourse, supported by church and state, that favours academic education. Academic education, translated into high Leaving Certificate honours, can be used by the advantaged to gain access to prestigious third-level and professional courses in fields such as law, medicine and dentistry; thus, social and economic power are maintained.

As pointed out earlier by Lynch and Lodge, the inequalities in Irish education have proved remarkably durable and knowledge about their existence has not led to a significant movement for change. There have been a number of innovative initiatives in recent years, such as the development of the Leaving Certificate Applied and the DEIS (Delivering Equality of Education in Schools) Scheme, yet considerable progress has yet to be made in tackling educational inequalities. The work of various sociologists of education over the last two decades helps us better understand the causes and consequences of this and how the education system fulfils its dual purpose of the socialisation and social mobility of the next generation.

8

Gender, Sexuality and the Family

A key development in the discipline of sociology over the last 50 years has been the rise to prominence of gender issues. This is related to two key processes: the reconstruction of Western (and also non-Western) societies in terms of occupational structures, secularisation and demographic change, as outlined elsewhere in this book; and the rise of the modern women's movement and the permeation of feminist and gender-oriented discourses into all aspects of social life.

Many of the major issues of public and private, social and political debate in Ireland for the past 50 years have related to issues of gender, sexuality and the family. At times, the country has been convulsed by conflicts around issues of contraception, adoption, abortion, censorship, homosexuality, sex education and divorce. In addition, the abuse of children – physical, sexual and psychological – has come to prominence in the media and legal and welfare systems. These revelations and debates have placed sex, gender, the body and the family at the centre of arguments that have also brought into play discussions of morality, freedom, personal integrity, authority and control. For many participants and observers, these conflicts and exposés have been central to the question of modernity and Irish society.

There are at least three common viewpoints about how relationships between men and women have changed in Ireland over the last three decades. One view is that there has been a huge amount of positive change and progress. Commentators point to the election of Presidents Mary Robinson and Mary McAleese as indicative of the more prominent role the Irish people have accorded women in public life. The two most senior legal positions in the country, the Attorney General and the Chief Justice of the Supreme Court, are both held by women. Female sports stars such as Katie Taylor and the golfing Maguire twins enjoy international reputations and many senior Irish journalists and academics are women. They may also cite the exposure of abuse against women and children, the conviction of the perpetrators and the calling to account of the institutions of church and state; the increasing involvement of men in housework and childcare; the cultural prominence of women in the visual and performing arts; and the huge shift of women into the paid workforce and into formerly male-dominated occupations. They may draw attention to the achievement of legal equality for men and women, the gradual development of women's health services, the growth of coeducational schools and so on. To such commentators, these factors are often seen as indicators that Ireland has become a 'modern European state'.

A second view is essentially opposed to the first, stressing how *little* has changed in Ireland and how much gender inequality and differentiation remain. This view propounds the continued real discrimination against women in many areas of employment and social life; women's inferior position with regard to wealth, property and income; the continuing economic dependence of women and children on men; and the additional burdens borne by women as primary carers, particularly during times of recession. We may be reminded of the fact that the highest echelons of Irish social institutions such as the law, medicine, the media, the churches, business and government continue to be largely dominated by males; of the persistence, indeed resurgence, of stereotyped images of masculinity and femininity within our culture; and of the failure of society and government to respond comprehensively to key issues such as childcare, domestic and sexual violence, abortion rights, care of older people and other social concerns.

A third and developing view is that the nature of gender inequality is changing and that *men* are increasingly disadvantaged within Irish society. This argument points to men's poorer health status and shorter life expectancy, the rising risk of suicide among young men, the academic underperformance of boys and suggestions that the educational environment has become 'feminised'. This approach can be summed up in the popular phrase 'boys are the new girls'. There is concern over males' higher level of exposure to violence, binge drinking and road trauma. Men have campaigned against their perceived marginalisation within the new forms of family and over legal decisions in relation to custody of and access to children after relationship breakdown. Overall, there are concerns over the inability of men to adjust to changes in society, education and the workplace and to formulate new, more modern models of masculinity. The existence of these three sets of views (and others) – which may all overlap and coexist – indicates something of the complexities of the gender issue.

The topic of gender is open to discussion and analysis from any number of vantage points. In recent decades, important gender-based geographies, histories, cultural studies and psychologies have emerged, along with numerous studies from within other disciplinary areas that have attempted to examine the position of women and men in the context of Irish society and its institutions. There has also been a concerted effort to change the paradigms within which we think about society, to move away from a male-centred or *androcentric* way of looking at the world and to adopt a view that reflects the experience of all people. We would argue that within this rethinking of the world, a sociological perspective is important and that the tools offered by sociology can provide us with useful knowledge about how society's structures, institutions, discourses and processes have helped to shape the relationships between men and women and how these relationships have been interpreted.

It would be impossible to produce a comprehensive sociology of gender in an Irish context, so in this chapter we limit ourselves to:

- Outlining the conceptual basis for a sociological examination of gender.
- Examining the sociology of the family in Ireland, focusing in particular on family life course.
- Exploring some aspects of the sociological study of sexuality in Ireland.
- Reviewing the emergent field of Irish masculinities studies.

Additionally, gender as an analytical category makes its presence felt in several other chapters of this book, for example in the chapters on education and work.

SEX AND GENDER

It is instructive at this stage to address some questions of definition. In particular, the differentiation between the concepts of *sex* and *gender* is important in the development of a sociological understanding of the relationships between women and men. Sex is commonly held to refer to the differing physical attributes, genital arrangements, chromosomal structures, reproductive systems and secondary sexual characteristics such as distribution of body hair, breast development and so on. Sex gives rise to two categories: *female* and *male*. Gender refers to the *meanings* that arise out of sexual classification and to the socially constructed experiences and identities that arise from assumed sexual differences. The clues to such gender identities are found in the physical attributes of sex and in a whole gamut of qualities and activities, ranging from social attitudes to style of dress, from appropriate career pathways to emotional make-up.

The categories that gender gives rise to in Western societies are *feminine* and *masculine*. Masculinity and femininity are constructs specific to historical time and place. They are categories continually being formed, contested, reworked and reaffirmed in social institutions and practices (as well as a range of ideologies). Amongst these conflicting definitions, there is always space for negotiation and change (Davidoff and Hall, 1987). We will maintain a focus on gender, as it is the socially constructed categories of masculinity and femininity that concern us. For simplicity we will use the terms 'men' and 'women' and 'female' and 'male', though we are aware that these tend to emphasise 'natural difference' more than we would like.

THEORISING GENDER

Sociobiology

There is a strong set of ideas, found both in common-sense and academic theories, that the differences between men and women are founded on a 'natural' or an 'inherited traits' basis. Writers point to *biological* differences such as those found in brain structure, hormones or body size, shape and strength. Men, for example, are typified as aggressive and goal driven and women as submissive and emotional.

It seems we have moved on from a time when women were seen to be naturally weak, emotionally unstable and believed to have smaller brains than men, but the belief in a direct biological basis for gender difference and inequality persists. For instance, some of the analysis of the causes of the financial meltdown in 2008 turned to sociobiological explanations, arguing that an excess of testosterone on the trading floor resulted in too much risk-taking, which proved disastrous in certain market conditions (Syed, 2008). The most recent research in this area tends to focus on genes (for example, a gene for 'aggressiveness') and on the nature of hormonal influences. But for sociologists, there can never be a simple or automatic link between any biological basis and social outcomes: even the most extreme biological variations must be mediated by social processes. Nevertheless, the interdisciplinary perspective known as sociobiology has sought to explain certain aspects of human social behaviour – including those aspects related to gender difference – in biological terms. Sociobiology has always been intensely controversial, as there is a fine line between explaining differences in terms of a biological basis and *justifying* them in these terms. When the differences concerned are expressed as social inequalities, this becomes a highly contentious field. Connell (2011) has argued for a rapprochement between biological and cultural approaches to gender analysis, specifically in the health domain. She suggests that while the traditional categorical nature of gender assumption relied too much on biological differentiation of sex, post-structural theories are too wedded to the cultural structuring of gender. A relational theory of gender, treating gender as a multidimensional structure operating in a complex network of institutions, would enable the consideration of both the biological and cultural structures underpinning gender.

Patriarchy

The concept of patriarchy has come to refer to the systematic patterning of society in such a way that men dominate, exploit and oppress women (O'Connor, 1998, p. 7). For O'Connor (1998, p. 13), a variety of everyday taken-for-granted practices reflect and reinforce patriarchal control, including practices and processes within the family, in interpersonal relationships, within the paid and unpaid workforce, in consumption and in the bureaucratic structures of the state and the economy. The problem with the concept of patriarchy is that it appears to be both universal and timeless. Though a number of matriarchal societies have been identified through anthropological studies and although some societies, such as hunter-gatherer societies, appear to display less gender inequality than our own, all known societies can be seen to be patriarchal to some extent. As patriarchy has been identified as a universal quality of extant human societies, it has been criticised as an essentialist and fatalistic concept that adds little to our understanding. For sociologists, it is a description rather than an explanation. It is certainly the case that all societies are differentiated by gender and have been dominated in various ways by men. The question is, *why?*

Sociological theories

It can be argued that theories derived from sociobiology and theories of patriarchy are non-sociological in that they are *essentialist*. In other words, they fail to examine how gender differences are created and expressed through social processes. Conversely, sociological theories attempt to trace how gender difference is constituted within particular types of social institutions, processes and historical contexts and to explain why it is that gender inequality exists and is reproduced within society. There are many varied sociological theories of gender, including broad-brush theories in relation to the historical origins and global experience of gender inequality; middle-range theories about how gender is structured in and through social institutions like the family, the educational system and the state; and micro-level theories that seek to explain how gender is constructed through and shapes phenomena such as conversation and everyday social interaction. Furthermore, sociological theories reflect the full range of political positions that exist in relation to gender, from conservative and reactionary to radical and revolutionary. It is therefore very difficult to summarise and convey the diversity of sociological approaches to gender. We can only briefly mention some of the main theoretical stances that sociologists adopt in relation to gender issues.

For *functionalists* such as Talcott Parsons, a dominant figure in American sociology in the mid-20th century, gender relationships and differences are seen as crucial to the effective functioning of society. Gender differences serve an integrative function in society: they help to bind members together. Thus, masculinity and femininity are seen as a complementary set of roles that span the family (in particular), the public sphere and the workplace. Women are responsible for the domestic arena, for the management of family life and the socialisation of children, while men are to be found in the public sphere, the world of paid work and making connections to the broader world outside the family. For functionalists, socialisation is, among other things, the preparation of people for the 'proper' fulfilment of such sex roles. Males are brought up to be rational, competitive and instrumental, females to be affective, empathetic and co-operative. Subsequent social interaction reinforces these gender scripts and sanctions are brought to bear on those who do not clearly reflect the appropriate role. A good example is the position of women in sport in Ireland. According to Liston (2002), sport exemplifies a cluster of values and expectations that reflect our ideas about ideal masculinity. As a result, non-conformists (women, gay men) do not fit in. Overall, women in sport tend to be valued for their femininity more than their sporting prowess. Conversely, Liston found that successful male participants in sport generate sporting capital that can be deployed to access social status as well as economic rewards.

While functionalist approaches (which share many assumptions with sociobiology) are out of favour with contemporary sociologists, they clearly continue to have resonances in everyday life and popular culture. Many jokes and throwaway remarks relate directly to the 'proper' roles of the sexes, while, perhaps more seriously, stereotypes in relation to the appropriate behaviour of males and females may adversely affect individuals' progress through the education system (see Chapter 7), employment and in public life. The functionalist concept of 'sex role' continues to be widely used, often in a non-critical way, in analyses of social phenomena.

Within Marxist thought, the oppression of women is an aspect of class conflict and antagonism. Marxists note how the unpaid work of women within the nuclear family allows the next generation of workers to be *reproduced* at a lower cost to the forces of capital (see Chapter 6). Women do the work involved in reproducing the existing labour force and the future labour force. They also may be called into the workforce as a reserve army of labour when the need arises. More broadly, the family is also a key site for the inculcation of ideologies favourable to capital. The family, and in particular women, who bear the brunt of this work, teaches children to be obedient, productive, healthy and communicative, the very values necessary for an efficient labour force. These sets of ideas have been brought together in sociology in *social reproduction theory*, an approach that argues for a systematic connection between the subordination of women and capitalist economic exploitation (Connell, 1987, p. 43).

Whether such reproduction takes place in ways that 'suit' capital is always contingent, always open to question. The family equally has the capacity to become a site of *opposition* to capitalism and the relationships between men and women are constantly reworked and redefined, not pre-set by the nature of the capitalist economy. Similarly, it is debatable whether gender inequality *does* favour capitalism. As we saw in Chapter 1, a key historical feature of capitalism has been that it breaks down what are seen as traditional relationships and structures and reconstitutes people as workers and consumers. In many respects the development of capitalist social relationships has seen a greater level of equality between men and women. Social progression means that women today are much more likely to be educated workers and enthusiastic consumers than was the case in any previous generation. Thus, higher levels of gender equality can be of great service to capital.

Feminist sociology is usually associated with the second wave feminist movement. (The first wave is usually taken to refer to the suffragist movements of the late 19th and early 20th century, but of course this does not mean that organised women's movements or systematic feminist thought did not precede this. There are many varieties of feminism – it is by no means a homogenous movement or system of thought.) It is common to divide modern feminist thinking into three main strands: liberal, socialist and radical feminism. Each overlaps with social theory in other fields – thus, socialist feminism shares many assumptions with Marxism, radical feminism with libertarian thinking. Similarly, intellectual currents in feminism are inextricably linked to competing political positions and strategies within the women's movement. *Liberal* feminists are concerned to uncover the immediate forms of discrimination against women and to fight for legal and other reforms to overcome them. They tend to focus on mainstream methods of bringing about social change, such as political lobbying, use of the media and working through existing political, business and bureaucratic structures. A good example in the Irish context would be Women's Aid, a voluntary organisation that provides support and information to women and their children who are being physically, emotionally and sexually abused in their own homes. It is self-defined as a feminist, political and campaigning organisation committed to the elimination of violence against and abuse of women.

Socialist feminists argue that women's oppression is both an aspect of capitalism and of patriarchy. An end to the current nature of capitalism does not in itself mean an end to the subordination of women, but is an essential part of it. The full liberation of women from oppression will also require a struggle against the control by men of private and public institutions. Socialist feminists often work through smaller left-wing political parties and groupings, trade unions, social movements and in academia and the media.

Radical feminists see male control of all women through patriarchy as the main problem. They argue that women must struggle to free themselves from the control of male institutions. They are most likely to work through women-only groups. Forms of action may span conventional lobbying techniques to innovative forms of protest such as the 'slut walk' rallies where women claim the right not to be stereotyped or judged by their display of sexuality (www.slutwalktoronto.com). Each of these approaches to feminism finds a reflection in the work of feminist sociologists.

In the 1990s, a body of writing arose that challenged the perceived orthodoxies of Western feminism, including the established divisions between the strands outlined above. Known as 'the new feminism' or third wave feminism, it rejected the oft-quoted precept that 'the personal is the political' and attempted to move feminism away from 'lifestyle' politics and back into the public sphere. British writer Natasha Walter suggested that the feminist focus on women's cultural and sexual behaviour has not led to the expected radical changes. Rather, she argued that:

> feminism has enunciated many, too many, critiques of dress and pornography, of poetry and film-making, of language and physical behaviour. It has sought to direct our personal lives on every level. And yet women have still not achieved fundamental equality; they are still poorer and less powerful than men. Rather than concentrating its energy on the ways women dress and talk and make love, feminism now must attack the material basis of economic and social and political equality. (Walter, 1998, p. 4)

The rise of the 'new feminism' expresses the tensions of a movement that has achieved remarkable success but still has to fully challenge the underlying realities of entrenched gender inequality. As such, it may represent a return to much of the style and substance of earlier models of feminism. The new feminism aims to tap into the concerns of younger women (and men), to draw on the vibrancy of popular culture (including fashion and music) and to make use of the new communications technologies of a globalising world: 'riot grrrls, guerrilla girls, net chicks, cyber chix, geekgirls, tank girls, supergirl, action girls, deep girls – this is the era of DIY feminism' (Bail, 1996, p. 3). Inevitably, the new feminism has had to confront suggestions of a 'sell-out' to patriarchy and capitalism and a lack of political purity. The debate between traditional and new feminists is a vigorous and challenging one for feminist thinking. Within sociology it may lead to a shift away from the concern with cultural issues of sexuality and representation and towards more main-stream sociological concerns with the structures of social inequality.

Ridgeway (2009) argues that gender continues to be one of the primary frames for organising social relations in society. Without acknowledging this, 'we cannot understand how the gendered structure of contemporary society both changes and resists changing' (2009, p. 145). The gender frame – constructed through institutionalised and taken-for-granted assumptions about gender differences – 'introduces implicit biases into expectations and behaviours that affect gender inequality' (2009, p. 151). She contends that gender frames crucially interact with institutional structures to produce gendered organisational practices that in turn sustain and reproduce shared cultural beliefs about gender.

THE SOCIOLOGY OF THE FAMILY

The family, in Ireland as elsewhere, has been identified as 'an important symbol of collective identity, unity and security' (O'Connor, 1998, p. 89). It is seen by many – from politicians, to priests, to some social scientists – as the 'natural' basis for society. It has also risen to prominence in commercial, political and social policy rhetoric, with much attention being given to 'the family' in political campaigns, media advertising and social policy initiatives. An understanding of the family is also central to any discussion of gender relationships, for it is through this institution, amongst others, that our experiences and understandings of gender and of sexuality are formed and mediated. But as the term 'family' has risen to prominence in public discourse, it has become more problematic and opaque. The rationalist economic discourse associated with neo-liberalism tends to focus on the *individual* primarily as worker and as consumer and secondarily as citizen. There is much focus on individual rights and actions in 'the market' and the family is seen in this context as anachronistic and limiting, as in 'family business', 'family farm' or 'family obligations'. The critique of hyper-individualism that has emerged in the wake of Ireland's economic collapse has to some extent prompted a renewed focus on traditional values, including those surrounding the family and family life.

Whether the focus is on individualism or familialism as its counterpoint, many questions to do with oppression and inequality of, and within, families have been largely ignored. But as Robertson (1991, p. 158) points out, we need to understand the family as the locus of much of what we define as social behaviour. Thus, 'if we are interested in such things as economic performance and social status, the interaction of life-cycles within the domestic group is much more informative than the life-cycle of each individual'. An understanding of the family is basic to a sociological understanding.

In Western societies there has been much debate over competing definitions of 'the family'. It is now widely accepted that there are many variations from 'the norm' of the nuclear family of married heterosexual couple plus children. For example, Irish social welfare policy and practice have now begun to recognise the validity of families based on cohabiting (not married) couples or lone parents (O'Connor, 1998, p. 90). There is far less agreement – in Ireland and elsewhere – over the possibility of families based on homosexual unions, although significant change has occurred in recent years in that respect. In 2006 the High Court rejected an action taken by a lesbian couple aimed at having their Canadian marriage recognised as valid under Irish law or securing the right to marry in Ireland. Dr Katherine Zappone and Dr Anne Louise Gilligan argued that the state acted unlawfully and breached their constitutional rights to equality, marriage, property and family. The High Court dismissed the case on the basis that the Irish Constitution does not allow for same-sex marriage (*Irish Times*, 14 December 2006). But in 2010, 17 years after the decriminalisation of homosexuality, the Oireachtas passed a Civil Partnership and Cohabitation Act that enables same-sex couples to enter into civil unions. The legislation was opposed by Catholic bishops but was passed nevertheless.

In Ireland and other Western countries, the range of family types is becoming increasingly diverse. While about two-thirds of family units are constituted by couples married for the first time, the other one-third is made up of lone-parent families, cohabiting couples and family units including couples who were previously married (also known as blended families) (Lunn and Fahey, 2011). Cohabiting couples are growing as a family unit and are often seen as a 'trial run' before marriage. Demographic trends are both a reflection and a determinant of ideas about gender and family. According to Fahey and Field (2008), marriage remains popular as an institution in Ireland, but the age at which people contract a marriage is increasing. In 2007 the average age of the groom was 33.4 years and 31.3 years for the bride. Correspondingly, the average age of giving birth has been increasing. The average age of first-time mothers during 2011 was just under 32 years (31.8) (*Irish Times*, 23 February 2012). Thirty-four per cent of births during that period were outside of marriage, one of the highest rates in Europe. For analysts such as Galligan (1998a, p. 27), such changes reflect the modernisation of Irish society, a growing level of secularisation and a more assertive attitude among women in relation to family formation. It is also possible that the wider economic transformation in Irish society is continuing to exert an effect, even after the downturn. Fahey and Layte (2007, p. 174) have argued that:

> the Celtic Tiger era was less transformational for famiy and sexual life than the decades that preceded it. What effect it did have seems to have been benign in important ways – economic growth encouraged more marriage, more children and thus, simply more family, the mirror image of how economic stagnation in the 1980s had done the opposite.

That upturn has stabilised during the 2000s with no evidence yet of a downturn in fertility, despite the recession.

O'Connor (1998, p. 120) observes that most lone parents have to an extent chosen their situation and overall enjoy routine parenting tasks and the independence of single parenthood. Nevertheless, lone parents form a significant proportion of those in poverty or at risk of poverty. There is an extremely strong relationship between low educational attainment and the likelihood of becoming a never-married lone mother (Lunn et al., 2010). At the same time, detailed analysis of the 2006 census figures confirm much more positive outcomes for highly educated women. Women in young couples are increasingly likely to earn more money and have a better standard of education than their male partners (Lunn and Fahey, 2011). Amongst young couples aged between 26 and 40 years, 42 per cent of women had a higher occupational level versus 28 per cent of men, and women in couples generally had higher levels of educational attainment than men. This exerts a direct challenge to the traditional notion of the man as the sole or key occupant of 'the good provider' role, beloved of functionalists such as Parsons.

While diversity of family types is not new (Irish history speaks of a number of types of domestic arrangement), the challenge to traditional conceptions is seen by many as further evidence of modernity. For example, the trends in relation to single parenthood, where women increasingly choose to bring up children without a permanent male partner, have been said by Irish sociologist Pat O'Connor (1998, p. 122) to suggest a new 'marginalisation of men within the family'. For O'Connor, this trend implies a 'radical challenge to our ideas about the family and to the cultural and social construction of heterosexuality'. Similarly, the greater acceptance of divorce and remarriage in Ireland signals a change in what can constitute a valid family arrangement. The Catholic Church was a key player in opposing and ultimately delaying the legalisation of divorce in Ireland. Despite the introduction of divorce in 1997, Ireland continues to have one of the lowest divorce rates in Europe, with most separated couples preferring legal separation to divorce (Burley and Regan, 2002).

The notion of the 'traditional' family continues to receive active support from many, if not the majority, in Irish society. In particular, most men, and women who are not working outside the home, tend to have more traditional views in relation to the family (Galligan, 1998b, p. 118). Such views are often expressed in self-conscious opposition to perceived changes in Irish society. Defence of a particular view of 'the family' is central to conservative thinking everywhere. This was the case, for instance, in relation to opposition to the passage of a civil partnership law that conservatives believed would undermine 'traditional' notions of marriage and the family.

Crucially, the family is implicated in relationships of power and inequality in Irish society. It is an important mechanism through which economic inequality is maintained and property rights are transmitted. It also provides a basis for access to, and success within, the education system. The experiences of women and men in Irish families may be shaped in important ways by the broader social relationships within which a family is located. Involvement in paid work, for example, may help to determine who has the 'power' within families, while at the same time women *and* men tend to underestimate and devalue the importance of unpaid work both 'inside' and 'outside' the family (P. O'Hara, 1998, p. 87).

By 2000 half of all couples in Ireland were dual earners (Russell, 2004), though the institutional and cultural context has not kept pace with this change, as evidenced by the strong gender segregation in the labour force, unequal domestic power relationships (McGinnity et al., 2007), poor childcare provision and lack of support for women in the public sphere. In everyday discourses, the Irish mother continues to occupy the role of primary carer and life-giver, leading to pressures and tensions in the attempt to manage both work and domestic spheres. For instance, a government agency's campaign to promote hygienic food in a hygienic environment deliberately played on women's insecurities about failing as 'mammies'. This was possible because while women's lives have changed dramatically in recent years, institutional change and cultural shift have been much slower. Thus, according to Collins (2006, p. 98):

> Women are torn between an ideology that contends that women should be in the workforce and an ideology that contends that women should be in the home. These contradictory pressures leave women feeling they are never good enough either as workers or mothers. In the family this leads to the well-known phenomenon of 'compensating' children with consumer goods for not spending enough time with them. In the home this means that women try to compensate for their absence by ensuring that it is a safe environment for their families. This, I believe, is behind the rise of anti-bacterial products, as women try to ensure a 'germ-free' home, and behind the anxiety about the safety of food.

It is important for sociologists to remember that the family is a *dynamic* concept. In Ireland, we have seen a considerable shift within a relatively short time in the nature and understanding of the family unit. There is evidence that the extended family was the norm within Irish rural society. Movement to urban and suburban areas does not necessarily mean that the extended family unit has disappeared (in O'Connor's analysis (2008, p. 42) of children's own accounts, about a quarter saw themselves as being part of an extended family), but it may be experienced in different ways. For instance, families may now use Skype and social networking sites to keep in touch with each other, even if they meet in face-to-face settings less often. In looking to the future we can begin to discern some important changes, for example a rise in numbers of single-person households, considerably smaller families, the rise of the one-child family, increasing levels of lone parenthood, more gay and lesbian couples and more voluntarily child-free people. Some researchers have suggested that non-familial ties with close friends, neighbours and so on are eclipsing family relationships in terms of closeness and necessity. However, reliance on family versus non-family relationships is a dynamic process that changes to meet specific needs during the life course. For instance, new research indicates that family is an important 'shock absorber' for people affected by the economic downturn in Ireland. Practices such as the giving of 'quick' loans to family members and new living arrangements such as three-generational households demonstrate the family's continued vitality as a resource (Changing Generation, 2012). Close friendships are becoming more important and more necessary for older people (Jamieson et al., 2006). Similarly, Pahl and Spencer (2004) recognise a social shift between those relationships that are given (kin) and those that are chosen (which may include kin and non-kin). When social ties move from given to chosen, this may or may not lead to greater commitment. The decline of close familial relations *does not necessarily* imply greater individualism if those family relations are replaced with friendship relations.

THE LIFE COURSE: FROM THE SOCIOLOGY OF CHILDHOOD TO THE SOCIOLOGY OF AGEING

Until relatively recently, children tended to be neither seen nor heard within mainstream sociology. Traditional views of the socialisation process reinforced the notion that children, in the context of their families and personal communities, play a passive role. Newer literature within the field of sociology of childhood has challenged traditional passive conceptualisations of the child and has argued for an interpretive reproduction approach. Such an approach holds that 'children are active, creative social agents who produce their own unique children's cultures while simultaneously contributing to the production of adult societies' (Corsaro, 2005, p. 3).

Corsaro (2005, p. 3) argues that childhood, as an embedded part of the social structure, is interrelated with other categories like social class, gender and age groups. A growing concern of Irish sociologists is how 'good' an experience childhood is in contemporary Ireland. Research suggests that children and families who are rich in social capital and sociability receive considerable social support and access to valued resources. The mechanism through which economic capital underpins and interacts with social capital gives rise to social inequalities in society (Bourdieu, 1986). Several studies in recent years, particularly those emanating from the Children's Research Centre at Trinity College Dublin, have raised questions about what kinds of resources are present in the family and in the community that will help bring about successful outcomes for the child. Likewise, the sociological literature on childhood is concerned to outline the benefits that a child brings to the family and community of which they form a part.

It is increasingly acknowledged that sociologists must move beyond the strictures of a narrow 'family structure effect' in trying to understand the everyday, lived experience of Irish children, since wider community, neighbourhood and structural effects will have an important bearing on their quality of life. This is particularly important for children in special situations – children with additional needs, children with different ethno-racial identities, poor children – because they have to manage 'their difference' from others in their schools and communities on an ongoing basis. In recent years a powerful discourse has emerged in Irish society around the rights of children, particularly those children who have special challenges to contend with in their lives. Notwithstanding the progress that has been made, a number of non-governmental organisations, along with the Ombudsman for Children, have been campaigning for several years for an amendment to the Constitution aimed at enhancing the protection of children's rights. It is argued that such an amendment would bring greater pressure to bear on the state to 'cherish all of its children equally'.

Within mainstream sociology, much of the research focusing on issues such as family life and well-being has taken a top-down view of the effect of parents on children and the ability of parents to invest in their children's well-being and future. A more active conceptualisation of children, Morrow argues, 'would explore how children themselves actively generate, draw on, or negotiate their own social capital, or indeed make links for their parents, or even provide active support for parents' (Morrow, 1999, p. 751). Thus, the emphasis within sociology is now on the transactional nature of the relationship between children, family, neighbourhood, community, media and culture because we allow for the fact that each has the capacity to influence and to be influenced by the other. Newer studies of childhood tend to be premised on the principle of children as active agents with the capacity to define their own situations. As Kelley et al. (1997, p. 305) argue, we should view children not simply as objects of adult socialisation, but rather as young people who are 'competent reporters of experience'.

Seventy-five per cent of children living in Ireland are in families with two parents, 18 per cent live with a lone parent and 6 per cent with cohabiting parents (Lunn and Fahey, 2011). Drawing on a nationally representative sample of nine-year-olds, the Growing Up in Ireland study reveals some key facts about what life is like for Irish children. In general, the researchers found that the majority of nine-year-olds have quite positive outcomes in terms of child development, although they noted differences in outcomes across the main social class groupings. For instance, they found significant associations between mothers' low educational level and prevalence of problems across all measures of child well-being. Most children grow up within a traditional family unit, with the majority of nine-year-olds (82 per cent) living in two-parent families. Over half of all mothers (54 per cent) worked outside the home, while 39 per cent were principally involved in looking after the home. The majority of parents favoured an authoritative parenting role, although gender differences in style emerged. Girls were more likely to experience an indulgent or uninvolved/permissive parenting style from both parents, whereas fathers were more likely to adopt an authoritarian style with boys than girls. Girls in general tended to be slightly more positive about themselves than boys, although girls tended to report more feelings of anxiety than boys. Nine-year-olds generally had a positive attitude toward school. The biggest problem they identified in their neighbourhoods was traffic, though generally speaking they felt safe where they lived (Williams et al., 2009).

Qualitative research with a sample of nine-year-olds participating in the Growing Up in Ireland study reveals that gender differentiation is very pertinent to their everyday lives. The study demonstrates that young boys and girls have a clear understanding of what is 'gender appropriate' behaviour for their sex. It is difficult to avoid gender stereotyping because there are many codes around gender in the culture that you would have to resist or challenge at every turn (blue for a boy, pink for a girl). Children can also defy these gender stereotypes by identifying more with the opposite gender (e.g. tomboys). In other words, these categories are socially defined and socially reproduced and therefore are always open to challenge and change. Not much has changed around gender stereotyping for small children and it is known that children prefer same-sex friends to opposite-sex friends up until the pre-teen/early teen transition. This might reinforce gender stereotypes. But children grow up in a highly mediated consumer culture that at every turn represents the sexes in markedly different ways (when leading London toy shop Hamley's decided to stop colour coding its floors as blue for boys and pink for girls in late 2011, it made the international news). As children get older, their interests in gender-specific toys fades and both boys and girls become more interested in clothes and electronic toys that are at least potentially more gender neutral.

Creative research methodologies provide us with some insight into the everyday lived experiences of Irish children. O'Connor's (2008) study of identity orientations among Irish Transition Year students shows how young people in Ireland relate to tropes of identity and to their local and global contexts. In response to an invitation to write a page 'describing themselves and the Ireland that they inhabit', the young people involved in the study produced texts that O'Connor has analysed. The young people in this study, born between 1982 and 1985, have grown up in a social and cultural context of rapid economic, social and cultural change. O'Connor identifies a number of different identity orientations among the group, including a global orientation, an individualisation ethos and a strong gender identity. She concludes that young people's accounts suggest that despite the highly globalised and rapidly changing nature of Irish society, their lifestyles, concerns and interests continue to be 'mapped' onto gender. Gender still matters in terms of self-definition.

Children growing up in a divided city

Leonard (2006) has carried out research into children's experience of growing up in North Belfast, in an interface area where Catholics and Protestants live close together but demarcate their own territories through a variety of symbolic means. One of the most striking features of the research was the tendency for the children to describe their daily lives in terms of growing up Protestant or Catholic. This badge of identity was employed more frequently than either gender or class. Leonard points out that the surrounding environment in which the children live their daily lives is highly segregated on the basis of religious identity. The majority of children did not have any friends from the other religious community and a substantial number had never interacted socially with anyone outside of their own religious grouping, demonstrating the closed nature of their immediate social world.

The research revealed the ongoing presence of sectarianism in the daily lives of children in the interface area. Leonard cites research carried out by Paul Connolly that found that from as young as three years of age, children are able to identify and negatively evaluate the other religious group and this process becomes more prevalent once children enter the segregated school system that characterises Northern Irish society.

The children's narratives revealed a propensity to denigrate members of the other community. They tended to define themselves socially and symbolically (through the use of jewellery, hairstyles, clothing and body piercing) in terms of members of 'in-groups' and 'out-groups'. But children also recounted some contexts in which they were able to produce more diverse identities. Some children spoke of interacting with the other religious community while on holidays outside of Northern Ireland or even at a skateboarding venue in the city centre of Belfast. Leonard thus concludes that even in highly constrained circumstances, children possess the ability to construct a range of identities that are negotiated and renegotiated across different spheres of interaction. Nevertheless, she notes that 'while the children in this research demonstrated the capacity to exhibit multiple identities, sectarianism still played a key and central role in the formation of their local identities' (p. 206).

AGEING

At the other end of the life course, sociologists and other social scientists are paying increased attention to the process of ageing in Ireland. A major demographic transformation is underway that has important economic, social and policy implications. Life expectancy at birth for males has increased from 57.4 years in 1926 to 76.7 years in 2005, representing a gain of 19.3 years over the 79-year period. The corresponding female rates were 57.9 and 81.5 years respectively, which represents a gain of 23.6 years. Improved living conditions coupled with further developments in medical care are considered to be the main contributing factors (CSO, 2008, p. 14). People are living longer and enjoying more active and engaged lifestyles. This has major implications for a range of social policies, from healthcare to housing to lifelong learning and new technology.

The Irish Longitudinal Study on Ageing (TILDA) is the most detailed study on ageing ever undertaken in Ireland. This interdisciplinary study explores the health, lifestyles and financial situation of a representative sample of older people, tracking them over a 10-year period. TILDA is specifically designed to develop a portrait of older people in Ireland that can inform planning and policy development into the future. The first results from the study (issued in 2011) indicate the heterogeneous nature of older people's experiences. These are determined to a great extent by the particular socio-economic conditions that prevailed for different age cohorts:

> Major social changes such as the introduction of free secondary schooling and the liberalisation of the contraceptive laws are evident in educational attainment and fertility differences by age. Social processes such as the intergenerational transmission of educational attainment are also seen. Low levels of economic growth which resulted in large-scale out-migration is evident in the remarkably high proportion of former emigrants in the older population. (TILDA, 2011, p. 1)

Older people as a whole experience a high quality of life. Most live with their spouse or with spouse and children, though the proportion of people living alone increases with age. Nearly a quarter of older people have lived abroad for more than six months. Three-quarters of adults aged 50 or over live in close proximity to at least one of their children. Half of older people provide care to grandchildren, while over one-third of older people provide practical help to their adult children. Neighbours and friends are the beneficiaries of help provided by older people, of whom a quarter provide on average 8 hours of such help per month. The majority of older people surveyed are socially engaged with their families and wider communities, though 6 per cent of older Irish women and 7 per cent of older Irish men are socially isolated.

A recent study (Corcoran, Grey and Peillon, 2010) of suburban living made some general observations about the lives of older people in suburban localities that dovetails with the portrait presented by TILDA. In general, senior residents of the suburbs under study who participated in focus group discussions displayed a strong sense of emotional rootedness to their local area. Taken as a whole, they were significantly more likely than younger respondents in the study to describe themselves as attached to the place where they lived. Sense of attachment was frequently predicated on a sense of the historical past and feelings of nostalgia often arising from the experience of a lifetime lived almost exclusively within the locale. In a study of older people in three English communities, Chris Phillipson and colleagues (1999) also found a strong relationship between people and place, with memories acting as a key mechanism in creating a sense of attachment to place. A key theme that emerged in the suburban study was the importance of neighbours to older residents: the survey data revealed that respondents aged 55 years or older were considerably more reliant on neighbours than were younger respondents. This result is consistent with Irish national data from the 1990s showing that 'about two-thirds of older people talk to their neighbours most days, with most of the rest doing so once or twice a week' (Fahey et al., 2007, p. 31).

For residents who were natives of the local area being studied or who had significant longevity there, strong social bonds had grown up over the years and neighbours were in some cases valued as much as kin (Corcoranet et al., 2010). Phillipson and his co-authors similarly point to the value of a community and locality perspective for understanding the impact of social changes in later life (1999, p. 715). In particular, residential stability across time facilitates social embedding and connections made at the early stage of family formation can provide a template for supportive friendship networks in later life. Neighbourliness is complemented by a pattern of localised kinship that is particularly important to older people as they move into a life stage when they will require more support. Most respondents in the suburban study reported that they had sons or daughters living either in the same locality or nearby. They could draw on this network in addition to the neighbourly network for the purposes of socialising and social support. National data (Fahey et al., 2007, p. 31) suggest that older people's frequency of contact with friends and relatives is about the same as contact with neighbours. While many older people may remain actively involved in their communities through retirement groups and similar associations, this does not preclude the existence of 'disaffiliated' older people whose lives are largely isolated and lonely.

Older people were also consulted by Corcoran et al. (2010) about their uptake of new technology. They recognised that the world is moving on technologically and that becoming technologically literate is a new challenge they faced. National data suggest that the digital divide is likely to manifest itself in age terms – older people (age 65 to 74) are significantly less likely to have used either a computer or the Internet than are younger adults (Fahey et al., 2007, p. 32). Children learn about new technology in school and at home, while adults are exposed to it in the workplace and use it at home. Non-working older people are the least likely to have exposure to information technology and when they do, they may lack the self-confidence and supports to engage with it fully.

SEXUALITY

In the words of Oliver J. Flanagan, TD, there was 'no sex in Ireland before television' (Tobin, 1996, p. 68). Similarly, sexuality is a topic that has been neglected within Irish sociology until relatively recently (Inglis, 1998d). This is unfortunate because since at least the early 1960s, debates over a range of issues linked to human sexuality have formed a key element of Irish society and of gender relationships. There is a commonly held perception that attitudes towards sexuality have seen a marked change in Ireland in recent years, and as Beale (1986, p. 87) argues, 'it is over issues to do with sexuality that the conflict between traditional and progressive forces in Irish society can be seen most clearly'.

As with constructions of gender more generally, our understandings, experiences and attitudes about sexuality are socially shaped – by the media, the education system, religious institutions, the family and social interaction with others. 'Sexuality' is not an unproblematic term. Like 'gender', it is a social construction.

We find not only one sexuality but multifarious sexual*ies*, discussion of which could fill a whole chapter of this book and more. In many ways sexuality permeates every aspect of our lives, though often in a subconscious or unremarked manner. It is built into how we experience aspects of life such as education, work, leisure and the media. In as much as we can perceive it as a unified field of practices, attitudes and institutions, it is, as British social historian (or historical sociologist) Jeffrey Weeks points out, 'an *historical* unity which has been shaped by a multiplicity of forces, and which has undergone complex historical transformations' (1989, p. ix). In other words, 'sexuality' is a diverse field of experience and behaviour that is brought together at certain times through a common body of language or discourse. There are many such discourses that help to mould our understandings of sexuality. Among the most powerful are those generated from within the family, the education system, medicine, popular culture and the churches. In Ireland, the legal and political systems have also been important as debates about various aspects of sexuality have erupted into the public sphere.

The pioneer in Ireland in terms of analysing sexuality from a sociological perspective has been Tom Inglis of University College Dublin. He has discussed the nature of Irish gender and sexual relationships in the context of the sociology of the Catholic Church in Ireland and in relation to the development of (and reaction to) sex education programmes (see in particular Inglis, 1998b). A key aim of Inglis's research is to 'break the silence' in relation to Irish sexuality and to question our assumptions. He is especially concerned (1998b, p. 3) about the ignorance of many Irish people on the topic and suggests that the failure of Irish people to confront the issue of sex leaves them lacking in confidence and competence.

Contrary to Oliver J. Flanagan's belief, talk about sex did not emerge in Ireland only in the time of modern communications technology. Foucault points out to us that sexuality in the past was not so much hidden or repressed, but talked about in a different sort of way. As Inglis suggests (1998e, p. 102), in 'traditional' Ireland, 'sex was real and demanding and it was rigorously inculcated in every church, school, hospital and home in the country'. This was a discourse that linked sex to ideas of sin, control, danger and regulation. As constituted by the churches (especially, but not only, the Catholic Church) and the state, sex was a powerful force that needed to be curtailed, particularly within the institution of marriage. In a fascinating discussion, Inglis has analysed the historical role and influence of the 'Irish mother', in particular how this has helped to shape attitudes to sexuality in Ireland. The basis of this process was laid in the 19th century with the restructuring of the rural economy towards pastoral farming. As women lost their productive role – for example, as weavers and spinners – they were increasingly confined to a powerless domestic position. A new basis of power was built through an 'alliance' between Irish rural mothers and the modernising Catholic Church, which was worked out as follows (Inglis, 1998e, pp. 198–9):

> The domination and control of women by the Church, and the necessity for women to ally themselves with that dominating power if they themselves were to have any power, led to their high level of marital fertility which, in turn, created the need for postponed marriage, permanent celibacy and emigration among their children. These practices were encouraged by the mother in the home through a devotion to the Church, a rigorous sexual morality, and a physical and emotional distance from her children.

The church imposed a strict discipline of sexual morality. Women were encouraged to feel ashamed of their bodies. The discourse of the church penetrated their everyday lives as the Catholic confessional became a site for the interrogation of women about their sexual feelings, desires and activities. Inglis suggests (1998e, p. 188) that 'sex became the most abhorrent sin'. Indeed, it came to dominate the notion of sin itself. On a broader plane, Inglis sees mothers as having an essential role in the 'civilising process' (as defined by German sociologist Norbert Elias). The modernisation of Irish society was reflected in the extension of disciplines of cleanliness, control and obedience into the Irish family and the key instruments of this process were the church, the school and the mother. The home, along with the school, became a site for supervision and surveillance by the church. The mores of the church and the practices of priests provided a powerful model for childrearing, as mothers imitated the social and moral perspective of the religious – 'through an imitation of their celibate lifestyle, their body discipline and morality [mothers] inculcated a sexual and emotional repression which was crucial to the attainment of postponed marriages, permanent celibacy and emigration' (Inglis, 1998e, p. 193).

In modern Ireland we now talk about sex in very different ways, with a complex range of public and private discourses that embrace 'news reports, feature articles, documentaries, panel discussions and talk radio' (Inglis, 1998b, p. 148). Many of these changes date from the 1960s and 1970s. Using the letters published by popular *Sunday Press* agony aunt Angela Macnamara between 1963 and 1980, Ryan (2011) offers a rare sociological insight into intimate relationships within family life in Ireland. He charts how dating and married couples negotiated a new understanding of their sexual lives against the backdrop of social change and shows how women rejected relationships where sex was a duty within marriage as opposed to an expression of love.

The church itself has also learned how to talk about sex in the new language of 'relationships', if not yet of pleasure. There is now a multiplicity of competing discourses that relate to issues of modernity, the public sphere and sexuality. For Inglis (1998b, p. 150), modern Ireland is now witnessing a conflict between two main opposing belief systems. One set of beliefs is based on traditional Catholicism and links contemporary manifestations of sexuality to materialism, consumerism and liberalism. Such a view sees modern expressions of sexuality as being intricately linked to the process of producing, buying and exchanging commodities. The other discourse of sexuality reflects 'a modern, or indeed post-modern, secular society based on liberal individualism'. It claims to be open about sexuality and to be non-judgemental about people's private and intimate behaviour or about depictions of sexuality in the media.

As Inglis has remarked (1998e), the context in which we understand Irish sexuality has changed markedly and this is bringing about an attendant change in attitudes. Two reports published by the Crisis Pregnancy Agency in 2004 illustrate the changing nature of sexual attitudes and at the same time point to the continuity of more old-fashioned ideologies about 'good girls' and 'bad girls'. A report on sexual attitudes by Rundle et al. (2004) focuses on a national sample of 3,000 men and women aged 18 to 45. The vast majority were sexually active and 80 per cent regularly used a method of contraception. Non-use of contraception was generally associated with older age, lower educational level, lower social class and casual relationship status. Forty per cent of men and 26 per cent of women admitted that drinking alcohol had contributed to having sex without contraception. Nearly one-quarter of participants (23 per cent) agreed that if a woman carries condoms while not in a relationship, it gives the message that she is looking for sex or is 'easy'. This theme is also visited in a report for the agency carried out by Murphy Lawless (2004), which constituted a qualitative study of the attitudes of young women to sexuality and fertility issues. Generally, the young women interviewed felt there was great openness in Irish society, that women's roles have evolved and that women had more life choices. Yet the researchers still found a strong discourse about women having sex outside of relationships being labelled in a certain way:

> I think, like, well for young people say around my age, I think the attitudes are still very backward like. Especially when it comes to men our age like, they still brand women 'slags' like, for sleeping around, and men 'studs', that's still very much alive (Nurse, 26, small city).

Furthermore, the greater openness and loosening of gender roles also brings greater confusion, as Inglis has argued, and as this respondent illustrates:

> I think there is more openness, you are able to discuss the very fact you are a sexual being, and things like the ability to enjoy sex. But there's also a sort of a level of insecurity and discomfort about that ... there are more 'shoulds'. You should enjoy sex. You should want to have it a lot, or more than you did. There's also the kind of *Cosmopolitan* culture that I think is going around, where young girls are under pressure to be a certain type of woman (Teacher, 30, Dublin).

The Crisis Pregnancy Agency has gone some way towards producing comprehensive accounts of sexual behaviour in Ireland, a topic that was long a neglected one. While Inglis reflects a liberal optimism about sexuality, some Irish feminists have stressed the complexities and contradictions inherent in its practices, especially where it concerns women. O'Connor (1998, p. 177), for example, indicates the distinguishing features of sexuality as experienced by young Irish women: an emphasis on active heterosexuality; continuing problems over the availability of contraception; the tangled concept of 'love'; the experience of sexual harassment; the stigmatisation of abortion; powerful and contradictory messages around body imagery; an emphasis on sex as a consumer product; and the pressures against 'saying no'. She points out that for women, 'love' can be a source of both power and vulnerability – a veil that hides the power within a relationship or a means of achieving a measure of equality. In Chapter 7 we have also pointed to some of the challenges that sexuality poses for young people in the Irish education system.

MASCULINITIES

Unfortunately, the slowly developing sociology of masculinity in Ireland has yet to provide a thoroughgoing critical analysis of the challenges that modern patterns and discourses of sexuality provide for Irish men. In response to the development of the women's movement and stimulated by the increased reflexivity of (post-)modern society, there has been a recent interest in the nature of *masculinity*. There has been a recognition that changing models of femininity may give rise to changes in the imagery, understanding or experience of masculinity. For a long time within society, and within sociology, masculinity has been 'invisible'. As British social psychologists Edley and Wetherell (1995, p. 2) suggest, 'masculinity has been regarded as the standard case, the usual pattern, synonymous with humanity in general'. Historically, men have had the capacity to define 'normality'; it is women who have been positioned as deviations from the norm and femininity that has required exploration and explanation. Thus, gender studies have tended to focus on women's experience and studies of men *as men* have been comparatively rare until recently.

The traditional image of the male breadwinner labouring in the male-dominated workplace of farm, factory or office now has a diminishing resonance in reality. Edley and Wetherell (1995) argue that a comprehensive understanding of contemporary masculinity requires an interdisciplinary approach. This combines a sociology of men with a social psychological understanding of male subjectivity and an appreciation of the discourses within which masculinity is defined and framed in our culture. Victor Seidler (1988) has explored the concept of masculinity and its development within the Western Enlightenment tradition. The Enlightenment bequeathed a vision of masculinity that equates reason with authority and that resulted in the devaluing of emotion. Authority ultimately was based around the concept of the father. During the Industrial Revolution, this image was elaborated to include the good provider role. Fathers were to inhabit the role of aloof and distant *pater familias*, the disciplinarian who left matters concerning family to his dutiful wife. Medicine and psychology colluded in legitimating and inculcating this image of appropriate masculinity, in the process labelling non-conformist masculine behaviour – such as homosexuality – as deviant.

How society responds to and shapes homosexuality is of importance not only for gays and lesbians – it is crucial to the formation of sexualities more generally. Homophobia, or fear of homosexuality, is a potent force in the development of dominant modes of masculinity and femininity. Indeed, gayness is seen as a negation of manhood and this is translated into anything that can be seized upon as evidence of feminine behaviour: involvement in domestic work, particular popular cultural choices or ways of walking, talking or dressing. Similarly, homophobic responses to lesbianism help to shape dominant notions of femininity. Moane (1997, p. 88) argues that '[homophobia] is damaging to all women because [it] involves extreme negative images and views of women, and induces fear in heterosexual women about their own feelings of affection for other women'.

The label 'lesbian' has been used as a weapon to silence and intimidate women who speak out assertively or defiantly and as a label to express an anti-feminist position. The failure of sociologists to adequately analyse the nature of masculinity has impoverished our understanding of gender as a whole. For McKeown et al. (1999), a full understanding of Irish masculinity is necessary to trace out, and to intervene in, fathering practices in Ireland. Drawing on research within the feminist tradition and from the rapidly expanding body of international research into masculinity, they place the practice of fatherhood within the context of the law, the 1937 Irish Constitution, psychoanalysis, work and, perhaps most interestingly, the division of domestic labour within the home. While the analysis and conclusions that McKeown et al. arrive at are in some ways controversial (for example, in their call for a constitutional amendment to protect paternal rights), they have provided a useful contribution to the understanding of gender relationships in Ireland.

The emergence of gay and lesbian sexualities into Irish public life has served to disrupt patterns of sexuality and gender relationships that have developed over centuries. Similarly, lesbian and gay activism has challenged dominant discourses of national and cultural identity. In Ireland, as elsewhere, gays and lesbians have been very much involved in the processes of building a community. While we discuss some of the problematic issues around the concept of 'community' elsewhere (see Chapter 4), it is notable that, particularly since the foundation of the Irish Gay Rights Movement in 1974 and the formation of separate lesbian organisations in 1978, Irish gays and lesbians have sought to develop a way to express and celebrate their sexuality – and to defend their rights – that is specifically Irish while also having a global context.

It is only recently that masculinity has moved centre stage in gender studies. This is partly as a result of the women's movement and the reconceptualisation of fatherhood that has followed in the wake of attempts to develop more egalitarian models of family formation and childrearing. Instead of focusing on binary oppositions between men and women, the trend now is towards exploring masculinities and femininities. The literature on masculinity in Ireland is limited but growing. In her introduction to the special issue of the *Irish Journal of Sociology* on masculinities, Cleary (2005, p. 1) quotes aptly from Harry Ferguson: 'while men were and are everywhere in Irish society, little attention was given to them as men, as gendered subjects'.

A 2001 National Economic and Social Forum (NESF) report on lone parents contained a chapter detailing the experiences of non-resident fathers, who hitherto tended to be written out of analyses of lone-parent families. A small study of non-resident fathers that was conducted as part of the preparation of that report identified a number of key issues that affected the development and maintenance of a fathering role after a relationship has ended. In particular, the research identified the contingent nature of fatherhood for young, marginalised men in Dublin. These fathers' experiences were compared to those of fathers who occupied estranged, committed and activist father roles. Key factors that militate against fathers maintaining an active role in their children's lives are identified. While the experiences of fatherhood vary across different categories of fathers, the majority of them aspire towards and value their fathering role, but their capacity to adopt a positive fathering role is affected by a range of institutional, economic and social barriers (Corcoran, 2005).

Weeks (2005, p. 64) argues that the new narratives of masculinity that are emerging 'speak of vulnerabilities as much as of power. They speak of fear and anxiety as much as of strength.' One Irish study (Cleary, 2005) that exemplifies this transition was carried out with a group of men who had engaged in suicidal behaviour. It revealed how socialisation of young men into traditional masculine roles inhibits their capacity to share their feelings with others, often with devastating consequences. According to Cleary (2005), non-disclosure of distress emerged as a key issue in examining pathways to suicidal action. Disclosure of difficulties was viewed as unmasculine, as implying weakness, and this was associated with feminine or homosexual-type behaviour. According to Cleary, 'constant performative work … was required to project an image of strength and to conceal growing levels of distress. When extreme, this challenged their sense of coherent self-identity' (2005, p. 155). For these men, the pressure to conform to traditional modes of masculinity was so overwhelming that they could not be true to themselves.

Other studies of masculinity have focused on its changing role within popular culture. The image of the 'child-centred father' has become a mainstay of contemporary advertising and nowadays men are almost as likely as women to be sexually commodified in the selling of consumer goods. Indeed, as women have become more dominant in the economy, both as the producers and consumers of goods and services, men have been portrayed more often as goofy, female-dominated losers. The markets for men's clothing, personal products and even plastic surgery have exploded and men are coming under increasing pressure to conform to gender stereotypes. The playbills at rugby internationals regularly carry advertisements for facial creams alongside the more traditional 'male' products. 'Metrosexuals' such as David Beckham – who combine both feminine and masculine qualities – take up extensive space in newspapers, magazines and on the web. Popular culture, in other words, is representing to us the fluidity and indeterminateness of notions of masculinity and femininity.

9

The Body, Health and Illness

Our everyday understanding of the body is that it is an organic entity, or perhaps even a machine or system, that is subject to occasional breakdown and gradual deterioration. When we think of our own body, or of health and illness, we tend to think in individual, personal terms. The contribution that sociology makes is to emphasise the social nature of the body and of the processes and conditions that we call health and illness.

For example, our likelihood of contracting hepatitis is partly an effect of the robustness of our immune system and our exposure to a particular virus, but it is also shaped by our age, sex, gender, occupation, geographical location, lifestyle, including our behaviours in relation to sex and drugs, previous involvement with medical systems (especially blood transfusions) and knowledge and attitudes. The same applies to any other form of illness or wellness, from our chances of having a 'trim, taut and terrific' body to our likelihood of developing malaria. All are the result of social processes.

This chapter opens with a discussion of the emergent discipline of the sociology of the body, for without human bodies there is no health or illness. It then outlines the main concerns of the sociology of health and illness, emphasising how the varying theoretical perspectives brought to bear influence the choice of object of study. We argue that the biomedical model of health remains dominant and, in an Irish context, continues to shape much of the sociological analysis of health and illness and the policy initiatives that are often based on such research. Finally, we look very briefly to the future, for ours is an era of dramatic change in the fields of medicine and the sciences of life and the body. What is the role for sociologists as society grapples with the social and ethical challenges of the Human Genome Project, cloning and transgenic transplants?

THE BODY

While sociologists often speak of individuals in abstract terms (as agents, actors, role-players and so on), there has been a strong shift in recent years towards recognising the social importance of the body – hardly surprising in a culture seemingly obsessed with physical bodies, with interests ranging from dieting to working out, from fashion to cosmetic surgery. Furthermore, as society becomes increasingly interested in the possibilities of virtual entities, there is also an increased focus on the corporeal, whether through technology, health or sport.

Sociological interest in the body is comparatively new. Sociological thinking has long emphasised the cultural, and consequently the natural, including the body, has been played down. There has even been considerable hostility towards approaches like sociobiology and genetics that have sought to incorporate biological processes into social analysis.

Recent sociological interest in the body has been stimulated by a number of factors (Nettleton and Watson, 1998, pp. 4–7). First, recent times have seen a politicisation of the body. Two groups have been of particular importance here. Feminists have focused on how women's bodies have been controlled and abused in a range of cultures. Works such as the landmark publication *Our Bodies, Ourselves* (Boston Women's Health Book Collective, 1973) and analyses of childbirth and eating disorders have critically examined how women's bodies are shaped by social factors and practices such as the medical industries, advertising and the fitness industry. Similarly, disabled groups have focused on how society discriminates against those that depart in any way from the dominant view of the normal body.

Second, demographic change, particularly in relation to the ageing or greying of the population in Western societies, has led to new issues. Increased lifespan has led to the emergence of new sets of questions. The incidence of some diseases, such as cancer and stroke, has increased while there are important issues related to the quality of life in later years. Many of these are directly linked to the body and its functioning. Ultimately, there are social and sociological questions related to death and the issue of euthanasia.

Third is the rise in consumer culture. There is a hugely increased focus on the body as part of this development. On the one hand, the body is a staple of advertising imagery and questions are constantly raised about the effects of images portrayed in the media. On the other hand, the body itself has become a major site of consumption, from cosmetics, fashion, diet and fitness to plastic surgery, tattoos and body piercing.

Fourth is the effect that the development of new technologies is having on our bodies and our experiences of them. Again, there are many areas of change here. New surgical techniques, including organ transplants, implants, prosthetics and cosmetic surgery, lead us to question the boundaries between humans and technology. One writer (Hayles, 1995, p. 321) suggests that up to 10 per cent of the American population may now be considered 'cyborgs': part human, part machine, in as much as their bodies are partly made up of pacemakers, plastic hips, penile implants, silicon breast implants, artificial skin, stomach staples or transplanted corneas. There are other areas of technological development that can only be listed here but which may have as yet unforeseen impacts on our personal and social lives: smart drugs (to improve memory or intelligence), genetic manipulation, cloning, dietary supplements (nutriceuticals) and transgenic implants (the use of animals' body parts).

Finally, the development of communications technologies, such as the Internet, digital cameras and computer viruses, have helped to raise questions about the nature of the virtual and the real. In an age where we can adopt multiple personas on the web or continuously retouch our family photograph album, the physical body may become a touchstone of reality and authenticity. This may increasingly be the case as other aspects of our identity, such as nation, class and religion, become less salient or defined.

Overall, we are now far more reflexive about our bodies. Rather than a vehicle (or encumbrance) for action that is taken for granted, our bodies are now sites of activity, always open to monitoring, improvement, alteration and concern (Jenkins, 1999). We no longer adopt a fatalistic approach to our bodies, but expect to be able to assert a greater degree of control. This translates into a wide range of behaviour, from working out and dieting, to yoga and aerobics, to cholesterol tests and pap smears. Our heightened consciousness of our bodies has undoubtedly driven the continual expansion in the field of health described below.

There is now a considerable sociological industry that focuses on the body (Nettleton and Watson, 1998, p. 2), much of it pitched at a very abstruse and abstract level and often with little analysis of how the body operates in everyday life. However, the renewed interest in the body and the self has stimulated new insights into the sociology of health and illness, calling into question in particular the assumptions made of many of its routine categories. The challenge for sociology now is to combine the new critical approach to the body with empirical analyses of how people view, use and feel about their bodies within a range of social settings and structural situations.

THE SOCIOLOGY OF HEALTH AND ILLNESS

A major aspect of our embodied existence is the health or illness that we experience individually and socially. Whereas the sociology of the body has tended to be neglected, there has long been an interest in medical sociology and in the sociology of health and illness. This can be traced back to Durkheim's work on suicide, which in many ways provided a model for the sociological study of illness and became one of the bases for the specific social science discipline of epidemiology.

Medical sociology has given much in the way of support to the medical industry by supplying data about patterns of disease and in attempting to deduce causal relationships from such observations. It has also provided an interpretation of the 'sick role': the process whereby people adopt the role of patient. Such a role requires stripping away many of our everyday beliefs and practices and allows us to expose ourselves to unquestioned subservience to professional instructions, outside observation of private bodily practices and invasive medical examinations and procedures. In return we can claim the status of patient and escape adherence to many of the norms of society, such as daily work, a cheerful countenance and appropriate dress. The sick role concept has been widely used in the training of doctors and other medical personnel.

The sociological analysis of health and illness has now moved beyond epidemiology and analysis of the sick role to embrace numerous aspects of social life. This reflects the increased interest in the body as well as the expansion of health to embrace an ever-increasing proportion of our everyday life and behaviour. According to Porter (1997, p. 15), 'the rise of sociology in healthcare can largely be explained by the gradual demise of ... the biomedical model of health and illness [see below] which saw health and illness as a purely mechanical, physical matter'. It is now recognised that issues of health and illness cannot be reduced to malfunctions of the individual body or the prevalence of germs or other causes of disease (although these of course are and remain factors). Rather, it is now recognised that health and illness are social entities – a sociology of health and illness is therefore necessary. Such a sociology can investigate many aspects of the medical field.

Sociology allows us to investigate patterns of health and illness. This embraces the branch of social research known as epidemiology. Epidemiology is the side of medical sociology that is closest to the medical professions themselves. It tends to use a positivist and highly quantitative approach that focuses on rates of illness or other factors, attitudinal research and the use of control groups and other aspects of scientific research. It has had an important role to play in the contemporary shift within the health services towards evidence-based practice.

Sociology has much to contribute to an understanding of the experience of health and illness. Here, both quantitative and qualitative techniques are used. How people define and experience pain, for example, has much to tell us about how they may or may not respond to the provision of healthcare services. Similarly, the exploration of how women have experienced childbirth and the medical interventions associated with it has helped to alter how maternity services are being provided.

The sociology of health and illness has also contributed much to our understanding of the medical industries and the medical professionals and other workers that operate within them. It has often been critical of the professions, laying bare the ways that professional groups create and sustain relations of power and domination over others in society, particularly through legitimated monopolies of knowledge and practice, such as the right to issue prescriptions or sign sickness certificates. Moreover, it can teach us a lot about how professional groups attain and maintain their privileged status.

Interpretative sociology has much of interest to say about how healthcare is provided and how members of the various groups involved in the practice of health and illness, such as doctors, nurses, patients and administrators, interact in ways that help to define each other's roles and the nature of health and illness themselves. Discourse analysts, drawing on the work of writers such as Szasz (1961) and Foucault (1973), have explored how the discourses of health are created and maintained through institutions such as hospitals, clinics, asylums and popular medical books. This approach emphasises the social constructedness of health and illness. Some of the most radical critiques of medical practice and medical knowledge stem from this approach. Categories such as health, madness and sickness are called into question and revealed to be fully social in nature. Medical knowledge is shown to be a particularly powerful discourse and this approach is critical to an analysis of the medicalisation of modern life.

THE BIOMEDICAL MODEL

The most powerful discourse within the field of medicine remains the biomedical model of health. This model dominates current thinking about wellness and illness as it appears in people's everyday beliefs and attitudes, in the practices of most health workers and in medical research and policy-making. The model holds that health and illness are caused by identifiable factors such as bacteria, viruses, toxins, chemical imbalances, genetic disorders or physical accidents. These factors can be identified most effectively by trained and professional personnel according to standardised tests and diagnoses. They can then be treated to varying degrees of success by specific practices, drugs and techniques. Medical research is a process of cumulatively discovering more about the causes of disease and ill health, and as society develops, medicine will gradually identify and cure an increasing number of ailments and conditions. At the same time, folk knowledge, traditional cures and superstitions will become increasingly less prevalent. As a result, the welfare of people in developed societies will gradually improve, longevity will increase and people will suffer less.

This is a very powerful discourse and one that appeals both to health consumers and to the medical industry. It supports the position of medical professionals, gives hope to patients and predictability to policy-makers. It justifies the activities of drug companies, medical researchers and builders of hospitals and other health facilities. It also aligns well with the theories of modernisation. It is a discourse taken so much for granted that it is very difficult to challenge or subvert.

Tucker (1997, p. 31) suggests that 'it is one of the characteristics of modern biomedicine that it has hegemonic designs and it has consistently discredited, marginalised or suppressed other systems or practices'. These include folk medicines, alternative medicines and other approaches, some of which have nevertheless managed to become more respectable and have been admitted to the field of 'real' medicine, for example chiropody, acupuncture and meditation.

Tucker reminds us that medical knowledge, like all knowledge, is socially constructed. The answers to health challenges are not just out there waiting to be discovered by scientists, doctors and researchers. Rather, medical knowledge is intrinsically tied up with social factors such as class, religion, gender difference and the interests and activities of commercial and political interest groups. This helps us to understand, at least partly, why so much money has been channelled into the development of drugs like Viagra while across the world millions of children die every year from diarrhoea.

The biomedical model tends to be individualistic, contrasting with a structural understanding of health behaviour privileging consideration of how social factors impinge upon health outcomes. Such a structural view has recently become more prominent in Irish health policy discourse, as reflected in the Department of Health's men's health policy, which while targeting smoking and alcohol consumption as major threats to men's health also explicitly acknowledges poverty as a key determinant of it (DHC, 2008). This structural understanding is not always evident in health debates, as dietary advice, for example, tends to be applied to the individual patient rather than being aimed at the food industry as a whole.

What might be the alternative to the biomedical model? Holism is often cited. This term can have various meanings and the boundaries between biomedical and holistic medicine overlap and are hotly contested. A holistic approach can apply to the individual where a broader range of systems, including 'the biological, the energetic, the psychic, the interpersonal and the spiritual' (Tucker, 1997, p. 42), are brought into view. More broadly, holism encompasses economic and political as well as biological and environmental systems; it reflects the idea that health and illness are not simply biological phenomena but are socially produced. Tucker (1997, p. 42) argues for a holistic medicine that does not privilege single explanations or therapies, which he contrasts with the reductionism of the biomedical model. He suggests that:

> The emergence of a holistic paradigm will require not only a change in the practice of medicine and healthcare, but also in the knowledge system and the model of science on which it is based. It will also require changes in the institutional fabric of healthcare.

What might this mean in practice? Perhaps it might mean providing the consumers of healthcare with more information, thus leading to greater choice of therapies. It may mean giving greater recognition and support to alternative medicine and therapies, such as homeopathy, herbalism or shiatsu. Or it may mean paying greater attention to social and environmental issues such as air pollution, workplace hazards or dietary intake. The spiritual dimension is also seen as important. This may mean providing ways for people to have more meaning in their lives.

The end result of a holistic approach may be to enhance the health of the population, but it may also serve to increase the level of surveillance of people and to extend the reach of medical dominance into ever more areas of everyday life. This is suggested by O'Donovan (1997a, p. 159), who argues that broader dissemination of medical information leads to 'an intensification of biomedical hegemony'. Similarly, the adoption of alternative therapies may result in a replication of the biomedical model, particularly as practitioners strive to become professionals (herbal medicine illustrates this).

The conflict between biomedicine and holism is intense, but also complex and dynamic. It is clear that one of the strategies used by professional medical groups has been the active exclusion of many forms of therapy and practice. In Ireland as elsewhere, the history of the medical profession as we know it today has been the marginalisation and negation of folk practices such as bone setting, herbalism and faith healing. The discourse of biomedicine has achieved much power and its supporters can hold up great achievements and point to any number of medical marvels. But popular choices seem to favour an increasing number of alternative therapies and many medical problems are dealt with through a broad variety of means of self-medication (MacFarlane, 1997) or attendance with alternative practitioners (Tucker, 1997, p. 31). Belief in the power of faith healers remains high, with 75 per cent of the Irish population reportedly expressing support for their efficacy (Ward, 2002, p. 75). It seems clear that both models of health and illness will continue to contend for public and official support.

DEFINING HEALTH AND ILLNESS

While we can usually say of ourselves that we are feeling well or sick, health itself is a difficult concept to define (Blaxter, 1995). In its 1946 Constitution, the World Health Organization defined health as a 'state of complete physical, mental and social well-being', but this understanding poses as many questions as it answers and seems to set up an impossible ideal – few of us could claim such a state for ourselves. Indeed, survey research has revealed that up to 95 per cent of the population experiences some sort of ill health in any two-week period (MacFarlane, 1997, p. 17).

What is 'health'? The health status of older Irish people
Empirical findings from the Irish Longitudinal Study on Ageing (TILDA) provides new insights into the health status of people over 50 in Ireland. Combining data gathered from interviews with health assessments of a representative national sample, this study found that the over-50 category in Ireland tends to experience physical and mental health problems, are engaged in their communities, utilise health services such as GPs and hospital care, have generally weak attachments to the labour market, especially as they reach 65, have variable material resources such as income, experience a good quality of life and have positive views of getting older (Barrett et al., 2011).

In many respects, health and illness are relative terms and thus are difficult to define. Furthermore, definitions are often dependent on the criteria and normative frameworks used by the observer. While the existence of a broken arm may be fairly unproblematic, conditions such as obesity, depression or hyperactivity are far more open to interpretation, and as Cleary (1997, p. 195) suggests, even for the understanding of diagnosis-specific data, methodological and conceptual considerations are crucial. Post-modern theorists, building on the work of writers such as Foucault, further problematise the notion of health. As Fox (1998, p. 11) suggests, 'all definitions [of health] have a politics associated with them; all try to persuade us to a particular perspective on the person who is healthy or ill'.

Medical policy-makers and epidemiologists use the term 'health status' to refer to the present state of illness or wellness in a community. It can be described in terms of 'rates of death and illness in a community, the prevalence of good and poor health practices, rates of death and disease (chronic and infectious) and the prevalence of symptoms/conditions of well-being' (Doorley, 1998, p. 17). Health status can be defined and measured by an outside observer, perhaps an expert such as a doctor or dietician, according to various criteria. Similarly, it can be based on the self-reported health-related perceptions of a person's physical functioning, emotional well-being, pain and so on. In reality, it is difficult to combine both measures.

We have seen that it is challenging to define health or well-being in any sort of holistic way. As a result, those that seek to measure such entities tend to use simpler indicators such as life expectancy, incidence of and/or death rates from specific diseases or availability and provision of specific health services. In terms of capturing the complex state that may constitute health, these are obviously fairly crude and indirect measures. However, there is a strong desire to establish and measure health in terms of these sorts of indicators. These include the desire to compare countries according to their health status, the need to inform health policy and expenditure, the ability to measure progress in a certain direction and a way to anticipate future health needs (Doorley, 1998, p. 18).

The most common indicators of health status used are life expectancy, death rates, morbidity rates (that is, rates of incidence of certain diseases), patterns of lifestyle and self-perceived health status. Ireland has lagged behind many countries in the availability of such data, especially at the localised level. This has made it difficult to analyse health patterns in Ireland, to identify causal patterns (for example, links between pollution levels and health outcomes) or to inform policy-making in a critical way. The launch of the All Ireland Cancer Atlas in December 2011 was thus a significant event in providing spatially defined epidemiological information that can shape future action in relation to health and well-being (National Cancer Registry Ireland & the N. Ireland Cancer Registry, 2011).

LIFE EXPECTANCY

Life expectancy is seen as one of the most important health measures. It is widely used to compare countries (for example, in United Nations reports) and to measure progress in a country, especially in terms of its modernisation. It is calculated by applying the death rates within a five- or one-year age group, and within each sex from the population under study, to a hypothetical birth cohort of 100,000 individuals (Doorley, 1998, p. 20).

Table 9.1: Life expectancy at birth (years) – Ireland in comparison with other European countries, 2009

Country	Males	Females
European region average	72	79
Austria	78	83
Belgium	77	83
Denmark	77	81
Finland	77	83
France	78	85
Germany	78	83
Greece	78	83
Ireland	**77**	**82**
Italy	79	84
Luxembourg	78	83
Netherlands	78	83
Portugal	76	82
Spain	78	85
Sweden	79	83
UK	78	82
Cyprus	78	83
Czech Republic	74	80
Estonia	70	80
Hungary	70	78
Lithuania	68	79
Latvia	67	77
Malta	78	82
Poland	71	80
Slovenia	76	82
Slovakia	71	79

Source: World Health Organization, 2011.

Compared to some other European countries (see Table 9.1), life expectancy in Ireland is high. For men in 2009, life expectancy was at 77 years, well above the European region average of 72. For women, the Irish figure of 82 is above the European average of 79. In all European countries women outlive men, though in both Ireland and other countries the gap is slowly narrowing.

While historically Ireland's performance could be seen as relatively poor in EU terms, there has been quite positive recent movement in the figures, with Irish people's life expectancy increasing in the 2000–2009 time period (Layte, 2010) by three years for both males and females. Looking further back, we can see quite a dramatic improvement in Irish people's life expectancy – the figures in 1960 were just 68.1 for men and 71.9 for women. At the turn of the 20th century (1902), a man or a woman, if they survived to the age of 25, could then expect on average to live to just 63 years of age. In 2009 (the most recent period for which figures are available), a 25-year-old can expect to survive until 77 (men) or 82 (women). This extension of life has major implications, for example in the area of retirement and pensions as well as in relation to health status and lifestyle. Demographic changes will mean that higher demands will be placed on current services, for example in terms of demand for long-term residential care (Layte, 2010).

CAUSES OF DEATH

Figures on the major causes of death are often used as an indicator of the health status of a society and even of its success in becoming developed. The reasons why people in a society die, and the stage of life at which they die, are determined by social factors. Thus, in less developed societies, major causes of death are likely to be infectious diseases (such as measles, typhoid, malaria) and malnutrition, while in more advanced societies, wealth, improved diet and sanitation and access to medical treatment means that such causes of death are far less likely. People, living longer, then succumb to the diseases of modernity, such as heart disease, stroke and cancer. It is predicted that as a result of such factors, Ireland will see a significant (72 per cent) increase in the incidence of cancer over the next two decades (WCRF, 2012).

Table 9.2: Causes of death in Ireland, 1947 and 2010

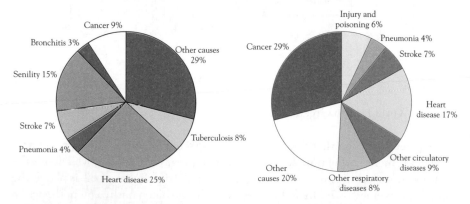

Source: Devlin, 1997, p. 14 for 1947 data and Department of Health, 2011 for 2010 data.

In Ireland, there have been major changes in the pattern of mortality in the past six decades. There has been a decline in deaths from infectious diseases such as influenza, measles and tuberculosis and an increase in deaths from cancer and cardiovascular disease (including heart disease and stroke) (Devlin, 1997, p. 19). There has also been a decline in deaths attributed to senility, as the coding of causes of death has changed over the years (see Table 9.2).

MORBIDITY

Morbidity data relates to the level of illness in society. As we have seen, illness, unlike death, is open to interpretation and contestation, thus the data is far less reliable. Furthermore, the collection and collation of such data is dependent on cases coming to the attention of the formal health services, which occurs with only a minority of medical conditions. Some, such as cancer, almost inevitably involve contact with the health services, so data are quite good; others are legally notifiable (such as certain infectious diseases like measles) and again, the information is relatively reliable; while others, especially minor ailments such as influenza or muscle sprains, are far less likely to be recorded or measured.

A more effective method of gathering data about morbidity is the health experience questionnaire, where people are asked about their health-related experience and activity over a defined period of time (for example, the last month). A number of internationally recognised questionnaire instruments have been developed and these allow for international comparisons. One of these is the SF-36 (as it comprises 36 questions), or the Short Form Health Survey. It reflects once again the complexity of what we term health (Houghton et al., 2010, p. 42) and attempts to capture this by measuring eight health concepts that are relevant across all social groups, including:

- Limitations in physical activities because of health problems.
- Limitations in usual role activities because of physical health.
- Bodily pain.
- General health perceptions.
- Vitality (energy and fatigue).
- Limitations in social activities because of physical and emotional problems.
- Limitations in usual role activities because of emotional problems.
- Mental health (psychological distress and well-being).

PROVISION OF HEALTH SERVICES

As in relation to health and illness, data on the provision of health services is also highly complex, open to interpretation and contestation and difficult to gather. However, there has been a long tradition of comparing countries on the level of services provided. The level of provision, in terms of numbers such as total and per capita health spending, hospitals, hospital beds and doctors, is one of the key pieces of information that is commonly used to measure the development of a country.

The continual expansion of the health field has meant that the health services provided by the public and private sectors have also developed. These range from the supply of drugs and medicines to the provision of many social services, such as care for children and the elderly through to the delivery of acute hospital care. In Ireland, the period from 2001 to 2010 saw more than a doubling in non-capital public health expenditure, from €7 billion to nearly €15 billion. This represented a significant quantitative increase in public health funding provision during this time (DHC, 2010). It would be a mistake to interpret such figures as providing an indication that the quality of health service provision in the country had universally improved. Such data veil significant inequities in access to health service treatment and the spatial organisation of these inequalities (Burke, 2009). The danger of relying on raw statistics, for Ireland as for any other society, is revealed.

HEALTH, ILLNESS AND SOCIAL CHANGE IN IRELAND

The sociology of health and illness in Ireland needs to be understood against the background of the significant social changes discussed in this book. For example, there have been major changes in fertility patterns, family size and composition and marriage rates. There have been substantial changes in the relationships between women and men and between adults and children. The involvement of the state in people's everyday lives has greatly increased. There have been dramatic alterations in the nature of the work people do and how they spend their leisure time. There have been changes in the food people eat, the drugs they use and the natural and built environment. All these factors have at least the potential to impact significantly on how we see and use our bodies and how we experience health and illness.

There has also been a huge expansion in the health infrastructure. The Department of Health was established in 1947 and since then there has been a development of public and private health provision that has been broadly in line with that of other Western countries. Ireland has developed a mixed health system based on public and private funding; in this way it is similar to other European countries such as France and Austria.

The changes in patterns of health in Ireland since the foundation of the Department of Health have been striking. As mentioned earlier, life expectancy increased significantly. Infant mortality has plummeted from 68 per 1,000 to just 3.8 per 1,000, now one of the lowest rates in the world (Department of Health, 2011), and maternal mortality, once frequent, is now a rare event. Beyond the statistics are the changes in attitudes, approaches, institutions and practices that have made for a greatly increased quality of life (Robins, 1997, pp. 5–6):

Fifty years ago many citizens with mental illness or mental handicap, elderly and infirm persons in need of care, unwanted and deprived children, outcast unmarried mothers, were being cared for en masse in large institutions of mainly nineteenth-century origin. Patients of little means needing basic medical care were subjected to the discriminating and restrictive requirements of the Victorian dispensary doctor system. Those of modest means requiring hospital treatment received no support from the state and often had to face intolerable financial burdens. Persons who were functionally, economically and socially disadvantaged by long-term disability were ignored, written off by society, with little effort made to integrate them in normal living activity.

By all these measures, the improvements in our healthcare system have been dramatic. For many analysts they are a clear indication that Ireland has become a fully developed society. The patterns of disease and mortality in Ireland resemble those of other Western nations and are very different to those of the developing world, where mortality levels are higher and deaths from infectious diseases remain the main cause of death.

More recent trends have started to reflect the significant changes that have taken place in Irish society and the broader international trends in how healthcare is delivered. Many of these reflect the pressures created by the expansion of the health field; the increased costs dictated by new medical technologies, procedures and drugs; the demographic challenge of the ageing of the population; heightened levels of legal and public accountability; and the increased incomes of an expanding range of health professionals and ancillary staff.

One response to increased costs that also reflects significant changes in the concepts underpinning suitable modes of care has been the shift from institutional to community care. This trend has been particularly noticeable in those areas previously structured around large residential institutions, such as mental health and care for young people, but it has also begun to change the way that healthcare is delivered to the aged and to other groups. The change reflects many sets of ideas in the healthcare field, and according to Saris (1997, p. 218), there exists:

a broad political consensus, encompassing such diverse elements as policy-makers interested in reducing the profile of big government and utopian visionaries valorising the community as a place of refuge from a heartless society, formed around the proposition that the time had come to close down these big institutions.

Community care is not without its controversies. Feminists in particular have pointed to the fact that 'care in the community' very often means 'care by women', whether family members or often poorly paid female staff (see Chapter 6). In the area of aged care, for example, fewer than 1 per cent of home helps in Ireland are men (O Donovan, 1997b, p. 150). Community-based services are seriously under-resourced, patchily provided and of low status, often focused on the needy and the down and out (Edmondson, 1997, p. 162). Much of the work is, like domestic labour, not seen by healthcare managers as real work. Rather, 'care has been constructed ... as charitable non-work provided by philanthropic women to their less fortunate neighbours' (O Donovan, 1997b, p. 153). Community care may be an opportunity to respond to health needs in a more holistic way, but at present it remains very much the poor relation of institutionalised healthcare.

There has been an increase in the numbers and varieties of health professionals, paraprofessionals and 'wannabe' professionals. Doctors, surgeons and nurses have now been joined by dieticians, physiotherapists, chiropractors, acupuncturists and medical social workers, not to mention foot reflexologists, iridologists and a panoply of alternative therapists. There is a burgeoning of specialists in all areas as medical knowledge becomes increasingly rationalised and fragmented.

The increasing rationalisation of medicine has seen a greater level of evaluation, performance measurement, research and monitoring built into the healthcare system (M. Butler, 2002). Increasing public and private resources are being channelled into healthcare and there are increasing demands for accountability within the system, involving concepts such as case mix and Diagnostic Related Groups whereby health systems are funded on the basis of identifiable and measurable conditions and practices. Moves in this direction may represent a shift in power from autonomous professionals to managers and bureaucrats, though there is a high level of collegiality and common purpose among management and practitioners within the Irish hospital system. Furthermore, the increasing attempt to rationalise medicine (see below) runs counter to the holistic philosophies that are becoming increasingly influential.

Controlling healthcare

A good example of the trend toward the increasing emphasis on cost-benefit efficiency in healthcare and the application of calculation, evaluation and planning principles is the work of the Health Information and Quality Authority (HIQA) (www.hiqa.ie). The function of this body is to exercise greater technical, bureaucratic and managerial control over how healthcare services are provided in Ireland. One aspect of HIQA's work involves the evaluation of hospitals by HIQA officials and the writing of formal published reports on their activities and progress in meeting national health goals.

Worldwide, medicine is increasingly experienced as big business – and a highly profitable one at that. The US represents one extreme – its largely private healthcare system consumes a greater proportion of financial resources than any other in the world. There are numerous opportunities for profit-making in healthcare:

- Fees-for-services for private practitioners (often working in publicly funded hospitals).
- Health screening and tests.
- Pathology services.
- Health insurance.
- Drug and appliance manufacture.
- Private hospitals, clinics and nursing homes.

Some have characterised this as the 'medical-industrial complex' (Davis and George, 1993, p. 185). The medical and healthcare industries provide significant employment in Ireland. According to the Industrial Development Authority (IDA, 2012), nine of the world's top 10 medical technology corporations have significant operations here, including firms such as Medtronic and Abbott. A similar proportion of the top pharmaceutical companies (such as Pfizer and MSD) have also invested in the country (with the industry concentrated in Co. Cork): overall, nearly 50,000 people are employed in the global 'life sciences' industries in Ireland and the sector makes a substantial contribution to Ireland's exports.

SOCIAL INEQUALITY AND HEALTHCARE

Despite the continuing expansion of medical services and infrastructure and, at least in terms of the biomedical model, an improvement in average health status, health and illness in Ireland are still very much determined by inequalities of class, gender, ethnicity, wealth and power. Indeed, there is a considerable body of evidence to suggest that the more unequally societal wealth is distributed, the poorer the health outcomes of a society (Wilkinson and Pickett, 2009). This societal distribution of wealth impacts on other outcomes as well and the 'spirit level' principle – that more equal societies are better societies – extends beyond health to the domains of education, crime and community life. Sociologists have long had an interest in these inequalities and in seeking to explain them.

As well as differential health outcomes in relation to social inequality, health systems themselves are structured by class, gender, location, age and ethnicity. In Ireland, as in many other countries, the system operates differently depending on where you are located in the social structure. Indeed, such is the level of inequality in the Irish healthcare system that it has been characterised as a form of 'Irish apartheid' (Burke, 2009). The causes of this are strongly related to deeply entrenched vested interests – of doctors, health providers and politicians – that combine to block attempts to reform the social organisation of healthcare.

CLASS

Our knowledge of how health and illness are related to social inequality is an outcome of social epidemiology. Such research has consistently indicated (for example, Wilkinson, 1996; Collins and Shelley, 1997; Nolan and Whelan, 1997; Balanda and Wilde, 2001; Burke et al., 2004; Wilkinson and Pickett, 2009) that in advanced industrial economies like Ireland, the UK, Australia and the US, poor health status is associated with variation in social class. Class difference has been shown to be related to overall mortality, infant mortality, disability and morbidity (Burke et al., 2004). Poorer than average health has also been shown to be strongly correlated with unemployment (Nolan and Whelan, 1997). The data reported in Balanda and Wilde (2001, pp. 29–31) indicates that with the sole exception of cancer of the kidney, all 64 other causes of death revealed a higher rate in the lowest social class compared with the highest. In many cases the variation is startling: those in the lowest class are 15 times more likely to die from homicide, six times more likely to die from respiratory disease and 17 times more likely to die of alcoholism.

Negative health factors and indicators associated with poorer and less powerful social groups include, but are not limited to:

- Higher levels of chronic physical illness.
- Higher levels of perinatal mortality.
- More financial problems that directly impact on health.
- Higher levels of smoking and drinking.
- Lower levels of breastfeeding.
- Lower levels of consumption of fruit and vegetables.
- Lower levels of exercise. (Burke et al., 2004, pp. 23–9)

Burke et al. (2004, p. 28) point out that health inequalities in Ireland can be dated back at least to early 19th-century reports that showed death rates among children in poor districts to be higher than in wealthier areas. Despite economic growth, political change and the extensive development of the health services, such types of differentials have largely persisted, as indicated by numerous studies and reports (Burke et al., 2004; Tussing and Wren, 2006). As Burke et al. conclude in an overview conducted for the Public Health Alliance:

> In Ireland, people who are poor and excluded get sick more often and die younger than people who are better off … Health inequalities are shown to exist when any measurement of income or wealth is used, i.e. socio-economic status, social class, poverty lines, deprivation, income and wealth indices, levels of education and age [see 'What is "health"? The health status of older Irish people' above] (2004, p. 22).

That such inequalities persist reveals much about the structured inequality of Irish society. The causes of such differences are briefly explored later in this chapter.

ETHNICITY

In many societies, a correlation has been demonstrated between ethnicity and health status. Such relationships may be asserted to be biological (for example, sickle cell anaemia in African-Americans) or are recognised as the outcome of inequalities of wealth and power, discrimination and racism. The relationships are often complex. Ethnicity and class interact with each other as well as with other social factors such as age, gender and place of residence.

One group that has been identified in Ireland as having particularly poor health status is the Travelling community.

The health status of Irish Travellers

The All Ireland Traveller Health Study provides new insights into the health and well-being of this group in southern Irish society as well as Northern Ireland. Based on qualitative and quantitative data gathered from Travellers and health service providers, this study found that life expectancy and general health status amongst Travellers are considerably lower than the general settled population, that Travellers' health status is interlinked with their educational and accommodation situations and that Travellers' engagement with health service providers tends to be patchy. A subset of the study involved an investigation of Traveller infant mortality, which found that Traveller infants are four times more likely to die compared to the settled population, that Travellers are less likely to avail of antenatal care and that first-time Traveller parents tend to be younger than the settled population. Notably, the study pointed to some positive developments in Traveller infant health since the late 1980s, such as a decline in neonatal mortality (Hamid et al., 2011).

The main cause of Travellers' inferior health status is to be found in poor living conditions, social exclusion and racism. In addition, health services have not been well adapted to the specific needs of Travellers; in particular, sensitivity to Traveller culture is not institutionalised in health services and tends to be confined to individual doctors who show good will toward Travellers (All Ireland Traveller Health Study, 2010).

Consultations with Traveller communities and organisations as part of the national health study indicated common sets of issues: individual prejudice and institutional discrimination; unsuitability of services; lack of confidence, education and support within Traveller communities; the changing roles of Traveller men; lack of trust; and incidence of stress, depression and mental health problems. The consultative process also indicated the desire of Travellers to be centrally involved in the shaping of the understandings and discourses of Traveller health (Institute of Public Health in Ireland, 2007).

The significant level of immigration into Ireland has given rise to considerable ethnic diversity. There has been little sociological research into the health needs and possible health inequalities that impact on new ethnic groups (Hyde et al., 2004, p. 82). It is likely that the health experience of ethnically defined groups may be influenced by cultural patterns that shape how the body, illness and health are conceptualised and expressed, the relationships between such groups and the existing health services, and how these may be shaped by cultural practices related, for example, to religion, language or models of gender-appropriate behaviour. Immigrants to Ireland also make a significant contribution to the health workforce and this will add further complexity (NCCRI, 2002). Prior studies have found evidence of a 'healthy immigration' effect in relation to large immigrant societies, but a recent study using data for Ireland found little or no evidence of this effect. This may be due to the cultural similarity between immigrants and the native Irish population, though additional research is needed to better understand this finding (Nolan, 2011).

There has been an interest in the health status of Irish people living abroad, particularly in Britain (Williams, 1996; Walls, 2006). It is only relatively recently that the Irish have been recognised as an 'ethnic group' for the purposes of public policy in the UK. Williams reports that although data on the Irish-born in Britain is very difficult to interpret, data on second and subsequent generations of the Irish community reveals higher than average mortality rates (1996, p. 59). A 2011 study found that the picture is more complex than sometimes assumed and that while earlier cohorts – with significant differences between the pre-1920 and 1920–1950 cohorts – of Irish immigrants experienced poor health status compared to the general English population, among recent Irish immigrants their health status tends to be better than their UK counterparts (Delaney et al., 2011). The inferior health status of earlier generations of Irish immigrants in Britain can be linked to selection effects among migrants – certain migrants select themselves to emigrate and they may cluster together in terms of certain traits such as health status – as well as to what might be termed the stress effect of migration – the life stresses associated with moving from one country to another (Delaney et al., 2011). As migration is such an important aspect of Irish society in historical and contemporary terms, the implications may be profound.

GENDER

Health status is clearly patterned by gender, in Ireland as in most other countries. Gender issues in health remain controversial and cannot be separated from broader questions about gender, power and inequality. On nearly all indicators, the health status of men is worse than that of women (Richardson, 2004, pp. 11–27). Men have higher death rates at all ages, from babyhood to older age groups. They are more likely to die in accidents, from suicide and from diseases like heart disease and all cancers, except those of the skin, the breast and the reproductive organs. In fact, the only other causes of death more likely to apply to women in Ireland are meningitis, congenital malformation of the nervous system and diseases of the skin and of the musculoskeletal system, such as rheumatoid arthritis and osteoarthritis (Balanda and Wilde, 2001, pp. 29–31). Moreover, in recent times the male suicide rate, already higher than the female rate, has increased sharply in many Western societies, including Ireland. Men are more than four times as likely to die from suicide (CSO, 2012c, p. 48) – they are also nearly twice as likely to die in an accident.

However, the statistics do not necessarily reflect the whole picture. As Kelleher (1997, p. vii) points out:

> While women do live longer, they also have a poorer quality of life as they age than men, bear the inequalities found in every society in the world more than men, carry the hidden un-prestigious and extensive responsibility for the iceberg of health need in every country, and strive throughout to bear and rear new generations of people in a complex and unjust world.

Furthermore, Irish women have rates of certain cancers (colon, breast, larynx and oesophagus) and ischemic heart disease that are among the highest in the EU (Mahon, 1997, p. 88; WHC, 2006). This may be attributed largely to lifestyle factors (diet, smoking, lack of exercise) and inadequate screening and preventative health strategies.

Irish sociologists of health and illness have attempted to identify and account for gender-based disparities in health status. Since 1997 a statutory body, the Women's Health Council (WHC), has carried out substantial research with a view to advising the government on women's health issues. There has been far less attention paid to men's health issues, though more recently the specific health issues that pertain to men have been placed on the agenda through the preparation of a national men's health strategy for the 2008–2013 time period (Department of Health, 2008).

Research carried out by the WHC has illustrated the complex relationships between health, gender and inequality. The WHC has pointed out (2003, p. 19) 'that women in less well-off socio-economic groups have consistently been shown to be at the greatest disadvantage with regard to many aspects of health'. It also admits that 'it is still almost impossible to say with any certainty how many women are disadvantaged and to gauge the extent of any health inequalities that may exist'. Unequivocal measurements of health, as we have seen above, are difficult to obtain, and the allocation of women to occupational, class or income categories is also fraught with difficulty.

The WHC points to a number of particular categories of women who are likely to suffer disproportionately from ill-health as a consequence of their overall economic and social disadvantage. One of these groups is carers in the home. The WHC (2003, p. 23) notes that carers 'have been found to receive little social, practical or financial support from formal health services, despite their common experience of isolation, reduced social interaction, high levels of strain and psychological distress, and compromised health status'.

Another group of women that suffers relatively poor health is women with disabilities, largely due to their exclusion from the labour market. Physical and social barriers to accessing health services, from poorly designed buildings and equipment to lack of sexual health awareness, compound such inequalities. Other categories of women more likely to suffer ill-health or difficulty in accessing services include older women, lone parents, lesbians, women who are homeless, rural women, drug and alcohol mis-users, asylum seekers/refugees and Travellers.

Specific men's health issues may relate to particular health problems unique to them, such as prostate or testicular cancer or, of perhaps greater sociological interest, to how the social construction of masculinities may shape males' experiences of health and illness. Richardson (2004, p. 3) argues that the former approach, which tends to focus on the differences between men and women, is problematic and that men's health needs to be addressed in its own right, with recognition that men's health, like women's, is patterned by issues of age, sexual orientation, ethnicity and social inequality. It is also shaped by experiences of maleness and expressions of masculinity: Richardson calls for less focus on the health aspect of men's health and for a more critical assessment of men.

Richardson (2004, p. 6) points to how men's health has been hijacked by the popular media (particularly websites and glossy magazines) and redefined as a largely aesthetic issue – of how to become and remain physically attractive (to women or other men) through the use of products and services provided by the pharmaceutical, fitness and cosmetics industries. The focus of such a discourse is inevitably on individual strategies of self-improvement and bodily maintenance and grooming rather than on the social determinants of men's health. While men are considerably more likely to suffer ill-health, from involvement in traffic accidents to diseases of the respiratory system, they perceive themselves to be healthier than women and are less likely to make use of health services. As Richardson (2004, p. 21) states, even where knowledge and awareness of health issues is high among men, the assumption cannot be made that this will impact on health behaviours. The reasons for this apparent mismatch are inevitably complex, but may reflect complex relationships between the body, health, vulnerability, control and masculinity.

Contemporary Irish constructions of masculinity may manifest themselves in patterns of behaviour that may contribute to poorer health outcomes for males. Examples include high levels of alcohol consumption that contribute to increased incidence of conditions such as cirrhosis of the liver, alcohol-related cancers and psychiatric illnesses, and involvement in accidents and violent incidents; men are also less likely to eat healthily, with much higher consumption of fried foods and meat/fish than women; they are also twice as likely to use illegal drugs (Richardson, 2004, pp. 16–19).

The complex issues related to gender remind us of the difficulty of defining health, especially as the biomedical model is increasingly open to critique. On the basis of indicators used by health managers and policy-makers, men are more unhealthy, but feminists have drawn attention to how women's experience of ill-health is broader, more diffuse and more hidden. There is a message here: sociological analysis of health and illness needs to reflect the difficulty and complexity of the issues involved and avoid simplistic interpretation of statistics that may be misleading or partial, or both.

Women have an important role as healthcare providers, particularly in the home, where much primary healthcare takes place. Four out of five state-recognised 'carers' are female (CSO, 2012c, p. 52). This is a dual role: maintaining good health of family members through, for example, food preparation and the maintenance of hygiene standards as well as direct provision through caring for others and mediation with healthcare services. In Irish society, there is a strong expectation that women, especially female family members, will take responsibility for healthcare tasks. Further, the caring role is intricately bound up with definitions and conceptions of femininity (Hodgins and Kelleher, 1997, p. 43).

The unpaid (and low-paid) work of women as healthcare providers is reinforced by community care policies that have seen a shift in emphasis away from the institutional delivery of some forms of healthcare like psychiatric care and care of the chronically ill. It has been shown that 'care in the community' usually means care by families and more often than not, care by women (MacFarlane, 1997, p. 19). The assumptions made of this gender division of labour underpin the perception of the nursing profession. Conversely, women are under-represented in senior and well-paid positions within the health services: while women comprise 80 per cent of employees in the health service, only 36 per cent of medical and dental consultants are women (CSO, 2012c, p. 53).

CAUSES

It is one thing to say that social inequality and health are related. It is another to tease out the many factors that help to create and sustain this relationship. Thus, in relation to unemployment (Nolan and Whelan, 1997, p. 103):

> It is extremely difficult, with the types of data usually available, to distinguish the role of different factors, or to isolate the impact of unemployment per se from that of the broader socio-economic background from which those experiencing unemployment generally come.

In the UK, the wide-ranging Black Report (Townsend and Davidson, 1982) offered four main explanations for the observed relationships between class and health:

- *Artefactual data:* The findings were a result of how the data was collected and the limitations inherent in this.
- *Selection:* Healthier people, as a result of their better health, were able to get better jobs or otherwise move into higher social class groups.

- *Materialist explanations:* Health was affected by material deprivation, including poor housing, poverty, pollution and hazards at work.
- *Cultural explanations:* Class shaped certain lifestyle factors, such as alcohol and tobacco consumption, diet and exercise.

The conclusion was that the last two explanations were the most likely; similar conclusions have been reached in other studies. In Ireland, the Kilkenny Health Project found that levels of smoking among unskilled and semi-skilled manual workers were almost twice those of non-manual workers. In general it found 'an association with social class for smoking prevalence, alcohol consumption, prevalence of obesity, [measurements of blood pressure] and [health] knowledge levels, but not for mean cholesterol levels or light leisure activity' (Collins and Shelley, 1997, p. 92).

It must be emphasised that the links between broader beliefs and attitudes, knowledge of health factors and everyday behaviour are very complex. Key sets of beliefs relate to whether or not one feels susceptible to particular conditions, in control in everyday situations and how one can reasonably behave in social settings. This may influence, for example, a person's decision whether or not to give up smoking, notwithstanding their knowledge that it is a health hazard. Meanwhile, others suggest that health inequalities are more directly related to material deprivation, for example to poor diet, housing, physical environment and access to leisure pursuits. Cumulative deprivation throughout the life-course may also be significant, including such factors as low birth weight, poor educational attainment and subsequent poor or hazardous employment conditions (Hyde et al., 2004, p. 71).

It is important not to fall into a 'blame the victim' mentality when addressing the issue of lifestyles. Morris (1995, p. 136) reminds us:

> These behaviours plainly are embedded in the social structure. When questions are asked not merely how people behave but why they behave as they do, lifestyles provide no release from the need to confront that structure which also has so many other effects on health.

Furthermore, Wilkinson (1996, 1999, 2005) has argued that the most important factor in determining health inequalities is not differential exposure to material hazards and risks (in particular, low income), but rather the level and nature of social inequality and cohesion. Thus, 'in more egalitarian societies, where differences in incomes and in social status are smaller, the average health standards of the population may be substantially improved ... [egalitarian societies] also seem to be more socially cohesive' (Wilkinson, 1999, p. 257). Putnam (2000, pp. 326–35) makes a similar argument in relation to the influence of what he calls social capital on health. According to this argument, it is the stress and psychosocial damage caused by relative inequality and low levels of social interaction that is the key to ill-health. Given that Ireland has a comparatively high level of economic inequality but also arguably a high level of social interaction and community cohesion, the determinants of health inequalities will inevitably be complex. This is an approach to health status that will repay further research in the future.

We have seen that the health field has expanded greatly in recent times. The concerns of modernist reformers were with ameliorating the health impacts of industrialism as these related to the incidence of infectious diseases, workplace hazards, poor housing and other social factors associated with mass society. Post-modernism sees an interest, both among sociologists of health and policy-makers, in other issues, particularly those to do with identity, rights and culture. An example may be found in the response of activists, sociologists and policy-makers to the issue of female genital mutilation (FGM), a practice widely carried out by some of the peoples of Africa and the Middle East. While the standard Western response to FGM has been one of horror and a high moral tone (Shaughnessy, 1997, p. 123), the issue is shown to be highly complex, involving a range of sexual, health-related, political, religious, economic and social factors. Any attempt to address the issue requires a sophisticated and multifaceted social understanding. Once again, we see a tension between the rationalist, positivist approaches to social issues that tend to be favoured by policy-makers and the more speculative, interpretative and qualitative approach of much of contemporary sociology.

POLICY RESPONSES TO INEQUALITY

Hederman O'Brien, reflecting the arguments of Wilkinson (above), reminds us that once a certain level of income is attained in a society, ill-health is usually a reflection of economic and social inequalities (1998, p. 81):

> Neither the total amount spent on health services nor the availability of sophisticated procedures will, of itself, offset the decreasing health standards and mortality rates of those at the bottom of widening differentials in a prosperous society.

The implication here – one that has been recognised in other societies (see Morris, 1995) – is that any attempt to tackle the persistent links between health and inequality must include action on broader issues of social inequality such as poverty, unemployment and gender discrimination. Doorley (1998, p. 38) concludes that a better distribution of economic resources would probably be the most effective way to reduce inequalities in health. The health sector thus needs to be more vocal in advocating stronger social policies to achieve this. However, these aspects of social inequality are deeply entrenched in Irish society.

One of the difficulties of responding to issues of social inequality is expressed in the paradox described by Bunton (1998, p. 25):

> The analysis of social policy process has become increasingly important in contemporary healthcare, especially due to an increased emphasis on the enhancement or promotion of health rather than simply the treatment of illness.

Yet at the same time the possibilities for coherent social policy are being increasingly restricted and our conceptions of social policy have undergone considerable change.

In other words, the extent to which the state can influence outcomes in society is increasingly open to challenge. The idea of a single one-size-fits-all health policy can be seen as a highly modernist notion – it is assumed that social life is predictable, rational and relatively homogenous (or predictably heterogeneous). All these assumptions are now called into question in Irish society.

Social policy is increasingly being determined by supranational bodies, in particular the agencies of the EU. Many of the factors that help to determine the notion of health are under the control of multinational corporations, for example in the drug, tobacco, food, insurance and healthcare industries. There have been significant changes in the organisation of work and employment that have rendered problematic the way that healthcare is funded. There is an increased heterogeneity of population and behaviour: Ireland is witnessing increasing ethnic and cultural diversity and there has been a rise in alternative lifestyles, medicines and therapies, many of which are widely dispersed (MacFarlane, 1997). Within consumer culture there is an increased emphasis on personal choice and the object of healthcare may now be seen as the customer rather than the patient. Furthermore, thanks to the availability of medical information on the Internet, the patient/customer is now likely to be highly informed (or misinformed) about their condition and treatment options.

It is also important to consider changes in the nature of the organisations and institutions that deliver healthcare. There has been much criticism of how Irish healthcare systems are managed. For example, McKevitt (1998, pp. 44–5) argues that in Ireland, the delivery of health services is typified by a strategic deficit and by poor performance measurement systems, inadequate professional supervision and underdeveloped management capability. Given the highly complex and conflicting nature of healthcare institutions, detailed and intrusive management and policy-making are indeed difficult. The model that appears to be emerging in Ireland as in other similar countries is one of facilitation and support for a range of diverse activities (McKevitt, 1998, p. 60). The emergence of government plans in 2011 to restructure the Health Service Executive can be seen as an attempt by the state to manage this diversity better.

IRISH HEALTHCARE INSTITUTIONS

There is extensive evidence that most healthcare issues are dealt with by people themselves, without reference to formalised healthcare services such as doctors and hospitals (MacFarlane, 1997, p. 18). Therefore, healthcare institutions only come into play in relation to specific events, conditions and situations. It should therefore be remembered that healthcare institutions represent only one, albeit important, part of the healthcare story.

The Irish healthcare system is based, like that in most Western countries, on a mixture of public and private funding. It is difficult to accurately identify how much of the funding is public, but it may range from 75 to 90 per cent. There are conflicting and mixed policy perspectives in relation to public and private elements (Smith, 2009). There has been considerable debate in Ireland in recent years in relation to the so-called two-tier health system, which sees differential services available to three categories of persons: those with private health insurance (about 50 per cent of the population), those with medical cards (about 30 per cent of the population) and those with neither of these (the remaining 20 per cent) (Wren, 2003; Tussing and Wren, 2006). According to the OECD, public spending in Ireland on health (which, as we have seen, includes some functions that in other countries would be defined as environmental services or welfare services) is at the level of 7.2 per cent of GDP, behind countries such as Germany (8.9 per cent) and Denmark (9.8 per cent) but ahead of Luxembourg (6.5 per cent) and Poland (5.3 per cent) (OECD, 2010).

The period since the early 19th century has seen a continual expansion in the provision of institutionalised health services. The first institutions were the workhouses, established in 1703; county infirmaries followed in 1765, which provided the basis on which the public health services were subsequently developed (O'Shea, 1998, p. 55). Among the earliest country-wide systems was that of asylums for the insane, first developed in the early 19th century as part of the general process of civilising the country (Saris, 1997, p. 214). Voluntary hospitals date back to the early 18th century. Jervis Street Hospital, now part of Dublin's Beaumont Hospital, opened in 1718 (O'Shea, 1998, p. 54). The churches, especially the Catholic Church, have been actively involved in the development of health services since the 1830s. Public health services in the community as we understand them today started in 1878 with the appointment of dispensary doctors and of county medical officers in 1925 (O'Shea, 1998, p. 55).

The Department of Health was established in 1947 and subsequent expenditure on healthcare expanded rapidly until the fiscal crisis of the 1980s. There was a sharp decline in spending in real terms during the 1980s, but since then there has been a gradual shift back towards expansion, though spending on health has not kept pace with the expansion in the economy or the population. Health policy and the structures that stem from it have increasingly been driven by expert groups within and outside government, in particular since 1995. There is now a very technocratic approach to the development of healthcare services. This can be perceived in the highly managerialist structures of the HSE.

The public system now plays 'a major role in the provision and funding of services, the regulation and setting of standards for inputs to the health system and in recent times [there has been] an increasing emphasis on setting standards and objectives' (T. O'Hara, 1998, p. 4). Despite the establishment of the HSE, it is still apparent that the management and planning of the healthcare system is not fully centralised, but rather, as T. O' Hara (1998, p. 5) suggests:

a combination of government, Department of Health and Children, advisory and executive agencies and voluntary organisations all play a role in service delivery and development, though their degree of power and influence varies.

MEDICALISATION

One factor driving the global expansion of health services is medicalisation: the process by which an increasing range of events and conditions are defined as being of interest to medicine. Many conditions previously taken to be non-medical are now grounds for consulting a doctor. Forms of behaviour previously seen as deviant are now defined as medical problems: bad behaviour by children is now hyperactivity or attention deficit disorder; shoplifting is kleptomania. Occasionally the process can operate in reverse – for example, alcoholism is now less likely to result in admission to psychiatric institutions in Ireland and more likely to be viewed as the result of personality or social factors.

The critique of medicalisation is most closely associated with the work of writers such as Thomas Szasz, Ivan Illich and Michel Foucault. Szasz (1961) was sharply critical of the regimes of psychiatry, in particular how psychiatric terminology and practice were being used to respond to social problems such as crime and poverty; Illich (1976) was critical of the whole medical industry/bureaucracy and highlighted the perverse role of medicine in creating illness and injury (iatrogenesis) through inappropriate and incompetent interventions; while Foucault saw the institutions, techniques and discourses of medicine, along with the penal and other state systems, as a means of surveilling and controlling populations. The level and efficacy of such surveillance has only increased as holistic medicine has become more favoured. Numerous lifestyle, social and even spiritual factors are now taken into account and subjected to comment, intervention and control. This has contributed to the expansion of medicalisation.

One part of life that has become increasingly medicalised and has attracted the attention of many sociologists is that of childbirth (Hyde et al., 2004, pp. 210–16). The discipline of obstetrics excluded and marginalised traditional midwifery practices, in particular through the monopolisation of specific technologies such as forceps. In the process, female practitioners were replaced by men (McDonnell, 1997, p. 70). The male-dominated profession of obstetrics has used a powerful discourse of risk and safety to exercise control over both women giving birth and midwives. It is argued, for example, that doctor-controlled hospital births are safer than midwife-controlled home births, though evidence for this is contentious to say the least (Hyde et al., 2004, pp. 214–15).

In an Irish study, Hyde (1997) shows not only how medicine has taken over the process of childbirth itself, but argues that the medical profession also makes moral judgments on the circumstances of pregnancy, particularly in relation to unmarried mothers, and justifies these on medical grounds. This then affects the interpretation of events such as post-natal depression or whether or not a baby should be given up for adoption. In Hyde's study, women were seen to be unable to decide what was in their own best interests, so medical staff, particularly paternalistic doctors, attempted to impose processes and activities (like seeing a social worker) upon them. This was related to class and age. Hyde concludes that along with other discourses such as economics and religion, 'medicine at least plays a part in the maintenance of social order around social arrangements for childbearing' (1997, p. 123).

Recently there has been a shift from medicalisation to what has been termed biomedicalisation (Clarke et al., 2003, cited in Hyde et al., 2004, p. 208). This refers to the extension of medico-scientific control from the external world to the internal, molecular and genetic level of the human organism. Scientists and medical researchers, especially through the development of the human genome programme, have a greater ability to manipulate and determine life itself. Genetic screening and gene therapy, if pursued within the current socio-political structures of medicine, are likely to refocus attention onto individual responsibility for health and well-being at the expense of more structural social and environmental factors (Hyde et al., 2004, pp. 207–10).

PROFESSIONALISATION

The issue of the professionalisation of healthcare is very much linked to that of medicalisation. Professionalisation is the process whereby an occupational group is able to claim special status for itself, for example through access to special knowledge or training, a monopoly over certain practices and the ability to exclude competing groups. The outcome is a greater measure of prestige, power and income. By the early 20th century, medicine had achieved dominance of the health field in North America, most countries of Europe and Australia (Daniel, 1998, p. 209).

Medicine has been able to create and sustain its professional status through a variety of strategies. The key process is that of closure: the ability to keep others out of the field of operation of the professional group. The most effective way to do this is through a process of registration, backed up by legislation. This requires the state to give legal backing to a range of occupational practices (Davis and George, 1993, p. 209):

- Access to restricted substances (for example, prescription drugs).
- Direct access to clients (fees-for-services).
- Control over the content of education and training.
- Self-regulation.
- Control of all others in the field.

Strategies to secure public acquiescence with the claim for professional status have largely been made through appeals to science and reason, according to the biomedical model. At the same time, the knowledge must retain a level of opacity and mystique so as to render it inaccessible to others.

The development of professional power does not rest only on securing rights over knowledge and practice – it is also crucially based on interactive relationships such as trust. As Daniel points out, if we do not accord a doctor or nurse trust, they have little power over us. Of course, the relationship of trust is built very much on the types of knowledge that are at stake (1998, p. 212):

> The complexity with which the expert [doctor, specialist] deals is typically baffling and alarming in the risks it poses. Trust reduces the client's apprehension of external complexity and uncertainty by substituting an inner confidence in the simplification of control held out by the expert.

Many of the accoutrements of professional practice, including the framed degree in the consultant's office, the letters after the name, the calm demeanour and the conservative dress, are props that aid in the building of a trusting relationship. At the same time, numerous distractions, such as disagreements over appropriate care, personal or social factors (such as ethnicity, dirty fingernails) or situational factors (a run-down office, a rude receptionist), can rapidly erode the relationships of trust that are so difficult to create. Access by clients to alternative sources of information, for example health information on the Internet, can also threaten the trust relationship. Trust is also sustained by the discipline itself: our belief in medicine as a rigorous, scientific practice that strives for the most effective outcome and its ethical basis (our belief that a doctor will not intentionally harm us).

NURSING

In contemporary Ireland, a particularly interesting site for the observation of professionalisation in medicine is the field of general nursing. The process of professionalisation has created an opportunity and a dilemma for this key group, which accounts for about 34 per cent of the Irish health workforce (DHC, 2009). Nursing is an almost exclusively female occupation; only about 8 per cent of nurses are men (CSO, 2012c, p. 53). Indeed, it has been one of the few secure professional careers open to women until relatively recently. Irish nurses have historically been recruited from middle-class and farming backgrounds and are well educated. Religious orders have played a significant role in the development of nursing and in recruitment and training, but functional differentiation (Dobbelaere, 2011) – the loss of religious control of healthcare and its takeover by the state – has led to a significant decrease in their role.

While medical practice has become the dominant profession within the healthcare system, nursing has historically been subordinated. Unlike most doctors, nurses work under supervision, for wages and for fixed hours, and usually in a fixed location. They lack real autonomy. They have also faced considerable gender discrimination and stereotyping within the workplace and the industry. As Davis and George remark (1993, p. 210), 'the emergence of nursing as a full-time occupation has occurred within a framework of gender inequality which has led to the subordination of nursing in the healthcare occupational hierarchy and resistance to attempts to change it'. McCarthy (1997, p. 176) reflects on how Irish nursing has been affected by the particular vision of femininity espoused by the founder of modern nursing, Florence Nightingale:

> It is true to say that Ms. Nightingale's ideas of vocation, discipline, diligence and obedience lived on in Irish nursing up to the 1970s and some remnants may still remain. They were perpetrated through an outdated method of education which included personal training and schools of nursing set within the hospital culture. The effects can be seen within the profession itself and in social appreciation and expectation. They have affected professional growth, and inhibited roles, education, accountability and management.

Historically, nurses have been largely excluded from management and policy-making positions but more recently have sought to escape such subordination by adopting a strategy of professionalisation.

The dramatic changes in recent times in the nature of nursing have contributed greatly to the thrust towards professional status. There has been considerable specialisation, with the emergence of numerous specialties within nursing, such as critical care, midwifery, oncology, anaesthetic and A&E (accident and emergency) nurses, to name just a few. Nurses now work with highly expensive and sophisticated technology, with complex medications and procedures and with a high level of autonomy and decision-making ability.

The changes in nursing have led to efforts to change the nature of nurse training, now increasingly carried out through the third-level education sector, and to develop an autonomous body of nursing knowledge, including a sociological component (Porter, 1997). This has not been without its difficulties, given the hostility of the existing medical professions and the lack of development in the field in the past. The shift towards the creation of a professional discourse for nursing has been accompanied by an increased use of industrial muscle. Unthinkable in the past, nurses have increasingly threatened and carried out industrial action and have resolutely pursued their claims through the industrial relations systems.

There are signs that the professionalising efforts of nursing are beginning to pay dividends. This may mean an increasingly professional and managerial role for nurses and there is some evidence that this is taking place in the Irish health system (Dwyer and Taaffe, 1998, p. 250). In 1998 the Irish government published the *Report of the Commission on Nursing*, a response to increasing industrial unrest in the nursing sector. Its recommendations in relation to a range of matters, from grading to education and training, have subsequently been implemented. Nursing education is now at honours degree level, professional clinical pathways have been established and nursing is increasingly represented in the management structures of the HSE. The development of an indigenous body of theoretical knowledge has proven to be more problematic: Hyde et al. (2004, p. 246) claim that this represents the single most difficult challenge for those aspiring to full professional status for nurses.

While there is evidence of some success in raising the power of nurses, the strategy has created some of its own difficulties. The change in the status of nurses may create some dilemmas for the emerging profession (McAdam, 2004). The shift in educational status may mean that the traditional hierarchies within medicine will need to be confronted. Will university-trained nurses be content to adopt the subordinate role of their hospital-trained predecessors, or will the improved status of nurses mean the emergence of additional levels of assistants and technicians, as is already the case in many countries? How will patients respond to nurses that may be more focused on technology and management than on the more traditional caring skills? Will the emerging discourse of professional nursing simply ape the biomedical model, or will it provide for a more holistic and patient-centred model of healthcare?

FUTURE CHALLENGES

During the last 60 years, the major social questions in relation to the body, health and illness in Ireland have changed dramatically. In the 1950s the issues were about the control and eradication of infectious diseases such as TB and polio. The major challenge was to build a modern public health infrastructure on the base of an often-despised system that had grown out of the workhouses of the 18th and 19th centuries. The major challenges for medicine in the years to come are posed by new medical technologies ranging from human genome marking to artificial body parts grown from embryonic stem cells. The challenges are financial and ethical and have the capacity to fundamentally alter our notions of the body, health and illness and the very nature of the self.

In the Irish context, particular ethical challenges have been raised by the way that technological advance has led to a redefinition of life in the areas of the conceptive technologies (for example, IVF) and the life-sustaining technologies (for example, life-support machines). Such technologies force us to consider issues about life, death and medicine that were formerly implicit. They reorder the boundaries between culture and nature and they raise fundamental philosophical questions about biological contingency. They alter the concept of the body itself (McDonnell, 1997, pp. 71–2). When life is dependent on a respirator, how then do we define death? Questions then arise about the right to die and the possibility of a 'good death'. Similarly, reproductive technologies raise legal, ethical and social dilemmas in relation to motherhood, the role of women and the nature of the human embryo.

Another major challenge relates to the management of the healthcare system. International trends reflect a tendency for the proportion of national resources consumed by healthcare to expand. In some ways Ireland benefits from this trend: the spectacular success of the impotency drug Viagra (the main ingredient for which is manufactured in Ringaskiddy in Co. Cork) and Botox, used in cosmetic surgery (manufactured in Westport, Co. Mayo), is an indicator of the substantial income industries located in Ireland derive from global healthcare expenditure. But the spiralling costs of healthcare provision also place strains on the Irish exchequer and there are major challenges in delivering efficient and effective healthcare to an ageing population. Increased efficiency and rationalisation may lead to a depersonalisation of healthcare, with the emergence of what Ritzer (2011, pp. 64–6) terms 'assembly line medicine' offering 'Docs-in-a-box'.

The dual tendencies of holism and biomedicine will continue to contend for public acceptance and support. The acute hospital sector, ever more sophisticated and high-tech, will demand a growing share of resources. At the same time, people are increasingly turning to alternative therapies and practitioners. There are demands for a community-based approach to health that embraces a more preventative role, focusing on health promotion rather than cure. It is likely that trends towards self-care will continue to intensify, with an ever greater interest in dietary matters, cosmetic surgery and exercise regimes. There is also an increasing recognition that control of environmental factors, from noise pollution to farm chemicals, is crucial in the maintenance of health. Overall, shifts in public images of health will also provide challenges of shifting resources and a threat to the entrenched power and status of some professional groups, as well as providing opportunities for the emergence of new types of practitioners, such as physical therapists and various types of counsellors. Health, illness and the body will continue to provide a fascinating area of research for sociologists, and sociologists have the potential to shape a healthcare system that is of benefit to all.

10
Crime and Deviance

For many Irish people, one of the most significant perceived social changes over the past 50 years or so has been in the extent and nature of crime. This chapter explores that perception, amongst other things. Discussing the topic from a sociological perspective allows us to raise some questions about change in Irish society as well as about how sociologists think about and define crime. A sociological approach challenges the received wisdom in this field, especially in relation to the apparent increase in crime rates. It also questions the definition of crime and raises issues about the links between crime and social inequality.

Crime has long been of interest to sociologists, not only because it is recognised as a major social issue, but also because it reflects much about the nature of society. This insight goes back at least to Durkheim, who was particularly interested in examining rates of crime and how they varied between different societies or in the same society across time. He argued that the rate of crime in a society reflected its balance between individualism and social regulation. In theory, a society that had got the balance right would display a 'normal' rate of crime. In practice, most societies have abnormal levels of crime – either too low, when there is too much regulation of the individual, or too high, when individualism becomes uncontrolled.

Durkheim's ideas remain influential in the sociology of crime. He reversed the assumption of criminologists that we need only study 'social factors' to explain crime; he stressed that crime itself was profoundly social. He also demolished the idea that societies can ever be, or even should be, crime free. He introduced the counter-intuitive notion that it is just as important to study a very low crime rate in a society as a very high one. This is a useful insight as we try to understand patterns of crime in Irish society.

Sociological research on crime in Ireland has been quite limited, though with a marked increase in research since the late 1990s. Much research has involved analysis of official crime statistics and has aimed to establish levels of crime and how they change over time. Researchers have also tried to show how crime is socially distributed in terms of both criminal actors and victims of crime. Comparatively little research has been published on other dimensions of crime, all of which have become major public issues in Irish society, such as white-collar crime, the operation of the criminal justice system, routine policing practices or the social processes of imprisonment. Nevertheless, there is now a greater willingness to facilitate research in the social aspects of crime and to welcome public enquiry and debate; consequently, the breadth and depth of sociological research have increased.

In this chapter we address a limited set of issues to do with crime. We open with an outline of how sociologists have viewed crime and 'deviant' behaviour. We stress the social constructedness of crime, and this stance is continued through an exploration of the nature of crime statistics. Our critical approach to the 'data' on crime shapes our discussion of crime trends in Ireland. Notwithstanding the issues in relation to statistics, it is clear that despite significant increases in crime since the 1950s, Ireland still has a lower than average crime rate compared to many similar societies. We look at the sociological explanations for the development of crime in Ireland and then at the social profiles of victims and perpetrators of crime, finishing with an overview of an emergent area of sociological and public interest: white-collar crime. Our case study looks at the sociologically fascinating history of incarceration in Ireland, which has much to say about the sort of society we have been, are now and may be in the future.

CRIME AND DEVIANCE AS SOCIAL PROBLEMS

What is 'crime' and how should we understand it sociologically? Until the 1950s, most sociologists took for granted that what they should study was, simply, crime: all they had to do was discover what behaviour was prohibited under the criminal law of their country, and that defined their object of study. Moreover, most early researchers in the field were motivated by a desire to respond to public concern about crime. The public saw crime as a major social problem about which something should be done, so sociologists and criminologists set out to study this problem in the hope that if they could discover its causes, they could help society to control or even eliminate it.

Much of this early work started from the assumption that crime is something done by criminals. Sociologists studied groups of convicted criminals, arguing that the cause of their criminal behaviour lay in the individuals themselves, in something that made them different from other law-abiding people. If they could find what it was that made criminals different, that would be the key step towards solving the problem of crime. The causes that researchers looked for varied considerably and have been the subject of much debate. In the early 19th century, it was common to look for physical causes of criminality; thus, 'phrenologists' argued that criminal tendencies could be detected in the shape of the skull or the size of the brain (Rafter, 2008, pp. 40–64). This 'biocriminological' approach still manifests itself in the search for genetic differences between 'criminals' and others (Rafter, 2008, pp. 227–34). Other researchers looked for psychological defects, such as personality problems or 'addictive personalities', often seen to derive from defects in the socialisation or childhood environment of the criminal.

As the study of 'crime' developed, so did a parallel interest in broader concepts of 'deviance'. The study of the latter rested on the recognition that in any society there is behaviour that is – statistically or normatively speaking – abnormal. There are things that very few people do, like running naked across football pitches or eating strict vegan diets. There are things that some, or many, people do that are seen to be 'wrong', from the very trivial, like picking your nose in public, to the very serious, like having sex with children. Nearly all people in society disapprove of these activities to varying degrees.

Sociologists of deviance set out to investigate any such rule-breaking that arouses public disapproval, whether or not it was criminalised. The impetus for research came from within sociology rather than from the demands of governments or policy-makers. It aimed to better understand the problem of social order: how did people manage their social relationships; how did they make their social world meaningful and intelligible? In short, how is society organised in a routine, regular way so that we can explain what has taken place and what might happen next? Rule-making is obviously an important element in our attempts to make society 'orderly', but so is handling and dealing with rule-breaking, and the concept of deviance is a way to research these issues.

The study of crime and of deviance shared similar challenges. Both had to confront the issue of whose disapproval counts: if some members of society strongly disapprove of a certain type of behaviour but others do not, should we regard the behaviour as criminal/deviant or not? Should sociologists simply endorse the view of the more 'respectable' and powerful groups? And how do we explain why an activity (e.g. consensual sex with an opposite-sex person aged 14) can be acceptable, or at least legal, in one European society (Italy) but a serious criminal offence in another one (Ireland)?

It became clear that both deviance and crime are *socially constructed*. To understand behaviour that was in some way unusual or wrong, we had to look not just to the person doing the behaviour, but also at how others perceived and responded to the behaviour at the immediate level of interaction and at the broader level of groups and institutions in society. Whether other people ignore, tolerate, disapprove or punish an action is crucial in determining whether someone achieves the social identity of a deviant or criminal or else continues to live a life that is to all outward appearances one of conventional conformity. Simply put, people who do something 'wrong', or even who break a criminal law, do not equate with convicted criminals. We have all broken a law, somewhere, at some stage of our lives. Whether we move from that status to the status of 'criminal' is a complex and profoundly sociological process. Further, the process of becoming a 'crime statistic' and formally registered as either a perpetrator or victim of crime is also a sociological phenomenon.

Coercive confinement in Ireland

Do we like to lock up criminals in Ireland? Well, it depends on what we mean by locking people up; it also depends on what we mean by a crime. On the one hand Ireland has had a comparatively small prison population until recently. On the other hand, until the late 1950s, the country had a huge number of people who were, to a greater or lesser extent, forcibly deprived of their liberty. That number has since fallen drastically. We have also moved from a society that locked up mainly women to one that mainly locks up men. How can we explain these surprising trends?

Eoin O'Sullivan and Ian O'Donnell (2007, 2011) have examined the phenomenon of 'coercive confinement' in Ireland. Their research is stimulated by the work of David Garland (2001), who has examined the emergence of an increasingly punitive 'culture of control' in advanced Western societies. While Garland sees an ever-increasing proportion of the population being imprisoned in such societies, O'Sullivan and O'Donnell suggest that the opposite has occurred in Ireland. How can this be when the prison population in Ireland has risen from less than 400 in 1958 to 4,400 in 2010?

The answer lies in the concept of 'coercive confinement'. At the same time (1951) as Ireland had just 443 prisoners in five prisons, it was locking up over 30,000 women, men and children in a broad range of other institutions. These included the places that have since become notorious to our 21st-century sensibilities as places of abuse, neglect and confinement. They were the industrial schools, the 'county homes' (former workhouses), the Magdalene laundries and, above all, the huge psychiatric hospitals. These places of 'coercive confinement' housed one in every thousand of the population – higher than the current rate of imprisonment in the US, one of the most punitive societies in the world.

Why were so many Irish people kept in such places? The 'usual suspects' of an uncaring state and an authoritarian Catholic Church certainly had a role to play. But O'Sullivan and O'Donnell point the finger squarely at the rural family. In a rural society of large families, strong views about property and a lack of viable alternatives (except emigration), the institutions of confinement provided a means whereby the 'surplus' rural population could be managed and the privileges of those who held property maintained:

> With limited alternatives for those who did not emigrate or were not financed to enter a limited range of professions, such institutions were an integral element in the maintenance of social order in 1950s Ireland. (O'Sullivan and O'Donnell, 2007, p. 33)

Thus, many people – the vulnerable, disabled, the sexually unreliable, the propertyless, the nonconforming, the 'difficult' – were sent to such institutions by their families, by the courts and by the other agencies of the state.

Following a pattern established in the early 19th century (Quinlan, 2011, p. 16), most of them were female. In many cases the confinement was, in theory, voluntary, but in practice it was much easier to get in than it was to get out.

Figure 10.1: Coercive confinement in the Republic of Ireland

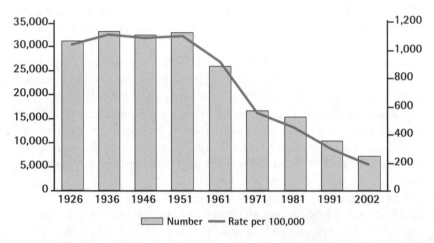

Source: O'Sullivan and O'Donnell, 2007, p. 41.

And then, as Figure 10.1 shows, the numbers plummeted. By 2002, fewer than 5,000 people were confined. The Magdalene laundries, industrial schools and 'mother and baby' homes had disappeared and there were only 1,000 involuntary patients in total in the psychiatric hospitals. We can see that the downward trend started in the 1950s and continued unabated into the new century. O'Sullivan and O'Donnell seek to explain why this dramatic change occurred. They dismiss explanations based on costs or that people were being confined elsewhere or in the community. Rather, they claim, the numbers declined with the 'drying up of the supply of potential entrants' (p. 43). The 'surplus' rural population was declining with smaller family size and the rise of alternative occupations through rural industrialisation and economic growth.

The story of Ireland's 'carceral archipelago' (a term coined by the French writer Michel Foucault) is a fascinating look back at a time when Ireland was, according to O'Sullivan and O'Donnell, 'a much less tolerant place'. Though 'crime', as we understand it today, was almost absent (much of it exported to Britain), Irish society was extremely harsh on what were seen as deviant forms of behaviour, condemning thousands (especially women and children) to regimes that were punitive, degrading and 'deliberately stigmatising' (p. 44).

We can be thankful that the punitive institutions of the past have mostly disappeared. They live on today through numerous commissions of enquiry, books, films and TV programmes, while many of the buildings themselves now serve as educational institutions or even hotels. Now the attention must turn to our current prison situation. There is evidence that Garland's punitive society is indeed emerging in Ireland, with record prisoner numbers, endemic prison overcrowding, longer sentences and proposals to build further prison places (Warner, 2011; Rogan, 2011, Ch. 9). The contemporary development of coercive confinement in Ireland demands a more intensive analysis from sociologists.

THE SOCIAL CONSTRUCTION OF CRIME STATISTICS

Crime statistics – such as those produced annually in Ireland by An Garda Síochána and released through the CSO – are a commonly used way to talk about crime amongst the public, in the media and by sociologists and criminologists themselves. The release of the most recent crime statistics is often the stimulus for news stories and discussion, especially if there is evidence of a significant rise in crime (falls in reported crime generally evince far less interest). Therefore, it is worth looking briefly at some of the processes involved in the construction of crime statistics.

Official statistics on crime are not a simple snapshot of what is happening at a point in time, but are the outcome of a complex series of social interactions and processes (CSO, 2007; WODC, 2010). First, a member of the public has to report to the police that a crime has been committed or the police themselves need to detect the commission of a crime, a fairly unusual event except for public order and traffic offences. Reporting rates for perceived crimes vary greatly and can be influenced by factors such as the requirements of insurance companies. Thus, for example, nearly all car thefts are reported to the Gardaí, whereas this does not apply to all thefts from the person. The incidence of crime can also be affected by the policing process itself, for example if the Gardaí decide to crack down on a particular activity, such as seatbelt-wearing, gang activity or recreational drug use.

What people are prepared to report to the police changes over time. Rape and child sex abuse, for example, are now much more likely to be reported than they were even 10 years ago, while a couple of generations ago they were reported very rarely indeed. This is partly to do with social recognition of such offences, but also that people have greater confidence that their act of reporting will have some positive consequences (CSO, 2007). Sometimes, as in the case of white-collar crime, as we will see later in this chapter, people are not even aware that they have been a victim of a crime and so no 'crime' is reported. It has been estimated in the UK that the so-called 'dark figure' of unreported crime may constitute about three-quarters of all criminal activity (NCC, 2004, p. 45).

Once a criminal event has been reported, the Gardaí have to record the crime as a crime, and in many cases this does not happen, for a number of reasons. Police will use their discretion, influenced by numerous social factors ranging from how busy they are to broader social attitudes, to guide whether they record a crime or not. For example, for a long time 'domestic violence' was often not treated as a crime, even though assault was illegal. A reported crime may, for administrative reasons, be aggregated with a number of others, or indeed one event may be divided into a number of discrete 'crimes' (e.g. 'drunk and disorderly' and 'resisting arrest'). A crime may be detected and recorded as 'cleared up' or it may be 'written off' when a suspect admits to a number of crimes. The Director of Public Prosecutions may decide not to bring a case to court or a judge may dismiss a case for lack of evidence or on a legal technicality. Given this complex set of processes, we may conclude that official statistics measure not the 'rate of crime' in society, but the outcomes of a complex process of reporting and recording. They tell us as much about how people respond to crime as about what criminals do.

If official statistics only include a selection of all 'crimes' committed, official statistics on 'criminals' are even less reliable. To officially become a criminal, a person must pass through a series of stages from arrest, to preparation of a case against them, to court appearances and finally a guilty verdict and the recording of a conviction. There is a high drop-out rate at each stage due to factors that may have little to do with whether the person actually committed the offence. Moreover, those who come to the attention of the Gardaí, are arrested or convicted are not a random sample of all criminal law-breakers, but a select social group: generally young, male, unemployed and from specific urban locations. The social characteristics that distinguish these people from the rest of the population are far more striking than any alleged physical or psychological 'defects' they might carry.

Other objections can be made to studies of crime that equate it with breaking the criminal law. First, laws are not static, but vary between societies and can change, sometimes quite radically, over time. What counts as a crime is relative to a particular time, place and culture. Second, if the assumption that criminals are different from conforming people is hard to sustain, so is the assumption that crimes (and criminals) resemble each other. Why should burglars have anything in common with those who live off immoral earnings, or illegal phone-tappers share anything in common with rapists, other than that they have all broken a law? Third, if our concern is with behaviour that harms society, there is little reason to confine ourselves to the study of crime, since much harmful behaviour (such as contribution to global warming) is not criminalised, and in addition, there are 'crimes' that most people would feel are not very harmful (such as keeping a dog without a dog license). We can conclude that the operation of the criminal law produces a rather narrow and biased measure of 'harmful rule-breaking'. In particular, as we will see, it mainly concerns itself with some of the harmful behaviour the poor or the powerless are likely to engage in, but is much less concerned with what the rich and powerful, or even the 'respectable', engage in.

MEASURING CRIME IN IRELAND

Having made a rather scathing critique of crime statistics, it is now a complex issue to discuss the experience of crime in Ireland. Much of the sociological analysis of crime is inevitably dependent on such statistics, both to describe the incidence of crime and to make comparisons across time and different nation states. Until 2006, the key official source of data was the annual report of An Garda Síochána. Since then, the Central Statistics Office (CSO) has compiled the statistics. Other useful data derives from criminal justice agencies such as the prison and probation services, crime victimisation data generated by the ESRI and specialised research data from bodies such as the National Advisory Committee on Drugs (NACD) and the National Crime Council (NCC, no date). Detailed crime statistics at the local level are now available to the public through the All-Island Research Observatory (www.airo.ie).

We must take such statistics at face value for the purposes of this discussion while keeping in mind the social processes that shape their production. Particular care should be taken in coming to any conclusions based on cross-national comparisons. It should also be noted that changes in the measurement and definition of crimes make it a hazardous exercise to compare crime rates in different years, even in the one country. In particular, there were major changes to the classification of offences in Ireland in the year 2000, associated with the introduction of the Garda PULSE computer system (CSO, 2007). The CSO (2007, s1.5) suggests that it is 'particularly unsafe' to consider broad figures in relation to 'crime' in general and that it is better to look at trends in particular crime types.

In very broad terms, the last few years have seen a total number of approximately 600,000 recorded crimes in Ireland per annum. In 2008 this figure jumped to around 840,000 but fell again in 2009 to around 760,000 (CSO, 2011). The substantial increase and subsequent decrease can mainly be accounted for by changes in traffic-related offences, which make up about two-thirds of recorded crimes. Such offences, which are nearly all detected by the Gardaí rather than reported by the public, are strongly influenced by police action, such as the operation of speed cameras or drink-driving checks. These statistics indicate the futility of looking at 'total crime' figures (which in fact are not provided by the CSO) – an increase of 1,000 crimes is not of major social concern if it is a result of people's failure to pay their car tax; it is another matter entirely if it reflects an additional 1,000 sexual assaults or kidnappings.

Rather than focusing on aggregate crime statistics, it makes more sense to look at the figures over time for particular types of crime. We initially look at the figures for homicide (unlawful killing). This is a type of crime that is less susceptible (though not immune) to statistical variation; it is also a source of major social concern and interest. In Ireland there is a perception that unlawful killing (particularly murder) has increased dramatically in recent years, specifically as a consequence of gangland killings in Dublin, Limerick and elsewhere, linked to feuds between criminal groups. What, then, do the figures for homicide tell us? Table 10.1 outlines the statistics for homicides in Ireland: these figures include murder, manslaughter and infanticide (very rare) but do not include the figures for death as a result of dangerous driving.

Table 10.1: Homicides in Ireland, 1951–2011

Year	Number of homicides
1951	7
1961	13
1971	14
1981	35
1991	31
1996	46
2000	56
2001	58
2002	59
2003	51
2004	45
2005	65
2006	67
2007	84
2008	55
2009	60
2010	58
2011	42

Note: The table does not include figures for 'dangerous driving causing death'.

Sources: National Crime Council; CSO.

Table 10.1 indicates that the number of homicides in Ireland was very low from the 1950s until the 1970s, with only three reported unlawful killings in the whole country in 1960. The figures increased slowly over the 1970s and 1980s, but there were still only 17 homicides in 1990. There was a significant increase in the mid-1990s and another jump at the start of this century, but since 2001 the annual number of unlawful killings has remained stable at around 55 to 60. A signficant drop in 2011 may or may not indicate a new trend.

Even if the number of cases of murder and manslaughter has not seen a great increase in recent years (in fact, a decline since 2007), what about serious crime more generally? Again, it can be difficult to discern the figures from the published statistics. While the Gardaí and CSO do not publish figures on 'serious crime' per se, they did (until 2007) release figures for 'headline' crimes. These include all the most serious crimes (such as murder, rape, assault, burglary, arson, particular types of theft) and exclude minor assaults and routine traffic offences (the latter being the sort of crimes 'we' rather than 'they' – the criminals – commit). Since 2007, the category of 'headline crime' is no longer used. There were also significant changes to how crimes were classified in 2000, which may well explain the apparent reduction in crime that year. For the years since 2007, it is possible to examine trends in non-traffic offences by removing two categories from the crime figures (4 and 14) that roughly equate to these.

Table 10.2: 'Serious crime' in Ireland, 1950–2010

Headline offences	
1950	12,232
1955	11,531
1960	15,375
1965	16,736
1970	30,756
1975	48,387
1980	72,782
1985	91,285
1990	87,658
1995	102,484
2000	73,276
2005	101,659
2006	103,177
2007	104,946
Categories excluding 04 and 14 – mainly traffic offences	
2008	242,700
2009	279,232
2010	272,455

Source: National Crime Council (nd).

Again, we can see from Table 10.2 that the incidence of crime in Ireland has gone through a number of phases. From 1950 to 1965 the reported incidence of crime was comparatively low and stable, by the mid-1970s it had quadrupled and there were further increases into the mid-1990s. Since then the crime rate has appeared to be relatively stable. While it is not possible to directly compare the most recent figures with those prior to 2007, we can see that the incidence of crime has remained relatively stable (indeed, has again seen a reduction) since that year.

How does Ireland's crime rate compare with other countries? While Durkheim was amongst those who pioneered the cross-cultural or comparative analysis of crime patterns, we now know that this is a much more complex and difficult endeavour than he perhaps appreciated. As outlined above, it is very risky to make firm claims about international comparisons when it comes to crime statistics (WODC, 2010, pp. 18–22 offers five pages of advice on the hazards). For example, offences are not defined in the same ways in different countries – what might be counted as an 'assault' in one country might be recorded as 'attempted murder' in another, with obvious implications for the incidence of 'serious' crime. There are also major differences in court systems, policing regimes and how different countries collect and present their statistics. For this reason, amongst others, there has been a move towards alternative, complementary ways to measure crime, for example through victimisation studies, which we discuss in the Irish context later on in this chapter.

Table 10.3 presents intentional homicide figures for selected countries, expressed as a rate per 100,000 of the population. The homicide rate for Ireland has varied from 1.3 to 2.0 (in 2007, as we know a peak year for unlawful killing in Ireland). In 2006 (a more typical year), the homicide rate in Ireland (at 1.6) was below the median (middle) figure of 1.7 and the rate in Ireland was similar to other western European countries such as Belgium (1.7), France (1.7) and the UK (except Scotland) (1.4). It was above a group of countries that apparently had very low homicide rates, such as Switzerland (0.8), Denmark (0.7) and Iceland (0.0), but was significantly below some countries, mainly in eastern and central Europe, that had very high (though declining) rates, such as Georgia (7.3), Lithuania (8.2) and the Ukraine (6.3). By way of comparison, the rate in the US in 2006 was 5.8, having declined from 9.8 in 1991 (FBI, 2009). For other areas of crime it is very difficult to take some of the comparison figures at face value – for example, is it likely that the rate of 'rape' is nearly three times higher (at 26 per 100,000) in Northern Ireland than in the Republic (9 per 100,000) (WODC, 2010, Table 1.2.1.13)? Given the strong similarities in culture between the two, it is more likely that definitional, policing and reporting processes explain this disparity.

Table 10.3: Homicide offences per 100,000 population

	2003	2004	2005	2006	2007	% change 2003–2007
Mean	2.4	2.5	2.4	2.1	2.0	
Albania	4.6	3.8	4.2	2.8	2.9	–38
Armenia	2.5	2.4	1.8	2.5	2.6	4
Austria	0.7	0.8	0.8	0.7	0.6	–10
Belgium	1.8	2.1	1.7	1.7	–	–

	2003	2004	2005	2006	2007	% change 2003–2007
Bosnia-Herzegovina	–	–	1.8	1.9	–	–
Bulgaria	3.0	2.9	2.3	2.2	2.2	–26
Croatia	1.8	2.0	1.6	1.8	1.6	–12
Cyprus	1.9	1.9	1.8	1.6	1.4	–28
Czech Republic	–	–	–	–	–	–
Denmark	1.4	1.0	1.1	0.7	–	–
Estonia	10.9	6.7	8.4	6.8	7.1	–35
Finland	2.5	3.3	2.5	2.6	2.9	14
France	2.0	1.9	1.9	1.7	1.6	–18
Georgia	7.0	8.8	9.2	7.3	–	–
Germany	1.3	1.2	1.2	1.1	1.0	–22
Greece	1.1	1.0	1.1	1.0	1.1	–3
Hungary	2.3	2.1	1.6	1.7	1.5	–31
Iceland	0.0	1.0	1.0	0.0	0.7	–
Ireland	**1.3**	**1.1**	**1.6**	**1.6**	**2.0**	**59**
Italy	1.3	1.3	1.1	1.1	–	–
Latvia	–	–	–	–	–	–
Lithuania	10.0	9.4	10.8	8.2	7.4	–25
Luxembourg	–	–	–	–	–	–
Malta	0.0	1.7	1.0	0.0	–	–
Moldova	–	–	–	–	–	–
Netherlands	1.5	1.2	1.2	0.9	–	–
Norway	1.1	0.8	0.7	0.7	0.6	–42
Poland	2.3	2.2	2.1	1.9	1.9	–20
Portugal	2.6	1.8	1.7	2.1	–	–
Romania	2.5	2.4	2.1	2.0	1.9	–26
Russia	–	–	–	–	–	–
Slovakia	2.7	2.3	2.0	1.7	1.6	–40
Slovenia	1.1	1.4	1.0	0.6	1.2	14
Spain	1.4	1.2	1.2	1.1	1.1	–24
Sweden	0.9	1.2	0.9	1.0	1.2	32
Switzerland	1.0	1.1	1.0	0.8	0.7	–32
TFYR of Macedonia	–	–	2.2	2.0	–	–
Turkey	–	–	–	2.8	2.5	–
Ukraine	–	7.4	6.4	6.3	–	–
UK: England & Wales	1.7	1.6	1.4	1.4	1.4	–15
UK: Northern Ireland	1.9	2.4	1.7	1.4	1.7	–12
UK: Scotland	2.1	2.8	1.9	2.4	2.3	8

Source: WODC, 2010, p. 41.

THE IRISH INCREASE IN CRIME: MODERNISATION OR EXPANDED CAPITALISM?

We have suggested that a focus on crime is a good way to think about change in Irish society. We have established that even if the statistics are open to debate and interpretation, there has been a significant increase in the incidence of crime in Ireland over the period since 1950. We see a nine-fold increase in the serious crime rate over the 40 years from 1955 to 1995, at a time when the population increased by just 25 per cent. But in the subsequent period (1995 to 2007), the Irish population rose by nearly a fifth while the incidence of reported indictable crime rate was virtually unchanged (it is difficult to compare later years due to changes in how crime is classified). When the change in population is taken into account, crime rates were remarkably stable over the period 1981 to 2007, notwithstanding fluctuations and variations in relation to particular types of criminal activity. There is no evidence to suggest that there has been any long-term increase in overall crime rates since the early 1980s and this experience is reflected in a number of other countries (McCullagh, 2011, p. 23).

The increase in crime in Ireland from the late 1950s to the 1970s came as Irish society was starting to modernise and industrialise. Sociologists argue that this is more than a coincidence: modernisation inevitably brings a rise in crime. In a sense, increased crime is the price we have to pay for the affluence and individual freedom we enjoy in modern society, but sociologists vary considerably in how they explain the connection between modernisation and rising crime.

One argument is that it is the experience of rapid change itself that leads to increased crime. Change produces *social disorganisation*, with disruption of societal values and of the institutions and methods of social control. In the transition from 'traditional' to 'modern' society, the shared values that maintained order are eroded, but new values have not yet developed to replace them. Consequently, there is no consensus about how to behave. As people become more mobile, especially as they migrate from rural areas into cities, the old institutions of family, church and local community lose their capacity to restrain behaviour while new institutions of control, such as education and the mass media, are not yet fully established. Social dislocation is widely experienced as old jobs disappear and people have to move in search of new ones. When people are left without clear values or controls, it is not surprising that the crime rate soars.

This explanation rests on a number of assumptions. First, that people need to be closely guided and regulated by society if they are to behave in a moral or sociable way; left to themselves, they are naturally anarchic and violent. This is a powerful argument that turns up frequently in discussions about crime, not just in sociology, but also in mass media treatments of crime. But does it really make much sense of either the European or the Irish experience? In Europe, rising crime rates occurred in most countries from the 1960s, including in those that we might regard as already 'modern' and highly regulated, such as Germany or Britain. This is odd, for if rises in crime are associated with the transition to modernity, the crime rates in these countries should have stabilised, not be increasing.

Second, the Irish experience of industrialisation and economic development since the late 1950s has *not* involved a massive level of social disorganisation compared to many 'late industrialising' societies. In Ireland, industrialisation was dispersed throughout rural areas rather than concentrated in cities. Dublin's population grew substantially, but due more to indigenous growth rather than to mass immigration from rural areas. Those who did in-migrate from the countryside were mainly educated people moving to secure middle-class jobs. Irish society did experience rapid social change, but not the social disorganisation or breakdown of 'the traditional social order' that could explain the rapid rise in crime. Some groups did experience severe dislocation: those who emigrated (and who have long made up a disproportionate number of prisoners in British prisons) and the urban working class whose jobs disappeared as older industries declined and who were consequently moved out of the centre of Dublin to the western suburbs (Moore, 2008, pp. 42–6). Disorganisation theories may help to explain the predominance of young people from new outer suburban estates in the criminal justice system of the 1970s and 1980s, but do little to explain general trends in crime over the period.

McCullagh (1996) discusses an alternative *social structural* way to explain the connection between modernisation and rising crime. This is concerned less with social change in itself and more with the type of society that is emerging. It emphasises that modernisation brings about a new social structure organised around *property*: ownership of property, social status based on property and careers in relation to property. In Chapter 15 we look at how contemporary consumer societies are structured around the production and consumption of a boundless supply of desirable goods.

Modernisation opened up a range of new, legitimate career opportunities in Irish society during the 1960s and 1970s based around the production, sale, advertising, management and protection of property and goods. But it also opened up a parallel range of *illegitimate* career opportunities, such as theft, burglary and fraud. In modern, urban, industrial society, property has become more widespread, visible, transportable and desirable, so that opportunities and motives for property crime increase. This explains why the crime rate continues to rise even in highly developed societies. Property keeps on expanding, taking on new forms and becoming more highly valued. This might help to explain why burglary rates are amongst the highest in countries (such as Austria, Denmark and the Netherlands) that have particularly advanced consumption-based economies (WODC, 2010, Table 1.2.1.18).

In addition to showing how the new society is structured around property, we need to address the issue of inequality in access to property. Access to desired goods is very unequal and certain groups in society are systematically barred from legitimately gaining such access. These conditions were described by the American sociologist Robert Merton (1938), following Durkheim, as 'anomic'. They provide an environment that will encourage property-related crimes and also make it likely that those who aspire to but cannot access such property will commit such crimes. Such an explanation of crime rests on different assumptions about human nature to those of the disorganisation thesis. It assumes that people are not naturally aggressive and selfish, but that these qualities are fostered in them by an anomic society. As a consequence, issues of income distribution and inequality, particularly access to employment opportunities, may have an important role in shaping the nature and extent of crime in modern societies.

More recently, a number of writers have sought to apply the work of influential criminologist David Garland to Ireland, including Campbell (2008). In his book *The Culture of Control* (2001), Garland sought to explore the landscape of crime in the US and the UK in the late 20th century: the period of 'late modernity' and its allied neo-liberal politics. As a society that is heavily influenced by these 'core' societies, it is worth examining the extent to which similar trends can be discerned in Ireland.

Campbell (2008) examines the relevance of Garland's thesis in the Irish context. For Garland, the current period is marked by a shift towards a free market, more punitive approach to crime and its control. This is manifested in the development of a number of indicators, such as a decline in rehabilitation of criminals as a social objective; a focus on penal sanctions and an increase in the use of imprisonment and longer sentences; a resurgent 'populism' in relation to crime, with a focus on the 'victim'; a focus on risk and its control through managerial strategies and enhanced surveillance; and finally, a sense of perpetual crime 'crisis' with a diminution of interest in the protection of human rights.

There is not space here to consider the pertinence of all Garland's arguments. There is certainly evidence both to support and to rebut his assertions in the Irish context. Certainly, some policy changes and projects reflect the emergent society predicted by Garland, such as stronger bail laws and fewer protections for suspects as well as a greater use of imprisonment and longer prison sentences, requiring an expansion of prison spaces. As in many countries, there has been an enhanced role for the 'victim', who has become a staple object of concern on, for example, talk radio and Internet forums. As in all areas of the public sector, there is undoubtedly a greater emphasis on managerialism and top-down control, with related concerns about 'risk management' and 'value for money'. The continuing gangland conflicts on the one hand and the perceived failure to tackle white-collar crime associated with the financial crash on the other may indeed lead to a heightened sense of panic or crisis about crime in general.

On the other hand, Campbell (2008) points out some of the weaknesses in applying Garland's thesis to Ireland. She notes that the Irish Prison Service remains committed to a rehabilitative goal and that the Irish state has not asserted that crime is 'out of control' – indeed, it regularly seeks to assure the population that it has achieved substantial reductions in crime. Notwithstanding changes to bail laws, the right to silence and some other changes, the fundamental constitutional basis of Irish law remains relatively intact. Campbell suggests that elements of Garland's late-modern 'crime complex' may be emerging in Ireland, but perhaps Garland's work is most useful as a warning in relation to the most regressive forms of response to crime that Irish society should seek to avoid. We now go on to look at some selected aspects of crime in Ireland.

THE SOCIAL DISTRIBUTION OF CRIME IN IRELAND

Victims of crime

We have argued that a level of crime is 'normal' in any society, but that is of little solace to those affected by crime and disorder. Who in Ireland is most likely to be a victim of crime and what are its impacts? Partly in response to the shortcomings of crime data outlined above, but also as a response to the contemporary political focus on the victims of crime (Campbell, 2008; Davies et al., 2007), there has been a concerted effort in recent years to measure the impact of crime in societies through the use of 'victimisation' surveys. Such surveys tell us much about who the victims of crime are, what their social and geographical characteristics are and how the experience has affected them. Such surveys can also reveal the impact of non-reported or under-reported crime, which may constitute the greater part of criminal activity. After a slow start, the Irish state has begun to generate victimisation data through a series of questions within the CSO's Household Budget Survey.

Victimisation surveys, not surprisingly, have their weaknesses and are no less socially constructed than other types of crime data. McCullagh (2011, pp. 27–8) has identified a number of issues related to victimisation surveys. These include: a) would all the incidents be considered 'crimes' if they had been reported to Gardaí, given that many incidents are of a relatively minor nature?; b) why are some 'crimes' reported to a researcher but not to the Gardaí?; c) surveys based on randomised sampling can miss out on how victimisation can be confined to specific areas; d) victim surveys are at a coarser grain of analysis (regional) than crime statistics (divisional), making comparisons difficult. Davies et al. (2007) point out further issues in their study of the sociology of victimology in England and Wales. They remind us that the likelihood, and the experience, of being a victim is shaped by interacting social divisions of age, class, gender, disability and ethnicity; that the nature of victimisation is strongly shaped by the media; and that victim surveys can easily miss criminal activities and social harm that are not necessarily visible to the individual, such as corporate and environmental crimes such as price-fixing or pollution. Nevertheless, victim surveys do provide us with an additional source of information about crime that can be combined with other sources to provide a more comprehensive picture.

An early victim survey in Ireland was that conducted by Breen and Rottman (1985) of the ESRI. It revealed crime as an urban phenomenon, concentrated in Dublin. The most likely to be victims were those in the higher social classes (self-employed or white-collar employees), generally younger (young middle-aged) and located in middle-class housing estates. These trends were supported by a subsequent survey (Watson, 2000) that also indicated specific gender patterns of victimisation: women were the most likely to be victims of theft, while men were more prone to being assaulted. Crimes related to vehicles helped to push the profile of victims towards middle age (being more likely to be car owners), but when this factor was removed from the analysis, it emerged that younger people (under 25) were disproportionately victimised. About a fifth of victims were institutions (mainly small businesses), while the other 80 per cent were individuals. The former were more likely to suffer from repeat victimisation.

The most recent victimisation survey carried out by the CSO was in 2010 (CSO, 2010). The survey asked respondents about their experience of crime in the last year and some questions about their perceptions of crime. The questions related to respondents' experience of household crimes, such as burglary and vandalism, and crimes against the person, such as robbery and assault. Questions about sexual assault or domestic violence were not asked, being deemed too sensitive, while there were no questions about corporate or white-collar crimes, such as fraud, price-fixing or environmental crimes.

A number of interesting findings emerged from the survey, which allowed for comparison with the earlier similar surveys of 2003 and 2006. First, the experience of crime had fallen, reflecting falls in reported crime. Second, only a small minority of the population had direct experience of crime as a victim: only 9 per cent of households experienced any crime (rising to 12 per cent in Dublin), while 4 per cent of individuals (rising to 6 per cent in the West) had experienced crime against the person. Even then, about a third of victims did not report incidents to the Gardaí as there was no loss or injury involved – raising the issue of whether these were 'crimes'. In terms of household-related crimes, those with children and those living in urban areas were more likely to be victims. For individuals, younger age groups, particularly students, were the most likely to experience crime, while the least likely were those over 65 years of age.

Perhaps most interesting, from a social constructivist point of view, was the wide disparity between people's experiences and their perceptions of crime. While the evidence showed that people were experiencing less crime now than previously, the number seeing crime as 'a very serious problem' increased slightly (from 47 to 49 per cent) over the three surveys. It may be that people are more influenced by the high-profile reporting of crime in the media than their own experiences. The most likely to see crime as a serious problem were those over 65 who, as we have seen, are the least likely to experience crime themselves. A more 'realistic' picture is perhaps found in the response to whether people see themselves as likely to be a victim of crime in the future: those saying 'no' increased from 43 to 59 per cent between 2003 and 2010 – a significant decline and perhaps reflecting the reality of their own experience and that of the people they knew.

Ideally, victim surveys can assist criminologists and sociologists in 'providing better estimates of the extent of crime and victimisation' (Davies et al., 2007, p. 11). The published data in Ireland does not make it easy to link the figures for 'reported crime' with the victimisation data, for reasons suggested above. Nevertheless, if the spatial units can be reconciled and the terminology for classification of crimes can be linked across both types of survey, then it may be possible to gain a better picture of phenomena such as unrecorded and unreported crime as well as the capacity to link people's worry about crime to the incidence of crime in their own communities. Even then, the statistical data will need to be complemented by ethnographic research at the community level to obtain a richer picture of how people may experience crime in their everyday life, especially in that relatively small number of Irish communities where criminality is an everyday part of life.

Antisocial behaviour

A major concern in many Irish communities, especially in 'disadvantaged' areas, is what has come to be called antisocial behaviour. It is a type of activity that is particularly difficult to capture in crime statistics, but one that is important in its social impact and which creates its own patterns of victimisation. The loosely defined term 'antisocial behaviour' has come to refer to a range of activities, from serious intimidation and harassment, to low-level drug-dealing, to children playing football in the street (Community Mediation Works, 2010). O'Higgins (1999) focuses on drug abuse, intimidation and vandalism, while in the context of disadvantaged areas of Limerick city, Hourigan (2011) shows how antisocial behaviour has come to incorporate activities that range from throwing stones and spraying graffiti through to systematic intimidation of many people in communities through the stealing and burning of cars and destruction of houses.

Antisocial behaviour is often associated with specific areas, usually housing estates or urban locations such as shopping centres, though theoretically it can take place anywhere. It is usually, though not always, associated with children and young people. In Ireland it has often been linked with public authority housing estates, where it can have a significant impact on the quality of everyday life (O'Higgins, 1999, p. 149; Fahey et al., 2011, p. 99). For Hourigan (2011, p. 131), 'residents of disadvantaged estates experience more fear and trauma on a daily basis because of the antisocial behaviour of children than the more serious activities of feuding gang members in their communities'.

Hourigan describes (2011, p. 50) how in Limerick since at least the early 1970s, 'teenagers from the more disadvantaged families ... viewed the street as the "stage" where they could assert themselves, exert control and demand respect from others'. While local communities were able to police and to a certain extent control such behaviour, this ability diminished as the social profile of the estates changed, largely through the out-migration of more prominent, socially active residents. This led to an increase in more serious forms of antisocial behaviour, such as joyriding in stolen cars, intimidation, open substance abuse and serious vandalism, including the burning of houses (2011, p. 53). The Gardaí seemed unwilling or unable to deal with these types of behaviour, which led to a vicious cycle of decline in certain areas of certain estates. In some cases, residents turned to local criminal gangs for protection, while in other cases the perpetrators of antisocial behaviour were linked to those gangs themselves. The antisocial behaviour helped to provide the type of environment – 'the water for the fish to swim in' – within which other serious criminal activities such as drug dealing and money laundering could take place relatively unimpeded (2011, p. 78). Similar connections between antisocial behaviour and serious drug- and feud-related crime have also been identified in areas of Dublin (Fahey et al., 2011, p. 48).

Residents of estates typically identify the fact that serious antisocial behaviour is limited to a relatively small proportion of residents – the 'few bad apples', 'certain families' or 'problem tenants'. Hourigan (2011, p. 136) refers to these as the 'disadvantaged of the disadvantaged' – young people who are closely connected to families involved in organised criminal behaviour or with severe addiction problems. But the activities of even a small number can lead to the severe stigmatisation of an entire estate, especially when the activities are amplified by media attention (Devereux et al., 2011). This will impact on the lives of other children and young people in the estate, for example in terms of educational and employment opportunities, thereby making it more likely that they too will be drawn into antisocial behaviour.

Sociological discussions of antisocial behaviour note the difficulties that the criminal justice system encounters when attempting to respond to the phenomenon. Hourigan notes that the system is 'almost powerless to act' in the Limerick context, partly due to the early onset of antisocial behaviour well below the age of criminal responsibility (12 years). Another factor is the fundamental weakness of the state's child protection systems, which are unable to respond at the required level for a range of reasons, including over-bureaucratisation and inappropriate training or supervision (Hourigan, 2011, pp. 140–9). Similarly, local government agencies, where much of the responsibility for action resides (Community Mediation Works, 2010; Fahey et al., 2011, p. 50), are often poorly resourced, lack expertise and may indeed make things worse.

There has been much discussion of the causes of antisocial behaviour amongst young people. One factor is the lack of public space available for use by young people, especially young men (Kelleher and O'Connor, 2011, pp. 173–8). Their attempts to claim space, such as green areas, boundary walls and shopping centres, inevitably bring these young people into conflict with others in the community and ultimately with the police. Young people also point to boredom – the familiar refrain 'there's nothing to do around here' (Griffin and Kelleher, 2010, p. 32; Community Mediation Works, 2010, pp. 11–15). Those lacking in educational or family resources may not have the capacity to deal with free time, especially if they have been excluded from or have left the school system and do not have legitimate employment. Hourigan (2011, p. 136) points to the excitement and feelings of power that involvement in antisocial behaviour can bring: 'getting away with' vandalism, personal abuse or shoplifting can create a 'buzz' that is similar to the potentially addictive effects of alcohol or gambling.

Attempts to address antisocial behaviour are often controversial, as they are dealing with a phenomenon that is not clearly defined, may be highly subjective in terms of how it is experienced and has the capacity to evoke both 'care' and 'control' (or both) responses. The study by Community Mediation Works (2010) of antisocial behaviour and the responses to it on a number of housing estates in the greater Dublin region illustrates this complexity. While members of the communities in question undeniably suffered the consequences of antisocial behaviour, the activities of the local government agencies also caused major problems for other residents – for example, for the family members of individuals who were involved in, or thought to be involved in, such behaviour. This included eviction from their local authority houses without any recourse to the law – effectively being made homeless by the state. There were concerns that some individuals were misidentified or scapegoated; unfairly targeted for what was seen to be 'normal' behaviour, such as playing football in the street; and that local council staff were insensitive to exceptional circumstances, such as family bereavements.

The phenomenon of antisocial behaviour illustrates many of the key issues in the sociology of crime and deviance. It is a complex issue; it is socially constructed and open to a variety of interpretations; it reveals key social divisions along the lines of class, gender and age; and it shows the variability of responses from the state and other social groups in attempting to respond. The sociological research into antisocial behaviour in Ireland shows that it has a major impact on certain groups in Irish society, is shaped to some extent by official and media responses and also has a certain rationality for those involved. It also shows that the attempts by various institutions in Irish society – local communities, health authorities, the Gardaí, local government – have not necessarily been very successful in adequately identifying the nature of or useful responses to the issue.

Perpetrators

We have some idea of who is likely to be a victim of crime, but what do we know about the perpetrators? Not surprisingly, there are no 'self-report surveys' in Ireland that ask people to report if they have ever been involved in criminal behaviour. At the same time, we know that there are processes that skew the identification of 'criminals' in specific ways, as we have seen in the earlier discussion of the social construction of crime. The data we have thus tends to identify those people who are most likely to be accused, apprehended and convicted of crimes. Statistically, these are most likely to be car drivers/owners, as the bulk of 'crimes' in Ireland are traffic related. Apart from these, 'criminals' are most likely to be people involved in publicly visible 'street crimes' like assault or burglary; those who conduct their crimes in private (such as 'white-collar criminals', discussed later on) are much less likely to be so defined.

In 1984, Rottman analysed data on those people 'apprehended' for indictable (roughly equivalent to 'serious') offences in the Dublin Metropolitan Area. He found that most were male (84 per cent), generally very young (one-quarter were under 16 and a further half between 17 and 20), economically extremely marginal (80 per cent of the 17- to 20-year-olds were unemployed and the rest were in unskilled or semi-skilled work) and drawn from specific locations in Dublin that were at that time places of great physical and social deprivation.

This particular pattern of young, poor, unskilled males from specific urban areas is one that has been confirmed by subsequent analyses of offenders. Thus, O'Mahony's later (1993, 1997) research on the inmates of Dublin's Mountjoy Prison and subsequent research by Dillon (2001) produced a broadly similar picture. Subsequent studies of other groups in custody have revealed similar patterns of experience of deprivation, including family breakdown, school problems and substance abuse, amongst other factors (Kilkelly, 2006, pp. 11–13). While we have to consider the possibility that some of these characteristics better explain why the person is in prison than why he broke the law, we can conclude that a significant proportion of offenders in Ireland come from extremely disadvantaged and marginalised groups.

Further evidence about this particular pattern comes from recent sociological research on crime in Limerick. Griffin and Kelleher (2010) conducted research with a group of '26 young men ... [who] live in some of the most disadvantaged areas in Ireland and are involved in, or at risk of becoming involved in, crime' (p. 25). The picture painted of this group of men is one of 'failure' within the education system (the majority left school without qualifications); consequent exclusion from a labour market where educational credentials are increasingly important; a lack of structured daily life and widespread experience of boredom; fear of violence, especially in relation to ongoing criminal feuds; and an overarching sense of 'hopelessness'. The researchers conclude that 'the barriers to social inclusion facing these men are enormous' (p. 43). The research conducted by Hourigan (2011, p. 148) in Limerick outlines the processes whereby such men can and do get involved in criminal activity, partly as a rational response to the situation in which they find themselves.

While there is much evidence that the perpetrators of crime are drawn from a fairly clearly demarcated social milieu, there are other groups of criminals that are significant within the Irish criminal justice system. These include sex offenders, who comprise a significant element of the prison population and who have a very different profile to the majority of those imprisoned – they tend to be older, more middle class and more likely to come from a rural background. Another significant group is those arrested for immigration-related offences, who, by definition, are more likely to vary in terms of nationality and ethnicity. A type of criminal who is rarely found in the prison environment, but may be socially significant, is the 'white-collar criminal'. There is further discussion of this issue later in this chapter.

WOMEN AND CRIME

As we have seen, the most common criminal offender profile in Ireland is that of a socially disadvantaged younger *male*. In fact, across all stages of the criminal justice process, whether for recorded crime, arrests or imprisonment, the overwhelming social category is maleness. It can also be noted that the majority of those involved in the criminal justice system, from police and prison officers to criminal lawyers and judges – even crime journalists – are men. Until the 1960s, criminologists and sociologists of crime tended to assume that criminals always *were* men – it could be said that they were 'gender blind'. They studied neither how masculinity nor femininity was relevant to crime. That situation has changed, largely as a consequence of feminist theory and research (Bacik, 2002, p. 134), and there is now a greater interest in issues of crime and gender. In this section we focus on the issue of women and crime, but as we saw in the previous section, there are also important things to be said about crime and masculinity (see Silvestri and Crowther-Dowey, 2008, Chapters 3 and 5 for more discussion on this issue).

In contemporary Ireland there are distinctive patterns in relation to gender and crime. Whether as criminals, victims or people involved in the criminal justice system, gender differences have an impact. At the same time, such differences intersect in complex ways with other aspects of social division and difference, such as class and ethnicity. Just as it does not make sense to say that all criminals are the same, there is no reason that all women (or men) will have the same experiences in relation to crime.

Nevertheless, there are numerous sociological questions that may arise when crime and deviance are approached from a gender perspective. For example: why do women continue to feature so much less than men in crime statistics, especially in an era of developing equality in so many other areas of social life? Why does the media treat male and female criminals so differently? Why is the administration of the justice system so male dominated? How are crime issues linked to broader gender and human rights issues? We can only scratch the surface in relation to such issues here.

Silvestri and Crowther-Dowey (2008, p. 26) maintain that 'the overriding consensus within criminology remains that while women do commit a broad range of offences they do commit less crime than men and are less dangerous and violent than their male counterparts'. This is borne out in the Irish experience. At this stage you would be right to be sceptical of crime statistics as a reliable indicator of criminal behaviour; nevertheless, an examination of the official statistics in Ireland does suggest that women are much less likely to be involved in crime. Thus, in 1998 it was predominantly men (87 per cent) that were *charged* with indictable offences (Bacik, 2002, p. 135). The further we move on through the criminal justice system, the fewer women appear. For example, the Garda crime statistical reports (available until 2004) show that around 10 to 15 per cent of those *convicted* of offences in any year are women. This varied by type of offence: women made up about a quarter of those convicted of larceny offences, but just 2 per cent of those convicted of 'offences against the person' or 'offences against property with violence'. Women are also most unlikely to be *imprisoned* for crime or to spend long periods of time in prison (Quinlan, 2011). According to the Irish Prison Service (IPS, 2010, p. 3), in 2009 women constituted just 3.4 per cent (132 individuals) of the total daily average of people in prison (3,881).

Why are women less involved in crime? This is a difficult and complex question to answer. We have seen that factors such as poverty and social exclusion have been broadly identified in Ireland and elsewhere as key determinants of criminal activity, yet women suffer disproportionately from poverty and are also excluded from many centres of power in our society. There must be other factors at play. It may be that women respond to poverty and powerlessness in ways that are not defined as criminal or that they do not choose such options. Or it may be that they do engage in criminal behaviour, but are less likely to be processed through the system of detection, arrest, conviction and imprisonment. If this is the case, we would need to explain why their rule-breaking may be ignored, dealt with more 'leniently' or seen as less serious.

Labelling theory has been a useful way to explore the links between gender, crime and deviance. It argues that deviance is a social role imposed on some in society, often for reasons that have less to do with behaviour than the sort of person they are. The labelling of someone as deviant (thief, prostitute, drug abuser) is often precipitated by factors such as where the rule-breaking act occurred, in front of whom or what sort of person the rule-breaker is thought to be. Gender is a highly visible and socially significant social characteristic that we are always aware of and respond to. It seems most likely that gender will enter into the labelling process that leads to the social construction of criminals.

Historical and contemporary research has shown that female criminality is often viewed through a particularly moralistic lens (Quinlan, 2011, pp. 33–40). Criminalised women are seen as 'doubly deviant', both for their crime and for also transgressing the norms of femininity (ACJRD, 2010, p. 26). We can see such processes at work, for example, in relation to juvenile offenders. In Ireland, one study indicates that girls are twice as likely as boys to be placed in secure care (cited in Kilkelly, 2006, p. 15). Magistrates usually justify this on the grounds that girls need 'care and protection'. Silvestri and Crowther-Dowey (2008, p. 44) argue that 'conceptualised as "wayward" and in need of "protection", girls are invariably harshly sanctioned for non-criminal offences and trivial misdemeanours'. Adult women who become criminalised are judged in terms of their adherence to conventional gender roles, especially motherhood and relationships with males, as well as their demeanour and appearance.

The portrayal of women criminals in the mass media assists in this construction. This has been the case in contemporary Ireland, North and South, where the few women convicted of serious crimes have been presented in a sensationalist and (especially in Northern Ireland) often highly sexualised way (Quinlan, 2011, pp.

77–84; ACJRD, 2010, p. 26). Rather than focus on the depressing, mundane and complex lives of the vast majority of female criminals, who almost invariably have experienced a life of abuse, poverty and exclusion, the media focuses on the very small number of 'black widows', 'evil mums-to-be' or 'sex-mad husband killers'. The effect of such narratives is to distort the nature of female criminality, of prisoners and of everyday prison life into a discourse of 'danger', increasing moral outrage and potentially fuelling an increased fear of crime.

The reality is that most crime committed by women in Ireland is 'petty, personal or sexual' (Quinlan, 2011, p. 84). It relates to crimes such as larceny, public disorder, non-payment of fines, soliciting, immigration offences, drug dealing and relational violence, much of which derives from the women's own situation of powerlessness. It is not the case that such women are dealt with more 'leniently' in the criminal justice system; rather, they are exposed to a 'gendered criminal justice system, characterised by gendered organisational logics and gendered agents of power' and suffer an 'oppressive and paternalistic form of individualised justice' (Silvestri and Crowther-Dowey, 2008, pp. 33, 34). As Quinlan's (2011) research in Dublin's Dóchas prison has revealed, women's experience of conviction and imprisonment may be different. To start, they are even more likely than men to experience multiple social problems such as abusive relationships, mental health issues, addictions, physical health issues, poverty, family and caring issues. When in prison they are particularly at risk of self-harm and suicide and often have to endure a fracturing of caring relationships with children or parents. The women in her study said that prison was more difficult and shaming for women than for men, as one prisoner remarked:

> In the prison you're just a number. You're stripped of your identity, your integrity and your honour. Your womanhood is taken away from you, and all you are left with is trying to keep your head up and yourself focused. ('Eithne' in Quinlan, 2011, pp. 166–7)

Within a human rights perspective, we can see that female criminals are often 'victims' of broader processes, such as domestic violence; poorly constructed health and welfare systems; globalisation that contributes to poor pay and working conditions, including in the illegal drugs industry; sexualised media portrayals; and a prison process that no matter how well-intentioned, positions women as powerless and worthless.

It is arguable that this situation is at least partly the consequence of a criminal justice system that continues to be dominated by men. For example, in Ireland there are eight Supreme Court judges, only two of whom are women; of 35 High Court justices, only five are women (www.courts.ie). Women make up around 16 per cent of prison officers (IPS, personal communication, 2011) and approximately a quarter of Gardaí (Clancy, 2009, p. 28). Women remain under-represented at the highest level in these bodies and in the legal profession. Furthermore, the institutions involved – Garda stations, law courts and prisons – remain highly male-centred environments with a distinctively masculine culture, symbolised in a myriad of ways, from paramilitary uniforms to lawyers' wigs to pornographic images on the walls of prison cells.

When we recognise how the criminal justice system may be socially constructed in relation to gender, we can see how it may also be involved in the construction and reproduction of class or ethnic inequalities. As we will see in our discussion of white-collar crime, so it is with crime and gender: we cannot treat the operation of the criminal justice system as if it were purely a reaction to crimes committed in society, but must recognise that it is involved in the creation of patterns and trends in relation to crime and in the social constitution of deviance.

Some of the most recent analyses of gender and crime have located the issues within an overt human rights framework (Silvestri and Crowther-Dowey, 2008). This is a useful approach for a number of reasons: it moves away from individualistic approaches and places crime issues firmly within a broad social framework; it allows for a global approach, as human rights are, by definition, universal; it decentres the issue of gender by focusing on rights for both men and women; and it does not confine itself to issues conventionally defined as 'crime', but looks more broadly at social harm and denial of basic rights. For example, the issue of domestic violence, which is intimately bound up with gender issues, can be understood in terms of the fundamental human rights to freedom, equality and dignity. Domestic violence is not then a matter of simple 'assault', but is bound up with issues of control, denial of identity and attacks on human dignity. A human rights approach may be far more productive in terms of the development of a holistic sociological approach to issues of crime – one that seeks solutions to the problems of crime not in individuals, but in the social structures and processes that shape rule-breaking across our society.

WHITE-COLLAR CRIME

Most sociological research takes for granted that crime is connected with poverty, disadvantage or powerlessness. Some of the more interesting sociological theories of crime, such as Merton's reworking of Durkheim's anomie theory, provide us with convincing accounts of why criminals are drawn overwhelmingly from the most deprived groups in society. But sociologists of deviance have raised a number of questions about this presumed connection. Labelling theorists ask whether the poorest in society are the most prone to breaking the law or whether they are the most prone to being caught, identified and publicly labelled as law-breakers. Marxists ask how we should understand the law in capitalist society: does it extend equal rights to all or is it partisan and biased, primarily concerned to protect the interests of the powerful? Perhaps we should ask not 'who commits most crime?', but 'who causes most social harm?' We may then find that much severely harmful behaviour is not defined as crime or, if so defined, that offenders are not subjected to criminal charges, proceedings or punishment. The behaviour that is most likely to escape the criminal justice system is what we have come to term 'white-collar crime'.

The recent and ongoing financial crisis in Ireland has drawn a lot of attention to this field. There have been consistent calls in the media and amongst the public for bankers, developers and other persons and institutions implicated in our financial problems to be prosecuted by the law. Comparisons are often made with other jurisdictions, especially the US, where high-profile 'white-collar criminals' such as the investment fraudster Bernard Madoff have been prosecuted and sentenced to extensive terms of imprisonment.

The study of 'white-collar crime' in sociology commenced with the work of American criminologist Edwin Sutherland, who coined the term in 1939 (Strader, 2002, p. 1). For Sutherland, white-collar crime was held to refer to 'a crime committed by a person of respectability and high social status in the course of his occupation' in order to make a profit for or otherwise benefit his company or employer. Sutherland was seeking to draw attention to the fact, socially unpalatable to many, that the practice of crime is distributed across society, rather than being confined to a low-status 'criminal' class. As Strader (2002) points out, the term has strayed beyond Sutherland's original conception and has come to be very broadly applied.

The term 'white-collar crime' now embraces many types of activity and is hard to clearly define. To a large extent it is defined as the opposite of publicly visible 'street' crime (Strader, 2002, p. 1). Maguire (2010), drawing on the work of Croall (2001), lists a number of types of white-collar crime. These include theft at work, fraud, employment offences, environmental crimes and state-corporate crime. Each of these areas can be further detailed. For example, fraud can include social welfare fraud, insider dealing in shares, bank fraud or the operation of price-fixing cartels. All of these have been witnessed and prosecuted in Ireland in recent years. There is an increasing recognition that such crimes 'undoubtedly cause serious harm' in society, perhaps more than 'street crime' (DJLR, 2010, p. 4).

Some forms of white-collar crime are carried out by individuals who gain the opportunity as a result of their occupation and are thus termed 'occupational crime'. An accountant in a firm may be in a good position to 'cook the books' and to embezzle money. A farmer may move animals around from farm to farm and claim additional subsidy payments. A call centre worker might sell confidential customer information to a competitor. As Maguire (2010, p. 175) points out, 'these types of crime accord with the general perception of crime, and differ only in the context in which they occur – theft and fraud are essentially the same animal in different forms'. Differences also occur, as we see below, in how the state responds to the same 'crime' in different contexts.

Another form of occupational crime is that committed to further the goals of an employer, often called 'corporate crime'. Examples might include price-fixing, illegal insider share dealing, evasion of health and safety regulations or breaches of food safety legislation. In some cases, it can be difficult to differentiate between criminal activity and 'normal business practice', especially in an era of what has been called 'light touch regulation' where a broad variety of formerly sanctioned business practices have been legitimised.

A further form of corporate crime is that carried out by state bodies. Globally, the failings of NASA (National Aeronautics and Space Administration) in relation to the 1986 *Challenger* space shuttle disaster represent a classic case of such 'state-corporate crime' – in this case, negligence. In Ireland, important cases relate to the health field, for example the hepatitis C scandal whereby over 1,000 Irish women suffered ill-health as a consequence of being administered contaminated blood products in the late 1970s. Again, professional and administrative negligence by public bodies was the central issue (O'Carroll, 1998; DoH, 1999). There has also been increasing concern about corruption within Irish state bodies, for example in the planning arena (Smith, 2010).

Finally, the rise of the Internet to a central role in global commerce and culture has brought a new range of criminal activities, some of which may also be defined as white-collar crime. These have been termed 'cybercrimes' and have become part of the global and Irish crime landscape (O'Connor and Gladyshev, 2006). Some of these are 'traditional' crimes of fraud, hate speech or identity theft that are facilitated by global electronic communications. Others are unique to the Internet environment, such as hacking, 'denial of service' attacks on company servers or the malicious spreading of computer viruses (DJLR, 2010, p. 32). Such crimes can be very difficult to combat, as they involve cutting-edge technologies and are often committed across state borders and in an environment (the Internet) that has no centrally controlling body.

McCullagh (1996, p. 60) suggests two reasons why sociologists should be particularly interested in white-collar crimes. First, they are primarily 'crimes of the middle class', not usually committed by people in disadvantaged or socially excluded situations. Second, they are crimes that have, until recently, been marginal to public consciousness: our perception of the 'criminal' has not embraced the 'respectable' businessperson engaged in fraud, negligence or misleading practices. Societal response to harmful or criminal behaviour varies greatly, so while certain types of illegal activities receive great public attention and disapprobation, others are hardly noticed. Similarly, sociologists and criminologists have paid less attention to white-collar crime in Ireland than to 'street crime', and official bodies such as the Garda Síochána and the CSO have been less likely to generate statistical data in this area – as we have seen, they are ignored in Irish crime victimisation surveys.

As previously noted, public consciousness of white-collar and corporate crime has expanded greatly since the global financial crisis of the last few years. It has been increasingly realised that 'criminal activity can occur in boardrooms as well as back alleys, and the same caution and judgment should be employed in both situations' (Maguire, 2010, p. 187). This shift does not necessarily reflect any increase in the incidence of such crimes; rather, it reflects a greater political and administrative willingness to define, detect and pursue such activities. There has been a political shift away from 'light touch regulation' and as a consequence, activities that were previously tolerated, even encouraged, are now regulated or even criminalised.

In Ireland, an increased public consciousness of white-collar and corporate crime dates back at least to the findings of the so-called 'Beef Tribunal', set up in May 1991 to investigate malpractice by the Goodman Group of beef-processing companies. The tribunal found evidence of occupational crime: the group was found to have '[abused] public funds on a large scale' by 'systematically taking meat that it was deboning under contract for the EC [European Communities] intervention system, meat that belonged to the EC, and packing it for its own commercial contracts with, for instance, the Tesco supermarket chain in England' (O'Toole, 1995, p. 264). It also discovered evidence of corporate crime: the group '[contrived] to cheat the public of taxes' (O'Toole, 1995, p. 281). Notwithstanding these findings, no member of the group was convicted of any criminal offence. Indeed, the only person prosecuted was a journalist [later senator], Susan O'Keeffe, for refusing to reveal her sources. Since the late 1990s the public proceedings of further tribunals of inquiry, and of the Dáil's Public Accounts Committee, have reinforced public concern and anger over white-collar crime.

Other types of white-collar crime have also come to prominence in Ireland over the past two decades through a number of serious and high-profile cases. These include:

- State-corporate crimes such as the hepatitis C and other health-related scandals, including the illegal retention and sale of children's organs, post-mortem, by a number of Irish hospitals.
- Financial scandals including the facilitation of large-scale DIRT tax evasion by Irish banks and their staff in relation to the so-called 'bogus non-resident accounts'; the activities of Allied Irish Bank 'rogue trader' John Rusnak, who lost nearly $700 million through bank fraud; and systematic overcharging and bank-sponsored tax evasion by National Irish Bank, revealed by RTÉ journalists Charlie Bird and George Lee in the late 1990s.
- Corruption of the planning process by developers and politicians, especially in relation to the rezoning of land, as revealed in the Mahon Tribunal findings published in March 2012.
- Price-fixing by the members of the Citroën Dealers Association, whereby car dealers were organised in such a way as to increase the costs of their products, in breach of competition law.
- A multi-million-euro 'carousel' VAT fraud across Ireland and the UK involving Irish-made computer chips.
- The long-running 'insider trading' court case involving Irish companies Fyffes and DCC.

In all cases, the process of prosecution or enquiry was long and complex; evidence was often drawn from internal 'whistleblowers' and the individuals, organisations and companies at fault generally did all in their power to prevent the truth from emerging.

Despite the emergent profile of the white-collar variety, crime continues to be routinely portrayed in the popular media, and even in much academic discussion, as intimately connected with, and explained in terms of, experiences of poverty, disadvantage and social marginalisation. Why is this? McCullagh identifies three processes that operate to emphasise working-class crime and conceal or play down middle-class crime. First is the process of law-making. How laws are made has the effect of sanctioning some kinds of harmful behaviour while ignoring others. For McCullagh (1995, p. 412), 'in Ireland the law has been written in such a way that the anti-social behaviour of those in business, corporate and commercial positions is inadequately regulated, or where it is regulated, it is generally not done so through the criminal law'. A government White Paper on corporate crime reveals (DJLR, 2010, p. 48) how many such cases are, for legislative reasons, pursued through 'administrative' processes rather than through the criminal courts.

The second process is that of law enforcement. Even where white-collar crimes are defined in law as crimes, enforcement tends to be selective and considerably less energetic than in the case of 'street' crimes. Maguire (2010, p. 179) identifies a 'reluctance to prosecute' white-collar crimes, 'attributed to the notion of what a crime is, and the specific requirements that have developed in relation to a crime'. Speaking in the High Court in 2011, Justice Peter Kelly was highly critical of the failure to effectively prosecute the suspects in white-collar crimes, noting that despite '*prima facie* evidence of criminal wrongdoing ... no prosecutions have ensued and little appears to have been done'. There was 'an apparent failure to investigate thoroughly yet efficiently and expeditiously possible criminal wrongdoing in the commercial and corporate sectors [and this] does nothing to instil confidence in the criminal justice system as applicable to that sector' ('Judge criticises Anglo investigation', *Irish Times*, 11 May 2011). Much of the public concern about white-collar crime relates to the slowness of the legal process when it comes to such infractions.

The third process is the workings of the court system. Research into the decision-making processes of Irish courts suggests that white-collar criminals, even in crimes aimed at personal benefit, such as embezzlement, are relatively unlikely to be convicted. If they are convicted, they are less likely to receive a prison sentence, or to have to serve it, than working-class 'professional' criminals are (McCullagh, 2006, p. 76). For example, despite a greater emphasis on identifying and pursuing tax evaders in recent years, in the period 2000 to 2010, only seven prison sentences for 'serious tax evasion' have been handed down (DJLR, 2010, p. 53) – this at a time when the rate of imprisonment and the prison population have increased substantially for other criminal activities. Similarly, as of July 2010, not one person prosecuted over the previous decade by the Office of the Director of Corporate Enforcement (the body that investigates entities such as banks, property developers and other companies) had been imprisoned ('Not one white-collar criminal ever jailed, admits watchdog', *Irish Independent*, 5 July 2010). Ten members of the Citroën Dealers Association, who were prosecuted in Ireland's biggest 'cartel' case related to price-fixing, received suspended prison sentences of up to nine months and fines up to €80,000 (DJLR, 2010, p. 52).

It would not be valid to label the differential treatment of 'street' and 'white-collar' crime as just a deliberate strategy or conspiracy to protect the powerful. There are complex social factors that shape the definition of white-collar crimes and how the state and the public respond to them. At the macrosocial level, the rise of the global financial industry has contributed significantly to the opportunity to commit such crimes, partly by making new sorts of crime (such as some of those related to share trading) possible, and also as a consequence of how the power of the global industry has impacted on the ability or willingness of governments – in the face of increasingly mobile investment capital – to effectively regulate the financial sector. This has had a major impact on Ireland, which has been a significant participant in the sector since the establishment of the International Financial Services Centre (IFSC) in 1987 (Maguire, 2010, p. 185). Similarly, the emergence of 'crimes' in the areas of the environment or food safety are at least partly the consequence of the development of relevant international regulatory bodies (especially at the EU level) that have helped to define and detect such crimes.

White-collar crimes can be difficult to detect. In many cases (such as certain types of 'regulatory crime'), victims may not even be aware that a crime has been committed or there may be no apparent 'victim'. It may also be difficult to identify intent, as the crime may result from a general failure of organisation or a sloppy approach to maintenance of standards – it is exactly because no one has acted responsibly that it is hard to find an individual person responsible for any breach of regulations. White-collar crimes may be relatively easy to hide, especially if computer technology is involved, and are often conducted alone and in private locations, where they are less likely to be observed by others. Put bluntly, we are far more likely to find a CCTV camera outside a nightclub than in the boardroom of a global corporation.

White-collar crimes are far more likely than 'street crimes' to be dealt with using administrative machinery (DJLR, 2010, p. 48). This may be because the financial penalties (such as fines) can be higher; also, there may be penalties, such as the loss of a license to operate, or reputational damage that can have a far greater impact on an individual or company than the imposition of fines or a period of imprisonment. It may also be argued that it is more constructive, from a social point of view, to impose different types of penalties on white-collar criminals, such as restitution for victims or restriction on the ability of the criminal to perpetrate further crimes by removing them from a position of power or influence.

Since being placed on the sociological and criminological map by Sutherland, white-collar crime has remained an interesting and challenging phenomenon for sociologists. It challenges common-sense, media and politics-led notions of what constitutes 'crime'. It also points to the close similarities between crime and 'business as usual', reinforcing our understanding of 'crime' as a socially constructed and highly contextualised entity. To date, apart from the pioneering work of

McCullagh, Irish sociologists have paid scant attention to white-collar crime, leaving the field largely free to journalists. As Ireland increasingly moves towards a knowledge and information-based economy, where the manipulation of financial data and intellectual property becomes ever more central, it is likely that white-collar crime will increase in significance, as will the sociological study of it.

Part III

Cultural Forms and Trajectories

11
Irish Identities

Global laughs
An Irish-born relative of one of the authors has been living outside the beltway in Washington, DC for more than 20 years. Recently, he emailed family members in Ireland a link to a YouTube site. The video clip features the UK-based group Fascinating Aida – three women comedians, two English and one Irish – performing in front of an Irish-American audience. They sing 'Cheap Flights', a parody of the traditional, heartrending Irish lament. The subject matter is thoroughly modern: the ordeal of a Ryanair flight from London Stansted to Tralee.

In directing us to the clip, this Irish emigrant is making clear his continuing transnational link with Ireland. He is expressing his 'knowingness' about what we in Ireland are likely to laugh at; he is demonstrating that he shares the national sense of humour. He is reaffirming his family ties that have remained steadfast over time despite decades spent out of the country. A comforting sense of local belonging is implied in this virtual exchange. Ryanair has a global presence, so the parody would be enjoyed by anyone who has ever travelled on the low-cost airline (or any low-cost airline, for that matter). But of course, it helps if you are Irish!

Each of us lives with a variety of potentially contradictory identities and which of them we focus on depends on many factors. At the centre are the values we share or wish to share with others. Identity is not simply imposed. It is chosen and actively used, though in specific social contexts and under particular constraints. Collective identities are not things we are born with, but are formed and transformed in our circuits of social relations and in the symbolic ways we choose to represent ourselves. Witness how *Riverdance* became the globally recognised shorthand for all things to do with Irishness and dance in the mid-1990s. Similarly, the vuvuzela entered the global lexicon after the soccer World Cup 2010, where it became synonymous with South African football fans.

We know what it is to be Irish because of how Irishness has come to be represented as a set of meanings within a national, and indeed a diasporic, culture.

A nation or a diasporic community is not only a political entity, but also a producer of meanings and a conduit for systems of cultural representation. A nation is a symbolic community, which accounts for its power to generate a sense of identity and allegiance. So how is the modern Irish nation imagined? What strategies do we use to construct our common-sense views of national belonging or identity? How has our understanding of nation and belonging changed in the recent past in response to the diversification of our population through immigration? How have our understandings of the nation evolved through the period of the Celtic Tiger and beyond into the period of economic crisis? Who are the primary custodians of our notions of Irishness and Irish identity?

Collective identities rely on memories of a common (and sometimes mythologised) past. They are also shaped by the processes we associate with modernity: intensified mobility, extensive use of technology and the attendant flexibilities and reflexivities that flow from those processes. In this chapter, we seek to address some of these issues. We begin by focusing on one of the defining features of Irish identity – Ireland's profile as an emigrant country. We note how that profile dramatically changed at the beginning of the 21st century and the attendant impact on identity, and in particular on transnational identities. We go on to explore aspects of identity in Ireland as viewed through media, youth, gender, racial and ethnic perspectives.

MOBILE IRELAND: FROM EMIGRATION TO IMMIGRATION TO EMIGRATION

Irish society has historically been concerned with emigration and the demographic and economic effects of the long-term haemorrhage of people from the country. Ryan (1990, p. 45) has argued that 'emigration is at the centre of the Irish experience of modernity'. It has been part of the process by which Ireland has been able to move from being a predominantly rural-based, agrarian society to an industrial state. Emigration has been closely related to other population patterns; indeed, it is inseparable from them. The forces that have led so many people to leave the country are derived from how families and communities have translated economic opportunities, property relations and religious and social attitudes into individual behaviour. The limits of economic opportunity available to (mainly) young people have led them to make decisions that have been shaped by the experiences of those that have gone before them. Others have felt compelled to escape the dominant frameworks of attitudes and behaviour that have governed religious, moral and social behaviour. The structures of families, the links that families have to property and opportunity and the patterns of birth and marriage have all fed into people's decisions about where they can and should live.

Over 60 years ago, Geary (1951, p. 400) pointed out that 'of no country in the world is it more true to say that the political and economic boundaries do not coincide'. It is true that for much of its history – and to the present day – many Irish-born people have chosen or have been forced to live outside the geographical confines of the island. Irish independence did not bring an end to emigration, as had been hoped. Indeed, after the effects of the Great Depression and the Second World War had passed, the stream of people leaving the country returned to 19th-century levels. The population continued to decline until 1961, apart from a small increase in the post-war years of 1946 to 1951. This decline can be clearly related to the failure of the country to economically develop in such as way as to provide a livelihood for its inhabitants. Not enough jobs were created in the non-agricultural sectors to compensate for the significant decline in agricultural jobs between 1926 and 1961.

Levels of emigration in the 1950s approached those of the 1880s: the net outward migration flow increased from a level of 16,600 per year in the period 1926 to 1936 to 42,400 per year in the 1950s (Drudy, 1995, p. 75). Remarkably, more than half of those who left school in the early 1950s had emigrated by 1961 (Guinnane, 1997, p. 279). For Hazelkorn (1991, p. 125), such people were 'reacting rationally to severe economic decline and labour surplus at home as well as widening differentials in welfare payments' between Ireland and Britain. While emigration continued in independent Ireland, there was a marked change in the destination of emigrants. From the mid-1930s, Britain became the main destination as opposed to the United States, partly following a tightening of entry regulations there. It is estimated that in the period 1890 to 1990, over 2 million Irish people emigrated to Britain, two-thirds of whom stayed (Ryan, 1990, p. 46). In the 1960s there were over 1 million Irish-born people there, making the Irish the largest ethnic minority group in Britain. The immigration of large numbers of Irish provided Britain with a convenient labour pool, thus reducing its dependence on workers from ex-colonies or the developing world. Those who emigrated from Ireland were largely unskilled, often from rural backgrounds. There were also a small but significant number of skilled professionals, for example doctors and engineers, who could not secure employment in Ireland and constituted a 'brain drain' (Hazelkorn, 1991, p. 128).

During the 1970s, Ireland experienced a net inflow of migrants, largely as a result of returners taking advantage of new job opportunities arising from the increased level of foreign direct investment in the country. Such opportunities contracted as Ireland entered the 1980s and an increased emigration flow once more reflected the parlous state of the Irish economy. The contraction in employment in indigenous manufacturing industries such as textiles and engineering and the inability to convert new investment into jobs saw emigration and unemployment spiral. The rate of unemployment reached 17 per cent (230,000) in 1993 (Drudy, 1995, p. 75). The outward flow of emigrants remained at between 33,000 to 35,000 per annum between 1991 and 1996, with two-thirds of the outflow aged between 15 and 24 years. Unemployment and poor economic conditions at home were significant 'push' factors in emigration, while 'pull' factors related to the strength of host country economies and the nature of their regulation of immigration. The increasing rate of in-migration from the mid-1990s onwards reduced the net migration flow substantially.

For Hazelkorn, the emigration flow accorded with the globalisation of the Irish economy. She suggests (1991, p. 131) that 'Irish governments facilitated emigration as a means of alleviating social and political tension, a possible means of providing additional skills and experience, and as a source of income through remittances and tourism'. As the nature of economic activity has changed – from labour intensive to capital intensive to knowledge intensive – so the demand for labour has changed. The development of 'global cities' as powerhouses of economic activity (such as London, an increasingly important emigrant destination) has also helped to shape the decisions of intending migrants (Lash and Urry, 1994; Skeldon, 1997, p. 187).

Changes in the nature of labour demand means that emigrants nowadays tend to be more skilled than previously. According to Hanlon (1991, p. 53), who has studied the emigration of Irish accountants, the 'upwardly mobile middle class were the most likely emigrants'. A National Economic and Social Council (NESC) report of 1991 showed that a third of emigrants in the 1980s and 1990s were already employed full time prior to departure. Hazelkorn (1992, p. 128) similarly argues that compared with those of the 1950s, more recent emigrants tend to be better educated, more urban, increasingly male and 'predominantly young, single and mobile'. A large proportion of graduates from the third-level education sector emigrated during the 1980s – up to two-thirds from some courses. Many subsequently returned during the 1990s.

At the turn of the 21st century, Ireland's population profile began to change dramatically. First, a pattern of return migration was established by the mid-1990s, with many Irish emigrants choosing to return home to a growing economy. Second, after 2000 there was a dramatic rise in immigration, accelerating after the accession of new countries to the EU on 1 May 2004. Between May 2004 and May 2006, for instance, 230,000 workers from Poland, Latvia and Lithuania arrived in the state and sought personal PPS numbers in order to be able to take up employment here (*Irish Times*, 25 November 2006). The number of immigrants from the EU12 (accession countries) remained strong in 2007 and 2008. As a result, by 2008 immigrants were estimated to make up 12 per cent of the labour force (McDonald, 2008).

The effect of the economic downturn from 2008 was dramatic. The numbers of immigrants from the accession countries plummeted from a high of more than 50,000 in 2007 to 9,000 in 2011. Indeed, considerably more people from the accession countries (15,000) left Ireland in that year (CSO, 2011d). At the same time, emigration began to creep inexorably upward. Net immigration peaked in 2006 at 71,000, but by the year ending April 2011, Ireland was recording net emigration flows of 34,000 – a figure redolent of the annual outward net migration flow in the 1980s. Furthermore, 2011 marked a sharp increase in the emigration of Irish nationals. Irish nationals were by far the largest constituent group among emigrants (almost 53 per cent) in the period to April 2011, followed by accession country nationals, who accounted for just a fifth of the emigrant population.

Table 11.1: Annual population change, 1987–2011

Components of population change (000)							
Year ending April	Births	Deaths	Natural increase	Immigrants	Emigrants	Net migration	Population change
1987	61.2	32.2	29.0	17.2	40.2	−23.0	5.9
1988	57.8	31.6	26.2	19.2	61.1	−41.9	−15.8
1989	53.6	31.0	22.6	26.7	70.6	−43.9	−21.2
1990	51.9	32.8	19.1	33.3	56.3	−22.9	−3.7
1991	53.1	31.1	22.0	33.3	35.3	−2.0	19.9
1992	52.8	31.4	21.4	40.7	33.4	7.4	28.8
1993	50.4	30.4	20.0	34.7	35.1	−0.4	19.6
1994	49.1	32.6	16.6	30.1	34.8	−4.7	11.8
1995	48.4	31.2	17.2	31.2	33.1	−1.9	15.4
1996	48.8	32.0	16.7	39.2	31.2	8.0	24.8
1997	50.7	31.7	19.0	44.5	25.3	19.2	38.2
1998	52.7	31.2	21.5	46.0	28.6	17.4	38.8
1999	53.7	32.4	21.2	48.9	31.5	17.3	38.5
2000	54.0	32.1	21.8	52.6	26.6	26.0	47.9
2001	55.1	30.2	24.8	59.0	26.2	32.8	57.7
2002	58.1	29.3	28.8	66.9	25.6	41.3	70.0
2003	60.8	28.9	31.9	60.0	29.3	30.7	62.6
2004	62.0	28.6	33.3	58.5	26.5	32.0	65.3
2005	61.4	27.9	33.5	84.6	29.4	55.1	88.6
2006	61.2	27.0	34.2	107.8	36.0	71.8	106.0
2007*	65.8	27.0	38.8	109.5	42.2	67.3	106.1
2008*	72.3	27.7	44.6	83.8	45.3	38.5	83.1
2009*	74.5	29.4	45.1	57.3	65.1	−7.8	37.3
2010*	74.1	28.2	45.9	30.8	65.3	−34.5	11.4
2011*	75.1	27.4	47.7	42.3	76.4	−34.1	13.6

*Preliminary.

Source: CSO, 2011c, p. 2.

It is clear that the recent period of Irish history has coincided with a particularly volatile pattern of migratory movements. Over a relatively short period of time, Ireland moved from a situation of net emigration to net immigration to net emigration again. According to Eurostat, Ireland now has the highest emigration rate in the European Union (*Irish Times*, 8 January 2011). The key countries that now attract Irish migrant labour are the UK, Canada, Australia and New Zealand. The latter two are actively seeking construction workers to contribute to major infrastructural projects in the aftermath of environmental disasters such as earthquakes and flooding. In the US, 2012 saw attempts to bring in a programme that would allow up to 10,000 Irish workers annually to obtain American work visas through a bill sponsored by Senator Charles Schumer. Fifteen years later, this recalls the Morrison and Donnelly visa lottery programmes of the 1990s, which also focused on Irish-American immigration (*Irish Times*, 14 December 2011).

What this short résumé of Ireland's migration history demonstrates is how deeply Ireland is implicated in global economic flows not only of capital, but also of labour. It is noteworthy that the labour tends to be differentiated between those migrants who are educated, skilled and equipped with cultural capital and those who are largely unskilled and whose choices are far more circumscribed. Corcoran (2002) suggests a model (see Table 11.2) for interpreting the impact of class differences on emigration. Highly educated emigrants – the professional or transnational elite – tend to be individualist and enjoy a considerable degree of personal agency in terms of their life plans and career choices. In contrast, the more traditional 'reserve army' of Irish emigrants, whose role is to fill the gaps in the secondary labour market of global cities, are much more constrained. Their decision-making is frequently contingent and inadequately thought through. They gravitate towards their ethnic group, where informal networks facilitate their entry into the labour market. They may be subject to a variety of constraints that range from prejudice and discrimination to the vagaries of the host country system of immigrant regulation, a particular problem for undocumented immigrants in the US.

Table 11.2: Emigrant typology

Process of migration	'Reserve army' emigrants	Professional elite
Decision-making	Contingent	Reflexive
Context	Ethnicisation	Self-actualisation migrant
Migratory persona	Situational ethnicity	Flexible subjectivity
Migratory experience	Structural constraint	Personal agency

Source: Corcoran, 2002, p. 188.

'Reserve army' emigrants make decisions that are primarily determined by the prevailing economic conditions. Furthermore, they are likely to be constrained in terms of opportunity structures because of low or non-transferable skills. Their professional counterparts make decisions that tend to be reflexive or based on an ongoing and self-conscious evaluation of personal and professional goals. The context of reception in the host country is also different for each group. The 'reserve army' emigrants tend to be absorbed quickly into the Irish ethnic niches in the labour market. Furthermore, they tend to live in the same neighbourhoods and congregate in the same bars. In contrast, the professionals tend to reject both symbolic and substantive ethnicity, preferring to make their way as individuals without unduly advertising their Irishness, particularly in the workplace. While the 'reserve army' emigrants find that to survive in the host country they must often develop an ethnic persona in a variety of strategic situations, the professional elite are busy deploying their flexible subjectivities across a range of work and leisure arenas. Finally, Corcoran argues that the experiences of the 'reserve army' emigrants most closely mirror those of previous generations of Irish emigrants (and eastern European immigrants in Ireland today), bounded as they are by structural constraints in the form of economic and social conditions as well as legal barriers. The Irish professional elite, in contrast, embody many of the attributes associated with modern individualisation.

TRANSNATIONALISM, MIGRATION AND IDENTITY

Whether we are thinking about the experience of the Irish abroad or new immigrants in Ireland, transnational practices create markers of identity and a means of identity formation. Transnational practices are both particulaiistic (in terms of their expression in time and place) and universalistic (in terms of their content and scope). For centuries, the Irish have been defined by their propensity to emigrate. Declan Kiberd once observed that the Irish understood and internalised the process of globalisation before the term was coined because of their history of diasporic diffusion throughout the 18th and 19th centuries. By the turn of the 21st century, the process of globalisation that had previously underscored migratory flows out of Ireland was enabling migratory flows into the country. Global migration chains now link Ireland with many more places around the world. Since 1990, people from more than 150 countries have settled in Ireland, bringing with them a new range of religions, cultures and experiences. The nation now encompasses almost 170 languages, from Acholi to Zulu. The presence of these new immigrants is felt in schools, churches, corner shops and community centres throughout the country.

If we use a transnational lens to focus on aspects of identity as expressed in national and diasporic spaces, we can see significant overlaps between the experiences of present day immigrants in Ireland, present day Irish emigrants and earlier generations of Irish emigrants. The central argument of transnational theorists is that in our globalised world it is increasingly the case that 'social life takes place across borders, even as the salience of nation-state boundaries remains strong' (Levitt and Jaworsky, 2007, p. 129). The new transnational studies span a range of disciplines that includes history, geography and sociology. It seeks to emphasise the dynamics of how people can live in one setting or country while maintaining strong emotional, economic and political ties with another. Indeed, scholars 'now recognise that many contemporary migrants and their predecessors maintained a variety of ties to their home countries while they became incorporated into the countries where they settled' (Levitt and Jaworsky, 2007, p. 120).

Transnational theory moves us beyond earlier assimilation models that advocated the incorporation of immigrants fully into the host society, even if that meant that ethnic, national and linguistic identities were lost. Transnationalism recognises that identity politics have become important to people's self-definition and that migrants operate across diverse social spaces. To understand global exchange processes (of capital, commodities or people), one has to understand relations *between* states or *across* borders. A transnational approach sees the migrant not as an outsider or marginal figure that belongs in neither the host society nor the society of origin; rather, the migrant is viewed as embodying the dual reality of being simultaneously part of both, in the process helping to shape and inform both contexts.

Contemporary Irish drama: Universalising the migrant experience

A kind of migratory 'memory trace' was at the heart of Arambe Productions' version of the Jimmy Murphy play, *Kings of the Kilburn High Road*, which premiered in Dublin in 2006. Murphy's play focuses on the lost dreams of a group of young men who left Ireland in the 1970s in the hope of making their fortunes and returning home. They meet to bid farewell to one of the group who is finally going home to Ireland – in a coffin – and spend the night musing on their memories, what has been lost and their essential placelessness in the new Ireland. Arambe Productions cast the play with African actors in order to illustrate the universality of the 'dislocated' migratory experience.

Just as Irish people left Ireland for a better way of life in Britain and the US in the past, eastern Europeans and Africans came to Ireland for much the same reason in the first decade of the 21st century. The preoccupations of the Irish men in the flat in Kilburn may be much the same as the preoccupations of the 'new immigrant communities' in Ireland today: 'the ordeal of the forgotten Irish in Britain was no less harrowing for being a reminder that it could just as easily be the plight of Africans in modern Ireland. Through casting alone the production functioned as a two-way mirror, allowing Irish and immigrant cultures to see each other through the same darkened glass' (Gibbons, 2007).

Subsequently, Arambe transposed J.M. Synge's 1907 play, *The Playboy of the Western World*, to a pub in the suburbs of West Dublin, casting the playboy as a Nigerian refugee. According to Gibbons, whereas the original drama hinged on the relationship between individual and community, the new version turns on the interaction between two communities. It is at this interface – between new immigrant community and host society, between one immigrant community and another – that identity is shaped, created, reproduced and represented.

TRANSNATIONAL PRACTICES: CIRCULATION OF PEOPLE AND CAPITAL

While transnationalism is considered a 'new' theoretical strand in migration studies, there is a rich history of transnational orientations and practices among the world's migrant populations. Levitt and Jaworsky point out that in the industrial and progressive era (1890s to 1920s), many US immigrants viewed themselves as sojourners and up to 40 per cent eventually returned home. When Irish emigrants to the US got the opportunity to return to Ireland in the 1990s, they did so. In Ireland, the 2011 census records that many eastern European migrants who came to Ireland in the last decade have already returned home.

Migrants have always saved money and remitted it to the home country in order to sustain the economy. Traditionally, emigrant remittances are used to support family members who stay behind, to fund small and large businesses, public works, social services and philanthropic exercises (Levitt and Jaworsky, 2007, p. 134). In the Irish case, it is well known that emigrant remittances played a vital role in sustaining the economy of the fledgling Irish state in the 20th century (Commission on Emigration and Other Population Problems, 1950, p. 140). In contemporary Ireland, these flows now work in the opposite direction. For example, Gort, Co. Galway, has played host to a significant Brazilian community since 1999 (McGrath, 2008). An Irish journalist who visited the hometown of many of these immigrants in Vila Fabril, Brazil, was struck by the connectedness between both places. He found that 'Gort was talked about as if it were a neighbouring townland and the trappings of Irish money could hardly stand out more'. Home renovations and makeovers were dependent on money remitted to Vila Fabril from Gort. One such home that had benefited from emigrant remittances was painted in the colours of the Irish flag (McCormac, 2007).

Two successive Global Irish Economic Fora convened in September 2009 and October 2011 in Dublin sought to draw on the Irish abroad as a transnational resource to help address some of the issues associated with the domestic economic crisis. The aim of these fora is to reconnect the diaspora with the home country in a very specific way by fomenting networks of high achievers in international business, the cultural or sporting worlds to assist in the promotion of Ireland. Kitchin et al. (2012) observe that the diaspora can act as a resource to a government that seeks to harness the expertise and experiences of those individuals who can enhance the reputation of the home country as a destination for investment, business start-ups and tourists. In the past, the Irish government has actively cultivated the transnational flow of investment: the current strategy is to exploit Irish identity as a means of enhancing that flow. The high-profile state visits by President Obama and Queen Elizabeth in 2011 are cases in point.

IDENTIFICATION WITH HOME

Emigrants are often talked about in the media as constituting a 'lost generation'. This harks back to the historical notion of emigrants as exiles and of emigration as a permanent dislocation. This emotive sobriquet has been applied most recently to those leaving as a result of the economic crisis that engulfed the country after 2008, though its contemporary appropriateness is questionable. Grabowska (2005) has described Polish workers in Dublin as exhibiting a 'backwards toward home' orientation. Similarly, undocumented Irish emigrants in the US of the 1980s retained strong ties with the country of origin. This was in part a consequence of their exclusion from the mainstream economic, social and political institutions of the host society. Like the eastern European, African and Filipina immigrants in Ireland today, they employed traditional symbols, norms and ideologies to enhance their own cohesion and distinctiveness and to assist them in maintaining the consciousness of their common interest and identity. They saw themselves primarily as transients, more oriented toward Ireland than either the established American-Irish ethnic community or the host society. For the Irish in New York, identification with home was maintained through high levels of media consumption. National and local papers were imported and sold widely in the new Irish community. Tapes of sports events and Irish current affairs TV programmes were regularly screened in the Irish bars, and for special events, live transmissions by satellite were arranged. The Irish bar – as a site for congregation, financial transactions, social networking, leisure, workplace – was at the heart of their transnational culture. Telephone charges at that time were relatively low and most immigrants phoned home on a regular basis. This communications network enabled the immigrant Irish community to continue to identify instantaneously with national and international events and issues from a distance. In short, the psychological distance from home was minimised by the range of mass media largely available to them through the neighbourhood bars.

Fast forward to the present day – the era of smartphones, Twitter, Skype, social networking and what Castells (2007) has called 'mass self-communication'. There is no doubt that the communications revolution of our time has profoundly altered the subjective experience of migration. Each new technological innovation further compresses time and space and enables transnationalism. This was already identified by the mid-1990s and the process has intensified since then. An *Irish Times* series on Irish emigration in 2011 reflected the impact that the Internet, Skype and social networks have on the lives of emigrants. Indeed, an editorial in the newspaper went so far as to suggest that 'the traditional roles played by the Irish pub and community centre in maintaining contacts and finding work have been supplemented, if not superseded, by modern communications' (*Irish Times*, 1 November 2011).

Anderson (1994) has asserted that legal documentation such as passports, immigrant visas, green cards and fake social security cards are less a testament of any given individual's allegiance to a particular nation state and more a claim for participation in a labour market. For Irish immigrants living in New York or eastern Europeans, Nigerians and Filipinas living in Ireland today, the host country may be their workplace, but home is still home. Despite the geographical distance from home, the psychological identification with Ireland and the international Irish community was (and is) readily maintained through the availability of the means of transnational communication. Indeed, in her study of contemporary Irish-born entrepreneurs in the US, Corrigan (2006) shows that Irish transnational connectivity is greatly enhanced by recent and emerging technological advancements. Cheap airfares and telecommunications, the availability of the Internet and new flexible work practices enable immigrants to engage with their homeland with greater frequency and intensity than ever before.

Chinese beauty pageants in Dublin

A sense of fixity is no longer of the essence in fomenting identity, and a sense of belonging need no longer be rooted to a particular place. Increasingly, identities can be chosen or rejected. They can be customised to serve the interests of the individual as he or she sees fit. A variety of resources can be drawn upon to help construct and perfect these identities. This is what Rebecca King-O'Riain found when she attended a Chinese beauty pageant in Dublin.

King-O'Riain (2006) sees the pageant as an exercise in identity construction occurring at the interface between the Chinese immigrant community and wider Irish society. Chinese immigrants use this vehicle of collective identification to simultaneously express their claim to belonging in Ireland. This claim is made within the field of popular culture, King O'Riain suggests, 'because the project of multiculturalism in both the Irish state and civil society has been relatively weak'. In the course of the pageant, diverse Chinese cultural identities are subsumed into a master identity of 'the Chinese in Ireland'. The production of a Miss China Ireland generates a culturally hybrid notion of what is understood as 'Chinese' that incorporates elements of global culture and Irish culture.

King O'Riain demonstrates how narratives of work, home and belonging among the Chinese in Dublin mirror the narratives of other diasporic groups, including those of the Irish abroad. As she notes, 'the production and reproduction of such universalising narratives in the pageant resonate with the diasporic history of Irish people and may help to encourage a point of intersection between Irish and Chinese cultures'.

STATE BUILDING AND IDENTITY POLITICS

Migrants have historically engaged in processes of nation-building and identity politics that have influenced many countries, including Ireland. The involvement of Irish-Americans in a range of transnational political activities, particularly since the second half of the 19th century, is well documented (Hanagan, 1998; Finnegan,

2002). When Éamon de Valera wanted to start a newspaper in Ireland in the 1930s as an instrument of the Fianna Fáil party, it was to the US that he travelled in order to secure the necessary investment – mainly garnered from ordinary Irish-Americans who became shareholders in the *Irish Press* company (O'Brien, 2001).

Political transnationalism is generally given expression through electoral participation, membership of political parties or campaigns, nation-building and advocacy. Currently, Irish emigrants do not have the right to vote in Irish elections. This has been a bone of contention amongst the diasporic Irish community for some time and has resulted in the establishment of an internationally based Votes for Emigrants Campaign. In contrast, Polish nationals living and working in Ireland are entitled to vote in Polish national elections. This resulted in the rather arresting sight of Polish presidential campaign posters adorning hoardings along Dublin's main thoroughfares in 2006. Polish emigrants were exhorted to exercise their franchise at the Polish embassy in Dublin. A year later, when a snap parliamentary election was called in Poland, around 21,000 Irish-based Poles registered to vote and queued to cast their ballots at the embassy in Dublin, in Cork and at the Irish-Polish Cultural Association in Limerick (*Irish Times*, 21 October 2007). Similarly, Americans living in Ireland may cast postal votes in the Democratic and Republican primary campaigns and in the American presidential election.

Though denied a formal voice in the politics of their country of origin, the Irish have been particularly successful at flexing their political muscles in the US. One of the most successful lobbying groups to emerge within the Irish-American community in recent years was the Irish Immigration Reform Movement (IIRM). Largely made up of undocumented emigrants, the lobbying group garnered support among key constituencies in the wider Irish-American community. In the 1990s, the IIRM was instrumental in bringing about the Donnelly and Morrison visa programmes that enabled thousands of undocumented Irish emigrants to regularise their status. The work of the IIRM is continued today through the Irish Lobby for Immigration Reform. Since its foundation in 2005, this organisation has lobbied for a legislative initiative that would allow for regularisation of those Irish who remain undocumented in the US and would extend more visas to prospective Irish immigrants.

IRISH CULTURAL HYBRIDITY

Transnationalism also challenges our understanding of the relationship between migration, the nation and culture. There is now a considerable literature on the literary, musical and artistic expressions of borderland identities. The mixing of cultural traits from the homeland and the host society creates the possibility of hybrid identities. In the Irish case, music has long been an intrinsic part of Irish culture and Irish emigrant culture. Indeed, Irish music itself is often seen as a hybrid of many different musical influences. Onkey (2005) develops a case study of this kind of hybridity focusing on the musical oeuvre of Van Morrison, who has had a successful international career spanning several decades. Onkey has argued that the profound and ambiguous impact of African-American music on Irish culture is embodied in this singer's life's work. Morrison's work provides evidence 'that the relationship between blackness and Irishness can be a modern, transatlantic and creative one that provides alternatives to fixed identity rather than one that re-inscribes colonial, racial stereotypes' (2005, p. 154).

Morrison is perceived here as a kind of troubadour version of globalisation, taking the global (soul music, diaspora experiences) and readapting and reworking it through his own locally grounded experience. He can draw on his lived experience of being a 'Paddy' in London in the 1960s and subsequent years spent in the US experimenting with black music. Onkey suggests that Morrison's facility with R&B music and his ability to seamlessly weave it with a quintessentially Irish musical style meant that for Irish-American audiences, 'Morrison could be a conduit, to an authentic, mysterious, ethnic Irishness' (p. 178). In essence, the singer has forged a musical version of transnationalism, so complex that we cannot disentangle the various cultural, social and ethnic filaments that weave together to produce his particular version of soul music. His work can be seen as a metaphor for migratory transnational practices.

RELIGION AND IDENTITY

Religion also constitutes a transnational domain for migrants. Scholars of civil society have demonstrated that religious networks, celebrations, rituals and organisations serve as an important way for individuals to build social capital (Levitt and Jaworsky, 2007, p. 141). This often takes place in a transnational context and helps migrants to be incorporated into the new society while remaining connected to their homelands. The role of Catholicism as an agent of social integration for Irish Catholic emigrants in the US has been well documented (Dolan, 2008), both historically and in a contemporary context. Religion similarly plays an important role for new immigrant groups in Ireland. Immigrant groups including the Chinese, Filipinos and migrants from central Europe have set up places of worship in the greater Dublin area. The large numbers of Catholic mass-goers from eastern Europe at St Audeon's church in Dublin's Liberties has reintroduced an overt religiosity into public space that had waned in recent years.

Ugba's (2007) study of the rise of Pentecostalism in Ireland reveals that for immigrants from Africa, religious affiliation is one of the first relationships that may be cultivated or reactivated once they have arrived in the country. In Ireland, many Africans have chosen to affiliate with African-led Pentecostal groups that resonate with their lived experience of Pentecostal practices. Members see the church as a place of refuge from the problems, hostilities and rejections they face in Irish society. For others, the church serves as a channel for identifying solutions to such problems. As was the case for Irish Catholics in 19th-century America and Roman Catholics of Irish origin in Scotland today, African immigrant membership of Pentecostal churches compensates for the lack of recognition or the diminished social status that they experience in the host society.

Irish identity has a fluidity of meaning both within the national and the diasporic culture. Since identity is socially constructed, it evolves and changes over time. Irishness has historically been defined through relations of transnationalism and continues to be so today, both within the diaspora and on the island of Ireland. Thinking about Irish identity as part of a transnational project allows us to move beyond narrow nationalistic and parochial understandings of Irishness. It creates a space in which we can begin to see the continuities (as well as discontinuities) across space and time. Finally, it enables us to see in the experiences of the present the memory traces of past migratory trajectories and the seeds of future ones. As suggested throughout this chapter, Ireland has long been recognised as part of a global economy and culture and this has been a central element of 'Irish identity'.

There has been an intensification of this discourse in recent years. From cultural theorists to media personalities, all have a view about how Irish identity has developed in the context of a wider integration into global society. In Ireland as elsewhere, the constitution of personal and social identity is a complex and highly dynamic process. It is suggested by many that in Ireland, key components of our identity can find their explanation in our colonial history, our history of emigration, the nature of our land(scape) and how we conceptualise others. It is further suggested that ideas about identity are translated into specific forms of social practice. In the remainder of this chapter we examine three instances of such understanding: in the media, among young people and in the context of intersecting gender and ethnic identities.

MEDIA AND IRISH IDENTITY

The media is a lens through which notions of identity are refracted. This is particularly the case in countries that have been colonised and which in a post-colonial context seek to create the 'imagined community' (Anderson, 1994) of the nation state. Kelly and Rolston (1995, p. 563) suggest that the Irish media have had to tread a fine line between seeking 'to represent the existing socio-cultural worlds' within Irish society and reproducing a particular version of cultural and national identity. They argue that the broadcasting media have been particularly successful in elaborating and developing a specific sense of Irish national identity without endangering social solidarity or losing touch with large sections of their listenership. But the elaboration has been 'within relatively narrow confines ... defined by class, gender and elite interests within Irish society and by the existing consensus which favours these groups' (1995, p. 576). Thus, the national broadcaster RTÉ reflects a picture of the Irish as a largely homogeneous people that live in family households; are largely uninterested in intellectual debate or in high culture; share interests in sport, current affairs and a limited range of 'traditional' and popular forms of music; and are fond of a chat. For Kelly and Rolston (1995, p. 570), 'the united phalanx of nation, state and church, reproduced on radio, did not encourage the development of alternative cultural practices or of a class-based cultural critique. On the contrary, the all-encompassing concept of nation functioned to hide class differences, as well as those based on gender.'

One example of this 'fixing of identity' around the notion of a shared national trope is the daily marking of the Angelus on RTÉ Radio and Television. An analysis of the revamped Angelus broadcast on RTÉ Television in the last decade directs us to the fact that while apparently modern, this newer Angelus relies on mythic and pre-modern versions of Irishness: 'it employs images of nature, craft labour, and reproduction to generate themes of the Irish as self-sufficient, hardy, unpretentious, industrious and intelligent' (Cormack, 2005, p. 272). Cormack argues that these themes are rooted in a 'race memory' of Celtic Ireland that was widely promoted in the 18th and 19th centuries but that resonates with Irish people today. Nevertheless, she concludes that the attempts to link these themes to national identity in the Angelus broadcast are at variance with the spatial and temporal realities that Irish people now live.

Selling versions of Irish identity

An interesting question might be posed in relation to how commercial advertising agencies' understandings of national identity might have changed in post-boom Ireland. During the boom years, for instance, advertisers tended to represent Ireland in terms of a new set of qualities: cosmopolitan, luxurious, wealthy and trendsetting. For example, a Bulmers commercial aired in 2006 featured beautiful, young 'Irish' people sitting around in an aesthetically pleasing garden, relaxing to music. They could have been young people anywhere. In 2010 the Bulmers Christmas commercial reverted to more traditional iconography featuring a distinctively Irish landscape with images of family, simplicity and domesticity. Similarly, a Guinness commercial aired in 2006, themed 'evolution', focused on drinkers going back in evolutionary (not Irish) time and forward into the future, and included dinosaurs, the Big Bang, futuristic scenery and fast pop music. Its 2010 signature commercial, 'Bring it to life', showed men toiling on the land, against a backdrop of natural scenery and to the strains of soft music. This may indicate that advertisers and the companies they represent are picking up on a re-evaluation of core values and identities among the audience.

It is undeniable that the media have had an important part to play in the development of an Irish identity. Yet they have also been important in linking that identity to others in complex and sometimes contradictory ways. Thus, while the Irish media institutions have been an important element in the development of an indigenous 'Irish' culture, the same institutions can also be seen to have played an important role in the integration of Irish culture into a broader Anglo-American culture and a particular vision of 'modernity' that became dominant in the second half of the 20th century. The pre-eminence of Anglo-American media forms, from action movies and soap operas to reality TV shows, has raised concerns about the effects that global (usually understood as Anglo-American) culture may have on local or indigenous cultures, especially in peripheral or semi-peripheral countries such as Ireland. There are concerns that the world's cultural diversity could diminish and that the result will be a homogeneous global culture.

An optimistic view of this process is that the intensification of contacts and communications across cultural boundaries will produce greater cultural hybridity from which may emerge a new global culture that is an amalgam of elements of the separate cultures it replaces. A more pessimistic view is that the dominant Anglo-American culture may usurp the role of other cultural forms and become *the* worldwide culture. Interestingly, those who adhere to the latter point of view miss the point that meanings in the global mediascape may move not only from the core to the periphery, but in the opposite direction. Ireland is an instructive case in point. A recent collection of essays has focused on the valorisation of Irishness in American consumer culture. Irishness, it seems, can be invented, imagined and consumed as heritage and culture, while simultaneously acting as a marker of ethnic identity. As Negra (2006, p. 4) observes:

> from the massive international success of the music/dance revue *Riverdance*, to the juggernaut of Celtic themed merchandising, and the spate of Irish themed material on Broadway, Irishness, it seems, circulates ever more widely in contemporary culture.

How then are we to interpret the success of U2, Enya and Jedward, the Irish soccer team, *Riverdance* and Roddy Doyle on the global stage? Has this led to an increased national confidence and strengthened national identity, or has Irish culture been undermined by globalisation? One answer has been provided by a study that focused on identity formation amongst Dublin teenagers in early 21st-century Ireland.

YOUNG PEOPLE AND IDENTITY

Moffatt (2011) carried out a study of identity amongst young people growing up in Dublin. Through a series of questionnaires and focus groups conducted in both private and public schools in the capital, he sought to trace the significance of paradigms of Irishness amongst the generation of young people coming of age during the Celtic Tiger years. The paradigmatic analysis of identity that Moffatt presents is intended to encapsulate the range of varied meanings attached to Irish identity that young people profess. One of his key findings is the essential fluidity of notions of Irishness and the ease with which young people segue from one position to another on Irishness depending on the situational context. Based on his close reading of the questionnaire responses and focus group contributions, Moffatt developed a typology for classifying the different, if overlapping, understandings of Irishness.

He argues that young people largely interpret Irishness through three dominant paradigms: traditional, modern and post-modern. For instance, under the rubric of *tradition*, Moffatt examines the symbolic and substantive meaning of the Irish language to young people. He found that the Irish language remains a significant symbol of Irish identity and a basis for constructing a sense of Irishness amongst a majority of young people. Crucially, the young people saw the language as more important as a signifier of Irishness for the generalised other rather than for themselves. Their attitudes to the Irish language were also laced with a utilitarian edge – they see no substantive role for the Irish language in society today. Moffatt suggests that the Irish language could be understood at one time to have constituted a hard boundary of identity – it was employed to mark a difference between having an Irish as opposed to an Anglo-Irish or British identity. Boundaries are not fixed but are subject to change over time. He concludes that the Irish language no longer marks a hard boundary of Irish identity. Not only has it become a soft boundary, but it also looks increasingly porous. The young people in the study demonstrate a remarkable capacity to oscillate freely between positive and negative attitudes toward the language and its role in constituting identity.

We might expect that given the changes wrought by modernisation, contemporary Irish identity has become 'not-what-it-was' Irishness. For Moffatt, a *modern* Irish identity strongly emphasises an Irishness expressed in the compass of being modern, affected by and engaged with modern social processes. Identity is perceived as non-bounded, floating and malleable. Young people display an inventiveness around Irish identity that allows them to customise their understandings of Irishness in a highly individualised way. They are willing to embrace themes that hark back to traditional notions of Irishness, such as a notion of Irish people as friendly, helpful and welcoming that re-embeds the concept of sociability at the core of Irish identity. At the same time, they represent themselves as secular, tolerant and urbane.

Moffatt argues that modern understandings of Irish identity admit to greater interrogation of the meaning of Irishness. The traditional paradigm mines the past for tropes of Irishness, while the modern paradigm engages in a more reflexive questioning and is also more open to influences emanating from without, such as from global sport, music and culture. Moreover, it admits to an inventive inconsistency in understandings of Irishness. For instance, while a majority of young people reported that they valued multiculturalism, over one-third of those who were affirmative would not welcome their schools teaching about other cultures. Moffatt also notes that while the most common complaint made by young people about contemporary Ireland centred on racism, 'some were more than able to operate within a rigid racialising frame that effortlessly racialised others and themselves' (2011, p. 413).

Moffatt concurs that the mobilising power of the nation and nationalism has changed. Young people operate very much within the contours of an Anglo-

American culture that provides many of their reference points. On the basis of his analysis of young people's views, he suggests that rather than fomenting a post-national identity, there are perhaps grounds for suggesting a *post-modern* identity. The collective markers of class, gender and nation still feature in identity formation, but the range of different, contradictory and overlapping interpretations of Irishness that have emerged destabilise traditional notions of identity and render it less fixed and secure.

O'Connor (2008) similarly provides some fascinating insights into the contours of adolescent identities in Ireland. Drawing on texts commissioned from Transition Year (TY) students invited to 'tell their life stories', to write a page 'describing themselves and the Ireland that they inhabit' for a national database, O'Connor traces the influences of individualism, localism, globalism and gender on identity construction. The social and cultural context in which the young people in this study, born between 1982 and 1985, grew up was one of unprecedented economic, social and cultural change. Growth rates outstripped those of Ireland's European partners in the 1990s, unemployment tumbled, consumer spending rose and for the first time in 200 years, Ireland became a country of immigration rather than emigration. The changes wrought over those years manifested themselves in a number of transitions: rural society to high-tech/post-industrial economy; a culture of localism to a greater openness to global influences; high levels of religiosity to widespread secularisation, consumerism and scepticism about 'our betters'; and mono- to multiculturalism.

It is against this backdrop that the TY students wrote about their everyday lives. O'Connor found that the sample responses could be clustered around four main types of identity:

- *Global* (19 per cent of sample), where respondents identified closely with global entertainment and technology.
- *Less global* (24 per cent), in which respondents alluded to global elements but only in passing.
- *Essentially gendered* (21 per cent), in which respondents (more girls than boys) viewed their lives primarily through a gendered perspective.
- *Individualised not global* (32 per cent), in which respondents typically made no attempt to locate themselves structurally but focused selectively and exclusively on one particular dimension of their lived experience (such as TY, school, sports, loss, etc.).

O'Connor concluded that despite their immersion in a highly globalised and rapidly changing Irish society, young people's lifestyles, concerns and interests continue to be 'mapped' onto gender (2008, p. 275). This dimension of identity remained highly significant in terms of self-definition. Moreover, O'Connor noted that global elements were frequently used to maintain rather than transform gender realities.

GENDER AND IDENTITY

It is not possible to write about the relationship between identity and modernity in Ireland without making reference to the issue of gender. The changes that have taken place in Ireland over the last few decades have been reflected in or shaped by the changing relationships between women and men. An understanding of contemporary gender relationships in Ireland (see Chapter 8) requires consideration of how such representations and identities have developed over time. In a sense, all history is a history of gender in that gender is implicated in all human activity. But it is also the case that until comparatively recently, historical writing tended to focus disproportionately on the experiences of men: women (and children) were marginalised or remained completely absent from written accounts (O'Dowd and Wichert, 1995). As a result, the lived, day-to-day experience of Irish women has been overlooked and its importance played down. The writing of history is in many ways a search for identity, an attempt to develop a coherent narrative that embodies the character of a people. In turn, 'history' becomes part of the context within which gender relations are lived out in the contemporary world and is therefore crucial to a sociological understanding.

A number of writers have attempted to trace the historical and discursive connections between gender, sexuality and 'Irishness'. For Ronit Lentin (1998, p. 11; 1999), the construction of Irishness has been 'disturbingly gendered'; the definition of Irish citizenship that has emerged since independence has actively marginalised women and indeed has sought to erase all expressions of difference. Lentin and other analysts have labelled the Irish Constitution as a conservative document that assigns a subordinate role to women. It places women essentially as wives and mothers within the context of the family. The model of femininity it espouses is 'passive, private and domestic'. Most notoriously, Article 41.2.1 of the Constitution has been identified as a patriarchal statement about the 'proper' place of women in Irish society in its recognition of the special contribution to Irish society of women 'within the home'. It closely reflected Catholic Church teaching at the time it was written (1937) but continues to exert an influence over policy and law.

A number of writers have argued that the *land* of Ireland – the central motif of our history – has been viewed historically in a gendered way: as a feminine entity (see Lentin, 1999, pp. 5–7). Ireland is not unique in this regard. Similar arguments have been made for other national landscapes, including those of Australia (Schaffer, 1988) and of Sweden (Åberg, 1999). The geographer Catherine Nash suggests that the land of Ireland has been depicted as female in a number of traditions and contexts that range from old Gaelic representations to colonialist viewpoints to nationalist myths (such as Dark Rosaleen, Caitlín ní Houlihán and the *aisling*). To 19th-century English colonialists, Ireland (and its people) was typified by 'supposedly ... feminine characteristics of sentimentality, ineffectuality, nervous excitability and unworldliness' that rendered it incapable of self-government; in contrast, for Irish-Ireland nationalists, 'avowals of heroic masculinity were made alongside the celebration of dependent, passive, domestic and selfless Irish femininity' (Nash, 1997, p. 114). In such discourses of nationhood, 'Ireland is raped, seduced or married and in turn features alternatively as virgin, wanton woman, bride, mother or old woman' (1997, p. 116). The idea that the gendered imagery of Ireland as a country is linked to the formation of gendered identities among its people is an intriguing one, but it needs to be further understood through research. One of the problems with such analyses, from a sociological point of view, is that they tend to essentialise both femininity and masculinity.

INTERSECTIONS OF GENDER, RACE AND ETHNICITY

It is only recently in Ireland that sociologists have begun to explicitly grasp the relationships between gender and *ethnicity*. Lentin has sought to focus on the inherent racism of the dominant constructions of 'Irishness', such as that expressed in the Constitution, and closer to home, within Irish sociology and women's studies. For her, 'the assumption that to be Irish is to be Roman Catholic (or, in a very limited sense also Protestant) settled and White, has not been adequately challenged by politicians, social scientists or the media' (Lentin, 1999, p. 9). Lentin mounts a strong argument that narrowly defined conceptions of 'Irishness', for example as expressed in the Constitution, serve to deny full citizenship to ethnic minority women, such as refugees and asylum seekers, Travellers, Muslim and Jewish people, and Black-Irish people. Tannam (1999, p. 31) points out that policy and academic texts on gender in Ireland tend to ignore the experiences of migrant women and those of minority ethnic groups. The rapid change that Ireland has recently undergone, particularly its transition to a multi-ethnic state, means that analysis of gender in Ireland needs to examine the specificity of Irish women – and men – of varying ethnic identifications and, inseparable from this, the nature and practice of racism in Ireland. Researchers have begun to problematise women's invisibility in migration studies in Ireland. Indeed, Carla De Tona's work on Italian women in Dublin argues that the silent presence that characterises migrant women 'is not the outcome of their existential condition, but the means through which the discrimination of their condition is perpetuated' (2004, p. 315).

Angeline Morrison has explored notions of Irish identity in the context of women of mixed-race backgrounds living in Dublin. She found their readings of their own bodies (and thus identities) as 'black' had largely to do with the way white, racialised Irish society read them (2004, p. 365). Furthermore, people had difficulty accepting their 'Irishness'. In other words, for these women, race was a category imposed on them, and in the racialised consciousness of the majority population, they could not really belong. Visible racial and ethnic signifiers often serve as the focus for a 'moral panic', as was the case in Ireland in 2004, when concerns about so-called 'maternity tourism' were expressed by the government and amplified by the media (Breen et al., 2006). The concerns centred on the perceived increase in pressure on maternity hospitals because of rising numbers of births to non-nationals. According to Luibheid (2004, p. 335), in an era of accelerated globalisation, the Irish government requires new strategies to construct the nation as a sovereign space. She argues that discourses and practices targeting child-bearing asylum seeker women, and culminating in the 2004 Citizenship Referendum, provided the government not just with an opportunity to reassert national boundaries, but also with the means through which to generate 'new modes of racialisation and racial hierarchies within Ireland'.

THE ONGOING CHALLENGE OF MULTICULTURALISM

Ireland's immigration bulge in the first half of the 2000s generated debates about refugee and labour rights, racism, integration and interculturalism. We must now address the reality of a multicultural Ireland – what that might mean for our social and personal identities and for social policy and practice. In this time of globalisation, migratory issues and particularly the transnational reality of many peoples' lives takes on a new importance. 'Multiculturalism' has become a familiar term in societies such as Canada, Sweden, Australia, the US and Britain, but can have very different meanings and resonances. In Canada and Australia it tends to have positive overtones and reflects official discourses about the need for those societies to meaningfully recognise the cultural diversity brought about by long histories of immigration. In the US and Britain, the term tends to be far more politically charged and tends to refer to the struggles of minority groups (most specifically black and, in Britain, Asian) in conflict with a majority white culture. In Ireland it is not clear what people are referring to when they talk about multiculturalism, though generally the term seems to embrace elements of both of these meanings. In addition, 'interculturalism' has become the favoured term amongst government and activist groups.

As Castles and Miller (1998, p. 212) point out, the experiences of immigrants are significantly shaped by the policies and practices of the state. As Ireland has historically been a country of emigration rather than immigration, it is perhaps understandable that it has had a relatively poorly developed immigration policy in contrast to 'immigration societies' like Australia or the UK. According to Mac Éinrí (2006, p. 238), Ireland is now faced with the difficulty of 'constructing immigration and integration policies against a background of a rapidly changing picture, limited experience, an often less than positive attitude toward difference, and a largely mono-cultural tradition'.

This was exemplified in the Citizenship Referendum held in 2004, when a large majority voted in favour of a constitutional amendment to remove the automatic right to citizenship of a person born in Ireland. The political debate surrounding the issue was largely framed in terms of a threat to national identity and a perceived (though unfounded) crisis in maternity hospitals, issues amplified through extensive media coverage (Breen et al., 2006). As Fanning (2002) shows, this negative attitude has long roots in the history of the Irish state. This stance has impacted negatively on those that have come to Ireland, in a period when migration activity has seen a dramatic shift. Policy responses have been reactive and piecemeal and generally have been in response to perceived crises, especially in relation to asylum seekers and refugees.

The academic response to Ireland's new demographic reality has been diverse and is still developing. The changed situation has stimulated a considerable amount of commentary and has opened up new areas of sociological analysis and research (MacLachlan and O'Connell, 2000; Farrell and Watt, 2001; Fanning, 2002; Lentin and McVeigh, 2002; Rolston and Shannon, 2002). Maguire (2004), for example, has shown how first-generation Vietnamese immigrants are transnational in the sense that they identify more with Vietnam rather than Ireland. They do not speak English and therefore do not communicate with Irish people. The second generation expresses a more 'hybrid identity', caught as they are between two cultures, Irish and Vietnamese. The question of belonging raises itself for second-generation immigrants. They perceive themselves to be Irish, yet they are always questioned as to where they come from. In many cases the voices of immigrants themselves are being heard in the academic literature, such as Sinha (2002), Mutwarasibo (2002), Wang and Chiyoko King-O'Riain (2006) and Kropiwiec and Choyoko King-Ó Riain (2006). The launch of the academic e-journal *Translocations* in 2006 provided another space for discussion of migration, 'race' and social transformation issues.

There is not space here to discuss all the issues related to Ireland's increased cultural and ethnic diversity. Rather, we conclude this section with a brief examination of some key academic and policy discourses that have emerged in the attempt to understand the new direction that Irish society has taken. Much of the discussion is couched in terms of the concept of 'racism'. The most immediate concern is with negative responses to immigrants: in terms of individual prejudice, biased or inflammatory media coverage and physical attacks, but also with what is termed 'institutional racism', which is embodied in the policies and practices of organisations, especially state bodies (Fanning, 2002, p. 180).

There has been considerable debate as to whether Ireland is a racist culture. Greeley (1999, p. 155) argues that international attitudinal research reveals the (southern) Irish to be 'the most tolerant people in the English-speaking world', while Aniagolu (1997) and Rolston and Shannon (2002) trace a long history of Irish racist attitudes and practices, particularly in terms of the role of Irish people within the British Empire. MacGréil (2011) has revisited attitudes of prejudice and tolerance he has been surveying since the early 1980s. He detects a growing level of inter-group tolerance between 1988–89 and 2007–08. He attributes this positive change to the resolution of the Northern Ireland conflict, the increase in social and economic security between 1995 and 2008 and the positive impact of in-migration of workers that foments favourable contact (2011, p. xvi). Yet he also noted a relatively high social prejudice score among the younger age cohort (18–

25 years), even though this group would have been expected to be less prejudiced given their high levels of educational attainment. Furthermore, he notes that while there is an amelioration of the social distance between the indigenous population and Travellers, almost one-fifth of respondents would deny them citizenship (2011, p. xvii). On the other hand, the level of homophobia in Irish society greatly decreased between 1988–89 and 2007–08. Focus group discussions with a sample of 15- to 18-year-olds who migrated to Ireland revealed that many of the participants had encountered racism on the street from strangers (including adults), peers in school, at work and in the search for work. They also reported that while they had been subjected to some overtly racist remarks from classmates, more commonly it was misunderstanding and misrepresentations that caused annoyance and frustration (Gilligan et al., 2010).

Farrell and Watt (2001, p. 13) stress that it is important to address the issue of racism in a holistic rather than reactive way. Reducing it to a discussion on migration and asylum policy can have the (albeit often unintentional) effect of reinforcing the myth that the only people in Ireland to experience racism are recent migrants and that ethnic and cultural diversity in Ireland is a consequence of recent migration. This draws attention to the need to look at the historical roots of racism in Ireland, including anti-Semitism, attitudes towards Travellers and towards Irish people of colour, before the most recent development of large-scale immigration. Fanning (2002, p. 179) critiques 'weak multiculturalism' where 'the imagery of diversity proliferates but where the aim is to manage diversity rather than contest inequalities'. Fanning sees this approach as typifying official responses in Ireland: there is a focus on 'liberal democratic rights' but little attempt to seriously address underlying structural inequalities and manifestations of institutional racism. Weak multiculturalism is an individualistic response to difference. It is this concept that Farrell and Watt (2001, p. 26) are presumably referring to when they assert that multiculturalism is an 'outmoded concept'. They favour the term 'interculturalism', which requires that:

> we focus attention and become aware of the accepted norms within the dominant culture ... The development of an intercultural approach implies the development of policy that promotes interaction, understanding and integration among and between different cultures and ethnic groups.

Interculturalism is what Fanning refers to as 'strong multiculturalism' – a multiculturalism that overtly addresses issues of structural inequality and institutionalised racism. By contrast, the term 'interculturalism' has contradictory meanings for Fanning. In as much as it used by the state and its institutions (such as the education system or the Gardaí), it refers to a very weak form of multiculturalism. On the other hand, when mobilised by activist groups (particularly grass roots Traveller organisations), interculturalism has been used in the sense of a strong multiculturalism that overtly challenges the status quo.

It emerges from this brief discussion that the use of terms such as 'multi-culturalism' and 'interculturalism' (and connected concepts such as 'racism' and 'integration') are, in the Irish context, both confused and hotly contested – as they are in many other societies. Multiculturalism is not a single doctrine, does not characterise one political strategy and does not represent an already achieved state of affairs. It is not a covert way of endorsing some ideal, utopian state. It describes a variety of political strategies and processes that are everywhere incomplete. There is no doubt that the debates over the meaning of the concepts of multiculturalism and interculturalism will be an important part of the continuing sociological analysis of the phenomena of identity, cultural diversity and inequality in Irish society.

12
The Culture of Everyday Life

[Everyday life] is work, hard work, in all the senses of the term – whether physical, economic or ethnomethodological. The fact of this work, of this concrete activity in specific situations, must be played up if we, as social scientists, are not to transform the people we meet into automatons, passive cogs in impersonal machines. The machines make conditions ... the people make their own lives, for themselves, the members of their households, kin and networks of friends and acquaintances. However overwhelming the constraints that frame the people, they must still perform the rest of their days, and, in the process, produce a particularity, a difference that the casual glance may miss. (Varenne, 1993, pp. 112–13)

The last chapter revealed the complexities that surround the notions of 'culture' and 'identity'. As Western societies, including Ireland, have experienced economic growth and an ever-greater involvement in the knowledge-based economy, emphasis on matters of culture increases. At one level, we now spend more time in 'cultural activities', from watching sport to visiting museums or eating in restaurants. Increasingly, people also make their livelihoods in such areas – the 'culture' industries – and the economic potential of culture has attracted more interest from business and policy-makers (Curran and van Egeraat, 2010). Reflexively, as (post-) modern people we are often engaged in thinking about, talking about and reading about our 'culture'.

Culture refers not only to a set of practices that take place in the 'public' world, but also to the texture of everyday life within households, families and workplaces. But the public and the private are not clearly demarcated social spheres of existence: they overlap and interpenetrate. A family meal out in a restaurant, for example, is both a 'private' and a 'public' event; part of culture, as defined by the cultural industries of tourism or catering, but also culture in terms of the patterns of people's everyday life. Going out for a meal is also one of the ways that we as tourists or visitors may sample, locally or abroad, the culture of a society that is not our own.

It is this combination of ideas about culture that we aim to investigate in this chapter. The title reflects a concern with two areas that are usually analysed separately in sociology: 'popular culture' and 'everyday life'. The idea of 'the culture of everyday life' (Fiske, 1992) is an attempt to reflect on both at the same time.

We do this through an examination of three aspects of life that have been relatively ignored by Irish sociologists: fashion and dress; food and eating; and pubs and drinking. We have selected these through our own interest and because there is some sociologically relevant information available. These activities and aspects of life do not, of course, exhaust the reality of people's everyday lives, nor capture their full 'particularity', as Varenne suggests in our opening paragraph. We could also very valuably look at aspects of everyday life such as commuting, sport, leisure, housing, shopping (see Chapter 15), tourism or waste, to name just some areas that justify (and need) more sociological analysis in the Irish context. Most of what we say here will be suggestive rather than in any way conclusive.

CULTURE

Following Williams (1976, pp. 87–93), we can identify three ways to define culture – these interpretations have evolved over centuries of use of the term. The first is culture as a process of intellectual, spiritual and aesthetic development. In this sense, the term is similar to our concept of 'civilisation'. We might contrast our society with that of the Dark Ages, when people in general were not exposed to fine art or literature, or indeed to what we now regard as 'good' table manners. We might see a person who had received a good upbringing and education and who was know-ledgeable and discerning as 'cultured'. This is a highly normative concept of culture.

A second interpretation reflects an 'anthropological' understanding – what Williams refers to as the 'particular way of life … of a people, a period or a group, or humanity in general'. It is in this sense that we might talk about the 'Maori culture of New Zealand' as a set of practices and attitudes typical of that people, such as language, dress, foodways, religion, kinship patterns and so on. This is the concept of culture that underpins the discussion of 'identity' in Chapter 11. Use of this concept may well involve debates about authenticity and boundaries. Does our conception of Maori culture embrace the fact that Maoris now speak English, use mobile phones, design websites, make and export wine and play rugby? How far can the idea of a Maori culture, or indeed of an 'Irish culture', stretch?

The third interpretation of culture pointed to by Williams is that of culture as 'works and practices of intellectual and especially artistic activity'. This is a widely accepted concept of culture, as reflected in the work of cultural practitioners such as painters, musicians or architects. Thus, for example, the 2011 Imagine Ireland series of events in the US, organised by a government agency called Culture Ireland (whose remit is to promote Irish arts abroad), featured, amongst a vast and eclectic panoply of events, an historical exhibition on Irish-American performance; an interactive science exhibition of 'sonic experiences'; the 'traditional' Irish music act Kila; paintings by London-born Irish artist Nick Miller; and a performance of a Seán O'Casey play, *The Silver Tassie*. There are vigorous debates as to what can, or should, be included in such a definition of culture, especially if it is a matter of providing financial support or official endorsement for such activities.

The broadest conception of culture derived from the above definitions would embrace 'everything' that a people does or thinks; as such, it dissolves as a useful concept. Thus we might wish to limit the boundaries of culture, but so inevitably the debate begins. Eating chips from a paper bag may not be 'cultured' behaviour according to the first definition; it may certainly be seen as a distinctively Irish way to behave (which the Irish also share with some other cultures); and it is unlikely that you could get a government grant to do it, unless it was part of a piece of 'performance art'. It is not really possible to pin down what 'culture' means. It may be more instructive to be aware of how the concept is being deployed in a particular context and why people are using it.

POPULAR CULTURE

Drawing on the concept of culture, sociologists have further sought to identify a field that may be termed 'popular culture'. As we have seen, the second part of this term is difficult enough to define: to go further and try to mark out particular aspects of culture as 'popular' is to add further problems. The concept is malleable, contested and may or may not even be useful, but this does not mean it is not widely used. A variety of interpretations of popular culture has been used in research and analysis and a useful checklist of these approaches is outlined by Storey (2001, pp. 5–16).

One way to think about popular culture is 'simply culture which is widely favoured or well liked by many people' (Storey, 2001, p. 6). Therefore, if a book sells 100,000 copies in the Irish market or a soft drink sells 50 million cans across the EU, we might think of it as 'popular'. This concept, while helping us to think about what popular might mean, has certain problems. First, we need to define a threshold over which the product in question has to pass (1,000 or 1 million downloads of a song, for example). Second, is the quantitative measure sufficient? Just about everyone in Ireland eats potatoes – does this make them an item of popular culture? A second way to think of popular culture is to define it in relation to its opposite – 'high culture'. High culture may include such phenomena as opera, sculpture or arthouse films, contrasted with a popular culture based on pop music, graffiti art or glossy magazines. This distinction relates to Bourdieu's concept of cultural capital wherein the 'value' of cultural practices is established through oppositions to other practices. Thus, he suggests:

> Distinction and pretension, high culture and middle-brow culture – like elsewhere high fashion and fashion, haute coiffure and coiffure, and so on – only exist through each other, and it is the relation, or rather, the objective collaboration of their respective production apparatuses and clients which produces the value of culture and the need to possess it. (Bourdieu, 1984, p. 250)

The distinction between these two types of culture may be made on various grounds. One might be 'difficulty'(a book that is easy to read might not be seen as literature); another might relate to complexity (a restaurant meal may be more elaborate than fast food); or the distinction may lie in the context in which an artefact is created or consumed (the original *Mona Lisa* in the Paris Louvre is high culture, but a poster of the same image on the wall of a flat in Galway is popular culture). This distinction may be very difficult to pin down in practice. Marilyn Monroe's films can be unambiguously thought of as popular, but what of the images of that same star in the art of Andy Warhol? And what then when that same image appears on a T-shirt?

Storey (2001, p. 8) also suggests that popular culture may be thought of as 'mass culture'. This view sees popular culture as the 'lowest common denominator', deliberately designed to appeal to the maximum number of people. As well as being contrasted with high culture, mass culture is also defined in opposition to 'authentic' folk culture, cultural expression that emerges organically from 'the people'. Thus, a reality-TV act such as Jedward is seen as a cynically produced and marketed product no different in essence to washing powder, whereas a rock or folk group that has emerged through years of touring and struggle (such as U2 or Dervish) is seen to be superior. This view is potentially condescending and dismissive of popular taste, but it may also draw attention to the processes whereby mass media and cultural industries package products, from music to food, for particular markets and audiences.

A further definition of popular culture, according to Storey, is based on Gramsci's notion of hegemony. Gramsci developed this term to explore how dominant groups in society could intellectually and culturally dominate others. The Gramscian approach to popular culture commonly sees it as a 'site' where dominant and dominated groups struggle for power and where dominated groups are able to express 'resistance'. Thus, just because a cultural product is created and distributed by a powerful entity (for example, a global company like Sony), this does not mean that the corporation has the power to determine how it is publicly consumed or interpreted, nor what resistant uses people may make of such products. Similarly, 'new feminists' have argued that women and girls can use the products of a sexist society (toys, clothes, cosmetics) to make their own cultural statements that may not be what the creators had in mind (see Rand, 1995, for an extensive discussion of how Barbie dolls have been used in such ways).

Finally, an understanding of popular culture may be shaped by theories of post-modernism. Post-modernism, in line with its dismissal of 'grand narratives', does not see a distinction between high and popular culture. In our contemporary world, the lines between art and entertainment, culture and commerce, authenticity and artifice are so blurred that the categories are fatally compromised. As Storey remarks (2001, p. 13), 'for some this is a reason to celebrate an end to elitism constructed on arbitrary distinctions of culture; for others it is a reason to despair at the final victory of commerce over culture'.

Culture, then, whether in general or 'popular', is a complex concept and may express a variety of relationships between people, objects and meanings. Often the concept is overtly or covertly normative, seeking to talk about how things *should* be, and suggests that certain ways of doing or being are 'better' than others. This is to enter territory replete with discourses of criticism and evaluation. From a sociological stance, it may be of more interest and value to examine how culture is lived in a real sense. This points us to the concept of everyday life. Such an approach may shift us away from an interpretation that sees culture as predominantly a set of texts or meanings and return us to a more materialist interest in how 'things' are used and produced, as well as consumed, in people's day-to-day interaction.

Briefly, the sociology of everyday life can be thought of as an area where 'the study of forms of social behaviour and social interaction [in] ... everyday social settings and the analysis of more general social processes and relationships meet and intermesh' (Bennett and Watson, 2002, p. ix). The second part of this definition relates to the macrosocial concerns that much of this book has been concerned with. But the idea of the 'everyday' calls for further unpacking. It may relate to the routine and familiar – literally things that happen 'every day' like shopping or eating. As Bennett and Watson (2002, p. x) point out, it also relates to the 'ordinary' things that ordinary people do, rather than the activities of the wealthy and powerful. In this sense, everyday life is closely linked to the second meaning of culture outlined above: the taken-for-granted ways of doing things within a society. It also connects with many notions of 'the popular'.

Everyday life also relates to the notion of the 'public' (Bennett and Watson, 2002, p. xi). This interpretation connects us to the idea of civil society (see Chapter 4), understood as that part of society outside of the state and the family. In contemporary times, the 'public' is synonymous with the ordinary people of society going about their daily business. We think of public opinion or public transport: each relates to everyday, non-elaborated ways of doing and being – reading the newspaper or taking the bus – carried out in company or in interaction with others. Again, the notion of public is closely related to many of the concepts of popular outlined above.

But the study of everyday life can reveal a more oppressive aspect. Foucault has analysed modernity's ever-increasing processes of surveillance of the ordinary person. This involves modern forms of discipline, such as the school, the asylum, the hospital and the prison – sites of institutional power within society intensely concerned with observing, recording and attempting to control and change the everyday life of the individual. This process does not only take place in easily identified institutional settings. Today, our movements on the street are monitored by CCTV, our supermarket purchases are logged through 'loyalty cards' and our telephone or Internet communications are tracked by ever more sophisticated electronic systems (Lace, 2005). Ironically, the process of surveillance has strong roots in sociology: much of the social science of the 19th century (such as that reflected in the SSIS; see Chapter 2) was concerned with gathering information about the everyday lives of the poor and the powerless in order to 'govern' them better.

In combining the perspectives of popular culture and everyday life, we can develop a framework that might allow us to understand and analyse people's routinised and informal activities, for example in relation to dress, food or drink. Each of these, as suggested, is part of our normal taken-for-granted daily activity, connected closely to ideas of domesticity and home, but also fundamental to our public being in the world. Wearing clothes, consuming food or visiting the pub are never just private personal activities – they are intensely social and are shaped by complex social forces. They relate strongly to the second conception of culture: that of the 'particular way of life' of a people. But in a globalised consumer society (see Chapter 15), our lives are at least partially shaped by commercially produced, often branded products that are heavily design laden and so intimately connected to popular culture. Thus, a pair of jeans can no longer be just an item of clothing – it connects to a broader set of meanings to do with youth, music and image. A ready-cooked 'Thai' meal is linked to visual representations through advertising, travel brochures, film or restaurants. Contemporary everyday life is intricately bound up with the products of popular culture. We may ask whether it is possible any more to create an 'authentic' everyday culture within a world that is saturated with media, products and consumerism. Or can we do little more than take the ingredients provided to us by the modern capitalist economy and recreate them in our own ways, as far as we can?

It is within this matrix of meanings and questions that we outline some salient features of everyday life in Ireland. Our discussion is limited by the available material. An analysis of everyday life ideally calls for an ethnographic approach that involves a close in situ study of social practices – the 'concrete activity in specific situations' referred to by Varenne (1993, p. 112) – but this type of research is sorely missing within Irish sociology. We will encounter versions of it in the material below, for example in Corrigan's analysis of clothing, or Curtin and Ryan's and Scarbrough's analysis of pubs. Unfortunately, though in-depth community studies have been a strong feature of sociological research in Ireland (see Chapter 4), such studies have tended to overlook the everyday cultural phenomena that we discuss here. Perhaps clothing, food and drink are so taken for granted that sociologists, and even anthropologists, do not really 'see' them, especially when they are looking for evidence of community, class or power.

FASHION AND DRESS

Perhaps more than any other element of consumer culture, clothing is the most efficient at announcing one's status to the world. At a broad level anyone will be able to read some useful social information from dress. At a narrower level, others will be able to read more complex messages from the same items. The street theatre of dress has not one audience, but many. (Corrigan, 1997, p. 176)

There has been comparatively little written about the sociology of fashion or of clothing in the Irish – or indeed international – context. As Corrigan (1988, p. vii) points out, there has been a long historical tradition of social and political commentary on dress and its relation to society (clothing as meaning), but little analysis of what people actually wear on an everyday basis (clothing as objects). But what people wear has long had social significance; many social movements, not least feminism, have focused on 'what not to wear' as a significant theme. Clothing is held to act in some ways as a mirror to society. For example, female fashions are thought to say something about women's position in society and economists have even produced serious studies that correlate economic cycles with skirt lengths.

There has been considerable interest in the nature of fashion as a system of meanings; somewhat less in the making of clothes themselves; and much less in people's experiences of choosing, wearing and using clothing. As with many popular cultural phenomena, there has been a tendency to separate studies of production, of interpretation and meaning and of consumption. The first may be studied by economists or industrial historians, the second by those in cultural studies or semioticians and the last by sociologists or even market researchers. This division of labour ignores the key roles to be played across the field by technological change, marketing, industry structures and so on in determining what gets worn by whom. As Entwistle (2000b) argues:

> Precisely what styles are deemed 'in fashion' depends on the circulation of meanings woven around clothes by a whole range of agents – fashion colleges and students, designers and design houses, tailors and seamstresses, models and photographers, as well as colour forecasters, fashion editors, distributors, retailers, fashion buyers, shops and consumers.

Entwistle reveals, for example, the powerful influence of the small number of industry personnel who decide which colours are going to be 'in' for a particular season. This influences what textiles manufacturers produce, the garments designers create and ultimately what is available to fashion commentators and those who purchase clothes in the shops.

A full study of clothing and fashion, as of any other type of cultural product, would analyse the 'system of provision' that ties consumption to production to meaning-creation in complex ways (Fine and Leopold, cited in Entwistle, 2000a, p. 209). No Irish sociologist has yet attempted such a task, though as we see below, McCrum (1996) does discuss some key elements of the Irish 'fashion system'. Our brief discussion of the sociology of fashion and dress in Ireland inevitably draws upon a small number of diverse, discrete and suggestive sources – a complete and systematic analysis of this fascinating topic is yet to be carried out.

Fashion

> Fashionable dress is dress which embodies the latest aesthetic, it is dress which is defined at a given moment as desirable, beautiful, popular. In articulating the latest aesthetic, and in making available certain kinds of clothes, fashion provides the 'raw material' of daily dress, produced by a multitude of people operating across a variety of sites. (Entwistle, 2000b)

Corrigan, an Irish sociologist now working in Australia, is one of the few that has taken seriously the sociology of fashion and dress. He notes that in 18th-century European society, clothing was used in a public way to demonstrate status and occupation. We still see traces of this in how hospital workers' uniforms clearly symbolise the wearer's place within the medical hierarchy. The emergence of mass industrial and urban society in 19th-century Europe saw an emphasis on how a person's individuality and character could be revealed. The result was not, as might be expected, a greater individuality in dress, but rather a concern for uniformity. It was now thought that clothing reflected what a person was like, rather than their social position. There was thus a concern to control public appearance: 'people started to dress in a very uniform and unindividual way, fearing that an unusual button or cuff would betray them as deeply flawed and deviant creatures' (Corrigan, 1997, p. 161). The 20th century saw further change with a greater desire to express individuality through clothing. It was now believed to reflect the creativity and style of the person who wore it.

The factors associated with changes in fashion and dress are inevitably complex and relate to technological development, broader values related to the body and its display, economic change and to trends in other areas of production and consumption, for example in relation to housing, transport and family structure. Sociological analysis of fashion attempts to connect broad societal change with the visible changes in what people wear. Key writers who remain influential within the field include Veblen and Simmel. Bourdieu, who had such an intense interest in the sociological meaning of material culture, has had comparatively little to say on dress, which is perhaps surprising given its intensely symbolic nature. The English sociologist Entwistle has sought to systematically draw together sociological work and theory in the field.

The sociological interest in fashion can be traced to the seminal analysts of modern consumption and everyday life: Veblen and Simmel (Sweetman, 2001, pp. 61–5). For Veblen, writing at the end of the 19th century, trends in fashion and dress within modern society were shaped by the phenomenon of 'conspicuous consumption'. Wealth was expressed both through the quality of material, but also in the way that clothing was distanced from what might be required for everyday physical labour. Thus, the starched white shirt and shiny top hat (for men) or the corset and high heels (for women) were indicators that the person did not – indeed could not – engage in the manual trades or domestic work. For Veblen, dress was associated with social difference, most specifically with class distinction.

For Simmel, fashion is also closely linked to class (Corrigan, 1997, p. 170). It reflects a tension between the desire for conformity and durability on the one hand and peculiarity and change on the other. This tension helps to shape fashion and ensure constant change: there are those that are imitators and those that are specialists and risk-takers. It is also the desire of lower classes to imitate the fashions of the wealthy – and the desire of the latter to look distinctive and not like the lower classes – that constantly drives fashion forwards. This is the process that McCracken (cited in Corrigan, 1997, p. 171) refers to as 'chase and flight'. Fashion helps to underpin social group identity and thus helps to solidify class differences. It 'brings together all those that have adopted the fashion of a particular class or group, and excludes those that have not. [It] produces similarity, union and solidarity within the group and the simultaneous segregation and exclusion of everyone else' (Corrigan, 1997, p. 170). Social hierarchies are now arguably far more complex than in Simmel's time, with many drivers of fashion besides what is worn by the wealthy. As a consequence, analysts of fashion find Simmel's approach less useful. But the contribution of both Veblen and Simmel to the understanding of 'how fashion works' has been influential within most subsequent sociological analysis of the phenomenon.

Bourdieu, in *Distinction* – his major work on consumption and everyday life – connects choices of clothing to social class, pointing (1984, p. 201) to the rather obvious 'opposition between the suit, the prerogative of the senior executive, and the blue overall, the distinctive mark of the farmer and industrial worker'. The distinction can also be seen (amongst both men and women) between the wearing of formal 'top coats' amongst the dominant classes and the more likely jacket or raincoat amongst workers or 'junior executives'. He is also significant in connecting fashion to how different social groups inhabit and use the body: this is an important if neglected aspect of fashion and dress (Entwistle and Wilson, 2001).

For Bourdieu, echoing earlier theorists, there are tensions and ambiguities within fashion and its connections to unequal social relationships. These help to stimulate innovation and change, as struggles for dominance amongst social groups are refracted through the symbolic oppositions of the fashion world. Fashion is based on the orchestration of struggles within the industry itself – between old/new, classical/practical, expensive/cheap, old/young and so on – and also on conflicts between those with power and those without. Thus, the established holders of power are associated with classical, tasteful and expensive clothing and with established labels or designers, while those challenging or up-and-coming within the social hierarchy are associated with the 'new', the 'young' and the avant-garde (Bourdieu, 1984, p. 233). There are clear echoes here of the high/popular culture dichotomy: 'haute couture' is akin to fine art, with expensive materials, painstaking attention to detail and its own arcane language. Mass-produced clothing is a cheap imitation of this: a disposable product produced for a mass market, shorn of the more outrageous elements of high fashion, aimed at the 'lowest common denominator'.

Unlike many of those who focus on interpreting the symbolism of fashion, Bourdieu does make some attempt to find out about what is actually happening at the everyday societal level – mainly through questionnaires about (French) people's practices and attitudes. Thus, he is able to discover (the perhaps not very surprising fact) that women who do not go out to work use less make-up, but also that those 'higher' in the social hierarchy have a greater degree of confidence about their looks. This is important, suggests Bourdieu, as the way we look is an increasingly important aspect of cultural capital that we bring to the workplace:

> the interest the different classes have in self-presentation, the attention they devote to it, their awareness of the profits it gives and the investment of time, effort, sacrifice and care which they actually put into it are proportionate to the chances of material or symbolic profit they can reasonably expect from it. More precisely, they depend on the existence of a labour market in which physical appearance may be valorised in the performance of the job itself or in professional relations, and on differential chances of access to this market and the sectors of this market in which beauty and deportment most strongly contribute to occupational value. (Bourdieu, 1984, p. 202)

As in his other analyses, Bourdieu attempts to connect a highly structuralist account of culture with patterns of social inequality and interaction. The result is some very suggestive discussion of what clothing and fashion might mean in an unequal capitalist society.

Entwistle suggests that while Veblen, Simmel and Bourdieu have been important in the development of a critical sociology of consumption and fashion, their analysis is now out of date and does not adequately reflect how fashion now operates in society. They each produce a symbolic analysis of fashion, where it can be 'read' like a text. Entwistle argues that fashion cannot now be reduced to the expression of a single societal theme (such as class distinction), but is a system made up of complex and sometimes contradictory elements. It is now, she suggests, 'the outcome of a range of intersecting practices: market and economic practices, labour relations and practices, technological developments and a range of more "cultural" practices such as marketing and design' (2000a, p. 227). Maynard (2004), in an analysis of fashion and globalisation, suggests that clothes themselves may be becoming less important as signifiers of 'being fashionable', with greater importance being attributed to contemporary consumer goods. She suggests (Maynard, 2004, pp. 41–2) that:

> wealth and position are more likely to be indicated by accessories, such as shoes, bags and watches, by the stylishness of owning the latest technology, by grooming, by the level of fitness, travel opportunities, membership of a gym, real estate, or even by owning intangible luxuries such as perfumes, rather than simply clothing alone.

As Maynard shows, on a global scale there has been a blurring of high fashion and 'street fashion': fashion no longer 'trickles down' from the 'upper echelons' to the lower social classes; it is just as likely to 'bubble up' from the street, to cross over from popular music or to emerge from art colleges. It is increasingly fragmented and flexible, with numerous fashion niches and no clear overall direction. At the same time, mass retailers – in Britain, Marks & Spencer and the Burton group sell a quarter of all clothes between them – have considerable power in (literally) shaping what people wear (Entwistle, 2000a, p. 225).

Aspers and Skov (2006, p. 802) make the interesting point that the fashion industry is 'both a creative sector and an old-fashioned manufacturing industry'. It embraces the high couture salons of Paris and Milan, the Sartorialist blog (www.the sartorialist.com) and branches of Penneys across the regional towns of Ireland. Its industrial and commercial processes span the sweatshops of China, artisan producers of Italy, fabric and button manufacturers, retailers, models, photographers, magazine editors, bloggers... It is inevitably a sprawling, global and difficult-to-grasp field of human endeavour that encompasses extremes of pleasure and misery. Key players/sites identified by Anders and Skov (2006, p. 804) include fashion fairs and buyers, art worlds and design schools, celebrities and catwalks, fashion magazines and street fashion as well as manufacturers, designers, producers, retailers and the consumers.

Entwistle (and other writers such as Sweetman, 2001) also stress the importance of linking fashion and dress to the body: in all cultures, the body is always the 'dressed body'. This draws our attention to clothes as objects that are worn, a point made strongly by Sweetman (2001, p. 66):

> When I wear a suit I walk, feel and act differently, and not simply because of the garment's cultural connotations ... but also because of the way that the suit is cut, and the way its sheer materiality both enables and constrains, encouraging and demanding a certain gait, posture and demeanour, whilst simultaneously denying me the full range of bodily movement that would be available were I clad in jogging-pants and a loose fitting t-shirt.

Fashion in Ireland

Fashion can be seen in two ways: as a specific style of dress in vogue at a particular time and place (as in '1920s London fashion') or as a specific industry – the fashion industry – that as Entwistle suggests embraces designers, manufacturers, distributors, retailers and commentators. The concept of an 'Irish fashion industry' is a relatively recent one and has attracted only two significant historical studies (McCrum, 1996; O'Byrne, 2000) and no extensive published sociological analysis.

For O'Byrne (2000, pp. 9–13), for much of their history the Irish have had 'little or no distinctive style of dress'. He suggests that this may be because Irish people lack a sense of fashion or style, based on what he terms their 'visual illiteracy', 'innate conservatism' and lack of 'discipline'. Together, these might add up to a more casual or less reflexive attitude to appearance. He argues that apart from in some isolated areas of the western seaboard, indigenous styles of clothing have been obliterated by British ways of dressing. Thus, 'as a rule, the inhabitants of Ireland dressed no differently from their nearest neighbours across the Irish sea'. The trade policies of the British government, which for a long period construed Irish manufacturers as rivals, did nothing to help the development of an indigenous Irish industry (McCrum, 1996, p. 2).

Conversely, O'Dowd (1990) suggests that until the 20th century there was much about the clothing of those on the Irish west coast and elsewhere that was 'particularly distinctive', including garments such as the black woollen shawl and the hooded cloak; the Aran Islands *crois* or belt; *troigthíní*, trews or soleless socks; and pampooties, a type of shoe. According to O'Dowd (1990, p. 7), 'it was clothing that was essentially uninfluenced and unaffected by high fashion and almost totally dependent on the availability of local resources and locally produced fabrics. Imported materials were only slowly adopted in areas near the large urban centres and by those who could afford to buy them.' McCrum (1996, p. xiii) similarly draws attention to distinctive aspects of the Irish clothing industry, including the key roles of fabrics like weatherproof wools and linen. She also argues that the Irish fashion industry has been distinctive and very successful for the size of the country.

This concept of traditional or 'authentic' dress is a complex one. In the 19th and early 20th centuries, Gaelic nationalists (paralleling the Russian revolution-aries) attempted to instil nationalistic modes of dress, drawing on the once typical clothing of the Irish rural dweller. O'Byrne (2000, p. 13) notes that such attempts to 'recreate what was believed to be native Irish dress' met with resistance, indeed derision, from the people; even Pádraig Pearse was sceptical, suggesting the proposed costume for men (which included trews) was 'fatal to … dignity' (quoted in Dunlevy, 1989, p. 176). More recently we can note that the 'traditional' Aran sweater dates only from the 20th century (O'Dowd, 1990, p. 8), when designers produced a highly elaborated version of the sweaters – originally introduced by British visitors – worn by fisherman and farmers of the west coast. Further elaboration came from continental Europe via returned emigrants from Boston (McCrum, 1996, p. 6). This specific garment is now closely associated with Ireland and Irish culture. Brought to worldwide attention in the 1960s by the Clancy Brothers ballad group, it remains a popular item on the tourist market. There are 65 outlets in France selling it and other 'traditional' Irish clothing such as tweed caps (O'Byrne, 2000, p. 170), not to mention numerous tourist shops the length and breadth of Ireland itself. To add a further twist, O'Byrne (2000, p. 165) shows how the Irish designer Cuan Hanley has produced a contemporary 'simplified' version of the Aran: completing the circle by designing a garment that looks remarkably like the original sweater. In clothing as in other aspects of Irish life, it can be unwise to take categories of 'traditional' and 'modern' at face value.

It is argued by the fashion industry that the image presented by the Aran sweater is no longer appropriate to a 'modern' Irish society. O'Byrne (2000, p. 170) remarks that 'just as dry stone walls and white-washed cottages do not reflect the reality of

Ireland in the new millennium, nor do Aran sweaters and tweed jackets provide an accurate view of Irish fashion today'. The irony is that numerous Irish fashion designers, from Sybil Connolly in the 1950s to Lainey Keogh in the 1990s, have drawn upon this discarded heritage in order to create an 'Irish' niche in the global fashion industry. O'Byrne sees the Irishness of the indigenous industry not in its motifs or fabrics, but in a specific set of ('traditional') skills and workmanship: he suggests (2000, p. 171) that 'the survival of these skills, perhaps more than anything else, is what sets Irish fashion apart'.

O'Byrne also looks to the success of the formerly 'peripheral' Belgian fashion industry as a model for Ireland, but admits that there is nothing, apart from the personnel involved, that is identifiably 'Belgian' about it. It is part of a larger global, or at least European, industry. Ireland is a small player in this industry, but fashion – like other image-based cultural industries such as film, popular music and tourism – has a growing economic influence. At the same time, the production of actual clothes, as opposed to designs for them, 'barely exists any longer' (O'Byrne, 2000, p. 168). The global economy has seen most aspects of the textile industries relocated to countries with lower labour costs.

Dress

> Irish people are the ones who never wear raincoats. We don't like planning and we don't like reality. (Hourihane, 2000, p. 99)

While there has been some interest in describing and accounting for the Irish fashion industry and the historical development of costume, there has been virtually no interest in the phenomenon of everyday dress. For example, while O'Byrne illustrates his account of Irish fashion with numerous images of Irish-designed clothes, all are worn by models: there are no pictures of what ordinary Irish people wear on a daily basis. We know little of how people live out this central aspect of their everyday lives.

Corrigan (1988) points out that most sociology of clothing focuses on its symbolic aspect rather than its uses in everyday social interaction, particularly as objects that are purchased, stored, worn and exchanged in a variety of social contexts. In research carried out in Dublin in the early 1980s, Corrigan sought to discover how people used clothing as part of their everyday lives. His sample embraced only a small number of families, but his findings are suggestive of people's complex relationships towards clothing and, through clothing, to each other.

Corrigan encouraged people to talk about the contents of their wardrobes and then, through repeated interviews and other interventions, sought to discover how items of clothing were linked to social relationships across and within families or groups of friends. He found that age, class and gender emerged as key 'sartorial variables' (1988, p. 71). It also emerged that the amount and variety of clothing available to people had increased considerably since the 1950s, when young people's clothing would have been confined to school uniform, 'Sunday best' and a nondescript outfit for everyday wear (Corrigan, 1988, p. 125).

People surveyed by Corrigan were generally happy to talk about their clothing, often linking particular items to specific people ('that skirt was a present from my sister') or to a specific phase of their life ('I wore that shirt when I was at college'). Gifts of clothing emerged as a significant element of people's wardrobes, and it was here that Corrigan focused, exploring the rationale for and consequences of gift-giving behaviour. He also systematically analysed patterns of exchange of clothing items, including transfers of 'cast-offs', and the 'borrowing' and 'stealing' of clothes amongst families and friends.

Not surprisingly, he found that clothing could be implicated in relationships of conflict and power, in particular between mothers and daughters – indeed, a 'state of war' could ensue between these family members in relation to what was worn, when and where. Typically such conflicts centred on issues of taste, appropriateness and 'niceness', as in when clothes were too revealing, not matching or inappropriate for age or weather conditions. This is how Corrigan describes aspects of this relationship:

> There are two phases of the mother-daughter relation: an earlier one where the mother, her direct family or friends act as more or less exclusive sources of clothes; and a later one (after about age 13) where daughters refuse clothes bought or made by the mother, sometimes begin to take clothes the mother acquired for herself, and almost invariably begin to swop clothes with non-familial girlfriends of their own age. (Corrigan, 1988, p. 116)

The males in Corrigan's sample were far less likely to share or exchange clothing: indeed, effort went into ensuring the separateness of their clothing from fathers or brothers.

In a study of the lives of low-income families, Daly and Leonard (2002, pp. 123–9; 138–9) also explore the importance of clothes in everyday life, especially of children. They stress how, for many children, wearing the 'right' (fashionable, brand name) clothes and (especially) footwear was socially very important. Not to have the appropriate clothes or runners could and often did lead to bullying in school, which in turn could contribute to academic underachievement and early school leaving. The pressure to purchase expensive branded clothing had real implications for everyday life, diverting resources from other purposes and creating strain within families. In some cases, it also determined the friendship networks that could be built and sustained. Clothing was seen very much as a mark of distinction between children. They sometimes devised stratagems to deal with this situation, as reported by one 14-year-old respondent (Daly and Leonard, 2002, p. 139):

> Well, there's about four [types of runners] you'd be alright with: Adidas, Nike, Ellesse and Reebok. Sometimes when my ma can't afford any of these, I try and get ones with no name. Having ones with no name is better than having a crap name. You can pretend with ones with no name. Sometimes I make them all

dirty so that it looks as if they're designer but you can't see the name right or I would cover up my feet so that it's hard to see the name.

Another child sewed brand name labels onto non-branded clothes in order to conceal her disadvantage. In a very real way, the clothing of the children in this study literally marked them out as poor and relatively powerless.

Sociological analyses of fashion and clothing are not well developed in Ireland. The work of Corrigan shows that such an analysis can reveal complex and fascinating information about social relationships, and the more recent research by Daly and Leonard indicates that issues related to clothing are not peripheral or frivolous: how people dress and how others respond have real social consequences. The development of sociological theory in relation to fashion, dress and the body (Entwistle, 2000a; Entwistle and Wilson, 2001; Anders and Skov, 2006) suggests that there is great scope for further research in this field within the Irish context.

FOOD AND DRINK

Inglis (2002, p. 27) has suggested that Irish people are becoming more rational, circumspect and educated about the pleasures of food and drink. They want to explore different tastes, products and services, and to eat and drink in new places. In this they are probably no different to other cultures where a diversification of food and drinking practices is taking place. Inglis suggests that such changes are related to the modernisation of Irish society. But what can we say about modernisation and food? On the one hand there is a strong view that the shift towards a more cosmopolitan and 'adventurous' diet is a modernising tendency. Yet other already 'modern' societies (such as Australia, the UK, the US) have seen similar trends in relation to diversification of food and drink, behind which are common factors: the activities of the food industry, global migration and travel. It is worth examining the issues of food and eating in a little more detail.

Food and eating

At the most banal level, consumption of food is a fundamental aspect of everyday life: if we don't eat we die, and hunger has been said to be amongst the most powerful of psychological drives. To a large (though perhaps diminishing) extent, everyday social life is structured around meals and mealtimes; similarly, the preparation and consumption of food has been identified by anthropologists as a fundamental basis of sociality. Along with dress, religious belief, language and kinship, food provides a key marker of cultural identity.

Sociological examination of food and eating reveals a field of great complexity. Topics for discussion range from the systems of provision within which food commodities – such as chicken or sugar – are produced, distributed and consumed; the symbolic meanings of food within families, communities, nations and the media; the connections between food and social inequality; the structure and meaning of meals or 'food events'; the nature of food choice; questions of nutrition, diet and health; and the complexities of food, gender and ethnicity (Beardsworth and Keil, 1997). The list is as broad as the discipline of sociology itself.

Contemporary Irish food systems mirror those of other Western economies in many ways, particularly those of English-speaking nations such as Britain and Australia. While a number of food systems intertwine and cross-cut at local, regional and national levels, the power of multinational retailers and distributors is increasingly significant. The activities of such corporations have long been exposed to critique from sociologists and other social scientists, but until the recent eruption of food scares – in relation, for example, to salmonella, *E. coli* and BSE as well as contaminated milk from China – such critiques found little acceptance. Now sociological critiques of food systems find a deeper resonance in a society that is increasingly sceptical of globalisation in general and has some suspicion about the food it eats (Boucher-Hayes and Campbell, 2009).

Food systems underpinned the earliest development of a global society, driving the migrations of early peoples and the explorations of 16th-century explorers and colonisers. International food regimes, based on the exchange of commodities such as meat, grain, sugar and slaves, formed the basis of global trade circuits that intimately tied the increasing consumption of tea, jam and white bread in 19th-century Ireland to the lives of plantation workers and farmers in India, Australia and the Caribbean. Now Ireland has some food multinationals of its own (Kerry Group, Aryzta, Fyffes) that span the world and compete with giant TNCs such as ConAgra, Nestlé and Cadbury-Schweppes.

But in whose interests are such developments? Tovey (1982) calls into question the transformation of Irish dairy co-ops into major food corporations. Organisations that had been established to develop solidarity and welfare for Irish farmers now provide stock market gains and profits to non-rural 'dry' shareholders. It is arguable that Irish farmers have lost out in the development of the Irish food industry. How does it favour the farmer in Dingle if Kerry Group becomes one of the world's largest producers of artificial flavours manufactured in factories off the New England Turnpike in the US? Schlosser (2001), in his analysis of the American fast food industry, reveals that the welfare of farmers, workers and consumers does not head the agenda for giant food corporations. Similarly, there is extensive evidence (Norberg-Hodge et al., 2000) that the global food system poses an increasing threat to both the economies and the ecologies of the South.

Sociologists are increasingly interested in the question of food choice. Filling a major gap in historical analysis, we now know a substantial amount about the history of Irish food, at least until the early part of the 20th century. It is a remarkable feature that the Irish diet as described in the law texts of the 7th and 8th centuries (Kelly, 1998, pp. 316–59) is not fundamentally different to that consumed in the 18th century (Clarkson and Crawford, 2001) or reported in recent food consumption surveys. Regardless of the massive changes that have taken place over the last 14 centuries, the Irish diet is still to a significant extent based on milk, grain, legumes and meat – with potatoes, tomatoes, sugar, tea and coffee amongst the most important contemporary additions.

What we eat

Across all income groupings, large amounts are spent on sweets, soft drinks, biscuits, crisps, sauces and creams, cakes and buns and tea. (Friel et al., 2004, p. 9)

Is a sociological interest in food choice anything more than intellectual voyeurism – a desire to know what the people next door are having for dinner? Or, perhaps more worryingly, could a managerialist interest in food and eating form the basis of an intensified monitoring and surveillance of the population – a desire to pry into people's everyday lives to ensure they are 'doing the right thing'? More promisingly, can it form the basis of a critique of existing food relationships – a way to challenge the power of the global food players? In Britain the state-funded Economic and Social Research Council sponsored a major interdisciplinary study of food choice entitled *The Nation's Diet*. In a summary of the findings, Murcott (1998, p. 2) reported that food choice is of interest to 'government departments, in sectors of the food industry, by professionals in health, in education and in catering, and many more'. Furthermore, it is 'a question that is self-evidently open to social scientific investigation'. It is also clear that the term 'food choice' itself is open to numerous interpretations and methodological approaches.

Nutritionists have an abiding interest in food choice. Increasingly they have moved away from crude measurements of food consumption towards methodological approaches drawn from sociology and anthropology. Such methods include food consumption diaries, analysis of household purchases, food frequency questionnaires and in-depth interviews (Roos and Prättälä, 1999; Miller and Deutsch, 2009). Not surprisingly, these methods reveal that food choice is shaped in many ways by questions of age, gender, ethnicity and class. This calls into question the biomedical basis of the nutritionist approach (see Chapter 9), which tends to focus on intakes of particular nutrients, such as minerals, vitamins or, more recently, antioxidants or amino acids.

In Ireland, there is a slowly increasing knowledge about the basic facts of food consumption. The North/South Ireland Food Consumption Survey indicates that in some respects the Irish diet has changed little since the 19th century, with the staples remaining potatoes, dairy products, bread and tea – items consumed every week by over 90 per cent of the Irish population. But not surprisingly, this basic menu has been supplemented with a broad range of food items from bananas (consumed by 27 per cent of respondents) to yoghurt (eaten by just one person in six) (Irish Universities Nutrition Alliance, 2001, pp. 16–17). The survey also revealed that four out of 10 of the population are 'overweight' and that the prevalence of obesity has increased sharply since 1990, especially amongst men.

The issue of obesity has, of course, become a major health policy issue, though with little agreement on how to address it.

There are major ethical questions to be asked in relation to the food that people choose to eat, and these inevitably concern sociologists. For example, who has the right to dictate what people 'should' eat? There is a long tradition of telling people, usually the poor, how to conduct their lives, and sociologists have sometimes colluded in this disempowering activity. In particular, is it correct to focus on individual choice and behaviour when the choices that people can make about what to eat are so powerfully shaped by the interests of food corporations? As Schlosser (2001, pp. 139–40) shows, the public had to be encouraged to embrace the hamburger as an ideal food; then when it was found that chicken could be produced at half the cost of beef, the Chicken McNugget was energetically promoted.

A challenge for sociology is to link the use of food in everyday life to the broader conception of the food system. Such an approach can link practices in relation to food to broader questions. For example, a study of how and why people increasingly choose to eat 'organic' food has the capacity to connect with questions about food regulation and issues of risk and trust (Share, 2002). The study of genetically modified (GM) food also links with issues about the practice of science, the influence of global TNCs over our food and broader ethical questions about 'nature' and the human manipulation of life. Perhaps these are the most crucial questions that sociologists can ask about food, involving as they do a genuinely fundamental change in the nature of what we put into our mouths and our bodies.

It is widely acknowledged that contemporary food systems are dominated and shaped by giant multinational corporations. Schlosser (2001) demonstrates how the American meat industry is controlled by a handful of firms, as is the French fry industry, the lettuce industry and so on. Dixon (2002) reveals similar trends within the Australian and global chicken industries. Ireland is moving along a similar trajectory, for example in the dairy, supermarket and alcoholic drinks sectors, each of which is dominated by a small number of large firms. It has even been shown that the jumbo breakfast roll, celebrated in Irish popular culture, is largely an expression of the strategies of global players in the food, oil and retail industries (Share, 2011; see 'The jumbo breakfast roll – Ireland's national dish?' below). It is arguable that such oligopolies and oligopsonies are unhealthy for the quality and diversity of our food and drink. Similarly, they may not be good for those who work in the food industry, as the reported situation of some of the immigrant workers in Ireland's mushroom industry has suggested ('In need of rescue from unscrupulous bosses', *Irish Times*, 12 November 2005).

How has 'the sociology of food' responded to such questions and how might it link to our discussion in Chapter 2 of approaches within Irish sociology? In a review of the field, Beardsworth and Keil (1997) point to the functionalist, structuralist and developmentalist approaches to food. In a later overview, Atkins and Bowler (2001) add the semiological, feminist, post-structuralist and post-modern. Each approach now commands an extensive bibliography and an expanding literature of its own.

Functionalist analyses of food and eating are most usefully placed within the 'managerial' approach. The most commonly manifest version of this approach is in the language of nutrition. As a quasi-medical discourse, nutrition has attracted a remarkably low level of critical attention. The ubiquitous food pyramid and the positive qualities of monounsaturated fats, dietary fibre and antioxidants have entered the popular consciousness with little apparent resistance. When a particular food element, such as monounsaturated fat, is shown to be less (or more) beneficial than had been previously thought, it is rare that the nutrition discourse itself is called into question. Coveney (2006) has shown how the 'nutrition landscape' is closely reflected in what he terms the domestic 'homespace'. Increasingly, people voice their food choices in the language of the nutritionists – it is perhaps not for nothing that their study of diet is often termed 'surveillance'.

Critical sociological approaches to food span a variety of positions. Drawing on Marxist theories of globalisation and commodity capitalism, food systems theorists such as Marsden (2000) outline the international networks of surplus accumulation and exploitation driven by TNCs and their political allies. Translated to the local level, such critical analyses examine the connections between diet, inequality and health (Friel and Conlon, 2004). Feminist approaches, not surprisingly, draw attention to gender inequalities in food provision, consumption and distribution, in particular within families and other domestic units. The critical approach also embraces the many ecological analyses of food systems, such as the developing 'food miles' critique (Norberg-Hodge et al., 2000).

Studies of food consumption patterns from a wide range of countries suggest links between social class and the sort of food that is eaten (Warde and Tomlinson, 1995; Crotty, 1999). An interesting aspect is the apparent influence of conceptions of 'healthiness' of food on consumption patterns by class (and by gender). Most studies indicate that the diet eaten by wealthier households corresponds closely to whatever is 'the nutritionally approved orthodoxy of the day' (Mennell et al., 1992, p. 54). In the 1980s, when health experts urged people to reduce their intake of salt, sugar and saturated fats and to increase their intake of fibre, 'a class-gradient is observed in the use of items such as skimmed milk, vegetables and brown bread' (1992, p. 54). There has long been an acceptance that higher-income groups are more likely to consume fresh fruit and vegetables (Warde and Tomlinson, 1995, p. 248), though evidence from the Slán survey (National Nutritional Surveillance Centre, 2003) suggests that in Ireland, for men at least, this relationship may be altering, with a significant increase in fruit and vegetable consumption amongst men in 'lower' social classes.

Sociologists and policy-makers have coined the phrase 'food poverty' to describe how food and diet may express relationships of inequality. As Friel et al. (2004, p. 3) point out, 'food poverty is multidimensional, referring not only to the lack of access to a nutritionally adequate diet but also to the related impacts on health, culture and social participation'. Food poverty may relate to the absolute lack of food or, more commonly in Western societies, to the lack of availability of a 'healthy diet'.

As suggested earlier, judgments about food are often shaped by issues of morality, taste and even disgust or fear. Thus, it may be difficult to assess the adequacy or quality of people's food intakes. For example, Belasco (2006) has pointed out how in Western societies, discussions about food and social welfare inevitably assume the centrality of meat (and especially beef) in the diet. This tendency is reflected in a study of the costs of healthy eating in Ireland (Friel et al., 2004), where suggested 'healthy' diets presuppose daily meat consumption. This presumption is of course open to critique from a vegetarian perspective. It reminds us that matters of nutrition are social as well as scientific questions (Coveney, 2006).

Notwithstanding such factors, Friel et al. (2004) provide a useful insight into the complexities of food poverty in Ireland. They construct daily menus for hypothetical low-income groups (two parents with two children, single parent with child, lone older person) based on 'typical' habitual dietary patterns and adjusted to reflect the recommendations of the food pyramid. The costs of providing such a menu from different types of retail establishments (such as big supermarkets like Tesco, 'symbol' stores like Centra or 'hard discounters' like Lidl) are calculated using real-world prices. The choice of brands (national versus home brand) is also brought into the equation. The accessibility of different types of retail outlet is considered (cheaper large stores are often only accessible by car).

Based on their calculations, Friel et al. (2004, p. 23) come to some disturbing conclusions, especially for those living exclusively on social welfare payments. They suggest that 'two adults with two children, a single mother with one child and an older person living alone, dependent on social welfare benefits as their only source of income, would have to spend 69 per cent, 80 per cent and 38 per cent respectively of their social welfare entitlements to eat healthily'. This finding suggests that exhortations to those on low incomes to eat healthy food (for example, in relation to the 'obesity epidemic') are misguided. Rather, for low-income groups, the money available to spend is a major influence on food choice and public health measures in relation to nutrition must also address questions of the distribution of wealth and income. Planning issues in relation to location and type of retail outlets are also important – the most easily accessible shops are the most likely to stock expensive and unhealthy foods (such as biscuits and snack foods) and least likely to stock fresh fruit and vegetables.

Echoing the work of Friel and her colleagues, Daly and Leonard (2002, p. 57) found that Irish low-income families were very constrained in the choices they could make about food, in particular about what variation or innovation in food purchasing could take place. What was bought was what 'would be eaten'. They concluded that 'the extent to which people lived out their family's poverty through practices relating to strict controls around food shopping and diet was very striking'.

The playful/intellectual sociological approach to food has been heavily influenced by the structuralist and semiotic approaches of Lévi-Strauss and Barthes. The latter's semiotic analyses of food, especially in his celebrated *Mythologies* (1973), have spawned many imitators, from systematic semiological analyses to weekend supplement journalism. This approach underpins the work of the increasing number of sociologists who study food for its own sake, rather than to provide the sort of directly 'useful' knowledge offered by nutritionists. At its worst such an approach offers little more than an extension of the vast body of writing about food that ranges from recipe books to restaurant reviews, with little that is systematic or theoretically informed. At its best this approach can open up useful debate and provide valuable information about how people think, talk and feel about food and how emotional and practical considerations can underpin food choice. For example, Collins (2006) analyses the campaign by Safefood (the Food Safety Promotion Board) to encourage Irish women to guard against Christmas food poisoning. Pointing out that in December 2004, no reported food poisoning was caused by Irish women in the home, Collins connects the food safety advertisements with the Good Friday Agreement, changing global notions of hygiene and the changing role of women in Ireland. As such, she critically assesses an increasingly dominant conception of food as risk in contemporary societies – including Ireland.

The jumbo breakfast roll – Ireland's national dish?

The jumbo breakfast roll (JBR) emerged publicly into Irish popular cultural consciousness through two specific cultural phenomena. On 6 January 2006, as the Irish bubble economy reached its zenith, a well-known comedian, Pat Shortt, went on Ireland's most popular television show, the *Late Late Show* and, in his persona of faded showband star Dixie Walsh, performed his new song, 'Jumbo Breakfast Roll'. It subsequently became the top-selling pop single of that year, though given its local sphere of reference it did not impact on any other nation's popular music market. Replete with references to building-related phenomena ('luminous jackets'; 'chippies' [carpenters]; 'sparkies' [electricians]; 'working up a ladder'), the song's refrain efficiently lists the key components of the JBR:

> Two eggs two sausage two rasher two bacon two puddin' one black one white
> All stacked like a tower on top of each other and rolled up good and tight
> If you're having some tea the milk's over there and sugar in a bowl
> Says she 'Do you want some sauce on that?' says I, 'I do in my roll.'

The JBR will forever be associated with the Celtic Tiger years, when Irish, Polish and Baltic construction workers, engineers and archaeologists cruised the expanding road networks of Ireland in their Hiluxes and Land Cruisers, speeding from site to site as Ireland's building frenzy continued unabated, stopping only to refuel on a Maxol or Statoil forecourt – diesel for the vehicle and a JBR, Coke and copy of the *Daily Star* for the occupants.

Breakfast Roll Man was a folk hero conjured up by popular economist David McWilliams in his best-selling book *The Pope's Children*, but the JBR itself was arguably the result of the specific intersection of traditional Irish foodways, global fast food systems, leading Irish technology, the Irish planning system and changes to the fuel retail sector.

The key drivers were:

- A booming construction industry that saw the employment of thousands of male manual and service workers in the 18–34 age group – the most likely to eat outside the home – all with plenty of disposable income and big appetites.
- An Irish company, IAWS (Cuisine de France), leaders in the development of the semi-baked baguette that can be finished off in any retail premises to create a 'fresh' crusty roll.
- An historical Irish love of pork meat that goes back at least 1,500 years and expressed today through the 'all day (Irish) breakfast'.
- A consolidation of the fuel industry that saw key players like Statoil expanding from petrol retailing into food, groceries and deli counters.
- A planning system that banned mega-supermarkets and encouraged the development of the convenience store sector – with its 5,000+ Centras, Maces and Galas, one of the most successful such sectors in Europe.
- A pragmatic approach to food that is more likely to see it as fuel than fancy cuisine.

All these factors came together to produce the phenomenon known as the jumbo breakfast roll. Of course other countries have similar products – from the Tex-Mex breakfast burrito to the Vietnamese bánh mi – but the particular combination, wrapped up in trusty tinfoil and clingfilm and perhaps washed down with a Lucozade, is unique to Ireland and, for a few years at least, could lay some claim to being our 'national dish' (Share, 2011).

Irish sociologists have tended to neglect the area of food, though there are signs that interest is increasing. But we know comparatively little about how people choose, obtain and consume food and in what settings. We do not know how taste is defined and experienced in the everyday lives of contemporary Irish households. A critical approach would also address the encroaching power of the major food-related companies operating in Ireland, such as Aryzta, Glanbia or Campbell Catering/Aramark. Increasingly, the power to influence the production, distribution, retailing and serving of Irish food is being handed over to the major global food companies, such as Tesco, Diageo and Unilever. It is most likely that this process will see a transfer of power away from the consumer and the independent producer towards the corporation and away from the local state to the multinational regulators such as the World Trade Organization. A critical sociology of Irish food that addresses such processes might allow for some sort of public response.

PUBS AND DRINKING

Alcoholic drink has long been seen by both external and indigenous observers as central to Ireland's social life and sociability. While there has been much debate over whether, statistically speaking, Ireland is a heavy-drinking country or not, the evidence points to a long history of alcohol consumption and to its central place within the culture (Molloy, 2002). Indeed, the consumption of drink and the influence of alcohol in Irish society appear to have been rapidly increasing since the early 1990s. But as with other aspects of popular culture and everyday life, the world of alcohol and its main site of consumption, the pub, have been comparatively neglected by Irish sociologists. Inglis (2002, p. 31) can validly assert that we still 'await a major social study and history of this important social institution'. Ireland is not alone in this regard. In the British context, Watson (2002, p. 191) has similarly remarked on the paucity of sociological analysis of the public house and of drinking. Drawing on available evidence, this section attempts to throw some light on this important aspect of Irish everyday life.

Watson (2002, p. 190) suggests that 'public drinking "houses" of one kind or another have been important sites of social, political and economic exchange in almost every type of society'. Ireland currently maintains over 7,500 pubs – or more accurately, pub licenses – one for every 600 of the population, man woman and child ('Who will mourn the loss of our pubs?', *Irish Times*, 10 January 2011). This figure compares with 21,000 in 1838 and 17,300 in 1896, though the definition of the pub has changed somewhat in the interim period (Competition Authority, 1998, p. 29). Until the mid-20th century, pubs performed many economic and social functions, from locations for trade and commerce, to transportation nodes, to bases for political and community-based organisations. In more recent times most of these ancillary activities have been transferred to other specialised entities, while pubs have increasingly been incorporated into the broader leisure and tourism industries (Scarbrough, 2008).

In Ireland, as in many other societies, pubs and alcohol have been seen both as a social problem and as an expression of national identity. Sociological research has tended to reflect this dual perception: analysis focuses either on 'problem' drinking and its links with poor health, delinquency and other social problems, or on the role that drinking and alcohol play in relation to group, community or ethnic identity. A third sociological (and anthropological) tradition seeks to explore the pub itself as a site of social interaction, one that is shaped by broader structural elements such as gender and class.

Irish social studies of pubs and the drinking of alcohol include a number of contributions by anthropologist Tanya Cassidy (1997, 1998); histories of the pub by Kearns (1996) and Molloy (2002); and studies of Irish Catholic temperance (abstinence) organisations, including a history of the Pioneer movement by Ferriter (1999). The most recent sociological study, by Gwen Scarbrough (2008), looks at how pubs changed during the Celtic Tiger years. Barich (2009) addresses the same topic from a journalistic stance. Given the centrality of pubs and drinking to Irish social life, they have been less than adequately reflected in studies of Irish communities, though community studies, most notably those by McNabb (1964), Brody (1986), Curtin and Ryan (1989) and Peace (2001), provide some information about the social meanings of public alcohol consumption. Analysis of drinking and pubs in other cultures somewhat similar to our own, for example England (Whitehead, 1976; Burnett, 1999; Watson, 2002), Australia (Fiske et al., 1987) and New Zealand (Fairweather and Campbell, 1990), can help us to understand the Irish experience in a comparative context, as can an understanding of the drinking practices of elements of the Irish diaspora (Stivers, 2000).

Alcohol

Ireland has been unusual in its expression of extremes – a culture of teetotalism coexists with one of high drink consumption; there is both 'abstinence and excess' (Ferriter, 1999, p. 166). Throughout the 20th century at least, the society maintained a high level of abstinence and as a predominantly Catholic country was unusual in this respect – teetotalism or temperance is usually associated with Protestantism. Conversely, it has also been suggested that heavy drinking was a response to the authoritarianism of a church-dominated culture (Inglis, 1998a, p. 170). It could be said then that Ireland, like many other societies, has a contradictory and ambivalent attitude towards alcohol: 'drink was both a pleasure and a curse, but the tirades against alcohol led to ambivalent attitudes and ambiguity as to whether it was a good or a bad thing' (Inglis, 2002, p. 33).

Surveys of consumption indicate the increasing importance of alcohol within contemporary Irish society. Coniffe (1993) has argued that it is very difficult to accurately compare alcohol expenditure across societies, but trends within one society can be instructive. In the 1950s it appeared that Irish alcohol consumption levels were low in the European context (Department of Health and Children, 2002d, p. 28). This may have reflected high levels of abstinence as well as demographic and economic factors. Ferriter (1999, p. 203) suggests that in 1961, middle-class Dubliners spent more on drink and tobacco than they did on housing, but a more careful examination of statistics suggests that the bulk of this expenditure was on tobacco. There was a marked rise in spending on alcohol over the second half of the 20th century: the Household Budget Survey indicates that expenditure on alcoholic drink amongst urban households rose from 1.1 per cent of total household expenditure in 1951–2 to 5.5 per cent in 1994–5 (CSO, 2000).

The two decades from 1980 to 2000 saw a dramatic increase in alcohol consumption in Ireland, as indicated in Table 12.1. This was at a time when per capita consumption in other countries was relatively static (e.g. Denmark, the UK) or declining (e.g. Italy, Australia). By 2001 Ireland had, together with France, the highest per capita alcohol consumption in the OECD (save for Luxembourg, where figures are distorted by cross-border and tourist traffic). The rate of consumption has since declined slightly, but Irish people are still amongst the heaviest drinkers in the world. The reasons for such a rapid increase are not easy to discern, but may be related to the relative youthfulness of the Irish population and a sustained period of economic growth.

A number of community studies have found that Irish attitudes towards alcohol consumption and alcoholism have been tolerant. Drink is seen to be 'essential as a means of initiating social contact, especially with strangers' (Ferriter, 1999, p. 205). Peace (2001, p. 75), in his study of Inveresk (see Chapter 4), found that those who suffered from drink problems were 'looked after' by the community. More broadly, the central role of alcohol and pubs in Irish oral and literary culture and as part of the built environment hardly needs to be stressed: they can truly be said to be 'part of what we are', from Flann O'Brien's celebration of the 'pint of plain' to the marketing of Dublin's Temple Bar.

The pub

> Drinking … is essentially a social act, subject to a variety of rules and norms regarding who may drink what, when, where, with whom and so on. Drinking does not, in any society, take place 'just anywhere', and most cultures have specific, designated environments for communal drinking. (SIRC, 1998)

In Ireland, three-quarters of alcoholic drink is consumed within the confines of a public house, or pub. An understanding of the pub is therefore crucial to an understanding of Irish people's relationship with alcohol. The pub is also central to Irish sociality and society. We can agree with Watson that the pub is something of an 'icon of the everyday' to which most people can relate. Pubs have much to do with habit and repetition, as expressed in the term 'regular'. They may offer a real sense of continuity, regularity and order that is 'fundamental to [a] sense of place, of time and of security' (Watson, 2002, pp. 188–9). In Irish society, pubs have been closely related to everyday community life. Conversely, perceived threats to the institution of the public house, whether through drink-driving legislation, the banning of tobacco smoking or changes in licensing laws, are often seen as an attack on the community or on popular practices.

The American sociologist Ray Oldenburg (1999) has stressed the importance within modern societies of the so-called 'third place'. This is a location that is not work and not home, but rather, a public place where people can easily meet, relax and interact. Such locations include not just pubs, but coffee bars, hairdressing salons, internet cafés, public libraries, amusement arcades and other similar but culturally specific locations. They are typified by their open, democratic nature, informality and ubiquity. For Oldenburg they are a major contributor to the maintenance of social capital and of healthy community life. His study of the 'third place' laments its passing in contemporary American society (echoing the concerns of Putnam, 2000).

Table 12.1: Alcohol consumption, 1960–2008, OECD countries

	1960	1970	1980	1990	2000	2008
Australia	9.4	11.6	12.9	10.5	9.8	–
Austria	10.9	13.9	13.8	12.6	11.1	12.5
Belgium	8.9	12.3	14.0	12.1	10.3	–
Canada	7.0	8.8	10.7	7.4	7.7	8.2
Czech Republic	–	–	11.8	11.3	11.8	12.1
Denmark	5.5	8.6	11.7	11.7	11.5	10.9
Finland	2.7	5.8	7.9	9.5	8.6	10.3
France		20.4	19.5	16.0	14.2	–
Germany	7.5	13.4	14.2	13.8	10.5	9.9
Greece	–	–	13.2	10.7	9.5	–
Hungary	8.2	11.5	14.9	13.9	12.0	–
Iceland	2.5	3.8	4.3	5.2	6.1	7.3
Ireland	**4.9**	**7.0**	**9.6**	**11.2**	**14.2**	**12.4**
Italy	16.6	18.2	13.2	10.9	9.0	–
Japan	5.0	6.1	7.1	8.0	7.6	7.5
Korea	–	–	–	9.1	8.9	8.1
Luxembourg	13.1	15.6	16.8	14.7	15.4	–
Mexico	–	–	3.4	4.9	4.8	5.9
Netherlands	3.7	7.7	11.3	9.9	10.1	–
New Zealand	5.3	9.8	11.8	10.1	8.9	9.5
Norway	3.4	4.7	5.3	5.0	5.7	6.8
Poland	6.3	8.0	8.7	8.3	8.3	10.8
Portugal	17.2	17.9	14.8	16.3	12.9	–
Slovak Republic	6.9	12.8	14.5	13.4	8.9	9.6
Spain	14.6	16.1	18.4	13.5	11.5	–
Sweden	4.8	7.2	6.7	6.4	6.2	6.9
Switzerland	12.1	14.2	13.5	12.9	11.2	10.2
Turkey	0.9	1.1	1.8	1.4	1.5	1.4
United Kingdom	–	7.1	9.4	9.8	10.4	10.8
United States	7.8	9.5	10.5	9.3	8.3	–

Source: www.irdes.fr.

Pubs are one of a number of such 'third places', which in Ireland in the past also included 'spirits grocers' (grocery shops that served alcohol, often frequented by women) and social clubs (which may or may not have facilitated alcohol consumption) – that have long provided a non-domestic social space (Curtin and Ryan, 1989; Kearns, 1996, p. 23). For Kearns (1996, p. 3), the pub is both the 'epicentre' and 'a true microcosm of social life, reflecting the socio-economic ethos of its host community'. Thus, the pub both helps to create and to reflect the society around it. Historically, Irish pubs, particularly those outside urban areas, tended to combine the sale of alcohol with other businesses, such as grocery sales, undertaking, drapery and so on that further increased their social influence (Lambe, 2001; Molloy, 2002, p. 77). Furthermore, publicans have played a central community role, for example in providing financial services in the form of credit or loans. According to Kearns (1996, p. 3), the pub has also served as a social support mechanism for men – an environment where 'they can openly share personal feelings about domestic life, work, health, finances and phobias'. Indeed, it may be argued that the pub shared many attributes with the church: the snug was often referred to as the 'confessional' and the barman as the 'curate'.

The pub provides for a particular type of freedom within modern industrial society. It was memorably described by the researchers of Britain's Mass Observation team in 1943 as 'the only type of public building used by large numbers of ordinary people where their thoughts and actions are not arranged for them' (cited in Watson, 2002, p. 201). Socially, pubs occupy a space somewhere between 'work' and 'home'; indeed, the pub's function, according to Fiske et al. (1987, p. 5), is to 'mediate their opposition by a complex set of repudiations and incorporations of both'. The pub can operate as a 'home away from home' or as an extension of the workplace, but also contains elements that are opposed to those locations. Indeed, it has often been seen as a threat to the stability of both these institutions and has been heavily regulated as a consequence.

For Fiske et al. (1987), speaking of Australian experience, the pub provides a strong symbolic alternative to the home, for example in its décor and in its acceptance of deviant behaviour, such as swearing or drunkenness. In Ireland, the gloomy and functional ambience of pubs was noted both by McNabb (1964, p. 233) in rural Limerick of the 1960s (though he found the local farmhouses generally uninspiring too) and by Curtin and Ryan (1989, p. 137) of urban Ennis pubs of the 1980s. But in both Australia and Ireland, as pubs have changed (in part to attract female customers) they have moved closer to the image of the home, with TV sets, carpets, food and familiar adornments. For Fiske et al. (1987, p. 10) this may change the symbolic function of the pub: the 'erosion of the boundary between home and pub threatens to make the pub no longer a specialised privileged space, where anti-social behaviour is sanctioned'. Indeed, there is now greater official pressure on publicans to restrict drunkenness on licensed premises.

While pubs may be seen as many things, they are pre-eminently places where alcohol is consumed. This helps to define the 'meaning' of pubs. Furthermore, they have tended to be associated with the consumption of particular types of alcohol, and in English-speaking countries, including Ireland, that drink has tended to be various forms of beer. Fiske et al. (1987, p. 16) suggest that as a drink, beer 'is cheap, egalitarian, masculine, social and, when drunk in pubs, significantly differentiated from both home (family/wife) and work (boss)'. This is not to suggest that in Ireland the consumption of spirits (in particular, whiskey) has not also been important, but until relatively recently, alternative, more 'domesticated' drinks, such as wine or coffee, were not an important element of Irish pub consumption.

Gender

> Pub culture is very important to men, particularly as their roles are challenged in modern society, often by women ... where else, if not to the pub, have many men to go to relax? (Psychiatrist Patricia Casey, quoted in S. Butler, 2002, p. 90)

Watson (2002, pp. 199–200) argues that 'what goes on in the pub is not separated from other areas of life but inextricably involved in it. Social relationships in the pub are intimately linked to social relationships outside and play a key role in reinforcing men's position of control and dominance in relation to wives and girlfriends.' Sociologists have noted that until recently, pubs have tended to exclude women and also that they may be associated with gendered attitudes and behaviour that have operated to maintain male power, for example through joking and wordplay that are specifically demeaning to women (Whitehead, 1976; Curtin and Ryan, 1989).

In many cultures, including Ireland, the pub has been recognised as a masculine domain. Thus, McNabb (1964, p. 233) reports that in rural Limerick of the 1960s, 'a respectable woman would never set foot inside one of these places unless there is a grocery shop attached. She certainly never drinks in the local bar.' According to Molloy (2002, p. 80), women were effectively excluded from most Irish pubs until the 1970s, and even then 'it was still common to see women and children sitting waiting outside a pub while husbands and fathers were drinking inside'. In 1989, Curtin and Ryan noted that Ennis pubs remained an almost exclusively male preserve. A consequence of the male domination of pubs has been the lack of adequate social spaces for women and children, though both Brody (1986, p. 162) and Curtin and Ryan note the importance of other 'third places' (though they do not use this term) such as the shop and the church.

There are strong links between pubs and masculinity. Taking the first alcoholic drink in a pub is seen as a 'coming of age'. In 1960s rural Limerick, 'a young man was initiated when he took his first drink in a public house. This was a sign that he had grown up, and was acceptable to the male community' (McNabb, 1964, p. 236). Similarly, Curtin and Ryan (1989, p. 140) draw out the manifold connections between the workplace, the pub, sport and the development of what gender theorist Connell (1987) would refer to as 'hegemonic masculinity' (see Chapter 9).

Female drinking has been almost universally negatively perceived. From time to time there have been moral panics about female alcohol consumption. Thus, in the 1950s 'pioneers writing about women were utterly unambiguous in asserting that females succumbing to drink were infinitely worse than drunken men, particularly in the context of the home' (Ferriter, 1999, p. 168). Women were traditionally confined to the snug or the lounge and until the 1980s it was not unusual for pubs to refuse to serve women a pint of ale or stout, as opposed to a half-pint 'glass'. More recently, particular concern has been raised about young women's consumption of 'alcopops' and other spirit-based drinks.

Despite such societal disapproval, a commonly noted trend has been the recent feminisation of drinking spaces. Women are now welcomed into pubs and the nature of the spaces themselves has changed to accommodate this new market (Molloy, 2002, p. 80). They have become increasingly domesticated:

> pubs have become carpeted and furnished. There are soft furnishings and household artefacts, magazines and newspapers, children's areas and tiled washrooms, all replicating, on a grander scale, elements of home and family life. (Watson, 2002, p. 209)

Associated with such changes, there has been an increase in Irish women's alcohol consumption (Cassidy, 1997, p. 447), probably related to increased disposable income as well as to changes in women's status and the availability of new styles of drinks. There have been significant changes in types of drink consumed, with a shift towards lighter beers (lagers) and white spirits, especially vodka (Molloy, 2002, p. 81). Consumption of such drinks was initially associated with women, but they have found increasing acceptance amongst males as well, suggesting that there has been a significant 'feminisation' of drinking.

The pub as site of interaction

When individuals enter a particular pub they are purchasing far more than a particular product, such as a drink or a meal. They are also purchasing an experience or ambience, which is associated with desire, and the creation and expression of identity and lifestyle. What is important is not so much the actual products that are consumed, but the meanings attached to those products (Watson, 2002, p. 207).

Pubs, not surprisingly, are the site of extensive social interaction. Much of this is overwhelmingly 'everyday' and routine, as revealed through participant observation (Mass Observation, [1943] 1987; Fairweather and Campbell, 1990). Aspects of pub life that have drawn sociologists' attention have been practices of reciprocity and ideologies of egalitarianism and, linked to these, pubs' distinctive oral culture.

The ideology of egalitarianism and reciprocity in Australian pubs has been extensively discussed by Fiske et al. (1987). Kearns (1996, p. 24) reports that the 'rounds system' was well entrenched in Ireland by the 19th century. Though it is certainly not unique to Ireland, Inglis (1998a, p. 170) sees in the strict rounds system evidence for Ireland's 'rule-bound' culture – part of a broader subservience to church and state. Egalitarianism, as expressed through such drinking practices, is for Inglis an expression of the desire to be accepted in the wider group. He maintains (1998a, p. 172) that pub drinking in Ireland has been closely associated with social control and that this is at variance with other European cultures where alcohol is seen as a vehicle of celebration and relaxation. The rounds system may also be seen as an aspect of mutual aid and obligation, mirroring but outlasting similar relationships within the sphere of production.

Irish pubs, like those in Britain and New Zealand, have been noted for their particular type of oral culture – termed 'slagging' in Ireland. This activity may be interpreted as an egalitarian, levelling process, where pretentiousness and selfishness may be challenged; alternatively, it may be seen as an exercise of power, where a particular worldview is enforced through verbal sanctions. In the Limerick Rural Survey, McNabb (1964) deplored the process of 'taking a rise out of some person' and saw it as damaging to the (male) community. Inglis (1998a, p. 172) sees in this process 'not so much a social problem but rather a practice by which the drinking group is maintained'. For Inglis, the traditional rural pub, with its dominant group of bachelor drinkers, was an associate of the church in the enforcement of a repressive social regime designed to protect private property and the family. Kearns (1996, p. 34), however, is more positive and argues that 'within the social dynamics of the pub each regular becomes valued for his distinctive personality and contributions to the group'. He is speaking of Dublin rather than rural pubs – there may be key differences between the two yet to be drawn out by sociologists.

For all sociological analysts, the pub is recognisable as a semi-public but highly regulated social space with its own codes of behaviour. Pubs, like the world within which they exist, are hierarchical and ordered. These arrangements can be expressed in the differences between pubs (Curtin and Ryan, 1989) and also through the geography of pubs themselves, for example as reflected in seating arrangements. Thus, according to Kearns (1996, p. 33), 'the most coveted social niche in the life of many Dubliners is their status as a "regular" in their local pub ... regulars are the privileged pub elite. They form an inner social circle as secondary groups defer to them in seating and conversational status.' Campbell and Phillips (1995) report similar findings for rural New Zealand pubs.

Curtin and Ryan, in their study of clubs and pubs in Ennis, argue that pubs both help to constitute and to reflect class inequalities. They detect (1989, p. 137) a 'distinct class pattern in their usage' and are able to identify 'middle-class' and 'working-class' pubs as well as a minority of 'mixed' ones. People are drawn to specific pubs on the basis that the pub offers a 'forum for [the drinker's] particular cultural and leisure interests'. Echoing the findings of Mass Observation in 1940s Britain, they also conclude (1989, p. 138) that the local pub 'takes on the character of a semi-exclusive "club" where the "inner circle" or regulars are clearly distinguished from casual patrons'. The parameters that define the clientele of a particular pub are strongly shaped by those in the workplace and reflect broader ideas about group identity. The sets of meanings that define 'working-class' and 'middle-class' pubs emerge from the interaction between customers and the environment:

> the discreet middle class bar, where the clientele speak in low educated tones of lofty issues, only recreates for the worker the formal rules of the workplace. He is not barred from these pubs and he can afford to buy his drink like the rest, but he cannot participate fully nor does he want to. 'Public' places such as pubs and lounge bars in this way become class specific according to 'informal' codes which are just as effective in shaping the character of social life in the town as were the 'formal' codes associated with 'members only' clubs of the 1930s. (Curtin and Ryan, 1989, p. 142)

Contemporary patterns

There have been significant changes in both the extent and style of alcohol consumption and the nature of the pub in the years since the early 1990s, a number of which have been alluded to above. The pub, and the use of alcohol more generally, is now increasingly associated with, to use a term popularised by Lash and Urry (1994, pp. 57–9), 'reflexive consumption'. In other words, both pubs and their customers are increasingly self-aware of the 'meanings' of the activity of going out (or staying in) for a drink and pay much greater attention to the symbolic aspects of the process. In the mid-20th century, Irish drinkers generally drank one of a small range of products from a nondescript glass; contemporary imbibers may select from a dazzling array of beers, wines, spirits, ciders, mixed drinks or even waters, often drinking straight from a bottle that bears a well-designed, highly visible and fashionable label.

There has been a rise in the so-called 'themed pub', both in terms of the phenomenal global popularity of the 'Irish pub' and in relation to the emergence of highly symbolised pubs serving niche markets. While themed pubs are not new, the number of them has increased greatly in recent years (Brown and Patterson, 2000). They are analysed briefly by Slater (2000, pp. 255–6), who points out that 'there are bars for young professionals, family bars, student bars, gay bars and sports bars. The market in Ireland and beyond is being segmented in ways similar to other consumer sectors, such as tourism and magazine publishing.' While the emergence of more heavily themed pubs such as those described by Slater may be a new phenomenon, we have already seen that particular pubs have long been associated with social groups that are shaped by gender, class, age and occupation.

More novel, certainly, is the rise of the constructed 'Irish pub' as a global commodity. As Molloy (2002, p. 91) reports:

you can now order a traditional Irish pub from firms such as the Guinness owned Irish Pub Company and the Irish Pub Design and Development Company, who will assemble your pub for you wherever you require. The second company offers six 'stylistic' choices: the cottage pub, the old brewing house, the shop pub, the Gaelic pub, the Victorian pub and the 'contemporary' pub.

By 2006 there were over 1,800 such 'Irish pubs' in 50 countries across the globe, including 400 in Germany, 300 in Britain and 200 in Italy as well as in more far-flung locations such as Dubai and Nepal (Brown and Patterson, 2000, p. 652; Kelley, 2006) and they must be counted as a highly significant aspect of 'Irish culture'. Brown and Patterson (2000, p. 651) report that 95 per cent of 'country themed' pubs in the UK are 'Irish', easily outstripping 'Australian' or 'Scottish' pubs. Slater, in an analysis of 'Irish' pubs in Singapore and Brazil, shows how 'Irishness' is self-consciously and deliberately created and re-created within such pubs through an over-the-top combination of visual symbolism (old street signs, packets of Barry's Tea, posters of Irish writers, chamber pots), Irish music, festivals and food and 'Irish' behavioural characteristics of relaxed informality. This last aspect involves a type of planned spontaneity: 'designing the Irish pub seems to involve a necessary illusion: it should appear that no design has gone into it at all' (Slater, 2000, p. 251). Indeed, it is the planned nature of themed pubs – where, unlike in 'real' pubs, the *craic* is guaranteed – that is a major part of their attraction (Brown and Patterson, 2000, p. 655; Kelley, 2006).

In the UK, a major change in government regulation of pubs has led to substantial shifts in how they operate and has led them to target new markets in new ways (Chatterton and Hollands, 2003). In Ireland, it could be argued that the lack of changes in regulation, and in particular the maintenance of existing licence numbers, has helped to shape the industry (Competition Authority, 1998). For example, recent years have seen the emergence, particularly in urban areas that are undersupplied with pub licenses, of so-called 'superpubs' that can accommodate over 1,000 people. More broadly, pubs are now firmly part of the entertainment industry and alcohol sponsorship underpins many aspects of Irish culture, from rock and pop music to the numerous summer festivals across the country. The comprehensive infiltration of Irish culture by the drinks industry has led to renewed concerns about economic, social and health impacts.

The end of the Irish pub?

The mid-2000s saw a sudden and worrying (for vintners) drop in the number of pub licenses in Ireland. From 2005 to 2006 there was a drop of 440. What was happening? Was it the workplace smoking ban, applicable in all workplaces but with its highest profile and impact in the pub sector? Was it the drink-driving laws, recently brought closer to the European norm? Was it cheap drink in supermarkets?

Gwen Scarbrough attempts to answer this question using Ray Oldenburg's concept of the 'third place'. The third place – a concept shamelessly adopted by a certain Seattle-based chain of coffee houses – is one of those places that are not home, not work, that people can hang out in, be themselves, perhaps be a part of a community and relax. They can include pubs, but also certain types of barbershops, coffee shops, hairdressers, Internet cafés, pool halls, bookshops and so on. As Scarbrough says, 'the pub is the ultimate third place', but in contemporary Ireland it is in real decline.

The legislation and the competition of cheap alcohol from the supermarkets or across the border are indeed factors. But there are other more social trends at work as well. These are related to changing concepts of space – public space, domestic space, 'themed space' and virtual space – and how we as Irish people relate to and make use of those spaces.

Scarbrough argues that contemporary Irish society has seen a relative 'disembedding' of space. It is now more fluid and less deterministic. Technology, mobility and heightened consumption mean that Irish people and communities are much less likely to be closely tied to a certain space and community – and to the pubs that have traditionally nestled, almost unnoticed, within those communities. People are now much more free to choose – and this includes the spaces where they wish to drink and to socialise. They are attracted to spaces that can mesh with their identities, whether this is expressed through elaborately 'themed' pubs such as sports bars, music, décor, furnishings and so on:

> Consumables (drinks and food, but also music, art and interior design, staff and clientele) available in the pub have become identity signifiers, selected on account of a perceived alignment to a particular concept of self (or 'self-brand').(Scarbrough, 2008, p. 60)

Scarbrough suggests that pubs have actually moved to become a 'fourth place' – locations that are specifically constructed to relate to a particular mode of reflexive consumption, like theme parks, tourist zones or shopping precincts. These are places that are consciously constructed to tap into the ideas individuals and social groups have about themselves. Though they may be festooned with 'authentic' artefacts, from old phone booths to fishing nets to the ubiquitous pre-metric signposts, they are in no way 'authentic' pubs, and their customers know that, and are often quite happy with things that way.

But there is a nagging feeling that these pseudo-places are perilously close to the 'non-places' of online communities; while they offer people the opportunity to interact with others based on interests rather than being tied to location, they threaten the basis of the face-to-face community of the third place, the one that can (in theory anyway) embrace all of the public, who can, just for the price of a pint, become part of a community of others for a while.

CONCLUSION

This chapter has attempted to sketch out some of the key approaches to popular culture and to everyday life and to suggest what an analysis of the 'culture of everyday life' in Ireland might look like. The point is made a number of times that Irish sociologists, like their colleagues in other societies, have largely tended to ignore the texture of everyday social life. When they have turned their attention to fashion, food or drink, it is more often to the symbolic aspects of these phenomena, rather than to the actual practices and attitudes of people as they make use of them in everyday social interaction.

It is arguable that a stronger ethnographic interest in the culture of everyday life would help to reveal a more comprehensive sociology of Irish society. But sociologists need to be aware of the tendencies within contemporary society that contribute to an ever-higher degree of monitoring and surveillance of people's everyday lives, whether directly as in CCTV and electronic data trails or more insidiously through the operation of 'expert' discourses such as nutrition and health promotion. It may be that the development of an increased knowledge about how and why people drink, eat and dress in certain ways may lead to enhanced efforts to control these aspects of people's behaviour, whether by institutions of the state, professional groups or private corporations.

It is also important to take note of the 'systems of provision' approach. Analysts of popular culture now stress that the use of artefacts in everyday life – eating a frozen dinner or wearing a pair of jeans – is just part of a longer chain of relationships that connects producers, marketers, distributors and 'meaning makers' of various types. In an increasingly globalised world, these connections can often span the globe, joining societies and institutions in increasingly complex ways. The culture of everyday life can be intensely domestic, but may also have wide-ranging ramifications.

13
Religion

Religion can be challenging to analyse sociologically due to the emotive nature of the concepts involved. At the same time, it is one of the key facets of Irish social life. In recent years, largely as a consequence of controversies involving the Catholic Church, it has become a major area of debate and discussion. Any sociological study of Ireland must reflect the importance of religion in shaping our contemporary society, its continuing relevance in terms of everyday social life and the still central role of religious institutions.

Remarkably enough, despite this centrality, Irish sociologists have failed to produce an extensive analysis of religious experience or of the power of the churches in contemporary Irish society. Until the late 1980s, the bulk of the sociological research was carried out by the churches themselves, predominantly by the Catholic Church (Irish Catholic Bishops' Conference, 2010; Conway, 2011a), and, not surprisingly, was rarely critical. Much of the questioning of the role of the churches, and of religion in Irish social life, has come from the pens of historians, novelists or visiting anthropologists.

Early sociological research into religion in Ireland tended to be positivist, focusing on statistical and attitudinal data. According to Inglis (1987, p. 2), it 'concentrated on gathering facts and data, usually through social surveys, and has avoided dealing with the larger, more general questions about the position and influence of the Church'. Conversely, as Akenson (1991) has argued, much historical research on religion in Ireland relied on anecdotal and skewed sources of evidence and lacked rigorous statistical or comparative analysis. Thus, our knowledge of many aspects of the role of religion in Irish social life has been less complete than it could – or should – have been. With the emergence of a new generation of researchers and a relative decline in the churches' own research activities, the sociological picture is gaining greater complexity.

Recent changes in the influence of the church in Ireland may have led many people, including sociologists, to discount its influence and to see religion as no longer of relevance (Cox, 2010, p. 101). Yet there are many manifestations of religion's enduring social presence. Public revelations and subsequent extensive documentation of decades of sexual and physical abuse within the institutions of the church (Smith, 2007; Keenan, 2011) have brought it to a heightened level of social and political relevance. It is also apparent that issues related to religion are resurgent at a global level, for example the continuing conflict between Christians and

Muslims in Nigeria. New religious movements are also increasingly attracting attention, and in the Irish experience have only very recently been studied sociologically (Cosgrave, Cox, Kuhling and Mulholland, 2011). It is likely, therefore, that religion will continue to be of major interest to sociologists and that in the years to come caution will be needed in interpreting changes in religion as evidence of its decline.

This chapter opens with a discussion of how sociology has defined and studied religion as a key element of social life. All the major founders of sociological thought were interested in religion as a phenomenon, if from different perspectives. Then, reflecting a key theme of this book, we trace the connections between religion and modernity in Ireland, focusing on the concept of secularisation. We examine the role of religion as a marker of social difference and an instrument of power, initially through an analysis of sectarianism in Ireland, then in terms of religion and gender, and then in terms of the emergent record of sexual and physical abuse that has had such an impact on the churches (particularly the Catholic Church) in recent years. Finally, we trace some of the indicators of religious change in Ireland and ask what the future holds for religious belief and structures.

WHAT IS RELIGION?

What exactly do we mean by 'religion'? This is a question that many of the early sociologists, in particular Durkheim and Weber, were drawn to. Across a range of analyses, we can see that key aspects of religion include the following.

- *Sacred symbols*: The crucifix, the star, holy statues, the sign of the cross and often certain colours such as red, green, purple and gold.
- *Rituals and special behaviour*: Pilgrimages, prayers, hand and body movements.
- A feeling of *reverence* towards and awe, even fear, of sacred symbols, practices, personnel and places.
- A *community of believers*: A parish, congregation, sect, cult, religious order or religious community.

Symbols provide a key to the development of religion and to understanding of what it might mean. They carry with them the emotional charge that arises from feelings of belonging – the excitement and fulfilment that come from being part of a crowd or of an intimate group. Symbols and the rituals associated with them emphasise and develop group solidarity.

The distinctive contribution of sociologists has been to move beyond the common-sense understanding of religion as dealing with mystery and the supernatural and to emphasise its social nature. Thus, as Émile Durkheim pointed out in his 1915 work *The Elementary Forms of Religious Life*, one of the first sociological studies of religion, 'if in the midst of these mythologies and theologies we see reality clearly appearing, it is none the less true that it is found there in an enlarged, transformed and idealised form' (cited in Bocock and Thompson, 1985, p. 1). Religious belief has a special nature and language but is clearly linked to underlying social patterns and structures.

The complexity of the religious symbolic universe may reflect the complexity of the society of which it is part. Functionalist sociologists stress how religious symbols (heaven and hell, good and evil) help to delineate the norms and values of society and how religious institutions and practices help to ensure adherence to those norms and values. They also show how religious symbols, and others including ethnic, 'racial' and linguistic ones, can be used to establish the boundaries of a society, thus helping to define who is 'in' and 'out'.

For Durkheim, a common feature of all religious systems is that they divide the symbolic world into the *profane* and the *sacred*. The profane is the matter-of-fact, everyday world that can be dealt with pragmatically, for example the supermarket bread and wine that we may consume with our dinner. The sacred refers to aspects of the world that must be approached in a special, controlled and self-conscious way, with special sorts of behaviour and attitudes, rituals and language – the bread and wine that appear and are consumed during a Christian communion ceremony.

Religions in modern societies, including Ireland, are the long-term outcome of historical processes that have seen the development of specialised and limited rites and cults into larger and more organised and institutionalised bodies of knowledge and practice. These processes include generalisation, abstraction, symbolisation and reification – all ways of organising knowledge about the cosmos – together with the development of specialised organisational and institutional structures such as churches, bodies of religious law, religious orders, seminaries and sacred works (Restivo, 1991, p. 151). Furthermore, despite their frequent appeal to the eternal and the unchanging, religious ideas and structures are also remarkably dynamic, reflecting (sometimes in advance of, sometimes lagging behind) other aspects of societal change.

THE SOCIOLOGICAL ANALYSIS OF RELIGION

The analysis of religion was of key importance to the early sociologists, both in terms of the influence and impact of forms of religious beliefs on society as a whole and in terms of the power and role of religious institutions in everyday social life. Restivo (1991, p. 150) reminds us that from a comparative sociological perspective, religions reflect much about the nature of the societies where they are found. He suggests that the sacred realm is like a:

> map of the social geomorphology, and the correlations between types of societies and types of religions illustrate the relationship between technological and economic development on the one hand and religious beliefs and institutions on the other.

Furthermore, religions are active instruments in the creation of societies. This approach to the relationship between belief systems and other aspects of social life can be found in particular in the works of Durkheim, Weber and Marx in relation to the development and evolution of religious belief.

Durkheim pioneered the functionalist analysis of religion as part of his broader attempt to develop a systematic sociology of modern society. For him, the functions of religion include social cohesion, social control and providing meaning and purpose. Religion helps to maintain the boundaries of society and creates a sense of belonging, especially through shared participation in religious rituals and recognition of shared symbols. Religious bodies typically lay down standards of acceptable behaviour, of good and evil, and these operate to govern the behaviour of populations. Religions also tell stories that relate to the origins, history and purpose of peoples and often speak of an afterlife. This helps to provide meaning and purpose for people over and above the mundane.

While Weber was not the first to connect religion and economic and social activity, his study of the links between Protestantism and capitalism was one of the most systematic. His work on the influence of religion, initially published in essay form in 1905 as *The Protestant Ethic and the Spirit of Capitalism* and later expanded into a comparative historical sociology of world religions, was an attempt to study the development of religion from an historical viewpoint and to methodically explore its sociological fundamentals through the application of 'ideal types' to a mass of complex empirical material on religious belief and practice (Swingewood, 1984, p. 151).

Weber did not posit a simplistic link between religion and economic activity; rather, he wanted to show that religious ideas were not mechanically linked to the economic structure but actively shaped how individuals lived out their day-to-day lives. His main concern was to explore how a set of beliefs about the world and the afterworld was linked to specific sorts of individual and group behaviour – beliefs that would ultimately underpin the development of the western European capitalist economic system. The kernel of his analysis was how adherence to an ascetic form of Protestantism – specifically, Calvinism – led people towards a particular way of thinking about work, social values and social action.

Weber was moved to describe this particular form of Protestantism as it developed in western Europe in the 16th and 17th centuries as 'the spirit of capitalism', for here was found an emphasis on the deferral of gratification, on self-control and on efficiency as a way towards salvation and away from eternal damnation. As it happened, these qualities were also those necessary for effective strategies of financial investment and capital accumulation (Swingewood, 1984, p. 155):

> The spirit of capitalism is expressed in the rationalising attitude to life, in such maxims of conduct as be prudent, diligent, punctilious in repayment of debts and loans, avoid idleness since time is money, be frugal in consumption and so

on. The spirit of capitalism is a social ethic, a structure of attitudes and behaviour closely identified with ascetic Protestantism and its associated religious sects such as the Puritans and the Calvinists. Weber went on to carry out wide-ranging comparative studies of world religions in order to explore how religion, as one of the many factors that shaped societies, operated in a range of settings.

Weber's analysis has been much criticised, not least for its empirical shortcomings (see Swingewood, 1984, p. 158). Nevertheless, in as much as it emphasises religion as a crucial element in the development of society, it clearly has great relevance to Ireland, for as the historian Donald Akenson (1991, p. 16) points out, during the last two centuries, it has been 'one of the most religiously sensitised nations in the western world'. Arguments similar to those of Weber have been mobilised from time to time in Ireland, especially in trying to explain why the (Protestant) north-east of the country industrialised while the (Catholic) remainder did not (Akenson, 1991, p. 18; Keating and Desmond, 1993; Garvin, 2004).

For Marx, religion was the 'opium of the people', a cultural phenomenon that served to blind people to their 'real' needs. For him, religion in the form of sets of ideas or institutional structures ultimately served the needs of the ruling class in society. While Marx did not carry out systematic analyses of religion in the manner of Weber or Durkheim, his views have been influential and have helped to shape the anti-clericalism of many socialist movements.

Contemporary sociologists have paid less attention to religion, perhaps in response to the perceived secularisation of society. In the Irish context, Inglis has successfully harnessed the work of French sociologist Pierre Bourdieu to help explain the *habitus* or 'lasting, general and adaptable way of thinking and acting in conformity with a systematic view of the world' that underpins the unique position of the Catholic Church in Irish society. It is due to the development of such a habitus that many Irish people know almost instinctively how to behave in accordance with the tenets of their religion. According to Inglis (1998a, p. 11), it is 'embodied in the home, school and church [and] produces specific Catholic ways of being religious and ethical'. Furthermore, Bourdieu's concept of 'cultural capital' helps to show how being a 'good Catholic' in Irish society could, until recently, translate into success at school, in the workplace, in business and political life and in the broader society (Inglis, 1997, pp. 79–80).

RELIGION IN IRELAND: FROM 'TRADITIONAL' TO 'MODERN'

In 1987, Inglis, in the first edition of his highly influential book Moral Monopoly: The Catholic Church in Modern Irish Society, was able to say that Ireland was a particularly religious country: 'one of the first impressions of the country that marks it out as different from other Western societies is that the [Catholic] Church is a strong and active force in everyday life' (p. 1). In the same vein, O'Toole (1998, p. 66) remarks that 'when it comes to belief in the existence of the soul, in life after death, in heaven, in prayer, the Irish score so much higher in surveys than the rest of the developed world as to seem not part of that world at all'. We can ask why, and how, has religion acquired such a central role in Irish social life? And is this influence now diminishing or even vanishing?

With its tag as 'the island of saints and scholars', there has been a perception that in some ways Irish people are *naturally* religious. Inglis (1987, p. 1) remarks that it is 'as if the Irish have always been a holy and religious people who are devoted to the Catholic Church'. Similarly, there have long been notions that as a 'Celtic' people, the Irish have some sort of affinity with superstition, spirituality, magic and religious belief. We now see this view reiterated in much New Age writing and practice related to Celtic mythology (Kuhling, 2004). Sociological and historical analysis show that there was nothing natural or inevitable about the development of religious beliefs, practices and institutions in Ireland; rather, these can be understood as the outcome of many complex social factors.

Within sociological thinking, there is a tendency to see the development of Irish religion as reflecting a move from a 'traditional', highly devotional society to a 'modern', increasingly secularised one where religion is of less consequence. But the modernisation approach may tend to oversimplify this process. In reality, the nature of religious belief and practice in Ireland has been very dynamic over the last two centuries and more, and its development has certainly not been unidirectional. For example, it was only with the rise of the Catholic middle class in the late 19th century that Mass attendance grew from its mid-century rate of approximately 35 per cent to its turn-of-the-century level of 90 per cent (Miller, cited in Akenson, 1991, p. 139). And, as we shall see later in this chapter, levels and styles of religious practice are continuing to change.

The picture that emerges from historical and sociological analysis is more complicated than a simple conception of modernisation would allow. For example, many of what may now be regarded as 'traditional' aspects of Catholic Church practice were introduced quite recently, in the period from the end of the 19th century to the 1950s. Furthermore, much of what is now seen as modern or even post-modern in evolving religious practice may represent a return to much older patterns of behaviour.

For example, historians of religion in Ireland highlight the existence of a long-established 'folk religion' that existed before the modern institutional churches we recognise today. In many respects, such as low attendance at formal religious events, a smaller gap between priests and people and a less centralised and dogmatic faith, this folk religion was closer to how many people (would like to) see the modern churches developing. Some critics of contemporary religion, such as Kirby (1984, p. 66), celebrate what they see as this expression of Irish spirituality:

A more authentic, gentle, tolerant and yet demanding faith was lived by (our) ancestors which had a deeply developed social conscience, a healthy anticleicalism and a complete absence of puritanism and prudery when it came to sexual matters.

Kirby suggests that the language of this pre-Famine folk religion reflected a more spiritual consciousness than that embodied in the 'stylised and sentimental prayer forms' associated with contemporary practice. It also embraced, he claims, a developed social conscience that expressed itself in everyday behaviour, for example in respect for the poor and in a form of social organisation that appears to approach a form of primitive communism or communitarianism.

Many explanations have been suggested for the almost unequalled growth in power of the Catholic Church in Ireland in the period between the Famine and the 1980s and the parallel growth in other organised religions (the Church of Ireland and Presbyterianism in particular) through much of the same period. There has been a great deal written on this topic, and space precludes an extensive discussion here. Historians and sociologists (see Kirby, 1984, pp. 55–64; Akenson, 1991, pp. 139–43; Fahey, 1994; Inglis, 1998a, pp. 102–28; Keogh, 1998, pp. 88–114; Halikiopoulou, 2011, pp. 43–53) suggest a range of key factors (see below), some of which, it must be noted, can appear to be contradictory.

Factors affecting the development of the churches in post-Famine Ireland include:

- The decline of the landless cottier class (where older alternative belief systems were prevalent) due to the development of new land tenure arrangements before, during and after the Famine.
- The nationalist political movement towards the development of a separate national identity, where 'Irish' increasingly came to be equated with 'Catholic'.
- The rationalisation of Irish society with increasing urbanisation and integration into a 'modern' and Anglophone society.
- The growth of religious belief and practice as a response to rapid social change.
- The 'civilising process' in western Europe, with the increasing 'respectability' and 'gentling' of Irish society accompanied by the growth of moral discipline.
- The successful centralisation and bureaucratisation of the various churches into more efficient administrative organisations – the 'devotional revolution'.
- The effective ceding of control over education from the state to the churches.
- From a class analysis perspective, the growth of religion suited both the British Empire and the Irish ruling class – as a distraction from class struggle and as a means of disciplining and controlling the working population.

The Catholic Church that very successfully developed in 19th-century Ireland went on to wield extensive power in the newly independent state until very recently, as succinctly described by O'Toole (1998, p. 70):

The groundwork laid down in the nineteenth century was the basis for the Church's triumph in independent Ireland. Once there was an Irish state, it became the effective arbiter of social legislation, having a ban on divorce inserted into the Constitution, encouraging the introduction of draconian censorship of books and films, delaying the legalisation of artificial contraception until 1979, retaining largely unquestioned control over schools and hospitals funded by the taxpayer, resisting the slow development of a welfare state.

It is common for critics to draw a pen picture of the 'traditional' (Catholic) Church in Ireland. This image is usually located somewhere around the 1920s to the 1950s: an age when 'devotional Catholicism' peaked with the popularisation of practices such as pilgrimages to Marian shrines, the building of grottoes, the practice of Novenas and the development of sodalities (MacCurtain, 1997, p. 247). It was also the time when the institutional church in Ireland was perhaps at its most influential (Fuller, 2005). Kirby (1984, p. 15) contrasts the early 1980s with a previous era when Ireland was 'a stagnant society, presided over by a repressive and sexually obsessed church, from which the young had to flee if they were to find any space to explore and satisfy their own needs'. Similarly, Inglis (1998a, pp. 1–2) contrasts the situation in Ireland today with the memory of his own childhood devotions. As we have seen, the churches did have significant ideological and social power in this period.

SECULARISATION: THE DISENCHANTMENT OF THE (IRISH) WORLD?

In February 1948, the first action of the newly elected inter-party cabinet, under Fine Gael Taoiseach John A. Costello, was to send a telegram to the Pope in the Vatican, stating its desire to:

> repose at the feet of your Holiness the assurance of our filial loyalty and of our devotion to your August Person, as well as our firm resolve to be guided in all our work by the teaching of Christ, and to strive for the attainment of a social order in Ireland based on Christian principles. (quoted in Whyte, 1971, p. 158)

On 20 July 2011, Fine Gael Taoiseach Enda Kenny spoke in the Dáil of 'the dysfunction, disconnection, elitism – the narcissism – that dominate the culture of the Vatican to this day'. He went on to say:

> thankfully … for us, this is not Rome. Nor is it industrial-school or Magdalene Ireland, where the swish of a soutane smothered conscience and humanity and the swing of a thurible ruled the Irish-Catholic world. This is the *Republic* of Ireland 2011. A republic of laws, of rights and responsibilities; of proper civic order; where the delinquency and arrogance of a particular version, of a particular kind of 'morality', will no longer be tolerated or ignored. ('This is a republic, not the Vatican', *Irish Times*, 21 July 2011, emphasis in original)

What had happened in the intervening 60 years to so change the attitude of the Irish political elite to the centre of Catholic Church power? What gave each of these Taoisigh the permission to say what they did? What do these statements say about the role and position of religion in Irish society?

Sociologists would argue that the contrast between the statements starkly reflects the *secularisation* of Irish society. Secularisation is a complex and contested concept, defined (by Berger, cited in Hornsby-Smith and Whelan, 1994, p. 8) as 'the process by which sectors of society and culture are removed from the domination of religious institutions and symbols'. Broadly, it is a set of social processes that entails a decline in the importance of religion in relation to non-religious roles and institutions, such as those of the state and the economy; a decline in the social standing of religious roles and institutions; and a decline in how people engage in religious practices, display beliefs of a religious kind and conduct their lives in a manner informed by such beliefs (Bruce, 2002, p. 3).

Secularisation reflects the separation of the profane and the sacred and the downgrading of the latter. It suggests a 'disenchantment' of society (Weber's evocative term), where the spiritual and the supernatural come to play less of a role in people's lives, to be replaced by more mundane, rational and scientific modes of thinking and expression. It means church attendance, prayer or the use of sacred objects become less important in people's daily lives. Finally, it refers to the reduced power and influence of religious institutions in public life and in the status and prestige of religious figures: this is what we can see in the changing orientation of Irish politicians to the Vatican.

In sociology, the concept of secularisation has been strongly linked with that of modernisation (Halman and Draulans, 2006, p. 264). A decline in the salience of religion was seen as a key element in the move towards a 'modern' society. When modernisation theory was at its most powerful, in the 1960s, secularisation was seen to be inevitable as societies became more urbanised and industrialised. While there have undoubtedly been moves towards markedly more secular societies, in countries such as Sweden, the Netherlands and Canada, the experience of the US, both intensely religious and highly 'modern', has led many to question the connection between the trends (Bréchon, 2007; Malesevic, 2010; Halikiopoulou, 2011). There is now a view that the 'classical' concept of secularisation is no longer useful (Aldridge, 2000, pp. 89–122) and the concept of 'neo-secularisation' has been posited (Malesivic, 2010). The new approach is specific to culture and history, focusing on the experiences of individual societies at different levels: individual, institutional and national. It does not assume a singular or universal direction of change, but recognises that changes in the role and power of religion are linked in complex ways with other aspects of social change and may follow different trajectories (Fahey et al., 2005, p. 31).

There is a general consensus that Ireland is, or was, a place 'where religion and churches matter' (Fahey et al., 2005, p. 30). It has been seen until recently as a society where the process of economic and cultural modernisation was not necessarily accompanied by substantial secularisation (Greeley, 1999; O'Toole, 1998, p. 66). This view has now largely altered, and it is agreed that Ireland is witnessing a substantive change in the role of religion (Inglis, 2007), one that is bringing it closer to the European mainstream.

There is a view that the public power and everyday influence of religion in the lives of Irish people peaked at some time in the late 1950s and has since been in almost continual decline (Fuller, 2005; Malesevic, 2010, p. 28). A key phase was the 1960s, when change in the churches at the global level, as manifested in Vatican II, was combined with a period of unprecedented economic growth in Ireland and a new openness to international influence. Kirby (1984, p. 19) suggests that this new era of prosperity and social change contributed to a new optimism for the future and a critique of the familiar institutions of Irish life, including the Catholic Church. Inglis (1998a, pp. 231–8) identifies the media – not least RTÉ's *Late Late Show* – as a major instrument of modernisation and stimulus of such change.

There was indeed evidence of a 'renewal' in the Christian churches in the second half of the 20th century. This was driven in part by a charismatic movement (Szuchewycz, 1989) that emphasised the role of lay people in the churches and was paralleled by more participatory and emotive types of religious practice, such as the 'folk mass'. Nevertheless, such innovations did not stem the long-term decline in church activity and influence. By the late 1990s the Moderator of the Presbyterian Church in Ireland, Dr Harry Allen, claimed Dublin to be 'one of the most secular cities in Europe, where vast numbers of people, especially those under 40, have no significant church connection' (*Irish Times*, 3 June 1998). Shortly thereafter, Cassidy (2002, p. 18) argued that 'to an outside observer, there is little to parallel the dramatic changes that have marked the Irish faith profile in recent years, changes that have revealed the folly of presuming that Ireland was or would always remain a type of spiritual oasis in an increasingly de-Christianised Europe'.

The period since the early 1990s in Ireland has been one of further social change and of considerable upheaval in the churches, especially the dominant Catholic Church. As in many other countries, a history of decades of physical and sexual abuse has been exposed, with cover-ups and legal and financial scandals. There has been a severe questioning of the doctrine of clerical celibacy, demands for a greater role for women in the church and widespread questioning of religious doctrine in relation to contraception, divorce and other questions of sexual morality (Hug, 1999; Fuller, 2002).

There has been a sustained 'crisis' in Catholic religious vocations and the church is unable to replace its ageing workforce. Religious vocations have experienced a sharp decline in Ireland (Conway, 2011b), as in the rest of western Europe. The closure in the 1990s of seminaries in Dublin, Thurles, Kilkenny, Waterford and Carlow and declining numbers in the only still operating seminary, St Patrick's College, Maynooth, from peaks of over 500 in the 1950s to a student priest body of about 70 in 2011 (Irish Catholic Bishops' Conference, 2011a), provides evidence of this decline in Catholic vocations.

The decline has severe implications for the laity as well as the religious workforce itself: it will result in parishes with few, if any, priests to administer the sacraments and increasing demands on the time and energies of the clergy who remain (Conway, 2011b). As Halikiopoulou (2011, p. 10) points out, this trend has major implications for the Irish Catholic Church in particular, as much of its institutional power has been based on its extensive personnel, for example across health, education and welfare services, as well as in the parishes.

Taken together, these trends suggest that even if Irish society resisted secularising tendencies until the 1980s, the process has now gained considerable momentum. A number of reasons for the decline in religious practice and influence in Ireland have been posited. One may be a general convergence with European and Western behaviour: figures for participation are even lower for other 'Catholic' countries like Spain and Italy and amongst the Catholic population in Britain. Second, the number and frequency of high-profile church-related scandals, while by no means unique to Ireland, have without doubt had a negative effect on the Catholic Church. Third, the media has operated as a supplier of alternative value systems (mainly associated with materialism, hedonism and consumerism) and also as an alternative way to pass time and socialise, an argument made strongly by Inglis (2007). Fourth, there has been a severe divergence between the churches (especially the Catholic Church) and much of the population in relation to social and 'moral' matters, such as contraception, celibacy, abortion and the role of women (Halikiopoulou, 2011).

In 1984, Kirby already perceived a 'major crisis' in the Catholic Church. It had 'not yet awakened to the major challenge that faces it if it is to find any significant role for itself in the fast-changing Ireland now taking shape' (1984, p. 10). It was, for him, a church unsure of the message it should preach and one that relied too much on a largely irrelevant set of principles and priorities. Kirby (1984, p. 66) suggested there had been a rupture between church and people, contributed to by the 'modern' church's own organisational success: 'where the old was intimate with God and saw his hand in the things of the world, the new was stylised and sentimental, encouraging a divorce between things spiritual and material'.

Halikiopoulou (2011) also sees a connection between secularisation and cultural modernisation, but of a different kind. In her view, it has been the Catholic Church in Ireland's resistance to modernising tendencies, or its inability to adjust to contemporary Irish life, that has seen its influence and popularity decline. This is partly due to the centralisation of power in the Vatican, which has reduced the possibility of a more flexible response. This is in contrast to the 'national' Greek Orthodox Church, which has been more integrated in and better able to adapt to changes in Greek society.

People may also combine various beliefs and attitudes, religious and non-religious, 'syncretically'. This anthropological term, used by Eipper, refers to how 'religious genres, allegiances, understandings and behaviours blur and blend in ways that require an acceptance of diversity, even a willingness to embrace it and enter into dialogue with it' (2011, p. 34). It is reflected in how people may combine elements of 'traditional' religions, 'New Age' ideas (for example, about alternative therapies) and aspects of what might be called 'superstition' or folk belief, together with what might be seen as 'modern' ideas about science (such as a belief in evolution) and economics – even when these different beliefs may be contradictory or logically inconsistent.

The apparent process of secularisation of Irish society is not straightforward to identify, measure or explain. As religion is complex and dynamic, so is its relationship to other aspects of social life. While keeping the complexity of secularisation processes in mind, it remains interesting to look at our knowledge of religious belief, 'conventional' religious practices, other religious practices and other indicators of institutional change.

RELIGIOUS BELIEF

Bréchon (2007, p. 466) suggests that we need to look carefully into indicators or religious identity, as they may 'not really measure a religious experience or a belief or a practice [but] sometimes convey attachment to a culture, to a nation or to an origin'. Thus, for example, Halikiopoulou (2011) has shown how in Greece, attachment to the Orthodox Church is strongly bound up with Greek nationalism. There is evidence that in Ireland, religious identification is also bound up closely with issues of culture and national identity. Thus, further probing of the nature of religious belief is justified.

According to the 2011 census, 84 per cent of the Irish population continues to identify themselves as Catholic. This represents a 4.89% increase from the 2006 census. Almost 6 per cent are prepared to assert that they have 'no religion' (AIRO, 2012), though the number so identifying has increased markedly since the option was first offered in 1961 (Mac Gréil, 2011, p. 439). In the 2011 census, the ranked order of growth (since the 2006 census) of religions identification is as follows:

Table 13.1: Growth of religious identification since the 2006 census

Atheist	320.34%
Lapsed Catholic	136.85%
Agnostic	132.41%
Orthodox	117.44%
Hindu	75.73%
Apostolic/Pentecostal	73.03%
Muslim	51.22%
Buddhist	33.56%

Source: AIRO (2012).

Similarly, recent research by Mac Gréil (2011, p. 462) indicates that just 4 per cent of respondents indicate that they do not believe in the existence of God. Thus, at the basic level of belief in a supernatural deity, Irish people could be said to be very religious. These findings may be compared with the UK, where, according to the International Social Survey Programme (ISSP), 32 per cent do not believe in God. Irish people are, in European terms, amongst a group of countries where the levels of religiosity are high; others include Portugal, Poland, Romania and Croatia (Halman and Draulans, 2006, p. 275). For Mac Gréil (2011, p. 465), the finding in his survey about Irish people's 'closeness to God' challenges 'the extent to which secularisation has penetrated Irish society'.

Table 13.2: Religious beliefs and behaviours of the Irish population (per cent), 1991–2008

	1991	1998	2008
God	92	93	90
Life after death	80	78	75
Heaven	87	85	79
Miracles	73	71	65
Hell	50	50	50
Feel very religious	14	13	11
Pray (every week)	9	25	10
Pray (never)	6	5	9
Attend church (once a week)	64	61	36
Attend church (once a month)	3.88	4.06	7.32
Attend church (several times a year)	6.87	11.78	17.03
Attend church as 11/12-year-old child (once a week)	79	80	69
Attend church as 11/12-year-old child (never)	0.3	0.4	1.9
Attend church (never)	5	4	10
Participate in church activity (every week)	4	6	5

Source: ISSP, 1991–2008.

It may be that people are prepared to 'sign up' to a religion without necessarily adopting the beliefs of a particular faith. What do we know about what Irish people believe and say they practice? The main source of information available to us is attitudinal research. This has been carried out in Ireland as part of broader European and international social science surveys or in surveys carried out for or on behalf of the churches themselves (Conway, 2011a). An early source of information we have on religious beliefs and practices in Ireland is the survey data reported in a landmark study in the 1970s by sociologist-priest Fr Micheál Mac Gréil and in a series of follow-up surveys he has carried out (published in 1977, 1996 and 2011). Mac Gréil's research has been complemented by a number of studies drawing on the European Values Survey (EVS) (Whelan, 1994; Cassidy, 2002; Fahey et al., 2005; O'Mahony, 2010), the International Social Survey Programme (ISSP) (Ward, 2002; Fahey et al., 2005) and by frequent opinion polls undertaken by media organisations, religious think tanks such as the Iona Institute (e.g. *Irish Times*, 2 November 2009) and the Association of Catholic Priests (Amárach Research, 2012).

Table 13.1 presents data from the ISSP relating to belief in God among the Irish population. The first thing that can be said is that in the Irish population there is a remarkably high level of belief in God, at over 90 per cent. In addition, between 1991 and 2008 there was a very slight decline in belief in God, from 92 per cent in 1991 to 90 per cent in 2008. Table 13.1 also shows that there are high levels of belief in such things as heaven, miracles and life after death. With respect to life after death and heaven, however, there has been a decline in levels of belief in the 1991–2008 time period.

Levels of belief in hell among the Irish population are much lower than levels of belief in these other items, with 50 per cent of the Irish population believing in the existence of hell. However, there has been considerable stability in levels of belief in hell in the 1991–2008 time period, with virtually no decline reported in belief in this item. Overall, there has been remarkable stability in levels of belief – but not religious behaviour – among the Irish population (Kerkhofs, 2005), suggesting that external practices are more prone to secularisation than internal beliefs (Fox and Tabory, 2008).

Table 13.1 also reports ISSP data relating to religious behaviours – including church attendance – in the 1991–2008 time period. To go back further in time to the early 1970s, it is necessary to turn to other data sources apart from the ISSP. Table 13.2 presents data relating to religious behaviours going back to 1974 drawn from these sources. Two important points can be made about the trend in weekly Irish church attendance. First, the decline in church attendance was from an initially very high level of participation. Second, the decline in weekly attendance was gradual in the 1980s, became more dramatic in the 1990s and then returned to a gradual decline in the 2000s. The proportion of the Irish population who say they never attend church has seen an increase from 5 per cent in 1991 to 10 per cent in 2008, which points to an increasing level of alienation from institutional religion.

While weekly church attendance declined between 1991 and 2008, attendance on a monthly basis and attendance several times a year increased rather than decreased. This suggests that Irish people are attending church less frequently than before rather than giving up church attendance altogether (Fahey, 2002).

Agreement with the tenets of the Catholic Church diverges sharply when issues related to socio-moral teachings are explored. As Cassidy (2002, p. 24) remarks, 'there is increasing evidence that Church teaching in key areas of sexual ethics is progressively less influential in determining lifestyle choices … on abortion, premarital sexual relations, extra-marital relationships and same sex relationships'. Attitudes to abortion have often been taken as indicative of the adherence to core Catholic teaching. According to the ISSP, in 2008, 31 per cent of respondents agreed with the statement that abortion is 'always wrong' in the case of a defect in the baby; this compares to 41 per cent in 1998. This suggests some weakening over time in commitment to church teachings in relation to abortion but also in relation to other socio-moral issues such as premarital sex, extramarital sex and same-sex relations (see Table 13.3).

Table 13.3: Attitudes toward socio-moral issues (per cent always wrong), 1991–2008

	1991	1998	2008
Premarital sex	36	30	14
Extramarital sex	71	63	58
Same-sex relations	68	60	26
Abortion (defect)	48	41	25
Abortion (poverty)	67	59	47

Source: ISSP, 1991–2008.

RELIGIOUS PRACTICE

There are many reasons why a person may attend a religious event, not all of which have to do with belief. As Bréchon (2007, p. 466) points out, occasional attendance at a religious institution for 'rites of passage' events, such as christenings, marriages or funerals, may 'measure the demand for social rituals to mark the major events of life rather than a true religious expectation'. Any attempt to 'measure' the extent of religious belief or practice is fraught with difficulty, as practices are diverse, culture specific and dynamic. For example, Halikiopoulou (2011, p. 6) points out that Catholicism and Orthodox Christianity have very different expectations in relation to attendance at religious services, which must then guide us in interpreting statistics in this area. Infrequent attendance has far less salience in Greece than it does in Ireland, where levels of participation in religious activities such as weekly Mass, communion and confession, as well as frequent prayer, are important indicators of attachment to the institution of the church.

The most recent analysis of the EVS shows that for Catholics, weekly attendance at Mass is limited to 34 per cent of the general population, a figure somewhat below Mac Gréil's figure (2011, p. 442) of 42 per cent. This figure has declined sharply since the 1970s (see Table 13.1), falling from 91 per cent in 1974 (Mac Gréil, 2011, 447). These levels may be compared to a European average, in the last decade, of 30 per cent (O'Connor, 1998, p. 61). Ireland, Poland and Malta are the only countries in Europe where monthly attendance at religious services exceeds 70 per cent (Fahey, 2002b, p. 53).

In Ireland, according to Mac Gréil's research, there are significant urban–rural differences in Mass attendance, ranging from a weekly rate of 29.5 per cent in urban areas with a population of over 100,000 to 62.7 per cent in rural village areas (Mac Gréil 2011, p. 449). This reinforces a long-established pattern. Mac Gréil suggests (2011, p. 451), in line with other analysts of secularisation from Durkheim onwards, that the urban–rural differences may be due to a 'lack of community' in the city, though offers no evidence to support this. Age is also a factor: according to one poll, in 2009, 31 per cent of 18- to 24-year-olds attended church weekly, while amongst the over-65s weekly attendance was at 70 per cent (*Irish Times*, 2 November 2009). Mac Gréil indicates an even lower rate of 20 per cent for the younger age group and 83 per cent for those over 71 years of age (2011, p. 448).

Prayer remains a popular activity. Fahey (2002b, p. 62) reports that only 9 per cent of Irish adults 'never pray', compared with 55 per cent in France and 48 per cent in Britain. Mac Gréil's 2007–8 study found that 72 per cent of respondents prayed weekly or more often (2011, p. 456). As with other aspects of religious practice, the least likely to pray are those that are most educated and most urbanised, the younger and those who have never been married. Mac Gréil surmises that there may be a decline in occasions like the family rosary or regular family prayers, to be replaced by the distracting 'intrusions' of the television and the Internet (2011, p. 457). Meanwhile, confession has almost died out as an activity for Catholics. According to Mac Gréil (2011, p. 445), one-third of Catholics 'never' go to confession and only a third would go as often as 'several times a year', while 44 per cent of those under 40 years of age 'never' go (p. 454).

The public image of the Catholic priest among Irish children
As part of the Growing Up in Ireland study, nine-year-old Irish children were asked about their role models. Specifically, they were asked a question about the person they most admired from a list including musicians, sports stars and church leaders. This question is an indirect measure of the public image of Catholic clerics among Irish children. Surprisingly, only 0.25 per cent of Irish children reported that a church leader was the person they most admired.

> This compares to 10.42 per cent who mentioned a pop star/rapper/singer, 23.05 per cent who mentioned a footballer or sports star and 44.66 per cent who said their mum or dad was the person they most admired.
>
> Two conclusions may be drawn from these findings. One is that Irish children tend to look to celebrity sports culture rather than to religious organisations for frames of reference to guide their everyday lives. Second, this finding suggests that the values embodied by celebrity icons such as sports stars and musicians – such as the pursuit of fame, wealth and 'the good life' – articulate more with Irish children than do religious values represented by church leaders. At the same time, Irish children clearly place the highest value on familial influences – which have a strong congruence with religious values – in shaping their future lives.

Can we conclude, then, that there has been a secularisation process in Ireland? It is certainly the case that religion, in various ways, remains important for a significant proportion of the population. It is also clear that the publicly expressed subservience of political discourse to religion has weakened considerably. The clearly articulated anti-clericalism that is most notable in France, but also in some other European countries, appears to be largely absent from Irish society. Rather, suggests Cox (2010, p. 100), Ireland is similar to Japan, where:

> a generalised religious sentimentality and near-universal biographical rituals mean rather that the practical salience of religion ebbs within individual lives than that whole sectors of the population become actively or consciously anti-religious.

Another possibility is that we are witnessing the emergence of 'civil religion' (Bellah, 1967) or a 'social church' where people seek and use religious values and symbols without the social commitment involved – often referred to (pejoratively) in Ireland as à la carte religion. For example, a former Moderator of the Presbyterian Church, Dr Allen, reported critically on 'social baptisms' among Spanish Anglicans, 'where families, suitably dressed, arrive at the church door, take photographs, and then proceed to the hotel for a meal, without ever going into the church. This also happens at confirmation time. They keep the custom but refuse the commitment' (*Irish Times*, 3 June 1998). There is little evidence yet whether such practices are becoming widespread in Irish society.

RELIGION, POWER AND SOCIAL INEQUALITY

Religion is always intertwined with structures of social inequality (Restivo, 1991, p. 154):

For the upper classes, it was a social activity intertwined with political ideologies and alliances, and a tool of oppression. For the lower classes, religion was a source of hope and release from the trials and uncertainties of everyday life. For the middle classes it was a source of rules about appropriate demeanour and deference.

There is a strong link in all societies between religion and power, including political power. The unity of religious and political power is weaker in more technologically advanced and complex societies, but the connections remain important. Religion has continued to be drawn upon by secular leaders in Ireland for legitimation and administrative organisation. Religious personnel continue to be involved in political activity to shore up their own hierocratic (worldly) power.

In Ireland, the exercise of church power has taken place through ideological power (the power of belief systems), through the control of resources (land, property, health, education and welfare systems) and, it is increasingly being revealed, through coercive physical power (usually described today as 'abuse'). Pioneering work by Whyte (1971, 1980) analysed the often close relationship between church and state in independent Ireland, while writers such as Inglis (1987, 1998a), Fuller (2005) and Halikiopoulou (2011) have drawn attention to the extensive institutional power and resources the Catholic Church has retained into the current century.

RELIGION, IDENTITY AND SECTARIANISM

The religious affiliation of the population of the Republic of Ireland remains overwhelmingly Roman Catholic. In recent years there has been an increase in those who do not identify with any religion, while there has also been a substantial increase in the numbers who identify as Muslim and Orthodox. There has been something of a revival in the Protestant religions, with increases in the numbers of adherents of the Church of Ireland, Methodists and Presbyterians (Mac Gréil, 2011, p. 439).

Prior to the recent turnaround, the long-term decline of the Protestant denominations in the Republic, against the durability of Catholicism, had been perhaps the main feature of the Irish religious landscape. This decline has been attributed by historians to a number of factors, including the return to Britain of many bureaucrats and servicemen and their families after independence; sectarianism directed against Protestants; lower rates of fertility amongst non-Catholics; the establishment of a theocratic Irish state; and the operation of the *Ne Temere* decree, whereby children of 'mixed marriages' were brought up as Catholics (Inglis, 1998a, pp. 18–20).

Akenson (1991, p. xi) claims that 'the cultural differences between Protestants and Catholics are so central to modern Irish history that to evade them leaves a great black hole in the nation's story'. He points out that the perceived 'fact' of difference between the two continues to be taken for granted, in relation to both the Irish living in Ireland and the Irish diaspora. Fahey et al. (2005, p. 31) conclude that the 'complex role of religion in defining relations of dominance and subordination between competing cultural traditions ... has proved deeply enduring and has undoubtedly played a part in maintaining a central place for religion in Irish life.' Halikiopoulou (2011) has identified the 'external threat' (religious and political) and consequent 'cultural defence' as key factors in the power of the Irish church.

From its earliest days, the independent Irish state began to define its people, through the state apparatus and official discourses, in terms of 'Catholic' and 'non-Catholic'. This dichotomy has always been attractive to commentators on Irish social issues. As Akenson points out, such contrasts 'were easily drawn in the nineteenth and early twentieth centuries and this was especially prevalent because it was an age that was given to thinking about cultural differences in racial terms' (1991, p. 10). Religious difference has become a central theme in thinking and writing about Irish history and contemporary society, not least because of the continuing, though now much reduced, conflict in the North of the country, which is widely perceived to be religious in nature.

Akenson's study of the historical differences between Irish Catholics and Protestants has gone a long way towards debunking many of the myths that have arisen about the two communities – both within Ireland itself and among the ethnic Irish of Australasia, North America and Britain. He focuses on a number of key areas where historians and sociologists have theoretically tied religion to other aspects of social life, specifically in relation to economic involvement, family size and structure and matters of sexuality and gender.

Akenson reports (1991, p. 26) that present-day variations in family structure began from very small differences that emerged in the 19th and early 20th centuries. Furthermore, there is evidence that the clergy of both religious groupings had similar attitudes to sexual morality; indeed, 'the image of the late nineteenth-century Catholic priest out beating the hedgerows for courting couples has become such a dominant motif that one forgets that the Protestant clergy had methods of enforcing sexual morality [for example, public shaming] that would have made the Catholic priests envious' (Akenson, 1991, p. 36).

In relation to other economic and social orientations, Akenson (1991, p. 108) is led to conclude that despite strong beliefs in Irish society about the social repercussions of Protestantism and Catholicism, there is:

> no empirically verifiable evidence that cultural factors caused a differentiation between the two religions on major social and economic axes. Neither in family structure, nor in economic behaviour, nor the treatment of women was there any compelling evidence for major differences, and, in some instances, there was positive evidence of fundamental similarities. What differences there were in these matters were much more plausibly ascribed to class than to culture.

Given these similarities, the question is: how and why were the two groups so clearly differentiated? McVeigh (1995) argues that this process can best be brought under the term 'sectarianism'. This is the process, familiar to nearly all Irish people, whereby religious differences are noted – through picking up clues from names, accent, school attended, sports played – then evaluated and sometimes acted upon in a way that is discriminatory.

The historical background of settler colonialism was obviously of key importance in the emergence of sectarianism: 'the triumph of the Protestant Reformation in England and its failure in Ireland meant that religion became the key signifier between settler and native – especially as second and third generation English and Scots planters became increasingly "Irish"'(McVeigh, 1995, p. 626). By the 19th century, religion, politics and identity were inextricably linked in Ireland. As a result, non-sectarian politics such as that espoused by the socialist James Connolly became the exception that proved the rule.

Sectarianism – like racism – must be seen in structural terms, not in terms of individual pathology. In other words, it is a quality of Irish society as much as of 'prejudiced' individuals. It provided a means of institutionalising inequality and conservatism north and south of the border. The more blatant forms of sectarianism in the North were reflected in the South by a 'pluralist theocracy' (McVeigh, 1995, p. 632) that recognised and entrenched religious difference. All major religious groups were explicitly recognised in Article 44 of the 1937 Constitution and they had high levels of control over 'their own' institutions, such as schools, hospitals and charities.

Sectarianism is about identity in the broadest sense of the term (McVeigh, 1995, p. 627):

> Sectarian labels are about more than religion ... they approximate more to notions of ethnicity – involving nationality, politics, culture, 'race', and boundary maintenance as much as faith and religious organisation. Religious identity ... remains the main signifier of ethnic difference in Ireland.

But these identities are complex: what makes an 'Ulster Catholic' or an 'Irish Protestant'? Religious conviction and organisation are an important part of the story, but what makes a Protestant a 'Protestant', a Catholic a 'Catholic' and a Jew a 'Jew' is determined by the interaction of historical, religious, social, cultural and political factors (Poole, 1997). Religion has operated in Irish society as an ethnic and cultural marker not necessarily related to beliefs or practices. Thus, suggests Akenson, 'it mattered not if an individual entered his church only to be baptised and to be buried, the life he lived between these two signal events was, in the eyes of those with whom he dealt, the life of either a Protestant or a Catholic' (1991, p. 129).

Religious boundaries are both self-defined and other-defined. Each identity provides a positive evaluation of its own characteristics, plus a negative denunciation of the other's. 'Otherness' was, and is, created and re-created through practices like endogamous marriage (marrying within the group and discouragement of 'mixed' marriages) and segregated or 'denominational' education. It has only been by keeping themselves segregated in family life and by separating the young that it has been possible for religious communities – in Ireland as elsewhere – to develop and perpetuate unique world views and, at the same time, sometimes grossly inaccurate views of each other.

The history of sectarianism in the North is broadly familiar. In the Republic, sectarianism was perhaps most vivid during the 1920s (Akenson, 1991, p. 4):

> Mostly a rural affair, it consisted of hectoring, intimidating, burning and murdering isolated Protestants, most, but not all, of whom were owners of small town businesses or of relatively large farms ... between early December 1922 and late March 1923 192 houses belonging to the Protestant minority in southern Ireland were destroyed. An outcome of the sectarian atmosphere that accompanied the establishment of the state was a reduction in the number of Protestants from 327,000 in 1911 to 221,000 in 1926.

It is also true that the sense of physical threat felt by Protestants in the South rapidly diminished as the state became more securely established. Meanwhile, at the political and cultural level, the first decades of the independent state saw an extension of Catholic hegemony that paid little heed to Protestant identity (Fanning, 2002, pp. 39–42).

There is also evidence of considerable anti-Semitism within Irish society (Keogh, 1998). Fanning (2002, p. 59) argues that the state's immigration policies were 'overtly anti-Semitic' in the period 1938 to 1956 and were aimed at producing a society that was 'without Jews'. He states (2002, p. 63) that in Ireland, Jews were perceived within the dominant discourse as 'enemies of the nation within a nationalism which drew upon religious sectarianism'. Both the Catholic Church and the Irish state, working in conjunction, expressed and put into practice anti-Semitic views.

GENDER AND RELIGION

Macionis and Plummer (2008, p. 614) point out that:

> All world religions are patriarchal. They have male gods at the centre of their cosmologies; favour men to be their officials on earth; and frequently devise ways of excluding women both from church and society. Many more recent sects and cults that are emerging seem to keep this patriarchal order.

Recent times have seen some change, most notably in Reform Judaism and most of the Protestant churches (O'Connor, 1998, p. 64). Some smaller groups, such as the Quakers, have always exhibited a high degree of equality of ministry (Wigham, 1992, p. 53). The Roman Catholic and Eastern Orthodox faiths still strongly resist any moves towards equality, while the Anglican Church has seen deep global divisions over the issue.

O'Connor (1998) reminds us that most analyses of the position of women in Irish society ascribe a strong causal element to the structure and nature of the churches, especially the Catholic Church. O'Dowd (1989, pp. 13–21) has outlined some of the key aspects of the evolving relationship between women and the churches in post-independence Ireland. He argues that 'to some degree all the churches shared an image of women's proper role, seeing it as familial, self-sacrificing and altruistic in the practical sense' (1989, p. 13). In Catholicism, the Marian cult, which idealised motherhood while abjuring all manifestations of female sexuality, held sway. Catholic social teaching emphasised 'the family ideal, the family wage, and the natural role of woman as mother and home-maker'. This viewpoint is outlined at length in Inglis's (1998a, pp. 178–200) discussion of the special role of the mother in the development of Irish Catholicism. The Protestant religions were more inclined to focus on the father as the senior figure in an economic and spiritual partnership.

O'Dowd (1989) lists a number of ways that Free State legislation entrenched elements of Catholic social teaching and this was accompanied by a range of other 'campaigns' and social initiatives, often (if not exclusively) aimed at women, for example the campaigns against birth control or 'jazz dancing'. It can also be argued that the political-commercial-religious elite in Ireland has been a very male-dominated one and that this is reinforced by the existence of exclusively male elite schools and an exclusively male religious hierarchy.

The relationship between gender and religion in Ireland is not a simple one. While undoubtedly patriarchal, the churches did provide opportunities and support for women when there were few other avenues (Fahey, 1987). By 1941, one out of every 400 women in Ireland was entering a convent (cited in MacCurtain, 1997, p. 248). Religious life was one of the only ways that women could access positions of power or responsibility in Irish society, for example in further education or in management positions within the fields of education, social welfare and health. There was a contradictoriness in this position, well expressed by MacCurtain (1997, p. 252):

> The image of the nun in midcentury Ireland (and elsewhere) was that of a docile and submissive figure clad in a black or white or blue sweep of garment with a medieval headdress who rarely raised her voice or eyes. Yet these same women were major players in church–state relations below the official level of the Catholic hierarchy. Owners and matrons of the main hospital systems in the country, they were entrusted by the state with the state's industrial schools and orphanages and with the responsibility of implementing the state's fragile and largely underdeveloped welfare policy.

At the level of the individual household and family, Inglis analyses in detail the role of the Irish (rural) mother in the development of the Catholic Church. His contention (1998a, p. 199) is that:

The domination and control of women by the Church, and the necessity for women to ally themselves with that dominating power if they themselves were to have any power, led to their high level of marital fertility which, in turn, created the need for postponed marriage, permanent celibacy and emigration among their children. These practices were encouraged by the mother in the home through a devotion to the Church, a rigorous sexual morality, and a physical and emotional distance from her children. It is this scenario, re-enacted over the generations, that is the essence of the dialectical relationship of power between the church and family in modern Ireland.

This neatly summarises Inglis's argument that the alliance of otherwise powerless mothers and the ever more powerful institutional church was the basis for the modernisation of Irish rural life and thus Irish society. The ascetic and constrained lifestyle enforced by a holy alliance of mothers and priests provided, according to Inglis, the conditions under which Irish property relations, occupational structure and demographic patterns altered in the post-Famine period. While Inglis's argument is fascinating, it is the case that similar discourses of femininity, rationalisation and control emerged in other societies where Catholicism was less influential, for example early 20th-century Australia (Reiger, 1985). Like Weber's suggestion of the link between Protestantism and the emergence of capitalism, Inglis's analysis of maternal power has the capacity to provoke interesting sociological analyses.

Inglis (1998a, p. 199) suggests that once women were able to access alternative sources of power through the workplace and public life (from the 1960s on), they were increasingly freed from the ideological power of the church. Gender issues have also been crucial in providing a site for oppositional discourses in relation to the church, in particular around matters of gender roles, reproduction and sexuality. While oppositional discourses to the hegemony of religion in Ireland have been few, Nic Ghiolla Phádraig (1995, p. 598) suggests that feminism has been an important critical force, for example through its central involvement in the various contraceptive rights, abortion and divorce campaigns.

IDEOLOGICAL CONTROL AND INSTITUTIONAL POWER

The extent of ideological control was and is reinforced by the churches' control of institutions such as education, health and social welfare and the generation of 'expert knowledge' such as medical discourses on childbirth or social studies discourses on attitudinal change.

A political discourse that focused on national identity based on difference from 'Protestant England' (and to a lesser extent Protestant Northern Ireland) helped to solidify the ideological control of Catholicism. There has been little organised (or even disorganised) anti-clericalism, unlike in France or Italy, for example. This has also been linked to the failure of left-wing politics to develop in Ireland (Mair, 1994, p. 404). This contributed to the phenomenal institutional power of the church in Ireland. As Fintan O'Toole has remarked (1998, p. 67):

An Irish person was, and is, likely to be born in a Catholic hospital, educated at Catholic schools, married in a Catholic church, have children named by a priest, be counselled by Catholic marriage advisors if the marriage runs into trouble, be dried out in Catholic clinics for the treatment of alcoholism if he or she develops a drink problem, be operated on in Catholic hospitals, and be buried by Catholic rites.

O'Toole is describing the 'cradle to grave' welfare system developed by the churches, particularly the Catholic Church, in Ireland during the 19th and 20th centuries. The historical development of welfare institutions, and so many of the service delivery aspects of the Irish welfare state, is intrinsically tied up with the expanding role of the churches in Irish social life during this period. Indeed, O'Toole suggests (1998, p. 65) that in the Republic, the Catholic Church became a 'surrogate state'. As Akenson (1991, p. 109) points out, the institutions of the different churches were also an expression of their self-perceptions: they 'crystallised in social practice what the Irish people believed to be the proper relationship between persons of differing Christian denominations. The institutional structures were the mechanisms whereby the Irish-Catholic and Irish-Protestant people kept themselves apart from one another.'

Historically, the Protestant churches had been involved in a number of philanthropic, educational and healthcare institutions. During the 19th and 20th centuries, the Catholic Church became increasingly involved in a wide range of institutions from hospitals to homes for 'unmarried mothers', elite boarding schools and residential homes for excluded young people. The rapid growth of these institutions – into an apparatus of 'containment' (Smith, 2007) – was facilitated by the large numbers of men and women who entered the religious life (Kirby, 1984, p. 56). This suited the state, as religious labour was cheap or free and the capital costs were met by fundraising from the flock and through 'dowries' brought in by the middle-class religious (MacCurtain, 1997, p. 248).

In education, a marriage of convenience was entered into between the emerging Irish state and the Catholic religious orders that already controlled significant elements of the education system (see Chapter 7 for more on the Catholic Church control of education). The existing denominational, single-sex schools provided a fertile ground for recruitment to the ranks of the religious, teaching costs were kept low through non-payment of full wages to religious staff and the school provided the sort of product desired by the state: young people schooled in orderliness, discipline, obedience and self-control (MacCurtain, 1997, p. 249). The church offered the state continuity and stability and in return sought its support for continuity and stability in its own work (Nic Ghiolla Phádraig, 1995, p. 609).

Though the operation of many religious institutions has now been opened up to critical examination, at the time of their operation there was little questioning of church control of welfare and educational institutions. As Nic Ghiolla Phádraig (1995, p. 601) suggests, 'belief in the altruism of the religious running them and the fear of challenging the church together with ignorance of conditions and the inmates' lack of powerful connections isolated them from public scrutiny'. In the last two decades there has been an intense critique of such bodies, in line with trends in other Western countries. The critique has taken many forms, from films and TV series to numerous government reports and statements by ex-'clients' themselves. The overall result has been a major shift in the public perception of religious institutions in general.

More recent times have seen a decline of religious involvement in public institutions. The causes have been various, but as well as the exposure of abuses of power mentioned above have included the sharp decline in vocations, especially in the religious orders; changes in church teaching about welfare and the role of the state; the expansion of the state itself and its penetration into social affairs; and an increased demand for the professionalisation of services.

SEXUAL SCANDALS IN RELIGIOUS INSTITUTIONS

The ideological and institutional power of the churches, and particularly the Catholic Church, have been severely impacted upon by the outbreak of a series of sex scandals in the Irish Catholic Church from the 1990s onwards with respect to clerical child sex abuse, church (mis)management of these scandals as well as sexual scandals involving individual Catholic clerics. These public scandals of individual clerics became 'institutional morality tales' (Gamson, 2001) and their institutional location in the church contributed to the specific charges of hypocrisy, loss of public trust and abuse of power. They also highlighted, via church–state clashes over their handling, the sometimes contested dynamic between the Catholic Church as a global transnational institution and sovereign national states as defenders of the rule of law (Casanova, 1994). After the first wave of the ISSP in 1991, revelations that a well-known Irish Catholic bishop, Bishop Eamonn Casey, had had an affair with an American woman and was the father of a child through this relationship were made public in 1992. In addition, from the early 1990s, a number of clerical child abuse cases and evidence of abuse of children in church-run institutions came into the public domain (Keenan, 2011).

Despite these scandals being a threat to the 'religious authority structure' of the church, through its front-line 'agency authority structure' (Chaves, 1993, p. 10) the church – through its day-to-day contact with poor and needy people – still speaks to public issues with some credibility (Yamane, 2003). Consider, for example, that the Irish hierarchy – itself embroiled at the time in a major crisis over its handling of clerical child sex abuse scandals – chose a Dublin city homeless service run by the Capuchin order as the location to launch a document about Ireland's economic crisis under the title *From Crisis to Hope: Working to Achieve the Common Good* (Irish Catholic Bishops' Conference, 2011b).

Table 13.3 presents data about levels of public confidence in churches and selected other institutions in Ireland, drawn from the Irish element of the

International Social Survey Programme (ISSP). That public confidence in organised religion has declined is not altogether surprising because of the major public institutions, it shared – along with the educational system – the highest level of public confidence. Churches, then, had farther to fall than other collective actors when public confidence in them did begin to decline (Hoffman, 1998). Nevertheless, a trend of increasing confidence (in this period) in key institutions is not reflected in a growing trust of the church and religious organisations.

Table 13.3: Confidence levels in Irish public institutions (per cent complete confidence/a great deal), 1991–2008

	1991	1998	2008
Confidence in church	48	26	28
Confidence in business/industry	16	27	66
Confidence in educational system	46	59	87
Confidence in legal system	30	31	64

Source: ISSP, 1991–2008.

THE FUTURE OF RELIGION IN IRELAND?

There is much evidence that rapid social change leads to a greater level of religious activity. While economic, social and technological change has the capacity to undermine religiosity, for some, religious belief and practice provide a framework for responding to change. Given that there is evidence of continual social and economic change in contemporary Ireland, how might the churches and religious practice change in the future?

This is a challenge that has been taken up in various ways by the churches in Ireland. In their attempts to respond to secularisation, they have tried to make themselves more relevant and 'in touch' by involving themselves more in social and political issues, embracing the media and changing their practices. This may help to attract more people but also risks blurring the sacred and profane and demystifying the nature of religion. As Taylor (1989, p. 3) points out, for religious regimes whose power and authority depend to some extent on the effectiveness of symbol and ritual, this can be a serious problem. Once the mystery has gone, what exactly is left?

One direction that the churches may take, important in countries like the US and Australia, is to claim a key role in the debate over emerging ethical dilemmas related to technological and social development. Many people are concerned about issues such as biotechnology, cloning, the Human Genome Project, medical ethics, reproductive technology and the general direction of the development of scientific knowledge. At this stage, the churches in Ireland have contributed little to the minimal public debate on these issues, apart from a rather narrow focus on the ethics of abortion. Similarly, there is a lot of concern about the effects of economic change, particularly as it may lead to greater social inequality and a generally less caring society. There has been more of a religious response in Ireland to these issues, particularly through bodies like Social Justice Ireland, and the rhetoric of equality and social justice informs much of the language of the contemporary churches at grass roots level.

An important trend has been the emergence of 'new' religions or new religious movements (NRMs) in Ireland. This is part of a global trend, though Bouma and Ling (2011, p. 509) caution that 'claims that we have more diversity now than in the past are dubious'. They write that it seems there is more diversity now because of past assumptions of religious denominations as homogenous entities. While 'alternative' spiritualities have had a long history in Ireland (for example, W.B. Yeats's interest in theosophy and other spiritualistic ideas), these have only begun to attract attention from Irish sociologists relatively recently (Cox, 2010; Cosgrove et al., 2011). A number of reasons underlie this interest. First, there has been an expansion of interest (especially amongst women) across the Western world in a whole range of 'New Age' practices and mind-body-spirit publishing (in books, magazines and on the Internet) that has embraced a huge range of topics and activities, from Chinese medicine to angelology to various types of yoga and meditation (Cox, 2010, p. 101). Second, the 2011 census indicates that many religions are increasing their number of adherents and that some, such as Buddhism, Islam and the Orthodox religions, have grown rapidly, though from quite low levels (AIRO, 2012). These increases are largely due to immigration (see box below), rather than to a sudden enthusiasm for these new creeds amongst the indigenous population, though 'conversions' have occurred. Third, there has been some expansion of certain global religious entities such as Mormonism and certain brands of evangelical Christianity that have attracted adherents across the globe, including in Ireland.

Whereas much of religious activity in Ireland has been about establishing and policing boundaries (between doctrines and communities of believers), it is suggested that the new religious landscape is about playing down institutional demarcation and creating more eclectic and personalised religious identities (Inglis, 2007; Cox, 2010, p. 102). There has been an increase in the number of people who claim to be 'spiritual' rather than religious and the notion of 'spirituality' (often 'Celtic') has become increasingly integrated into mainstream church practices (Cox, 2010, p. 105).

As Ireland becomes an increasingly multicultural society, the emergence of new ethnically based and globalised religions, such as the Orthodox faiths, Islam and Pentecostalism, will become far more significant. As in other countries of Europe, it is such religions that are growing most rapidly. At the moment there is little knowledge about how such religions may impact on the older, established ones, though heretofore almost moribund faiths such as Presbyterianism and Methodism have been invigorated by an influx of new worshippers, both as a consequence of immigration and a shift towards a less formal evangelical style. It is quite likely that as such faith groups expand their influence, there will be debates about their public role, for example in the area of schooling and the delivery of welfare services – areas where the established churches have had something of a monopoly.

Religion and the immigrant experience

Religion has long been recognised as playing an important role in helping migrants adapt to a new society. Available research suggests that the Catholic Church in Ireland plays an important role in promoting an ethnic sense of belonging to the church among Polish Catholics through the provision of ethnic parishes and chaplaincies. This can be said to represent an example of institutional adaptation by the dominant religion as it seeks to respond to changes in the broader society. A 2008 study by the Young Christian Workers Movement found that among some Polish migrants, religion is an important resource in helping them negotiate their everyday lives.

One respondent spoke of this influence:

'I know that God cares about me, that He leads me on His ways. When I didn't know where to find a Polish church in Ireland, I felt bad. When I came here at Easter, to this Polish church for the very first time, I had to cry. I felt like a lost sheep that had found its home!' (Young Christian Workers Movement, 2008, p. 17)

Some respondents in this study expressed dissatisfaction with the ethnic ministry provided by the Catholic Church in Ireland, mentioning the importance of having native ethnic translators of the Mass rather than translators from the host country.

Another study of religion among recently arrived African migrants in Ireland found that Pentecostalism also fulfils an important role in people's lives. One member of the Christ Apostolic Church related the role it (along with other social institutions such as schools) plays in integrating Africans into Irish society:

'The church is about inclusion and oneness. The church is open. The church's door is open to everybody … these same people who are in the church belong to the society, to an ethnic organisation or society, they derive some benefits there … People who come here also socialise in other places, they socialise at work. Some of them have other ways of meeting and knowing people, they throw parties, the so-called African parties. Places of education are other avenues for socialisation. They meet a lot of people.' (Ugba, 2009, p. 96)

At the same time, some respondents spoke of the challenges their religion posed in terms of their social integration. One Pentecostal church leader related that religion can also act as a barrier to integration with the host society by contributing to the construction of group difference:

> 'Unfortunately we don't at the moment have an environment that is conducive for the work we've been called to do, where we can really get our message across to the Irish people. Our people ... because of some challenges they face in this society – verbal abuse, racial abuse and everything – they are really hiding in their shells, they are afraid, they are withdrawn from society and people even without realising it sometimes.'
> (Ugba 2009, p. 95)

Aldridge (2000, pp. 103–6) has pointed out that it is liberal capitalist societies – such as the US – that are most open to the growth of new religious forms, citing the Mormons and the Jehovah's Witnesses as examples of such dynamic religions. European societies, where the state is far more closely aligned with established religions, have been less fertile ground for this kind of religious entrepreneurship and consequent expansion. But it is quite possible that the embrace of neo-liberal economic orthodoxy in Ireland will be reflected in the expansion of these 'modern' global religious entities as the 'market' for alternative religious belief and expression develops.

THE FUTURE?

Drawing on social survey evidence, denominational data and historical material, the purpose of this chapter has been to map the major changes and continuities in the Irish religious economy over the last 50 or so years by examining trajectories of religious growth and decline at the individual, organisational and societal levels. This analysis pointed to relative stability in individual-level belief (but not behaviour), a contracting institutional presence and a weakening of religious authority.

In the sociology of religion literature, Irish religiosity tends to be characterised as peculiar among western European societies. Sociologist Michael Carroll, for instance, opens his historical study of pre-Famine Irish Catholic devotion with this claim about Irish religious exceptionalism: 'Ireland has the dubious distinction of being a case that is forever subverting patterns that are otherwise well established in the study of Catholic societies' (Carroll, 1999, p. 5). Similarly, using a more empirical approach applied to the contemporary situation, Michael Hornsby-Smith adds grist to the mill of Irish religious peculiarity by claiming that 'a comparison of Ireland with Western European countries as a whole shows that the scores of Irish respondents on the religious dimensions are well above the European average' (Hornsby-Smith, 1992, p. 282).

In response to this exceptionalism claim, one can say that at least with respect to the general direction of change over time, Irish people are becoming more like other western European societies in terms of their levels of church attendance and in terms of their beliefs in such things as heaven, hell and miracles. The peculiarity of Irish religiosity, however, is borne out – notwithstanding processes of secularisation, urbanisation and modernisation – by the continuing high levels of belief in God and the high level of church attendance when placed alongside trends and patterns evident in other specifically European Catholic societies. Overall, it might be more accurate to say that Irish religiosity is different rather than exceptional.

After a period of growth from the mid-19th century right up until the 1950s, the survey and historical evidence presented in this chapter suggests that the influence of the Catholic Church in Irish society is unlikely to be as significant now and into the future as it was in the past. The answer to the 'what future for religion in Ireland?' question is not, however, simple or straightforward. In earlier periods of its history, the Catholic Church in Ireland had poor physical plant, few regular devotees and a disorganised workforce, but over a period of time managed to organise itself into a strong social institution. Indeed, religious organisations often tend to follow cycles of decline and growth rather than linear trajectories in one direction or another (Demerath, 1998).

At least in the short term, the Irish religious landscape is likely to be characterised by lower levels of church attendance compared to earlier periods as well as relative stability in religious beliefs. The increasing delegitimation of religious control of state-funded hospitals and schools means that in the future, the church's public presence and ability to shape people's ideological development will likely diminish significantly. While some personnel declines may be offset by recruitment of lay employees, it is unlikely that the Catholic workforce will ever again reach the peak levels of the 1950s.

A large majority of Irish people will continue to report that they believe in God and a sizable minority will continue to attend church/religious services on a regular basis, have regard for their local priest/religious leader and socialise their children into the Catholic or another faith. A mass exodus of laity from the churches seems unlikely even in the face of the ongoing and lengthy processing of historical memories of Catholic institutional child abuse. This will mean that the 'losses' of the church will likely be greater at the macro and meso levels than at the micro level.

The Irish religious landscape will also likely be characterised by modest growth in some new religious movements, such as Protestant evangelicalism and Islam, giving these global religious traditions a peculiarly Irish inflection. The 2011 census reported a 51% increase in the Irish Muslim population. Some of this growth will be among relatively new migrants as well as people disaffected by the majority religion. Native Irish Catholicism will also likely be reshaped by new migrant groups as well as by the challenges of exerting an influence in an increasingly liberal, secular and pluralistic society in which the relationship between Irish identity and Catholicism can no longer to be understood as a taken-for-granted cultural given.

14
Media and New Technologies

The relationship between the media, technology and society is a central concern in the social sciences. Media analysts pay attention to issues of ownership and control, the social organisation of media production, the nature of media audiences and the media's political and social effects. Analysts of new media similarly try to assess the underlying political economy of new media platforms and the degree to which they bring about change in economic, social, political and cultural life. Historically, it has been a matter of some debate as to whether or not the media play an agenda-setting role with regard to the shaping of attitudes and the formation of public opinion. Early studies, for example, focused on elections and public health campaigns and noted a correspondence (although not a causal connection) between the significance of issues as identified by the print and broadcast media and their salience to politicians and the general public (McCombs and Shaw, 1972; Blumler and Gurevitch, 1981; Cook et al., 1983).

Such studies tend to overlook the fact that the priorities of three key constituencies – the media, the public and the policy-makers – may not coalesce but may, in fact, interact in complex ways and in different directions (Rogers and Dearing, 1987). While the media may not play an overt agenda-setting role, it is nevertheless deemed to be particularly effective because of its capacity to construct meanings and to offer those constructs in a systematic way to audiences where they are likely to be incorporated, to one degree or another, into personal meaning structures (Gamson and Modigliani, 1989; McQuail, 2005). So while the media may not tell us what to think, it does tell us what to think about.

The proliferation of new media platforms – the Internet, social networking, smartphones – has raised new concerns in the field of mass communication studies. Buckingham (2000) observes that current debates about the perceived impact of new digital technologies in society tend to display the same sort of ambivalence that characterised earlier debates about the arrival of cinema, radio and television. These debates broadly fall into two strands: those that argue that new media technology have the capacity for dehumanisation and a general dumbing down of culture and those that see the technologies as tools for enhancing creative expression, political activation, communal bonding and individual self-fulfilment.

In Ireland, as elsewhere, the mass media have become ubiquitous, pervasive and a part of our existence that is largely taken for granted. On any given day, a typical Irish person may make and receive texts and calls by mobile phone, vote via mobile phone for a contestant on a reality TV programme, update their Facebook profile and comment on other people's profiles, communicate via instant messaging on a PC, play a multiplayer computer game with unknown others across the world, check road directions on a satellite navigation device and watch a favourite TV programme, perhaps on a tablet.

In some ways it is impossible to separate out 'the media' as a discrete entity within our society. Many of the issues and aspects of social life we have discussed in this book are permeated by media processes and technological diffusions. For example, our knowledge and understanding of crime is almost entirely determined by the media; the political process takes place largely through the newspapers, radio and television; our notion of ourselves as a modern society is expressed through advertising imagery, film and popular music; even the contours of class and inequality are reflected in the choices we make (and can make) about what sorts of films to watch, books to read, radio stations to listen to, websites to frequent or music to download. Moreover, given the growing significance of personalised Internet use in everyday life, we increasingly have to think about audiences not just as consumers and interpreters of the media, but also as producers in their own right.

It is possible to apply a sociological imagination and critically examine the history, nature and development of media *institutions* as organisations that pursue particular ends, from the creation of a national identity to the maximisation of profit. We can analyse the implications of recent changes in the media business landscape, the convergence of previously separate 'old' and 'new' media platforms and the new genres that have emerged on television that depend on greater audience participation. We can investigate how people, as *audiences*, consume the media and how they make their own sense of what they see on the screen, read on the page or hear on their smartphones. The enormous success of Internet-based social networking sites such as Facebook and the viewer-driven YouTube website demonstrate how the media and technology are helping not only to reconfigure how we construct and manage our personal identities, but also how we navigate our way through everyday life.

SOCIOLOGY AND THE STUDY OF THE MEDIA

Sociology has much to offer in the analysis of the media and new technologies that can complement other disciplinary approaches. In particular, sociologists can help to look at how people create, use and interpret the media and media content. In this way, they can balance analyses that tend to focus on the media as text, such as those derived from literary and film theory. They can also challenge asocial analyses from a psychological perspective, which have been influential in the study of media 'effects'. Sociologists can make use of social theories and concepts to examine how media processes are underpinned by relationships of power and inequality.

According to Kelly and O'Connor (1997, p. 1), in one of the few published collections of sociological analyses of the Irish media, 'access to and mode of participation in [media] cultures are structured and limited by social class, by gender, by ethnicity, by location in space, and by generation'. Sociological analyses can help us to understand how people use and interpret the media – how television, cinema, radio, the Internet and other media forms are integrated into the textures of everyday life. One of the newest forms of multimedia to diffuse through society is digital game playing. According to Kerr (2006, p. 128), digital games are now an intrinsic part of contemporary global flows of cultural goods, services and images. Digital games, which Kerr suggests fuse digital technology and cultural creativity, should be seen as 'a socially constructed, dynamic and diverse cultural practice'. Like Kelly and O'Connor, Kerr points out that a number of social factors, such as age, gender, race, income and class, act as a constraint on digital game players.

There are many ways to study and analyse the media. Devereux (2003, p. 9) points out that the media can be approached from a number of different and contrasting sociological perspectives that may focus on the following units of analysis:

- Communication between senders and receivers.
- Media as industries and organisations.
- Texts as commodities.
- Texts as cultural products.
- Media as agents of social change and globalisation.
- Media as agents of socialisation and sources of meaning.

Any one of these foci could form the basis of a sociological examination of the media that would require a chapter in itself. We have chosen to highlight a number of important historical and contemporary elements in the development of media in Ireland. We start with a brief review of theoretical approaches to the media. We follow this with an overview of the development of the mass media in Ireland. In particular, we focus on the media in relation to the issues that have formed a key theme of this book: the experience of modernity and the challenges Ireland faced in the early years of state formation and nation building. This is followed by a perusal of the changing media landscape in Ireland and an examination of some significant sociological and public policy challenges they imply. We conclude with a brief review of how the media, technology and communications industries may develop in the future and what the sociological implications of such developments might be.

THEORETICAL MODELS FOR UNDERSTANDING THE MEDIA

There are many theoretical models for understanding how the mass media 'work'. With limited space here, we briefly outline some main points, but for an exhaustive but accessible discussion of the numerous approaches, see McQuail (2010). Functionalist sociological approaches to the analysis of the media aim to describe and understand what it is that people, and society, 'get out of' the media; in other words, what functions the media performs and what desires it fulfils for users. In psychology this is known as the *uses and gratifications approach*. For functionalist sociology, the media have a broad range of functions in society. These include a *surveillance* function, whereby the media allow us to know what is going on around us – everything from the best new phone to the fate of democracy protestors in all corners of the world – and a *status conferral* function, whereby the media reflect high-status individuals and groups in society, from top sports stars to the latest C-list reality show celebrity. The media also function to help *apply social norms*, partly through direct provision of information (for example, crime prevention campaigns) but also through the negative portrayal and censure of deviance, such as overeating or robbing banks. This is part of the media's broad function of the *transmission of culture*. This ranges from the socialisation of children, for example through television programmes such as *Dora the Explorer* and websites such as Club, to the maintenance and passing on of national heritage and culture (Irish-language programmes and films like *Michael Collins* and *The Guard*). Finally, the media have been seen to have a *narcotising* function (or dysfunction) – they can flood society with too much information, thereby making it difficult for people to agree on norms and values or to know how best to act (Macionis and Plummer, 1998, p. 587).

Criticisms of the functionalist approach of the media centre on the fact that such analyses tend to be highly descriptive. They are good at categorising and listing various effects and uses of the media, but not very useful as a way to understand the crucial dimensions of power, conflict and inequality in relation to the media, nor for understanding change. More critical approaches to the media have tended to dominate sociological work in the area, particularly those derived from Marxist and feminist perspectives. A key issue is the *political economy* of the media – in other words, who owns and controls the media institutions; how are media companies integrated into other forms of capitalist enterprise; and what are the relationships of power involved? A second focus is on the content of the media, especially in terms of *ideology*. Does the media provide a distorted or biased view of the world and why might this be the case? Sometimes there is an attempt to link the two concerns: to show how particular patterns of media ownership and control lead to the dissemination of particular messages, but this is notoriously difficult to demonstrate unless something happens to disrupt the relationship. Famously, recent prime ministers in Britain – Tony Blair, Gordon Brown and David Cameron – all courted Rupert Murdoch, the long-standing CEO of News Corporation and a dominant player in the global media field, because they believed endorsement by his newspaper titles was crucial to gaining electoral advantage. The phone hacking scandal involving the Murdoch flagship *The News of the World* in 2011, and the public enquiry that followed it, provided a rare insight into the use and abuse of power by a media organisation.

As in other areas of sociological investigation, the theoretical lens that is used will determine, to a large extent, the knowledge that is generated. In sociological studies of the media we can discern a pattern where a fascination with the power of technology has given way to a highly critical stance, to be in turn replaced by an acknowledgement of the complexity and diversity of the phenomenon being studied and the potential to shape technology in our own interests. This reflects how new media technologies themselves are received with various combinations of enthusiasm and fear, before they either fade away (the Sony Walkman) or are assimilated into the textures that are taken for granted in everyday life (Facebook, smartphones). The challenge for sociologists, then, is to analyse the place of the media and new technology in social life without ascribing them a greater influence than they might merit.

NATION BUILDING AND THE IRISH MEDIA

The mass media embrace a broad range of institutions and activities, content and audiences. Traditionally, perhaps, they are seen to refer to newspapers, magazines, film, radio and TV. They may also expand to include book publishing, the recorded music industry, numerous aspects of advertising, digital games and arcades, theme parks and, most recently, social networking sites and online services. Historically, numerous popular media sectors and formats have come and (almost) gone, from cinema newsreels, radio soap operas and weekly comics to 8-track cartridges, VCRs and analog cameras. In this section we briefly examine some aspects of the development of the Irish media landscape historically, which was closely allied with the project of nation building throughout the 19th and 20th centuries. The state in particular occupied an influential role in the development of the Irish media, for example in relation to broadcasting policy.

During the 19th century, newspapers were actively mobilised in support of nationalist and unionist politics; in the early part of the 20th century, radio was central to the formulation of the newly independent state; film has been mobilised as a carrier of messages about national identity; and later, national television has been seen as an overarching symbol and carrier of modernity. Pervading many of the debates about the mass media has been the issue of domination by outside forces and the extent to which the Irish media can, or should, be a means of fostering, developing or reflecting a distinctively Irish culture. There has been long-standing concern about the influence of British and American cultural products, particularly mass media products such as magazines, films, TV and radio programmes and popular music. It formed part of the early debates over the establishment of a national radio service (McLoone, 1991) and the creation of a national television service and was revisited in the Rainbow Coalition government's *Green Paper on Broadcasting* in 1995 (Department of Arts, Culture and the Gaeltacht, 1995, pp. 132–6).

There is evidence that the early days of the Irish state saw a strong ideological element to media policy. The development of aspects of the media, for example some newspapers and radio and to some extent film, were tied to particular ideas about national identity and culture. In this regard the emerging Irish state was no different to others attempting to nation build through 'imagining communities' (Anderson, 1993). As in many countries, the relationship between state and media has also involved religious bodies, and Inglis (1998a) has stressed the powerful influence of the Catholic Church, especially in relation to issues of censorship. Here we give two brief examples of early media forms that contributed to nation building and the fomenting of a particular Irish identity.

The *Irish Press* and nation building

As a mass medium, newspapers have had a long history in Ireland, with the first newspaper being published in 1649 and the oldest in continuous publication being the *Belfast Newsletter*, founded in 1737 (Oram, 1993, pp. 53, 105). The development of newspapers has been intertwined with social and political struggle. For much of their history, newspapers have been associated with particular political groupings or positions or have reflected the concerns of economic and social interests.

An interesting example of the development of newspapers in relation to their social context is found in the now-defunct *Irish Press* newspaper group, which embodied the desire of many nationalists to break free from British cultural domination. This motive was one of those underpinning the foundation of the *Irish Press*, which constituted a communications medium for the Fianna Fáil party – in the face of hostility from existing papers – and was 'central to [the party's] struggle for hegemony in the early 1930s' (Curran, 1996, p. 8). The interests behind the paper were a complex mix of American supporters of the party, prominent members of the Irish bourgeoisie, local party organisations and activists and the leadership of the party itself, in particular Éamon de Valera. There was also tacit support from the Catholic Church and the party used the church's campaign against popular British newspapers as a way to assist the development of the *Irish Press*.

According to Curran (1996, p. 13), the *Irish Press* was a populist paper. It sought to channel working-class radicalism towards the Fianna Fáil party. In line with dominant Catholic thinking of the time, it presented rural culture as the 'authentic culture of the people'. Conscious of the dependency on Great Britain, it also pursued an anti-imperialist line. As the independent Irish state developed, the *Irish Press* continued to reflect the position of Fianna Fáil, which was to become the dominant political force in the state. It attempted to appeal to the same coalition of interests as did the party: a sometimes uneasy mix of small farmers, the urban working class, indigenous industrialists and the nationalist political position. To many it reflected the voice of 'official' Ireland, with support for nationalist politics, the Catholic Church, rural life, the Irish language and private property. O'Brien (2001) has argued that the *Irish Press* ultimately was de Valera dominated rather than party dominated. He chronicles the disintegration of the relationship between the Fianna Fáil party and the newspaper. Over time, the *Irish Press* company found itself alienated from its traditional readership base in a modernising Ireland and a changing Fianna Fáil party. Its closure in the mid-1990s marked the end of 'the old certainties of Catholicism, nationalism and republicanism .... replaced by the vulgarities of consumerism, pragmatism and a brand of consensual politics' (2001, p. 230).

Television and modernity

Television arrived in Ireland at 7:00 p.m. on New Year's Eve 1961, though for some time prior to that, enthusiasts on the east coast were able to pick up British TV signals (Tobin, 1996, p. 63), albeit through a curtain of electronic 'snow' on the screen. RTÉ was set up under the Broadcasting Act 1960, which not only established the television service, but removed broadcasting as a whole from the direct control of the Department of Posts and Telegraphs. By 1966, 85 per cent of Irish homes had a television set (Sheehan, 1998, p. 138). The development of television in Ireland has been very important in relation to debates about modernity. In the 1960s, a national TV network, like a national airline, became an important symbol of development. Hazelkorn (1996, p. 28) describes how TV in Ireland has been associated with modernising tendencies:

> The arrival of Radio Telefís Éireann in 1960 coincided with a phenomenal growth rate of economic change, transforming Ireland within a decade from an agricultural to an industrial society. Over the years it has powerfully challenged traditional cultural forms and vented the aspiration of an emergent middle class, whose allegiances are increasingly attuned to continental Europe, undermining the primacy of the countryside in national life.

For Inglis, television was also instrumental in bringing about the gradual decline in the power and authority of the Catholic Church: 'the social process where moral discourse was limited to what was taught in the school, read in the occasional newspaper, heard on the radio and from the pulpit every Sunday, was changed by the little box which appeared in the corner of Irish homes' (1998a, p. 93). RTÉ came to produce an impressive amount of drama and other programming that often attempted to relate directly to the social changes that were taking place in Irish society (Sheehan, 1987). Of particular importance were debates over economic development and the liberalisation of family law (Kelly and Rolston, 1995, p. 574).

In the two media forms briefly mentioned here, we can see a common involvement in issues of national identity. Such debates tend to be most intense in the period around and shortly after the introduction of a new medium, when provision is likely to be limited and the state is most involved. As the medium becomes more ubiquitous and as commercial considerations become more dominant, the medium often tends to become taken for granted. Few people, except for 'moral entrepreneurs' and perhaps media studies academics, get very worked up about what is on TV in Ireland today, radio is virtually ignored and the most voluble public discourse is reserved for the new mass medium: the Internet. Let's now take a closer look at the current media landscape in Ireland.

Fifty years of Irish television

Writing about the fiftieth anniversary of RTÉ Television in the *Irish Times*, Hugh Linehan (2012) observes that the history of Irish television is not one that can be easily simplified. He suggests that from its inception, RTÉ 'had to face both ways' as it competed for audience share with UK broadcasting channels. As a result, RTÉ is often 'simultaneously criticised for behaving like an arrogant monopolist in its own market and being a pale imitation of its British counterpart'.

Linehan questions whether Irish audiences are as loyal to their national broadcaster as national audiences are elsewhere. He accepts that in many respects RTÉ has succeeded in imagining the national community through its 'great national setpieces' (such as the stellar coverage of Gaelic games down through the years), its early children's television programmes and its tradition of drama and documentary making. But he also notes that as a monopolistic operator in the marketplace for a long time, RTÉ often relied on the fact that it was 'the only show in town'.

Much has been made of the significance of RTÉ as an agent of modernity in Ireland, but Linehan suggests that that role may have been overblown: 'Irish produced television was just one of the windows which opened up the outside world, along with the dismantling of censorship and the arrival of consumerist popular culture'.

Linehan draws our attention to what he sees as 'the sins of omission rather than those of commission'. For the most part, he says, RTÉ avoided clashes with government (and indeed, rather meekly succumbed to the political censorship imposed by government during the Northern Ireland Troubles in the late 1980s). It did not on the whole encourage a vibrant, independent production sector. But RTÉ, like other national television stations, now stands on the cusp of further transformation and change: 'you no longer need a television (for which the Irish citizenry still pay a licence fee) to watch television; you can already watch any free-to-air Irish television channel on line', notes Linehan. Web-enabled television sets are the next 'new thing'.

The primary role of a national public service broadcaster is, in the words of President Michael D. Higgins, to deepen, widen and enrich the lives of the public. How well RTÉ Television has done this in its 50 years is clearly a matter of debate. Linehan concludes by warning against a preoccupation with the commercial market at the expense of the market of ideas: 'the strongest arguments in favour of continuing to fund public service content are cultural, not commercial. In a globalised, media saturated world, the need for Irish people to hear and see their own stories and experiences reflected and explored on screens of whatever sort or size remain.'

MEDIA PLATFORMS: CONTINUITY AND CHANGE

In recent years there has been a dramatic multiplication in terms of the media platforms available to provide both information and entertainment content. Alongside the newer media, many older, venerable media institutions have continued to hold on to market share. But in the wake of the economic crisis that beset Ireland in 2008, the media landscape has shifted once again. As Foley (2010) suggests, 'the boom and subsequent downturn have had a profound impact on the media environment with implications for ownership, employment as well as media diversity'. In Ireland, as elsewhere, newspapers, magazines and radio stations are increasingly owned by large conglomerates, often with other interests in areas such as the food industry or other branches of the entertainment industry. Little research has been carried out in Ireland into media ownership or the impact of cross-media ownership (where a company has interests, say, in newspapers, TV and telecommunications). Concern has been expressed from time to time about these issues and other effects of media monopoly, such as political interference and below-cost selling of newspapers. Such has been the pace of innovation and change in these dynamic industries that any account of ownership risks becoming immediately out of date, so this section will sketch out a snapshot of the media landscape as of 2011.

The print media

Historically, Ireland has had a flourishing newspaper culture. According to the Joint National Readership Survey (JNRS), in 2010, 86 per cent of the country's population still regularly read a paper and most of them read more than one title a week. At the national level, readers have had access to a broad range of views from Irish and imported newspapers, particularly on Sundays. This has changed in recent years with the disappearance of some significant titles. The demise of the *Irish Press* group in the mid-1990s took three titles out of the marketplace and signalled the end of the hitherto profitable relationship between a newspaper group and a political party (Fianna Fáil). More recently, the *Sunday Tribune*, which had a reputation for strong investigative journalism, ceased trading. According to Foley (2010), a unique feature of the Irish print media scene is the strength of the British press. He estimates that 25 per cent of daily newspaper sales in Ireland are for newspapers published in London, rising to one-third of market share on Sundays. During the boom years British titles (often bringing out Irish editions of largely British content-driven newspapers) targeted Irish audiences, thus increasing their advertising revenue. In line with the international trends, however, newspaper sales are generally on the decline. In the period January to June 2010, all the major titles – both daily and weekly – lost market share. The *Irish Times* reported a 7.6 per cent drop in circulation and the *Irish Independent* a 4.8 per cent drop in circulation during that time period (Greenslade, 2010b).

As is the case for most other mass media in Ireland, the press is dependent on advertising, with at least 43 per cent of its income coming from this source (Rapple,

1997, p. 70). The major titles have diversified in recent years, developing online services to complement their printed versions and stave off competition from magazines, radio, TV and online information services in an attempt to hold on to advertising, which has been migrating from offline to online services. As Greenslade (2010a) has observed, 'the net has not eradicated old media but it has certainly hollowed out the profits of newspapers and commercial TV and radio outlets by attracting the advertisers who funded their content'. The newspaper market continues to be highly segmented, with particular newspapers targeting, for example, well-off businesspeople, while others define their readership in terms of broader class categories. Research carried out in the Netherlands (d'Haenens et al., 2004) that compared the experiences of readers of online and print versions of newspapers found no significant difference in terms of reader consumption or recall. This would suggest that one is not necessarily replacing the other, but rather that people attend to both versions in more or less the same way. This is borne out in research by Hoffman (2006), who found readers to be mobilised at the same rate to find out more information arising from a particular story, whether read in the newspaper or online.

Ireland has boasted a strong local newspaper industry and most were family owned until the 1990s. Today, however, most regional newspapers are owned by media groups such as Independent News and Media (INM) (Foley, 2010). The group has a dominant position in the Irish newspaper industry, accounting for two-thirds of all daily Irish newspaper sales and a large proportion of Sunday newspaper sales. It owns the highest-selling daily newspaper, the *Irish Independent*, plus the *Sunday Independent*, *Evening Herald*, *Star* and *Sunday World*. It also owns a number of regional weekly newspapers (including the *Kerryman* and the *People* newspapers). The INM group's Internet website, Unison.ie, supports 27 national and regional newspaper titles and is the leading news portal in Ireland, with almost 17 million page impressions per month (*INM Annual Report*, 2005).

Diverse media

Metro Éireann is Ireland's first and only weekly multicultural newspaper. It was set up by two Nigerian journalists, Chinedu Onyejelem and Abel Ugba, in April 2000. Published by Metro Publishing and Consultancy Limited, *Metro Éireann* is the primary source of news and information on Ireland's immigrant and ethnic communities. Apart from supplying up-to-date news and analysis, *Metro Éireann* has become a forum for intercultural communication, showcasing the rich cultural diversity of Ireland (www.metro eireann.com).

Radio and television

The radio landscape is diverse, with five national broadcasters, six multi-city/regional stations, seven commercial stations operating in Dublin, five operating in Cork and 18 local stations operating around the country. RTÉ remains a dominant player in both radio and television in Ireland. The public media sector embraces TV, radio, teletext and the weekly *RTÉ Guide*. RTÉ has also developed successful online media services and has an interest in digital broadcasting. Nevertheless, its monopolistic position has been diluted somewhat since the advent of commercial and community alternatives in the sector. Nowadays, RTÉ serves a diversified and differentiated audience in conjunction with local and national privately owned stations. Since the late 1970s, the dominant position of RTÉ has been challenged by these commercial radio stations, particularly at the local level. Independent radio was legalised in 1989, in the face of concerted opposition from the national broadcaster, after over a decade of almost unfettered activity by illegal pirate radio stations that developed a loyal local listenership.

Despite early financial and programming problems, local radio is in a healthy state, with some local stations commanding a higher listenership than the market leader, RTÉ. The JNLR figures released in May 2011 indicate that 85 per cent of the adult population was listening daily to a mix of national, regional, multi-city and local radio throughout the country in the period April 2010 to March 2011. The weekday reach figures were RTÉ Radio 1 (25 per cent), Today FM (13 per cent), RTÉ 2FM (12 per cent), Newstalk (8 per cent) and RTÉ Lyric FM (3 per cent). Local radio listenership was strongest on the western seaboard, with Highland radio in Donegal reaching 66 per cent of listeners, Shannonside reaching 53 per cent and Midwest Radio, Radio Kerry, WLR FM and Limerick Live all scoring between 48 per cent and 51 per cent in terms of reach. Despite the apparent diversity in the sector, Foley (2010) points out that Communicorp, run by businessman Denis O'Brien, owns several radio stations operating in Dublin and two nationally (Today FM and Newstalk).

RTÉ Television broadcasts three channels: RTÉ1, Network 2 and the Irish language station, TG4. It is funded by both a license fee and advertising. It is arguable that RTÉ's public service remit has been somewhat compromised by its dependence on advertising, as this has inevitably limited its ability to push beyond the limits of popular taste (Cullinane, 2012). Inglis (1998a, p. 232) sees the commercial element as very important and links the development of television to the expansion of advertising and the creation of a consumer society in Ireland. More recently, RTÉ has tended to follow successful commercial templates from elsewhere, such as reality-type programming and talent-spotting shows. According to Corcoran (2004, p. 3), a strong public service broadcasting system is the best hope for original Irish production (about half of broadcast material is domestically produced), given the rather weak television economy and the unregulated commercial television system. 3e is the privately owned commercial alternative to RTÉ Television, but nowadays terrestrial television must also compete with a wide range of digital TV channel competitors.

In Ireland, as elsewhere, public service broadcasters have been affected by the developments in broadcasting and communications technology. Partly as a result of such changes and partly as a response to increased competition in a less regulated environment, they have been forced to adopt the methods of commercial broadcasters, including new technologies and work practices. According to Hazelkorn, who has studied the changes in work practices in RTÉ, digital technology in particular has broken down the demarcations between journalistic, presenter and engineering skills. Some positions have been largely eliminated (sound operators, lighting electricians) while new areas have opened up, for example for IT experts and multi-skilled engineers. Some jobs have been 'reskilled' – journalists, for example, are now more directly involved in the presentation and publishing process. Competition and commercialisation have necessitated cost reduction, which has fomented greater casualisation and flexibilisation in the media sector (see Chapter 6). The changes have had differential gender effects. As in the newspaper industry, women have disproportionately benefited from the changes, with greater job loss in male-dominated 'craft' areas like electrical work and expansion on the 'creative' and administrative side, such as research. It is interesting that the 'newest' TV channel, TG4, is predominantly staffed by women (Horgan, 2001, p. 181). These changes have broad implications for media in general. Hazelkorn (1996, p. 37) highlights in particular the development of the 'independent production sector' as a key outcome. Increasing proportions of the output of public service broadcasters is undertaken by such companies. They are especially good at producing the relatively cheap and flexible 'infotainment' programmes (talent shows, house and holiday programmes, entertainment news) that are such a staple of TV programming.

CONVERGENCE

A feature of media ownership across the world is the *convergence* of formerly separate companies into large, multi-platform media conglomerates. Some of the names of these conglomerates are also familiar global brands, such as Sony, Disney and Philips, while others may be less well known in the public arena (Viacom, Bertelsmann, Vivendi). The business pages of the press frequently report on takeovers and mergers as formerly nationally based companies like Eircom, Disney or Bertelsmann seek out 'strategic partners', joint venture opportunities or are involved in takeover bids.

Increasingly, media companies seek to control the emergent players in the new media sector. Rupert Murdoch, CEO of News Corporation, who describes himself as a 'digital immigrant', purchased the (then) highly popular Myspace.com online community for US$580 million in 2005 (*BBC News/Business*, 19 July 2005). In 2006, Google, the Internet search engine, acquired YouTube, another social networking site whose content is uploaded by its users, for US$1.65 billion. The convergence of media production operates at two important levels. On the one hand, there is the coming together of previously disparate companies into giant business conglomerates. A media conglomerate will typically embrace interests in the production, distribution and/or marketing of some or all of the following: film, video, TV, recorded music, book, magazine and newspaper publishing, business information and consultancy, satellite services, computer software, mobile telephony and perhaps consumer electronics, toys or theme parks. Thus, it is not unsurprising for a particular media product, such as *Harry Potter*, to be produced and distributed through multiple platforms and multiple arms of the same global conglomerate.

The convergence at the business level has been facilitated by technological convergence, especially through the development of *digital technologies*. Digitisation means that formerly separate technologies, such as computers, photocopiers, cameras, printers, telephones and TVs, now 'talk' to each other and have been combined to form new products such as smartphones. Similarly, digital production and recording have broken down the boundaries that previously existed between film, television, music or computer software. Any of these is now easily convertible into another, and entities such as digital movies, computer games and social networking sites are types of media that could not have existed until relatively recently. There is considerable debate over the effects of the changes that have taken place. For example, the foreign ownership of most of the Irish telephony industry serves to reduce the capacity of the Irish people to control their 'own' telecommunications and media. Convergence is linked to the marketisation of the media industries, with a perceived reduction in the public service ethos that has typified European (and Irish) broadcasting. The dominance of News Corporation in digital television is a case in point. News Corporation, headed by Rupert Murdoch, wholly owns Italy's most popular pay-TV company, SKY Italia, which has more than 4 million subscribers. The company also has significant holdings in British Sky Broadcasting, the UK's largest digital pay-TV platform, reaching a third of all homes and a leading broadcaster of sports, movies, entertainment and news; Germany's leading Sky Deutschland; Asia's Tata Sky; and Foxtel in Australia and New Zealand.

On the other hand, it is possible to see how the processes of industrial and technological convergence can 'open up' the media. The emergence of giant conglomerates and the decline in the monopoly of public service organisations may provide space for the development of smaller, 'niche' players in the interstices of the mega-media corporations. In Ireland, for example, there has been a significant expansion in the number of independent production companies in the TV, film and audio-visual fields. Furthermore, the digitisation and miniaturisation of production technology means that people can now make videos, publish books or produce music recordings, and distribute them, without the need for a large production infrastructure like a record company, publishing house or film studio. Partly as a consequence of such technological change, but also due to financial pressures, public service broadcasters like RTÉ and TG4 are increasingly acting as facilitators and *publishers* of programming, with their core production activities being stripped back to such activities as news and current affairs.

IRISH MEDIA GO GLOBAL

In recent years, Irish companies have spread their holdings abroad while foreign companies have extended their interests in the Irish marketplace. Independent News and Media (INM) is a global media player with a global workforce of more than 2,900. The INM group manages gross assets in excess of €841 million. Spanning four continents, INM has market-leading newspaper positions in the Republic of Ireland as well as South Africa and Northern Ireland. It is also a major shareholder in APN, which is the largest newspaper publisher in New Zealand and in regional Australia, the biggest radio broadcaster in Australia and a major player in the outdoor advertising (billboard) business in Australia, Hong Kong and Indonesia. It also operates the largest newspaper print facility in Ireland as well as the Independent Colleges, a private third-level college specialising in law and accountancy (INM, 2011).

Communicorp is a media holding company, founded in 1989 by Irish entrepreneur Denis O'Brien. It has significant media holdings, including radio stations, Internet portals and service companies. Communicorp Group owns and operates various media channels with a strong focus on radio broadcasting. Headquartered in Dublin, the company operates one of the largest independent radio groups in central and eastern Europe. On the other hand, Ulster Television (UTV), Granada and Scottish Radio Holdings have been significant players in the media of the Republic at different times. British media giant Emap previously owned Today FM, Ireland's leading national commercial radio station, as well as other Irish radio stations. 3e, the main private TV network, is owned by a British-German private equity company. As previously noted, many British-owned newspapers, such as the *Daily Mirror* and the *Sun*, have a strong presence in the Irish market, producing 'local' editions with some 'Irish' content.

THE SHIFT TOWARD NEW MEDIA

For the first time in history, the amount of television being watched by younger generations is decreasing rather than increasing annually. This is because people are shifting their allegiance away from the box in the corner and toward interactive media, particularly online activities (Shirky, 2010). Irish people have embraced the new media technologies that have become available in recent years. Most Irish families have access to at least one computer in the home. Three out of every five children between the age of eight and 12 own a mobile phone, with almost every child owning one by the time they reach sixth class (*Irish Times*, 30 January 2006). The Growing Up in Ireland study tracking the experiences of Irish children across time found that watching TV is an almost universal activity among nine-year-olds. Two-thirds of nine-year-olds usually watched one to three hours of TV each evening, with 10 per cent watching three hours or more. Furthermore, three-quarters of boys and 54 per cent of girls spent some time each day playing video games and 45 per cent of children had a TV in their bedroom (Williams et al.,

2009, p. 20). Amongst the population at large, social networking has become a regular part of daily life. There are just under 2 million Irish profiles on Facebook and 49 per cent of the population aged over 15 years are signed up to the social networking site. More than 80 per cent of all Irish Internet users used social network sites in the month of December 2010. The average Irish user spends just over four hours a month on Facebook (Irish Social Media Statistics, May 2011).

What does this shift toward digital culture mean? Buckingham (2000) observes that debates about new digital technologies display the same sort of ambivalence that characterised debates around the arrival of cinema, radio and television. Television was originally seen as an educational medium, then as a source of cultural and moral decline. Similarly, promoters of computers focus on their educational potential while detractors focus on their entertainment function. Many of the arguments levelled against computers were once levelled against television: computer games are accused of causing imitative violence, excessive use of technologies is seen as detrimental to physical and mental health, the PC or games console represents an anti-social rather than pro-social activity and a moral panic often underpins concerns about pornography, sexism and paedophilia on the net.

On the other hand, advocates of new technology argue that computers have an important educative function that transcends the limitations of earlier pedagogic models associated with print and television. For instance, James Paul Gee, author of *What Video Games Have to Teach Us About Learning and Literacy*, argues that the best games offer a model learning experience and suggest teachers can learn useful lessons by looking at how games draw players in and motivate them to concentrate and tackle complex problems in new and creative ways (*Guardian*, 2 June 2006). At a more basic level, Nintendo can prove a useful device for helping children to learn. Irish teachers have used the Nintendo DS in class to help national school children with maths. They found that children concentrated and applied themselves when using consoles, making it easer for them to enjoy maths learning. Success on the DS unblocked negative feelings about maths and has had a ripple effect on other areas of learning (*Irish Times*, 10 November 2009).

While older media like TV are viewed as passive, the net and digital technologies have at least the potential to be active. Computers offer the possibility of bringing the means of expression and communication within everyone's reach, seen as facilitating the individual to unleash their imaginative potential. This is reflected in the ubiquitous commitment made by politicians and public policy-makers to create a 'smart economy' or 'digital revolution'. Both sets of arguments, Buckingham notes, connect a mythology about childhood with a mythology about technology. Thus, children are seen to simultaneously possess a natural, spontaneous creativity that is somehow released by the machine and they are seen as vulnerable, innocent and in need of protection from the damage that the technology can inflict on them. The technology is seen as transformative, both in negative and positive ways.

SOCIAL NETWORKING

The first decade of the 21st century witnessed the meteoric rise of social networking. Facebook, with half a billion members worldwide, is the dominant social networking platform in terms of number of users and frequency of use. There has been considerable speculation about the possible social impact of such sites on the quality of people's relationships with each other and their propensity to participate in their communities and in face-to-face activities such as volunteering or political organising. Keith Hampton, lead author of a study carried out on behalf of the Pew Research Center's Internet and American Life Project, suggests that people who use sites like Facebook actually have more close relationship and are more likely to be involved in civic and political activities (University of Pennsylvania, 2011). The survey found that regular users of Facebook have more close relationships, are more trusting and get more social support than other Internet users. While researching the world of social networking is a relatively new phenomenon, much of the work carried out thus far has been on young people who are seen as 'early adapters' of this technology. The setting up of a social networking page is highest between the ages of 16 and 24 years and those most likely to use Facebook are between 18 and 24 years old (Office of Communications Social Networking Research Document, 2008).

Emerging research on social networking sites suggests that they are used to reproduce and reinforce existing relations online (Boyd, 2006; Livingstone, 2008). Danah Boyd (2006) has explored the expansion of social network sites and their diffusion into youth culture. She observes that social network sites provide a space for 'a public' to gather, but are also constituted as 'a public' in and of themselves. Teenagers have always used their peers as a reference group, but crucially, their interactions, encounters and social experimentation took place 'off stage'. Nowadays, through social networking sites like Facebook, 'friends are publicly articulated, profiles are publicly viewed and comments are publicly visible' (Boyd, 2006). A form of 'networked public' is created as teenagers seek to create and embellish portraits of themselves and their friendship groups against the backdrop of an imagined audience. Social networking sites are increasingly important to young people, Boyd argues, as they are sites of identity formation, status negotiation and peer-to-peer sociality. The sites enable the presentation of 'possible selves' that may be a mixture of true self or ideal self, as opposed to 'now selves', and in which the characteristics of popularity, well-roundedness and thoughtfulness are valorised (Zhao et al., 2008).

According to Livingstone (2008), the changing nature of childhood and the greater capacity nowadays for young people to conduct the task of adolescence online raises issues of both opportunity and risk. There are opportunities, or what she calls 'affordances', associated with new technology that encourage self-expression, sociability, new forms of technological literacy, creativity and engagement. For Livingstone, social networking sites enable the expression of identity through display and connection with peers. But there is also the potential for these sites to socially isolate users, to enable transgressive representations of the self, to permit abuse and to erode principles of privacy and morality. In a similar vein to Boyd, Livingstone suggests that for young people there is a conflict or tension around what is permissible to show to others and what should remain private. Both authors see a connection between the activities of teenagers in the past (hanging out together in public spaces, decorating bedroom walls) as displaying a continuity with the present. Social networking sites similarly provide a canvas upon which to paint a persona, engage with like-minded others and develop identity, but the distinction between the public and private realms has now become much more attenuated.

As social networking sites have gained popularity, the issue of privacy has come to the fore. Web users are becoming increasingly concerned about how private data are made public. In December 2009, Facebook changed the default settings on its privacy controls so that individuals' personal information would be shared with 'everyone' rather than selected friends. According to the *Economist* (22 May 2010), Facebook argued that this reflected a shift in society towards greater openness and noted that users could still adjust privacy settings back again. If people are encouraged to share more information (rather than keep it private), it increases the traffic on the network, thus enabling Facebook to sell more advertising. This reminds us that behind the soft-focus image of Facebook as a 'social good', there are important economic rationales that underpin the design and development of the site. If we want to fully understand the meaning of new technology in everyday life, then we have to pay attention to its political economy: who owns, who controls and what are the implications for users of a service that is market driven and profit oriented?

MEDIA AUDIENCES

Consideration of the media process indicates how important a knowledge of the audience is. We may claim that the producer of a media message has a certain intention or that a text has specific overt or covert meanings, but how people themselves interpret and understand media messages is of crucial importance if we are concerned about, say, the effects of the media or how the media form a part of people's everyday lives.

Furthermore, the audience has been shown to be very important in the development of the media. Technologically oriented stories about the development of radio, television or other mass media tend to focus on the invention of the technology and its gradual development and dissemination into society, but as Sorlin (1994, pp. 47–55) has shown, the audience is a significant part of the media development process. For instance, the worldwide web was largely developed by a community of computer programmers and individual users who helped to develop browser software, search engines and other applications that were subsequently picked up and commercialised by major companies.

One of the most dramatic trends in recent years has been the diffusion of Facebook from an amateur website set up by Harvard students to a mainstream subscriber service with global reach. Social networking technologies have proliferated across the Internet, changing the landscape of computer-mediated communications and reconstituting the audience as producers as well as consumers of content. As media and technology commentator Lillington puts it, 'from mashups to wikis, Flickr to Bebo, MySpace to YouTube, blogs to Facebook, the web's hottest spot is where people converge to create and share their own content' (*Irish Times*, 29 December 2006). An important question to ask is what role the Internet is playing in the reconfiguration of social relations, particularly in the context of the constitution of audiences.

Researching audiences

All media companies are intensely interested in the topic of audiences. After all, as many critics have pointed out, the key role of the media institution is to *sell audiences to advertisers*. The company needs to know the size of its audience, its composition and nature (often seen in terms of consumers with particular levels of spending power) and, increasingly, *how* the audience consumes the product. Highly sophisticated methods of researching audiences have been developed by international companies such as Nielsen, incorporating technology such as 'people meters' that measure exactly who is watching what and when on the TV screen. The technology is being continually developed to enable it, for example, to track people's purchases (via packaging bar codes) and to link these to demographic categories and to particular advertising campaigns. Morozov (2011) observes that information-sharing on the Internet may seem trivial, but once information that we provide is analysed alongside data from similar services, it can generate insights about individuals and groups that are of interest to marketers and intelligence agencies. This process, known as 'data mining' – the basis of Google's business – creates the possibility for companies to customise their products and target their advertising at tiny (but potentially receptive) niche audiences. Morozov sees the Internet propelling us toward 'a future where privacy becomes a very expensive commodity'.

While demographics have been the main interest of the commercial media, psychological studies of the audience have dominated academic research in the area. As well as the uses and gratifications approach that has attempted to define and measure why people consume the media, there has also been a focus on media effects, often on those perceived to be more susceptible to its messages, particularly children. Within this tradition there has been a great deal of interest in the issues of violence, health and welfare and, more recently, sexist imagery. Much of the research has been carried out using experimental techniques and questionnaires. In recent years, the approach to audience research has been based on the notion of the viewer or reader of the media as an interpreter of messages within a social environment, rather than a person with a particular mental orientation or a consumer within a demographic group. This approach often focuses on the 'fan' – the dedicated user of specific media products, such as comic books, *Star Trek* or romantic fiction. The methodology is usually ethnographic, in the sense that the researcher tries to get close to the experience of media consumption and to enter the world of the media consumer. The data gathered is often rich and complex, though inevitably difficult to generalise to larger groups of media users. The interest in ethnographic and socially situated research reflects something of how we typically use the media: often less as a series of individual media events and more as a continuous *flow* of messages, images and information, into which we may dip in and out during the day with varying degrees of attention (a point first made by the British Marxist critic Raymond Williams).

The concept of *mass* media implies a large and relatively undifferentiated audience. It is very much tied in to the development of the technologies of newspaper publishing, cinema, radio and, above all, television – technologies that have compressed time and space in such a way that very large numbers of people (up to several billion for events like the soccer World Cup or Olympic Games) can experience the same messages and images at virtually the same moment. But to a certain extent, the 'mass media audience' is a fiction, brought into being through the process of talking about, measuring or analysing it. In reality, people experience the media alone, in close domestic and family environments or in relatively small public groups. The media is thus, as Sorlin (1994) has suggested, inevitably linked with other aspects of our everyday social interaction.

A good example of the type of audience research that reflects a concern with everyday lived experience is that of the British researcher Marie Gillespie, who has studied how television is part of the lives of a group of London Punjabi teenagers. She argues (1995, p. 205) that 'TV talk, though it may seem esoteric and trivial, is an important form of self narration and a major collective resource through which identities are negotiated'. In other words, how people think about, respond to and talk with others about what they see on TV makes up a part of their process of defining themselves and others. Given that people may spend more time watching TV every week than going to work or being with family members, this is hardly surprising.

Gillespie's research is part of a group of studies that has shown how people across the world are able to make sense of global media products in their own ways. For example, Ang (1985) has studied how the US soap, *Dallas*, was watched by a group of women in the Netherlands, Gripsrud (1995) has traced the reception of another US soap, *Dynasty*, in Norway and Miller (2011) has examined how Facebook use has helped to strengthen and revive community in Trinidad. Such detailed and culturally integrated consideration of audiences can address issues like the extent to which indigenous or local cultures may resist or be undermined by global media penetration.

Audience research in Ireland

For both theoretical and practical reasons, sociological audience research in Ireland has adopted a qualitative methodology, as opposed to the quantitative methods used by the media industry or the experimental methods favoured by psychologists. Qualitative audience research, according to Kelly and O'Connor (1997, p. 3), can 'explore the rich cultural terrain at the interface between media, power and subcultural discourses and identities'. In *Media Audiences in Ireland*, Kelly and O'Connor (1997) provide a good overview of academic audience research, though 'qualitative research' has been interpreted as open-ended or semi-structured interviews with people *about* their media use; there is little evidence of observational or participative studies that attempt to establish in situ how people use the media in their ordinary everyday environment. Underpinning many of the studies is a concern with *power*: who has it – the audience or the media institutions? Is there a 'dominant ideology' at work, basically leading people to think in particular ways, or does the notion of the 'active audience' make more sense, where people can take what they wish from the media and interpret it in their own ways, even in an oppositional fashion? Kelly and O'Connor (1997, p. 10) conclude that both these tendencies are apparent. The media confirm the ideological and symbolic power of some powerful and high-status groups while weakening and disorganising those with little power. And yet it is possible for the latter to use the media creatively for their own psychological, pleasurable and cultural purposes. However, the pleasures of the text can be highly seductive and hide the symbolic power of the media to confirm the status quo, in particular, perhaps, by ignoring voices and cultures 'from below' and its non-articulation of alternative and radical perspectives. This theme is returned to below in our discussion of the audience for reality television.

There is also a question as to whether, given the (limited) power that the media hold over the creation and dissemination of meanings, they have any responsibility to their audience(s). This issue is linked closely to the concept of the 'public sphere'. The question can be asked whether the modern mass media allow – or should allow – a space for disinterested public debate. This is a topic that is addressed in Sara O'Sullivan's analysis of RTÉ 2FM's *Gerry Ryan Show* (GRS). The GRS was one of the first of the talk radio genre to gain a substantial audience in Ireland. The genre remains robust, with programmes like Joe Duffy's *Liveline* on RTÉ Radio 1 and the *Adrian Kennedy Show* on FM104 demonstrating strong audience reach as well as numerous similar programmes on local radio stations. O'Sullivan suggests (1997, p. 167) that talk radio, 'provides a rare opportunity for Irish audiences to participate in mass mediated debate and discussion'. In particular, and given the success of TV shows like *Oprah* and even *Big Brother*, is the significance of the public discussion of what were formerly seen as 'private' matters, for example sexuality, domestic relationships and personal opinions. This may be of particular importance in the Irish context, where so many recent political and social debates (over the economic crisis, the housing bubble, child sexual abuse and so on) have engendered huge public interest. O'Sullivan found that people called in to a radio show to express their views, seek help, offer support or get things off their chests. She concludes that while the show allows for these sorts of expression, it does not encourage critical discussion of social and political issues. One reason is that access to shows such as GRS is relatively tightly controlled by RTÉ staff: 'this control on participation makes it difficult to see how the show might have a contribution to make to the public sphere, where, in theory at least, access should be open to all' (1997, p. 177).

PEOPLE POWER? THE RISE OF REALITY TELEVISION

The focus on the active audience in sociological research has been propelled in part by the advent of reality television and the proliferation of the talent show genre that allows audiences to offer their views and opinions on participants and to play a part in the show's outcome. It offers a means for the public to scrutinise and evaluate others' bodily and emotional performances (Skeggs, 2009). According to Griffin-Foley (2004), the depiction of programmes like *Big Brother* or *I'm a Celebrity Get Me Out of Here* as a 'phenomenon' have obscured their direct connection to older print and media outlets. Griffin-Foley surveys the history of participatory media from the late 19th century to the present day and identifies a number of genres that allowed for audience participation, including periodicals that featured readers' contributions, confessional magazines, women's magazines, true lives publications, talkback radio and 'real life' genres. She notes that attempts to engage the audience by soliciting their feedback and contributions and creating dialogues with readers was a significant factor in the 'attempt to consolidate an audience, give readers a sense of agency and project a feeling of communality'.

The role of the ordinary public as television participants as well as audience members has intensified in recent years with the global proliferation of the reality television genre. Writing in the *Observer* in 2010, journalist Elizabeth Day notes that reality television turns the private lives of ordinary people into a daily public spectacle. The shows are based on comprehensive surveillance of the key protagonists, whether living in a house together (*Big Brother*) or competing on a reality TV show (*X Factor*). The audience ultimately determines the outcome through voting people to remain in contention or to be eliminated from the show. 'It's always going to be popular,' Peter Bazalgette, the former creative director of production company Endemol and the man who brought *Big Brother* to UK screens told Day:

the average show takes members of the public and sends them on a journey. We love to follow that because it's a cracking story which engages our emotion. It's not unlike a soap opera, except that these are real people and you get to vote them out one by one. That simple premise dominates everything from *Britain's Got Talent* to *Big Brother* and *The Apprentice*. What it creates is an extraordinarily powerful story arc where we get involved in the characters. That's why we watch it. (Day, 2010)

For Rose (2005), the popularity of reality television programming represents a sophisticated quest for greater authenticity within the traditional fiction-oriented entertainment sphere. He suggests that there is a paradox at the core of this quest: although authenticity is desired, consumers of reality television revel in the ironic mix of the factitious and the spontaneous. A subtle blend of the genuine must be combined with the aspiration to capture what viewers desire or fantasise about in their own lives.

According to Skeggs, reality television represents a shift towards the individualisation of human experience while obscuring the real and significant class boundaries that still shape individual life chances. She suggests (2009, p. 628) that:

> 'ordinary' people doing 'ordinary everydayness' with new levels of televisual representational play [offers] the perfect site for exploring self-making, self-legitimation and the supposed demise of class.

Skeggs argues that one of the subterfuges of reality television is to gloss over the advantages (and disadvantages) of class groupings in terms of their access to social, cultural and educational capital. The format suggests that 'skill and disposition are all that is needed to become socially mobile' (p. 637), whereas in reality, social mobility in the UK has been atrophying and getting ahead is hugely dependent on 'access to a different inheritance, a different economical location and a different education system' (2009, p. 637). It is not just the core inequalities and power differentials that stem from class that are ignored. Other social categories like race and gender are also reduced to matters of individualised self-performance in front of the cameras. The self-transformation narrative at the core of much reality television has to entertain in order to garner an audience. Yet the audience is not necessarily supine. Skeggs notes that despite the focus on working-class participants as inadequate and in need of self-investment (they must transform themselves in order to be better), black and white working-class audience groups revealed strong defensive reactions to the demonisation of characters such as the late Jade Goody and Jordan (Katie Price).

MEDIA AND THE PUBLIC SPHERE

One of the basic principles of democracy is the ideal of the public sphere – that notional space where the public formulate, debate and exchange opinion. The concept has been most fully developed by the German social theorist Jürgen Habermas. For Habermas, the public sphere is a place for discussion oriented towards the common good, untainted by commercial or governmental interests. The ideal location of the public sphere was the coffee shops and salons of 18th-century Europe. Public opinion ideally is conceived as the outcome of the cut and thrust that occurs in the public sphere. There is now a widespread view that while the democratic public sphere may be more necessary than ever, it is increasingly difficult to locate.

The rise of infotainment programming (such as reality television) and the concomitant 'dumbing down' of culture, the expansion in the number and range of media platforms and the proliferation of news managers and news management techniques have combined to fracture the notion of a body politic, alienating us from the public sphere. Conglomeration, commercialisation and commodification characterise the media landscape today, with negative consequences. As former Minister for the Arts and Communications and now President of Ireland, Michael D. Higgins, has observed (2004, p. 139):

> The main tendencies in communications at the present time include convergence of technology, concentration of ownership in a number of international conglomerates and fragmentation of audiences. These tendencies occur at a time when the prevailing ideology guiding economic policy decisions is one that places an emphasis on unrestricted market adjustments. The circumstances of these transitions are different from other historical shifts of the industrial era. It is very difficult to question, indeed identify, the assumptions upon which they are based. We are drifting into, rather than choosing, this new condition of our unfreedom – our existence as consumers rather than citizens.

In these circumstances, public service broadcasting has often been held up as the last refuge of the public sphere, a far cry from Habermas's 18th-century coffee house, but an enduring forum nevertheless for promoting reasoned argument and disputation. It is to the public service broadcasters that we have traditionally repaired when seeking balance, objectivity and impartiality in the reporting of the issues of the day. But public service broadcasting is no more immune than it has ever been to the machinations of its political masters: witness the unrelenting pressure to which the British Broadcasting Corporation (BBC) was subjected by the British government in 2003 over its coverage of the war in Iraq.

Politicians, and the 'spin masters' working on their behalf, to a greater or lesser extent seek to control access, to shape 'their message' and to determine where and how that message is diffused. When public service broadcasting loses something of its reputation for independence, journalists baulk at covering 'difficult' and 'dangerous' stories, a chill wind blows through the newsroom and the audience inevitably is short-changed. Furthermore, public service broadcasting in Ireland and across Europe has come under increasing commercial pressure as technology delivers more and more media platforms. It has had to follow the market, resorting increasingly to programme-making of the infotainment variety. As President Higgins has argued (2004, p. 136), 'broadcasting now stands to be judged as a production space for commodified entertainment products rather than that public space where citizens listened and viewed to be informed, educated or entertained'. We now inhabit a world where time and space differences are being obliterated by the sheer flow of information through multiple media platforms. The notions of a 'national audience' and a 'body politic' are increasingly questionable in a media-saturated world.

Rubberbandits: An Internet sensation

Towards the end of 2010, a comedy duo from Limerick, the Rubberbandits, uploaded a music video on YouTube. Their performance of 'Horse Outside' went on to receive 7 million hits. The video and song seemed to capture the public imagination as it riffed mercilessly on some of the vanities associated with the Celtic Tiger years. The appeal of the Rubberbandits is at least in part attributable to their versatility and their razor sharp political edge. According to Byrne and Keohane:

> Horse Outside is many things: a satire of Celtic Tiger mimetic consumerism, released just at the moment when this corrupt form of living had become fully visible ... Horse Outside is a song, a rap with witty, incisive lyrics; a dance, a video, a live performance – a multidimensional artistic production. Horse Outside is presented in the form of play, a play not just in a formal theatrical sense, but a political-anthropological dramaturgy that recovers and reactivates an ancient technique of social renewal and redemption.

It is arguable that for many people in Ireland and beyond, this YouTube clip represents a more effective critique of the failings of Irish society than the commentary in the opinion pieces of the broadsheets or the chambers of the Oireachtas.

According to Stevenson (1999), a number of key features shape the contemporary relationship between the public and the mass media. First, most of us, most of the time, engage with the media in privatised contexts where we are largely passive. The media's capacity to make us aware of common concerns (for example, the global news reach of the story of the September 11th attacks on New York) is mitigated to some degree by the comparative isolation in which we make our interpretations. There are fewer opportunities for people to pursue a collective response to either the terrorist attacks or to the US retaliation; we feel rather powerless and maybe even fearful a lot of the time. Fragmentation of the media audience means that rather than constituting a national audience of citizens, we are increasingly composed of targeted audience segments, delivered to advertisers and programme sponsors. At the same time, Stevenson points out that the very fragmentation of the national audience makes it more difficult for governments and information managers to control and censor debate. The rapid expansion of new media made available by technological change means our public culture will become increasingly based on individual choice.

Second, the rapid development of media technologies has increased the volume of information available, but more information does not necessarily mean a better-informed citizenry. Indeed, Peillon (2000, p. 181) has described how the use of public opinion polls and mass surveys by the political class, and increasingly by media professionals, enables them 'to remain within the confines of a predictable public opinion in order to find its political action validated, justified'. In other words, the audience can become 'the news' through extensive use of opinion polls, exit polls, straw polls, email polls and so on. The delivery of information is now almost simultaneous and a wealth of new interactive mechanisms is available to news producers and their audiences through the Internet. Indeed, the Internet helps to blur the distinction between producer and consumer since it facilitates two-way interactions.

Writing in the *Irish Times* on the fate of newspapers in the age of the new media, Roy Greenslade quotes Jay Rosen's maxim that 'the people formerly known as the audience will play a key role in the gathering and transmission of news events' (Greenslade, 2010a). Such input is likely to appear online, on independent sites that do not necessarily form part of the traditional global media empires. The arrival of the Internet and the diffusion of technology that allows people to participate through blogging, tweeting and social networking heralds, says Andreas Kluth, the beginning of a new era, an era that might be called the age of personal or participatory media (*The Economist*, 20 April 2006). Albrechtslund (2008) terms this, somewhat more sinisterly, the possibility to engage in 'participatory surveillance'. People can now upload to as well as download from the web. The Pew Internet and American Life Project found that 57 per cent of American teenagers create content for the Internet, from text to pictures, music and video (cited in Kluth, 2006). Kluth points out that this transformation has huge implications for traditional business models within the mass media that were based around a mass audience held captive during advertising breaks and/or required to pay a fee for access. In the new media era, it is predicted that audiences will become more and more fragmented. Except for occasional events such as a World Cup football match, the Olympics or a royal wedding, audiences will be smaller.

Across Europe there has been an erosion of the commitment to public service broadcasting as the commercial imperative comes to dominate. In the US, it is the commercial right-wing channel Fox Television News that dominates the airwaves. If there is no longer a place for public service broadcasting, is there a place for the public sphere? Even in countries like Britain, where public service broadcasting has historically been strong, it has been subjected to a bruising. The Hutton inquiry in Britain (after the Iraq War) may turn out to mark a watershed in terms of the relationship between government and public service broadcasting. The BBC, an institution trusted and respected all over the world, found itself under sustained criticism from government. Though accusations of a 'whitewash' quickly circulated in the media, polls conducted in the aftermath of the event showed that respondents were more inclined to believe the public service broadcaster than the British government. But most public service broadcasters now face an uncertain future. It may well be the case that the public will look increasingly to new digital technologies as a means to constitute a new kind of 'public sphere'.

However, some commentators have sounded a note of caution in that regard. Malcolm Gladwell has argued that far from promoting activism and citizen participation, the Internet makes it easier for people to feel connected but without any personal cost. Gladwell (2010) suggests that the platforms of social media are primarily built around weak ties, which are useful for being networked but not for advancing change: 'Twitter is a way of following (or being followed by) people you may never have met. Facebook is a tool for efficiently managing your acquaintances, for keeping up with the people you would not otherwise be able to stay in touch with.' Weak ties that are not based on shared experience, intense commitment and willingness to suffer for a cause do not lead to high-risk or strategic activism oriented toward social change.

In a similar view, Eygeny Morozov argues in *The Net Delusion: How Not to Liberate the World* (2010) that the Internet's public sphere potential has been grossly overrated. He contends that online political acts – such as 'liking' a particular Facebook page or signing an Internet petition – involve no commitment or risk. He goes so far as to suggest that rather than democratisation, the Internet may end up entrenching authoritarian regimes. In particular, he challenges what he sees as two fundamental delusions about the Internet: 'cyber-utopianism' – the idea that the Internet is emancipatory – and 'Internet-centrism' – the belief that the Internet can provide a framing device for every important question in modern society. In reality, people actually use the Internet not for political or public good purposes, but for entertainment and self-validation. Meanwhile, authoritarian regimes such as the Chinese administration engage in a range of activities to block or limit access to the Internet, to infiltrate protest groups and to seed their own propaganda online.

15
Consumption

Consumerism: a way of living that revolves around the wanting of things, a way of life in which having, desiring, and wishing for more and more things have become significant preoccupations for late modern subjects whose identities are increasingly bound up with what and how they consume. (Smart, 2010, p. 5)

What is consumption and why is it of interest to sociology? Consumption refers to how we use material objects, like smartphones or T-shirts, and services, like getting a haircut or going to the doctor, and even how we interact with facilities like transport systems or landscapes. Consumption is a central part of everyday life. It has a lot to do with how we meet our material needs but includes much more, including our personal and social identities, our interactions with others, even the future of our planet. How we consume goods and services also makes up much of what we think of as culture, for in consuming goods and services we consume culture and we also create and re-create it.

Despite the significance of consumption, sociology has paid it relatively little attention until quite recently. While the term 'consumer society' is often used to describe modern, capitalist society, its analysis has largely been left to economists and psychologists. However, a more comprehensive sociology of consumption has begun to emerge as a greater sociological interest in culture and everyday life has displaced an earlier preoccupation with social structure and structural processes. This interest also reflects the growing impact of globalisation and the neo-liberal economic policies that have massively stimulated consumption across the world, including the so-called developing world.

This chapter outlines some of the key ideas in the sociology of consumption and then examines what sociologists have had to say about the topic in the Irish context. It suggests some reasons for its comparative neglect in 'classical' sociology, then, drawing on the work of Campbell, Veblen and Simmel, it explores some of the factors behind consumption in contemporary societies. It goes on to examine connections between economic development, class and consumption before focusing on the particular expressions and analyses of consumption in Irish society. Reflecting on one of our key themes in this book, it looks at how consumption has been linked to conceptions of modernity. It concludes with a discussion of the key way that we now consume: through shopping, with an overview of trends in the retail industries and a snapshot of that modern temple of consumption, IKEA.

Sociology embraces a range of approaches to consumption. One view sees it as a threat to satisfactory human relationships. Sociologists have long engaged in a moral critique of consumerism, found, for example, in the work of the critical theorists of the Frankfurt School, Adorno and Horkheimer (2002). Since the 1970s, the ecological critique of consumerism has also been increasingly significant (Gorz, 1975; Smart, 2010). More recently, some sociologists (and other social scientists such as social anthropologists and social historians) have expressed a keen interest in the nature of everyday life and lifestyles (Bennett and Watson, 2002; Shove et al., 2007; Stewart, 2007; Miller, 2008). They have recognised that consumption forms a major element of the daily round and is also a significant contributor to people's making of meaning and expression of personal and social identities. They have begun to focus on the routine practices of consumption, seeking to develop an interpretation that is closer to consumers' own practices and understandings.

In many ways, the experience of consumption in Ireland has been similar to that in other developed societies, but has also evolved in its own way, related to our historical, cultural and economic development. As we shall see, these differences stem from a particular experience of late or disrupted urbanisation and industrialisation; nationalist and religious ideologies; and patterns of sociability and community. More recently, it might be argued that globalising tendencies in the production, promotion, distribution and retailing of consumer goods have seen Ireland follow a pattern more similar to the core industrial societies, as reflected in the development of our retail sector.

THEORETICAL PERSPECTIVES ON CONSUMPTION

As we have stressed throughout this book, sociology developed as the study of modernity. Its comparative neglect of consumption is rather curious, as for many, increased consumption is a key distinguishing feature of modern society and a 'consumer society' is seen as a 'modern' society. We can find a reason for this blind spot in how the early sociologists structured the understanding of modernity.

In his materialist approach to history, Marx focused on relationships of production. While he saw capitalism as a system that encouraged people to consume and to 'fetishise' commodities, his work helped divert sociological attention away from consumption by arguing that capitalism would inevitably lead towards the increasing impoverishment and 'immiseration' of working people, to the extent that this would provoke a socialist revolution. He argued that by the time capitalism had become fully established in the world, the experience of the working class would be one of such reduced consumption that they would be unable even to buy the necessities of food and clothing, let alone the more aspirational goods from which a lifestyle and personal identity might be created. As far as the developed world is concerned, this prediction has turned out to be wrong, but it meant that Marxist sociologists were relatively uninterested in the study of consumption. Consumerism tended to be seen as a way to 'buy off' the working class or to create 'false needs' rather than a body of practices worth examining in its own right.

Weber also helped to direct sociological attention away from consumption. He argued that the development of capitalism was significantly shaped by the emergence, in early modern Europe, of a particular type of 'ascetic Protestantism' (see Chapter 13) that stressed self-denial. Ascetic Protestants were committed to an ethic of hard work and success in their working lives, but saw this as a way to honour God, not to acquire a luxurious lifestyle. This encouraged Protestant businessmen to accumulate capital, but this was reinvested in their businesses rather than spent on luxury goods. Many became wealthy capitalist producers but lived domestic lives of frugality or modest comfort. Their success encouraged others to follow their example. Weber thus provides a fascinating explanation for the growth in early modern Europe of a 'culture of capitalism' that, in promoting dedication to work and entrepreneurial success, substantially accounted for the spread of capitalism. But he did not explain how, as capitalism developed and matured, this asceticism came to be replaced by the contemporary enthusiasm for consumption.

FROM LEISURE CLASSES TO MASS SOCIETY

For Weber, capitalist development is linked to a repression of the desire to consume, rather than its expansion. In response, Campbell (1987) aims to develop a theory to explain the parallel revolution in consumption. He initially asks: why do we need an explanation at all? Surely it is natural to human beings to consume and all that holds them back is a lack of opportunity? Have there not always been examples of greed and extreme desire for material possessions in all societies?

Campbell argues that there are some significant issues about consumption that need to be explained. First, consumers seem to be insatiable: 'rarely can an inhabitant of modern society, no matter how privileged or wealthy, declare that there is nothing that they want ... It is a central fact of modern consumer behaviour that the gap between wanting and getting never actually closes' (1987, pp. 37–8). Second, as well as being continually re-created, wants are also continually extinguished: 'a natural corollary of endless wanting is the high rate of product (and hence want) obsolescence' (1987, p. 38). As a result, modern society is 'symbolised at least as much by the mountains of rubbish, the garage and jumble sales, the columns of advertisements of second-hand goods for sale and the second-hand car lots, as it is by the ubiquitous propaganda on behalf of new goods' (1987, pp. 38–9). We could now add eBay and other Internet auction sites to this list as well as those services (such as Freecycle) that help people to give away their surplus possessions.

Although we take these phenomena for granted, they are historically neither normal nor natural. In pre-industrial societies, consumption was governed by custom and tradition that set limits to the range of wants a person would have, though these were socially variable. We therefore need to explain how the pattern of consumption found in modern industrialised societies developed and how it is maintained. Campbell surveys three theories of consumption in his search for an adequate explanation, and we now briefly review these.

The first approach he terms *instinctivist*. This suggests a biologically based desire to consume. Human wants are seen to be inherent and 'triggered off' by goods that enter the individual's environment. We are thought to have a 'latent demand' for goods, unleashed when new goods come onto the market. A problem with this approach is that it cannot distinguish between biological needs (food, warmth, sex) and culturally mediated wants (diamonds, Porsches, iPhones). Nor can it explain how wants vary across societies or over time. In particular, it cannot explain how we can rapidly 'stop wanting' perfectly usable – and to others, still desirable – consumer goods.

Campbell calls the second approach *manipulationist*. Consumers are led to develop wants by outside agents, particularly advertisers. They do not have an inborn capacity to seek out specific goods or satisfactions but are relatively passive objects of external influences. Campbell believes this approach overstates the power of others, even of advertisers, to create wants. Much research suggests that consumers are not passive recipients of advertisements, but can actively evaluate the messages they receive. They can do this because they live in a world that has already been given meaning by their culture. Advertisers may try to exploit 'the desires and dreams of the consumer' (1987, p. 47), but they do not create these in the first place, or at least not in a cultural vacuum. What they try to manipulate are not the wants of consumers, but the symbolic meanings that consumers attach to goods and products.

This idea is central to Campbell's third perspective, that *acts of consumption are themselves signs or symbols*. This approach derives from the work of American sociologist Thorstein Veblen, remembered today for his book *The Theory of the Leisure Class* (1925) and the phrase 'conspicuous consumption'. Veblen studied the 'new rich' in the US of the late 19th century and was interested in how they sought to gain social acceptance among established elites. He argued that acts of consumption were a way to signal or lay claim to social status, as they reflected the level of wealth the consumer possessed. Commodities not only satisfy wants or needs, but also convey meanings about oneself to others.

Veblen assumed that human beings are motivated by the desire for 'emulation': to compete with others in displays of wealth and prestige. He also assumed that the significant message contained in a commodity was its price – in purchasing it, a consumer sends the message 'see how rich I am, that I can afford this!' But Campbell points out that consumption goods also carry other meanings, particularly about taste and style, that may have little to do with price. An overriding concern with price and 'conspicuous consumption' may be peculiar to newly wealthy groups that need to validate their social position; it may not be so important for those whose status is secure or have no interest in upward social mobility.

Does Veblen explain why consumption is characterised by restless insatiability? He claims that humans strive constantly to emulate those higher up the status ladder. They must be constantly prepared to change their consumption habits and styles. Those they emulate must also constantly invent new lifestyles or fashions in order to maintain their superiority: 'drinking champagne or malt whiskey, once the preserve of the aristocracy, has moved down the social status ladder ... so that the upper echelons either cease to drink those drinks, or consume more exclusive and expensive vintages' (Bocock, 1992, p. 127). This may explain the restless nature of consumption among those around the top of the social hierarchy, but not how a concern with consumption and style is widespread across the mass of the population.

For Simmel, the answer to this question lay in the rapid urbanisation of Western societies. Simmel is perhaps best known for his analyses of the contemporary urban human, in particular how people's behaviour has altered in response to living in a rationalised, depersonalised and busy city environment. The city produces a person who must develop a 'blasé outlook' – a calculated lack of interest in the numerous people one will share space with every day at work, on public transport or in the city streets. Consumption is a way for people to reassert their identity and individuality in the face of this depersonalisation of modern life (Paterson, 2006, p. 21). Yet this personal identity always exists in tension with broader society: we wish to be individual but also to be accepted as part of the community. What we see in the cycles of fashion is 'a continual cycle of establishing the norm, challenging it, and thereby deriving a newly altered norm which hastily abandons the previously established norms' (Paterson, 2006, p. 23). We recognise here the restlessness of consumption that Veblen alluded to. There is also clearly an antagonism between personal and societal or community needs, a conflict we will see in contemporary Irish responses to consumption.

For Campbell, patterns of consumption can only be explained in relation to cultural movements that present some ways to behave as valuable and intelligible, with others as bizarre or irrational. He traces our contemporary responses to commodities to the Romantic movement of the early 19th century. For Campbell, it was this movement that introduced a new 'consumer ethic' into developing capitalist society, expressed through notions of sentiment, feeling, individualism and a commitment to pleasure. It manifests itself in a peculiar orientation towards goods: not a utilitarian one, but one typified by dreaming and anticipation and a shift from having to 'wanting'. Consequently, 'goods are thought of as bridges to displaced meanings – bridging the gap between present lived reality and the set of ideals one keeps in mind', which may be 'a golden past or even a bright hope for the future' (Paterson, 2006, pp. 24–35).

MASS CONSUMERISM AND THE AFFLUENT WORKER

Early sociological work on consumption, such as Veblen's, focused on the upper classes. It was not until the mid-20th century that sociologists began to ask questions about consumption among the industrial working class. They focused on one key question: does a rising standard of living and increased availability of consumer goods lead to a blurring of class divisions in industrialised societies? More bluntly, do well-paid industrial workers become more like middle-class people and thus less likely to challenge the status quo of capitalist society? The boom in Western economies after the Second World War led to rising wage levels for industrial workers, especially skilled workers in 'new' industries such as car-making and the manufacture of consumer durables (such as TVs and washing machines). Compared with those in the older, heavy industries like coal-mining and ship-building, it appeared that workers in the new industries were not only better off, but seemed to be the forerunners of a new type of employee who no longer fitted easily into the traditional view of the industrial working class.

A major British study of such 'affluent workers' (Goldthorpe et al., 1968–9) set out to explore this question. It did find differences in lifestyle and consumption behaviour between workers in the old and new industries. The latter tended to be more home centred, spent less time with other men in traditionally male pursuits such as football or the pub, were interested in spending money on the home (house decorating, domestic gadgets) and generally had at least one car in the household. But this did not imply that affluent workers were becoming more middle class: they still saw work as a way to finance consumption rather than as a source of personal satisfaction, and so had more in common with other members of the working class. Rather, what was happening was the emergence of a *mass consumer* society, where consumption patterns were being generalised across social classes rather than being sharply differentiated along class lines.

'Conspicuous consumption' was moving down the status hierarchy as societies became more industrialised. Smart connects the emergence of such mass consumption with the development of mass industrial production, which sociologists have termed 'Fordism' in recognition of the revolutionary impact of the Ford Motor Company's assembly line (see Chapter 6). In Fordism, mass consumption is inextricably linked to mass production: 'consumerism became an increasingly essential cultural corollary, vital for engendering continual increases in consumer demand, which became more and more necessary as productivity grew rapidly through the twentieth century' (Smart, 2010, p. 10).

More recent analyses of consumption have drawn heavily on theories of identity, in particular those associated with French writers such as Barthes, Bourdieu and Baudrillard. These analyses focus strongly on how *meanings* are constructed in and through material goods and services and also stress the significance of consumption in everyday life. As Paterson (2006, p. 30) suggests:

> in a late capitalist consumer society ... meanings and signs are inextricable from, but not simply reducible to, the consumption and display of commodities; and the habitual, everyday use we make of them in constructing and maintaining aspects of our identity.

According to this view, consumption, as for Simmel, is about expressing one's individuality within broader cultural patterns of similarity. Consumption can be seen as a form of communication: 'this is who I am, not the same as you, but not so different either'. At the same time, our 'identity' is not a fixed entity, but rather may change according to the circumstances or social situations in which we locate ourselves; our workplace identity may be quite different to the one we express when out at the weekend. Modern consumption allows us some choice around how we present ourselves, but this then raises further questions about authenticity – who or what we really are. As Paterson (2006, p. 56) remarks, 'new identities may be bought and worn as if trying on outfits at the mall, to be discarded later ... but in such a case you are not what you wear'. This tension between authenticity and artificiality is one that underpins Irish discussions about consumption.

CONSUMPTION AND SOCIAL DIFFERENCE: CLASS

As consumption occupies an ever more central position in our social lives, it increasingly becomes a marker of and arguably a source of social difference and inequality. Differences of class, gender, ethnicity and age can be expressed through what we wear, what we eat and how we move around. Such differences may be a result of our exercise of choice or they may be forced on us through lack of the resources (such as money or education) to make such choices.

A central issue is the relationship between consumption and social class. Sociologists have generally assumed that social class determines consumption patterns – that if we know what occupational, educational and income bracket a person fits into, we can fairly accurately estimate the consumer behaviour they will display and, indeed, vice versa: that we can tell a lot about the social positioning of a person by looking into their shopping trolley or at what they are wearing.

On the face of it, social class differences in wealth and income can be seen to directly impact on consumer behaviour. As Scott points out (2009, p. 149), income differentials mean that many of the goods advertised are not equally accessible to all, and so social class determines the type, quantity and quality of the products we consume. The great majority of the population in a country such as Ireland are not in a position to easily purchase Hermés handbags, Mercedes cars or Château Lafite wines. Many will be able to choose alternatives from Zara, Toyota or Jacob's Creek, while for others these choices are also beyond their means. We explore the class impact on Irish consumption patterns in more detail below.

While the purchasing power of consumers is shaped by occupation and economic position, class by itself cannot fully explain how people use that power, or whether they use it at all. Between the capacity to consume an item and its consumption lies a range of factors to do with taste, style and aspiration. This is a controversial area, as statements about the taste and choices of others are inevitably seen as judgemental. But, as argued by Australian sociologists Bennett et al. (1999, p. 1):

> our likes and dislikes have a definite pattern, one which emerges from the roles played by social class, age, gender, education, and ethnicity in distributing cultural interests and abilities differentially across the population.

In the mid-1990s, Bennett and his colleagues asked a large representative sample of Australians about their use of a broad range of 'cultural' phenomena from food to opera to gambling. They also sought their views about cultural activities, such as what was a suitable subject for a photograph, and about their attitudes to consuming certain goods. At the same time, they surveyed them on their social background. The overall aim was to develop 'a richly textured cartography of cultural tastes'. The conclusions were clear: when it came to the consumption and use of a broad range of consumer goods and activities, Australians' choices and tastes were shaped by their membership of broad social groupings. The most significant differences were, as we might expect, between 'professionals' and 'manual workers', with the former disproportionately favouring cultural products and activities such as opera, while the latter were strong supporters of rock concerts. But Bennett et al. warn (1999, p. 263) against any suggestion of a simple divide within society, stressing that:

> watching the football on a Saturday, playing beach cricket, growing giant pumpkins for the show, driving a stock car, walking a bush trail, doing voluntary work for a service club, playing bridge, gardening, working out, going to the movies or a dance club, each of these is diversely configured and specifically valued in ways that do not sustain generalisation.

In all cases, factors such as gender, rurality, age, ethnicity and education are influential to varying degrees. In other words, as the researchers conclude, 'cultural distinction is as complex as social life itself' (1999, p. 269). Nevertheless, they do find an important link with educational attainment and type of school (private vs. state/Catholic) that emerges as the most significant element of class distinction.

The approach adopted by Bennett et al. finds its sociological origins in the work of Max Weber and, more overtly, in the highly influential work in this field of French sociologist Pierre Bourdieu. Weber distinguished between class and status as outcomes of the distribution of power in society. While he defined class primarily in terms of material resources or educational credentials, social status was based on the degree of social respect or esteem that people are accorded due to their social group membership. Status groups may be based on ethnicity, religion or profession, or may simply be groups that display a particularly valued lifestyle. For Weber, most of the conflicts around inequality in modern society were the result of rivalry and competition between status groups rather than between classes. Subsequent discussion of his ideas has generally focused on ethnic or professional status groups, but Weber's inclusion of 'styles of life' suggests that groups differentiated by patterns of consumption – or what we now term 'lifestyles' – are also relevant to social stratification.

Perhaps the most influential sociologist to pick up on this idea has been Bourdieu. He starts from a Marxist position on class and locates the cause of social inequality in the social structure, especially the economic structure. But he adds to this a quite Weberian concern to understand differences between groups in terms of status. Bourdieu's main work on this topic is his monumental study *Distinction: A Social Critique of the Judgement of Taste* (1984), based on 1960s and 1970s research into stratification in French society. One of Bourdieu's main purposes is to establish that 'taste' is not a purely individual or idiosyncratic quality, but is socially derived and socially utilised. Bourdieu says that the exercise of taste, as evidenced in patterns of consumption, is the main way that social groups distinguish themselves from one another. Here he is echoing ideas we have already seen in Veblen, but in emphasising the making of distinctions Bourdieu suggests that a focus just on conspicuous consumption is too crude to express the complexities of the stratification process.

Both Marx and Weber link class position to the ownership of capital. One of Bourdieu's major contributions has been to distinguish between different types of capital. One is the traditional concept of economic capital that refers to material wealth, such as property, land, shares and money. To this concept Bourdieu adds the notion of symbolic or *cultural capital*, which refers to the intellectual resources that exist in society, from particular educational qualifications to the capacity to appreciate, critique or create new cultural forms and objects. Social groups differ not only in the access they have to these sorts of capital, but also in the extent that they aspire to either. Society is characterised by continual struggle, not just between groups in a stratification system, but also over the stratifying mechanisms themselves – over whether knowledge or wealth, taste or property, should be the main ways to divide between individuals and groups and to arrange them in a hierarchy of value.

For Bourdieu, making such distinctions is an important part of maintaining social inequality. They are part of how dominant groups try to retain their position. This process has become increasingly subtle and sophisticated as consumption has become democratised and access to valued lifestyles appears to be open to broader sections of the population. Bourdieu's perspective, it should be noted, remains essentially structuralist: society is organised around the distribution of economic and cultural capital and the structural position an individual occupies greatly influences their capacity to choose between and adopt alternative lifestyles.

But Bourdieu also emphasises that individuals are not entirely determined by structures. People respond to and act on the symbolic meanings attached to different commodities and different patterns of consumption and may develop beliefs and aspirations that are relatively independent of their structural position in society. In consuming, or in exercising their taste, people create differences between social groups rather than just expressing them. Bourdieu's work shows us how shopping reproduces society – or rather, how choosing to purchase one item over another contributes to the validation or otherwise of a social structure based on status hierarchy. Whether Bourdieu can ultimately combine a structuralist emphasis with an image of the consumer as a creative and relatively autonomous actor is still much debated, but he has firmly established the issue of *taste* in the contemporary sociology of consumption, and other sociologists have adopted and developed this theme, particularly to explore how individuals use taste and style to establish or create a specific personal identity.

CONTEMPORARY PATTERNS OF CONSUMPTION

We have seen some arguments as to why consumption now forms such a central activity in contemporary human experience, one that is diffusing across the globe at a rapid pace. Much consumption behaviour remains linked to inequalities of class, gender and age and is used to express and reinforce such social divisions. But in a world characterised increasingly by what Giddens (1994, p. 91) calls 'life politics', where such social divisions may be becoming less salient, personal identity is also increasingly tied to our consumption behaviour. This may be because, as Marx predicted, capitalism tends to devalue the experience of work, leading us to find fulfilment in purchased commodities. Or it may be, as French philosopher Baudrillard argues (1998 [1970]), that consumption is now fundamentally about the consumption of symbols and meanings. In consuming these symbols we *become* those meanings: our identity is constructed through our consumption. I shop, therefore I am!

On the other hand, Smart (2010, p. 169, citing Schor, 2002) asks whether sociology has moved away from the real material issues in relation to consumption. In a world where massive social inequality persists, where much production takes place in grossly exploitative situations and where over-consumption threatens the ecological future of the planet:

> social analysis of consumption has not been well-served by a 'cultural turn' which has led to 'increasingly marginal postmodern theories of fantasy consumption, an under-theorised notion of identity consumption, emphasis on "simulacra" and spectacle … the positing of the consumer as sovereign agent' and a simultaneous neglect of influential, if not determining, 'structural constraints' and 'economic processes'.

The sociological debate on consumption has moved well beyond Veblen's concepts of emulation and conspicuous consumption, but there remains continued scope for lively debate over its features and impacts.

CONSUMERISM AND CONSUMPTION IN IRELAND

As Dolan (2009, p. 118) points out, we cannot only talk about the consumer in the abstract, as 'each society has undergone distinct, though interrelated, processes of social development'. Consumers in Ireland will have experiences that are similar to those in other societies and economies, but there will also be distinctive features that relate to other aspects of Irish society. Now that we have explored something of the sociology of consumption, what can we say about the Irish experience in relation to our specific history and cultural experience?

Much of our analysis in this book draws connections between changes in Irish society and the experience of modernity. This is very much the approach adopted by Linehan (2007) and Dolan (2009), who are amongst the few writers to critically examine Irish consumption patterns from a sociological perspective. More historically focused works have been quicker to make the connection between consumerism and the emergence of 'modern' Ireland (Charleton, 2007; Rains, 2010; Walsh, 2011).

Consumption, modernisation and dependent development

Consumption processes in Ireland need to be understood in the context of the uneven development of global capitalism. This unevenness applies as much to the spread of modern consumption patterns as it does to the diffusion of modern capitalist economic relations. As we have seen in Chapter 3, dependency theory has provided one way to understand uneven development and continues to be used to explain the Irish experience, most recently by Kirby (2010). But dependency theory has focused on how capitalism has developed as a structure of *production*, with little to say about how being a post-colonial or late-developing semi-peripheral society in Europe may have shaped our practices or values in relation to *consumption*.

The dependency perspective suggests that incorporation into multinational capitalism reinforces or increases social division in the incorporated society. Penetration of multinational companies into Ireland creates a local business elite (Eipper, 1986) who can aspire to a level of consumption like that of equivalent groups in core societies. With its cross-national contacts and networks, this elite may adopt 'conspicuous consumption' values or emulate international colleague groups in lifestyle and purchasing behaviour. Dependent development simultaneously generates a marginalised low-waged sector, condemned to relative poverty and excluded from much discretionary consumption.

This analysis – as applied to a great variety of dependent economies across the globe – raises as many questions as it answers. In particular, connections between dependency and consumption are generally discussed in the context of relations between the developed (the global North) and developing (the global South) worlds. Such analyses tend to ignore uneven development *within* the developed world or the presence of 'semi-peripheral' societies, like Ireland, that have a distinctive historical trajectory on the margins of developed cores.

The dependency approach fails to adequately account for the consumption experience of most Irish people: those who are neither part of the internationalising elite nor of the socially and economically excluded. It does not help us to trace the specific effects of trends such as the urbanisation and suburbanisation of Irish society. We know that sociologists such as Simmel and another influential German writer, Walter Benjamin (1999), tended to see a close association between consumption and the city. Cities are seen as places that provide the best opportunities to buy desired goods and services and to flaunt one's consumption choices. Urbanisation in turn is linked to capitalist development and industrialisation. Thus, it is argued, less developed, predominantly rural countries like Ireland should have been slower to develop modern consumption practices.

But the experience in Ireland had its own specific patterns. Far from being backward in the ways of shopping, the country has had a complex experience of consumption, reflecting the different ways of being incorporated into the global economy, since at least the 18th century. For example, in the early 1900s Ireland was an integral part of the broader United Kingdom market for consumer goods. Dublin was a major consumption centre, albeit oriented mainly towards London as fashion leader (Brady, 2001; Rains, 2010). This story is revealed in historical studies of noted, but now disappeared, Dublin retailers such as the Switzers department stores (Cooney, 2002; Spiller and Linehan, 2006), the Findlaters grocery chain (Findlater, 2001) and the Irish operations of the American/British Woolworth Company (Walsh, 2011). Other cities such as Belfast and Cork were important regional centres of consumption and fashion. But provincial towns and rural areas – largely as a consequence of Ireland's once-extensive railway network – were also very much a part of national and international consumption processes (Lambe, 2001; Charleton, 2007; Walsh, 2011) in a way that was not necessarily the case in many peripheral or semi-peripheral societies. Thus, it is wrong to assume that consumerism is a relatively new feature of Irish society.

Dolan (2009) has been one of the few sociologists to examine the broad development of consumption in Ireland. Working within the macrosociological 'figurational' perspective developed by German sociologist Norbert Elias, he aims to link emerging concepts of the consumer with broad patterns of social change over extended periods of time. In particular, he is concerned with how Irish society has, over generations, moved from one where our consumption choices were largely shaped by the communities in which we lived to one based on the individual's 'felt needs and wants in the market' (2009, p. 123). He suggests this is related to modernisation, in particular the differentiation of roles and extension of complex relationships that accompany this process. Similar processes have been identified in other modern societies, where 'production [and consumption] of a seemingly limitless range of new goods appeared to offer the prospect of new possibilities, new meanings, and new forms of human expression and being' (Smart, 2010, p. 18).

This approach reminds us of Durkheim's interest in how modern societies become more complex, specialised and differentiated and how this influences people's attitudes and behaviours. Thus, for Dolan, as Irish society became more complex and diverse, the opportunities for community surveillance and social control, including of consumption, were reduced. In a 'traditional' and relatively undifferentiated society, where there were strong bonds of community, there was a strong 'social duty' to abide by communal standards of consumption. Variation from agreed norms of consumption behaviour would lead to public comment and perhaps sanction. With a shift towards a 'modern' society that is increasingly differentiated, mobile and complex, there is a parallel shift in consumption towards 'the proclaimed sovereign right of each individual to follow their own dispositions and predilections'. People were freer to make their own consumption choices, shaped by their own desires and wants, rather than what they thought was 'right'. Through the market, 'personal identity superseded the earlier emphasis on group identity' (Dolan, 2009, p. 125).

The shift suggested by Dolan was not a smooth one. In fact, the issue of consumption was an important area of social and political debate in Ireland after independence. In the 1930s, with the coming to power of a long series of Fianna Fáil governments, there was a significant restructuring of the discourses and experiences of consumption. Up to the 1950s, at a time when much of the Western world experienced strong nationalistic and protectionist policies and politics, Irish society was also shaped by a dominant discourse of national independence and self-sufficiency, often described as 'inward looking'. Faced with heavy financial debts to Britain and later to the US, Fianna Fáil governments urged restraint on consumption as part of a deliberate development strategy. But it was also clearly more than that. As Dolan (2009, p. 125) notes, 'consumption was to be as nationalistic as other social activities; people were expected to buy and use Irish goods'.

A lifestyle of modest comfort, combined with hard but healthy manual work, assumed the status of a distinctively Irish ideal. Limiting consumption was part of a broader strategy to establish cultural as well as economic and political independence from Britain, along with parallel attempts to revive the Irish language and even to develop distinctively Irish dress codes. If British society was seen to be urban, then it was the lifestyle of the frugal but relatively secure small farmer that was to symbolise Irish identity. If British society was characterised by materialism and consumerism, then Irish society would develop in the opposite way, through an emphasis on spirituality and non-material enjoyments. There was also an element of social egalitarianism 'inimical to displays of refinement and social superiority' (Dolan, 2009, p. 127). This worldview was expressed in Taoiseach Éamon de Valera's celebrated Radio Éireann speech of St Patrick's Day, 1943, popularly entitled 'The Ireland That We Dreamed Of':

> The ideal Ireland that we would have, the Ireland that we dreamed of, would be the home of a people who valued material wealth only as a basis for right living, of a people who, satisfied with frugal comfort, devoted their leisure to the things of the spirit – a land whose countryside would be bright with cosy homesteads, whose fields and villages would be joyous with the sounds of industry, with the romping of sturdy children, the contest of athletic youths and the laughter of happy maidens, whose firesides would be forums for the wisdom of serene old age. (RTÉ, nd)

The extent to which the Irish people fully 'bought into' this ascetic ideal is debatable. Charleton's (2007) analysis of the social and historical development of Henry Lyons's department store in Sligo town suggests that even from the early 19th century (the shop was established in 1835), a strong and pervasive discourse of consumerism emerged, with a 'thriving shopping culture' apparent (Charleton, 2007, p. 5). Nevertheless, in the 1920s a 'cosmopolitan' enthusiasm for 'Parisian' and other international styles was complemented (rather than challenged) by a strong promotion of 'Irish-made' products such as tweed and linen goods. Similarly, the US/British Woolworth Company, which had expanded into Ireland during the 20th century, also made good strategic use of 'Buy Irish' campaigns (Walsh, 2011, pp. 41–4).

Charleton also reports that at the turn of the 20th century, a government inspector of social conditions was moved to remark that 'the younger female portion of the [Sligo] community spent a great deal too much on dress' (2007, p. 30), while Linehan (2007, pp. 294–5) notes that in the 1920s, there were further concerns about the consumption patterns of women. The 'consumption behaviour of the "modern girl" or "the flapper" on the streets of Dublin – hair products and cosmetics, fashionable clothes and cigarettes – came to represent everything that was disorderly and morally dangerous to the strict values of the conservative elite' (2007, pp. 294–5). This concern reflected the fact that, in some urban areas at least, women were beginning to enter the paid workforce and to obtain a measure of economic independence that allowed them to make consumption decisions for themselves. Nevertheless, in this response Ireland would not have differed greatly from other European countries.

The Fianna Fáil discourse of anti-consumerism and self-reliance was a version of what dependency theorist Sklair (2002, p. 165, citing Wells, 1972) has termed 'ascetic developmentalism', where a society aims to increase production but limit consumption as a way to build up national wealth and productive capacity. This approach has also been witnessed in centrally planned societies such as the former Soviet Union and China (until the mid-1980s) and also in some societies that have transformed rapidly from rural to industrial economies, such as South Korea. Thus, the absence of mass consumerism in a society may not indicate poverty or a lack of economic resources, but a specific ideological or cultural stance on consumption.

For many Irish people, an experience of 'ascetic developmentalism' continued well into the 20th century – even into the 1980s. Taxation policies (high taxes on labour, low taxes on land and capital) and generous support for multinational companies left much of the workforce with relatively modest increases in their standard of living, despite continually rising levels of productivity at work and increasing wages. For much of the century, such restraints on consumption could retain some validity as a marker of Irishness, but with the emergence of the so-called Celtic Tiger economy, attitudes towards consumption, and consumption practices themselves, changed dramatically.

Consumption: The Celtic Tiger and beyond

Since the experience of rapid economic growth and the accompanying growth in consumer activity, sociological analyses such as those of Inglis (2002) and Keohane and Kuhling (2004b) have addressed the tension between the perceived asceticism of the past and the contemporary enthusiasm for consumption. Inglis (2002, p. 30) notes that formerly, 'self-indulgence was a sin and pleasure had to be legitimated within an overall habitus of self-denial'. He sees the public expression of pleasure in consumption as a new feature of Irish life, linked to the declining influence of religion. For Irish women, Inglis suggests, 'I'm worth it!' has replaced 'Lord I am not worthy' (2002, p. 25). But he detects a residual lack of comfort with such conspicuous consumption.

Linehan (2007, pp. 291–2) links recognition of Ireland as a 'high consumption' society with the contemporary unease about (too much) consuming and its potential impact on established patterns of Irish society:

> changes in patterns of consumption and its effects on way of life have raised concerns about the social conditions of Irish society. Consumption appears to represent the contradictions of increased prosperity and the loss of community … amongst public commentators, these shifts in values are a matter of acute anxiety.

At the height of the economic boom, denunciations of 'runaway consumerism' were common and it was suggested that in some way, authentic 'Irish values' were being lost as a consequence. Anxieties over excessive or ill-advised consumption have also been reflected in state policies such as the national obesity and alcohol strategies.

Keohane and Kuhling also perceive this unease, but ask 'why is there such a contradiction between what people are actually spending, and the generalised condemnation of over-inflated spending?' (2004b, p. 47). The answer, for them, lies in French sociologist Marcel Mauss's concept of the reciprocal 'gift relationship'. Mauss sought to show how societies are held together by reciprocal relationships of obligation, partly cemented by the giving and receiving of gifts. For Keohane and Kuhling, such reciprocity is important in Irish culture, which stresses generosity to others as a basis of community, as reflected in giving to charity, Christmas gift-giving and in wedding ceremonies. Historically this system operated in the context of relative scarcity; it now takes place in a time of abundance, giving rise to high levels of expenditure relative to other societies, but also to spiralling consumer debt. Unlike for other critics, for Keohane and Kuhling (2004b, p. 51), 'far from indicating the devaluation of traditional values of community, Irish consumerism shows paradoxically how the traditional value of community remains central'. But the 'combination of acquisitive accumulation and generosity, of possessive individualism and collective commitment' (2004, p. 48) is ultimately destructive, as it does not allow for a more rational system of social redistribution to take place. It is interesting that Irish people continue to be amongst the highest spenders in the Western world come Christmas time, spending twice as much per capita as the Germans (*Economist*, 2011).

When it comes to close-grained analysis of everyday patterns of consumption in Ireland, there is little available sociological work and detailed work on the purchase and use of particular goods or items is rare (Drazin and Garvey, 2009, p. 7). Linehan does remind us that consumption trends are related to broader trends in the economy: 'household expenditure rises and falls in relation to job losses, employment growth and sense of job security, all of which are well known to affect the size of, and predisposition to spend, personal disposable income'. Thus, 'the dynamics of lifestyle change … are not to do with "irresponsible individualism" but shifts in the economy and new sources and patterns of demand and supply of goods and services' (2007, p. 296). It is thus important to move away from the overly moralistic critique of consumption implicit in so much sociological analysis. Changes in consumption can reflect trends such as new household formation. As household size in Ireland declines, each household requires its own washing machine, couch, fridge, car and so on. Similarly, 'if [people] "splash out" on a barbecue or a gas patio heater … to enjoy time with friends and family, it can hardly be represented as the decline of Irish values' (2007, p. 297).

Consumption, inequality and class

Consumption activity is necessarily shaped by levels of income and wealth. Crudely put, the rich spend their money differently to the poor. In Ireland, research conducted in the early 1990s by the since-abolished Combat Poverty Agency (Murphy-Lawless, 1992) suggested that income had a major impact on consumer spending. A study compared the weekly spending patterns of two household types, one with an income of £200 to £250 (€250 to €320) per week, described as an 'average' family, and the other relying on unemployment payments. After paying for food and fuel, housing and transport, the 'average' family had 37 per cent of its income left over while the other family had 34 per cent. Out of this surplus, each family spent about the same proportion on consumer durables and other goods (10 to 11 per cent). The family on unemployment payments spent a higher proportion of its income (but a lower absolute amount) on drink and tobacco than the 'average' family, but the 'average' family spent a much higher proportion on clothing, shoes and services of various kinds (mainly related to leisure and recreation, such as going to the cinema or out for a meal, getting clothes dry cleaned or hair cut, caring for a family pet). Neither family could be described as high consumers; even the 'average' family had very little surplus income after standard items in the family budget, such as professional haircuts, were accounted for, but they did have more than the other family, as one might expect, and used it on different forms of consumption.

A decade later, a further study of the income and expenditure patterns of low-income households was carried out in 2000 (Daly and Leonard, 2002). The researchers discovered that people often found it difficult to account for all expenditure, especially in relation to infrequent or unexpected outlays. On the basis of the information that was available, the findings to a large extent replicated those of the earlier research. The main expenditure category was still food, followed by fuel and light, then by cigarettes and alcohol. Compared to average households, poor households spent a much greater proportion of income on necessities (Daly and Leonard, 2002, p. 22). Unfortunately, at the very period in recent Irish history when levels of consumption exploded, sociologists apparently did not continue to trace the connections between consumption, class and poverty.

SHOP TILL YOU DROP

> In many ways the shopping centre and mall best represent the change in the material, social and cultural fabric of everyday life. Where once the churches dominated the streetscapes of village and town life, now it is shopping centres and malls that dominate and lay claim to the status of Mecca, Cathedral and Temple. Not only are they centres of social and consumer activity, but they are represented as places of pilgrimages and worship, as centres of meaning. For many consumption is a new religion. (Cunningham, 2008, p. 232)

When people think about consumption, in practice what they are often thinking about is *shopping*. According to time-use surveys, shopping is an activity that occupies, on average, about half an hour per day of an Irish adult's time (McGinnity et al., 2005) – 45 minutes a day for women. This is more time on average than is spent on childcare, in pubs/restaurants or on religious activity and does not include the time spent travelling to the shops, planning the visit or unpacking goods on return.

Shopping has become an important leisure activity, but for many people it is also a basis for livelihood: it employs approximately one in seven of the Irish workforce, similar to the proportion in other EU countries (Forfás, 2010, p. 2). Retail sales represent approximately 45 per cent of consumption, with spending on transport, communications, services and housing making up most of the remainder (FinFacts, 2010). Private consumption of goods and services constituted €81 billion in 2009 out of a gross national product (GNP) of €131 billion (CSO, 2010a), so shopping is a significant economic activity as well as a key component of everyday life.

Yet as in other aspects of consumption, there has been relatively little academic study of shopping in the Irish context. Perhaps this is because, as Scott notes (2009, p. 139), 'there is something of a stigma attached to shopping: it is regarded as trivial, vacuous, a sign of moral weakness, and arguably a feminine activity that is not really important … it is implicitly contrasted with the socially useful work that is performed in the "male" sphere of production'.

Nevertheless, after a neglect of Irish retailing history (Crawford, 1995, p. 222), there has recently been something of a publishing boom in this field, with a number of studies of individual retailers and retail chains, such as grocery chain Findlaters (Findlater, 2001); department stores such as Switzers of Dublin (Cooney, 2002) and Lyons of Sligo (Charleton, 2007); and chains such as Woolworths (Walsh, 2011). There have also been broader studies of shopping districts such as Dublin's Grafton Street (Brady, 2001) and Cork's English Market (Ó Drisceoil and Ó Drisceoil, 2005). But it is only very recently that Irish writers have turned to an analysis of the experience of shopping itself, either from an historical or sociological perspective. Even Walsh's detailed analysis (2011) of Woolworths' Irish stores focuses far more strongly on the activities of the company and its staff, and media coverage, than on the experiences of shoppers themselves. The potentially most interesting work is just beginning to emerge from anthropology, where Garvey is focusing on the experience of shopping in the Irish branch of Swedish furniture giant IKEA (see below).

IKEA

On 27 July 2009 a significant retail and sociological event took place in Ballymun, north Dublin: the opening of the Republic of Ireland's first IKEA store (a store had opened in Belfast 20 months previously). IKEA is a global phenomenon – the world's largest furniture retailer, with a global turnover in 2009/10 of €23 billion, employing 127,000 people in 36 countries. The Dublin store, located on the M50 ring road near the city's airport, was the 301st in the world.

While the opening of the Dublin store did not lead to the hysteria and mild civil disorder that has occurred in some other countries, it did introduce a highly popular retail destination to the Irish market, with over 15,000 visitors and turnover of €450,000 a day in its first month of operation ('Ikea clocks up early sales of over €15m', *Irish Times*, 4 June 2010). It has since become one of IKEA's most profitable stores, even in a time of economic recession.

From one perspective, IKEA is just a chain of very successful furniture shops, most famous for its 'flatpack' self-assembly products. From another, it is a unique phenomenon. It has been linked with notions of 'Swedishness'; of 'democratic design'; of a particular notion of the family; of environmental pillage; of 'disposability' and a 'throw-away culture'; and with the cutting edge of retailing psychology and supply chain management. It has attracted a substantial academic literature across business, marketing and design studies.

Surprisingly, sociologists have paid comparatively little attention to IKEA, reflecting a neglect of analysis when it comes to consumer goods in general (Molotch, 2011). In his well-known sociology text *The McDonaldization of Society*, George Ritzer (2010, pp. 18–20) offers a brief analysis of IKEA, stressing his signature themes of calculability, predictability, control and irrationality. Like much popular commentary on IKEA (Shell, 2009; Stenebo, 2010) Ritzer's tone is negative, stressing alleged poor quality of the product, the cunning psychological control exerted by the store layout and the frustrations of self-assembly.

In Ireland, the only social scientist to seriously examine IKEA has been NUI Maynooth anthropologist Pauline Garvey. She has a more nuanced approach than many critics, showing how people's experiences of IKEA are inevitably linked to broader sets of ideas and social practices, for example in relation to family, home-making or design. Her research has involved observing and interviewing IKEA customers in Stockholm, where the company's largest flagship store is located, and in Ballymun.

Garvey finds that Irish consumers do not share the negativity of sociological critics such as Ritzer. Rather, they embrace IKEA in a positive approach to 'home-making' in general: 'the home is still such a fundamental expression of who we are and what we are, so anything that gives us an outlet for that expression is inevitably looked upon favourably' (quoted in Duncan et al., 2010, p. 59). Customers also like to feel they are saving money: 'the feeling of saving through spending, combined with the provision of practical, functional solutions for storage "problems" provides a magic combination for their brand of furniture retail' (ibid).

What makes IKEA so successful, apart from the obvious factors of price and convenience? Garvey talks about how IKEA sells its customers the opportunity for 'inspiration'. IKEA stores are set up like a series of theatrical sets, but ones you can enter and interact with – actively imagining yourself, and your family or workmates, in the 'new' home or office space you might design for yourself from relatively cheap elements. As Garvey (2011, p. 146) suggests:

> behind these practices is the framework of 'inspiration', a nebulous idea based on the co-location of people and scene, envisioning oneself in these spaces, physically interacting with the furnishing, and somehow emotionally responding to them.

In IKEA, unlike many other stores, customers are actively encouraged to 'use' the furniture and household objects on display: to lie on the beds, sit in the chairs or switch the lamps on and off. Then when they bring their purchases home, there is further interaction, as they finalise the assembly of the product. Retail psychologists have shown that when people can help to shape a product, they gain more satisfaction from it – even if only to add an egg to an instant cake mix. This process has been dubbed the 'IKEA effect' (Norton et al., 2011) and points to the pleasures people gain from 'making' the world around them (Shove et al., 2007).

> Lots of people go to IKEA at turning points in their domestic lives, like buying a first home, going off to college or setting up a separate household after divorce. It is no surprise, then, that IKEA is closely linked to idealised notions of the family, romance and relationships: a Swedish TV drama only has to show a couple ascending an IKEA store's escalator to suggest a promising romantic entanglement. Often a trip to IKEA is an outing for family or friends, where other domestic arrangements can be observed and commented upon. As Garvey notes, 'the IKEA showroom provides an interactive space for the consultation, browsing, and occasional keen awareness of other domestic arrangements, other people, other couples and families' (2011, p. 151).
>
> There is certainly much that can be said about IKEA from a critical sociological perspective. We can look to the environmental impact of its manufacturing and distribution; the financial and taxation structures of the company; or the experiences of its workforce. But an analysis of people's pleasures and motivations is also sociologically interesting. An examination of IKEA can teach us a lot about consumption more generally, particularly how people actively integrate 'products' into their personal and family biographies and living situations. Consumption need not necessarily make us into passive, unquestioning beings – we can still strive to be active agents in our own lives.

Kennedy (cited in Lambe, 2001, p. 207) reports that 'Ireland has always suffered from a plague of small shopkeepers'. Irish society has long featured a numerous and influential family business/small proprietor sector. In the 19th and for most of the 20th century, Irish shops were small and traditionally run in conjunction with pubs, sub-post offices or other service businesses, such as funeral undertaking or petrol retailing. Shops in rural areas were the precursor of today's convenience store (Lambe, 2001, p. 214) and were used on a frequent, often daily, basis. As a consequence they had an important social role, not unlike that enjoyed by pubs – a parallel noted by Brody (1986, pp. 157–74). Thus, the shopkeeper was an important person in the community, where:

> [extensive] contacts, combined with the physical location of the shops within the community, made them transmitters and receivers of information, news and gossip. These advantages, together with the significance of their economic role and strong kinship ties in the community enabled shopkeepers to enjoy an important social and political role, and to wield power and patronage at local level. (Lambe, 2001, p. 222)

Irish retailing evolved slowly over the 19th and 20th centuries, reflecting the increasing marketisation of society and improved systems of distribution, packaging and advertising (Lambe, 2001). Spiller and Linehan (2006) have examined the development of department stores in the mid-20th century. They see the emergence of such stores (e.g. Switzers and Arnotts in Dublin, Cash's in Cork) as part of the development of modernity in Ireland. They point out that in the 1930s, 'an Irish urban culture was awakening that had the financial freedoms to embrace a culture that warmly accepted modern commodities or cosmopolitan fashions' (2006, p. 147). This predominantly middle-class cohort embraced new emblems of modern consumerism such as cinema and dancehalls as well as the new type of shops. They were also exposed to international trends, and this could lead to tensions when juxtaposed with more traditional and conservative values and mores: 'during the 1950s the Catholic magazine *The Fold* encouraged women to cover their cleavage and upper arms when choosing a dress. Yet Cash's in Cork, for instance, sold revealing swimwear by leading European designers' (2006, p. 154). Spiller and Linehan argue that the Irish population (especially men) took time to adjust to the 'freedom' of such stores, initially feeling awkward and self-conscious when entering just to browse.

On the more everyday front, Crawford (1995, p. 223) suggests that the country saw a 'retailing revolution' in the period 1958 to 1988, stimulated by the arrival of the supermarket. In this period the number of supermarkets increased fourfold while grocery shops declined by 60 per cent. 'Family grocers' could not compete with the scale of the multiples' operations. They responded by forming collective voluntary groups that allowed them to achieve greater economies of scale and the result was that the relentless expansion of the supermarkets was halted (temporarily) by the late 1980s. By 1989, 60 per cent of families used a major supermarket at least once a week for their shopping (Crawford, 1995, p. 224). Small neighbourhood shops, especially those that will provide credit, remain important for many customers.

Parker (1999, p. 70) has described the suburbanisation of shopping since the 1960s. He identifies four stages to this process, which involve the gradual shift out of city and town centre areas of the following types of retailers. Similar patterns can be determined in most Irish cities and larger towns and have included developments such as:

- Convenience goods retailing – this saw the development of the first shopping centres. In Ireland the first was the Stillorgan Shopping Centre in south suburban Dublin, opened in 1966.
- Durable goods retailers, such as DIY stores and carpet sellers, moved into old factories or warehouse parks, in areas such as Dublin's Long Mile Road.
- Fashion retailers and other specialist shops – these were to be found in particular in new suburban shopping centres. They provided direct competition with more exclusive city centre boutiques and department stores. This trend has reached its greatest expression in mega-complexes such as the Dundrum Town Centre in South Co. Dublin and Cork's Mahon Point Shopping Centre.
- New styles of retail operation, such as outlet stores (e.g. Kildare Village), big box outlets (e.g. Dixons), petrol station forecourt stores (e.g. Applegreen) and retail parks (such as that at Dublin's Liffey Valley).

The latter two stages can be seen as evidence of the increased 'malling' of Ireland. According to Langman (1992, p. 43), the shopping mall is 'the signifying and celebrating edifice' of consumer culture in the contemporary world. Langman (1992) suggests that contemporary society is best described as 'amusement society': with leisure now central to the experience of selfhood, shopping has become the pivotal leisure activity. Shopping malls are physically designed to promote various forms of loitering, parading and strolling as part of the consumption experience as well as providing additional forms of entertainment (fun fairs, fashion shows, cinemas). They are constructed to present both 'an enchanted space [and] a theatre of dreams' and simulated experiences as well as being – in a more practical way – a locale for entertainment for family groups (O'Connor, 2011). Contemporary shopping practice centres on strolling, browsing and 'gazing'. As the shopping mall becomes a leisure centre, those who visit it are likely to spend as much of their time gazing at the goods on display and fantasising about them as actually buying. At the same time, systems of both overt (store detectives and security guards) and covert (physical layout and closed circuit TV) control ensure the mall is not open to everyone; it excludes the very poor, the potentially disruptive (bored teenagers) and those with no capacity or inclination to buy.

The rapid rise of the shopping mall has been analysed in the Irish context by Corcoran (2000). She suggests (2000, pp. 91–2) that 'since the 1960s Dublin has been turning itself inside out' as retail activity has shifted to the suburbs and the land along new motorways. Indeed, as Corcoran points out, 'the new shopping malls are predicated on a consumer class with spending power and access to private vehicles'. The development of shopping malls indicates a point where public and private interests can meet and collide. The state has had a major role in underpinning new models of retail development, as in the Tallaght Town Centre. But the major beneficiaries are arguably property developers and the mainly British-based retail corporations (such as Tesco and Marks & Spencer) that have seen Ireland emerge, at least until the economic crash, as a particularly profitable territory.

A massive expansion in the development of both shopping malls and retail parks took place in Ireland from 2004 to 2010. In this period, the total shopping centre space doubled to 2 million square metres while space in retail parks increased from under half a million square metres to 1.3 million square metres (CB Richard Ellis, 2010). Most of this has been outside of the existing major urban centres, to the suburbs and 'edge city' locations. Such development has often closely followed road developments, with shopping centre and supermarket development linked, for example, to Dublin's M50 and also to bypasses of such towns as Athlone, Donegal and Mullingar. The attraction of such retail locations is outlined by Parker (1999, p. 72):

> the M50 has provided rapid access around the city, enabling affluent and highly mobile suburbanites to extend their range of shopping choice to one or other of the larger regional-scale centres. By comparison to the effort involved in trying

to access the city centre by private car and find (and pay for) parking, the ease with which the relatively free-flowing motorway leads to large-scale retail alternatives with extensive and free parking is considerable.

Other key trends in retailing identified by Parker include the continued strength of Dublin city centre as a retail location, particularly traditional shopping areas such as Grafton and Henry Streets, which have long been the most popular and prestigious shopping areas in the city (Brady, 2001). This is reflected in the very high rentals that – until the economic crash – could be secured by the owners of properties in such areas. This is linked to another important trend: the internationalisation of Irish retailing. It is often remarked that a walk down Dublin's Grafton Street is now little different to that of any British city, such is the dominance of British and other international retail brands.

Globalisation of the retail sector, allied with economic growth in Ireland, means that there are now numerous foreign-based retailers operating in Ireland. These include not just major supermarket operators like the UK-based Tesco, but specialist stores like PC World and the Body Shop (both UK); discount supermarkets Aldi and Lidl (Germany); fashion retailers (Zara – Spain; H&M – Sweden) and major department stores such as Debenhams (UK). The influx of such global retailers is helping to change the landscape of shopping in Ireland – for example, in their demand for larger store premises.

Ireland is also relatively unusual in the strength of its so-called 'convenience store' or 'c-store' sector – outlets such as Centra, Daybreak and SuperValu (all part of the Cork-based Musgrave group); Mace and Spar (both part of the BWG group) and Londis. There are over 5,000 such stores in the Republic of Ireland (Bord Bia, 2010) and though the sector felt the impact of the economic crash more strongly than most, it still accounts for around 5 per cent of total grocery shopping expenditure. The increasing prevalence of these 'symbol' stores reflects a rapid decline in 'independent' retailers, whose numbers halved from nearly 7,000 in the state to approximately 3,500 in the Celtic Tiger years 2001 to 2006 (Oireachtas, 2011, p. 9), itself an indication of the growing concentration and integration of the retail sector.

Others trends that are shaping the future of retailing in Ireland include the increasing crossover amongst formerly separate areas. This is already happening in the UK, where Tesco has become a major petrol retailer, while in Ireland petrol companies are increasingly becoming involved in the supermarket and c-store business. Other areas of change and development are in airport shopping and the establishment of new shops on third-level campuses, Internet and TV selling, party-selling (goods sold in private homes such as Avon, Amway and Herbalife) and farmers' markets and box schemes for organic food.

Within the context of these structural changes to retailing, we must remember that the degree of affluence in a society and its distribution across classes continues to constrain the extent to which shopping and the shopping experience can provide a new source of individual identity. In addition, it is important not to uncritically accept the retail industry's drive to redefine shopping as entertainment. Shopping is also work – obviously enough for those, generally young, often immigrant, female and poorly paid, who are employed in retail – but also for many consumers who must budget, list, drive, negotiate car parks and shopping trolleys, and physically shift goods from place to place. For those without private transport, the burdens can be considerable.

We may also question whether it is true that in late modern or post-modern society individuals lack a strong sense of identity and are therefore free (or forced, depending on your point of view) to construct one through shopping. In most developed societies, even if class is less salient than before, people still derive significant personal identities from where they live and their cultural, ethnic and familial ties. In Chapter 4 we have seen how modern Irish society has been characterised by connections to broader social entities: these may offer identities based in location, ethnicity, religious ideology or gender. Among certain social groups across the world, identity may have come to depend very heavily on the exercise of consumer choice, but it would be a mistake to assume that this provides the only model towards which the rest of the world is inexorably moving. Unfortunately, we have as yet scant sociological evidence in relation to the experiences and meanings of shopping itself for Irish consumers. Hopefully it is a topic that will excite the interest of future Irish researchers and writers.

16
Sociological Futures

'All time past is forced to move on by the incoming future; that all the future follows from the past; and that all, past and future, is created and issues out of that which is forever present.' – St Augustine, Book Eleven, Chapter Six, Confessions

INTRODUCTION: MOVING FORWARD, MOVING BACK

Imagine the future. All kinds of clever and interesting things have been said and written by poets, philosophers and prophets about the academic category of the future. Indeed, you may recall that in the earlier sections of this book the classical social theorists themselves all made important predictions about the direction of evolution of modern society – Marx foretelling the rise of class stratification and the collapse of capitalism, Durkheim predicting the death of the old gods and Weber warning moderns about becoming iron-caged by rationality. Each of these alternative futures was based on a careful and critical analysis of the past and present circumstances of our social lives.

To think about the future, which this chapter invites you to begin doing as students of Irish society, culture and politics, involves a kind of heightening or intensification of the sociological imagination, as futures are imagined before they are lived. This chapter, then, can best be understood as a sociological thought experiment involving thinking hard and seriously about what the future of our society might look like 15 to 20 years from now. These 'not yet' futures strongly influence our identities and human actions in the present (Weigert, 2010). Indeed, all human action is oriented toward the future (Weigert, 2005).

To be sure, it is difficult to imagine the future. A major trend in our society is an emphasis on short-term thinking and practices that militate against taking the long-run view. We are very much a 'here and now' people, which means that our temporal horizons do not routinely extend much beyond the present. A focus on sociological futures thus helps to increase our long-range time sense and perspective. Doing so at a time of crisis and flux in contemporary liberal capitalism and governance in relation to its ability to sustain economic growth and social harmony may bolster our sense of passive hopelessness, but it may also fuel a sense of active possibility.

A second challenge of glancing forwards is that social change tends to unfold not in the form of straight-line arrows, but in the shape of curved circles. This means that we may not encounter the future as some brave 'new' world, but rather as the repetition of earlier experiences from before. The future is usually a throwback to the past – the new Ireland may well be an old Ireland that has come back again. A third important point that can be made in relation to the category of the future is the degree of agency we exercise in relation to it. In our everyday lives this takes the form of an amalgam of an activity mode (some aspects of the future are controllable and subject to human agency) on the one hand and an expectation mode (other facets of the future are not controllable and lie largely outside the bounds of our agentic powers) on the other (Kern, 1983). Which mode becomes dominant in the future is uncertain, as it is difficult to judge whether the future will be a story of the unfolding of a coherent set of changes or a tale of isolated, independent and chance developments.

In this chapter we are sensitive to these challenges as we engage in a 'sociology of the future' that identifies the key developments, trends and shifts likely to shape modern Ireland in the next decade or so in light of the major changes and continuities mapped out in the former chapters. This exercise in looking to the future is thus grounded in what is already known about the social world (Tilly, 1997). Some of these futuristic changes are likely to play out at the level of the individual, such as how we engage with the use of technologies to communicate with others in our lives; other changes will take place at the meso level of the community, such as how we plan and design our urban spaces; while still others bring us right up to the level of society by influencing how we go about interacting with the natural world around us.

Before going further, a few basic preliminary points require brief elaboration about our approach to – and what we mean by – a sociology of the future. First, we take as a starting point that the future is not a singular thing – rather, it is best understood as involving multiple possibilities or 'futures' ranging from the positive utopias of equality, social justice and peace right through to the negative dystopias of economic recession, ecological crisis and political chaos. There are also possibilities for what are termed 'endtime' futures – the possibility that our lives as we know them now will come to a sudden or unexpected end. Nuclear disasters and ecological crises are implicated in 'endtime' (Weigert, 2010). Human actions (and inactions) will play a critical role in steering the direction of evolution of our society in one imagined future rather than another.

Second, a sociology of the future calls for a consideration of the sociology of time. As a sociological category, times consists of the (recalled) past, the (experienced) present and the (imagined) future (Lewis and Weigert, 1981). As sociologists, we are often more explicitly concerned and comfortable with the past and the present tenses, yet our understanding of these is always in relation to some anticipated future tense. Indeed, the present and past function as reference points for imagined sociological futures. When we say, for example, that people are 'less' religious, we mean this in relation to the past but also in relation to some anticipated future. Just as comparison involves some frame of reference – we must compare something in relation to something else and declare the historical context of our comparisons (Fischer, 2010) – imagining the future involves some assessment of change in relation to the present or the past or both. Put differently, Who I (We) are now and before is tied up with Who I (We) will be (Weigert, 2010). At the same time, because the future is not yet, it is always uncertain and ambiguous, though religious and secular interpretations vary in their degree of certainty about it (Weigert, 2005).

Third, imagined futures implicate human emotions and hope and despondency are its dominant polar feelings (Weigert, 2010). Our critical analyses of society in the past and present build toward the creation of a better society of the future and improvement in the human condition. As such, they are inspired by a sense of hope about the 'not yet'. Contemporary political discourse frequently makes reference to the relationship between this emotion and the future. Consider, for example, the story President Barack Obama told when he came to Ireland in 2010. Speaking in College Green, Dublin, President Obama addressed himself to the realities of austerity Ireland but also urged his audience to claim the future as one of hope:

> And, Ireland, as trying as these times are, I know our future is still as big and as bright as our children expect it to be. I know that because I know it is precisely in times like these – in times of great challenge, in times of great change – when we remember who we truly are. We're people, the Irish and Americans, who never stop imagining a brighter future, even in bitter times (Obama, 2011).

Another President, Michael D. Higgins, also spoke of claiming the not yet future – without liquidating the past – at his inauguration address in Dublin Castle in November 2011:

> A common shared future built on the spirit of co-operation, the collective will and real participation in every aspect of the public world is achievable and I believe we can achieve it together. In our rich heritage some of our richest moments have been those that turned towards the future and a sense of what might be possible. It is that which brought us to independence. It is that which has enabled us to transcend our present difficulties and celebrate the real Republic which is ours for the making (Higgins, 2011).

Access to the future emotions of hope and despair are, however, unequally distributed (Weigert, 2010). There are sharp global differences in access to them as well as internal differences within single societies, including Ireland.

In the face of this message of hope, we are aware of strong currents of despondency. The futures we imagine may not always be the futures we create, as human actions generate unintended as well as intended consequences (Weigert,

2005). A growing body of literature on 'risks' alerts moderns to the destructive possibilities of the future and the risks, some known (such as environmental destruction, global terrorism, nuclear explosion) and others unknown (such as volcanic explosions) (Weigert, 2005), that transcend national borders.

Having laid out these three basic points, we develop this with reference to three domains of social life. Specifically, we have organised this chapter around three orienting themes – how societies relate to nature, technology and culture. These domains can best be viewed not in terms of a ranked order of importance, but as nodal points on a concentric ring. For each theme we give a brief capsule summary of what we mean by each and then relate this to contemporary Irish society with relevant examples, applications and scenarios. We see certain dominant creative and opposing tendencies operating or playing out within each set of relations – between interdependence and exploitation in the case of nature-society relations, alienation and attunement in regard to technology-society relations and the dual tension between individualisation/collectivisation and inclusion/exclusion with respect to the case of culture-society relations – in a time of crisis in global politics and economics that Ireland has not experienced before.

In turn, different conceptions of human actors directly follow from each of these contrary tendencies. In the case of nature-society relations, human actors in the future will confront the choice of being 'leavers' or 'takers', people who view the natural world as an ally and asset versus those who view it as a site of exploitation. Moderns' relation to technology will be likely to take the form of engagement with it on the one hand or alienation from it on the other. In the domain of culture-society relations, the future is likely to reinforce patterns of exclusion and individualisation or to create more possibilities for inclusion and emphasis on the collectivity. Schematically, Table 16.1 presents our framework for a sociology of the future. We do not attempt to synthesise all – or even most – of the topics covered in this book, nor do we examine every aspect of future social change within this threefold organising scheme. Instead, we have chosen to focus on a few select and salient examples within each domain. After discussing each of these three sets of relations – and mainly with reference to the Irish experience in order to make the account as familiar as possible – the third part of the chapter examines the connection between a sociology of the future and the future of sociology. The final part of the chapter offers some brief concluding remarks.

One final point by way of orientation to this concluding chapter: in discussing each domain, we briefly set forth how we think each is likely to play out in the 15 to 20 years ahead. We are careful not to engage in an exercise in fantasy – the imagined Ireland of the future will not eradicate all of the social divisions of today, nor will it be conflict free. Our imagined Ireland is both realistic and idealistic. As we glance forward, what we envisage is not all disaster, but neither is it without problems, disappointments and challenges.

Table 16.1: An analytical framework for exploring the sociology of the future

Domain of relations	Opposing tendencies	Human actor
Nature-society	Interdependence-exploitation	Leaver-taker
Technology-society	Attunement-alienation	Technophile-Luddite
Culture-society	Individualisation-collectivisation, inclusion-exclusion	Citizen-consumer

IMAGINING IRELAND IN THREE DOMAINS: THE MANY FACES OF THE FUTURE

Domain #1: Nature-society relations and related challenges

One of the most important and urgent problems confronting humankind today is the ecological crisis. This is a crisis about the natural physical world but with real social origins and consequences. Many of the problems associated with recent changes in the natural world – the loss of plant and animal species, the depletion of stocks of water and the decline of soil quality, for example – arise from human behaviours. Despite the increasing urgency of dealing with global challenges to the earth's survival, sociologists have been relatively slow to respond. This owes something to the dominance of the nature-culture dichotomy in the discipline that has tended to preclude sociological inquiries of nature by opposing it too much to the social. Only recently has sociological understanding of nature spiked and resulted in a proliferation of studies of the social bases of nature and of society-nature interactions. As sociological interest has risen, media interest has waned. Big natural processes unfolding slowly over time – such as environmental change – do not easily fit into the issue attention spans of media organisations, making it difficult to keep environmental concern a live issue in the public consciousness (Anderson, 2009).

In thinking about the nature-social relation, the 'tragedy of the commons' provides an important lesson – when one person decides to step over to one side of a ship to look out to sea, this in itself is not dangerous, but when all the passengers on a ship do it, it certainly is. Likewise, when individuals act to damage the environment by not disposing of waste, for example, the accumulation of their individual actions has important and negative consequences for the collectivity in different spaces but also in different times.

The destruction of nature in many parts of the world alerts us to the fact that more and more, we view the natural world as an end rather than a means to an end. Instead of harnessing the natural world to serve human needs and interests, we increasingly seek to master and colonise it. In his book *Ishmael*, Daniel Quinn captured this well by characterising moderns as either 'leavers' or 'takers'. By 'leavers', Quinn means people who relate to the planet as stewards of its rich resources and thereby seek to preserve it for future generations. 'Takers', on the other hand, colonise the planet for their own ends and engage in a kind of scorched earth policy in relation to it (Quinn, 1992). Only by winning as many of the general populace over to the side of 'leavers' can the future of humanity be secured. Environmental organisations will have a critical role to play in this as they seek to attune moderns to the collective planetary implications of their individual human behaviours.

'Global warming' was the environmental watchword of the 1990s, but now 'climate change' is the next big global challenge, displacing earlier international challenges such as nuclear disaster. This is not an abstract challenge, but one with real practical consequences at an everyday level. We see this evident, for instance, in the increasing frequency of severe weather conditions that only a few years ago were very rare. Sociologists know well that environmental changes such as this are unequally distributed in their impact and tend to reproduce existing patterns of social stratification (Laszewski, 2008). People who live in the poorest parts of the world, for instance, are often the most prone to environmental shifts.

Although there is broad consensus about the human behaviours influencing nature, there is considerably less agreement about what should be done about this and by whom (Anderson, 2009). Climate change may be a diffuse target – and scientists may disagree about its stage of progression and the factors enabling and disabling it (Anderson, 2009) – but future solutions will involve individual and collective action on both local and global flanks. The diffuse nature of big environmental challenges makes it difficult to organise for change – the slow melting of ice regions is much less observable on a day-to-day level than the polluting fumes of a burning landfill site in a Co. Kildare village. On the local level, change is possible and there may even be a partly Irish solution to climate change. For example, the preservation of Irish bogs could play a role in counteracting this. By acting as a sponge for human-made gases that pollute our planet, bogs have the potential to reduce their release into the atmosphere (Viney, 2011). Other local actions can become more politicised.

Environmental problems to government, government to environmental problems – the case of Kerdiffstown

In early 2011, residents in the County Kildare village of Kerdiffstown – and in response to a fire in a local dump – came together and lobbied their local councillors 'to do something' about the fire and its impact on the health and well-being of local people. This led to meetings with the Environmental Protection Agency and the ratcheting up of the environmental stakes. It culminated in the fire services tackling the landfill blaze. This Kildare story follows a familiar script replicated in other parts of the world: problem–

problem to government–no action–further mobilisation–government to problem (Laszewski, 2008). Local solutions on their own, however, are insufficient. What is also needed is global action. International environmental agreements, such as the 1997 Kyoto Protocol, can help to institutionalise environmental concern as a key element of government activity and legitimise political action on behalf of those seeking to save the planet from destruction ('Local community rages as dump that turned into a nightmare still burns', *Irish Times*, 4 February 2011).

Much future nature-society political agitation is also likely to come from non-state actors or civil society organisations such as Greenpeace and other environmental groups that collectively organise across national borders as ecological 'watchdogs' of governmental and non-governmental actions. Recent times have seen the emergence of a relatively new trend toward the use of celebrity culture to raise awareness of environmental change. Irish golfer Rory McIllroy visited Haiti in 2011 as a UNICEF Goodwill Ambassador to highlight the plight of children in a country devastated by the natural disaster of an earthquake. Beyond Ireland, former US vice-president Al Gore has stimulated renewed interest in environmental change (Anderson, 2009). Leadership for environmental change will also likely come from religious institutions (Laszewski, 2008) – as custodians of long-standing civilisational norms (Tucker, 2011) – as they seek to urge devotees and non-devotees alike to act as concerned stewards of the earth's resources. The Irish Catholic bishops, for example, published a pastoral reflection in 2009 under the title *The Cry of the Earth* (Irish Catholic Bishops' Conference, 2009) calling for 'ecological conversion' to the problems and challenges of environmental change.

Such leadership, however well-meaning, often runs up against the problem of a reluctant world. Many people, while self-identifying as environmentally aware, often make individual choices that close off possibilities for engaging in wider socio-political change. Consider, for example, people who routinely recycle their household waste in green bins or decide to buy an electronic car instead of a petrol-powered one. These individual actions are laudable and have important positive impacts on the environment, but rarely do they lead to the realisation that there is a world still to be won by agitating for national government oversight of large corporations and how they relate to the environment. As people resort to the comfort blanket of their own solipsism, they are often de-politicised, and frequently people who are materially advantaged are best positioned to make these kinds of constricted individual choices (Laszewski, 2008). Ultimately, this can be viewed as a form of self-protection rather than planetary concern in so far as it does not move people up to the level of the collectivity. The future challenge is to make this individual to collective leap.

Another problem future organised leadership for ecological change faces is the perception that things have changed when in fact they haven't. Consider, for example, the high-tech computer industry – a significant presence in Ireland's 'knowledge economy' and likely key engine of future growth in the national economy and society. The common-sense view tends to be that 'new' high-tech sectors are free of the environmental impacts associated with 'old' industries of the past, such as steel. Some research has found, however, that the production of high-tech items such as mobile phones involves two processes associated with earlier heavy industries – the mining of metals and the dumping of dangerous metal products (Laszewski, 2008) – that involve potential future environmental hazards.

Ultimately, whatever actor is involved, only a sociological understanding of the planet – a realisation that one's own actions and inactions interact and conjoin with those of real and imagined others in near and far-away places – can rescue humanity from these challenges and the worst-case dystopia of environmental destruction.

Domain #2: Technology-society relations and related challenges

Humankind's relation to the natural world does not exhaust the range of relationships we have to the world around us. Going back to the earliest hunting and gathering societies, human beings have developed and interacted with various technologies. Will the technologies of the modern world – gadgets and gizmos like iPhones and iPads – dominate us or will we learn to adapt them to human purposes? With what consequences for our individual and collective identities?

Two possibilities suggest themselves about the influence of technology across the domains of work, family and leisure. One negative scenario is that new technologies will displace or substitute for real human interaction and that they will endanger the formation of human relations. Consider, for example, that moderns increasingly spend time engaged in watching television or virtual spaces, leaving less and less time for meaningful interaction with real significant others. Or that the sit-down family meal has increasingly become a casualty of ready-made, microwaved meals (Halton, 2008) and that people shop online instead of shopping in their local supermarket (Banerjee, 2001). The use of technologies can also de-tune us from awareness of our immediate natural (and social) environments. In this model, human beings are reduced to Luddites – people for whom technology is experienced as a remote and alien presence in their lives. Even as we claim more leisure time, we seem to make use of more and more technologies to pass it (Halton, 2008).

A positive scenario may also be operative. There are several examples of this. Acting as a labour-saving device, technology has the potential to free up our time to engage with others. As moderns live increasingly busy and harried lives, the availability of technologies like microwaves, washing machines and more means that less human labour is invested in the performance of everyday tasks of cleaning and cooking, freeing it up, potentially, for the development and strengthening of social relations.

One of the ironies of our technological age is that while it potentially releases moderns from everyday tasks, it also contributes to the increasingly harried pace of our lives. The average Irish person in 2005 spent over 70 minutes travelling, over two hours watching television, nearly four hours working and just half an hour on breaks (McGinnitty et al., 2005). Against this background the future might see a trend toward an emphasis on slowness. Instead of seeing speed as a virtue, we might well valorise slowness as the preferred temporal pace of the years to come. Already there are signs of this taking hold. Consider, for example, the emergence of a slowness movement (Honoré, 2004), manifest in a growing interest in incorporating such bodily practices as yoga and Pilates into our daily lives.

New technologies such as Skype are being increasingly used to bring Irish families separated by thousands of miles into real-time social interaction and allowing them to maintain and sustain emotional connections across old and new generations (Kenny, 2011). The return of emigration to Ireland in the wake of economic recession means that this may become more important than ever in the future in connecting to the global Irish diaspora across time and space.

In the future, emerging technologies may increasingly operate in the other direction as well by leading to the individualisation of our lives and the emergence of a 'personal communication society' (Campbell and Park, 2008, p. 380). For example, consider the ubiquity of the mobile phone. According to an agency of the United Nations, the International Telecommunications Union, 99 per cent of 15- to 24-year-olds in Ireland have the use of a mobile phone (International Telecommunications Union, 2008). Compared to desk-bound computers, mobile phones are highly personalised, footloose technologies and many people consider them an appendage of the self (Campbell and Park, 2008). This personalisation has important social consequences. One of these is that mobile phones play an increasingly significant role in identity formation as people express their sense of self – by choosing phone designs and covers, for example – through them. Another is that mobile phone usage contributes to the personalisation of social spaces such as parks and shopping malls when people use them to connect with others, whether co-present or not (Campbell and Park, 2008). Some consequences are less positive, however, and one of these is that the personalisation of technology may allow global media corporations to track patterns in the consumption behaviours of individual users and thereby extend the reach of surveillance technologies – already at high levels through the use of CCTV footage in public spaces – into our everyday lives.

In the area of travel and mobility, electronic cars will likely reduce our dependence on oil as a resource as well as reducing human contributions to environmental emissions (Mitchell et al., 2010). As 'greener' modes of transportation take hold, such as the use of publicly provided bicycle schemes in our cities, we may well see the emergence of a stronger bike culture in Ireland and a return of earlier modes of transportation. As an example of this, a Co. Limerick-based company is restoring old high nelly bicycles for Irish and international markets (see below). This 'green' imperative may also mean that people will engage more with the public spaces of their lives – streets, parks and playgrounds – thus generating new possibilities for social engagement (Connerton, 2009). The great American urban critic Jane Jacobs celebrated the street as the locus of social capital and bemoaned the creeping loss of this public realm in US cities (Jacobs, 1989; Banerjee, 2001). One of the best ways to learn about a city, Jacobs felt, was simply walk its streets. While concerns about the loss of the public street may be less acute in western Europe, there are signs of the increasing commodification of Irish urban streetscapes that threaten to purge them of their unique traditional features and encourage a kind of forgetting of the city (Connerton, 2009). As in the US, the vitality and sense of place of Irish streets will also come under threat from the growth of indoor shopping malls, displacing the spontaneous public activity of Main Street Ireland with the controlled and sanitised behaviour of private indoor spaces of consumption.

Back to the transportation future

GoEco, a family-owned company based in Cappamore, Co. Limerick, collects old high nelly bicycles discarded by people in sheds and garages around the country and restores them as bikes in working order. This restoration involves converting the traditional bike into a 36 volt battery-powered electric bicycle called an e-bike. This allows users to reach a speed of up to 40 km/h. Restored high nellies cost about €999. Demand for the high nelly bike is strong and orders for the newly restored bike come from Irish consumers but also from other western European countries, especially Holland, which has a strong bicycle culture ('Get on yer bike as "High Nelly" makes electric comeback', *Irish Independent*, 8 February 2010).

Even 'third places' (Oldenburg, 1989) – those public spaces in between our private domestic home spaces and the public square of the street – such as Irish pubs are not immune to the intrusion of the homogenising effects of consumption and technological culture (Scarbrough, 2008). Increasingly, Irish pubs are becoming more and more like one another, as evidenced by the almost ubiquitous presence of plasma screen televisions broadcasting the latest sporting events. The spectator culture that this gives rise to tends to undercut the participant culture of singing and dancing associated with pubs and bars in the past, though it also provides a common currency for everyday social conversation. Self-styled 'super pubs' may also reduce intergenerational personal contact.

A sense of connection to urban space is also under threat from the rise of the sprawling city (Connerton, 2009). Cities of the future may become de-centred places as they extend outwards in ever increasing ways. This process is more advanced in other parts of the world – Asia, for example – but is taking place in Ireland as well. Such is the sprawl that has taken place in Dublin that it is difficult now – compared to even 30 years ago – to see all of the city from the vantage point of the Dublin Mountains.

Domain #3: Culture-society relations and related challenges

A third domain in which human action takes place is at the level of culture. In this book we have considered a wide range of cultural identities, objects and practices spanning gender, class and racial differences. The concept of culture encompasses these things, but also issues to do with politics and power. As such it is a catch-all category, so we have selected here a few aspects of it that we see as salient in the future.

Let's begin with gender. One of the key challenges for young adults in the future is the extension of young adulthood into the late twenties and early thirties (Kimmel, 2009). In the past, young people left school, found a job and typically got married in their early twenties. Today's emerging generation is different. The average young Irish adult today spends most of their early to mid-twenties in college, is likely to be financially dependent on his/her parents well into their young adult lives and is unlikely to be married until their early to late thirties (Lunn et al., 2009). One of the consequences of this is not just the delaying of marriage and child-bearing, but the elongation in the length of parenting done by earlier generations. It may also contribute to the solidifying of relations between generations so that when the young adult generation does marry and initiate families, they will do so with the support of strong familial bonds to their parents, whose influence on them is likely to be greater than with any previous generation. For still other young people it may be that the maintenance of same-sex friendships competes with marriage in their definition of normative masculinity and femininity and thus contributes to this extension of this period of young unmarried adulthood.

The economisation of social life is manifest in different aspects of everyday life, but one notable example relating to gender has to do with dating practices. Increasingly, dating – either in early adulthood or later life – has become financialised through the proliferation of dating agencies, many with online locations, to which members pay a fee in exchange for introductions to potential future earth mates. This means that emotions such as love have become more and more marketised, but it also reflects – and may even reinforce – existing patterns of social division relating to class and race. Access to online dating, for example, requires financial resources which most poor and disadvantaged people do not have. As a result, people with high levels of economic capital are more likely to take advantage of dating services, in turn reinforcing existing social divides. A further possible consequence of online dating services is the reinforcement of patterns of homogamy (Brynin et al., 2008), that is, the tendency of people to marry people socially like themselves in terms of educational background and economic resources, though the Irish evidence suggests that homogamy – or tendency not to cross cultural fault lines – is not highly pronounced in Ireland (Lunn and Fahey, 2011).

Advances in health mean that moderns are living longer lives, with important consequences for work and leisure. The future is likely to see an extension of people's working lives beyond the traditional retirement age of 65 as well as a much greater emphasis than before on active retirement, as people take advantage of leading healthier lives well into old age and perhaps even adding a new career or more civic participation or more childcare responsibilities. Indeed, what it means to be 'old' will be different in the future compared to now. This will likely be the lead labour market story of the next generation, as the entry of females into employment was for the generation of the Celtic Tiger years in the 1990s.

For those at the other end of the labour market, the work world in the future will not be the same as before (Moen, 2010). As single work 'careers' break down into multiple jobs with indefinite timeframes over an adult life, the next generation's labour market experiences will be characterised by more flexibility but also by less security and more precarity. These structural changes will put a premium on the ability of workers to develop job skills that can be transposed from one job to another rather than developing highly specialised knowledge unique to one particular job role.

Although few contemporary sociologists would agree with the classical social theorists' predictions about the long-term demise of religion, it is clear that how people relate to God, faith and the sacred is also likely to change significantly in the future. The trend of people dis-identifying with institutional religion is likely to continue, but it will be accompanied by a greater emphasis on individualised experiences of the sacred and the expression of religious identities outside the formal structures of churches. The 'I'm spiritual but not religious' formulation is thus likely to gain increasing currency among future Irish generations who may not wish to be seen – or see themselves – as church-goers but who are equally adamant that their lives are not empty or meaningless either. This may be seen by some as a watering down of traditional forms of religiosity or, alternatively, as taking religious meanings and experiences in a new direction (Ecklund and Long, 2011). In the past, social control tended to operate by exerting pressure on people to attend church and religious services, but in the future it is likely to operate the other way around as people come under social pressure from others not to be seen as someone who regularly darkens the door of a church. The emergence of more religious options, the shift from ascribed toward achieved religious identities and the trend toward disaffiliation with organised institutional religion are all possibilities in regard to what religion might look like in the future.

More broadly, the future will likely see shifts in the values moderns hold to be important in their lives. Three value axes – left-right, materialist-postmaterialist and religious-secular – represent the dominant value orientations of our society. Of these fault lines, perhaps the most attention has been given to the shift toward 'postmaterialist' values, by which is meant a shift from value systems – associated with a rise in general societal prosperity – emphasising material advancement and deference toward authority toward values of non-materiality and self-expression and self-fulfilment (Van Deth and Scarbrough, 1995). What available research tells us, however, is that people do not neatly line up on one side of these fault lines – making it difficult for governments to 'weapon' their policies toward specific values

– and that these value orientations are shaped by the structural realities of people's day-to-day lives (Van Deth and Scarbrough, 1995). As national societies and economies struggle during times of crisis and cross-national structural inequalities become deeper, it is likely that leftist, materialist value orientations will become increasingly salient as people try to negotiate and make sense of their difficult life circumstances and bring about political change. This suggests that in terms of value systems, the future will not be a straightforward story about the rise of new values and the jettisoning of older ones, but the reassertion of older values – such as the importance of people's material security – interacting with newer ones – such as the significance of ecological awareness (Van Deth and Scarbrough, 1995).

The final – and related – element of culture that we consider is politics. Politics is essentially about the future, as it asks what is likely to happen to humankind if we follow one path rather than another (Tilly, 1997). If we imagine Ireland as a better society in 15 to 20 years' time, the way we make decisions about the distribution of government resources in society will play a critical role in this. In recent times, a debate has emerged in Ireland about how Irish society might go about this. This debate has tended to focus on critiquing liberal capitalism and reorganising the political institutions of the state so as to achieve a better balance between national priorities and local needs. It has also sought to initiate debate about a value-led future (O'Toole, 2009) – to articulate the values that will guide policy and decision-making in the future. Should we develop a society that is more equal? Should we develop a society that has less conflict? Should we develop a society that is more democratic?

Yet it is still unclear what the institutional profile of a new Ireland should look like or how one might get there. The increasing fragmentation of value systems in the general population means that national governments can no longer rely on the existence of a single dominant value system for adjudicating between colliding interests (Van Deth, 1995). It also suggests that value-led change directed from below by non-state actors may be more difficult than is often assumed. How other societies are organised, politically and socially, provides a useful frame of reference for thinking about the possible direction of evolution of Irish society and politics. The Nordic countries are notable for the quiet and peaceable nature of their peoples but also for their emphasis on social equality and concern for the common good. These countries have pioneered democratic practices in relation to citizen deliberation – consistent with value orientations emphasising the de-legitimation of traditional sources of authority – in order to reduce the distance between politicians and citizens and have high rates of female participation in their national parliaments. Such societies are not without problems, of course (Denmark has higher crime rates and lower life expectancy than Ireland), but their experience – notwithstanding the significant socio-cultural differences with Ireland – shows that greater equality, more effective democracy and peace and social harmony are realisable goals generated by human political decision-making processes. The larger payoff of this is considerable – not only would it help to create a better society, but it might also help to sustain a greener planet (Wilkinson and Pickett, 2009).

A SOCIOLOGY OF THE FUTURE AND THE FUTURE OF SOCIOLOGY

In this chapter we have engaged in an anticipatory exercise of looking forward to what is 'not yet'. The ability of the discipline to engage in this 'sociology of the future' is partly bound up with the future of sociology itself – sociology and the future and sociology in the future go together (Tilly, 1997). As mentioned already, as a social science discipline, sociology struggles to compete with older disciplines such as history and economics whose academic practitioners are more readily called upon to offer insight into contemporary issues and debates and who seem to have more influence among power elites. A browse of the shelves in most Irish bookshops will tell you how much attention history and economics get compared to sociology, usually subsumed into a generic category like 'contemporary Irish society'. There are a few reasons why sociology has been marginal in Irish intellectual debate. The commitment of sociologists to data-driven research is sometimes viewed as too 'empirical' by other, more literary-oriented scholars. But sociology, as a science of social life, has been guided by theory and a sense of history and employs qualitative evidence as much as other cognate disciplines. Sometimes sociologists are seen as carriers of leftist ideas and there may be an ideological bias in other disciplines against this orientation. A third criticism sometimes levelled at practitioners of the discipline is their tendency to be faddish – their inclination to study 'hot' topics or to be oversensitive to dominant current trends – but this is to ignore their long-standing preoccupation with topics such as religion and organisations, going back to the work of the classical theorists.

In its past, Irish sociology has been shaped by a curious succession of forces, influences and markets – foreign travel writers and statistical experts from the mid to late 19th century, Catholic sociologists from the early 20th century to the 1950s, civil service and policy bureaucrats from the 1960s to the 1990s (Conway, 2006), and perhaps higher education managers and auditors from the 1990s onwards and into the future – that has given it a distinctive, if somewhat marginal, place in Irish intellectual culture. Marginality in the past may be no bad thing for the future – indeed, it might be the very impetus sociology needs to move itself (Burawoy, 2009a).

Sociology may be said to have a number of things going for it that give grounds for hope in this regard. For example, it is institutionally well positioned to engage in a tentative forward-looking into the future. It is taught in nearly every third-level institution in Ireland, is an attractive subject matter for many third-level students, is integrated into second-level civic, social and political education curricula, is the recipient of government and international funds with important social consequences and its legions of past students provide a ready audience for sociological insight and reflection.

Beyond these institutional resources, the discipline is also intellectually ahead of other disciplines in its ability to contribute to debates about the future evolution of Irish society. By emphasising the connectedness of our individual and collective lives, the influence of context on human action and the social divisions that constrain or enable human capabilities, sociologists bring a vantage point that other disciplines do not. Sociology's stress on empirical data – and not just relying on untested assumptions or unsubstantiated speculation about the social world around us – also gives the discipline an advantage over others (Gans, 2010). Sociologists of Ireland – sociologists whose work has focused on studying the national experience – and sociologists in Ireland – sociologists whose work involves little or no attention to the Irish situation – have added significantly to what we know about the major topics of culture, health/illness, education, family and more addressed in this book.

The beginnings and endings of significant timeframes, such as millennia or centuries, often provide a stimulus for reflection on the direction of evolution of sociological knowledge. In this context it is not surprising that sociologists generally have recently begun to reflect on and write about how the discipline should respond well into the next century. This can be understood in terms of theory, data, methods and public engagement.

Over the past few years, some of this reflection has taken the form of delineating some 'big idea' that sociologists ought to take up in the years to come. John Urry, for example, writes that a 'mobile sociology' ought to be the future of sociology. By this he means that the central task of sociologists of the future will be a concern with the theme of mobility applied to the full range of human experience – objects, images, people, information, travel, waste and so forth (Urry, 2010). This theme of mobility involves a new emphasis in sociology on understanding mobilities, networks and fluidities across borders, displacing an earlier emphasis on the national 'society' as the basic unit of analysis. As a big idea, Urry's claim would appear to have particular appeal for Ireland given the country's embrace of globalisation (O'Sullivan, 2006).

Urry has less to say about the methodological challenges of this kind of sociology – the relative lack of a strong social science data-gathering tradition in many poor and underdeveloped non-Western societies – and whether some methods, such as extended live-in ethnographies, may be better suited to studying mobilities across borders than others. Along similar lines, US sociologist Michael Burowoy asks whether sociology can develop a 'global sociology' that transcends national boundaries and that would involve much more cross-national collaborative research projects (Burawoy, 2009a). Burawoy's point about developing cross-cultural understandings and rethinking narratives in the discipline toward a hemispheric emphasis is a good one, but as Peter Beyer points out, 'the global always has to "come down" somewhere concretely' (Beyer, 2006, p. 411) and this implies paying attention to future global–local interactions as well.

At a theoretical level, future developments need not necessarily be a matter of constructing some new grand theories that will rise to the fore, but of endeavouring to create middle-range concepts or useful classifications, typologies and models that have a more restricted empirical scope but that also allow sociologists to make certain generalisations. Such conceptual innovation is likely to come from one of two possible sources – existing concepts and theories and careful consideration of the empirical world (Abbott, 2000).

Theoretical innovation might also come from greater debate and exchange across disciplinary sub-fields. Although sociologists tend to identify with particular sub-fields – and this book reproduces this in its treatment of major topics separately – there is much to be learned by importing concepts and theories from one field to another and going in the other exporting direction as well. To take one example, future studies of religion stand to benefit from drawing on insights from the sociology of organisations by examining the organisational aspects of religion, such as their tendency to become more technocratic, bureaucratised and professionalised (Demerath et al., 1998).

The sharing of disciplinary insights with scholars working in other disciplines – and without losing sociology's distinct disciplinary identity – is another source of conceptual development. This would mean identifying the theories and empirical foci in sociology that are shared with other disciplines as well as those peculiar to sociology. Curiously, sociology has not figured prominently in Irish Studies – whose object of study is Irish society and culture – although this field offers considerable scope for making publics interested in Irish history and literature aware of sociological research and writing. Already it is clear that Irish historians are increasingly influenced by and responsive to the work of Irish sociologists (Ferriter, 2009) and even in relation to topics that sociologists have tended to shy away from. Sociologists themselves could fruitfully benefit from other social science disciplines such as geography in deepening their understanding of nature-society relations (Anderson, 2009).

There is also considerable scope for innovation in the data sociologists employ in the future. One example is the use of visual data in sociology, not as an alternative to more traditional kinds of data like observation, documents, statistics and interviews, but as a supplement to them. Their chief merit is their capacity to capture context (Becker, 2000) – a photographer who took photos of certain places and people in Ireland in 2012 and came back again 50 years later to photograph the very same places and people would generate rich data beyond what the written text could do. A second virtue of the photo is its immediacy – it presents information about the detail of social phenomena at a particular moment in time. Indeed, there may be some sociological truths that are best, or maybe even only, told via the visual.

In terms of methods, the use of comparative approaches would also seem to be an important part of Irish sociology's future. While Irish society and culture are sometimes seen as unique, exceptional or different, only a comparative analysis can allow us to locate the Irish experience in relation to other societies. Indeed, one can only fully understand one society by placing it in relation to trends, patterns and dynamics in other societies. The ready availability of underutilised large-scale social survey datasets in quantitative data archives such as the Irish Social Science Data Archive – going back to the 1980s in some cases – offer rich possibilities for students of Irish society in terms of answering important sociological questions – across the full range of disciplinary sub-fields – within a comparative framework. Advances in data analysis techniques as a result of the availability of computer software packages mean that carrying out research combining qualitative and quantitative methods will be more realisable than ever.

Empirically, there are some residual topics that have not received nearly enough attention from sociologists or other humanists. Consideration of what sociologists have not so far studied and written about may be a portent of future concerns (Borgatta and Cook, 1988). While sociologists pay attention to the intellectual endeavour of studying 'down' by investigating the lives of disadvantaged, disempowered and marginal groups, they spend considerably less time studying 'up' by turning their critical gaze to the systematic study of social and political elites. Elites are those people at the top level of social structures who make decisions with important consequences. Bishops, bankers, millionaires, public intellectuals and military generals all belong to this category. Admittedly, there are methodological challenges here – gaining access to hard-to-reach or difficult-to-find groups – but these are hardly insurmountable for a serious and discerning sociologist.

The notion of sociology as a publicly engaged discipline has gained some renewed attention in recent times and has been presented as a means of rescuing sociology from isolation and lack of relevance in the future (Burawoy, 2009b). This issue of the 'publicness' of sociology brings the discipline's boundaries to the fore. Admittedly, certain sub-fields – such as education and health – have a stronger applied/policy orientation than others (Borgatta and Cook, 1988), so we should be careful about making blanket claims about its possibilities across different fields. In general, though, what would a public sociology in an Irish key look like? There is a diversity of ways in which this engagement can be expressed, ranging from making contributions to policy decision-making to getting sociological insights into the news. Each tends to lend itself to certain preferred formats of presenting sociological ideas. The journal article and monograph, for example, tend to be the most effective means of communicating sociological research to fellow sociologists. Non-conventional formats – straddling the academic journal and popular magazine genres – are arguably more useful for sociologists seeking to get their research taken up by mass media outlets and research reports tend to be the preferred format of policy-makers. *Contexts*, a journal of the American Sociological Association, is a good example of this. In the Irish context, the long-running *Irish Sociological Chronicles* series attempts to make sociological insight publicly available using an easy-to-read, non-jargon approach.

The use of a diversity of academic writing genres is likely to become increasingly relevant in the years to come as sociologists attempt to make their work more 'applied' and read by wider publics. In every case, the imperative of writing in a clear and accessible manner will be important and there are many exemplars to work with here, ranging from Erving Goffman's *Asylums* (Goffman, 1961) to Howard Becker's *Outsiders* (Becker, 2008). Compared to the other areas though, sociologists may exercise less control over the application of their research than they would like (Borgatta and Cook, 1988) – increasingly, funding agencies with a strong policy orientation exert influence not only in relation to the goals of applied research, but also its mode of presentation.

One of the key venues for public engagement is the seminar room and lecture hall and thus the teaching of sociology is an important, if rarely discussed, aspect of the project of making sociology more socially useful and relevant. While recognising that sociology is entangled in curriculum politics in Irish higher education institutions, teaching the discipline well to large numbers of students should be a priority for the next generation of sociologists. This would mean helping students apply sociological insights to their everyday lives and developing active rather than passive forms of engaging with sociological writing and research, such as student-led class discussions rather than the traditional stand-up lecture method (Yamane, 2006).

Future changes and developments in theory, data, methods and public engagement will likely occur at an uneven rate. Mainly because theoretical innovation requires more effort, tends to be more difficult and involves jettisoning earlier conceptual commitments, it is likely to occur at a slower rate compared to changes in other areas such as public engagement.

CONCLUSION: FACING THE FUTURE

Sociology has – and will have – an important contribution to make to the advancement of knowledge and understanding of race, class, gender, religion, media, politics and more. Much work remains to be done, however, and future sociological work in/of Ireland should address and capitalise on the methodological, theoretical and empirical challenges – and opportunities – we identified earlier in this chapter. In particular, our understanding of all types of social phenomena will be enhanced by greater cross-currents – between sub-fields and specialities within the discipline as well as across disciplinary boundaries and even occupational identities – in the future. Moving forward in the future does not mean that past issues and concerns should be abandoned altogether. Rather, it means thinking about old puzzles in new ways as well as developing new puzzles as an impetus for fresh and innovative theorising and empirical analysis. Institutionally, Irish sociology is relatively well placed to take up these future intellectual challenges, though we are aware of growing bureaucratic changes and pressures in and outside of higher education that are likely to pose challenges for our collective disciplinary future.

Irish society represents a particularly interesting case study of social change for future sociologists and other humanists because of the relative suddenness of many changes that have already taken place, but also because of the elements of Irish culture – religious identity, political identity and local identity – implicated in it.

Our exercise in engaging with possible sociological futures likely raises as many questions as it answers. A chapter with the title of 'sociological futures' is inevitably more speculative, aspirational and provisional than the earlier chapters in this lengthy textbook. At the same time, we argue that the framework we laid out earlier – focusing on relations and opposing creative tendencies in three domains of social life – helps us understand the Ireland that might emerge in the years to come and could usefully be applied to national settings beyond Ireland as other sociologists seek to understand and predict the future long-term evolution of contemporary societies and follow in the footsteps of the classical theorists.

During his lifetime, Karl Marx wrote some of the most influential studies in sociology, including some relating specifically to Ireland. One section from Marx's *Eighteenth Brumaire of Louis Bonaparte* communicates directly to the emphasis on sociological futures developed in this chapter: 'men make their own history, but they do not make it just as they please; they do not make it under circumstances chosen by themselves, but under circumstances directly encountered, given and transmitted from the past' (Marx, 1970, p. 96). This wise and timeless comment remind students of Irish society, culture and politics that while we exercise agency in fashioning the future, we are also tradition-bound in our individual and collective capabilities, influenced and constrained as much by the exigencies of the past as by the limits of our own forward-looking imaginations.

References

Abbott, A. (2000) 'Reflections on the future of sociology'. *Contemporary Sociology* 29(2), pp. 296–300.

Åberg, A. (1999) 'Modern nature? Images of nature and rurality in Swedish cinema'. Paper to European Rural Sociological Society conference, Lund.

ACJRD (Association for Criminal Justice Research and Development) (2010) *Women in the criminal justice system*. Proceedings of 13th ACJRD conference, Dublin, October. [www.acjrd.ie/files/Women_in_the_Criminal_Justice_System_(2010).pdf]

Akenson, D. (1991) *Small differences: Irish Catholics and Irish Protestants, 1815–1922*. Montreal and Kingston: McGill-Queen's University Press/Dublin: Gill & Macmillan.

Albrechtslund, A. (2008) 'Online social networking as participatory surveillance'. *First Monday* 13(3). [firstmonday.org/article/view/2142/1949]

Aldridge, A. (2000) *Religion in the contemporary world*. Cambridge: Polity.

Alexander, J. (1998) 'Civil society I, II, III — constructing an empirical concept from normative controversies and historical transformations' in J. Alexander (ed.) *Real civil societies: Dilemmas of institutionalisation*. London: Sage.

All Ireland Traveller Health Study Team (2010) *All Ireland Traveller Health Study: Summary of findings*. Dublin: Department of Public Health, Physiotherapy and Population Science, University College Dublin. [www.dohc.ie/publications/traveller_health_study.html]

All-Island Research Observatory (2012) 'Table 35: Percentage change in population by sex, religion, census year and statistic 2002–2011'. Maynooth: AIRO. [www.airo.ie/spatial-indicators/view/2498]

Allen, K. (1997) *Fianna Fáil and Irish Labour: 1926 to the present*. London: Pluto.

Allen, K. (2000) *The Celtic Tiger: The myth of social partnership in Ireland*. Manchester: Manchester University Press.

Allen, M. (1998) *The bitter word: Ireland's job famine and its aftermath*. Dublin: Poolbeg.

Amárach Research (2012) *Contemporary Catholic perspectives*. [commissioned by the Association of Catholic Priests] Dublin: Amárach Research.

Anderson, A. (2009) 'Media, politics and climate change: Toward a new research agenda'. *Sociology Compass* 3(2), pp. 166–82.

Anderson, B. (2006) *Imagined communities: Reflections on the origin and spread of nationalism*. [rev. ed.] London: Verso.

Ang, I. (1985) *Watching Dallas: Soap opera and the melodramatic imagination*. London: Methuen.

Aniagolu, C. (1997) 'Being black in Ireland' in E. Crowley and J. Mac Laughlin (eds) *Under the belly of the tiger: Class, race, identity and culture in the global Ireland*. Dublin: Irish Reporter.

Arensberg, C. and S. Kimball (2001) [1940] *Family and community in Ireland*. 3e. Ennis: CLASP.

Armstrong, P. and H. Armstrong (2005) 'Public and private: Implications for care work' in L. Pettinger et al. (eds) *A new sociology of work?* Oxford: Blackwell/*The Sociological Review*, pp. 169–87.

Aspers, P. and L. Skov (2006) 'Encounters in the global fashion business: Afterword'. *Current Sociology* 54(5), pp. 802–13.

Atkins, P. and I. Bowler (2001) *Food in society: Economy, culture, geography*. London: Arnold.

Bacik, I. (2002) 'Women and the criminal justice system' in P. O'Mahony (ed.) *Criminal justice in Ireland*. Dublin: Institute of Public Administration.

Bail, K. (ed.) (1996) *DIY feminism*. Sydney: Allen & Unwin.

Baizán, P. (2005) 'The impact of labour-market status on second and higher-order births. A comparative study of Denmark, Italy, Spain and the United Kingdom'. [Paper no. 2005-11] Barcelona: Department of Political and Social Sciences, Universitat Pompeu Fabra. [www.upf.edu/demosoc/_pdf/DEMOSOC11.pdf]

Baker, J., K. Lynch, S. Cantillon and J. Walsh (2004) *Equality: From theory to action*. Basingstoke: Palgrave.

Balanda, K. and J. Wilde (2001) *Inequalities in mortality 1989–1998: A report on all-Ireland mortality data*. Dublin: Institute of Public Health in Ireland.

Banerjee, T. (2001) 'The future of public space: Beyond invented streets and reinvented places'. *Journal of the American Planning Association* 67(1), pp. 9–24.

Barich, B. (2009) *A pint of plain: Tradition, change and the fate of the Irish pub*. London: Bloomsbury.

Barrett, A., S. McGuinness and M. O'Brien (2008) 'The immigrant earnings disadvantage across the earnings and skills distributions: The case of immigrants from the EU's New Member States in Ireland'. Dublin: Economic and Social Research Institute. [www.esri.ie/UserFiles/publications/20080501123344/WP236.pdf]

Barrett, A., G. Savva, V. Timonen and R. Kenny (2011) *Fifty plus in Ireland 2011: First results from the Irish Longitudinal Study on Ageing (TILDA)*. Dublin: The Irish Longitudinal Study on Ageing.

Barthes, R. (1973) *Mythologies*. St Alban's: Paladin.

Baudrillard, J. (1998 [1970]) *The consumer society: Myths and structures*. London: Sage.

Bauman, Z. (2001) *Community: Seeking safety in an insecure world*. Cambridge: Polity.

Bauman, Z. (2002) 'Individually, together' in U. Beck and E. Beck-Gernsheim, *Individualization: Institutionalised individualism and its social and political consequences*. London: Sage.

Beale, J. (1986) *Women in Ireland: Voices of change*. Basingstoke: Macmillan.

Beardsworth, A. and T. Keil (1997) *Sociology on the menu: An invitation to the study of food and society*. London: Routledge.

Beck, U. (1992) *Risk society: Towards a new modernity*. London: Sage.

Beck, U. and E. Beck-Gernsheim (2002) *Individualization: Institutionalised individualism and its social and political consequences*. London: Sage

Becker, H. (1967) 'Whose side are we on?' *Social Problems* 14(3), pp. 239–47.

Becker, H. (2000) 'What should sociology look like in the (near) future?'. *Contemporary Sociology* 29(2), pp. 333–6.

Becker, H. (2008) 'Above all, write with clarity and precision'. *Sociological Inquiry* 78(3), pp. 412–16.

Begley, M., D. Chambers, P. Corcoran and J. Gallagher (2004) *The male perspective: Young men's outlook on life.* Dublin: National Suicide Research Foundation.

Belasco, W. (2006) *Meals to come: A history of the future of food.* Berkeley: University of California Press.

Bell, D. (1982) 'Community studies: The new anthropological heritage and its popularity in Ireland'. *International Journal of Anthropology and Social Policy* 1, pp. 22–36.

Bellah, R. (1967) 'Civil religion in America'. *Daedalus* Winter, pp. 1–19.

Benington, J. (2001) 'Partnerships as networked governance?' in M. Geddes and J. Benington (eds) *Local partnerships and social exclusion in the European Union: New forms of local social governance?* London: Routledge, pp. 198–219.

Benjamin, W. (1999) *The Arcades project.* [ed. R. Tiedermann]. Cambridge, MA: Harvard University Press.

Bennett, T. and D. Watson (2002) 'Understanding everyday life: Introduction' in T. Bennett and D. Watson (eds) *Understanding everyday life.* Oxford: Blackwell/Open University.

Benson, M. (2007) 'Changing cityscapes and the process of contemporary gentrification: An examination of the transformation of Ringsend within the context of post-industrial growth in Dublin'. Unpublished PhD thesis, Department of Sociology, NUI Maynooth.

Beyer, P. (2006) 'Globalization' in H. Ebaugh (ed.) *Handbook of religion and social institutions.* New York: Springer, pp. 411–29.

Binchy, A., M. McCann, S. Ó Síocháin and J. Ruane (eds) (1994) 'Travellers' language: A sociolinguistic perspective' in *Irish Travellers: Culture and ethnicity.* Belfast: Institute of Irish Studies, Queen's University Belfast, for the Anthropological Association of Ireland.

Blaxter, M. (1995) 'What is health?' in B. Davey, A. Gray and C. Seale (eds) *Health and disease: A reader.* Buckingham: Open University Press.

Blumler, J. and M. Gurevitch (1981) 'Politicians and the press: An essay on role relationships' in D. Nimmo and K. Sanders (eds) *Handbook of political communication.* London: Sage, pp. 467–93.

Bocock, R. (1992) 'Consumption and lifestyles' in R. Bocock and K. Thompson (eds) *Social and cultural forms of modernity.* Cambridge: Polity/Open University.

Bocock, R. and K. Thompson (eds) (1985) *Religion and ideology.* Manchester: Manchester University Press/Open University.

Bollier, D. (2011) *The future of work: What it means for individuals, businesses, markets and governments.* Washington, DC: Aspen Institute. [www.aspeninstitute.org/sites/default/files/content/docs/pubs/The_Future_of_Work.pdf]

Bonner, K. (1996) Review of P. Clancy et al. (eds) 'Irish society: Sociological perspectives' in *Irish Journal of Sociology* 6, pp. 212–20.

Bord Bia (2010) 'Servicing the Irish convenience retail sector' [presentation]. [www.bordbia.ie/eventsnews/ConferencePresentations/ServicingIrishConvenienceRetailSector2010]

Borgatta, E. and K. Cook (eds) (1988) *The future of sociology.* London: Sage.

Boston Women's Health Book Collective (1973) *Our bodies, ourselves: A book by and for women.* Boston: Boston Women's Health Book Collective.

Boucher-Hayes, P. and S. Campbell (2009) *Basket case: What's happening to Ireland's food?* Dublin: Gill & Macmillan.

Bouma, G. and R. Ling (2011) 'Religious diversity' in P. Clarke (ed.) *The Oxford handbook of the sociology of religion.* Oxford: Oxford University Press, pp. 507–22.

Bourdieu, P. (1984) *Distinction: A social critique of the judgement of taste.* London: Routledge and Kegan Paul.

Boyd, D. (2008) 'Why youth love social network sites: The role of networked publics in teenage social life' in D. Buckingham (ed.) *Youth, identity, and digital media.* [The John D. and Catherine T. MacArthur Foundation Series on Digital Media and Learning] Cambridge, MA: MIT Press, pp. 119–42.

Boylan, T. (1996) 'Rural industrialisation and rural poverty' in C. Curtin et al. (eds) *Poverty in rural Ireland.* Dublin: Oak Tree.

Boylan, T. and T. Foley (1992) *Political economy and colonial Ireland: The propagation and ideological function of economic discourse in the nineteenth century.* London: Routledge and Kegan Paul.

Brady, J. (2001) 'The heart of the city: Commercial Dublin, c.1890–1915' in J. Brady and A. Simms (eds) *Dublin through space and time (c.900–1900).* Dublin: Four Courts.

Breathnach, P. (1985) 'Rural industrialisation in the West of Ireland' in M. Healey and B. Ilbery (eds) *The industrialisation of the countryside.* Norwich: Geo.

Breathnach, P. (1993) 'Women's employment and peripheralisation: The case of Ireland's branch plant economy', *Geoforum* 24(1), pp. 19–29.

Bréchon, P. (2007) 'Cross-national comparisons of individual religiosity' in J. Beckford and N. Demerath (eds) *The Sage handbook of the sociology of religion.* London: Sage.

Breen, M., A. Haynes and E. Devereux (2006) 'Citizens, loopholes and maternity tourists: Media frames in the citizenship referendum' in M. Corcoran and M. Peillon (eds) *Uncertain Ireland: A sociological chronicle, 2003–2004.* Dublin: Institute of Public Administration.

Breen, R. and D. Rottman (1985) *Crime victimisation in the Republic of Ireland.* Dublin: Economic and Social Research Institute. [Paper no. 121]

Breen, R. and C. Whelan (1996) *Social mobility and social class in Ireland.* Dublin: Gill & Macmillan.

Breen, R., D. Hannan, D. Rottman and C. Whelan (1990) *Understanding contemporary Ireland: State, class and development in the Republic of Ireland.* London: Macmillan.

Brenner, N. (2004) *New state spaces: Urban governance and the rescaling of statehood.* Oxford: Oxford University Press.

Brody, H. (1986) *Inishkillane: Change and decline in the west of Ireland.* London: Faber & Faber.

Brown, S. and A. Patterson (2000) 'Knick-knack Paddy-whack, give a pub a theme'. *Journal of Marketing Management* 16, pp. 647–62.

Bruce, S. (2002) *God is dead: Secularization in the West.* Oxford: Blackwell.

Brynin, M., S. Longhi and M. Pérez (2008) *The social significance of homogamy.* [Working Paper No. 2008-32] Colchester: Institute for Social and Economic Research, University of Essex. [www.iser.essex.ac.uk/publications/working-papers/iser/2008-32.pdf]

Buckingham, D. (2000) *After the death of childhood: Growing up in the age of the electronic media*. Cambridge: Polity.

Bunton, R. (1998) 'Inequalities in late-modern health care' in A. Petersen and C. Waddell (eds) *Health matters: A sociology of illness prevention and care*. Buckingham: Open University Press.

Burawoy, M. (2005) 'For public sociology' [2004 American Sociological Association presidential address] *American Sociological Review* 70(1), pp. 4–8.

Burawoy, M. (2009a) 'Challenges for a global sociology'. *Contexts* 8(4), pp. 36–41.

Burawoy, M. (2009b) 'Public sociology in the age of Obama'. *Innovation: The European Journal of Social Science Research* 22(2), pp. 189–99.

Burawoy, M. (2011) 'Universities in crisis: A public sociology perspective'. Paper to the Royal Irish Academy, Dublin, 13 January in M.P. Corcoran, K. Lalor and J. Maguire (eds) *Public intellectuals at a time of crisis*. Dublin: Royal Irish Academy.

Burke, S. (2009) *Irish apartheid: Healthcare inequality in Ireland*. Dublin: New Island.

Burke, S., C. Keenaghan, D. O'Donovan and B. Quirke (2004) *Health in Ireland: An unequal state*. Dublin: Public Health Alliance Ireland.

Burley, J. and F. Regan (2002) 'Divorce in Ireland: The fear, the floodgates and the reality'. *International Journal of Law, Policy and the Family*, 16, pp. 202–22.

Burnett, J. (1999) *Liquid pleasures: A social history of drinks in modern Britain*. London: Routledge.

Butler, M. (2002) *Evaluation in the Irish health sector*. [CPMR Discussion paper 21] Dublin: Institute of Public Administration.

Butler, S. (2002) *Alcohol, drugs and health promotion in modern Ireland*. Dublin: Institute of Public Administration.

Byrne, A., R. Edmondson and T. Varley (2001) 'Introduction to the third edition' in C. Arensberg and S. Kimball, *Family and community in Ireland*. Ennis: CLASP.

Byrne, D. and E. Smyth (2010) *No way back? The dynamics of early school leaving*. Dublin: The Liffey Press.

Byrne, L. and K. Keohane (forthcoming) 'The Rubberbandits' "Horse Outside": Towards a redemptive art for post-Celtic Tiger Ireland' in M. Corcoran and P. Share (eds) *Irish Sociological Chronicles Vol 8*.

Calhoun, C. (1996) 'Social theory and the public sphere' in B. Turner (ed.) *The Blackwell companion to social theory*. Oxford: Blackwell.

Campbell, C. (1987) *The romantic ethic and the spirit of modern consumerism*. Oxford: Blackwell.

Campbell, H. and E. Phillips (1995) 'Masculine hegemony and leisure sites' in P. Share (ed.) *Communication and culture in rural areas*. Wagga Wagga (NSW): Centre for Rural Social Research, Charles Sturt University.

Campbell, L. (2008) 'The culture of control in Ireland: Theorising recent developments in criminal justice'. *Web Journal of Current Legal Issues* 1. [webjcli.ncl.ac.uk/2008/issue1/campbell1.html]

Campbell, S. and Y. Park (2008) 'Social implications of mobile telephony: The rise of personal communication society'. *Sociology Compass* 2(2), pp. 371–87.

Care Alliance Ireland (2010) *Family caring in Ireland*. Dublin: Citizens Information Board. [www.carersireland.com/library_research.php]

Carroll, M. (1999) *Irish pilgrimage: Holy wells and popular Catholic devotion*. Baltimore: John Hopkins University Press.

Casanova, J. (1994) *Public religions in the modern world*. Chicago: University of Chicago Press.

Cassidy, E. (2002) 'Modernity and religion in Ireland, 1980–2000' in E. Cassidy (ed.) *Measuring Ireland: Discerning values and beliefs*. Dublin: Veritas.

Cassidy, T. (1997) 'Sober for the sake of the children: A discussion of alcohol use amongst Irish women' in M. Leonard and A. Byrne (eds) *Women in Ireland: A sociological profile*. Belfast: Beyond the Pale.

Cassidy, T. (1998) 'Just two will do' in M. Peillon and E. Slater (eds) *Encounters with modern Ireland: A sociological chronicle 1995–1996*. Dublin: Institute of Public Administration.

Castells, M. (2007) 'Communication, power and counter power in the network society'. *International Journal of Communication* 1, pp. 238–66.

Castles, S. and M. Miller (1998) *The age of migration: International population movements in the modern world*. Basingstoke: Palgrave.

Catholic Schools Partnership (2011) *Catholic primary schools in the Republic of Ireland: A qualitative study*. [www.catholicschools.ie/wp-content/uploads/2011/10/Report-on-Research-on-Catholic-Primary-Schools.pdf]

CB Richard Ellis (2010) *Market view: Dublin retail Q2 2010*. [www.cbre.ie]

Changing Generations (2012) *Study of intergenerational solidarity in Ireland*. Irish Centre for Social Gerontology, NUIG and the Social Policy and Ageing Research Centre, TCD.

Chamberlain, G. (2011) 'Apple's Chinese workers treated "inhumanely, like machines".' *The Guardian*, 30 April. [www.guardian.co.uk/technology/2011/apr/30/apple-chinese-workers-treated-inhumanely]

Charleton, M. (2007) 'Cosmopolitanism and nationalism: A cocktail for consumer craving in a rural Irish department store'. MA thesis, National College of Art and Design, Dublin.

Chatterton, P. and R. Hollands (2003) *Urban nightscapes: Youth cultures, pleasure spaces and corporate power*. London: Routledge.

Chaves, M. (1993) 'Intraorganizational power and internal secularization in Protestant denominations'. *American Journal of Sociology* 99(1), pp. 1–48.

Clancy, C. (2009) '50 years later: Women in policing'. *Communique: Garda Síochána Management Journal* December, pp. 22–8. [www.garda.ie/Documents/User/Communique%20Final%20DEC%2009%20Reduced.pdf]

Clancy, P. (1982) *Participation in higher education: A national survey*. Dublin: Higher Education Authority.

Clancy, P. (1988) *Who goes to college? A second survey of participation in higher education*. Dublin: Higher Education Authority.

Clancy, P. (1995) 'Education in the Republic of Ireland: The project of modernity?' in P. Clancy et al. (eds) *Irish society: Sociological perspectives*. Dublin: Institute of Public Administration in association with the Sociological Association of Ireland.

Clancy, P. (2001) *College entry in focus: A fourth national survey of access to higher education*. Dublin: Higher Education Authority.

Clancy, P., N. O'Connor and K. Dillon (2010) *Mapping the golden circle*. Dublin: TASC. [www.tascnet.ie/upload/file/MtGC%20ISSU.pdf]

Clarkson, L. and M. Crawford (2001) *Feast and famine: A history of food and nutrition in Ireland 1500–1920*. Oxford University Press.

Cleary, A. (1997) 'Gender differences in mental health in Ireland' in A. Cleary and M. Treacy (eds) *The sociology of health and illness in Ireland*. Dublin: University College Dublin Press.

Cleary, A. (2005) 'Death rather than disclosure: Struggling to be a real man' in *Irish Journal of Sociology* 14(2) [Special issue on Masculinities], pp. 155–76.

Clegg, M. (2003) 'Trusteeship: A model in progress' in N. Prendergast and L. Monahan (eds) *Reimagining the Catholic school*. Dublin: Veritas.

Clinch, P., F. Convery and B. Walsh (2002) *After the Celtic Tiger: Challenges ahead*. Dublin: O'Brien.

Cohen, R. (2010) 'Rethinking "mobile work": Boundaries of space, time and social relation in the working lives of mobile hairstylists'. *Work, Employment and Society* 24(1) pp. 65–84.

Collins, C. and E. Shelley (1997) 'Social class differences in lifestyle and health characteristics in Ireland' in A. Cleary and M. Treacy (eds) *The sociology of health and illness in Ireland*. Dublin: University College Dublin Press.

Collins, G. (2006) 'Germs, globalisation and gender: The making of a food scare' in M. Corcoran and M. Peillon (eds) *Uncertain Ireland: A sociological chronicle, 2003–2004*. Dublin: Institute of Public Administration.

Commission on the Points System (1999) *Consultative process: Background document*. Dublin: Stationery Office.

Community Mediation Works (2010) *The state of anti-social behaviour policy and practice in working class communities*. Dún Laoghaire: Community Mediation Works. [www.iprt.ie/files/The_State_of_Anti_Social_Behaviour.pdf]

Competition Authority (1998) *Interim study on the liquor licensing laws and other barriers to entry and their impact on competition in the retail drinks market*. Dublin: Competition Authority.

Conniffe, D. and D. McCoy (1993) *Alcohol use in Ireland: Some economic and social implications*. Dublin: Economic and Social Research Institute [Report no. 160].

Connell, R. (1987) *Gender and power: Society, the person and sexual politics*. Sydney: Allen & Unwin.

Connell, R. (2011) 'Gender, health and theory: Conceptualizing the issue, in local and world perspective'. *Social Science and Medicine*. [doi:10.1016/j.socscimed.2011.06.006]

Connerton, P. (2009). *How modernity forgets*. Cambridge: Cambridge University Press.

Connolly, B. (1997) 'Women in community education and development – liberation or domestication?' in A. Byrne and M. Leonard (eds) *Women and Irish society: A sociological reader*. Belfast: Beyond the Pale.

Conway, B. (2006) 'Foreigners, faith and fatherland: The historical origins, development and present status of Irish sociology'. *Sociological Origins* 5(1) [special supplement] pp. 5–35. [available at www.sociological-origins.com]

Conway, B. (2011a) 'Catholic sociology in Ireland in comparative perspective'. *The American Sociologist* 42(1), pp. 34–55.

Conway, B. (2011b) 'The vanishing Catholic priest'. *Contexts* 10(2), pp. 64–5.

Conway, B., M.P. Corcoran and L. Cahill (2011) 'The "miracle" of Fatima: Media framing and the regeneration of a Dublin housing estate'. *Journalism* 13(6), pp. 1–21.

Conway, P. (2002) 'Learning in communities of practice: Rethinking teaching and learning in disadvantaged contexts'. *Irish Educational Studies* 21(3), pp. 61–91.

Cook, F. et al. (1983) 'Media effects and agenda setting'. *Public Opinion Quarterly* 47(1), pp. 16–35.

Cooney, D. (2002) 'Switzer's of Grafton Street'. *Dublin Historical Record* 55(2), pp. 154–65.

Corcoran, M. (2000) 'Mall city' in E. Slater and M. Peillon (eds) *Memories of the present: A sociological chronicle of Ireland, 1997–1998.* Dublin: Institute of Public Administration.

Corcoran, M. (2002) 'On the waterfront' in M. Corcoran and M. Peillon (eds) *Ireland unbound: A turn of the century chronicle.* [Irish Sociological Chronicles, vol. 3] Dublin: Institute of Public Administration.

Corcoran, M. (2005) 'Portrait of the absent father: The impact of non-residency on developing and maintaining a fathering role'. *Irish Journal of Sociology* 14(2) [Special issue on Masculinities] pp. 134–54.

Corcoran, M., J. Gray and M. Peillon (2010) *Suburban affiliations: Social relations in the Greater Dublin Area.* New York: Syracuse University Press/Dublin: University College Dublin Press.

Cormack, P. (2005) 'Angels, bells, television and Ireland: The place of the Angelus broadcast in the Republic'. *Media Culture and Society*, 27(2) pp. 271–87.

Corrigan, Á. (2006) 'Irish immigrant entrepreneurs in the United States: Ethnic strategies and transnational identities'. Unpublished PhD thesis, Department of Sociology, NUI Maynooth.

Corrigan, P. (1988) 'Backstage dressing: Clothing and the urban family'. Unpublished PhD thesis, Department of Sociology, Trinity College Dublin.

Corrigan, P. (1997) *The sociology of consumption: An introduction.* London: Sage.

Corsaro, W. (2005) *The sociology of childhood.* California: Pine Forge Press.

Cosgrove, O.L. Cox, C. Kuhling and P. Mulholland (eds) (2011) *Ireland's new religious movements.* Newcastle-upon-Tyne: Cambridge Scholars' Press.

Coveney, J. (2006) *Food, morals and meaning: The pleasures and anxieties of eating.* London: Routledge.

Cox, L. (2010) 'Current debates: New religion(s) in Ireland. "Alternative spiritualities, new religious movements and the New Age in Ireland". Conference report, NUI Maynooth, 30–31 October 2009'. *Irish Journal of Sociology* 18(1), pp. 100–11.

Crawford, E. (1995) 'Food retailing, nutrition and health in Ireland, 1839–1989: One hundred and fifty years of eating' in A. den Hartog (ed.) *Food, technology, science and marketing: European diet in the twentieth century.* East Lothian: Tuckwell.

Cresswell, R. (1969) *Une communaute rurale d'Irlande.* Paris: Institut de Ethnographie.

Croall, H. (2001) *Understanding white-collar crime.* Buckingham: Open University Press.

Crothers, C. (2008) 'New Zealand sociology textbooks'. *Current Sociology* 56(2), pp. 221–34.

Crotty, P. (1999) 'Food and class' in J. Germov and L. Williams (eds) *A sociology of food and nutrition: The social appetite.* Melbourne: Oxford.

Crowley-Henry, M. (2010) 'Twenty-first-century international careers: From economic to lifestyle migration' in J. Hogan, P.F. Donnelly and B.K. O'Rourke (eds) *Irish business and society: Governing, participating and transforming in the 21st century*. Dublin: Gill & Macmillan.

CSO [Central Statistics Office] (2000) *That was then, this is now: Change in Ireland 1949–1999*. Dublin: Central Statistics Office.

CSO [Central Statistics Office] (2006) *Statistical yearbook of Ireland 2006*. Dublin: Stationery Office. [www.cso.ie/releasespublications/statistical_yearbook_ireland_2006.htm]

CSO [Central Statistics Office] (2007) *Interpreting crime statistics: A background briefing note*. Dublin: Central Statistics Office. [www.cso.ie/releasespublications/documents/crime_justice/current/interpretingcrimestats.pdf]

CSO [Central Statistics Office] (2008) *Population and labour force projections 2011–2041*. Dublin: Central Statistics Office.

CSO [Central Statistics Office] (2010a) *National income and expenditure: Annual results for 2009*. Dublin: Central Statistics Office. [www.cso.ie/releasespublications/documents/economy/current/nie.pdf]

CSO [Central Statistics Office] (2010b) *Crime and victimisation: Quarterly National Household Survey 2010*. Dublin: Central Statistics Office. [www.cso.ie/releases publications/documents/crime_justice/current/crimeandvictimisation_qnhs2010.pdf]

CSO [Central Statistics Office] (2010c) *Quarterly National Household Survey: Union membership. Quarter 2, 2009*. Dublin: Central Statistics Office. [www.cso.ie/en/media/csoie/releasespublications/documents/labourmarket/2009/qnhsunionmembership_q2 2009.pdf]

CSO [Central Statistics Office] (2011a) *Garda recorded crime statistics 2005–2009*. Dublin: Central Statistics Office. [www.cso.ie/releasespublications/documents/crime_justice/2009/gardacrimestats_2009.pdf]

CSO [Central Statistics Office] (2011b) *Statistical yearbook of Ireland 2011*. Dublin: Government Publications. [www.cso.ie/en/releasesandpublications/othercsopublications/statisticalyearbookofireland2011edition]

CSO [Central Statistics Office] (2011c) *Population and migration estimates*. [http://www.cso.ie/en/media/csoie/releasespublications/documents/population/2011/Population%20and%20Migration%20Estimates%20April%202011.pdf]

CSO [Central Statistics Office] (2012) *Women and men in Ireland 2011*. [www.cso.ie/en/media/csoie/releasespublications/documents/otherreleases/2011/Women%20and%20Men%20in%20Ireland%202011.pdf]

Cullen, L. (1987) *An economic history of Ireland since 1600*. London: Batsford.

Cullinane, M. (2012) 'RTÉ, the newstandard and the search for news in the public interest'. Paper to Sociological Association of Ireland Postgraduate conference, Sligo, December 2011. [markcullinane.wordpress.com/2012/01/26/rte-the-newstandard-and-the-search-for-news-in-the-public-interest]

Cunningham, T. (2008) 'Jesus in Dundrum: Between God and Mammon' in M. Corcoran and P. Share (eds) *Belongings: Shaping identity in modern Ireland*. [Irish Sociological Chronicles, vol. 6] Dublin: Institute of Public Administration.

Curran, C. (1996) 'Fianna Fáil and the origins of the Irish Press'. *Irish Communications Review* 6, pp. 7–17.

Curran, D. and C. van Egeraat (2010) *Defining and valuing Dublin's creative industries*. Dublin: Dublin City Council, Office of International Relations and Research. [www.dublincity.ie/Planning/EconomicDevelopment/Documents/Creative_Industries_Final_Report._05.05.10.pdf]

Curry, J. (2003) *Irish social services*. Dublin: Institute of Public Administration.

Curtin, C. (1988) 'Social order, interpersonal relations and disputes in a West of Ireland community' in M. Tomlinson, T. Varley and C. McCullagh (eds) *Whose law and order? Aspects of crime and social control in Irish society*. Belfast: Sociological Association of Ireland.

Curtin, C. (1996) 'Back to the future? Communities and rural poverty' in C. Curtin et al. (eds) *Poverty in rural Ireland*. Dublin: Oak Tree.

Curtin, C. and C. Ryan (1989) 'Clubs, pubs and private houses in a Clare town' in C. Curtin and T. Wilson (eds) *Ireland from below: Social change and local communities*. Galway: Galway University Press.

Curtin, C. and T. Varley (1986) 'Bringing industry to a small town in the West of Ireland'. *Sociologia Ruralis* 26(2), pp. 170–85.

Curtin, C. and T. Wilson (1989) *Ireland from below: Social change and local communities*. Galway: Galway University Press.

Curtis, B. (2007) 'Working' in S. Matthewman, C. Lane West-Newman and B. Curtis (eds) *Being sociological*. Basingstoke: Palgrave Macmillan, pp. 67–86.

D'Andrea, A. (2010) 'You shouldn't bring the BlackBerry to the bedroom at night: Mobility and flexibility of high-tech professionals in the National Technology Park'. Field report, Nomadic Work/Life in the Knowledge Economy Project. Limerick: University of Limerick. [nwl.ul.ie/publication/DAndrea_2010_NTP_Report.pdf]

d'Haenens, L., N. Jankowski and A. Heuvelman (2004) 'News in online and print newspapers: Differences in reader consumption and recall'. *New Media and Society* 6(3), pp. 363–82.

Daly, M. (1997) *The spirit of earnest inquiry: The Statistical and Social Inquiry Society of Ireland 1847–1997*. Dublin: Institute of Public Administration.

Daly, M. (1998) 'The Statistical and Social Inquiry Society of Ireland' in K. Kennedy (ed.) *From famine to feast: Economic and social change in Ireland 1847–1997*. Dublin: Institute of Public Administration.

Daly, M. and M. Leonard (2002) *Against all odds: Family life on a low income in Ireland*. Dublin: Combat Poverty Agency.

Daniel, A. (1998) 'Trust and medical authority' in A. Petersen and C. Waddell (eds) *Health matters: A sociology of illness, prevention and care*. Buckingham: Open University Press.

Darmody, M. and S. McCoy (2011) 'Barriers to school involvement' in M. Darmody, N. Tyrrell and S. Strong (eds) *The changing faces of Ireland: Exploring the lives of immigrant and ethnic minority children*. Rotterdam: Sense, pp. 145–63.

Davies, B. (1990) *Frogs and snails and feminist tales: Preschool children and gender*. Sydney: Allen & Unwin.

Davies, P., P. Francis and C. Greer (2007) 'Victims, crime and society' in P. Davies, P. Francis and C. Greer (eds) *Victims, crime and society*. London: Sage.

Davis, A. and J. George (1993) *States of health: Health and illness in Australia*. Sydney: HarperCollins.

Day, E. (2010) 'Why reality TV works'. *The Observer*, 21 November. [http://www.guardian.co.uk/tv-and-radio/2010/nov/21/why-reality-tv-works]

Day, G. (1998) 'A community of communities? Similarity and difference in Welsh rural community studies'. *Economic and Social Review* 29(3), pp. 233–58.

de Guistino, D. (1995) 'Finding an archbishop: The Whigs and Richard Whately in 1831'. *Church History* 64(2), pp. 218–36.

De Tona, C. (2004) '"I remember when years ago in Italy": Nine Italian women in Dublin tell the diaspora'. *Women's Studies International Forum* 27(4). [Special Issue: Representing Migrant Women in Ireland and in the EU] pp. 315–34.

Delaney, L., A. Fernihough and J. Smith (2011) *Exporting poor health: The Irish in England.* [RAND Working Paper #863] [www.rand.org/content/dam/rand/pubs/working_papers/2011/RAND_WR863.pdf]

Demerath, N. (1998) 'Snatching defeat from victory in the decline of liberal Protestantism: Culture versus structure in institutional analysis' in N. Demerath, P. Hall, T. Schmitt and R. Williams (eds) *Sacred companies: Organizational aspects of religion and religious aspects of organizations.* Oxford: Oxford University Press, pp. 154–71.

Demerath, N., P. Hall, T. Schmitt and R. Williams (eds) (1998) *Sacred companies: Organizational aspects of religion and religious aspects of organizations.* Oxford: Oxford University Press

Department of Arts, Culture and the Gaeltacht (1995) *Active or passive? Broadcasting in the future tense.* [Green Paper on broadcasting] Dublin: Stationery Office.

Department of Education (1965) *Investment in education. Report of the survey team appointed by the Minister for Education in October, 1962.* Dublin: Stationery Office.

Department of Education and Science (2000) *Learning for life: White paper on adult education.* Dublin: Stationery Office.

Department of Health and Children (2002) *Strategic taskforce on alcohol: Interim report.* Dublin: Department of Health and Children. [www.doh.ie/pdfdocs/stfa.pdf]

DES [Department of Education and Science] (2005) *Survey of Traveller education provision: Inspectorate of the Department of Education and Science.* Dublin: Department of Education and Science.

DES [Department of Education and Skills] (2009) Department of Education and Skills statistics website. [http://www.education.ie/servlet/blobservlet/web_stats_08_09.pdf]

DES [Department of Education and Skills] (2011a) *National strategy for higher education to 2030.* [http://www.hea.ie/files/files/DES_Higher_Ed_Main_Report.pdf]

DES [Department of Education and Skills] (2011b) Department of Education and Skills statistics website. [http://www.education.ie/servlet/blobservlet/stat_web_stats_10_11.pdf]

DES [Department of Education and Skills] (2012) Department of Education and Skills statistics website. [www.cso.ie/px/des/database/des/des.asp]

Department of the Taoiseach (2006) *Report on active citizenship consultation process.* Dublin: Task Force on Active Citizenship, Department of An Taoiseach.

Department of the Taoiseach (2008) *Building Ireland's smart economy: A framework for sustainable economic renewal.* Dublin. [http://www.taoiseach.gov.ie/BuildingIrelands SmartEconomy_1_.pdf]

Devereux, E. (2003) *Understanding the media.* London: Sage.

Devereux, E., A. Haynes and M. Power (2011) 'Beyond the headlines: Media coverage of social exclusion in Limerick city – the case of Moyross' in N. Hourigan (ed.) *Understanding Limerick: Social exclusion and change*. Cork: Cork University Press.

Devlin, J. (1997) 'The state of health in Ireland' in J. Robins (ed.) *Reflections on health: Commemorating fifty years of the Department of Health 1947–1997*. Dublin: Department of Health.

DHC [Department of Health and Children] (2008) *National men's health policy 2008–2013*. Dublin: Stationery Office. [www.dohc.ie/publications/pdf/en_mens_health_policy.pdf?direct=1]

DHC [Department of Health and Children] (2009) *An integrating workforce planning strategy for the health services*. Dublin: Stationery Office. [www.dohc.ie/publications/pdf/workforce_planning_strategy.pdf?direct=1]

DHC [Department of Health and Children] (2010) *Health in Ireland: Key trends 2010*. Dublin: Stationery Office. [www.dohc.ie/publications/pdf/key_trends_2010.pdf?direct=1]

DHC [Department of Health and Children] (2011) *Health in Ireland: Key trends 2011*. Dublin: Stationery Office. [www.dohc.ie/publications/pdf/key_trends_2011.pdf?direct=1]

Dillon, L. (2001) *Drug use among prisoners: An exploratory study*. Dublin: Health Research Board.

Dixon, J. (2002) *Changing chicken: Chooks, cooks and culinary culture*. Sydney: University of New South Wales Press.

DJLR [Department of Justice and Law Reform] (2010) *White Paper on crime discussion document no. 3: 'Organised and white collar crime'*. Dublin: Department of Justice and Law Reform. [www.justice.ie/en/JELR/Pages/WPOC_Discussion_Doc_3]

Dobbelaere, K. (2011) 'The meaning and scope of secularization' in P. Clarke (ed.) *The Oxford handbook of the sociology of religion*. Oxford: Oxford University Press, pp. 599–615.

DoH [Department of Health] (1999) *Report of the tribunal of inquiry into the infection with HIV and hepatitis C of persons with haemophilia and related matters*. Dublin: Stationery Office. [www.dohc.ie/publications/lindsay.html]

Dolan, J. (2008) *The Irish Americans: A history*. London: Bloomsbury.

Dolan, P. (2009) 'Developing consumer subjectivity in Ireland: 1900–80'. *Journal of Consumer Culture* 9, pp. 117–41.

Doorley, P. (1998) 'Health status' in E. McAuliffe and L. Joyce (eds) *A healthier future? Managing healthcare in Ireland*. Dublin: Institute of Public Administration.

Dörre, K. (2006) 'Precarity – the cause and effects of insecure employment'. *Arbeit(s)leben im wandel*. Goethe Institut. [www.geothe.de/soz/arb/pre/en1870532.htm]

Drazin, A. and P. Garvey (2009) 'Design and having designs in Ireland'. *Anthropology in Action/Irish Journal of Anthropology* 16 [special issue on 'Anthropology, design and technology in Ireland'] pp. 4–18.

Drudy, P. (1995) 'From protectionism to enterprise: A review of Irish industrial policy' in A. Burke (ed.) *Enterprise and the Irish economy*. Dublin: Oak Tree.

Drudy, S. (1991) 'Developments in the sociology of education in Ireland 1966–1991'. *Irish Journal of Sociology* 1, pp. 107–27.

Drudy, S. and K. Lynch (1993) *Schools and society in Ireland*. Dublin: Gill & Macmillan.

Duffy, M. (2011) *Making care count: A century of gender, race, and paid care work*. New Brunswick, NJ: Rutgers University Press.

Duncan, M, P. Rouse and E. Reilly (2010) 'Dr Pauline Garvey' in *Mosaic: A celebration of Irish research in the humanities and social sciences*. Dublin: Irish Research Council for the Humanities and Social Sciences, pp. 56–9. [www.irchss.ie/IRCHSS%2010%20 Event%20Page/Mosaic%20(Dublin,%202010).pdf]

Dunlevy, M. (1989) *Dress in Ireland*. London: Batsford.

Durkheim, E. (1964) *The rules of sociological method*. New York: The Free Press.

Dwyer, M. and P. Taaffe (1998) 'Nursing in 21st century Ireland: Opportunities for transformation' in A. Leahy and M. Wiley (eds) *The Irish health system in the 21st century*. Dublin: Oak Tree.

Ecklund, E. and E. Long (2011) 'Scientists and spirituality'. *Sociology of Religion* 72(3), pp. 253–74.

Economist (2011) 'The embarrassment of riches: Which nation is the most generous giver of Christmas presents?' [Daily chart, 12 December] [www.economist.com/blogs/ graphicdetail/2011/12/daily-chart-1]

Edley, N. and M. Wetherell (1995) *Men in perspective: Practice, power and identity*. London: Prentice Hall.

Edmondson, R. (1997) 'Older people and life-course construction' in A. Cleary and M. Treacy (eds) *The sociology of health and illness in Ireland*. Dublin: University College Dublin Press.

Eipper, C. (1986) *The ruling trinity: A community study of church, state and business in Ireland*. Aldershot: Gower.

Eipper, C. (2011) 'The spectre of Godlessness: Making sense of secularity'. *Australian Journal of Anthropology* 22(1), pp. 14–39.

Entwistle, J. (2000a) *The fashioned body: Fashion, dress and modern social theory*. Cambridge: Polity.

Entwistle, J. (2000b) 'Fashion as culture industry'. *Consumers, commodities, and consumption newsletter* 1(2). [web.archive.org/web/20040413132555/http://socrates. berkeley.edu/~nalinik/newslett/n0004_entwistle.html]

Entwistle, J. and E. Wilson (eds) (2001) *Body dressing*. Oxford: Berg.

Etzioni, A. (1995) *The spirit of community*. London: Fontana.

Eurofound [European Foundation for the Improvement of Living and Working Conditions] (2008) *Who stays, who goes?* Dublin: Eurofound. [www.eurofound. europa.eu/pubdocs/2008/892/en/1/EF08892EN.pdf]

Eurofound [European Foundation for the Improvement of Living and Working Conditions] (2011) *Youth and work – Foundation findings*. Dublin: Eurofound. [www.eurofound.europa.eu/pubdocs/2011/40/en/2/EF1140EN.pdf]

Eurostat (2011) *Labour market statistics* [Eurostat pocketbook]. Luxembourg: Publications Office of the European Union. [epp. eurostat.ec.europa.eu/cache/ITY_OFFPUB/KS-32-11-798/EN/KS-32-11-798-EN.PDF]

Evans, J. (2008) 'A brave new world? How genetic technology could change us' in J. Goodwin and J. Jasper (eds) *The Contexts reader*. New York: Norton, pp. 353–60.

Fagan, H. (1995) *Culture, politics and Irish school dropouts*. Westport, CT/London: Bergin & Garvey.

Fahey, T. (1987) 'Nuns in the Catholic Church in Ireland in the nineteenth century' in M. Cullen (ed.) *Girls don't do honours: Irish women in education in the 19th and 20th centuries*. Dublin: Women's Education Bureau.

Fahey, T. (1994) 'Catholicism and industrial society in Ireland' in J. Goldthorpe and C. Whelan (eds) *The development of industrial society in Ireland*. Oxford: Oxford University Press/The British Academy.

Fahey, T. (2002) 'Is atheism increasing? Ireland and Europe compared' in E. Cassidy (ed.) *Measuring Ireland: Discerning values and beliefs*. Dublin: Veritas, pp. 46–66.

Fahey, T. and C. Field (2008) *Families in Ireland: Analysis of patterns and change*. Dublin: Stationery Office. [www.welfare.ie/EN/Policy/PolicyPublications/Families/Documents/Familes%20in%20Ireland%20-%20An%20Analysis%20of%20Patterns%20and%20Trends.pdf]

Fahey, T. and R. Layte (eds) (2007) 'Family and sexuality' in T. Fahey, H. Russell and C. Whelan, *The best of times? The social impact of the Celtic Tiger*. Dublin: Institute of Public Administration.

Fahey, T., B. Hayes and R. Sinnott (2005) *Conflict and consensus: A study of values and attitudes in the Republic of Ireland and Northern Ireland*. Dublin: Institute of Public Administration.

Fahey, T., B. Maitre, B. Nolan and C. Whelan (2007) *A social portrait of older people in Ireland*. Dublin: Stationery Office.

Fahey, T., M. Norris, D. McCafferty and E. Humphreys (2011) *Combating social disadvantage in social housing estates: The policy implications of a ten-year follow-up study*. [Combat Poverty Agency Working Paper Series 11/02] Dublin. Combat Poverty Agency.

Fairweather, J. and H. Campbell (1990) *Public drinking and social organisation in Methven and Mt Somers*. Canterbury (NZ): Agribusiness and Economics Research Unit, Lincoln University.

Fanning, B. (2002) *Racism and social change in the Republic of Ireland*. Manchester: Manchester University Press.

Farrell, F. and P. Watt (eds) (2001) *Responding to racism in Ireland*. Dublin: Veritas.

FBI [Federal Bureau of Investigation] (2009) *Crime in the United States*. Table 1. [www2.fbi.gov/ucr/cius2009/data/table_01.html]

Ferriter, D. (1999) *A nation of extremes: The Pioneers in twentieth-century Ireland*. Dublin: Irish Academic Press.

Ferriter, D. (2009) *Occasions of sin: Sex and society in modern Ireland*. London: Profile.

Findlater, A. (2001) *Findlaters: The story of a Dublin merchant family, 1774–2001*. Dublin: Farmar.

FinFacts (2010) 'Irish GDP will expand 0.6% in 2010 and GNP will contract 0.5%'. [www.finfacts.ie/irishfinancenews/article_1018904.shtml]

Finnegan, R. (2002) 'Irish-American relations' in W. Crotty and D. Schmitt (eds) *Ireland on the world stage*. London: Longman.

Fischer, C. (2010) 'Compared to what?' *Contexts* 9(4), p. 84.

Fisher, A. (2009) 'When Gen X runs the show' in *Time* magazine feature 'The future of work'. [www.time.com/time/specials/packages/article/0,28804,1898024_1898023_1898086,00.html]

Fiske, J. (1992) 'Cultural studies and the culture of everyday life' in L. Grossberg, C. Nelson and P. Treichler (eds) *Cultural studies*. London: Routledge.

Fiske, J., B. Hodge and G. Turner (1987) *Myths of Oz: Reading Australian popular culture*. Sydney: Allen & Unwin.

Fitzpatrick Associates and P. O'Connell (2005) *A review of higher education participation in 2003*. Dublin: Higher Education Authority.

Fives, A., D. Kennan, J. Canavan, B. Brady and D. Cairns (2010) *Study of young carers in the Irish population: Main report*. Dublin: Stationery Office. [www.dcya.gov.ie/documents/publications/StudyofYoungCarers-Main.pdf]

Foley, M. (2010) 'Media landscape: Ireland'. European Journalism Centre. [www.ejc.net/media-landscape/article/Ireland]

Forfás (2010) *Future skills needs of the wholesale and retail sector*. [Expert Group on Future Skills Needs] Dublin: Government Publications. [www.forfas.ie/media/EGFSN%20Wholesale%20Retail%20ONLINE%20FINAL.pdf]

Foucault, M. (1973) *The birth of the clinic: An archaeology of medical perception*. New York: Vintage.

Fox, J. and E. Tabory (2008) 'Contemporary evidence regarding the impact of state regulation of religion on religious participation and belief.' *Sociology of Religion* 69(3), pp. 245–71.

Fox, N. (1998) 'Postmodernism and "health"' in A. Petersen and C. Waddell (eds) *Health matters: A sociology of illness, prevention and care*. Buckingham: Open University Press.

Fox, R. (1978) *The Tory Islanders: A people of the Celtic fringe*. Cambridge: Cambridge University Press.

Frank, A. (1967) 'The development of underdevelopment'. *Monthly Review*, September, pp. 17–30.

French, J. and B. Raven (1959) 'The bases of social power' in D. Cartwright and A. Zander (eds) *Group dynamics*. New York: Harper & Row.

Friel, S. and C. Conlon (2004) *Food poverty and policy*. Dublin: Combat Poverty Agency/Crosscare/St Vincent de Paul. [www.cpa.ie/health/foodpoverty/]

Friel, S., O. Walsh and D. McCarthy (2004) *The financial cost of healthy eating in Ireland*. [Working paper 04/01] Dublin: Combat Poverty Agency.

Fuller, L. (2002) *Irish Catholicism since 1950: The undoing of a culture*. Dublin: Gill & Macmillan.

Fuller, L. (2005) 'Religion, politics and socio-cultural change in twentieth century Ireland'. *The European Legacy* 10(1), pp. 41–54.

Gaffney, M. (2011) *Flourishing*. Dublin: Penguin.

Gallie, D. (2011) 'Changing perspectives in British economic sociology'. *Sociological Research Online* 16/3/19. [http://www.socresonline.org.uk/16/3/19.html]

Galligan, Y. (1998a) *Women and politics in contemporary Ireland*. London: Pinter.

Galligan, Y. (1998b) 'The changing role of women' in W. Crotty and D. Schmitt (eds) *Ireland and the politics of change*. London/New York: Longman.

Gamson, J. (2001) 'Normal sins: Sex scandal narratives as institutional morality tales'. *Social Problems* 48(2), pp. 185–205.

Gamson, W. and A. Modigliani (1989) 'Media discourse and public opinion on nuclear power: A constructivist approach'. *American Journal of Sociology* 95(1), pp. 1–37.

Gans, H. (2010) 'Making sociology more socially useful'. *Contexts* 9(2), p. 88.

Garavan, M. (2006) 'Seeking a real argument' in M. Corcoran and M. Peillon (eds) *Uncertain Ireland: A sociological chronicle, 2003–2004*. Dublin: Institute of Public Administration.

Garvey, P. (2011) 'Consuming Ikea: Inspiration as material form' in A. Clarke (ed.) *Design anthropology: Object culture in the 21st century*. Vienna/New York: Springer.

Garvin, T. (1998) 'Patriots and republicans: An Irish evolution' in W. Crotty and D. Schmitt (eds) *Ireland and the politics of change*. London/New York: Longman.

Garvin, T. (2004) *Preventing the future: Why was Ireland so poor for so long?* Dublin: Gill & Macmillan.

Garvin, T. (2012) 'The assault on intellectuals in Irish higher education' in M.P. Corcoran, K. Lalor and J. Maguire (eds) *Public intellectuals at a time of crisis*. Dublin: Royal Irish Academy.

Garvin, T. and A. Hess (2006) 'Introduction: Tyranny in Ireland?' in G. de Beaumont, *Ireland: Social, political and religious*. Cambridge, MA: Harvard University Press.

Geary, R. (1951) 'Irish economic development since the Treaty'. *Studies* Xl(160), pp. 399–419.

Geddes, M. (2000) 'Tackling social exclusion in the European Union: The limits of the new orthodoxy of local partnership'. *International Journal of Urban and Regional Research* 24(4), pp. 782–800.

Geddes, M. and J. Benington (2001) 'Social exclusion and partnership in the European Union' in M. Geddes and J. Benington (eds) *Local partnerships and social exclusion in the European Union: New forms of local social governance?* London: Routledge, pp. 15–45.

Gibbon, P. (1973) 'Arensberg and Kimball revisited'. *Economy and Society* 4, pp. 479–98.

Gibbons, L. (2007) 'Finding integration through engaging with our past'. *Irish Times*, 29 October.

Giddens, A. (1994) *Beyond left and right: The future of radical politics*. Cambridge: Polity.

Giddens, A. (2006) *Sociology*. Cambridge: Polity.

Gillespie, M. (1995) *Television, ethnicity and cultural change*. London: Routledge.

Gilligan, R. et al. (2010) *In the front line of integration: Young people managing migration to Ireland*. Dublin: Trinity Immigration Initiative.

Gladwell, M. (2010) 'Small change: Why the revolution will not be tweeted'. *The New Yorker*, 4 October. [www.newyorker.com/reporting/2010/10/04/101004fa_fact_gladwell]

Gmelch, S. (1989) 'From poverty subculture to political lobby: The Traveller rights movement in Ireland' in C. Curtin and T. Wilson (eds) *Ireland from below: Social change and local communities*. Galway: Galway University Press.

Goffman, E. (1961). *Asylums*. Harmondsworth: Penguin.

Goldthorpe, J. and others (1968–9) *The affluent worker in the class structure*. [3 vols] Cambridge: Cambridge University Press.

Grabowska-Lusiska, I. (2005) 'Changes in the international mobility of labour: Job migration of the Polish nationals to Ireland.' *Irish Journal of Sociology* 14(1), pp. 27–44.

Greeley, A. (1999) 'The religions of Ireland' in A. Heath, R. Breen and C. Whelan (eds) *Ireland north and south: Perspectives from social science*. Oxford: Oxford University Press.

Greenslade, R. (2010a) 'Newspapers in peril as trends change in age of new media'. *Irish Times*, 4 January.

Greenslade, R. (2010b) 'Irish newspapers fall away'. Greenslade blog. [www.guardian. co.uk/media/greenslade/2010/aug/19/newspapers-ireland]

Gregg, M. (2011) *Work's intimacy*. Cambridge: Polity.

Griffin-Foley, B. (2004) 'Reality TV: From *Tit-Bits* to *Big Brother*: A century of audience participation in the media'. *Media, Culture and Society* 26(4), pp. 533–48.

Griffin, M. and P. Kelleher (2010) 'Uncertain futures: Men on the margins in Limerick city'. *Irish Probation Journal* 7, pp. 24–45.

Grint, K. (2005) *The sociology of work*. Cambridge: Polity.

Gripsrud, J. (1995) *The Dynasty years: Hollywood television and critical media studies*. London: Routledge.

Guinnane, T. (1997) *The vanishing Irish: Households, migration and the rural economy in Ireland, 1850–1914*. Princeton: Princeton University Press.

Habermas, J. (1971) *Towards a rational society*. London: Heinemann.

Habermas, J. (1989) *The structural transformation of the public sphere*. Cambridge: Polity.

Halikiopoulou, D. (2011) *Patterns of secularization: Church, state and nation in Greece and the Republic of Ireland*. Farnham: Ashgate.

Halman, L. and V. Draulans (2006) 'How secular is Europe?'. *British Journal of Sociology* 57(2), pp. 263–88.

Halton, E. (2008) *The great brain suck and other American epiphanies*. Chicago: University of Chicago Press.

Hamid, N., L. Daly and P. Fitzpatrick (2011) *All Ireland Traveller Health Study: Our geels – the birth cohort study follow up*. Dublin: Department of Public Health, Physiotherapy and Population Science, University College Dublin. [www.dohc.ie/ publications/aiths_follow_up.html]

Hanagan, M. (1998) 'Irish transnational social movements, deterritorialized migrants and the state system: The last one hundred and forty years'. *Mobilization* 3(1), pp. 107–26.

Hanlon, G. (1991) 'The emigration of Irish accountants: Economic restructuring and producer services in the periphery'. *Irish Journal of Sociology* 1, pp. 52–65.

Hannan, D., B. McCabe and S. McCoy (1998) *Trading qualifications for jobs: Overeducation and the Irish labour market*. Dublin: Oak Tree/Economic and Social Research Institute.

Hannan, D., E. Smyth, J. McCullagh, R. O'Leary and D. McMahon (1996) *Coeducation and gender equality: Exam performance, stress and personal development*. Dublin: Oak Tree/Economic and Social Research Institute.

Harris, L. (1984) 'Class, community and sexual divisions in North Mayo' in C. Curtin et al. (eds) *Culture and ideology in Ireland*. Galway: Galway University Press.

Haughton, J. (1995) 'The historical background' in J. O'Hagan (ed.) *The economy of Ireland*. Dublin: Gill & Macmillan.

Hayes, M. (2006) *Irish Travellers: Representations and realities*. Dublin: Liffey.

Hayles, N. (1995) 'The life cycle of cyborgs' in C. Hay (ed.) *The cyborg handbook*. London: Routledge.

Hazelkorn, E. (1980) 'Capital and the Irish question'. *Science and Society* 44(3), pp. 326–56.

Hazelkorn, E. (1991) 'British labour and Irish capital: Evidence from the 1980s' in Galway Labour History Group (ed.) *The emigrant experience: Papers presented at the second annual Mary Murray Weekend seminar*. Galway: Galway Labour History Group.

Hazelkorn, E. (1996) 'New technologies and changing work practices in the media industry: The case of Ireland'. *Irish Communications Review* 6, pp. 28–38.

Hederman O'Brien, M. (1998) 'Healthcare – the context' in E. McAuliffe and L. Joyce (eds) *A healthier future? Managing healthcare in Ireland*. Dublin: Institute of Public Administration.

Held, D., A. McGrew, D. Goldblatt and J. Perraton (1999) *Global transformations*. Cambridge: Polity.

Hess, A. (2000) 'Introduction: After success – the politics of civil society'. *Soundings* 16, pp. 90–5.

Hess, A. (2007) 'Against unspoilt authenticity: A re-appraisal of Helmuth Plessner's *The Limits of Community* (1924)'. *Irish Journal of Sociology* 16(2), pp. 11–26.

Hettne, B. (1990) *Development theory and the three worlds*. Harlow: Longman.

Higgins, M. (2004) 'Culture, democracy and public service broadcasting' in M. Corcoran and M. O'Brien (eds) *Censorship and the democratic state*. Dublin: Four Courts.

Higgins, M.D. (2006) 'The limits of clientelism: Towards an assessment of Irish politics' (1982). Reprinted in *Causes for concern*. Dublin: Liberties Press, pp. 73–96.

Higgins, M.D. (2011) 'Presidential inauguration', *Irish Times*, 12 November.

Hill, M. (2005) *Bibliography of Martineau's writings on Ireland*. [www.sociological-origins. com/HMSSIrishCD.html]

Hillery, G. (1955) 'Definitions of community: Areas of agreement'. *Rural Sociology* 20(2), pp. 111–23.

Hochschild, A. (2003) *The managed heart: Commercialization of human feeling*. [rev. ed] Berkeley: University of California Press.

Hodgins, M. and C. Kelleher (1997) 'Health and well-being in social care workers'. *Women's Studies Review* 5, pp. 37–48.

Hoffman, J. (1998) 'Confidence in religious institutions and secularization: Trends and implications'. *Review of Religious Research* 39(4), pp. 321–43.

Hoffman, L. (2006) 'Is internet content different after all? A content analysis of mobilizing information in online and print newspapers'. *Journalism and Mass Communication Quarterly* 83(1), pp. 58–76.

Honoré, C. (2004) *In praise of slow*. London: Orion.

Horgan, J. (2001) *Irish media: A critical history since 1922*. London/New York: Routledge.

Hornsby-Smith, M. (1992) 'Social and religious transformations in Ireland: A case of secularisation?' in J. Goldthorpe and C. Whelan (eds) *The development of industrial society in Ireland*. Oxford: Oxford University Press, pp. 265–90.

Hornsby-Smith, M. and C. Whelan (1994) 'Religious and moral values' in C. Whelan (ed.) *Values and social change in Ireland*. Dublin: Gill & Macmillan.

Houghton, F., N. Keane, N. Murphy, S. Houghton and C. Dunne (2010) 'Tertiary level students and the Mental Health Index (MHI-5) in Ireland'. *Irish Journal of Applied Social Studies* 10(1), pp. 40–8. [arrow.dit.ie/ijass/vol10/iss1/7]

Hourigan, N. (ed.) (2011) *Understanding Limerick: Social exclusion and change*. Cork: Cork University Press.

Hourigan, N. and M. Campbell (2010) *The TEACH report: Traveller education and adults: Crisis, challenge and change*. Athlone: National Association of Travellers' Centres. [cora.ucc.ie/bitstream/10468/254/1/NMH_TEACHPV2010.pdf]

Hourihane, A. (2000) *She moves through the boom*. Dublin: Sitric.

Hug, C. (1999) *The politics of sexual morality in Ireland*. London: Macmillan.

Humphreys, A. (1966) *The new Dubliners: Urbanisation and the Irish family*. London: Routledge and Kegan Paul.

Humphreys, E. (2007) 'Social capital in disadvantaged neighbourhoods: A diversion from needs or a real contribution to the debate on area-based regeneration?' *Irish Journal of Sociology*, 16(2), pp. 50–76.

Hyde, A. (1997) 'The medicalisation of childbearing norms: Encounters between unmarried pregnant women and medical personnel in an Irish context' in A. Cleary and M. Treacy (eds) *The sociology of health and illness in Ireland*. Dublin: University College Dublin Press.

Hyde, A. and E. Howlett (2004) *Understanding teenage sexuality in Ireland*. [Report no. 9] Dublin: Crisis Pregnancy Agency.

Hyde, A., M. Lohan and O. McDonnell (2004) *Sociology for health professionals in Ireland*. Dublin: Institute of Public Administration.

IDA [Industrial Development Authority] (2010) *IDA Ireland annual report and accounts 2010*. [www.idaireland.com/news-media/publications/annual-reports/pdfs/IDA-Annual-Report_2010.pdf]

IDA Ireland (2012) [www.idaireland.ie]

Illich, I. (1976) *Limits to medicine*. London: Marion Boyars.

Inglehart, R. (2009) 'Cultural change, religion, subjective well-being, and democracy in Latin America' in F. Hagopian (ed.) *Religious pluralism, democracy, and the Catholic Church in Latin America*. Notre Dame: University of Notre Dame Press, pp. 67–95.

Inglis, T. (1987) *Moral monopoly: The Catholic Church in modern Irish society*. Dublin: Gill & Macmillan.

Inglis, T. (1998a) *Moral monopoly: The rise and fall of the Catholic Church in modern Ireland*. Dublin: University College Dublin Press.

Inglis, T. (1998b) *Lessons in Irish sexuality*. Dublin: University College Dublin Press.

Inglis, T. (1998c) 'A religious frenzy' in M. Peillon and E. Slater (eds) *Encounters with modern Ireland*. Dublin: Institute of Public Administration.

Inglis, T. (1998d) 'Foucault, Bourdieu and the field of Irish sexuality'. *Irish Journal of Sociology* 7, pp. 5–28.

Inglis, T. (1998e) 'From sexual repression to liberation?' in M. Peillon and E. Slater (eds) *Encounters with modern Ireland*. Dublin: Institute of Public Administration.

Inglis, T. (2002) 'Pleasure pursuits' in M. Corcoran and M. Peillon (eds) *Ireland unbound: A turn of the century chronicle*. Dublin: Institute of Public Administration.

Inglis, T. (2007) 'Individualisation and secularisation in Catholic Ireland' in S. O'Sullivan (ed.) *Contemporary Ireland: A sociological map*. Dublin: University College Dublin Press.

INM [Independent News and Media] (2011) *Annual report 2010*. [www.inmplc.com/reports/uploads/INM_Annual_Report_2010.pdf]

Institute of Public Health in Ireland (2007) *Consultations in relation to all-Ireland Traveller health study*. [www.publichealth.ie]

IPS [Irish Prison Service] (2010) *Annual report 2009*. Dublin: Stationery Office. [www.irishprisons.ie/documents/AnnualReport2009PDF.pdf]

Irish Catholic Bishops' Conference (2009) *The cry of the earth*. Dublin: Veritas. [www.catholicbishops.ie/wp-content/uploads/images/stories/features/Cry_of_the_Earth/env_pastoral_09_long_final.pdf]

Irish Catholic Bishops' Conference (2010) *40 years of social research*. [www.catholicbishops.ie/2010/11/05/feature-40-years-of-social-research]

Irish Catholic Bishops' Conference (2011a) '22 new seminarians begin studies for the priesthood for Irish dioceses'. Press release. [www.catholicbishops.ie/2011/08/29/22-seminarians-studies-priesthood-irish-dioceses]

Irish Catholic Bishops' Conference (2011b) *From crisis to hope: Working to achieve the common good*. Maynooth: Council for Justice and Peace. [www.catholicbishops.ie/2011/02/21/from-crisis-to-hope-working-to-achieve-the-common-good]

Irish Social Media Statistics (2011) May 2011. [www.neworldblog.ie]

Irish Universities Nutrition Alliance (2001) *North/South Ireland food consumption survey: Summary report on food and nutrient intakes, anthropometry, attitudinal data physical activity patterns*. Dublin: Food Safety Promotion Board.

ITU [International Telecommunications Union] (2008) *Use of information and communication technology by the world's children and youth*. Geneva: International Telecommunications Union. [www.itu.int/ITU-D/ict/material/Youth_2008.pdf]

Jackson, J. (1998) 'Social science in Ireland'. Unpublished paper for the Sociology Department, Trinity College Dublin.

Jackson, J. (2004) 'Research policy and practice in Ireland: A historical perspective' in M. MacLachlan and M. Caball (eds) *Social science in a knowledge society: Research policy in Ireland*. Dublin: Liffey.

Jacobs, J. (1989) *The death and life of great American cities*. New York: Vintage.

Jacobson, D. (1989) 'Theorising Irish industrialisation: The case of the motor industry.' *Science and Society* 53(2), pp. 165–91.

Jamieson, L., D. Morgan, G. Crow and G. Allan (2006) 'Friends, neighbours and distance partners: Extending or decentring family relationships?' *Sociological Research Online* 11(3). [www.socresonline.org.uk/11/3/jamieson.html]

Jenkins, E. (1999) *Tongue first: Adventures in physical culture*. London: Virago.

JNLR (2011) Figures for April 2010 – March 2011. Dublin: Ispsos MRBI.

Jones, B. (1982) *Sleepers wake! Technology and the future of work*. Melbourne: Oxford University Press.

Jorgensen, A. (2006) 'Fields of knowledge' in M. Corcoran and M. Peillon (eds) *Uncertain Ireland: A sociological chronicle, 2003–2004*. Dublin: Institute of Public Administration.

Kane, E. (1996) 'The power of paradigms: Social science and intellectual contributions to public discourse in Ireland' in L. O'Dowd (ed.) *On intellectuals and intellectual life in Ireland*. Belfast: Institute of Irish Studies/Royal Irish Academy.

Kavanagh, J. (1954) *Manual of social ethics*. Dublin: Gill.

Keane, J. (1988) *Civil society and the state*. London: Verso.

Keane, J. (1998) *Civil society: Old images, new visions*. Cambridge: Polity.

Kearns, K. (1996) *Dublin pub life and lore: An oral history*. Dublin: Gill & Macmillan.

Keating, P. and D. Desmond (1993) *Culture and capitalism in contemporary Ireland.* Aldershot: Avebury.

Keenan, M. (2011) *Child sexual abuse and the Catholic Church: Gender, power, organizational culture.* New York: Oxford University Press.

Kelleher, C. (1997) 'Preface'. *Women's Studies Review* 5, pp. vii–viii.

Kelleher, P. and P. O'Connor (2011) 'Men on the margins: Masculinities in disadvantaged areas in Limerick city' in N. Hourigan (ed.) *Understanding Limerick: Social exclusion and change.* Cork: Cork University Press.

Kelley, A. (2006) 'Ireland's "crack" habit: Explaining the faux Irish pub revolution'. *Slate* 16, March. [www.slate.com]

Kelley, P. et al. (1997) 'Children's accounts of risk'. *Childhood* 4(3), pp. 305–24.

Kelly, F. (1998) *Early Irish farming: A study based mainly on the law-texts of the 7th and 8th centuries AD.* Dublin: Dublin Institute of Advanced Studies.

Kelly, M. and B. O'Connor (eds) (1997) *Media audiences in Ireland: Power and cultural identity.* Dublin: University College Dublin Press.

Kelly, M. and B. Rolston (1995) 'Broadcasting in Ireland – issues of national identity and censorship' in P. Clancy et al. (eds) *Irish society: Sociological perspectives.* Dublin: Institute of Public Administration.

Kennedy, F. (2001) *Cottage to crèche: Family change in Ireland.* Dublin: Institute of Public Administration.

Kenny, C. (2011) 'Starting today: Generation emigration'. *Irish Times*, 21 October.

Keogh, B. and C. O'Lynn (2007) 'Gender-based barriers for male student nurses in general nursing education programs: An Irish perspective' in C. O'Lynn and R. Tranbarger (eds) *Men in nursing: History, challenges, and opportunities.* New York: Springer, pp. 194–204.

Keogh, D. (1998) *Jews in twentieth century Ireland: Refugees, anti-Semitism and the Holocaust.* Cork: Cork University Press.

Keohane, K. and C. Kuhling (2004) 'The "gift" relationship and Irish consumerism' in M. Peillon and M. Corcoran (eds) *Place and non-place: The reconfiguration of Ireland.* Dublin: Institute of Public Administration.

Kerkhofs, J. (2005) 'Reorganizing the parish: A horizon of kindly light.' *The Furrow* 56(4), pp. 195–207.

Kepel, G. (1994) *The revenge of God: The resurgence of Islam, Christianity and Judaism in the modern world.* Cambridge: Polity.

Kern, S. (1983) 'The future' in *The culture of time and space 1880–1918.* Cambridge, MA: Harvard University Press, pp. 89–108.

Kerr, A. (2006) *The business and culture of digital games: Gamework/gameplay.* London: Sage.

Kilkelly, U. (2006) *Youth justice in Ireland: Tough lives, rough justice.* Dublin: Irish Academic Press.

Kimmel, M. (2008) *Guyland.* New York: HarperCollins.

King-O'Riain, R. (2006) 'Miss China Ireland' in M.P. Corcoran and M. Peillon (eds) *Uncertain Ireland.* Dublin: Institute of Public Administration.

Kirby, P. (1984) *Is Irish Catholicism dying?* Cork: Mercier.

Kirby, P. (1997) *Poverty amid plenty: World and Irish development reconsidered.* Dublin: Gill & Macmillan/Trócaire.

Kirby, P. (2002) *The Celtic Tiger in distress: Growth with inequality in Ireland.* Basingstoke: Palgrave.

Kirby, P. and M. Murphy (2011) *Towards the second republic: Irish politics after the Celtic Tiger.* London: Pluto Ireland.

Kitchin, R., M. Boyle and D. Ancien (2011) 'Ireland's diaspora strategy: The quiet policy of obligation and opportunity' in M. Gilmartin and A. White (eds) *Ireland's migrations: Ireland in a global world.* Manchester: Manchester University Press.

Kluth, A. (2006) 'Among the audience'. *The Economist,* 20 April.

Komito, L. (1984) 'Irish clientelism: A reappraisal'. *Economic and Social Review* 15(3), pp. 173–94.

Kropiwiec, K. and R. Chiyoko King-O'Riain (2006) *Polish migrant workers in Ireland.* Dublin: National Consultative Committee on Racism and Interculturalism. [Community Profiles Series]

Kuhling, C. (1998) 'New Age Travellers on Cool Mountain' in M. Peillon and E. Slater (eds) *Encounters with modern Ireland.* Dublin: Institute of Public Administration.

Kuhling, C. (2004) *The New Age ethic and the spirit of postmodernity.* Cresskill, NJ: Hampton.

Kuhling, C. and K. Keohane (2007) *Cosmopolitan Ireland: Globalisation and quality of life.* London: Pluto.

Kumar, K. (1995) *From post-industrial to post-modern society.* Oxford: Blackwell.

Lace, S. (2005) *The glass consumer: Life in a surveillance society.* Bristol: Policy/National Consumer Council.

Lambe, M. (2001) 'At the cross: A shop in rural Ireland 1880–1911' in D. Cronin, J. Gilligan and K. Holton (eds) *Irish fairs and markets: Studies in local history.* Dublin: Four Courts.

Langer, J. (1992) *Emerging sociology: An international perspective.* Aldershot: Avebury.

Langman, L. (1992) 'Neon cages – shopping for subjectivity' in R. Shields (ed.) *Lifestyle shopping: The subject of consumption.* London: Routledge.

Larragy, J. (2006) 'Origins and significance of the community and voluntary pillar in Irish social partnership'. *Economic and Social Review* 37(3), pp. 375–98.

Larsson, A. (2008) 'Textbooks, syllabuses and disciplinary formation in Sweden'. *Current Sociology* 56(2), pp. 235–51.

Lash, S. and J. Urry (1994) *Economies of signs and space.* London: Sage.

Laszewski, C. (2008) 'The sociologists' take on the environment'. *Contexts* 7(2), pp. 20–5.

Layte, R. (2010) *A good news story about Irish health care.* ESRI Bulletin. Dublin: Economic and Social Research Institute.

Layte, R., H. McGee, A. Quail, K. Rundle, G. Cousins, C. Donnelly, F. Mulcahy and R. Conroy (2006) *The Irish study of sexual health and relationships.* Dublin: Crisis Pregnancy Agency.

Lee, J. (1989) *Ireland 1912–1985: Politics and society.* Cambridge: Cambridge University Press.

Lee, J., F. Bean and K. Sloane (2003) 'Beyond black and white: Remaking race in America'. *Contexts* 2(3), pp. 26–33.

Leeuwis, C. (1989) *Marginalisation misunderstood: Different patterns of farm development in the west of Ireland.* Wageningen: Wageningen Agricultural University.

Leith, W. (2010) 'Why it doesn't add up'. *Financial Times,* 8–9 May.

Lentin, R. (1998) '"Irishness", the 1937 Constitution, and citizenship: A gender and ethnicity view'. *Irish Journal of Sociology* 8, pp. 5–24.

Lentin, R. (1999) 'Racializing our Dark Rosaleen: Feminism, citizenship, racism, antisemitism'. *Women's Studies Review* 6, pp. 1–17.

Lentin, R. and R. McVeigh (eds) (2002) *Racism and anti-racism in Ireland*. Belfast: Beyond the Pale.

Leonard, M. (2006) 'Sectarian childhoods in North Belfast' in M. Corcoran and M. Peillon (eds) *Uncertain Ireland*. Dublin: Institute of Public Administration.

Levitt, P. and B. Nadya Jaworsky (2007) 'Transnational migration studies: Past developments and future trends'. *Annual Review of Sociology* 33, pp. 129–56.

Lewis, J. and A. Weigert (1981) 'The structures and meanings of social life'. *Social Forces* 60(2), pp. 432–62.

Leyden, B. (2002) *The home place*. Dublin: New Island.

Leyton, E. (1966) 'Conscious models and dispute regulation in an Ulster village'. *Man* [new series] 1, pp. 534–42.

Leyton, E. (1975) *The one blood: Kinship and class in an Irish village*. Newfoundland: Institute of Social and Economic Research.

Linehan, D. (2007) ' "For the way we live today" consumption, lifestyle and place' in B. Bartley and R. Kitchin (eds) *Understanding contemporary Ireland*. London: Pluto. [www.ucc.ie/en/media/Linehan0701.pdf]

Linehan, H. (2012) 'A window on the nation or a mirror of our own society?' *Irish Times*, 7 January.

Liston, K. (2002) 'The gendered field of Irish sport' in M. Corcoran and M. Peillon (eds) *Ireland unbound: A turn of the century chronicle*. Dublin: Institute of Public Administration.

Livingstone, S. (2008) 'Taking risk opportunities in youthful content creation: Teenagers' use of social networking sites for intimacy, privacy and self-expression'. *New Media and Society* 10(3), pp. 395–411.

Lodge, A. (2005) 'Gender and children's social world: Esteemed and marginalised masculinities in the primary school playground'. *Irish Journal of Sociology* 14(2), pp. 177–92.

Lodge, T. (2009) *Response comments at symposium on public intellectuals at a time of crisis*. Dublin: Royal Irish Academy.

Luibheid, E. (2004) 'Childbearing against the state? Asylum seeker women in the Irish republic'. *Women's Studies International Forum* 27(4). [Special Issue: Representing Migrant Women in Ireland and in the EU], pp. 335–49.

Lunn, P. and T. Fahey (2011) *Households and family structures in Ireland: A detailed statistical analysis of census 2006*. Dublin: Economic and Social Research Institute.

Lunn, P., T. Fahey and C. Hannan (2010) *Family figures: Family dynamics and family types in Ireland, 1986–2006*. Dublin: Economic and Social Research Institute. [www.fsa.ie/fileadmin/user_upload/Files/Familly_Figures.pdf]

Lynch, C. (1997) 'Literacy is a human right: An adult underclass returns to education' in E. Crowley and J. Mac Laughlin (eds) *Under the belly of the tiger: Class, race, identity and culture in the global Ireland*. Dublin: Irish Reporter.

Lynch, K. (1987) 'Dominant ideologies in Irish educational thought: Consensualism, essentialism and meritocratic individualism'. *Economic and Social Review* 18(2), pp. 101–22.

Lynch, K. (1999a) *Equality in education*. Dublin: Gill & Macmillan.

Lynch, K. (1999b) 'Equality studies, the academy and the role of research in emancipatory social change'. *Economic and Social Review* 30(1), pp. 41–69.

Lynch, K. (2007) 'Love labour as a distinct and non-commodifiable form of care labour'. *Sociological Review* 55(3), pp. 550–70.

Lynch, K. and A. Lodge (2002) *Equality and power in schools: Redistribution, recognition and representation*. London: Routledge.

Lynch, K. and C. O'Riordan (1999) 'Inequality in higher education: A study of social class barriers' in K. Lynch, *Equality in education*. Dublin: Gill & Macmillan.

Mac an Ghaill, M., J. Hanafin and P. Conway (2002) *Gender politics and exploring masculinities in Irish education: Teachers, materials and the media*. Dublin: National Council for Curriculum and Assessment.

Mac Gréil, M. (2011) *Pluralism and diversity in Ireland: Prejudice and related issues in early 21st century Ireland*. Dublin: Columba.

MacCurtain, M. (1997) 'Godly burden: The Catholic sisterhoods in twentieth-century Ireland' in A. Bradley and M. Valiulis (eds) *Gender and sexuality in modern Ireland*. Amherst: University of Massachusetts Press.

MacFarlane, A. (1997) 'The changing role of women as health workers in Ireland'. *Women's Studies Review* 5, pp. 18–36.

Macionis, J. and K. Plummer (1998) *Sociology: A global introduction*. London: Prentice Hall.

MacLachlann, M. and M. O'Connell (eds) (2000) *Cultivating pluralism: Psychological, social and cultural perspectives on a changing Ireland*. Dublin: Oak Tree.

Maguire, M. (2004) *Differently Irish: A cultural history exploring twenty-five years of Vietnamese Irish identity*. Dublin: Woodfield.

Maguire, R. (2010) 'White-collar crime: The business of crime' in J. Hogan, P.F. Donnelly and B.K. O'Rourke (eds) *Irish business and society: Governing, participating and transforming in the 21st century*. Dublin: Gill & Macmillan.

Mahon, E. (1997) 'The development of a health policy for women' in J. Robins (ed.) *Reflections on health: Commemorating fifty years of the Department of Health 1947–1997*. Dublin: Department of Health.

Mair, P. (1994) 'Explaining the absence of class politics in Ireland' in J. Goldthorpe and C. Whelan (eds) *The development of industrial society in Ireland*. Oxford: Oxford University Press/The British Academy.

Malesevic, V. (2010) 'Ireland and neo-secularisation theory'. *Irish Journal of Sociology* 18(1), pp. 22–42.

Marsden, T. (2000) 'Food matters and the matter of food: Towards a new food governance?' *Sociologia Ruralis* 40(1), pp. 20–9.

Marshall, T. (1950) *Citizenship and social class, and other essays*. Cambridge: Cambridge University Press.

Marx, K. (1970) 'The Eighteenth Brumaire of Louis Bonaparte' in *Marx and Engels: Selected works*. London: Lawrence and Wishart.

Mass Observation Library (1987 [1943]) *The pub and the people: A Worktown study*. London: Cresset.

May, T. (1997) *Social research: Issues, methods and processes*. Buckingham: Open University Press.

Maynard, M. (2004) *Dress and globalisation*. Manchester: Manchester University Press.

McAdam, M. (2004) 'A paradoxical dilemma in nurse education' in A. Ryan and T. Walsh (eds) *Unsettling the horses: Interrogating adult education perspectives*. Maynooth: MACE.

McBrierty, V. and R. Kinsella (1998) *Ireland and the knowledge economy: The new techno-academic paradigm*. Dublin: Oak Tree.

McCann, M., S. Ó Síocháin and J. Ruane (eds) (1994) *Irish Travellers: Culture and ethnicity*. Belfast: Institute of Irish Studies, Queen's University Belfast, for the Anthropological Association of Ireland.

McCarthy, G. (1997) 'Nursing and the health services' in J. Robins (ed.) *Reflections on health: Commemorating fifty years of the Department of Health 1947–1997*. Dublin: Department of Health.

McCarthy, P. (1971) 'Itineracy and poverty: A study in the subculture of poverty'. Unpublished MA thesis, University College Dublin.

McCarthy, P. (1994) 'The sub-culture of poverty reconsidered' in M. McCann, S. Ó Síocháin and J. Ruane (eds) *Irish Travellers: Culture and ethnicity*. Belfast: Institute of Irish Studies, Queen's University Belfast, for the Anthropological Association of Ireland.

McCombs, M. and D. Shaw (1972) 'The agenda-setting function of the press' in *Public Opinion Quarterly* 36, pp. 176–87.

McCormaic, R. (2007) 'Faraway fields give Vila Gort new gloss', *Irish Times*, 11 April.

McCoy, S. and D. Byrne (2011) '"The sooner the better I could get out of there": Barriers to higher education access in Ireland', *Irish Educational Studies* 30(2), pp. 141–57.

McCoy, S., A. Quail and E. Smyth (2012) *Growing up in Ireland: Influences on 9-year-olds' learning: Home, school and community*. Dublin: Economic and Social Research Institute/Trinity College Dublin/Department of Children and Youth Affairs. [http://www.esri.ie/UserFiles/publications/BKMNEXT204.pdf]

McCrum, E. (1996) *Fabric and form: Irish fashion since 1950*. Stroud: Sutton/Ulster Museum.

McCullagh, C. (1995) 'Getting the criminals we want – the social production of the criminal population' in P. Clancy et al. (eds) *Irish society: Sociological perspectives*. Dublin: Institute of Public Administration.

McCullagh, C. (1996) *Crime in Ireland: A sociological introduction*. Cork: Cork University Press.

McCullagh, C. (2011) 'Getting a fix on crime in Limerick' in N. Hourigan (ed.) *Understanding Limerick: Social exclusion and change*. Cork: Cork University Press.

McDonald, H. (2008) 'Ireland immigrants return home as slump sharpens fear of racism', *The Observer*, 4 May.

McDonnell, O. (1997) 'Ethical and social implications of technology in medicine: New possibilities and new dilemmas' in A. Cleary and M. Treacy (eds) *The sociology of health and illness in Ireland*. Dublin: University College Dublin Press.

McGinnity, F. and H. Russell (2008) *Gender inequalities in time use: The distribution of caring, housework and employment among women and men in Ireland*. Dublin: Equality Authority/Economic and Social Research Institute. [www.esri.ie/UserFiles/publications/20080612164547/BKMNEXT113.pdf]

McGinnity, F., H. Russell and E. Smyth (2007) 'Gender, work life balance and quality of life' in T. Fahey, H. Russell and C. Whelan (eds) *The best of times? The social impact of the Celtic Tiger.* Dublin: Institute of Public Administration.

McGinnity, F., H. Russell, J. Williams and S. Blackwell (2005) *Time-use in Ireland 2005: Survey report.* Dublin: Economic and Social Research Institute.

McGrath, B. (2008) 'They had already prepared the way ... social capital formations and combinations in the lives of Brazilian migrants to Ireland'. Paper to the Sociological Association of Ireland conference, NUI Galway, 9–11 May.

McGuinness, S., E. Kelly, T. Callan and P. O'Connell (2009) *The gender wage gap in Ireland: Evidence from the National Employment Survey 2003.* Dublin: Equality Authority/Economic and Social Research Institute. [www.equality.ie/index.asp?docID=817]

McKeown, K., H. Ferguson and D. Rooney (1999) *Changing fathers? Fatherhood and family life in modern Ireland.* Cork: Cork University Press.

McKevitt, D. (1998) 'Irish healthcare policy' in E. McAuliffe and L. Joyce (eds) *A healthier future? Managing healthcare in Ireland.* Dublin: Institute of Public Administration.

McKevitt, P. (1944) *The plan of society.* Dublin: Catholic Truth Society of Ireland.

McLoone, M. (ed.) (1991) *Cultural identity and broadcasting in Ireland: Local issues, global perspectives.* Belfast: Institute of Irish Studies, Queen's University.

McLoughlin, D. (1994) 'Ethnicity and Irish Travellers: Reflections on Ní Shúinéar' in M. McCann, S. Ó Síocháin and J. Ruane (eds) *Irish Travellers: Culture and ethnicity.* Belfast: Institute of Irish Studies, Queen's University Belfast, for the Anthropological Association of Ireland.

McNabb, P. (1964) 'Social structure' in J. Newman (ed.) *The Limerick rural survey, 1958–1964.* Tipperary: Muintir na Tíre.

McQuail, D. (2010) *Mass communication theory.* London: Sage.

McSorley, C. (1997) *School absenteeism in Clondalkin: Causes and responses.* Clondalkin: Clondalkin Partnership.

McVeigh, R. (1995) 'Cherishing the children of the nation unequally: Sectarianism in Ireland' in P. Clancy et al. (eds) *Irish society: Sociological perspectives.* Dublin: Institute of Public Administration.

McVeigh, R. (1998) 'Irish Travellers and the logic of genocide' in M. Peillon and E. Slater (eds) *Encounters with modern Ireland.* Dublin: Institute of Public Administration.

McWilliams, D. (2005) *The pope's children: Ireland's new elite.* Dublin: Gill & Macmillan.

Mennell, S., A. Murcott and A. van Otterloo (1992) *The sociology of food: Eating, diet and culture.* London: Sage.

Merchant, C. (1980) *The death of nature: Women, ecology and the scientific revolution.* San Francisco: HarperCollins.

Merton, R. (1938) 'Social structure and anomie'. *American Sociological Review* 3(5), pp. 672–82.

Messenger, J. (1969) *Inis Beag: Isle of Ireland.* New York: Holt, Rinehart & Winston.

Miles, I. (2005) *Ireland and the knowledge society.* Dublin: Eurofound [European Foundation for the Improvement of Living and Working Conditions]. [www.eurofound.europa.eu/pubdocs/2004/08/en/1/ef0408en.pdf]

Miller, D. (2008) *The comfort of things*. Cambridge: Polity.

Miller, D. (2011) *Tales from Facebook*. Cambridge: Polity.

Miller, J. and J. Deutsch (2009) *Food studies: An introduction to research methods*. Oxford: Berg.

Mingione, E. (1997) 'Enterprise and exclusion'. *Demos Collection* 12, pp. 10–12.

Mingione, E. (2005) 'Urban social change: A socio-historical framework of analysis' in Y. Kazepov et al. (eds) *Cities of Europe: Changing contexts, local arrangement and the challenge to urban cohesion*. Oxford: Wiley-Blackwell, pp. 67–89.

Mingione, E. (ed.) (1996) *Urban poverty and the underclass: A reader*. Oxford: Blackwell.

Mitchell, W., C. Borroni-Bird and L. Burns (2010) *Reinventing the automobile: Personal urban mobility for the 21st century*. Cambridge, MA: MIT Press.

Moane, G. (1997) 'Lesbian politics and community' in A. Byrne and M. Leonard (eds) *Women and Irish society: A sociological reader*. Belfast: Beyond the Pale.

Moen, P. (2010) 'Redefining retirement'. *Contexts* 9(1), p. 86.

Moffatt, J. (2011) *Paradigms of Irishness for young people in Dublin*. PhD thesis, Department of Sociology, National University of Ireland Maynooth.

Molloy, C. (2002) *The story of the Irish pub*. Dublin: Liffey.

Molotch, H. (2011) 'Objects in sociology' in A. Clarke (ed.) *Design anthropology: Object culture in the 21st century*. Vienna/New York: Springer.

Moore, N. (2008) *Dublin's Docklands reinvented: The post-industrial regeneration of a European city quarter*. Dublin: Four Courts.

Moran, J. (2008) *Queuing for beginners: The story of daily life from breakfast to bedtime*. London: Profile.

Morozov, E. (2011) *The net delusion: How not to liberate the world*. London: Allen Lane.

Morris, J. (1995) 'Inequalities in health: Ten years and a little further on' in B. Davey, A. Gray and C. Seale (eds) *Health and disease: A reader*. Buckingham: Open University Press.

Morrison, A. (2004) 'Irish and white-ish mixed "race" identity and the scopic regime of whiteness'. *Women's Studies International Forum* 27(4) [Special Issue: Representing Migrant Women in Ireland and in the EU], pp. 385–96.

Morrow, V. (1999) 'Conceptualising social capital in relation to the well-being of children and young people: A critical review'. *The Sociological Review* 47(4), pp. 744–65.

Murcott, A. (ed.) (1998) *The nation's diet: The social science of food choice*. Harlow: Longman.

Murphy, M. and P. Kirby (2008) *A better Ireland is possible: Towards an alternative vision for Ireland*. Dublin: Community Platform

Murphy-Lawless, J. (1992) *The adequacy of income and family expenditure*. Dublin: Combat Poverty Agency.

Murphy-Lawless, J., L. Oaks and C. Brady (2004) *Understanding how sexually active women think about fertility, sex and motherhood*. Dublin: Crisis Pregnancy Agency.

Murphy, M. (2009) 'The politics of redirecting social policy: Towards a double movement' in D. Ging, M. Cronin and P. Kirby (eds) *Transforming Ireland: Challenges, critiques, resources*. Manchester: Manchester University Press, pp. 174–89.

Murray, M. (2007) 'Cosmopolitans versus the locals: Community-based protest in the age of globalisation'. *Irish Journal of Sociology* 16(2), pp. 117–35.

Murray, P. (2005) 'The pitfalls of pioneering sociological research: The case of the Tavistock Institute on the Dublin buses in the early 1960s'. [NIRSA working paper, 25] Maynooth: National Institute for Regional and Spatial Analysis, National University of Ireland Maynooth. [www.may.ie/nirsa/publications/wps25.pdf]

Murray, P. (2009) *Facilitating the future? US aid, European integration and Irish industrial viability*. Dublin: University College Dublin Press.

Murray, P. and M. Feeney (2009) 'The market for sociological ideas in early 1960s Ireland: Civil service departments and the Limerick Rural Survey, 1961–64.' [NIRSA working paper, 53] Maynooth: National Institute for Regional and Spatial Analysis, National University of Ireland Maynooth. [www.nuim.ie/nirsa/research/documents/ LRS_working_paper.pdf]

Murray, P. and M. Feeney (2010) 'Muintir na Tíre seeks funding for rural sociology in 1960s Ireland'. [NIRSA working paper, 63] Maynooth: National Institute for Regional and Spatial Analysis, National University of Ireland Maynooth. [www.nuim.ie/nirsa/research/documents/wp63_murray_feeney_muintir_na_tire.pdf]

Mutwarasibo, F. (2002) 'African in Ireland'. *Studies* 91(364), pp. 348–58.

NALA [National Adult Literacy Agency] (2010) 'Adults count too'. Press release, 6 September.

Nash, C. (1997) 'Embodied Irishness: Gender, sexuality and Irish identities' in B. Graham (ed.) *In search of Ireland: A cultural geography*. London: Routledge.

Nash, T. (1995) *Who's counting? Marilyn Waring on sex, lies and global economics* [film]. National Film Board of Canada. [http://www.nfb.ca/film/whos_counting]

National Cancer Registry Ireland and the N. Ireland Cancer Registry (2011) *All Ireland cancer atlas 1995–2007*. Belfast: N. Ireland Cancer Registry, Queen's University Belfast. [www.qub.ac.uk/research-centres/nicr/Publications/AllIrelandReports]

National Nutrition Surveillance Centre (2003) *Dietary habits of the Irish population: Results from SLÁN Annual Report 2003*. Dublin: National Nutritional Surveillance Centre, Department of Public Health Medicine, University College Dublin.

NCC [National Crime Council] (2004) *Report of the Expert Group on Crime Statistics*. Dublin: National Crime Council. [www.crimecouncil.gov.ie/downloads/Expert GroupStats.pdf]

NCC [National Crime Council] (no date) *Criminal justice system statistics*. [www.crimecouncil.gov.ie/statistics_cri.html]

NCCRI [National Consultative Committee on Racism and Interculturalism] (2002) *Cultural diversity in the Irish health care sector: Towards the development of policy and practice guidelines*. Dublin: National Consultative Committee on Racism and Interculturalism.

Negra, D. (ed.) (2006) *The Irish in us: Irishness, performativity and popular culture*. Durham, NC: Duke University Press.

Nettleton, S. and J. Watson (1998) *The body in everyday life*. London: Routledge.

Ní Shúinéar, S., M. McCann, S. Ó Síocháin and J. Ruane (eds) (1994) 'Irish Travellers, ethnicity and the origins question' in *Irish Travellers: Culture and ethnicity*. Belfast: Institute of Irish Studies, Queen's University Belfast, for the Anthropological Association of Ireland.

Nic Ghiolla Phádraig, M. (1995) 'The power of the Catholic Church in the Republic of Ireland' in P. Clancy et al. (eds) *Irish society: Sociological perspectives*. Dublin: Institute of Public Administration.

Nolan, A. (2011) 'The "healthy immigrant" effect: Initial evidence for Ireland'. *Health Economics, Policy and Law*. [DOI:10.1017/S174413311000040X]

Nolan, B. and C. Whelan (1997) 'Unemployment and health' in A. Cleary and M. Treacy (eds) *The sociology of health and illness in Ireland*. Dublin: University College Dublin Press.

Norberg-Hodge, H., T. Merrifield and S. Gorelick (2000) *Bringing the food economy home: The social, ecological and economic benefits of local food*. Dartington: International Society for Ecology and Culture [ISEC].

Norton, M., D. Mochon and D. Ariely (2011) 'The "IKEA effect": When labor leads to love'. Harvard Business School, Working paper 11-091. Cambridge, MA: Harvard Business School. [www.hbs.edu/research/pdf/11-091.pdf]

Ó Baoill, D. (1994) 'Travellers' Cant – language or register?' in M. McCann, S. Ó Síocháin and J. Ruane (eds) *Irish Travellers: Culture and ethnicity*. Belfast: Institute of Irish Studies, Queen's University Belfast, for the Anthropological Association of Ireland.

Ó Buachalla, S. (1974) 'Permanent education in the Irish context'. *Studies* Winter, pp. 355–65.

Ó Drisceoil, D. and D. Ó Drisceoil (2005) *Serving a city: The story of Cork's English Market*. Cork: Collins.

Ó Maitiú, S. (2001) *W&R Jacob: Celebrating 150 years of Irish biscuit making*. Dublin: Woodfield Press.

Ó Riain, S. (2000) 'Soft solutions to hard times' in E. Slater and M. Peillon (eds) *Memories of the present: A sociological chronicle of Ireland, 1997–1998*. Dublin: Institute of Public Administration.

Ó Riain, S. (2004) *The politics of high tech growth: Developmental network states in the global economy*. Cambridge: Cambridge University Press.

Ó Riain, S. (2006) 'Social partnership as a mode of governance: Introduction to the special issue'. *Economic and Social Review* 37(3), pp. 311–18.

Ó Riain, S. (2010) 'Snatching defeat from the jaws of victory: Ireland rediscovers crisis' in P. Share and M.P. Corcoran (eds) *Ireland of the illusions*. Dublin: Institute of Public Administration, pp. 23–35.

Ó Riain, S. and P. Murray (2007) 'Work transformed: Two faces of the new Irish workforce' in S. O'Sullivan (ed.) *Contemporary Ireland: A sociological map*, Dublin: University College Dublin Press, pp. 248–64.

Ó Siocháin, S. (ed.) (2009) *Social thought on Ireland in the nineteenth century*. Dublin: University College Dublin Press.

O'Brien, M. (2001) *De Valera, Fianna Fáil and the Irish Press: The truth in the news?* Dublin: Irish Academic Press.

O'Byrne, R. (2000) *After a fashion: A history of the Irish fashion industry*. Dublin: Town House.

O'Carroll, J. (1985) 'Community programmes and the traditional view of community'. *Social Studies* 8(3/4), pp. 137–48.

O'Carroll, J. (1998) 'Blood' in M. Peillon and E. Slater (eds) *Encounters with modern Ireland*. Dublin: Institute of Public Administration.

O'Carroll, P. (2010) 'A dam burst of indignation: The GAA, the Cork County Clubs and the players' strikes' in P. Share and M.P. Corcoran (eds) *Ireland of the illusions*. Dublin: Institute of Public Administration.

O'Clery, C. (2007) *The billionaire who wasn't: How Chuck Feeney secretly made and gave away a fortune*. Philadelphia: Perseus.

O'Connell, D. (2009) 'Public intellectuals in times of crisis: What do they have to offer?'. Paper to Symposium organised by the RIA Committee for Social Sciences. Royal Irish Academy, Dublin, 27 November. [www2.lse.ac.uk/humanRights/articles AndTranscripts/OConnellRIANov09.pdf]

O'Connell, J. (1992) 'Working with Irish Travellers' in DTEDG File. *Irish Travellers: New analysis and new initiatives* (originally 1989). Dublin: Pavee Point.

O'Connell, M. (2001) *Changed utterly: Ireland and the new Irish psyche*. Dublin: Liffey.

O'Connor, B. and C. MacKeogh (2007) 'New media communities: Performing identity in an online women's magazine'. *Irish Journal of Sociology* 16(2) pp. 97–116.

O'Connor, O. and C. Dunne (2006) 'Valuing unpaid care work' in T. O'Connor and M. Murphy (eds) *Social care in Ireland: Theory, policy and practice*. Cork: Cork Institute of Technology Press.

O'Connor, O. and P. Gladyshev (2006) *ISSA/UCD cybercrime survey 2006: The impact of cybercrime on Irish organisations*. Dublin: University College Dublin and Information Systems Security Association. [www.issaireland.org/ISSA%20UCD %20Irish%20Cybercrime%20Survey%202006.pdf]

O'Connor, P. (1998) *Emerging voices: Women in contemporary Irish society*. Dublin: Institute of Public Administration.

O'Connor, P. (2006) 'Globalization, individualization and gender in adolescents' texts'. *International Journal of Social Research Methodology* 9(4), pp. 261–77.

O'Connor, P. (2008) *Irish children and teenagers in a changing world: The National Write Here, Write Now Project*. Manchester: Manchester University Press.

O'Connor, P. (2011) 'Virtual worlds: The shopping centre and the commodification of meaning'. *Research West Review* 1(2). [greenlinkwest.webs.com/RWR%20 POCONNOR.pdf]

O'Connor, P. (2012) 'Public intellectuals in times of crisis: What do they have to offer? Reflections on the public intellectual's role' in M.P. Corcoran, K. Lalor and J. Maguire (eds) *Public intellectuals at a time of crisis*. Dublin: Royal Irish Academy.

O'Donovan, O. (1997a) 'The plan for women's health and the politics of knowledge: A brief commentary'. *Women's Studies Review* 5, pp. 159–62.

O'Donovan, O. (1997b) 'Contesting concepts of care: The case of the home help service in Ireland' in A. Cleary and M. Treacy (eds) *The sociology of health and illness in Ireland*. Dublin: University College Dublin Press.

O'Donovan, O. and C. Curtin (1991) 'Industrial development and rural women in Ireland' in T. Varley, T. Boylan and M. Cuddy (eds) *Rural crisis: Perspectives on Irish rural development*. Galway: Centre for Development Studies, National University of Ireland, Galway.

O'Dowd, A. (1990) *Common clothes and clothing 1860–1930*. Dublin: National Museum of Ireland.

O'Dowd, L. (1988) *The state of social science research in Ireland*. Dublin: Royal Irish Academy.

O'Dowd, L. (1989) 'Church, state and women: The aftermath of partition' in C. Curtin, P. Jackson and B. O'Connor (eds) *Gender in Irish society*. Galway: Galway University Press.

O'Dowd, L. (1992) 'State legitimacy and nationalism in Ireland' in P. Clancy, M. Kelly, J. Wiatr and R. Zoltaniecki (eds) *Ireland and Poland: Comparative perspectives*. Dublin: Department of Sociology, University College Dublin.

O'Dowd, L. (2012) 'Public intellectuals and the "crisis": Accountability, democracy and market fundamentalism' in M.P. Corcoran, K. Lalor and J. Maguire (eds) *Public intellectuals at a time of crisis*, Dublin: Royal Irish Academy.

O'Dowd, L. (ed.) (1996) *On intellectuals and intellectual life in Ireland*. Belfast: Institute of Irish Studies/Royal Irish Academy.

O'Dowd, M. and S. Wichert (eds) (1995) *Chattel, servant or citizen: Women's status in church, state and society*. Belfast: Institute of Irish Studies, Queen's University Belfast.

O'Hara, P. (1998) *Partners in production: Women, farm and family in Ireland*. New York and Oxford: Berghahn.

O'Hara, T. (1998) 'Current structure of the Irish health care system – setting the context' in A. Leahy and M. Wiley (eds) *The Irish health system in the 21st century*. Dublin: Oak Tree.

O'Hearn, D. (1992) *Putting Ireland in a global context*. [Occasional Papers Series 8] Cork: University College Cork, Department of Sociology.

O'Hearn, D. (1998) *Inside the Celtic Tiger: The Irish economy and the Asian model*. London: Pluto.

O'Higgins, K. (1999) 'Social order problems' in T. Fahey (ed.) *Social housing in Ireland: A study of success, failure and lessons learned*. Dublin: Oak Tree.

O'Higgins-Norman, J. (2009) 'Still catching up: Schools, sexual orientation and homophobia in Ireland'. *Sexuality and Culture* 13(1) pp. 1–16.

O'Loingsigh, D. (2001) 'Intercultural education and the school ethos' in F. Farrell and P. Watt (eds) *Responding to racism in Ireland*. Dublin: Veritas.

O'Mahony, E. (2010) 'Religious practice and values in Ireland: A summary of European Values Study 4th wave data'. Maynooth: Council for Research and Development, Irish Catholic Bishops' Conference.

O'Mahony, E. (2011) 'Being religious and becoming secular in Ireland and France: Rescaling secularisation theory'. *Symposia: The Graduate Student Journal of the Centre for the Study of Religion at the University of Toronto* 3(1), pp. 14–30. [symposia.library. utoronto.ca/index.php/symposia/article/viewFile/14385/12250]

O'Mahony, P. (1993) *Crime and punishment in Ireland*. Dublin: Round Hall.

O'Mahony, P. (1997) *Mountjoy prisoners: A sociological and criminological profile*. Dublin: Stationery Office.

O'Shea, D. (1998) 'A particular problem in the East …' in A. Leahy and M. Wiley (eds) *The Irish health system in the 21st century*. Dublin: Oak Tree.

O'Sullivan, D. (1989) 'The ideational base of Irish educational policy' in D. Mulcahy and D. O'Sullivan (eds) *Irish educational policy: Process and substance*. Dublin: Institute of Public Administration.

O'Sullivan, D. (1992) 'Shaping educational debate: A case study and an interpretation'. *Economic and Social Review* 23(4), pp. 423–38.

O'Sullivan, E. and I. O'Donnell (2007) 'Coercive confinement in the Republic of Ireland: The waning of a culture of control'. *Punishment and Society* 9(1), pp. 27–48.

O'Sullivan, M. (2006) *Ireland and the global question*. Cork: Cork University Press.

O'Sullivan, O. (1997) *The silent schism: Renewal of Catholic spirit and structures*. Dublin: Gill & Macmillan.

O'Sullivan, S. (1997) '"The Ryanline is now open…" Talk radio and the public sphere' in M. Kelly and B. O'Connor (eds) *Media audiences in Ireland: Power and cultural identity*. Dublin: University College Dublin Press.

O'Sullivan, S. (2007) 'Gender and the workforce' in S. O'Sullivan (ed.) *Contemporary Ireland: A sociological map*, Dublin: University College Dublin Press, pp. 265–82.

O'Toole, F. (1995) *Meanwhile back at the ranch: The politics of Irish beef*. London: Vintage.

O'Toole, F. (1998) *The lie of the land*. Dublin: New Island.

O'Toole, F. (2009) *Ship of fools: How stupidity and corruption sank the Celtic Tiger*. London: Faber.

O'Toole, F. (2010) *Enough is enough: How to build a new republic*. London: Faber.

Obama, B. (2011) 'Remarks by the President at Irish celebration in Dublin, Ireland'. [www.whitehouse.gov/the-press-office/2011/05/23/remarks-president-irish-celebration-dublin-ireland]

OECD [Organisation for Economic Cooperation and Development] (2009a) 'Information note: Irish students' performance in PISA 2009'. [www.oecd.org/dataoecd/19/13/46971917.pdf]

OECD [Organisation for Economic Cooperation and Development] (2009b) *Programme for International Student Assessment, 2009*. [www.oecd.org/document/0,3746,en_2649_201185_46462759_1_1_1_1,00.html]

OECD [Organisation for Economic Cooperation and Development] (2010) *Health expenditure and financing*. [stats.oecd.org/Index.aspx?DataSetCode=DECOMP%20]

OECD [Organisation for Economic Cooperation and Development] (2011) *Education at a glance*. [www.oecd.org/dataoecd/61/2/48631582.pdf]

Ofcom (2008) *Social networking: A quantitative and qualitative research report into attitudes, behaviour and use*. London: Office of Communication.

Oireachtas (2011) *Matters concerning the retail trade in Ireland*. [Joint Committee on Enterprise, Trade and Innovation, 12th report. Parl. No. A11/0132] Dublin: Government Publications. [www.oireachtas.ie/documents/committees30thdail/j-enterprisetradeemp/reports-2011/20110208.pdf]

Oldenburg, R. (1999) *The great good place: Cafes, coffee shops, bookstores, bars, hair salons, and other hangouts at the heart of a community*. New York: Marlowe.

Onkey, L. (2005) 'Ray Charles on Hyndford Street: Van Morrison's Caledonian soul' in D. Negra (ed.) *The Irish in us: Irishness, performativity, and popular culture*. Durham, NC: Duke University Press.

Oram, H. (1993) *Paper tigers: Stories of Irish newspapers by the people who make them*. Belfast: Appletree/RTÉ.

Pahl, R. (1985) *Divisions of labour*. Oxford: Blackwell

Pahl, R. and L. Spencer (2004) 'Personal communities: Not simply families of fate or choice'. *Current Sociology* 52(2), pp. 199–221.

Parker, A. (1999) 'Retail trends and the suburbanisation of Dublin's retailing: Into the twenty-first century' in J. Killen and A. MacLaran (eds) *Dublin: Contemporary trends and issues for the twenty-first century*. Dublin: Geographical Society of Ireland. [Special Publication 11]

Paterson, M. (2006) *Consumption and everyday life*. London: Routledge.

Peace, A. (1986) '"A different place altogether": Diversity, unity and boundary in an Irish village' in A. Cohen (ed.) *Symbolising boundaries*. Manchester: Manchester University Press.

Peace, A. (1993) 'Environmental protest, bureaucratic closure: The politics of discourse in rural Ireland' in K. Milton (ed.) *Environmentalism: The view from anthropology*. London: Routledge.

Peace, A. (2001) *A world of fine difference: The social architecture of a modern Irish village*. Dublin: University College Dublin Press.

Peillon, M. (1995) 'Interest groups and the state' in P. Clancy et al. (eds) *Irish society: Sociological perspectives*. Dublin: Institute of Public Administration in association with the Sociological Association of Ireland.

Peillon, M. (1998) 'Community of distrust' in M. Peillon and E. Slater (eds) *Encounters with modern Ireland*. Dublin: Institute of Public Administration.

Peillon, M. (2000) 'Information overload' in M. Peillon and E. Slater (eds) *Memories of the present*. Dublin: Institute of Public Administration, pp. 165–81.

Peillon, M. (2001) *Welfare in Ireland: Actors, resources and strategies*. Westport, CT: Praeger.

Pereyra, D. (2008) 'Sociological textbooks in Argentina and Mexico, 1940–60'. *Current Sociology* 56(2), pp. 267–87.

Pettinger, L., J. Parry, R. Taylor and M. Glucksmann (eds) (2005) *A new sociology of work?* Oxford: Blackwell/*The Sociological Review*.

Phillipson, C., M. Bernard, J. Phillips and J. Ogg (1999) 'Older people's experiences of community life: Patterns of neighbouring in three urban areas'. *Sociological Review* 47, pp. 715–43.

Plender, J. (2008) 'Shut out'. *The Financial Times*. [www.ft.com/cms/s/0/b63025ca-9cad-11dd-a42e-000077b07658.html#axzz1nHzeOdLm]

Plummer, K. (2010) *Sociology: The basics*. London: Routledge.

Pollack, A. (1999) 'An invitation to racism? Irish daily newspaper coverage of the refugee issue' in D. Kiberd (ed.) *Media in Ireland: The search for ethical journalism*. Dublin: Open Air.

Poole, M. (1997) 'In search of ethnicity in Ireland' in B. Graham (ed.) *In search of Ireland: A cultural geography*. London: Routledge.

Porter, S. (1997) 'Why should nurses bother with sociology?' in A. Cleary and M. Treacy (eds) *The sociology of health and illness in Ireland*. Dublin: University College Dublin Press.

Powell, F. (2000) 'State, welfare and civil society' in F. Tonkiss and A. Passey (eds) *Trust and civil society*. Basingstoke: Macmillan.

Powell, F. (2012) 'Think globally, act locally: Sustainable communities, modernity and development'. *Geojournal*. [www.springer.com/geography]

Putnam, R. (2000) *Bowling alone: The collapse and revival of American community*. New York: Simon & Schuster.

Quinlan, C. (2010) *Inside: Ireland's women's prisons, past and present*. Dublin: Irish Academic Press.

Quinn, D. (1992) *Ishmael*. New York: Bantam.

Rafter, N. (2007) *The criminal brain: Understanding biological theories of crime*. New York: New York University Press.

Rains, S. (2010) *Commodity culture and social class in Dublin 1850–1916*. Dublin: Irish Academic Press.

Rand, E. (1995) *Barbie's queer accessories*. Durham, NC: Duke University Press.

Rapple, C. (1997) 'Ownership, standards, diversity: A way forward' in D. Kiberd (ed.) *Media in Ireland: The search for diversity*. Dublin: Open Air.

Reich, M., D. Gordon and R. Edwards (1973) 'Dual labor markets: A theory of labor market segmentation'. *American Economic Review* 63(2), pp. 359–65.

Reich, R.B. (2007) *Supercapitalism: The transformation of business, democracy and everyday life*. New York: Knopf.

Reiger, K. (1985) *The disenchantment of the home: Modernizing the Australian family 1880–1940*. Melbourne: Oxford.

Restivo, S. (1991) *The sociological worldview*. Oxford: Blackwell.

Richardson, N. (2004) *Getting inside men's health*. Kilkenny: Health Promotion Department, South Eastern Health Board.

Ridgeway, C. (2009) 'Framed before we know it: How gender shapes social relations'. *Gender and Society* 23, pp. 145–60.

Ritzer, G. (2010) *The McDonaldization of society* 6. Thousand Oaks, CA: Pine Forge.

Robertson, A. (1991) *Beyond the family: The social organization of human reproduction*. Oxford: Polity.

Robins, J. (ed.) (1997) *Reflections on health: Commemorating fifty years of the Department of Health 1947–1997*. Dublin: Department of Health.

Rogan, M. (2011) *Prison policy in Ireland: Politics, penal-welfarism and political imprisonment*. London: Routledge.

Rogers, E. and J. Dearing (1987) 'Agenda-setting research: Where has it been? Where is it going?' in J. Anderson (ed.) *Communication yearbook*. London: Sage.

Rolston, B. and M. Shannon (2002) *Encounters: How racism came to Ireland*. Belfast: Beyond the Pale.

Roos, G. and R. Prättälä (1999) *Disparities in food habits: Review of research in 15 European countries*. Helsinki: National Public Health Institute.

Rose, M. (1991) *The post-modern and the post-industrial*. Cambridge: Cambridge University Press.

Rose, R. (2005) 'Paradox and the consumption of authenticity through reality television'. *Journal of Consumer Research* 32(2), pp. 284–91.

Ross, A. (2009) *Nice work if you can get it: Life and labor in precarious times*. New York: New York University Press.

Ross, S. (2009) *The bankers: How the banks brought Ireland to its knees*. Dublin: Penguin.

Rostow, W. (1960) *The stages of economic growth*. Cambridge: Cambridge University Press.

Rottman, D. (1984) *The criminal justice system: Policy and performance*. Dublin: National Economic and Social Council.

Rottman, D., D. Hannan, N. Hardiman and M. Wiley (1982) *The distribution of income in the Republic of Ireland: A study in social class and family-cycle inequalities*. Dublin: Economic and Social Research Institute.

RTÉ (no date) 'The Ireland that we dreamed of'. [Audio recording] [www.rte.ie/laweb/ll/ll_t09b.html]

Ruane, J. (1989) 'Success and failure in a West of Ireland factory' in C. Curtin and T. Wilson (eds) *Ireland from below*. Galway: Galway University Press.

Rundle, K., C. Leigh, H. McGee and R. Layte (2004) *Irish Contraception and Crisis Pregnancy [ICCP] study: A survey of the general population*. Dublin: Crisis Pregnancy Agency.

Russell, H. et al. (2004) *Work poor households: The welfare implications of changing household employment patterns*. Dublin: Economic and Social Research Institute.

Russell, H., P. O'Connell and F. McGinnity (2007) *The impact of flexible working arrangements on work-life conflicts and work pressure in Ireland*. Dublin: Economic and Social Research Institute. [www.esri.ie/UserFiles/publications/20070427094523/WP189.pdf]

Ryan, A. (1997) 'Gender discourses in school social relations' in A. Byrne and M. Leonard (eds) *Women and Irish society: A sociological reader*. Belfast: Beyond the Pale.

Ryan, L. (1990) 'Irish emigration to Britain since World War 2' in R. Kearney (ed.) *Migrations: The Irish at home and abroad*. Dublin: Wolfhound.

Ryan, P. (2011) *Asking Angela MacNamara: An intimate history of Irish lives*. Dublin: Irish Academic Press.

Sabel, C. (1996) *Ireland: Local partnerships and social innovation*. Paris: OECD.

Sacks, P. (1976) *Donegal mafia: An Irish political machine*. New Haven, CT: Yale University Press.

Saris, A. (1997) 'The asylum in Ireland: A brief institutional history and some local effects' in A. Cleary and M. Treacy (eds) *The sociology of health and illness in Ireland*. Dublin: University College Dublin Press.

Scarbrough, G. (2008) 'New places, non-places and the changing landscape of the Irish pub' in M.P. Corcoran and P. Share (eds) *Belongings: Shaping identity in modern Ireland*. Dublin: Institute of Public Administration, pp. 57–70.

Schaffer, K. (1988) *Women and the bush: Forces of desire in the Australian cultural tradition*. Melbourne: Cambridge University Press.

Scheper-Hughes, N. (1979) *Saints, scholars and schizophrenics: Mental illness in rural Ireland*. California: University of California Press.

Schlosser, E. (2001) *Fast food nation: What the all-American meal is doing to the world*. London: Allen Lane/Penguin.

Seidler, V. (1988) 'Fathering, authority and masculinity' in R. Chapman and J. Rutherford (eds) *Male order: Unwrapping masculinities*. London: Lawrence & Wishart.

Seligman, A. (1992) *The idea of civil society*. New Jersey: Princeton University Press.

Sennett, R. (2008) *The craftsman*. New Haven, CT: Yale University Press.

Share, M. and L. Kerrins (2009) 'The role of grandparents in childcare in Ireland: Towards a research agenda'. *Irish Journal of Applied Social Studies* 9(1), pp. 33–47. [http://arrow.dit.ie/ijass/vol9/iss1/5/]

Share, P. (2002) 'Trust me: I'm organic' in M. Corcoran and M. Peillon (eds) *Ireland unbound: A turn of the century chronicle*. Dublin: Institute of Public Administration.

Share, P. (2011) 'The rise and fall of the jumbo breakfast roll: How a sandwich survived the decline of the Irish economy'. *Sociological Research Online* 16(2). [www.socresonline.org.uk/16/2/2.html]

Shaughnessy, L. (1997) 'Female genital mutilation: Beyond mutilating mothers and foreign feminists'. *Women's Studies Review* 5, pp. 123–34.

Sheehan, H. (1987) *Irish television drama: A society and its stories*. Dublin: Radio Telefís Éireann.

Shell, E. (2009) *Cheap: The high cost of discount culture*. New York: Penguin.

Shirky, C. (2010) *Cognitive surplus*. London: Allen Lane

Shove, E., M. Watson, M. Hand and J. Ingram (2007) *The design of everyday life*. Oxford: Berg.

Shutes, M. (1991) 'Kerry farmers and the European Community: Capital transitions in a rural Irish parish'. *Irish Journal of Sociology* 1, pp. 1–17.

Silverman, M. (1993) 'An urban place in rural Ireland: An historical ethnography of domination, 1841–1989' in C. Curtin, H. Donnan and M. Wilson (eds) *Irish urban cultures*. Belfast: Institute of Irish Studies, Queen's University.

Silvestri, M. and C. Crowther-Dowey (2008) *Gender and crime*. London: Sage.

Simmel, G. (1971) *Georg Simmel on individuality and social forms*. [D. Levine, ed.] Chicago: University of Chicago Press.

Sinha, S. (2002) 'Generating awareness for women of colour in Ireland' in R. Lentin and R. McVeigh (eds) *Racism and anti-racism in Ireland*. Belfast: Beyond the Pale.

SIRC [Social Issues Research Centre] (1998) *Social and cultural aspects of drinking: A report to the Amsterdam Group*. Oxford: Social Issues Research Centre.

Skeggs, B. (2009) 'The moral economy of person production: The class relations of self-performance on "reality" television'. *The Sociological Review* 57(4), pp. 626–44.

Skeldon, R. (1997) 'Of migration, great cities and markets: Global systems of development' in W. Gungwu (ed.) *Global history and migrations*. Boulder: Westview.

Sklair, L. (2002) *Globalization: Capitalism and its alternatives*. New York: Oxford University Press.

Slater, E. (2000) 'When the local goes global' in E. Slater and M. Peillon (eds) *Memories of the present: A sociological chronicle of Ireland, 1997–1998*. Dublin: Institute of Public Administration.

Slater, E. and T. McDonough (2008) 'Marx on 19th century colonial Ireland: Analyzing colonialism beyond dependency theory'. [NIRSA working paper 36] Maynooth: National Institute for Regional and Spatial Analysis, National University of Ireland, Maynooth. [eprints.nuim.ie/1151/1/cover36slater_V2.pdf]

Slowey, M. (1987) 'Education for domestication or liberation? Women's involvement in adult education' in M. Cullen (ed.) *Girls don't do honours: Irish women in education in the 19th and 20th centuries*. Dublin: Women's Education Bureau.

Smart, B. (2010) *Consumer society: Critical issues and environmental consequences*. London: Sage.

Smith, G. (2010) 'Political corruption in Ireland: A downward spiral' in J. Hogan et al. (eds) *Irish business and society: Governing, participating and transforming in the 21st century*. Dublin: Gill & Macmillan.

Smith, J. (2007) *Ireland's Magdalen Laundries and the nation's architecture of containment*. Notre Dame: University of Notre Dame Press.

Smith, S. (2009) *Equity in health care: A view from the Irish health care system*. [An Adelaide Health Policy Brief] Dublin: Adelaide Hospital Society. [www.adelaide.ie/cms/cms/uploads/files/Equity%20in%20Healthcare%20Apr09.pdf]

Smyth, E. (2009) *Religious education in a multicultural society: School and home in comparative context*. Dublin: Economic and Social Research Institute. [www.esri.ie/research/research_areas/education/Remc/final_report_-_publishabl/REMC_Final_Report_Publishable_Summary.pdf]

Smyth, E. (2010) 'Single-sex education: What does research tell us?' *Revue française de pédagogie* 171, pp. 47–55.

Smyth, E. and M. Darmody (2011) 'Religious diversity and schooling in Ireland' in M. Darmody, N. Tyrrell and S. Song (eds) *The changing faces of Ireland: Exploring the lives of immigrant and ethnic minority children*. Rotterdam: Sense Publishers.

Smyth, E. and D. Hannan (1997) 'Girls and coeducation in the Republic of Ireland' in A. Byrne and M. Leonard (eds) *Women and Irish society: A sociological reader*. Belfast: Beyond the Pale.

Smyth, E. and S. McCoy (2009) *Investing in education: Combating educational disadvantage*. Dublin: Economic and Social Research Institute.

Sorlin, P. (1994) *Mass media*. London: Routledge. [Key Ideas series]

Sparks, C. and K. Duke (2010) '"All that is solid melts into air": Empty hopes and empty houses in Leitrim' in P. Share and M.P. Corcoran (eds) *Ireland of the illusions*. Dublin: Institute of Public Administration.

Spiller, K. and D. Linehan (2006) '"Beacons of modernity": Department stores, modernity and the urban experience in mid-twentieth century Ireland'. *Irish Geography* 39(2), pp. 143–58.

Stein, M. (1964) *The eclipse of community*. New York: Harper & Row.

Stenebo, J. (2010) *The truth about IKEA: How IKEA built its global furniture brand*. London: Gibson Square.

Stevenson, N. (1999) *The transformation of the media*. London: Longman.

Stewart, K. (2007) *Ordinary affects*. Durham, NC: Duke University Press.

Stiglitz, J. (2003) *Globalisation and its discontents*. New York: Norton.

Stiglitz, J. (2006) *Making globalization work: The next steps to global justice*. New York: Norton.

Stivers, R. (2000) *Hair of the dog: Irish drinking and its American stereotype*. New York: Continuum.

Storey, J. (2001) *Cultural theory and popular culture: An introduction*. Harlow: Prentice Hall.

Strader, J. (2002) 'Introduction to white collar crime'. *Understanding white collar crime*. LexisNexis. [www.lexisnexis.com/lawschool/study/understanding/pdf/WhiteCollar Ch1.pdf]

Sugrue, K. (2000) 'Sex in the city' in M.P. Corcoran and M. Peillon (eds) *Ireland unbound: A turn of the century chronicle*. Dublin: Institute of Public Administration.

Sweeney, P. (1998) *The Celtic Tiger: Ireland's economic miracle explained*. Dublin: Oak Tree.

Sweetman, P. (2001) 'Shop window dummies? Fashion, the body and emergent socialities' in J. Entwistle and E. Wilson (eds) *Body dressing*. Oxford: Berg.

Swingewood, A. (1984) *A short history of sociological thought*. Basingstoke: Macmillan.

Syed, M. (2008) 'What caused the crunch: Men and testosterone'. *The Times*, 30 September.

Symes, D. (1972) 'Farm household and farm performance: A study of twentieth century changes in Ballyferriter, Southwest Ireland'. *Ethnology* 11, pp. 25–38.

Szasz, T. (1961) *The myth of mental illness: Foundations of a theory of personal conduct.* New York: Harper & Row.

Szuchewycz, B. (1989) '"The growth is in the silence": The meanings of silence in the Irish Catholic charismatic movement' in C. Curtin and T. Wilson (eds) *Ireland from below: Social change and local communities.* Galway: Galway University Press.

Tannam, M. (1999) 'At home from abroad: The experiences of some migrant women in Ireland'. *Women's Studies Review* 6, pp. 19–32.

Taylor, L. (1989) 'The mission: An anthropological view of an Irish religious occasion' in C. Curtin and T. Wilson (eds) *Ireland from below: Social change and local communities.* Galway: Galway University Press.

Therborn, G. (1991) 'Cultural belonging, structural location and human action: Explanation in sociology and in social science'. *Acta Sociologica* 34, pp. 177–91. [asj.sagepub.com/content/34/3/177.abstract]

Thompson, E. P. (1982) 'Time, work discipline and industrial capitalism' in A. Giddens and D. Held (eds) *Classes, power and conflict.* London: Macmillan.

TILDA [The Irish Longitudinal Study on Ageing] (2011) Executive summary. [www.tilda.ie]

Tilly, C. (1997) *Roads from past to future.* Lanham: Rowman & Littlefield.

Time (2009) 'The future of work'. [series of articles, various authors] [www.time.com/time/specials/packages/article/0,28804,1898024_1898023_1898169,00.html]

Timoney, N. (2010) 'Labour and employment in Ireland in the era of the Celtic Tiger' in J. Hogan et al. (eds) *Irish business and society: Governing, participating and transforming in the 21st century.* Dublin: Gill & Macmillan.

Tobin, F. (1996) *The best of decades: Ireland in the 1960s.* Dublin: Gill & Macmillan.

Tönnies, F. (2001 [1887]) *Community and civil society [Gemeinschaft und Gessellschaft].* Cambridge: Cambridge University Press. [Cambridge Texts in the History of Political Thought]

Tovey, H. (1982) 'Milking the farmer? Modernisation and marginalisation in Irish dairy farming' in M. Kelly et al. (eds) *Power, conflict and inequality.* Dublin: Turoe.

Tovey, H. (1985) '"Local community": In defence of a much-criticised concept'. *Social Studies* 8(3/4), pp. 149–64.

Tovey, H. (1992) 'Rural sociology in Ireland: A review'. *Irish Journal of Sociology* 2, pp. 96–121.

Tovey, H. (1993) 'Environmentalism in Ireland – two versions of development and modernity'. *International Sociology* 8(4), pp. 413–30.

Tovey, H. (1999) '"Messers, visionaries and organobureaucrats": Dilemmas of institutionalisation in the Irish organic farming movement'. *Irish Journal of Sociology* 9, pp. 31–59.

Townsend, P. and N. Davidson (eds) (1982) *Inequalities in health: The Black Report.* Harmondsworth: Penguin.

Tucker, M. (2011) 'Religion and ecology' in P. Clarke (ed.) *The Oxford handbook of the sociology of religion.* Oxford: Oxford University Press, pp. 819–35.

Tucker, V. (1987) 'State and community: A case study of Glencolumbcille' in C. Curtin and T. Wilson (eds) *Ireland from below: Social change and local communities*. Galway: Galway University Press.

Tucker, V. (1997) 'From biomedicine to holistic health' in A. Cleary and M. Treacy (eds) *The sociology of health and illness in Ireland*. Dublin: University College Dublin Press.

Turkle, S. (1999) 'Cyberspace and identity'. *Contemporary Sociology* 28(6), pp. 643–8.

Turner, B. (1996) 'Introduction' in B. Turner (ed.) *The Blackwell companion to social theory*. Oxford: Blackwell.

Tussing, A. and M. Wren (2006) *How Ireland cares: The case for health care reform*. Dublin: New Island.

TWG [Technical Working Group] (1995) *Interim report to the Steering Committee on the Future of Higher Education*. Dublin: Higher Education Authority.

Ugba, A. (2007) 'African Pentecostals in twenty-first century Ireland: Identity and integration' in B. Fanning (ed.) *Immigration and social change in the Republic of Ireland*. Manchester: Manchester University Press, pp. 168–84.

Ugba, A. (2009) 'A part of and apart from society? Pentecostal Africans in the "New Ireland"'. *Translocations* 4(1). [www.imrstr.dcu.ie/volume_4_issue_1/index.html]

Ungar, S. (2008) 'Ignorance as an under-identified social problem'. *British Journal of Sociology*, 59(2), pp. 301–26.

University of Pennsylvania (2011) 'Facebook users are more trusting, have more close friends, are more politically engaged, and get more support from their friends'. [Press release] Annenberg School for Communication, University of Pennsylvania. [www.asc.upenn.edu/news/NewsDetail.aspx?nid=933]

Urry, J. (2010) 'Mobile sociology'. *British Journal of Sociology* 61, pp. 347–66.

Van der Bly, M. (2007) 'Globalization and the rise of one heterogeneous world culture: A microperspective of a global village'. *International Journal of Comparative Sociology* 48(2–3), pp. 234–56.

Van Deth, J. (1995) 'Introduction: The impact of values' in J. van Deth and E. Scarbrough (eds) *The impact of values*. Oxford: Oxford University Press, pp. 1–18.

Van Deth, J. and E. Scarbrough (eds) (1995) *The impact of values*. Oxford: Oxford University Press.

Varenne, H. (1993) 'Dublin 16: Accounts of suburban lives' in C. Curtin, H. Donnan and T. Wilson (eds) *Irish urban cultures*. Belfast: Institute of Irish Studies, Queen's University.

Veblen, T. (1925) *The theory of the leisure class: An economic study of institutions*. London: Allen & Unwin.

Viney, M. (2011) 'Irish peatlands: The last stand against climate change', *Irish Times*, 8 October. [www.irishtimes.com/newspaper/weekend/2011/1008/1224305438093.html]

Walls, P. (2006) *The 2006 Irish in Brent health profile report: A report of research undertaken for Brent Irish Advisory Service and Brent Health Action Zone*. Brent: Brent Irish Advisory Service. [open.charityblog.org.uk/wp-content/uploads/2006/03/BIASreport jan06.pdf]

Walsh, B. (2011) *When the shopping was good: Woolworths and the Irish Main Street*. Dublin: Irish Academic Press.

Walsh, J., S. Craig and D. McCafferty (1998) *Local partnerships for social inclusion?* Dublin: Oak Tree/Combat Poverty Agency.

Walter, N. (1998) *The new feminism.* London: Little, Brown.

Wang, Y. and R. Chiyoko King-O'Riain (2006) *Chinese students in Ireland.* Dublin: National Consultative Committee on Racism and Interculturalism. [Community Profiles Series]

Ward, C. (2002) 'Intimations of immorality: An analysis of the International Social Survey Programme (ISSP) 1998' in E. Cassidy (ed.) *Measuring Ireland: Discerning values and beliefs.* Dublin: Veritas.

Warde, A. and M. Tomlinson (1995) 'Taste among the middle classes, 1968–88' in T. Butler and M. Savage (eds) *Social change and the middle classes.* London: UCL.

Waring, M. (1989) *If women counted: A new feminist economics.* Basingstoke: Macmillan.

Warner, K. (2011) 'Regimes in Irish prisons: "inhumane" and "degrading". An analysis, and a solution'. Paper to 7th North/South Irish Criminology Conference, Institute of Technology, Sligo, 21–23 June.

Watson, D. (2000) *Victims of recorded crime in Ireland.* Dublin: Oak Tree/ESRI.

Watson, D. (2002) '"Home from home": The pub and everyday life' in T. Bennett and D. Watson (eds) *Understanding everyday life.* Oxford: Blackwell/Open University.

WCRF [World Cancer Research Fund] (2012) 'Press release: Number of UK cancer cases up 30% by 2030'. [www.wcrf-uk.org/audience/media/press_release.php?recid =175]

Weber, M. (1970) [1920] *The Protestant ethic and the spirit of capitalism.* [Trans. Talcott Parsons] London: Unwin.

Weeks, J. (1989) *Sex, politics and society: The regulation of sexuality since 1800.* London: Longman.

Weeks, J. (2005) 'Fallen heroes? All about men'. *Irish Journal of Sociology* 14(2) [Special issue on Masculinities] pp. 53–65.

Weigert, A. (2005) *Religious and secular views on endtime.* Lewiston, NY: Mellen.

Weigert, A. (2010) 'Metatheoretical theses on identity, inequality, time, and hope: Toward a pragmatic cosmopolitanism'. *Journal for the Theory of Social Behaviour* 40(3), pp. 249–73.

Wellman, B. and K. Hampton (1999) 'Living networked on and off line'. *Contemporary Sociology* 28(6), pp. 648–54.

WHC [Women's Health Council] (2003) *Women, disadvantage and health: A position paper of the Women's Health Council.* Dublin: Women's Health Council. [www.whc.ie/publications/31657_WHC_Disadvantage.pdf]

WHC [Women's Health Council] (2006) *Women and cancer in Ireland 1994–2001.* Dublin: Women's Health Council. [www.whc.ie/publications/WomenCancer.pdf]

Whelan, C. (1994) *Values and social change in Ireland.* Dublin: Gill & Macmillan.

Whelan, C. and B. Whelan (1984) *Social mobility in the Republic of Ireland: A comparative perspective.* Dublin: Economic and Social Research Institute.

Whitehead, A. (1976) 'Sexual antagonism in Herefordshire' in D. Barker and S. Allen (eds) *Dependence and exploitation in work and marriage.* London: Longman.

WHO [World Health Organization] (2011) *World health statistics: Part 2 Global health indicators.* [www.who.int/gho/publications/world_health_statistics/EN_WHS2011_Part2.pdf]

Whyte, J. (1971) *Church and state in modern Ireland 1923–1970*. Dublin: Gill & Macmillan.

Whyte, J. (1979) 'Church, state and society, 1950–70' in J. Lee (ed.) *Ireland: 1945–70*. Dublin: Gill & Macmillan.

Wickham, J. (1986) 'Industrialisation, work and unemployment' in P. Clancy et al. (eds) *Ireland: A sociological profile*. Dublin: Institute of Public Administration/Sociological Association of Ireland.

Wickham, J. (1997) 'Where is Ireland in the global information society?' *Economic and Social Review* 28(3).

Wickham, J. (1998) 'An intelligent island?' in M. Peillon and E. Slater (eds) *Encounters with modern Ireland*. Dublin: Institute of Public Administration.

Wickham, J. (2006) *Gridlock: Dublin's transport crisis and the future of the city*. Dublin: Tasc/New Island.

Wickham, J. (2007) 'Irish mobilities' in S. O'Sullivan (ed.) *Contemporary Ireland: A sociological map*, Dublin: University College Dublin Press, pp. 48–64.

Wigham, M. (1992) *The Irish Quakers: A short history of the Religious Society of Friends in Ireland*. Dublin: Historical Committee of the Religious Society of Friends in Ireland.

Wilkinson, R. (1996) *Unhealthy societies: The afflictions of inequality*. London: Routledge.

Wilkinson, R. (1999) 'Putting the picture together: Prosperity, redistribution, health and welfare' in M. Marmot and R. Wilkinson (eds) *Social determinants of health*. Oxford: Oxford University Press.

Wilkinson, R. (2005) *The impact of inequality: How to make sick societies better*. London: Routledge.

Wilkinson, R. and K. Pickett (2009) *The spirit level: Why more equal societies almost always do better*. London: Penguin.

Williams, J., S. Greene, E. Doyle, E. Harris, R. Layte, S. McCoy, C. McCrory, A. Murray, E. Nixon, T. O'Dowd, M. O'Moore, A. Quail, E. Smyth, L. Swords and M. Thornton (2009) *Growing Up in Ireland. National Longitudinal Study of Children: The lives of 9 year olds*. Dublin: Office for the Minister for Children and Youth Affairs.

Williams, R. (1976) *Keywords: A vocabulary of culture and society*. London: Fontana.

Williams, R. (1996) 'The health legacy of emigration: The Irish in Britain and elsewhere'. *Irish Journal of Sociology* 6, pp. 56–78.

Willis, P. (1977) *Learning to labour: How working class kids get working class jobs*. Farnborough: Saxon House.

Wilson, T. and H. Donnan (2006) *The anthropology of Ireland*. Oxford: Berg.

WODC [Wetenschappelijk onderzoek- en documentatiecentrum] (2010) *European sourcebook of crime and criminal justice statistics – 2010*. Den Haag: Ministry of Justice Research and Documentation Centre (WODC). [www.europeansourcebook.org/ob285_full.pdf]

Wollman, H. (2004) 'Good local government and the local community'. Paper presented at the Resurgent City conference, London School of Economics, 19–21 April.

Woolgar, S. (1988) *Science: The very idea*. Chichester: Horwood/London and New York: Tavistock.

Wren, M. (2003) *Unhealthy state: Anatomy of a sick society*. Dublin: New Island.

Yamane, D. (2003) 'Bishops' political influence and the Catholic Watergate'. *American Sociological Association Sociology of Religion Section Newsletter* 9(3), pp. 1–4. [www2.asanet.org/section34/previousnews/spring2003.pdf]

Yamane, D. (2006) 'Course preparation assignments: A strategy for creating discussion-based courses', *Teaching Sociology* 34(3), pp. 236–48.

Young Christian Workers Movement (2008) *What's the story? Experiences of young migrant workers in relation to work, faith and social integration in Ireland*. [www.ycw.ie/downloads/Whats_the_story_Report%20for%20web.pdf]

Young, I. (1990) 'The ideal of community and the politics of difference' in L. Nicholson (ed.) *Feminism/postmodernism*. London: Routledge.

Zhao, S., S. Grasmuck and J. Martin (2008) 'Identity construction on Facebook: Digital empowerment in anchored relationships'. *Computers in Human Behaviour* (24), pp. 1,816–36.

Index